NEW THOUGHTS ON THE BLACK ARTS MOVEMENT

NEW THOUGHTS ON THE BLACK ARTS MOVEMENT

Edited by Lisa Gail Collins and Margo Natalie Crawford

Rutgers University Press
New Brunswick, New Jersey, and London

Library of Congress Cataloging-in-publication data

New thoughts on the Black arts movement / edited by Lisa Gail Collins and Margo Natalie Crawford.

    p. cm.

  Includes bibliographical references and index.

  ISBN-13: 978-0-8135-3694-1 (hardcover : alk. paper)

  ISBN-13: 978-0-8135-3695-8 (pbk. : alk. paper)

1. Black Arts movement. 2. African-American arts–20th century. 3. Arts–Political

aspects–United States. I. Collins, Lisa Gail. II. Crawford, Margo Natalie, 1969-

  NX512.3.A35N49 2006

  700'.89'96073--dc22

                                        2005011269

A British Cataloging-in-Publication record for this book is available from the British Library

Book design by Karolina Harris

Manufactured in the United States of America

To William E. and Joyce Collins and Bob and Margo Crawford for bringing up their daughters in Cleveland and Chicago, respectively.

CONTENTS

Acknowledgments   ix

Introduction: Power to the People!: The Art of Black Power   1
LISA GAIL COLLINS AND MARGO NATALIE CRAWFORD

I.   CITIES AND SITES

1. Black Light on the *Wall of Respect*: The Chicago Black Arts Movement   23
   MARGO NATALIE CRAWFORD

2. Black West, Thoughts on Art in Los Angeles   43
   KELLIE JONES

3. The Black Arts Movement and Historically Black Colleges and
   Universities   75
   JAMES SMETHURST

4. A Question of Relevancy: New York Museums and the Black Arts
   Movement, 1968–1971   92
   MARY ELLEN LENNON

5. Blackness in Present Future Tense: Broadside Press, Motown Records,
   and Detroit Techno   117
   WENDY S. WALTERS

II.   GENRES AND IDEOLOGIES

6. *A Black Mass* as Black Gothic: Myth and Bioscience in Black
   Cultural Nationalism   137
   ALONDRA NELSON

7. Natural Black Beauty and Black Drag   154
MARGO NATALIE CRAWFORD

8. Sexual Subversions, Political Inversions: Women's Poetry and the Politics of the Black Arts Movement   173
CHERISE A. POLLARD

9. Transcending the Fixity of Race: The Kamoinge Workshop and the Question of a "Black Aesthetic" in Photography   187
ERINA DUGANNE

10. Moneta Sleet, Jr. as Active Participant: The Selma March and the Black Arts Movement   210
CHERISE SMITH

11. "If Bessie Smith Had Killed Some White People": Racial Legacies, the Blues Revival, and the Black Arts Movement   227
ADAM GUSSOW

III.   PREDECESSORS, PEERS, AND LEGACIES

12. A Familiar Strangeness: The Spectre of Whiteness in the Harlem Renaissance and the Black Arts Movement   255
EMILY BERNARD

13. The Art of Transformation: Parallels in the Black Arts and Feminist Art Movements   273
LISA GAIL COLLINS

14. Prison Writers and the Black Arts Movement   297
LEE BERNSTEIN

15. "To Make a Poet Black": Canonizing Puerto Rican Poets in the Black Arts Movement   317
MICHELLE JOAN WILKINSON

16. Latin Soul: Cross-Cultural Connections between the Black Arts Movement and Pocho-Che   333
ROD HERNANDEZ

17. Black Arts to Def Jam: Performing Black "Spirit Work" across Generations   349
LORRIE SMITH

Afterword: This Bridge Called "Our Tradition": Notes on Blueblack, 'Round'midnight, Blacklight "Connection"   369
HOUSTON A. BAKER, JR.

Notes on Contributors   375

Index   379

ACKNOWLEDGMENTS

Collaboration and dialogue were at the heart of the Black Arts Movement. This collection continues this necessary work. As co-editors, we came together from our respective departmental homes in English and art history to the essential interdisciplinary field of African American studies to hone and share our mutual interest in the arts and politics of the 1960s and 1970s. The response to our call for others immersed in this crucial period was extraordinary; we were inundated with fresh research. In the end, we selected essays that creatively addressed several new avenues of inquiry. What were the principal cities and sites of the movement? How were art forms fused and synthesized, and why were criteria for creating and evaluating art so hotly contested during the period? And what are the links between the Black Arts Movement and other sociocultural movements? Who are the movement's predecessors and peers, and what are its legacies?

Support for this dialogue and collaboration was indispensable. Leslie Mitchner, editor in chief at Rutgers University Press, offered crucial early support, encouragement, and guidance. Simply put, Leslie Mitchner and her colleagues at the press made this book possible. Our contributors inspired us with their originality and accessibility. We are honored to be in conversation with them, and we thank all of them for generously sharing their brand new work with us. Two of our intellectual role models, Houston A. Baker, Jr., Susan Fox Beischer and George D. Beischer Arts and Sciences Professor of English at Duke University, and Haki Madhubuti, Distinguished University Professor of English at Chicago State University and founder of Third World Press, graciously offered their supreme wisdom and valuable time. Bob Crawford, another vital role model, gallantly lent his visionary photography that so eloquently engages the movement and serves as the backbone of this book. The work of artists inspired these pages, and we are deeply grateful to them as well as to the institutions that make sharing their work possible.

We were also fortunate to have hearty support from our colleagues at Vassar College and Indiana University, respectively. Warm thanks to Lee Bernstein, Uma Narayan, Nikki Taylor, Molly Shanley, Meg Stewart, Judith Weisenfeld, and the Faculty Research Committee in Poughkeepsie, and Paula Bryant, Purnima Bose, Susan Gubar, George Hutchinson, De Witt Kilgore, and Steve Watt in Bloomington. At Indiana University, Margo Crawford teaches a graduate course on the Black Arts Movement. At Vassar, Lisa Collins regularly offers a seminar that compares creations kindled by the pursuits for Women's Liberation and Black Power. Students in both of these courses have enabled us to approach the Black Arts Movement with heightened clarity. We genuinely salute our students for their critical insights and contagious enthusiasm.

During the early stages of this collaboration, the wise counsel of Jeff Donaldson (1932–2004) was absolutely invaluable and this collection greatly benefited from the late artist and teacher's creative and humane brilliance. We sincerely hope it honors his memory.

NEW THOUGHTS ON THE
BLACK ARTS MOVEMENT

Introduction
Power to the People!
The Art of Black Power

Lisa Gail Collins and
Margo Natalie Crawford

CITIES AND SITES

Harlem (1964), Brooklyn (1964), Philadelphia (1964), Watts (1965), Chicago (1966), Cleveland (1966), San Francisco (1967), Tampa (1967), Cincinnati (1967), Atlanta (1967), Boston (1967), Milwaukee (1967), Newark (1967), Detroit (1967), Baltimore (1968), Kansas City (1968), Chicago (1968), Pittsburgh (1968), Washington, D.C. (1968).

On July 29, 1967, President Lyndon B. Johnson issued Executive Order 11365 establishing a National Advisory Commission on Civil Disorders to investigate the explosion of "racial disorders" in American cities. President Johnson's mandate for the eleven-member appointed commission was to answer three crucial questions about the recent upsurge in urban violence: "What happened? Why did it happen? And what can be done to prevent it from happening again?"[1] After conducting extensive field research, hearings, surveys, and interviews, the bipartisan commission published its detailed findings in a hefty government document known as "The Kerner Report." Released on March 1, 1968, the 425-page report was informally named for the commission's chairman Governor Otto Kerner of Illinois.

Focused on 1967, the National Advisory Commission on Civil Disorders found that over 120 U.S. cities had reported disturbances in "minority" neighborhoods—especially in predominantly African American communities—during the first nine months of the year (fig. I. 1).[2] Ranging from minor disturbances such as broken windows to major outbursts that included arson, looting, and sniping, these disturbances—which were typically fueled by real and perceived crimes of discriminatory or abusive police actions—reached a peak in July 1967. Newark and Detroit were the sites of the most explosive violence.

Cartography by: M.E. Stewart, Vassar College

Fig. I-1. Sites of urban uprisings in the United States, January-September 1967. Based on data in the Report of the National Advisory Commission on Civil Disorders (March 1, 1968). Map by Meg Stewart.

After five days of unrest, twenty-three people had died in Newark. And after almost a week of unrest in Detroit, forty-three people had been killed, most at the hands of police officers and National Guardsmen.[3] In addition to the violent deaths, 600 people had been injured during the Michigan rioting and fire had destroyed or badly damaged over one hundred Detroit homes.[4]

The widely available 1968 Kerner Commission Report opened with a dire warning about the current course of the nation: "This is our basic conclusion: Our Nation is moving toward two societies, one black, one white—separate and unequal."[5] Explaining that poverty, prejudice, segregation, discrimination, and feelings of powerlessness were the underlying causes of the recent "civil disorders," the commission saw the solution as the elimination of barriers to decent jobs, quality education, and affordable housing. Calling for the "enrichment" of riot-battered central cities, it also stressed the need for increased integration of outlying metropolitan areas. Expressing both a concern with the charged "polarization of the races" and a deep faith in the nation's founding ideals, the commission declared:

> Discrimination and segregation have long permeated much of American life; they now threaten the future of every American. This deepening racial division is not inevitable. The movement apart can be reversed. Choice is still possible. Our principal task is to define that choice and to press for a national resolution. To pursue our present course will involve the continuing polarization of the American community and, ultimately, the destruction of basic democratic values. The alternative is not blind repression or capitulation to lawlessness. It is the realization of common opportunities for all within a single society.[6]

Recommending that America commit to "national action on an unprecedented scale" by curbing unemployment and underemployment, eliminating *de facto* segregation in the public schools, reforming the welfare system, overcoming racial discrimination in federal housing programs, and making adequate living spaces accessible to those in need, the President's National Advisory Commission on Civil Disorders stressed their vision of a nation aligned with its ideals: "It is time to make good the promises of American democracy to all citizens."[7] Underlying the commission's sweeping recommendations was also the desire for a unified America. "The major goal is the creation of a true union—a single society and a single American identity," the report asserted.[8]

The backdrop for the Kerner Report and its urgent plea for increased integration and national unity was the loud call for "Black Power" which had first been publicly proclaimed and embraced during the summer of 1966. Within earshot of the mainstream media, Student Nonviolent Coordinating Committee (SNCC) organizer Willie Ricks and SNCC chairman Stokely Carmichael had unleashed the deep hunger of many African Americans for righteous militancy and collective self-determination with their explosive cry for "Black Power." On the night of June 16, 1966, in Greenwood, Mississippi, during the volatile "March Against Fear," Carmichael had given voice to this latent yearning in his fiery speech:

> Don't be afraid. Don't be ashamed. We want black power. We want black power. We want black power. We want black power. We want black power. That's right. That's what we want, black power. And we don't have to be ashamed of it. We have stayed here and we've begged the President, we've begged the federal government. That's all we've been doing, begging, begging. It's time we stand up and take over. Take over.[9]

Initiated by James Meredith—the man who had integrated the University of Mississippi in 1962—the March Against Fear was originally conceived of as a daring but small southward walk through Meredith's home state as a way to embolden black Mississippians—following the 1965 passage of the Voting Rights Act—to register to vote and, in this way, to participate in the political process. Yet after Meredith was shot and injured by a white sniper near Hernando, Mississippi (just across the border from Memphis, Tennessee), on June 6, 1966, the second day of his journey, prominent civil rights leaders arrived at the scene and resumed his march. This greatly expanded march took on a very different character from the original one, and it quickly became a site of charged ideological debate among major civil rights organizations. In direct conflict with the more moderate philosophies of the National Association for the Advancement of Colored People (NAACP) and the Southern Christian Leadership Conference (SCLC), SNCC and the Congress of Racial Equality (CORE) began pressing for more militant political strategies and social goals during the hot and heated walk from Memphis to Jackson.

Challenging the notion that nonviolence was the only viable path to progressive change, rejecting the liberal understanding of integration as the ultimate social goal, critiquing capitalism, and doubting the efficacy of interracial alliances, many young black activists in SNCC and CORE, as well as in other activist groups such as the emerging Black Panther Party, began to rethink the traditional tactics and visions of the black freedom struggle. Inspired by the late Malcolm X's call for collective self-definition, self-determination, self-reliance, self-respect, and self-defense, these resolute activists began to call for racial solidarity and black pride, independent black leadership and freedom from white authority and, in some cases, armed defense and/or struggle under the rubric of "Black Power."

Although the first bellows for "Black Power" came from the Deep South, the phrase and its array of connotations quickly captured the imagination of the urban North. On July 26, 1967—on the heels of the Newark riots and in the heat of the Detroit riots—H. Rap Brown, Stokely Carmichael's successor as SNCC's chairman, employed the strident language of the new black militancy to assert the meaning of the uprisings igniting the American urban landscape. He declared the rebellions precursors to armed revolution:

> We stand on the eve of a black revolution. Masses of our people are on the move, fighting the enemy tit-for-tat, responding to the counter-revolutionary violence with revolutionary violence, an eye for an eye, a tooth for a tooth, and a life for a life. These rebellions are but a dress rehearsal for real revolution . . . . A stable and just society cannot mount a successful offensive action against a black youth who breaks a window and at the same time plead that it is powerless to protect black youth who are being murdered because they seek to make American democracy a reality. Each time a black church is bombed or burned, it is an act of violence in our streets. Each time a black body is found in the swamps of Mississippi or Alabama, that is violence in our land. Each time black human rights workers are refused protection by the government, that is anarchy. Each time a police officer shoots and kills a black teenager, that is urban crime. We see America for what it is, and we recognize our course of action.[10]

H. Rap Brown, as well as other fierce advocates of Black Power, saw the recent unrest as political protest and believed urban rebellion would lead to black revolution. These activists viewed the revolts as climactic expressions of frustration, anger, and resolve and sure signs that the black freedom struggle had shifted from a nonviolent struggle for equality, exemplified by the slogan "Freedom Now," to more militant tactics for political potency and autonomy implied by the "Black Power" rallying cry.

On July 27, 1967, the day after H. Rap Brown's dramatic foretelling, President Johnson delivered an address to the nation on, what he called, the "civil disorders" enflaming U.S. cities. Directly countering Brown's characterization of the rioters as emerging revolutionaries, the president insisted that the "disorders" were the work of "criminals" and were not in any way related to "civil rights protest."[11] The Kerner Commission, however, disagreed with President Johnson's characterization of the rioters, particularly his attempts to depoliticize them. In their report, the president's appointees claimed the rioters were "informed about politics" and that the largely young African American male participants were "more likely to be actively engaged in civil rights efforts" than their non-involved peers.[12] The bipartisan committee, however, was far from aligned with the SNCC chairman's premonition of black revolution, for while they understood the rioters to be politically minded, they saw the riots as desperate cries for inclusion in mainstream American society. Regarding their thoughts on the meaning of the riots, the commissioners wrote: "What the rioters appeared to be seeking was fuller participation in the social order and the material benefits enjoyed by the majority of American citizens. Rather than rejecting the American system, they were anxious to obtain a place for themselves in it."[13]

By claiming that the message behind the unrest was a frustrated longing for inclusion in America's capitalist democracy and that the solution to the misplaced despair was increased integration, the Kerner Commission stood at dramatic odds with the militant advocates of Black Power. Although the brash phrase quickly became attached with numerous contradictory political strategies—from the development of black capitalism and the election of African American politicians to the ignition of a Marxist-inspired revolution and the creation of a new black nation—the collective yearnings lodged behind the fiery slogan were in direct conflict with the leanings of the liberal report. Whereas the appointed commission sought integration and national unity, Black Power activists typically advocated for Black nationalism, particularly the strains of nationalist thought attributed to Malcolm X that stressed racial separatism, sovereignty, and revolution. Concerning the vital link between Malcolm X and Black Power, Black Arts Movement founder LeRoi Jones asserted, in November 1966, nearly two years after Malcolm X's murder: "The concept of Black Power is natural after Malcolm. Malcolm's legacy was the concept and will toward political power in the world for the Black Man."[14]

Malcolm X and his legacy played pivotal roles in the growing racial consciousness and militancy of African Americans during the mid- to late 1960s. Reflecting on the charismatic leader's brutal and confusing assassination in Harlem's Audubon Ballroom on February 21, 1965, Larry Neal, the Black Arts Movement's key theorist and advocate, wrote:

> But even though Malcolm's death—the manner of it—emotionally fractured young black radicals, there were two central facts that *all* factions of the movement came to understand. And they are: that the struggle for black self-determination had entered a serious, more profound stage; and that for most of us, nonviolence

as a viable technique of social change had died with Malcolm on the stage of the Audubon .... Malcolm's ideas had touched all aspects of contemporary black nationalism: the relationship between black America and the Third World; the development of a black cultural thrust; the right of oppressed peoples to self-defense and armed struggle; the necessity of maintaining a strong moral force in the black community; the building of autonomous black institutions; and finally, the need for a black theory of social change.[15]

Malcolm X's powerful contributions to contemporary Black nationalism were sources of intense anxiety for the Kerner Commission. Defining the movement "toward racial consciousness and solidarity reflected in the slogan 'Black Power'" as evidence of the "frustrations of powerlessness," the commission was quite wary of confident calls for racial pride and black unity.[16] This wariness was perhaps based on the commission's primary data that linked tenets of Black nationalism, namely racial consciousness and black solidarity and pride, to unrest. For example, in an effort to assess the "racial attitudes" of rioters in comparison to those who claimed to be uninvolved in the riots, surveys in Detroit and Newark had asked both African American participants and non-participants in the recent urban uprisings who they found "nicer" and "more dependable" "Negroes" or "Whites"? When a much higher percentage of the self-reported riot participants than those who purported not to have been involved in the riots affirmed that indeed "Negroes" were "nicer" and "more dependable" than "Whites," the commission revealed its discomfort with its "racial conscious-ness" findings by quickly claiming that "rioters have strong feelings of racial pride, if not superiority."[17] Likewise, in an attempt to gauge the level of "black consciousness" of riot participants, a survey of African American participants and non-participants in Newark asked each group what they preferred to be called—"Black," "Negro," or "Colored"—and found that the self-reported ri-oters, in line with the unapologetic new militancy and somewhat in contrast to those uninvolved, preferred to be called "Black."[18] The same Newark survey also asked participants and non-participants if they agreed with the statement "All Negroes should study African history and language."[19] In line with Mal-colm X's Pan-African emphasis on the study of the ancient continent and its diverse cultures, nearly 80 percent of self-reported riot participants vigorously affirmed the statement. And reflecting the logic and reach of Black nationalism during the period, almost 70 percent of those purportedly uninvolved in the urban uprisings also agreed.[20]

With its faith in liberalism and capitalist democracy and its desire for na-tional unity, the Kerner Commission feared Black nationalism, especially its tenets that affirmatively claimed blackness, emphasized the African origins of "New World" black identities, advocated Pan-African political thinking, and fearlessly sought autonomy from white America. Although the commission had concluded that the nation was "moving toward two societies, one black, one white," they saw this course as the problem, as exactly what needed to be reversed through wide-reaching social programs and committed national will. The idea that African Americans in the United States could understand themselves as constituting a viable nation—and a potentially glorious and righteous one at that—fell beyond the commissioners' faith. It was precisely this ambitious vision, however, that lay at the core of the Black Arts Movement. Concerning the links between Black Power, Black Arts, and nationhood, Larry Neal, the quintessential theorist of the cultural movement, explained in 1968:

> The Black Arts and the Black Power concepts both relate broadly to the Afro-American's desire for self-determination and nationhood. Both concepts are nationalistic. One is concerned with the relationship between art and politics; the other with the art of politics. Recently, these two movements have begun to merge: the political values inherent in the Black Power concept are now finding concrete expression in the aesthetics of Afro-American dramatists, poets, choreographers, musicians, and novelists. A main tenet of Black Power is the necessity for black people to define the world in their own terms. The black artist has made the same point in the context of aesthetics. The two movements postulate that there are in fact and in spirit two Americas—one black, one white.[21]

Whereas the Kerner Commission lamented the creation of "two societies," Larry Neal saw possibility in this split. For him, the Black Power call for political potency and autonomy was coupled with a related desire for artistic potency and autonomy. Neal firmly believed that the search for new political directions would be enabled by a search for new aesthetic directions.

Dubbed "spiritual leader" of the Black Arts Movement posthumously by Amiri Baraka (formerly LeRoi Jones), Larry Neal penned many of the movement's most passionate position papers.[22] A poet, dramatist, essayist, and activist, Neal viewed the Black Arts Movement as the cultural wing of the struggle for black nationhood. Inspired by Malcolm X's calls for self-definition, self-determination, and self-defense, Neal saw the arts as ripe terrain on which to graft lofty ideals—ideals that would enable black people to envision and force change. While he did not see the arts as capable of liberating black people on their own, he did believe that their ability to provide vision and cohesion made them a necessary component of a successful social revolution. In his 1969 *Ebony* manifesto, "Any Day Now: Black Art and Black Liberation," he explained:

> A cultureless revolution is a bullcrap tip. It means that in the process of making the revolution, we lose our vision. We lose the soft, undulating side of ourselves—those unknown beauties lurking rhythmically below the level of material needs. In short, a revolution without a culture would destroy the very thing that now unites us; the very thing we are trying to save along with our lives.[23]

Championing the expression of a "black aesthetic" that would ignite a black sociocultural revolution, Larry Neal first pressed African American cultural workers to reconceive of their audience. In particular, he encouraged them to shift from creating "protest" art—which he saw as art that "screams and masturbates" for a white audience—to creating art that directly addressed black people.[24] This shift, he prompted, would enable African American artists to free themselves from "white standards" of judgment under which their work was usually deemed lacking. Neal also called for new aesthetic standards that would inspire and value art that reflected "black realities," affirmed black culture, spoke to the masses of black people, and aligned itself with liberation struggles throughout the world. Finally, Neal insisted that this new art express what he defined as a "Vision of a Liberated Future." Of this last requisite, he explained:

> Liberation is impossible if we fail to see ourselves in more positive terms. For without a change of vision, we are slaves to the oppressor's ideas and values— ideas and values that finally attack the very core of our existence. Therefore, we must see the world in terms of our own realities.[25]

In his initial charge to the National Advisory Commission on Civil Disorders, President Lyndon Johnson asked his appointees about the images created by the mainstream media and their impact: "What effect do the mass media have on the riots?" he inquired.[26] In its final report, the Kerner Commission placed heavy blame on the mainstream media for failing to communicate "the causes and consequences of civil disorders and the underlying problems of race relations."[27] Yet, the commission was less troubled by the actual riot coverage than by the pervasive lack of coverage of the daily complexities of black life. Concerning this palpable lack, the report found that mainstream newspapers and television programming neglected both African American subject matter and viewers. The report stated: "They have not shown understanding or appreciation of—and thus have not communicated—a sense of Negro culture, thought, or history. Equally important, most newspaper articles and most television programming ignore the fact that an appreciable part of their audience is black. The world that television and newspapers offer to their black audience is almost totally white, in both appearance and attitude."[28] In short, the commission criticized the mass media for exacerbating race relations by stating "the communications media, ironically, have failed to communicate."[29]

Participants in the Black Arts Movement, in a sense, wholly agreed with the Kerner Commission's heavy charge against the mainstream media for failing to illuminate black life. Two years before the report was released, in 1966, LeRoi Jones had characterized American television as "a steady deadly whiteness beaming forth."[30] Black Arts workers like LeRoi Jones and Larry Neal, however, turned their spirited energies away from the mass media and mainstream society, for they held deep faith in art and black community. Amidst bullets and flames, they took matters into their own mighty black hands and artistically fought to transform the cities of explosive unrest into sites of regenerative creativity.

Black Arts Repertory Theater/School (Harlem), Free Southern Theater (Jackson, Mississippi), BLKARTSOUTH (New Orleans), Organization of Black American Culture (Chicago), Black Arts West (San Francisco), *Liberator* (New York City), Association for the Advancement of Creative Musicians (Chicago), Watts Writers' Workshop (Los Angeles), Concept East Theater (Detroit), Karamu Playhouse (Cleveland), Wall of Respect (Chicago), Institute of Black Studies (Los Angeles), Wall of Dignity (Detroit), Sudan Arts Southwest (Houston), Museum of the National Center of Afro-American Artists (Boston), Conference on the Functional Aspects of Black Art (Evanston, Illinois), *Journal of Black Poetry* (San Francisco), Umbra Workshop (New York City), Black Power Conference (Newark), Du Sable Museum of African American History (Chicago), Institute of the Black World (Atlanta), Weusi (Harlem), Spirit House (Newark), *Soulbook* (Oakland), "Where We At," Black Women Artists, Inc. (New York City), Broadside Press (Detroit), Third World Press (Chicago), Gallery Toward the Black Aesthetic (Milwaukee), *Negro Digest/Black World* (Chicago), *Black Scholar* (San Francisco), *Black Dialogue* (San Francisco/New York City), Black House Theater (Oakland), Nyumba Ya Sanaa Gallery (Harlem), Congress of African Peoples (Atlanta).

GENRES AND IDEOLOGIES

The urban explosion of "Black Power" ignited an explosion of "Black is Beautiful." This explosive black aesthetic led to an eruption of new criteria for creating and evaluating art. In the opening essay of *Black Fire* (1968), the signal text of the Black Arts Movement, cultural theorist James Stewart evokes the notion of a black cosmos as he expands the notion of a black nation. As he asserts that a new cosmology offers a fresh way of "looking at the world," he decries the limits of "white models" and "white forms."[31] "The models must be non-white. Our models must be consistent with a black style our natural aesthetic styles and our moral and spiritual styles," he writes.[32] This tension between a new cosmology of blackness and the suffocating vacuum attributed to whiteness reflects the Black Arts ethos. The sheer rhythm within the performance poetry of the period often evokes a blackness that cannot stand still. The anti-white rhetoric and the attacks against the non-revolutionary "Negroes" (the "jive revolutionaries") are stumbling blocks within this explosive motion.

This love affair with blackness often led to an obsession with images of pernicious whiteness and non-enlightened blackness. As poet and critic A. B. Spellman explains in his poem, "The Beautiful Day #9," "the mirror was blackness," and this "black mirror" often revealed images of that which was imagined as not black.[33] These demonized figures are those that must be purged within the re-conditioning process imagined by these Black Arts rhetoricians—a re-conditioning process in which they wonder if the mind itself can be decolonized.

Any re-conditioning process must counter dominant ideology with a bold barrage of new signs and new images. The aesthetic warfare of this movement was often the conscious attempt to deprogram the hypnotic effects of anti-black ideology. Don L. Lee (who later changes his name to Haki Madhubuti) depicts this alternative hypnotism in his poem "Awareness" (1966):

BLACK	PEOPLE	THINK
PEOPLE	BLACK	PEOPLE
THINK	PEOPLE	THINK
BLACK	PEOPLE	THINK—
THINK	BLACK.	

Amiri Baraka imagines this deprogramming process when he implores black people to "try to see your own face, when you close your eyes" and then "get up and go."[34] As Baraka gives these orders in *In Our Terribleness* (1970), he is the hypnotist aiming to help his subjects learn to become their own hypnotists. Ideally, the "resurrection of blackness" would include many black magicians— "black magic" being one of the recurring motifs of the movement.[35]

As Jeff Donaldson, one the founders of AFRI-COBRA (African Commune of Bad Relevant Artists), thinks about this deprogramming process, he insists, "Check out the image," as he revels in "our image making," the new visual images of blackness.[36] One element of this new image making is "Color color Color color that shines, color that is free of rules and regulations."[37] Donaldson's celebration of the "shine" of blackness is the bold decision to love blackness unabashedly and unapologetically. No other African American cultural movement has revolved so entirely around the purging, from the African American psyche, of racial self-hatred, the internalization of anti-black ways of seeing and thinking. Clearly, the visual culture of the Black Arts Movement directly underscored the new ways of seeing. Jeff Donaldson crystallizes this new black gaze:

> We strive for images inspired by African people/experience and images which African people can relate to directly without formal art training and/or experience. Art [is] for people and not for critics whose peopleness is questionable. We try to create images that appeal to the senses—not to the intellect. . . . It is our hope that intelligent definition of the past, and perceptive identification in the present will project nationfull direction in the future—look for us there, because that's where we're at . . . . Among our roots and branches we have selected these qualities to emphasize in our image making . . . . Superreal images for SUPERREAL people. Check out the image.[38]

Donaldson envisions black "roots and branches" as inseparable from black images. This conjoining of cultural heritage and aesthetics was a principal part of Black Arts. "Culture," within this movement, is not only what you do or practice, but also who you are. Baraka understands this new cultural identity as the putting on of new clothes: "I can take off these clothes and wear some others," he writes.[39] On the one hand, blackness was celebrated as primal and essential. Yet on the other hand, there were strident critiques of the very notion of an essential blackness. In the play *The Theme is Blackness* (1966), Ed Bullins imagines a predominantly white audience waiting for the appearance of blackness, but the anticipated performance never happens. As the audience sits in silence for twenty minutes, their own conceptualization of blackness is the truth of blackness that Bullins aims to make visible.

Theories of ideology and the aesthetic gained a down-to-earth public forum during this cultural movement. In *The Ideology of the Aesthetic* (1990), Terry Eagleton states, "[T]he aesthetic, one might argue, is [. . .] the very paradigm of the ideological."[40] During the Black Arts Movement, the inseparability of the ideological and the aesthetic was considered intuitive and self-evident. These revolutionaries recognized that "ideology and style are the same thing."[41] This proclamation, made by Baraka in *In Our Terribleness*, can only be fully appreciated when we remember that the ideology of blackness became a way of thinking (exemplified by "Think Black," the title of one of Don L. Lee's [Haki Madhubuti's] volumes of poetry) as well as a stylizing of the body (an interviewee remembers that "in those days, we wore our culture, our Africa").[42] The black aesthetic of this period was a bold re-envisioning of life itself as a work of art dedicated to the advancement of black people. This type of art *engagé* defined beauty as "black," hence the power of the words that became so much more than a slogan—"Black is Beautiful." What did it mean, at this particular historical moment, to define beauty itself as black? Blackness emerged as a veritable liberation theology: to be free one had to love one's blackness. Black self-love was publicly expressed during this period with an unprecedented loudness akin to James Brown's mantra, "Say it loud, I'm black and I'm proud."

The efforts to smash dominant aesthetic models is proclaimed loudly in *Think Black* (1967), when poet and publisher Don Lee asserts, "We must destroy Faulkner, dick, jane, and other perpetuators of evil. It's time for DuBois, Nat Turner and Kwame Nkruma [sic]."[43] In the opening essay of *Black Fire*, James Stewart presents the new aesthetic models as motion opposed to any fixity: "Art is not fixed. Art can not be fixed. Art is change, like music, poetry, and writing are, when conceived. They must move (swing)."[44] The breaking of boundaries during the movement is perhaps best appreciated by remembering the types of collaborations that happened in the artistic collectives. Collaborations between poets, musicians, theorists, dancers, painters, and photographers defined Black Arts. The Black Arts Repertory Theater/School, Spirit House, the Organization of Black American Culture (OBAC), and BLKARTSOUTH were all spaces where this collaborative energy thrived.[45] The 1967 Chicago mural *The Wall of Respect* was created by the visual arts component of OBAC, whose visual artists later formed AFRI-COBRA (fig. I. 2). At the *Wall*, there was a fusion of poetry and music, theater and dance, painting and photography.

Fig. I-2. Bob Crawford, Photograph of the *Wall of Respect*, Chicago, Illinois, 1967. Courtesy of the artist.

The openness of the cross-genre work within the collectives did not always lead to openness in ideology. The mixed media was sometimes used to express singular visions of a monolithic blackness. Sexism and homophobia were often a part of the Black nationalism that shaped the movement. Nikki Giovanni wrestles with sexism in the poem, "The True Import of the Present Dialogue, Black vs. Negro" (1968). When she ends with the words, "Learn to be Black men," after the injunction "Can you kill the nigger /in you/ Can you make your nigger mind/ die," she articulates black women's rage even as she focuses on black men.[46]

Killing the ghosts of oppression is at the core of the Black Arts ethos. In Ed Bullins' *A Short Play for a Small Theater* (1970), killing the ideology of whiteness (white power) is performed in the following manner: an audience that is two-thirds black and one-third white watches a black actor shoot white people in the audience and then re-load his gun "if there is need."[47] This imaginary gunfire made visible, onstage, the real violence shaping the volatile 1960s race relations. Bullins' script insists on the "ratio" of two-thirds black/one-third white as he specifies that people should be "turned away" if necessary. The performative gunfire, the aesthetic warfare, reveals either a close-minded understanding of whiteness (whiteness as that which must be annihilated) or an open explosion of the power of blackness, which Haki Madhubuti screams in the following litany:

black doubleblack purpleblack blueblack beenblack was / black daybeforeyesterday blackerthan ultrablack super / black blackblack yellowblack niggerblack blackwhi-teman / blackerthanyoueverbes 1/4 black unblack coldblack clear / black my momma's blackerthanyourmomma pimpleblack fall / black so black we can't even see you black on black in / black by black technically black mantanblack winter / black coolblack 360degreesblack coalblack midnight / black black when it's convenient rustyblack moonblack /black starblack summerblack electronblack spaceman / black shoeshineblack jimshoeblack underwearblack ugly / black auntjimammablack, uncleben'srice black williebest / black blackisbeautifulblack I justdiscoveredblack negro / black unsubstanceblack.[48]

Within this explosion, blackness is both open and fixed, motion and stasis. This tension between possibilities and constraints fueled the fire of the Black Arts Movement.

PREDECESSORS, PEERS, AND LEGACIES

FIRE . . . flaming, burning, searing, and penetrating far beneath the superficial items of the flesh to boil the sluggish blood.

FIRE . . . a cry of conquest in the night, warning those who sleep and revitalizing those who linger in the quiet places dozing.

FIRE . . . melting steel and iron bars, poking livid tongues between stone apertures and burning wooden opposition with a cackling chuckle of contempt.

FIRE . . . weaving vivid, hot designs upon an ebon bordered loom and satisfying pagan thirst for beauty unadorned . . . the flesh is sweet and real . . . the soul an inward flush of fire . . . Beauty? . . . flesh on fire—on fire in the furnace of life blazing. . . .

"Fy-ah,
Fy-ah, Lawd,
Fy-ah gonna burn ma soul!"
Foreword to *Fire!!*, 1926

The fire of the Harlem Renaissance kindled the fire of the Black Arts Movement. This kindling is clearly evoked by the very shift from the publication of *Fire!!* in 1926 to the publication of *Black Fire* in 1968. This line of descent, however, was vexed. Participants in Black Arts often belittled their predecessors for—what they saw as—the Harlem Renassiance's disconnection with African American people at large. Haki Madhubuti, in his 1971 essay "Renaissance I to Renaissance III?: An Introduction," boldly asserts: "[T]he black arts movement in the twenties was of a minimal influence and virtually went unnoticed by the majority of black people in the country. More whites knew about what was happening than brothers and sisters. One of the main reasons for the short life of renaissance I is that no black people, other than the artists themselves, were involved in it. No lasting institutions were established."[49] Other Black Arts Movement cultural workers critiqued what they perceived as the reliance on dominant aesthetic criteria and white patrons during the Harlem Renaissance. In his recent essay, "The Last Movement," poet and cofounder of BLKART-SOUTH, Kalamu ya Salaam, argues that Harlem Renaissance artists "were always on the leash of white patrons and publishing houses."[50]

In critical contrast to this widespread perception, many black-owned publishing presses were established during the Black Arts Movement. Broadside Press, founded in 1965 by Dudley Randall, and Third World Press, founded by Don Lee in 1967, were two of the period's most successful Black Arts publishing houses. Importantly, however, mainstream publishers produced many of the central Black Arts Movement texts. William Morrow & Company, for example, published LeRoi Jones and Larry Neal's crucial collection *Black Fire*. In their preface, however, the two editors chafe at this predicament: "[B]ut these devils claim it costs too much to reprint. Hopefully, the 2nd edition of the paperback will have all the people we cd think of. The frustration of working thru these bullshit white people shd be obvious."[51] Though Black Arts leaders repeatedly critiqued the white patronage and presumed irrelevancy of the Harlem Renaissance, key New Negro Movement texts were brought back into circulation during the period. For example, in 1968, the same year *Black Fire* was published, a new edition of the definitive Harlem Renaissance anthology *The New Negro* (1925) was released. And in 1969 *Cane* (1923) was revived and celebrated as a Harlem Renaissance classic. Thus, the New Negro Movement was both belittled and revived during the Black Arts Movement.

The fire was lit during the Jazz Age 1920s and spread to the hotly charged clime of the 1960s and 1970s. This fire was a part of a simultaneous combustion. The flames of the Student Movement, the Chicano Movement, the American Indian Movement, the Women's Liberation Movement, the Anti-Vietnam War Movement, the Prisoners' Rights Movement, the Gay Liberation Movement, the Environmental Movement, and the counterculture all reacted vigorously with the flames of the Black freedom struggle, especially the Black Power Movement and its corollary, Black Arts. In his 1978 essay, "The Shadow World: New York's Umbra Workshop and Origins of the Black Arts Movement," poet and critic Lorenzo Thomas charts how the African American writers who formed the Umbra Workshop in 1962, and who in 1963 launched its journal *Umbra*, directly mined the aesthetic and political terrain that a few years later became known as Black Arts.[52] Members, he argues, "provided the core membership and intellectual direction" of the Black Arts Movement.[53] Thomas, a former member, also notes how the group's site—New York City's Lower East Side with close ties to Harlem—as well as its "concerns and orientation" made the circle open to influences from and exchanges with neighbors who shared or propelled their sense of outrage, urgency, and creative energy.[54] Downtown and uptown alliances with Puerto Rican poets and orators were particularly vital. Umbra members, for example, were delighted when Pedro Pietri, whom

Lorenzo Thomas remembers as "the 'people's poet' of East Harlem's barrio and of 14th Street" and who later became central to the Nuyorican Poetry Movement, joined Umbra's poetry gathering at the spring 1965 inauguration of the Black Arts Repertory Theater/School in Central Harlem.[55]

The simultaneous combustion of the 1960s and 1970s is explored in a gathering of essays that examine links between the Black Arts Movement and other aesthetic and socio-cultural movements. Two essays, for example, explore artistic collaborations, as well as political coalitions, between African American and Puerto Rican cultural workers during the period. Largely focused on the Umbra Workshop and the performance poetry troupe The Last Poets, and especially interested in the work of poet and *Umbra* contributor Victor Hernández Cruz and the work of Last Poet Felipe Luciano, these essays offer fresh insight into how Puerto Rican writers, particularly poets, drew from a "black aesthetic" and a Puerto Rican cultural consciousness to advance the Black Arts Movement and to launch the Nuyorican Poetry Movement, a peer to Black Arts, as well as the New York City Chapter of the Young Lords Party, a peer to the Black Panther Party.[56]

Focusing on links, another essay explores how incarcerated people translated and transformed the Black Power and Black Arts Movements from behind prison walls. Drawing from the period's interest in prisoners and prisons, their strong ties to political and cultural workers outside prison walls, and their own creative talents and social commitments, incarcerated people both energized the Black Arts Movement and launched a vital but short-lived Prison Arts Movement. Another essay explores the parallels between the Black Power and Women's Liberation Movements, as well as their cultural corollaries, the Black Arts and Feminist Art Movements. Exposing their close resemblances in terms of traits, tendencies, tactics, and goals, this essay argues that—though strikingly few cultural workers were able to concretely bridge them—these two parallel movements were ideologically linked by their shared common goal for their imagined allies and kin—social and psychological liberation and freedom from oppression. Both Black Power activists and Women's liberationists, kindled by the same flame that ignited many radical movements of the 1960s and 1970s, dared to create a world where they could thrive, be safe, and feel connected, authentic, and whole.

This fire is still burning. AFRI-COBRA remains active. It has gained an international dimension and a diasporic focus. In a 2002 interview, Jeff Donaldson explained: "We found that there were groups all over the world, that wanted a group that would express the same ideals--in Nigeria, in Martinique, in Senegal, in Côte d'Ivoire, in Mozambique. All of the names [countries] had a relation to an atavistic vision of tomorrow, a worldview that is consistent with our heartbeats. We now have shows with sixty-eight artists from twenty-two countries."[57] Haki Madhubuti's Third World Press is another luminous legacy of the Black Arts Movement. It is now the preeminent publishing press owned by African Americans. The most emblematic sign of the ongoing fire, however, may be the direct connection between the orality and performance-oriented nature of Black Arts poetry and contemporary African American poetry. The last section of *Role Call*, a recent anthology of young African American poets, fiction writers, and visual artists, is titled "Black Fire." Clearly a legacy of the Black Arts Movement, Third World Press published this anthology in 2002. In his foreword, "The Generation Now," Madhubuti introduces these descendants of the Black Arts Movement: "*Role Call* is to this generation what *Black Fire* was to mine."[58] In his poem "Identification Please," Bryant Smith exclaims, "I am light and shadow."[59] As opposed to Larry Neal's insistence in *Black Fire* that the "light is black," this contemporary poet takes "Black is Beautiful" for granted to such an extent that he can identify with both light and shadow.[60] The impulse to mix forms and cross genres is one of the looming legacies of the Black Arts Movement and *Role Call* feels this tug as it mixes poetry, prose, music, and art.

Role Call is a response to Baraka's "calling all black people" in his poem "SOS," published in *Black Magic* (1969). The young editors present the call as an open invitation to create and share. The elongation and repetition of words within Black Arts performative poetry was bequeathed to the younger generation. The words "It's nation ti eye ime" in Baraka's legendary poem "It's Nation Time" (1969) continue to enchant as the younger poets find space within this long sustained chant to improvise new chants.[61] At the end of their opening statement in *Role Call*, the three editors playfully assert, "*Say it loud! I'm black and I'm . . .*" Instead of filling in the blank space, they tease, "Uh huh. Thought so."[62] Within the creative space dug by black pride practitioners, contemporary art has flourished. This signals that the fire is still burning. The fire is still felt in some sites and the embers warm all of our hands.

NOTES

1. *Report of the National Advisory Commission on Civil Disorders* (Washington, DC: U.S. Government Printing Office (March 1, 1968), 1.

2. *Report*, 65.

3. Ibid., 60–61.

4. Ibid., 197.

5. Ibid., 1. The report was available for $2 through the U.S. Government Printing Office. In addition, *The New York Times*, in conjunction with E. P. Dutton, republished the report, with an introduction by Tom Wicker, in April 1968.

6. Ibid.

7. Ibid., 2.

8. Ibid., 11.

9. Stokely Carmichael, *Will the Circle Be Unbroken?: An Audio History of the Civil Rights Movement in Five Southern Communities and the Music of Those Times*, audiocassette, tape 7, episode 20. Atlanta, GA: Southern Regional Council, 1997.

10. Statement by H. Rap Brown, July 26, 1967; reprinted in *Black Power: SNCC Speaks for Itself: A Collection of Interviews and Statements* (Ann Arbor, MI: Radical Education Project, 1967), 5.

11. President Lyndon B. Johnson's Address to the Nation on Civil Disorders, 27 July 17, 1967; reprinted in *Report of the National Advisory Commission on Civil Disorders*, 297.

12. *Report*, 4.

13. Ibid.

14. LeRoi Jones/Amiri Baraka, "November 1966: One Year Eight Months Later," *Onyx* (1966); reprinted in *Raise Race Rays Raze: Essays Since 1965* (New York: Random House, 1971), 29. See also LeRoi Jones, "The Legacy of Malcolm X and The Coming of the Black Nation," chap. in *Home* (New York: William Morrow & Company, 1966). LeRoi Jones was honored with the Arabic name Ameer Barakat ("Blessed Prince") in 1967. Soon after, he changed the spelling and pronunciation of his name slightly to Amiri Baraka.

15. Larry Neal, "New Space/The Growth of Black Consciousness in the Sixties," in *The Black Seventies*, ed. Floyd B. Barbour (Boston: Porter Sargent, 1970), 27. In terms of his "cultural thrust," Malcolm X had forcefully called for the launching of a "cultural revolution" at a Harlem rally devoted to announcing the aims and objectives of his Organization of Afro-American Unity (OAAU). On June 28, 1964, Malcolm X declared from the stage of the Audubon Ballroom: "Our culture and our history are as old as man himself and yet we know almost nothing of it. We must recapture our heritage and our identity if we are ever to liberate ourselves from the bonds of white supremacy. We must launch a cultural revolution to unbrainwash an entire people. Our cultural revolution must be the means of bringing us closer to our African brothers and sisters. It must begin in the community and be based on community participation. Afro-Americans will be free to create only when they can depend on the Afro-American community for support and Afro-American artists must realize that they depend on the Afro-American community for inspiration." Malcolm X, Statement of Basic Aims and Objectives of the Organization of Afro-American Unity," in *New Black Voices: An Anthology of Contemporary Afro-American Literature*, ed. Abraham Chapman (New York: Penguin, 1972), 563.

16. *Report*, 5.

17. Ibid., 76, 333.

18. Ibid. In the survey of "black consciousness" in Newark, those not involved in the riots preferred to be called "Negro" over "Black" and "Colored."

19. Ibid.

20. Ibid. 79.8 percent of participants and 68.8 percent of those not involved affirmed the statement.

21. Larry Neal, "The Black Arts Movement," *The Drama Review* 12: 4 (1968): 29–39; reprinted in *Visions of a Liberated Future: Black Arts Movement Writings* (New York: Thunder's Mouth Press, 1989), 62.

22. Amiri Baraka, "Foreword: The Wailer," in *Visions of a Liberated Future*, x.

23. Larry Neal, "Any Day Now: Black Art and Black Liberation," *Ebony* 24:10 (August 1969): 56.

24. Ibid.

25. Ibid., 54.

26. *Report*, 201.

27. Ibid.

28. *Report*, 210.

29. Ibid.

30. Amiri Baraka, "Work Notes—'66," chap. in *Raise Race Rays Raze: Essays Since 1965* 12.

31. James Stewart, "The Development of the Black Revolutionary Artist," in *Black Fire: An Anthology of Afro-American Writing* (New York: William Morrow & Company, 1968), 3.

32. Ibid.

33. In his poem "The Beautiful Day #9," A. B. Spellman muses, "what if his mirror was blackness." *Black Fire*, 245.

34. Imamu Amiri Baraka and Fundi (Billy Abernathy), *In Our Terribleness: Some Elements and Meaning in Black Style* (Indianapolis: Bobbs-Merrill, 1970), 160.

35. "Black Magic" is the name of a 1969 book of poetry written by Amiri Baraka. The role of the black magician is also a principal theme in Baraka's play *A Black Mass* (1966). The very idea of "black magic" became a key part of the Black Arts Movement reclamation of the "black primitive." The "science" undergirding racial primitivism is defied when magic is connected to reason and intelligence as the old primitivist binaries are destroyed. In her poem "Of Liberation" (1970), Nikki Givoanni celebrates "The Resurrection of Blackness," Nikki Giovanni, *Black Feeling Black Talk/ Black Judgement* (New York: Morrow Quill, 1979), 48.

36. Jeff Donaldson, "Africobra 1: African Commune of Bad Relevant Artists," *Black World* 19 (October 1970): 83–86.

37. Ibid., 85.

38. Ibid., 80–89.

39. Baraka, *In Our Terribleness*, 122.

40. Terry Eagleton, *The Ideology of the Aesthetic* (Oxford: Blackwell, 1990), 93–94.

41. Baraka, *In Our Terribleness*, 131.

42. In a 2003 interview, this interviewee articulated this idea of "wearing our culture, our Africa" as she explained her memories of body politics during the Chicago Black Arts Movement.

43. "Introduction," Don L. Lee, *Directionscore: Selected and New Poems* (Detroit: Broadside Press, 1971), 29.

44. Stewart, "The Development of the Black Revolutionary Artist," 4–5.

45. In 1965, The Black Arts Repertory Theater/School (BARTS) in Harlem was organized by LeRoi Jones, and followed by the creation of Spirit House in Newark, New Jersey. In 1967, the Organization of Black American Culture (OBAC) was founded in Chicago; its legendary members included Gwendolyn Brooks, Haki Madhubuti, and Hoyt Fuller, the editor of *Negro Digest/ Black World*. An artistic workshop named BLKARTSOUTH, in New Orleans, gradually blossomed between 1967 and 1970 once an artistic collective named Free Southern Theater lost its funding to recruit Northern actors. One of the founders of BLKARTSOUTH, Tom Dent, remembers discovering the specificity of his black Southern identity during the Black Arts Movement.

46. Nikki Giovanni, *Black Feeling Black Talk/ Black Judgement*, 20.

47. Ed Bullins, *The Theme is Blackness: "The Corner" and Other Plays* (New York: William Morrow & Company, 1973), 182.

48. "Gwendolyn Brooks," in Lee, *Directionscore*, 89–90.

49. Ibid., 12.

50. Kalamu ya Salaam, "The Last Movement." *Mosaic* 13 (Spring 2002): 40.

51. Jones and Neal, *Black Fire*, xvi.

52. Lorenzo Thomas, "The Shadow World: New York's Umbra Workshop and Origins of the Black Arts Movement," *Callaloo* 4: 1 (October 1978): 54. For more on how the Umbra Workshop served as a "predecessor" to the Black Arts Movement and "anticipated" its cultural directions, see Tom Dent, "Umbra Days" *Black American Literature Forum* 14: 3 (Autumn 1980): 105–108.

53. Lorenzo Thomas, "Umbra Writers Workshop," in *Encyclopedia of African-American Culture and History*, ed. Jack Salzman, David Lionel Smith, and Cornel West (New York: Macmillan, 1996), 2696.

54. Thomas, "The Shadow World," 54.

55. Ibid., 68.

56. After a year performing with the Last Poets (1968–69), Felipe Luciano cofounded and became Deputy Chairman of the New York City Chapter of the Young Lords Party during the summer of 1969.

57. Interview of Jeff Donaldson, by Margo Crawford, December 12, 2002, Washington, D.C.

58. Haki R. Madhubuti, "Foreword: The Generation Now," in *Role Call: A Generational Anthology of Social and Political Black Art and Literature*, ed. Tony Medina, Samiya A. Bashir, and Quraysh Ali Lansana (Chicago: Third World Press, 2002), xv.

59. Bryant Smith, "Identification Please," in *Role Call*, 487.

60. In his afterword to *Black Fire*, Larry Neal exclaims, "We are not Kafkaesque creatures stumbling through a white light of confusion and absurdity. The light is black (now, get that!) as are most of the meaningful tendencies in the world"; *Black Fire*, 652.

61. Imamu Amiri Baraka, *It's Nation Time* (Chicago: Third World Press, 1970), 24.

62. Tony Medina, Samiya A. Bashir, and Quraysh Ali Lansana, "Introduction: Call & Response," in *Role Call*, xviii.

I.
CITIES AND SITES

1

Black Light on the
Wall of Respect
The Chicago Black Arts
Movement

Margo Natalie Crawford

The subtleties and nuances of the Chicago Black Arts Movement emerged in the intersections of poetry and visual art. In his essay, "Toward a Definition: Black Poetry of the Sixties" (1971), Chicago-based poet and publisher Haki Madhubuti recounts that "[b]lack art of the sixties, on the national scene, started with the advent of LeRoi Jones ([Amiri] Baraka) and the black theater" and "[w]e in the Midwest felt the pressures from both the west and the east coasts."[1] In "Two Schools, New York and Chicago: Contemporary African-American Photography of the 60s and 70s," a 1986 exhibit of African American photography, curated by Deborah Willis, the distinguishing traits of the Chicago Black Arts Movement photographers and the New York photographers emerge as subtle differences in the representations of black urban style.[2] In order to uncover the specific texture of the Chicago Black Arts Movement, it is necessary to unveil the full significance of the legendary mural, the *Wall of Respect*. This 30 x 60' outdoor mural that was completed in 1967 and destroyed in 1971 became a locus of cultural activity (dance, poetry, drama, and public speaking). In order to understand the specificity of the Chicago Black Arts Movement, we must remember the significance of 43rd and Langley, the economically depressed, culturally rich site of the *Wall of Respect*. In the groundbreaking text, *Black Arts: An Anthology of Black Creations* (1969), poet Askia Muhammad Touré proclaims, "Look at the progress of the Chicago artists—the Wall of Respect plus the community workshops in the arts that they formed. . . . [E]very large Black community should have a Wall of Respect."[3] The *Wall of Respect* was a cultural production that included people who lived in the neighborhood, the artists who painted the mural, the poets who read their work at the *Wall*, the photographers whose art reproduced and preserved the *Wall*, and the many Black Arts participants who lived in other parts of Chicago's "South Side" but gravitated toward this cultural center. In order to understand the significance of the transformation of a brick wall of a building into a veritable cultural center without walls, we must zoom in and zoom out in order to appreciate both the intensely local flavor of the Chicago Black Arts Movement and the national scope of this local movement.

Amiri Baraka's collaboration with a Chicago Black Arts Movement photographer, Fundi (Billy Abernathy), to produce *In Our Terribleness* (1970), signaled the national scope of the Chicago Black Arts Movement. During Baraka's frequent visits to Chicago in the 1960s, he befriended Fundi Abernathy who, after the publication of *In Our Terribleness*, lived for a few years in Spirit House, the Black Arts collective that Baraka spearheaded, in Newark, New Jersey, after founding the Black Arts Repertory Theater School in 1965.[4] Baraka's enchantment with Abernathy's photographs of black Chicago led to the production of *In Our Terribleness*, a call and response between Baraka's poetic narrative and Abernathy's black and white photographs of black Chicagoans. Photography is one of the most neglected genres of the Black Arts Movement. *In Our Terribleness*, an "imagetext," a dialogue between words and visual images, is one of the unsung masterpieces of the Movement. Published by Bobbs-Merrill, *In Our Terribleness* continues the black narrative photography tradition that begins with *12 Million Black Voices* (1941), with Richard Wright's prose and photography edited by Edwin Rosskam, and *The Sweet Flypaper of Life* (1955), co-authored by Langston Hughes and the photographer Roy DeCarava.

One sign of the particular black aesthetic that gained momentum between the Chicago Renaissance in the 1940s and the Chicago Black Arts Movement of the 1960s and 1970s is the trajectory from *12 Million Black Voices* to *In Our Terribleness*. *12 Million Black Voices* is a black and white collaboration, a collaboration between Richard Wright and white photographers working within the New Deal's Farm Security Administration project. The photographs of Chicago's Black Belt in *12 Million Black Voices* were created by Edwin Rosskam, born in Germany, and Russell Lee, born in Illinois. As Rosskam remembered many years later the tour of Chicago's Black Belt that Richard Wright gave them, he mused, "I don't know if many white men had the opportunity to see it the way we saw it."[5] In contrast to this black-led interracial tour that led to the memorable merging of image and text, *In Our Terribleness* is a much less acclaimed "black on black" imagetext, Baraka and Abernathy's imaging of the beauty that emerges when a black gaze implodes.

Sylvia (Laini) Abernathy, who arranged the layout of the *Wall of Respect*, also arranged the layout of *In Our Terribleness*. As Jeff Donaldson, one of the founders of AFRI-COBRA and one of the painters who created the *Wall of Respect*, thinks about the "terribleness" of the *Wall*, he insists that the mural was "guerrilla art."[6] In a 2002 interview, as the layers of Donaldson's memory assume a collage effect comparable to the layers of the mural, he explains the "guerrilla" nature of this community centered art that sparked a mural movement in Chicago and throughout the nation. In the first layer of his collage-like memory, he remembers painter William Walker's spearheading of the decision to create the *Wall* and the leader of the gang that gave the approval for the *Wall*. He explains:

> William Walker was caught in the tail end of the WPA; he was a little bit older than the other artists. He had already decided that he was going to paint a mural in the neighborhood of 43rd and Langley and then we [the other artists who become part of the OBAC visual arts workshop] said why don't we all do this. Walker said, we can do this building because I have permission from Herbert [the gang leader]. Herbert liked the idea and Herbert actually purchased the paint. Herbert and his friend painted the wall white. I remember, once when Herbert was ten feet up the ladder, he fell down.
>
> The gang may have been the Blackstone rangers, Egyptian cobras, or a more regional gang. This same gang banger approved the list of people, the heroes, who would be painted on the wall. Herbert's dead body was propped against the wall, maybe in 1968. Herbert and the other gang leaders rejected King and we agreed with them. The people in the neighborhood didn't believe in nonviolence. By 1968, 102 cities were in flames, not in the South where they were praying. After King's death, the politicians took the worst streets and named them "King." They used the elevation of King to "calm them down."[7]

Donaldson's memory of the gang leader's instrumental role in the creation of the *Wall* is invaluable oral history that reveals that the OBAC (Organization of Black American Culture) members were aiming for art that would, in the words of poet Gwendolyn Brooks, "rouse" as opposed to politicians' attempts to quell black protest.[8] The painters of the *Wall of Respect* agreed that artists' names and signatures would not be included on the *Wall*. The collective vision that led to the *Wall*, including academicians and gang leaders, could not be reduced to an individual signature.

The OBAC visual arts workshop decided to shape the mural around the following categories: rhythm and blues, jazz, theater, statesmen, religion, literature, sports, and dance. In each of these categories, the workshop members created a list of the black cultural "heroes" who would be represented on the Wall. The rhythm and blues category included Billie Holiday, Muddy Waters, and James Brown. The statesmen category included Malcolm X, Stokely Carmichael, and Marcus Garvey. Chicago Black Arts Movement photographer Bob Crawford captures the early stages of the creation of the images in the sports category (fig. 1.1). This photograph reveals that the very process of creating the mural was a work of art. The milk crates that were the temporary display stand of the paintings and the hair roller worn by the little girl sitting next to the paintings become a part of the aesthetic sensibility that shaped the *Wall*.

The grassroots community involvement was one of the guerrilla tactics that led to the creation of the *Wall of Respect*. The artists and the gang leaders shared a common list of heroes. The artists did not live in the immediate neighborhood

Fig. 1.1. Bob Crawford,
An early detail of the
Wall of Respect, 1967.
Courtesy of the artist.

surrounding 43rd and Langley but the neighborhood was not the "slum" they invaded. Donaldson explains:

> We knew that if we didn't get the approval, they would mark it up. Plus we agreed with them. We didn't put the Supremes up, or Whitney Young, the head of Urban league, and no Roy Wilkins. Elijah Muhammad wanted his image removed because Malcolm was there. The heroes chosen were those who did not compromise their humanity, black people charting their own course, using art to forward the movement of the people, putting art to the service of the movement.[9]

Jeff Donaldson and Elliot Hunter painted the "jazz" category. The chosen heroes included Charles Parker, Ornette Coleman, and Nina Simone. Donaldson remembers his painting of Nina Simone being deeply influenced by one particular woman who lived on 43rd and Langley:

> I was painting Nina Simone when this old lady who lived across the street asked me to come over. She said, 'I got to look at that ugly mothafucka you just painted everyday.' So I changed it. She had all kinds of collages and doilies that she starched so that they took on sculptural forms. Art was all around her house and the walls were painted different colors.[10]

The viewpoint of the "old lady" mattered. Donaldson reshaped his image of Nina Simone because he wanted this most local critic to approve of the art that he was forcing her to "look at . . . everyday." Like this most local critic, the OBAC visual art workshop members were folk artists—artists who understood that "art was all around" and aesthetic judgments could sometimes take the simple form of "that ugly mothafucka."

Jeff Donaldson directed the OBAC visual arts workshop that had close ties to both the OBAC writers' workshop and AACM, the Association for the Advancement of Creative Musicians. The *Wall* was painted in one intense month in the summer of 1967. There were impromptu poetry readings and dance performances as the *Wall* was being created. Donaldson recounts that "while we were painting, while the work was being done, people would come dance or read."[11] During one of the many "dedications" of the *Wall*, Gwendolyn Brooks read poetry. Brooks wrote a poem, "The Wall," in commemoration of this event. In this poem, Brooks celebrates the "Black Power!" that the *Wall* embodied.[12] The meaning of "Black Power!" is defined in this poem as "the old decapitations. . .revised/ the dispossessions beakless."[13] These words underscore the revolutionary sensibility of the creators of the *Wall*, their revision of the old script of African American dispossession. The "slum" building that becomes the site of the mural is simply a sign of the larger dispossession that African Americans have suffered. Looking through the lens of Bob Crawford, one of the Chicago Black Arts Movement photographers in Kenkeleba Gallery's "Two Schools, New York and Chicago: Contemporary African-American Photography of the 60s and 70s" exhibit, we can more fully understand the "Black Power!" that overwhelms Brooks as she thinks about the significance of the *Wall*. In Crawford's photographs of Brooks at the *Wall*, Brooks is the mother figure, the legendary Pulitzer Prize winning poet, embraced by the younger generation (fig.1.2). Brooks is one of the "heroes" painted on the *Wall*. Crawford's photograph of her at the *Wall* presents a double image, a layering of his photographic image and the image of Brooks painted on the *Wall*.

The "thickness" of this double image is a profound testament of the depth of Brooks' involvement in the Chicago Black Arts Movement. In 1950, Brooks won the Pulitzer Prize for Poetry. During the 1960s, she became a mentor for younger poets in the Chicago Black Arts Movement. In *Report from Part One* (1972), Brooks remembers how greatly the younger poets affected her.[14] Brooks and Haki Madhubuti greatly influenced each other during the Black Arts Movement. In the poem "In the Mecca" (1968), after Brooks represents a black poet who wants desperately to create art but lacks "talent" because he is suffocated by the burden of a white literary tradition, she announces that, unlike this poetaster, Don Lee "wants / new art and anthem."[15] With this overt reference to "new art," Brooks demands that we understand her own poetry as situated in the prism of "new [black] art." She imagines the uniqueness and pain of the black people living in "The Mecca," the former white-occupied building in Chicago that becomes an "all-black" space. Brooks' poetry, during the years leading to her Pulitzer Prize, appears in journals targeting a black audience and also occupies an exceptional space within a predominantly "whites only"

Fig. 1.2. Bob Crawford, Gwendolyn Brooks at the *Wall of Respect,* 1967. Courtesy of the artist.

publishing edifice. During the Black Arts Movement, her poetry is reclaimed as an "all-black" space. In the poem "Gwendolyn Brooks" (1969), Madhubuti describes the acclaim that Brooks received in this predominantly "whites only" publishing edifice. The speaker in "Gwendolyn Brooks" inveighs against Brooks' reception by white literati. Madhubuti states sardonically, "[A] whi-te critic said: / 'she's a credit to the negro race.'"[16] During the 1960s Brooks gains a large black readership. In "Gwendolyn Brooks" Madhubuti directly connects Brooks' evolution from a "negro poet" to a "black poet" to the black aesthetic that emerged in the 1960s. The second stanza, in which Madhubuti presents the explosive nature of this black aesthetic, begins with the words, "into the sixties / a word was born . . . BLACK/ & with black came poets/ & from the poet's ball points came:/ black doubleblack purpleblack blueblack beenblack was / black daybeforeyesterday blackerthan ultrablack" (89). The speaker in the poem understands blackness as that which is not "negro." The word "black" that "was born" in the 1960s signified a political and cultural awakening of the "negro." As opposed to the label "fine negro poet" given to Brooks by white literary critics, Madhubuti attributes the intensity of "ultra-black[ness]" to Brooks (89). The final line in this poem is "[B]ro, they been calling that sister by the wrong name" (90).

Baraka's poem "SOS" (1966) also underscores the "calling" or hailing of "black" subjects.[17] The poem begins with the words, "Calling black people / calling all black people, man woman child / Wherever you are."[18] As Baraka repeats the words "calling black people," he reminds us, like the philosopher Louis Althusser, that the enactment of ideology seems as natural as a person, upon answering the telephone, stating, "Yes, speaking" or "This is . . . "[19] Ideology makes the person assume the subject position that seems as natural and instinctual as these responses to the question, "Hello, may I speak to . . . ?" In "SOS," Baraka urges the conscious assumption of a new ideology, "blackness," that will overthrow the ideologies of slavery, anti-black racism, and racial self-hatred. In *In Our Terribleness*, Baraka reminds us that "ideology and style are the same thing."[20] The blackness that Baraka "hails" is ideology and style, both the content and the form of the art produced during the Black Arts Movement.

Edward Christmas painted the poem "SOS" on the *Wall of Respect* (fig. 1.3). The painting of the poem testifies to the concerted effort during the Black Arts Movement to make poetry concrete. In "Black Art" (1968), Baraka insists that "[p]oems are bullshit unless they are / teeth or trees or lemons / piled on a step."[21] When Edward Christmas paints "SOS," he insists that "poems are bullshit unless" they are painted on the *Wall* for an entire community to experience as both visual art and the written word. Christmas demonstrates that the written word itself must become visual art. In the left panel of the painting,

Christmas includes the profile of a pensive black man. The words "calling black people" are painted near the closed lips of the venerable face. Edward Christmas responds to Baraka's "call" as he paints the words in "SOS." The painting of this key Black Arts Movement poem signals the fusion of forms at the heart of this movement. Christmas reveals that, within the Black Arts ethos, poetry should be concrete enough to be painted and visual art should be concrete enough to articulate the "call." The blurred words in Edward Christmas' painting of "SOS" force the viewer to squint in order to read this "call." The *Wall* was a prime example of "black light," one of the recurrent metaphors for the dazzling new ways of seeing evoked during this movement.

MADHUBUTI, BROOKS, AND THE METAPHOR OF BLACK LIGHT

In "The Negro" (1968), Madhubuti muses on the possibility of "black light" as he thinks about the racist underpinnings of the associations of light with enlightenment. Madhubuti writes, "Swinging, Swinging, / into aberration where there is a black light trying to penetrate that whiteness called mr. clean" (65). In the seminal Black Arts Movement anthology, *Black Fire* (1968), Larry Neal unpacks this "black light." He explains, "We know who we are, and we are not invisible, at least not to each other. We are not Kafkaesque creatures stumbling through a white light of confusion and absurdity. The light is black (now, get that!) as are most of the meaningful tendencies in the world."[22] Neal denaturalizes "white light" as he reveals that optics itself has been tainted by the racist privileging of whiteness. This discussion of white versus black light is omnipresent in *Black Fire*. In "Pome. For Wierd. Hearts. & All you mothers" (1968), Ahmed Alhamisi refers to "white light" as that which teaches black people to hate themselves (428). In "The Tide Inside, It Rages!," one of the essays in *Black Fire*, the novelist Lindsay Barrett theorizes about black light in the following manner: "Today, what the artistic sensibility of the black man spreads before the world as evidence of his social and historic dilemma, is really the articulation of a protest against the white denial of the possibility or existence of black light, and the superimposition, on his knowledge of this black light, of the hostile white light of Western history" (150). Barrett recognizes that the very "possibility" and "existence" of black light is hard to imagine due to the glare of white light.

Black light became the movement's trope for an imagined resolution of an imagined contradiction. Black Arts Movement poets, photographers, and theorists wrestled to imagine new aesthetic experiences of light itself. A veritable meditation on black light is embedded in the poetry and photography of the Chicago Black Arts Movement. The photography of Crawford and Abernathy illuminates the black light that Brooks and Madhubuti celebrate in their poetry. In the poem "An Aspect of Love, Alive in the Ice and Fire" (1971), Brooks describes a "black is beautiful" sensibility that experiences "Afrikan velvet" skin as "a physical light in the room" (479). The idea that Afrikan velvet skin is the embodiment of light subverts the deep-seated connection of light and whiteness. In "Intermission" (1949), one of Brooks' pre-Black Arts Movement poems, the speaker admits, "It is plausible. The sun is a lode," after she implores the "daughter of the dusk" to "[s]tand off. . ./ And do not wince when the bronzy lads / Hurry to cream-yellow shining" (137). The use of the word "lode" conveys the idea of the sun being akin to a layer of minerals in the body, perhaps just underneath the surface skin, making some skin tones "bright." The word "lode" can also signify a rich supply. As demonstrated by Baraka's reference to the "sun people," dark-skinned blackness is often imagined as "having" the most sun.[23] As the speaker of the poem confesses that desire for light-skinned blackness is not surprising, we hear Brooks herself wince as she realizes that if the sun is a rich supply, desire for dark-skinned blackness should be just as "plausible" as desire for "cream-yellow shining." In "Ballad of Pearl May Lee" (1945), Brooks fully unveils the pain light-skinned privilege causes dark-skinned black women. In one of the most scathing stanzas the speaker taunts Sammy with the following words, "At school, your girls were the bright little girls. / You couldn't abide dark meat. / Yellow was for to look at, / Black for the famished to eat. / Yellow was for to look at, / Black for the famished to eat" (61). Brooks critiques the sexual "consumption" of dark-skinned blackness and the beauty attributed to light-skinned blackness. In *The Sexual Politics of Meat* (1990), feminist critic Carol Adams argues that, when people consume meat, what they are eating is an "absent referent" (14–15), the reality of blood and slaughter sanitized by the supermarket packaging of meat. Brooks imagines the horror of "yellow" women becoming the "absent referent" as dark-skinned blackness is consumed, the horror of a black male gaze that places "yellow" women on a beauty standard pedestal and views dark-skinned black women as sexual prey ("black for the famished to eat" [61]).

This consumption of blackness begs to be contrasted with Baraka's response, in *In Our Terribleness*, to one of Abernathy's photographs of a dark-skinned young man: "You shd been there man / like you shda been eatin sun" (17). The reclamation of racial primitivism embedded in Baraka's celebration of the black "sun people" leads Baraka to fetishize the darkest shades of blackness. If fetishism is always the huge overcompensation for a notion of lack that has often been naturalized, the dark skin tone of the subject photographed in the image that accompanies the words "you shda been eatin sun" is the huge overcompensation for the lack of whiteness. The photograph is a "close-up" that accentuates all the features that antiblack racism has vilified. Dark-skinned blackness, in so many Black Arts Movement texts, becomes an embodiment of the "black light" that many of the poets and visual artists were discovering. In "The Self-Hatred of Don L. Lee" (1968), Madhubuti, formerly known as Don L. Lee, describes the trajectory from the privilege of light-skinned blackness to "pitch-black paragraphs of 'us, we, me, I' awareness" and "hatred of [the] light brown outer."[24] The speaker confesses, in the final stanza of the poem, "i began to love only a part of me—my inner self which is all black" (55–56). In a post-Black Arts Movement essay, "Race, Rage, and Intellectual Development: A Personal Journey" (1995), as Madhubuti explains the insidiousness of colorism (the privileging of lighter shades of blackness within the palette of shades of blackness), he remembers his mother's beauty as "illuminated by very light skin color that attracted the darkest of black men" (249). It is significant that Madhubuti muses on this "yellow light" three decades after the Black Arts Movement. He and other Black Arts poets focused on the possibility of a "black light" illuminating the beauty of dark-skinned blackness. The very words "black light" circulated between writers such as Madhubuti and Larry Neal and visual artists such as Faith Ringgold.[25]

This "black light" becomes the modus operandi of the black and white photography produced during the Black Arts Movement.[26] Cultural critic Kobena Mercer, while analyzing the photography of Robert Mapplethorpe, has argued that black and white photography is racial fetishism, the fetishism of the contrast between whiteness and blackness. Since dark skin absorbs light, the "black" subject of black and white photography, depending on the amount of light used, can be lightened or darkened. In the poem "Judy-One," Haki Madhubuti reveals that, during the Black Arts Movement, black and white photography was reclaimed as the process of embodying darkness as opposed to entering light, the racially inflected understanding of photography crystallized in the following passage written by the French psychoanalyst, Jacques Lacan: "It is through the gaze that I enter light and it is from the gaze that I receive its effects. Hence it comes about that the gaze is the instrument through which light is embodied and through which—if you will allow me to use a word, as I often do, in a fragmented form—I am *photo-graphed*" (106).

In the first two stanzas of "Judy-One" (1970), Madhubuti writes, "She's the camera's / subject: / the sun for colored film / her smile is like / clear light bouncing off / the darkness of the / mediterranean at nighttime" (75). As opposed to dark skin absorbing light, our normal understanding of what happens when dark skin is photographed, Madhubuti imagines "light bouncing off / the darkness," as if the skin itself becomes a projector instead of an absorbent of a white gaze. When Madhubuti begins the poem by announcing that Judy is the "sun for colored film," it is clear that there is a conscious assumption of a new metaphysics of darkness, one in which darkness is a "way of seeing and being seen," and dark skin when photographed is not "captured" by light but, rather, a projector of light—"black light."[27]

In "The Wall" (1968), Madhubuti's commemoration of the *Wall of Respect*, black light is figured as the "black beauty" that "hurts" (66). In the opening lines of "The Wall," the black aesthetic is presented as a "weapon": "sending their negro / toms into the ghetto / at all hours of the day / (disguised as black people) / to dig / the wall, (the weapon) / the mighty black wall (we chase them out—kill if necessary)" (66). The "negro [uncle] toms" are the subject of Madhubuti's poem "The New Integrationist" (1968): "i seek integration of negroes with black people" (51). In "The Wall," the word "negro" as opposed to "black" signifies those who are not consciously fighting "white power." In a 2002 interview, Jeff Donaldson remembers this "white power" as the FBI surveillance during the creation of the Wall: "FBI and Cointelpro infiltrated the movement. I received a note once that warned me what would happen 'the next time you climb that ladder.'"[28] In "The Wall," Madhubuti also thinks about the white power structure's attempt to stop the creation of the *Wall*. The *Wall of Respect* terrified the white power structure that feared the type of "black power" and grassroots community organization that the *Wall* represented. In Gwendolyn Brooks' poem "The Wall" (1968), there is an explicit equation of the *Wall* and "black power": "Black / boy-men on roofs fist out 'Black Power!' Val, / a little black stampede / in African / images of brass and flowerswirl, / fists out 'Black Power!"[29] As Brooks recalls Val Gray, a dramatist and poet, performing at the *Wall*, the meaning of the *Wall of Respect* becomes comparable to the meaning of the "black power" fist in 1967—black self-determination, black solidarity, and "black rage," the name of William Grier and Price Cobb's influential 1969 treatise. During the Black Arts Movement, the black power fist was often accompanied by the words "Power to the People!" In the poem "The Wall" Madhubuti makes the *Wall of Respect* emblematic of the words "art for people's sake."

Madhubuti muses, "[B]lack on gray it's hip," as he thinks about the color scheme of this mural.[30] The black and white photography that was mounted on it complemented this black and gray color scheme. In "The Wall," Madhubuti writes, "[B]lack photographers deal blackness for / the mighty black wall" (67). The photography of Robert Sengstacke, Darrell Cowherd, Billy Abernathy, and Roy Lewis was framed and mounted on it. The mural became a gathering point for Chicago Black Arts Movement photographers. As it was photographed, the process of creating it became inseparable from the final product. The photographers of the mural also reveal the relationship between "space and identity," the ways that the identities and styles of the people who lived in the neighborhood of 43rd and Langley shaped the cultural production of the *Wall*. In the photographs of the second phase of the mural, during which some parts of the original *Wall of Respect* are altered and buildings on the opposite side of the street are painted as an extension, the photographer Bob Crawford makes it impossible to separate the artistry of the mural from the style of the people interacting with it (fig. 1.4).[31] As the subjects in this photograph lean against the *Wall*, their style (the way they stand, the way they dress) complements the images painted on the mural. The *Wall* isn't the background; the photographer makes the *Wall* become as "alive" as the subjects he photographs. The "coolness" of the subjects photographed somehow merges with the anger and rage in the painting depicting the confrontation of the white and black profiles. The "coolness" of the subjects photographed becomes the bridge between the

Fig. 1.4. Bob Crawford,
Detail of the second
phase of the *Wall of
Respect,* 1967.
Courtesy of the artist.

rage in the painting and the words "peace" and "salvation" painted in the oval
border.

The second phase of the *Wall* included the creation of the *Wall of Truth*
across the street from the *Wall of Respect.* A sign posted on the *Wall of Truth*
announced, "We the people of this community claim this [building] in order
to preserve what is ours." The Black Arts Movement was often a reclamation
of black urban style and a bold seizure of public property. In *In Our Terribleness,* when Baraka insists, "We know these cities are ugly. We know they are
examples of white art, white feeling (?) . . . . The Empire State Building is a
white man," it is clear that Baraka understands the connection between space
and identity.[32] The creation of the *Wall of Respect,* and its extension, the *Wall of
Truth,* is one prime example of the Black Arts Movement's conscious attempt
to create new spaces from which new identities would arise. In "The children
of the poor" (1949), Gwendolyn Brooks implores the oppressed to "First fight.
Then fiddle / . . . Rise bloody, maybe not too late/ For having first to civilize a
space."[33] During the Black Arts Movement, Brooks gains a new appreciation of
free verse poetry, however, her earlier adept use of the sonnet enables the sonnet itself to become the site where she "first . . . civilize[s] a space" (118). Just
as Brooks "civilizes" the savage elitism that the sonnet can signify, the artists
who create the *Wall of Respect* "civilize" the savage poverty of the urban jungle
in Chicago's "South Side."

REMEMBERING THE AESTHETIC WARFARE IN CHICAGO

Ebony magazine articles, published between 1967 and 1970, celebrated the *Wall of Respect*, Gwendolyn Brooks, Haki Madhubuti, the Affro Arts Theater, and the emergence of "natural black beauty." *Ebony* magazine, like *Negro Digest/ Black World*, was a vital part of the cultural production of the Chicago Black Arts Movement.[34] *Ebony* announced the emergence of the Chicago Black Arts Movement to a national audience.[35] In a 1967 issue of *Ebony* magazine, an article on the *Wall of Respect* is preceded and followed by advertisements for bleaching cream and straight hair wigs. The aesthetic warfare between the bleaching cream advertisements and the signs of "Black is Beautiful" on the *Wall of Respect* reminds us that the mission of the *Wall of Truth*, the "[re]claim[ing] of [buildings] in order to preserve what is ours," included the reclamation of black bodies unaltered by bleaching cream and straight hair wigs (fig. 1.5). In one of the advertisements for bleaching cream, in the same 1967 issue of *Ebony* that celebrates the revolutionary "Black is Beautiful" aesthetic of the *Wall of Respect*, an image of "brighter, clearer skin!" is used to market "Dr. Fred Palmer's Skin Whitener."[36] The cover story in this 1967 *Ebony* issue is the emergence of the "natural" hairstyle.[37] The magazine cover announces "Natural hair—New symbol of race pride"; another story title listed on the cover is "New Trend toward Black Beauties." The bleaching cream aesthetic and the black aesthetic that celebrated the "natural" and undergirded the creation of the *Wall of Respect* were literally part of the same cultural text, the pages of *Ebony* magazine.

Just as the national scope of the Chicago Black Arts Movement was signaled by the merging of New York/New Jersey and Chicago when Baraka and Abernathy collaborated in order to produce *In Our Terribleness*, the black celebrities and public figures who visited the *Wall of Respect* are evidence of the national scope of this local movement. Nina Simone, one of the jazz "heroes" painted on the *Wall*, traveled to Chicago in order to see this legendary mural. The famous black actress Eartha Kitt also visited the *Wall*. Eartha Kitt's interaction with the Chicago Black Arts Movement is represented in Bob Crawford's 1968 photograph of Kitt in Ellis bookstore (fig. 1.6). Like the *Wall of Respect*, the OBAC meetings, and the Affro Arts Theater, Ellis bookstore, located on 65th and Cottage Grove Avenue, was one of the cultural centers of the Chicago Black Arts Movement. In Crawford's photograph of Kitt, the celebrity face looks away from the camera as the lens focuses on the "black culture" she holds tenderly. The books she holds, *The Books of American Negro Spirituals* and *The Lost Cities of Africa*, become signs, in this photograph, of "black consciousness." The psychological journey from the "American Negro" to the "lost cities of Africa" is the "spiritual" being sung in this photograph.

Like Ellis bookstore, Third World Press, founded in 1967 by Haki Madhubuti, becomes a cultural center of the Chicago Black Arts Movement. In the 1971 introductory essay to *Directionscore: Selected and New Poems*, Madhubuti asserts that Black nationalism "means publishing our own books" (21). In 1987, Third World Press publishes *Blacks*, a compilation of the wide range of

Fig. 1.5. Bob Crawford, Detail of the *Wall of Truth,* Chicago, Illinois, 1968. Courtesy of the artist.

Gwendolyn Brooks' poetry, published thirty-seven years after Brooks wins the Pulitzer Prize. When the definitive anthology of her work is published by this black-owned press and entitled "Blacks," Brooks and Madhubuti guarantee that Brooks' work will be enshrined in the canon of Chicago Black Arts Movement literature.

There is a call and response, between Madhubuti and Brooks, in their 1960s descriptions of the black aesthetic. In "A Further Pioneer," the opening essay in Madhubuti's volume of poetry *Don't Cry, Scream* (1968), Brooks meditates on the meaning of a black literary aesthetic. She writes:

> Sometimes there is a quarrel. Can poetry be "black"? Isn't all poetry just POETRY? The fact that a poet is black means that his life and the histories of his ancestors have been different from the histories of Chinese and Japanese poets,

Eskimo poets, Indian poets, Irish poets. The juice from tomatoes is not called merely juice. It is always called TOMATO juice. If you go into a restaurant desiring tomato juice you do not order the waiter to bring you "juice": you request, distinctly, TOMATO juice . . . . The poetry from black poets is black poetry. Inside it are different nuances AND outrightnesses. (82–83)

This passage begs to be compared to Madhubuti's insistence, in "Toward a Definition: Black Poetry of the Sixties" (1971), that:

Just as there are the French writer, the Jewish writer, the Russian writer, the African writer, we have the black, or African-American, writer. Black poets have discovered their uniqueness, their beauty, their tales, their history, and have diligently moved to enlighten their people and the world's people in an art form that's called poetry, but to them is another extension of black music. (223)

In this passage, we hear echoes of Langston Hughes' critique, in "The Negro Artist and the Racial Mountain" (1926), of the young poet who wants to be a poet as opposed to a "negro" poet. Both Brooks and Madhubuti emphasize that the specificity of a black literary aesthetic need not be understood as a pigeon-holing or a trap. In a post-Black Arts Movement tribute entitled "The Good Man" (1987), Brooks implores Madhubuti to "[r]ouse our rhyme" in "the time of detachment, in the time of cold."[38] Her use of the word "rouse" recalls her poem "The Wall" in which she describes the creation of the *Wall of Respect* as "the Hour of ringing, rouse, of ferment-festival."[39]

The Chicago Black Arts Movement itself was an "hour of ringing." The *Wall of Respect* was one of the most resounding bells. With the framed photography, paintings, painted poetry, poetry readings, dance performances, and political speeches, the *Wall of Respect* epitomized the breaking of boundaries between genres that defined the Black Arts Movement. The *Wall of Respect* also involved the crossing of boundaries between black people who, in the 1960s, had a middle-class status due to educational opportunities and black people who were economically disenfranchised due to the lack of these educational opportunities.[40] The site of the *Wall of Respect*, the corner of 43rd and Langley, is now undergoing a slow but steady process of gentrification. Condominiums and townhouses have replaced the buildings on which the *Wall of Respect* and its extensions, the *Wall of Truth* and other murals, were painted. In a 2002 interview, Jeff Donaldson explained that the mural was "never meant to be a permanent thing; it was meant to be something that changed with the movement."[41] After interviewing Donaldson, my father, Bob Crawford, and I went searching for a plaque that Donaldson recalled, one that announced "this is where the Wall of Respect was."[42] We didn't find this plaque. Once the gentrified housing was built, the plaque itself must have been demolished. Hoping that this street corner would remain a site of memory, I asked my father to photograph the street sign, 43rd and Langley. I noticed the name of the bus stop has changed from "43rd—ROOT" to "43/43rd." If nostalgia is, as critic Susan Stewart explains, a "sadness without an object," I knew my father and I were guilty.[43]

NOTES

1. Don L. Lee, "Toward a Definition: Black Poetry of the Sixties" in *Within the Circle: An Anthology of African American Literary Criticism from the Harlem Renaissance to the Present*, ed. Angelyn Mitchell (Durham and London: Duke University Press, 1994), 216. This essay first appeared in Addison Gayle, Jr., ed., *The Black Aesthetic* (New York: Doubleday, 1971).

As the Black Arts Movement was unfolding, regional differences were often discussed. In the essay, "The Crisis in Black Culture," in *Black Arts: An Anthology of Black Creations*, ed. Ahmed Alhamisi and Harun Kofi Wangara (Detroit: Black Arts Publications, 1969), 33, Askia Touré argues, "It's a shame that our main journals—*Soulbook*,

Black Dialogue, Journal of Black Poetry—are all located on the West Coast! There should be some kind of regular literary publication representing each area—East Coast, Mid-West, South, and West Coast—as well as publications geared for national and international circulation. The writers in each region should make it their responsibility to organize workshops to train young thinkers and writers in Black Consciousness and New Black writing" (33).

2. This exhibit was held April-May 1986 at the Kenkeleba Gallery, 214 East Second Street, in New York City. In the catalog of this exhibit, Deborah Willis explains, "During the early 1960s, a large number of Black photographers began to study and explore the art of photography in workshops, art schools and community centers in both New York and Chicago . . . . The common thread among the Chicago-based photographers is documentary and/or social landscape photography. The emphasis on the social concerns of the Black community and the experiences of its people is prevalent in the works of the Chicago school."

3. Alhamisi and Wangara, *Black Arts*, 36.

4. After founding the Black Arts Repertory Theater/School on West 130th Street in Harlem, Baraka creates "Spirit House" in Newark, New Jersey. This collective included a performance group, the Spirit House Movers, and a school that Amina Baraka founded in 1967, the African Free School.

5. Maren Stange, *Bronzeville: Black Chicago in Pictures 1941–1943* (New York: The New Press, 2003), xvi.

6. In "The Rise, Fall, and Legacy of the Wall of Respect Movement," *International Review of African American Art* 15:1 (1998): 22–26, Jeff Donaldson explains, "[T]he single most important factor in convincing the group [the OBAC Visual Art workshop] to adopt the project was the idea of a 'guerilla mural.' While Mr. Baker, occupant of the grocery and liquor store, welcomed the idea, the absentee owner of the building was never consulted. The unauthorized action was revolutionary in and of itself, even beyond the effects the project would engender" (22).

7. I interviewed Jeff Donaldson in Washington, D.C., on December 12, 2002. Before beginning his long teaching career at Howard University, Donaldson was a central participant in the Chicago Black Arts Movement.

8. Gwendolyn Brooks, *Blacks* (Chicago: Third World Press, 1987), 511.

9. Author's interview with Jeff Donaldson, December 12, 2002, Washington, D.C.

10. Ibid.

11. Ibid.

12. Brooks, *Blacks*, 444.

13. Ibid., 445.

14. Gwendolyn Brooks, *Report from Part One* (Detroit: Broadside Press, 1972)

15. Brooks, *Blacks*, 423–24.

16. Don L. Lee (Haki Madhubuti), *Directionscore: Selected and New Poems* (Detroit: Broadside Press, 1971), 89.

17. The legendary poem "SOS" was first published in *Black Art* (1966): LeRoi Jones, *Black Art* (Newark: Jihad Productions, 1966), 4.

18. Amiri Baraka, *The LeRoi Jones/Amiri Baraka Reader*, ed. William J. Harris, (New York: Thunder's Mouth Press, 1991), 218.

19. In "Ideology and Ideological State Apparatuses (Notes towards an Investigation)," in *Lenin and Philosophy and Other Essays* (New York: Monthly Review Press, 1971,

first published in *La Pensée*, 1970), 127–186, Louis Althusser explains, "We all have friends who, when they knock on the door and we ask, through the door, the question, 'Who's there?,' answer (since 'it's obvious') 'It's me.' And we recognize that 'it is him,' or 'her.'"

20. Imamu Amiri Baraka and Fundi (Billy Abernathy), *In Our Terribleness* (Indianapolis and New York: The Bobbs-Merrill Company, Inc., 1970), 131.

21. LeRoi Jones and Larry Neal, ed. *Black Fire: An Anthology of Afro-American Writing* (New York: William Morrow & Company, 1968), 302–303.

22. Ibid., 652.

23. As the field of "race and psychoanalysis" continues to emerge, we need to think about the relation between the psychoanalytic idea of "having" the phallus (the male body) versus "being" the phallus (the female body) and the tension, cemented by the American idea of the "one drop rule," between "having" visual signs of whiteness and "being" black. In the psychoanalytic fiction, the woman "is" the phallus in the sense that, once she is objectified, her body is a substitute phallus. In the Freudian story about castration anxiety, the male child sees the mother as both lacking and possessing the male sexual organ. When the male child fetishizes the mother's femininity, supposedly, her body becomes the peculiar site of both presence and absence. The psychoanalytic language of the male who "has" the phallus and the woman who "is" the phallus can be applied to the light skin/dark skin "narcissism of minor differences" that sometimes structures the way black people look at black people. If the phallus is the signifier of cultural power and cannot be reduced to the male sexual organ, it includes white skin. The idea of lack being covered might apply in a literal way to the fetishism of gradations of nonwhite skin color. In psychoanalytic theories of the sexual fetish, "having" the phallus is the position of power whereas "being" the phallus, the reflection of the phallus, is the site of disempowerment. The one drop rule makes "being" white the privileged term and refuses to make "having" whiteness a reflection of the phallus. Anti-black racism is constantly being both internalized and subverted by African Americans so that an imagined phallus of blackness sometimes emerges in addition to a certain dilution anxiety, the sense that dark-skinned blackness is the visual signifier of "roots" and cultural authenticity and that light-skinned blackness is a visual signifier of assimilation and cultural hybridity. In order to understand black fetishism of blackness, the emergent field of race and psychoanalysis needs to focus more on the coexistence, in the African American visual imagination, of desire for "whiteness" and dilution anxiety (fear of loss of "blackness").

24. Lee, *Directionscore*, 55–56.

25. In 1967, Faith Ringgold started her exploration of "black light." There was a "Black Light" exhibit of Ringgold's work at Spectrum Gallery in 1969. Ringgold explains, "In 1967 I had begun to explore the idea of a new palette, a way of expressing on canvas the new 'Black is Beautiful' sense of ourselves. The way we see color is influenced by the colors that surround us. Our own color for instance is indelibly etched in our mind and, unless someone tells us otherwise it influences overall sense of color. As an artist and women of color I had become particularly interested in this idea. I had noticed that black artists tended to use a darker palette. White and light colors are used sparingly and relegated to contrasting color in African-American, South Africans and East African Art. In Western art, however, white and light influence the entire palette, thereby creating

a predominance of infinite, pastel colors and light and shade or chiaroscuro" (162). Dan Cameron, Richard Powell, Michele Wallace, eds., *Dancing at the Louvre: Faith Ringgold's French Collection and Other Story Quilts* (Berkeley: University of California Press, 1998).

26. In the poem "The Convert" (1960), Margaret Danner, a Chicago-born poet who becomes one of the central figures in the Detroit Black Arts Movement, crystallizes the new metaphysics of darkness that became such a principal part of the 1960s and 1970s "Black is Beautiful" sensibility. In the poem, Danner imagines black light in the following manner: "until, finally, I saw on its stern / ebony face, not a furniture polished, shellacked shine, / but a radiance, gleaming as though a small light / had flashed internally" ("The Convert," 5). The "shellacked shine" is the image of dark-skinned blackness created by minstrel shows and their legacies. This poem appears in Danner's *Impressions of African Art Forms* (Detroit: Broadside Press, 1960), a series of poems exploring an African American's process of "falling in love" with African art. Danner imagines a "radiance" that would subvert the glossy minstrel images of dark-skinned blackness. In the opening poem of *Impressions of African Art Forms*, Danner revels in the beauty of "velvet black" after a series of stanzas that begin with the word "Africa" (1). As Danner "falls in love" with African art, she "falls in love" with the darker shades of blackness. As she embraces African art, she embraces the primitivist modernism associated with Picasso's use of African masks. In "The Christmas Soirée and the Missing Object of African Art," she imagines a woman at an artists' party waiting for someone who never arrives: the embodiment of African art. The speaker of the poem muses that, if this embodiment did arrive, the "dean of aesthetics would have echoed/ Picasso in praise" (8). This embodiment of African art has a "symmetrical sheen" and a "smoother-than-panther / and almost as beautifully dark, face" (9), as opposed to the "shellacked shine" of blackface minstrelsy.

27. In *Sent for You Yesterday*, John Edgar Wideman imagines a character Samantha discovering a non-essentialist understanding of "Black is Beautiful" when she discovers that blackness is a "way of seeing and being seen," both a way of thinking and a bodily enactment (135). John Edgar Wideman, *Sent for You Yesterday* (London: Flamingo, 1981), 135.

28. Author's interview with Jeff Donaldson, December 12, 2002, Washington, D.C.

29. Brooks, *Blacks*, 444.

30. Lee, *Directionscore*, 67.

31. As Jeff Donaldson explains that this second phase of the wall was a "horrible alteration," he insists that "art must have an attraction for its own sake" in addition to delivering a political message. (Author's interview with Jeff Donaldson, December 12, 2002, Washington, D.C.)

32. Baraka and Abernathy, *In Our Terribleness*, 136.

33. Brooks, *Blacks*, 118.

34. In 1970, the journal *Negro Digest*, first issued in 1942, is renamed "Black World."

35. An article on Gwendolyn Brooks, "Gwendolyn Brooks—Poet Laureate: Noted Literary Figure is Patron of Young Black Artists," appears in Phyl Garland, "Gwendolyn Brooks—Poet Laureate: Noted Literary Figure is Patron of Young Black Artists," *Ebony* 23: 9 (July 1968): 48–56. An article on Haki Madhubuti (Don Lee), "Black Don Lee: Young Creator of Black Art is Writer-in-Residence at Cornell," appears in *Ebony* 24: 5

(March 1969), 72–80. An article on the Affro-Arts Theater, "Mecca For Blackness: Chicago's Affro-Arts Theater Celebrates African Culture," appears in *Ebony* 25: 7 (May 1970), 96–102.

36. This advertisement appears immediately after an article on Haki Madhubuti (Don Lee) entitled "Black Don Lee," 72–80. The full text in this advertisement is: "nicer things happen with brighter, clearer skin! His admiring glances . . . that look in his eyes! This and more can come true with Dr. Palmer's wonderful, exclusive formula. Your skin will be shades lighter, brighter . . . and a smoother, lovelier, more radiant complexion will be yours. So easy and pleasant to use . . . for removing discoloration from face, neck, hands, elbows, and knees. Its medically prescribed ingredients are also recommended as an aid in eliminating blackheads and refining pores. Women of all skin tones, everywhere, have proven it indispensable . . . so start using it today for a happier, more glowing you" (80).

37. This 1967 issue of *Ebony* includes an article on the Wall of Respect, "Wall of Respect: Artists Paint Images of Black Dignity in Chicago Ghetto," *Ebony* 23: 2 (December 1967): 48–50.

38. Brooks, *Blacks*, 511.

39. Ibid., 445.

40. The crossing of class boundaries was coupled with the local residents' fight against the nonresidents' appropriation of their community as cultural capital. Donaldson explains, "Kids in the neighborhood began to charge people to take pictures. 'I'll mess your car up,' they would tell white and black tourists, anybody who had a camera. They knew, 'If you make money, we ought to too.'" (Author's interview with Jeff Donaldson, December 12, 2002, Washington, D.C.)

41. Author's interview with Jeff Donaldson, December 12, 2002, Washington, D.C.) Donaldson explains that parts of the Wall were moved to Malcolm X City College in Chicago, and DuSable Museum. According to Donaldson, the demolition of the Wall was "an official act of the city." He elaborates, "Ultimately that whole community was condemned by the city as buildings were demolished. Art is dangerous. Once the Wall became a rallying point for a lot of things, the city's powerbrokers were nervous. For example, Ralph Metcalfe, a great athlete, chose to break from the Daley democratic machine, and made the announcement in front of the Wall."

42. Donaldson remembers the plaque being at the top of "three steps that led into the building."

43. In *On Longing: Narratives of the Miniature, the Gigantic, the Souvenir, the Collection*, Susan Stewart writes, "Nostalgia is a sadness without an object, a sadness which creates a longing that of necessity is inauthentic because it does not take part in lived experience. Rather, it remains behind and before that experience. Nostalgia, like any form of narrative, is always ideological: the past it seeks has never existed except as narrative, and hence, always absent, that past continually threatens to reproduce itself as a felt lack" (23). Susan Stewart, *On Longing: Narratives of the Miniature, the Gigantic, the Souvenir, the Collection* (Durham & London: Duke University Press, 1993), 23. In *Bodies that Matter*, Judith Butler echoes this idea when she thinks about the "loss of nostalgia's referent" (101). Judith Butler, *Bodies that Matter: On the Discursive Limits of "Sex"* (New York & London: Routledge, 1993), 101.

2
Black West, Thoughts on
Art in Los Angeles

Kellie Jones

BLACK SPACE/BLACK PLACE

Generally periodized between 1965 and 1976, the Black Arts Movement has
been primarily theorized as literary though like its most recognized forerunner,
the Harlem Renaissance, it encompassed visual, music, theater, and all the arts.
Among its hallmarks were: social and political engagement; a view that art had
the ability to encourage change in the world and in the viewer; separatism—a
belief in a self-contained "black aesthetic" walled off from white culture; forms
that were populist, that could be easily distributed and understood by audiences (broadsides, pamphlets, one-act plays, concerts, representational painting, posters, etc.).

The Black Arts Movement championed the aesthetic pleasure of blackness
and focused on reception by black audiences. It was art with African American
specificity that reflected "the special character and imperatives of black experience."[1] Again as in the Harlem Renaissance the wellspring of African American
creativity was found in vernacular form, the creativity of "the folk" who by the
1960s were recognized as the urban working class and underclass rather than
inhabitants of the rural south. There was also the ancestral legacy of Africa that
became ever more palpable in the ongoing independence struggles of the period. A premium was placed on orality and performativity. Literary forms, like
poetry, that could be "built around anthems, chants, and political slogans"[2]
were favored. Black speech and music were privileged. Music could be popular,
social, sacred, and entertaining; in music one could see more clearly the African
American cultural connections to Africa; music was egalitarian and participatory,
it did not "stress roles of performer and audience but rather of mutual participation in an aesthetic activity."[3] As literary critic David Lionel Smith has theorized, the result of transposing the literary into a musical form was theater.[4]

In the realm of visual art perhaps the most defining voice of the movement was the collective AFRI-COBRA from Chicago which, in 1970, offered some guidelines for artmaking through a set of aesthetic principles; these included: representational imagery, fragmented planes combined with organic form (called free symmetry and rhythm), bright colors (augmented by "shine"), and embedded words which clarified message and content. Thematically, the works should define the past—through a consideration of African heritage; identify the present—in contemporary black heroes; and offer direction for the future—with images of the black family. As AFRI-COBRA was overwhelmingly composed of painters, these tenets, not surprisingly, seem more focused on qualities of two-dimensional art. Mary Schmidt Campbell has also identified other works that dismantled "icons of racism" (including the American flag) and thus fulfilled their role as "weapons" of the black cultural revolution.[5]

The founding of Broadside Press in Detroit, the Association for the Advancement of Creative Musicians (AACM) in Chicago, and the Black Arts Repertory Theater/School (BARTS) in Harlem, all in 1965, makes it the watershed year for the start of the Black Arts Movement. Mirroring these cultural signposts were even more visible social ones, the assassination of Malcolm X and the rebellions in Watts. In roughly the same epoch—1965–1966—we also see the initiation of activism by the US Organization in Los Angeles and the Black Panther Party for Self Defense in Oakland.[6] These groups would prove to be the most influential black nationalist organizations in the coming period. Both emerged from a "militant intellectual culture" that presaged the call for black studies nationwide, and were connected to the Afro-American Association which had branches possibly as early as 1962 at University of California, Los Angeles, headed by Ron Everett (later Karenga), and in the Bay Area centered around University of California, Berkeley, and Merritt College in Oakland which had Huey Newton as one of its members.[7]

While the Black Panthers and US shared the goal of African American empowerment, the approaches were different; the Black Panthers called for immediate armed struggle to this end, while US championed a revolution in black cultural life and thought as a precursor to radical material transformation. Both US and the Panthers took the strict view that art must be "a tool for liberation,"[8] that it "must expose the enemy, praise the people, and support the revolution."[9] Or to use Karenga's famous three criteria, it must be "functional, collective, and committing."[10] Though based in Los Angeles, Karenga's program of black cultural nationalism became more widespread among artists because of its adoption by the poet and playwright Amiri Baraka (the former LeRoi Jones), one of the most influential voices of the time who, in fact, gave the Black Arts Movement its name.[11] While more has been written about activities on the East Coast and in the Midwest, indeed much of the ideological force behind the Black Arts Movement came from California.[12]

In writing about art practices in the 1960s and 1970s and site-specific art in particular, Miwon Kwon has spoken of art that ceded to its environment, placed itself in the context of the world, and became enamored of a public role which penetrated social frameworks and concerned itself with contemporary life and issues (rather than solely with internal dynamics).[13] All of these qualities could be found in the precepts and artwork of the Black Arts Movement. Considered more broadly, such ideas—a concern with the social/political landscape, and individuals' relationship to the polis and the larger world—were what many African Americans, artists and non-artists, were grappling with during this era. Like the practices Kwon names, these people insinuated themselves in the environment in a quest to claim and hold space. The Watts rebellions, the activities of US, the Black Panthers, the Black Arts Movement, and other social, political, and cultural formations of African Americans in the 1960s were all about opening a larger arena for black culture and life, insisting on its visibility, its place as human and equal, and its viable contribution to the existence and history of the United States.

Kwon has identified the concept of "site" as simultaneously "phenomenological, social/institutional, and discursive."[14] While the first two iterations are fairly self-explanatory, site in its discursive sense threads itself through all types of spaces, concrete, ethereal, as well as those of memory. Kwon's formulations share similarities with poststructuralists such as Henri Lefebvre who outlines a theory of space that is at once mental, physical, and social, defined through "knowledge and action," outlined through a collection of social practices, and that is a social product;[15] or Michel Foucault's heterotopia that is more trace, "the habitus of social practices."[16] In the example of the Watts rebellions we see this marking and claim of territory through violence. Yet, the same action of defining and asserting one's place in the world is also found in the Black Panthers' championing of self-defense, communications, and social programs, in the development by US of new cultural traditions such as Kwanzaa, and the poems, theater, music, and art gathered under the rubric of the Black Arts Movement.

In Los Angeles, artists and other social actors delineated space and place in a rapidly changing and increasingly globalized society. The city's fortunes shifted as it went from being one of the world's largest areas of growth in the immediate postwar period, to a scarred map of urban deindustrialization in the 1960s and 1970s, demonstrating signs of crisis and conflict as it devolved into a militarized enterprise zone for world capital.[17] Many of the African American artists discussed here (and/or their parents) had migrated to California from the South and the Midwest seeking opportunity and a less restrictive life. Like theorist Saskia Sassen's classic protagonists that fuel globalized urban economies, they were "new city users" staking their claim through imaginative cultural forms and identities.[18] It was this energy that artists in Los Angeles would transform into a visual language for their time.

ODE TO WATTS

After 1910, Los Angeles became the center of California's black population and a vibrant cultural mecca.[19] A lively music scene grew up along Central

Avenue as well as in Watts into the 1950s. At mid-century, visual artists—like William Pajaud, Curtis Tann, Betye Saar, Camille Billops, and even Charles White—began to create informal networks, producing exhibitions in churches and homes. White had relocated to Los Angeles in 1956, bringing with him a practice inspired by social realism and progressive politics. A younger generation of artists, those more fully a part of the Black Arts Movement, connected directly with White's activist voice when he began teaching at Otis Art Institute in L.A. in 1965.[20]

Around 1962, Ruth Waddy started a more formal artist organization called Art West Associated. Formed in dialogue with the Civil Rights Movement, Waddy's intention was a civic activism that would create more opportunity for African American artists. Some of those involved with the group included Dale and Alonzo Davis—who in a few years time would start Brockman Gallery—and Chestyn Everett, elder brother of Ron Karenga. It was Chestyn with whom Karenga first stayed when he arrived in Los Angeles from rural Maryland in 1958 upon his graduation from high school.[21]

Other influential figures in the evolution from 1950s types of art practices to those that more fully embodied the goals of the Black Arts Movement included Melvin Edwards and Jayne Cortez. Edwards had a meteoric rise in the burgeoning mainstream Los Angeles art scene before he was thirty. His growing political consciousness led him to make his first *Lynch Fragments* there in the mid-1960s using the welding technique that would become his signature. At that same moment, Cortez was creating works that can be referred to as performance pieces, combining literature, jazz, visual art, and politics (in 1963 she worked with the Student Non-Violent Coordinating Committee (SNCC) in Mississippi and with founding a branch in Los Angeles). Cortez is one of the figures who first embodies what is understood as the aesthetics of the Black Arts Movement with its base in oral poetry and verse and its connection to political struggle and black communities.[22]

The rebellions in Watts during August 1965 changed things; changed people's expectations and the way they looked at the world; changed artists' approach to their craft, and their materials, and led them to question what art might be and do. The Watts rebellions galvanized people to write about these experiences, sing and play about them, create objects about them; to take what had happened and turn it into something else called art. In the post-1965 era there was an outpouring of creativity from African Americans in Los Angeles in all areas. Given that poetry was one of the key expressive forms of the Black Arts Movement, it is not surprising that Los Angeles became home to numerous writers in the late 1960s.

Immediately after the rebellions, screenwriter Budd Schulberg began a writers workshop as a way to bridge the divide between white and black Los Angeles. Known as the Watts Writers' Workshop, it eventually published an anthology under the title, *From the Ashes: Voices of Watts*.[23] Quincy Troupe was already a published poet by the time he arrived in Los Angeles in the mid-1960s.[24]

His earliest book-length work was the edited collection *Watts Poets: A Book of New Poetry and Essays* (1968) which included some of the Watts Writers' collective (Ojenke and Emory Evans) as well as others such as K. Curtis Lyle, Eric Priestly, and Stanley Crouch; another contributor was Elaine Brown who was a singer and songwriter before dedicating her energies to the Black Panthers.[25] These artists and others like Wanda Coleman and Kamau Daaood, performed their poetry at places such as the Watts Happening Coffee Shop—a former furniture showroom that was transformed into a performance space after the rebellions. Another regular there was Horace Tapscott, a pianist and leader of the Pan-Afrikan Peoples Arkestra begun in 1961 to preserve and perform black music for the benefit of African American communities; Jayne Cortez figured among the group's early collaborators. [26]

The Watts Summer Festival became one of the most well known cultural institutions in the community. Among its founders was Ron Karenga, head of the recently formed US Organization, which, with its cultural nationalist profile, was thus identified with the event from the outset.[27] Starting with its own members US set out to educate African Americans about African history, language and traditions, and through its program "construct a new black culture."[28] US members (known as "advocates") wore African-inspired attire, and took African (Swahili) names. Indeed, a key aspect of Karenga's program was the creation of rituals that focused on contemporary milestones in African American life. These were acknowledgements of "status elevation" and "status reversal" which sought to replace an apparently bankrupt black cultural inheritance.[29] The institutionalization of the *Kwanzaa* celebrated in December is the most visibly lasting part of the US legacy. Other events included *Dhabihu* (sacrifice)—commemorating Malcolm X's sacrifice of life for African Americans; held February 22, 1966, it also marked the first public appearance of US.[30] *Uhuru* (freedom) Day—celebrated on August 11—marked the Watts rebellions.

Begun a year after the rebellions, the Watts Summer Festival embodied ideas of rebirth and celebration as well as commemoration. While some law enforcement officials rejected it because of the seeming tribute to acts of violence and uprising against the state, the Los Angeles County Commission on Human Relations fostered the idea of an "anti-riot coalition" and the event as a way to curtail future hostilities and activism.[31] Featuring an array of African and African American cultural displays including art, crafts, and music, the Watts Summer Festival was held from 1966 through the mid-1980s. Its heyday, however, was from 1966 to 1973, the high point of the Black Arts Movement.

Over the years, the Watts Summer Festival always hosted exhibitions of visual art, placing focus on supporting community artists who often made work specifically for the venue. This tradition was perhaps related to how art had initially appeared there, in an exhibition called "66 Signs of Neon," comprised of work created from the material evidence of the Watts uprising.

Among the earliest as well as the longest lasting evidence of Watts as a cultural hub are the famed "Towers" that have marked the site for most of the twentieth century. Created by Simon Rodia, an Italian immigrant and laborer, between 1921 and 1954, they are composed of a series of interconnected spires of steel rods and concrete embedded with shells, stones, broken glass and all manner of refuse brought together in a mosaic-style surface. The structures, including fountains and birdbaths, reach almost 100 feet at their highest point. After Rodia abandoned the property in the mid-1950s, the Committee for Simon Rodia's Towers was formed to protect this amazing landmark.[32]

In 1964, Noah Purifoy was hired by the Committee to look after the towers and the small school that was run there and is credited as the founding director of Watts Towers Arts Center. The 1960s saw the beginning of the renaissance of the site as a home for classes in visual and performing arts primarily for youth, as well as exhibitions and concerts. It also became a place where artists found employment.

While Purifoy records some of his own earliest work as collage, he was eventually drawn to assemblage because of the accessibility and availability of materials—it was made from discarded things. In his eyes such junk was democratic; it didn't discriminate against those with less advantage (or access to art materials) because it was free. Assemblage also had its relationship to narratives of poverty in a way as it reflected communities ravaged by a social system that cared little for them.[33]

Though he received his BFA from Chouinard Art Institute some years before, Purifoy contends that it was the rebellions at Watts in 1965 "that made me an artist."[34] He experienced them from the "back door" of the Center, the destruction, the looting. He and Judson Powell, another artist on the Center staff, "while the debris was still smoldering, we ventured into the rubble like other junkers of the community, digging and searching, but unlike others, obsessed without quite knowing why. By September, working during lunch time and after teaching hours, we had collected three tons of charred wood and fire-moulded [sic] debris."[35] A year later this detritus had been transformed into the exhibition "66 Signs of Neon," part of the first Watts Summer Festival. The show was composed of sixty-six assemblages created by various artists. In the catalogue for the exhibition one gets a sense of how Purifoy's philosophy affected the show's overall concept where "creativity is the only way left for a person to find himself [sic] in this materialistic world," where junk creates order from disorder and "beauty from ugliness."[36] In the reworking of charred remnants of society was found the transformative power of art, its ability to affect change in the individual and the psyche.

Examples of Purifoy's own work created in the aftermath of the rebellions include *Sir Watts*, c. 1966 (now lost), which graced the frontispiece of the catalogue for "66 Signs of Neon" (fig. 2.1). As its title seems to suggest, the piece is modeled after medieval armor. What we see, however, is only a partial torso molded out of metal, with abbreviated arms and head. Where a face might be a small purse of metal mesh was affixed, which was sometimes opened and gaping as a hungry mouth. The belly was a series of wooden drawers, while

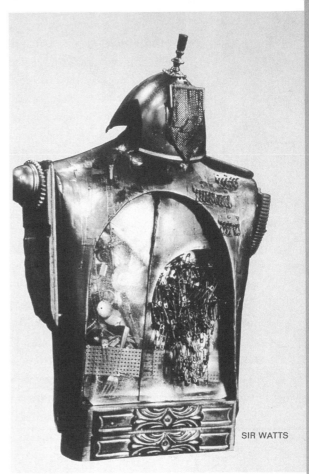

SIR WATTS

the chest cavity was covered with a scarred piece of glass revealing a complicated agglomeration of small personal objects (hair pins, a fork, buttons). The heart was an open hole through which poured hundreds of tangled safety pins, dripping down the front of the sculpture. Again the image of violence, of the warrior—the knight as sign for "people in battle"[37]—was turned into a figure simply in want of love and care.

For some artists, including Noah Purifoy, Betye Saar, John Riddle, and John Outterbridge, assemblage was a clear metaphor for the process of change—the transformation of psyche and social existence—required of art in the rhetoric of the Black Arts Movement, art that "advance[d] social consciousness and promote[d] black development."[38] While numerous times he thought of abandoning such parameters for artmaking John Riddle realized that the world was such, that politics was such that "there's always, every day, some resource" when one was working in a socially based mode.[39]

A Los Angeles native, Riddle began to meet a community of African American artists around the time of the Watts rebellions, some while poking through the post-rebellion rubble. While he had been drawn to assemblage before that time, August 1965 as well as Noah Purifoy's influence put a new spin on things, made him think hard about "what the purpose of art should be."[40] *Ghetto Merchant*, c.1966, was created from physical remnants of the rebellions and most probably shown in the "66 Signs of Neon" exhibition. Anthropomorphic in sensibility, it incorporates a burned-up cash register as its core element, its wiry keys a skeletal torso. This is topped by an "empty" head formed from the negative space in a metal fragment and held up by spindly steel legs, an apt metaphor for a figure that preyed on the Watts community.

John Outterbridge who arrived in Los Angeles from Chicago in 1963, saw the beginnings of the Black Arts Movement as a visionary time for artists because it took into consideration "how art and culture could effectively participate to help build a community, break existing moulds [sic] and create an interest in social change. . . . Artists were challenged to think among themselves in new ways."[41] For Outterbridge, art with social commentary evolved naturally from the climate of the times. It was indeed part of the aesthetic of assemblage, "how you use whatever is available to you, and what is available to you is not mere material but the material and the essence of the political climate, the material in the debris of social issues."[42] Catalyzed by the times, Outterbridge came to think of himself as an "activist-artist" whose "studio was everywhere."[43]

Working typically in series, Outterbridge's Rag Man group (1970–1976) was inspired by a figure from his youth in the South and Midwest who would come by to collect cast off clothes for reuse and resale. By alluding to an African American vernacular method here, Outterbridge makes a subtle comparison between black tradition and assemblage as a fine art practice, creating a dialogue between high and low forms, and showing how African American creativity, in fact, even predated this modernist mode of artmaking.

Born in Watts, Betye Saar began her career as an artist in the 1950s making fine crafts and jewelry. By 1960 she had turned to printmaking and early on developed a number of thematic threads and artmaking strategies that she has continued to explore; among these are the centrality of images of women, alternative spiritual practices and cosmologies, and the collision of textures. Beginning in 1966, the prints became meshed with found window frames which provided a new kind of support but also set up a fresh narrative structure, which like a film *storyboard*, allowed the action of the picture plane to unfold incrementally, as in *Mystic Window for Leo*, 1966.

As has been argued elsewhere, the mystical arena evoked by Saar and others like Sun Ra during this period represented a surrogate space of liberation, and for Saar one that pointed back to the self.[44] *Black Girl's Window*, 1969, seems to be a turning point in this regard where we see Saar re-embrace the black body and make the connection between the black female form and her surrogate, the lion (emblem of Saar's zodiac sign, Leo). As the window frame device gave way to shallow boxes and small altars, the work became at once more theatrical and increasingly grounded in traditional African-American belief systems.[45] In two of what she refers to as her "ancestral boxes"[46]—*Ten Mojo Secrets*, 1972, and *Gris-Gris Box* 1972—Saar uses words (mojo and gris-gris)

alluding to African-American ritual or conjuring practices often identified with
Louisiana, homeland of her paternal grandparents. A small altar-like *Mti*, 1973,
takes its title from the Swahili word for wood, engaging in this way with a
lexicon of the Black Arts Movement. However, it is perhaps the link between
Gris-Gris Box and what is arguably Saar's most famous work, *The Liberation of
Aunt Jemima*, 1972, made the same year, that we see how the personal—in the
form of an active yet private spirituality—indeed becomes political, how the
mystical represents the will to power (fig. 2.2). In both works the central figure

is a black woman in a headscarf, linking her iconographically to the stereotypical mammy. Yet each is laden with props of power, guns in the latter and strong magic in the former.

Engagement with the idea of exploding stereotypes was a trope of visual arts practice clearly connected to Black Arts Movement theory. It allowed artists to create figurative, representational work that was recognizable and thus available "to the masses" yet at the same time demonstrated art's role as weapon by enacting the destruction of negative imagery. Other artists creating work in this vein included Murray DePillars, Jeff Donaldson, and Joe Overstreet. As art historian Jane Carpenter and Betye Saar argue, however, Saar was the first to integrate *actual* historical objects, so-called "black collectibles," into her pieces.[47] By incorporating them Saar sought to consume their power, to enact physical and artistic cannibalization and thus drain their negative magic.

In the 1950s, Watts was perceived as "the bottom of the social and economic ladder"; Eldridge Cleaver, who grew up in Los Angeles at that time, observed that to say someone was from Watts was a put down, a way of saying that person was uncool.[48] After 1965, the reverse was true, having any connection with Watts was seen as a badge of honor as it came to connote a new course for black identity, one that embodied power, strength, and uncompromising behavior. Indeed, Watts seemed to epitomize site in the discursive sense as outlined by Kwon. It denoted a tangible place, a symbol, and a way of thinking; it was (re)constructed and (re)born through violence, assemblage, language, as well as physical and institutional structure.

SHOWING OUT

If the Black Arts Movement embodied a search for a black aesthetic, it also sought out alternative institutional structures that could nurture and support these new art forms. Historically, the majority of African American artists were certainly not welcomed with open arms, if at all, within mainstream museums and galleries in Los Angeles or the rest of the country. In the post-WWII period, we begin to see a slow shift in African American relations to artworld structure, a trend that picked up momentum in the 1960s. We can consider these changes in terms of different types of activity, actions that were more "integrationist" in focus (i.e., penetrating preexisting institutions) paired with those creating autochthonous formations (i.e., new galleries, periodicals, etc.).

This advance began with African Americans' growing attendance in BFA and MFA programs, fueled by the disintegrating barriers to *de jure* segregation as well as the G.I. Bill. Riddle, Purifoy, and Outterbridge were all veterans of the Korean War who used their educational benefits to attend art school. Each of them also ended up working in new institutional settings that supported the work of African American artists. Riddle moved to Atlanta in the mid-1970s, becoming the head of the Neighborhood Arts Center that gave David Hammons one of his first solo shows. Outterbridge assumed the directorship of the Watts Towers Arts Center in 1975, the year that it officially became a municipal art space. Purifoy, the first director of Watts Towers between 1964 and 1966, eventually joined the newly created California Arts Council, where he remained an arts administrator for eleven years.

Around 1969 several non-municipal, independent establishments were also formed. Brockman Gallery, Gallery 32, and The Gallery were all venues run by and largely for African American artists. While Brockman Gallery had the longest life span of the three—1967–1990—the other two enterprises were very active in the first half of the 1970s. At their core these were spaces run by artists for artists.

Besides creating or managing sites for the display (and sale) of art or places where people could perform or just congregate, another institutionally directed aspect of Black Arts Movement activity was agitating and protesting against public organizations that refused to admit, exhibit, or hire African Americans but yet benefited from the tax dollars of these same citizens. One Los Angeles group that concerned itself with such issues was the Black Art Council.

Like Art West Associated before it and the Black Emergency Cultural Coalition in New York, the Black Art Council served in part as a watchdog organization, the thorn in the side of mainstream art institutions demanding that they be more fully representative of the city that they served.[49] Cecil Fergerson, one of the Black Art Council's founding members, had begun working at the Los Angeles County Museum of Art (LACMA) as a janitor in 1948. By the mid-1960s he had risen through the ranks to the position of preparator. With the climate of social change alive in the United States and the rising prominence of the Black Arts Movement and growing consciousness about the importance of culture, Fergerson and Black Art Council (BAC) co-founder Claude Booker, "both realized how important arts were to people. Up until that point, I just looked at art as a [nice club] for the rich. Because you have no point of reference—right?—being black. No black museums. No black people in the collection."[50]

During the first half of the 1970s continuous lobbying of LACMA by the BAC brought about three major exhibitions focused on African American artists.[51] "Three Graphic Artists" (1971) featured works on paper by Charles White, David Hammons, and Timothy Washington.[52] It was from this exhibition that LACMA purchased Hammons' seminal *Injustice Case*, 1970 (fig. 2.3). The next year the museum presented "Los Angeles, 1972: A Panorama of Black Artists," a group show of contemporary art curated by African American art historian Carroll Greene.

The last very visible project that LACMA undertook in the 1970s involving African American artists was the large historical exhibition "Two Centuries of Black American Art" (1976). It provided much needed historical context to the contemporary art scene, reminding the world that African- descended peoples in the United States had been around hundreds of years and in that time had been creative, and that amazingly, given their circumstance for much of that time, had made some beautiful things, including art. Curated by renowned

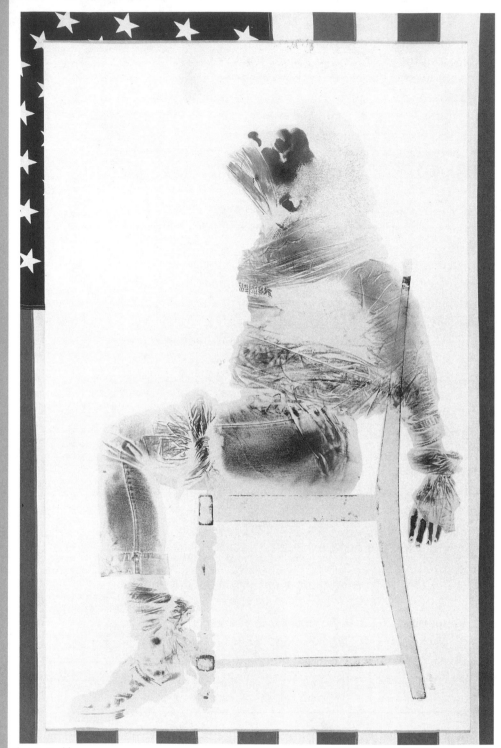

Fig. 2.3. David Hammons, *Injustice Case,* 1970. Los Angeles County Museum of Art.

professor, artist, and curator David Driskell, the show traveled extensively and was a huge success. The exhibition catalogue often served as a key text in courses on African American artists that were beginning to be taught at this time.

While much of the focus of the Black Art Council was on correcting the oversights of the Los Angeles County Museum of Art, the group also involved itself in other projects in the larger community. Fergerson and Booker, preparators at LACMA and the real driving force behind the BAC, lent their installation skills to the visual arts portion of the Watts Summer Festival between 1970 and 1975. Black Student Unions at colleges and universities in the area also engaged the services of the Black Art Council to create a black visual presence on campus. The group helped out hanging shows at emerging black-owned galleries such as Gallery 32 as well. The gallery, in turn, opened its space for the organization's meetings and at least once for a fundraising exhibition.[53]

A year after a cross-country road trip led them to experience the United States and "see artists of color, that they were out there, that they were doing it, they were making a significant statement," Alonzo and Dale Davis opened the Brockman Gallery.[54] Named for their maternal grandmother who had been a slave, the Davises dedicated Brockman primarily to the work of African American artists. The gallery was located on the Westside of Los Angeles in its wealthiest black enclave, a bid to attract that clientele.

The Davises opened their gallery in 1967 with shows of their own work. Early on, Brockman represented Timothy Washington and David Hammons. Brockman was, in fact, the place where Hammons first showed the now classic *Injustice Case*, 1970, in its original guise as a mixed media installation: a body print bordered by an actual American flag and enclosed in a lighted, glass, museum display case along with a gavel (this larger container was later destroyed). Elizabeth Catlett had her first U.S. solo show in many years at Brockman. In addition to exhibitions of works by African Americans, Brockman also organized group shows that were more integrated including work by Chicano, Japanese, and white artists.

The Davis brothers had always envisioned Brockman Gallery as a commercial venture. Yet they were also very active in the community helping with other exhibitions and programs. To handle their growing community-focused activities they set up Brockman Productions in 1973, a nonprofit entity that was eligible for public funding. By 1976, Alonzo was able to quit all the other jobs he held to keep the gallery afloat and concentrate his energies on running these enterprises.[55] Brockman expanded its reach to outdoor exhibitions, mural projects, and concerts, as well as a film festival; it was able to support more artists than ever before because commercial viability was not so much of an issue.

Suzanne Jackson was a professional dancer before moving to Los Angeles in 1967. She initially supported herself working concurrently for the Los Angeles Unified School District as an elementary school art instructor, and at Watts Towers Arts Center teaching dance and visual art. She was a model for other classes at Watts Towers and for Charles White's courses at Otis Art Institute. She sat in as a student on some of White's sessions, as well, which was how she first met other artists such as David Hammons, Dan Concholar, Alonzo Davis, and Timothy Washington. Searching for a new studio space in the vicinity of both Otis and Chouinard, Jackson found a beautiful place on Lafayette Park and was encouraged by friends to turn it into a gallery. And so Gallery 32 was born.[56]

Though barely in operation for two years Gallery 32 was visible, progressive, and full of energy. It was not necessarily a "black gallery" though its proprietor and the majority of the artists who showed there were. There was a healthy competition between Brockman Gallery and Gallery 32, though they often shared opening weekends (Brockman debuting new shows on Friday and Gallery 32 on Saturday), and some artists (Hammons, Washington, Concholar). However, Brockman was known for exhibiting more established practitioners while Gallery 32 specialized in a younger, more eclectic, and in some ways more political group.

Jackson considered her effort more alternative, a space for artists who weren't really showing elsewhere; it was not a serious effort at a commercially viable venture. Elizabeth Leigh-Taylor's exhibition focused on the Greek resistance (1969); "The Sapphire Show" (1970) presented black women artists including Betye Saar, Yvonne Cole Meo, Gloria Bohanon, and Senga Nengudi. The invitation for John Stinson's exhibition of photographs—showing him standing in the doorway of his mail truck—drew crowds of politicos as well as everyday folk.[57] But, arguably, the best attended of all Gallery 32 shows was a 1969 solo by Emory Douglas, Minister of Culture of the Black Panther Party, and principal illustrator of the *Black Panther* newspaper (fig. 2.4). By late 1970 Jackson had closed Gallery 32 and moved on. Like many artists during this period she was harassed and seen as subversive; the gallery as a meeting place, as a place to debate the artist's relevance to the black community came under scrutiny, particularly one with a higher political profile such as hers.[58]

Samella Lewis arrived in Southern California in 1966, as a forty-four-year-old artist and academic, with a Ph.D. from Ohio State University and fifteen years of teaching under her belt. She initially took a position at California State University, Long Beach, but by 1968 she had joined the Los Angeles County Museum of Art as coordinator of education. This position was the result of agitation by forces such as Art West Associated and the Black Arts Council seeking greater visibility for African Americans in this large municipal art center which their tax dollars went to fund but which provided them with little access and even less inspiration. It was Lewis' own disenchantment with the institution, combined with the social energy of the time, that led her to develop her own groundbreaking projects which would distinguish her as a major force in African American art in the twentieth century. The amazing projects—three books, a magazine, two galleries, and a museum—all came to fruition in the decade between 1969 and 1978 and flowered in the California landscape.

The first of the two-volume *Black Artists on Art* was published in 1969 and hatched somewhat earlier by Lewis, Ruth Waddy, and E. J. Montgomery in the latter's Bay Area living room.[59] It featured introductory texts by Lewis and Waddy reflecting the rhetoric of the Black Arts Movement, attesting to the unique vision of African American artists and the need for the mainstream to expand notions of aesthetic beauty. Each artist was also represented by a brief statement and at least one image. Many of the contributors, not surprisingly,

SEE REVOLUTIONARY
ART EXHIBIT
BY EMORY DOUGLAS
Minister of Culture, Black Panther Party

October 17, 18
(3 to 8)
and 19 (1 to 6)

*Gallery 32;
672 So. Lafayette
Park Place
Los Angeles, Calif.*

HEAR
ELAINE
BROWN
*Deputy Minister of Information,
Southern California, B.P.P.*

*Singing Revolutionary Songs
from soon to be released
album, "Seize the Time"*

DONATION:
$2.00 PER PERSON

FOR FREE BREAKFAST FOR CHILDREN,
FREE HEALTH CLINIC,
AND FOR POLITICAL PRISONERS

For More Information, Call
235-4127

Fig. 2.4. Emory Douglas, *Revolutionary Art Exhibit* (Gallery 32), 1969. San Diego Archive.

were from California, and, in effect, the book reproduces those networks of African American artists stretching from the 1950s to the contemporary moment. In Lewis' eyes the publication legitimized the work of these practitioners, demonstrating that they were worthy of exhibitions, jobs, and general support by the larger culture. A second volume of *Black Artists on Art* appeared in 1971. Both were self-published. Together they highlighted the work of almost 150 contemporary African American artists, an amazing number given Lewis' resources, and the one or two figures often showcased in mainstream contexts (even today). As a way to keep the ideas in the books updated, Lewis along with Val Spaulding and Jan Jemison began the magazine *Black Art*. This first periodical devoted to African American and African Diaspora artists would later change its name to *International Review of African American Art*.

The first half of the 1970s found Samella Lewis putting her mark on Los Angeles as a curator, however she did so through sheer force of will and in spaces that she herself created. Lewis first opened The Gallery on Redondo Boulevard near Olympic, later moving it to Pico Boulevard.[60] In addition to organizing shows for The Gallery, in 1976 Lewis founded the Museum of African American

Art. For a while both gallery and museum shared the same building. Eventually Lewis relinquished the gallery space to focus on the museum. In its third year of existence, The Museum of African American Art moved to its current space in the May Company Department store. Mary Jane Hewitt eventually joined Lewis in this endeavor.[61]

All during this period Lewis continued to work fulltime in academia. She was hired as a professor of art history and humanities by Scripps College in 1970. Scripps was part of the Claremont University Center (CUC)—a consortium of colleges—that provided support for several of Lewis' projects, particularly the museum and the magazine. She also worked with CUC's Black Studies program mentoring students and giving lectures on African American art. In 1978, Lewis transformed these lectures into a book, *Art: African American*. This survey joined only two others, James Porter's *Modern Negro Art* (1943) and Cedric Dover's *American Negro Art* (1960). Until the mid-1990s this book was the standard academic text to introduce new students of all ages to the field of African American artists and their histories.[62]

Institutional structures of the Black Arts Movement related to the visual arts revitalized and revalidated African American art history at the same time as they supported contemporary practitioners. It was perhaps the younger generation of artists active in this era that would benefit most from the embrace of black aesthetics and organizational support and who would also take these forms to the next level and to their endpoint.

SHOWING UP

The path opened up by assemblage and other multimedia art forms in the post-WWII visual landscape led away from traditional practices of painting and sculpture. These styles instead placed value on the recycling of everyday objects of human facture in new juxtapositions which retained echoes of their use, recontextualized, and often reinscribed in the mirror of metaphor. Such strategies found a comfortable home with Los Angeles artists working within Black Arts Movement rubric such as Noah Purifoy, John Otterbridge, John Riddle, and Betye Saar. These artists (and others) engaged with bits and pieces of their environment, in particular the remnants of the Watts rebellions, through which they could refer to African American culture and life without relying on simplistic painted representations of the black figure. David Hammons, Houston Conwill, Maren Hassinger, and Senga Nengudi followed the trajectory of these and other contemporary bricoleurs. Yet, they were of a slightly younger generation that employed such devices as part of a more conceptual, active, and participatory practice.

Conceptual art privileged ideas. Art was a "metaphysical vehicle for an idea intended";[63] it was human thought made visible. No longer defined by its physical attributes, art dematerialized into "the melted down . . . status of evidence,"[64] remains, concepts, words. Conceptualism like Black Arts Movement forms emphasized audience, the reception of and interaction with aesthetics. Art was not just to be seen but experienced. Eventually these methods would separate from autonomous form altogether and live as performance. If, as David Lionel Smith has suggested, the Black Arts Movement's flow of poetry into music created theater, then we can also see the gestures of theater and material culture combining to produce performance art. Post-WWII temporal aesthetics led away from the specter of world annihilation (in wartime destruction, nuclear menace, and cold war countermoves), *and* formalism's impasse (art solely concerned with the status of itself) back to a reaffirmation of human existence.[65] In African American communities, threats to the physical and social body continued into the 1960s and 1970s (as they had for hundreds of years) making such practices in some ways even more appropriate. Performance could also be "placed" anywhere, dispersed quite effortlessly into the flow of everyday life, as "spectacle or political act,"[66] and offered unmediated connection to the viewer, again qualities favored by the Black Arts Movement.

Of the younger group of Los Angeles artists, it is perhaps through the work of David Hammons that we can most clearly chart the evolving visual aesthetics of the Black Arts Movement, and the move from more didactic formulas to those that rely to a greater extent on abstraction, dematerialized practices, and performance. Hammons arrived in Los Angeles from Illinois in 1963 at the age of twenty. He attended art classes at various institutions throughout the city but in particular sought out Charles White at Otis Art Institute.[67] White's influence on Hammons can be seen in his early choice of the graphic medium as well as in his works' political content. In pieces such as *Black Boy's Window*, 1968, and *Injustice Case*, 1970, the commentary on African American exclusion from opportunity (in the first instance) and persecution by the American system (in the second) is clear. They classically embody Black Arts Movement style in their figurative presentation and commentary on U.S. racism. Hammons is also clearly working within the California assemblage aesthetic. In *Black Boy's Window*, Hammons applies a photo silkscreen process to a discarded window frame using the bar-like structure of panes to suggest jail-like connotations. The piece also demonstrates the influence of Betye Saar who had begun creating similar constructions in 1966. However, there is a dialogue between the two artists as well. Saar made her *Black Girl's Window*, 1969, the year after Hammons' piece appeared; her *Self-Window with Reflection*, 1970, like *Black Boy's Window*, also included a functional window shade in a nod to the performative.

It was the development of the printing process in Hammons' early works that was most fascinating. He used himself as the printable "plate," oiling his body, leaning or lying on a piece of paper or board, then sprinkling the grease infused areas with powdered pigment. Silk-screened embellishments were often added to these emblematic indexes, but it was clear that the fulcrum of signification revolved around the performative body. The body prints share similarities with the Anthropometries of Yves Klein.[68] But rather than using the female form as a titillating paintbrush, Hammons was the dynamic agent, collapsing the position of auteur with those of signifier *and* signified.

With his Spade Series (c.1971–1974) Hammons moved more fully into a multimedia and performance practice. Of equal interest was the artist's manipulation of language. Hammons took a derogatory term for African Americans—Spade—and reversed and opened up meaning. In showing the spade in so many permutations, he attempted to deconstruct the image and divest it of its power, again a classic trope of Black Arts Movement practice and one also employed by Saar at the same moment.

In a vintage 1970s photo, Hammons poses with *3 Spades*, 1971, a body print showing a black man (the artist "in print") holding two familiar (if enlarged) emblems taken from a deck of playing cards. The conflation between symbol, slur, and human being reveals an approach to speech and use of taboo language clearly influenced by Black Arts Movement poetics. In sculptural pieces such as *Laughing Magic* and *Bird* (both 1973), Hammons takes a more celebratory stance, again locating his method stylistically within Black Arts Movement commemoration of black heroes and heritage. Each pays homage to respective African and African American legacies, one through the use of the mask form, the other as a quiet monument to the musical genius of alto saxophonist Charlie "Bird" Parker.

In his interaction with "Spade" objects, Hammons created some of his earliest performance works. Interestingly, using the Spade as a performative device lent a more violent edge to his concept. Shapes cut from cardboard or leather are props used by the artist, but they also become stand-ins for black bodies. One piece from this period, *Spade Covered with Sand or Buried Spade* (no date), has been referred to by Hammons as an "earth work," the action is as the title suggests: Hammons digs a hole and entombs the form in the ground.[69] Documentation of *Murder Mystery*, 1972 (also known as *Spade Run Over by a Volkswagen*), shows a cardboard Spade "crushed" under the wheel of a Volkswagen Beetle, painted blood pouring forth. Another performance consisted of Hammons hanging leather spade forms from trees. Given the violent repression of African Americans agitating against injustice—both historical and contemporary, some witnessed and experienced firsthand by the artist—it would not be a stretch to see Hammons' Spade performances as his own coded response to the climate of the times, in the same vein as Melvin Edwards' *Lynch Fragments* (and perhaps even as a homage to them). It wasn't merely formal exploration that led Hammons to hang these pieces (which he dubbed "skins") from trees.[70]

After meeting at Howard University where they both were art students, Houston and Kinshasha Conwill moved to Los Angeles in the early 1970s to attend graduate school at the University of Southern California (USC).[71] There Houston created an artistic vocabulary for objects and performances that referenced both African and African American visual and ritual heritage. Performances often took place within a different solo exhibition of objects. These included the shows "JuJu Funk" (1975) at the Lindhurst Gallery of USC, "JuJu" (1976) at the Pearl C. Woods Gallery, and "JuJu III" (1976) at The Gallery, the space on Pico Boulevard run by Samella Lewis. Hybrid painted/sculpted elements hung from the walls and were laid out on the floor, but in each installation the focus was drawn to "the ceremonial space at the center of the room."[72]

The action revolved around a central sculptural tableau: a narrow strip of red carpet connecting a stool and a pail that were both elaborately adorned. Perched on the stool during the performance, Houston's painted body became a medium, calling his forbearers with an evocative litany. This base held the seated energy of the African ancestors in much the same way stools do in the Akan traditions of Ghana.[73] The pail became a "gutbucket"—antebellum container of "the food remains given slaves," sign of "the base level of emotion or experience," and inspiration for that down-home blues.[74] Here allusion to African American foodways celebrated heritage but also vernacular practice, the creation of delicacies (such as chitterlings) from discards; yet another approach to and comment on the practice of assemblage. These live works were often collaborations with artists like Kinshasha and Hammons as well as musicians. Other significant performances by Houston in this period included *Warrior Chants, Love Songs and New Spirituals* (with poets Kamau Daaood, Charles Dickson, and Ojenke) performed at the Watts Towers Art Center in 1979, and *Getup* written by Senga Nengudi in 1980.

Both Senga Nengudi and Maren Hassinger came to performance from dance, though they were discouraged by their respective colleges from majoring in it on the undergraduate level. To a great extent, this rejection had to do with what was (is?) perceived as the correct body type for the discipline, a formula that didn't include black women.[75] Hassinger, a Los Angeles native, was a neighbor of Alonzo and Dale Davis growing up on the Westside of Los Angeles. In graduate school at UCLA in the early 1970s, she discovered what would become a pivotal medium for her: wire rope. In her hands, this material came to embody the changing landscape of American sculpture from minimal to post-minimal: it was a synthetic substance that, with subtle intervention, could echo organic form. These solid and industrial, yet process-driven sculptures become the "initiators of activity," lending themselves to the temporality of performance.[76] Though she showed at Brockman Gallery and was certainly a part of this group of younger artists in Los Angeles experimenting with dematerialized practices and performance, Hassinger's work seemed the least concerned with rhetorics of African American or African aesthetics. However, in retrospect she did feel there was a connection:

One thing I think I have discovered along the way, after years of feeling compelled to do things and many of those years doing them in collaboration with Senga [Nengudi] and Ulysses [Jenkins] and Frank Parker, and then recently looking at slides from African performances and masquerades and reading . . . . I realized that in Africa . . . time-based movements are not separated from the static work in the same way . . . . You know, it's the flip side of one coin. And I really do think that it's the impulse that moves through all of our work . . . . [This gives a context to] my impulse to take the sculpture and expand it so that the idea exists in time and includes movement and includes people, sound and voices, and things.[77]

Like Conwill, one of Hassinger's first performances took place within one of her gallery installations.[78] *High Noon*, 1976, performed at the Arco Center for Visual Art in Los Angeles, extended sculptural notions into time and motion. Another early performance took place on Easter Sunday, 1977, at David Hammons' Slauson Avenue studio. This time Hassinger was not performing among her own works, but those of Hammons' certainly provided an environment for the action.[79] An ensemble of performers (including Senga Nengudi) is linked through the interchange of objects, in this case actual wood saplings. Like *High Noon*, the title of the piece, *Ten Minutes*, is blandly descriptive in the mode of classic, language-driven conceptualism. The spareness of the branches, the performers' light colored and soft clothing, and their simple actions capture the minimalist edge that Hassinger's sculptures tread as well. A third work, *Diaries (Part 1 of Lives)* (1978), was performed at the Vanguard Gallery, a newly opened alternative space in downtown Los Angeles and finds corollaries in the anthropomorphic connotations of her major sculptures from that year, *Walking* and *Whirling*.

While studying at California State University, Los Angeles, Senga Nengudi worked both at Pasadena Art Museum and Watts Towers Arts Center drawing inspiration from mainstream sources as well as others that privileged black creativity.[80] As David Hammons recalls, Nengudi was rejected for the most part by the then burgeoning West Coast Black Arts Movement due to her non-representational tendencies. Speaking of the *Water Compositions*, he observed, "she used to put colored water in plastic bags and sit them on pedestals. This was the Sixties. No one would even speak to her because we were all doing political art. She couldn't relate. She wouldn't even show around other Black artists her work was so 'outrageously' abstract. Senga came to New York and still no one would deal with her because she wasn't doing 'Black Art.'"[81]

Yet, in New York, Nengudi did create what would become her signature works, free form sculptures constructed primarily of pantyhose and sand. Their "skin-like forms . . . stretched and pulled linear extensions and append-ages . . . "[82] were tied and knotted, shaped, twisted, and suspended from walls and ceilings. Their very material and anthropomorphic form certainly sug-gested the body in motion. However, their pliant nature was not just part of an anti-sculptural, environmental orientation, or feminist bearing. They were supposed to be interacted with: caressed, fondled, and stroked by the art-ist as well as viewers. It was through participatory three-dimensional works that movement and finally performance (re)entered her work as an important creative force (fig. 2.5).

Some of Nengudi's early forays into performance were done in the com-pany of other artists who formed the core of Studio Z. This loose group came together at Hammons' studio on Slauson Avenue—sometimes weekly—to

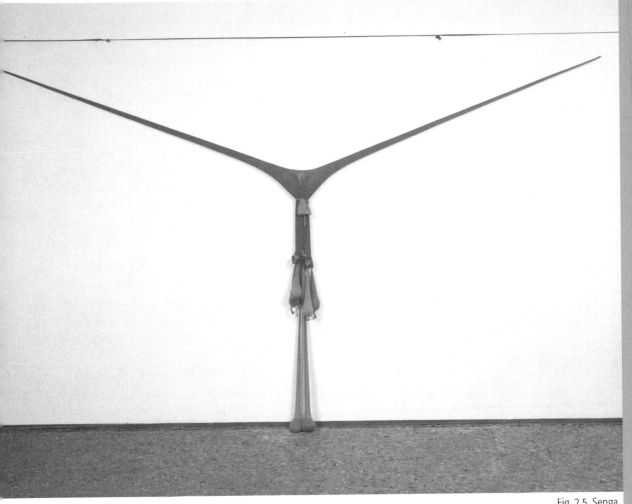

Fig. 2.5. Senga
Nengudi, *RSVP Series,*
1975–1977. Thomas
Erben Gallery.

engage in spontaneous actions; these might be performed in the streets of
L.A. as well. Studio Z had a changing membership (if one could call it that),
including at various times Franklin Parker, Houston Conwill, Ulysses Jenkins,
and RoHo, along with Hassinger, Hammons, and Nengudi. Hammons' space,
a huge old dance hall with a wooden floor, was a perfect place to work out
ideas.[83]

Nengudi's first full-length work of performance took place in March 1978.
Ceremony for Freeway Fets was a public art project supported by a CETA grant
and sponsored by Brockman Gallery along with Cal Trans (the Los Angeles
transportation system).[84] The one-time event took place under a section of the
freeway near the Convention Center. A small orchestra composed of students
and artists played saxophone, flute, drums, and other less traditional instruments. Nearly everyone was equipped with a form of Nengudi's sculpture,
from Franklin Parker's knotted and twisted headdress, to RoHo's full mask.
Nengudi, Hassinger, and Hammons provided the work's major movement and
most elaborate costume.

Ceremony for Freeway Fets shares certain aesthetic conventions with West African masquerade. For instance, there is the crew of masked performers, some in full-body gear. Nengudi's version of her wearable sculpture culminates in a crown that appears to be placed on top of the head, calling to mind the elaborate wooden superstructures found in Nigerian Gelede masquerades, among others. In some African productions, the actual faces of performers are covered with mesh or folds of fabric, comparable in affect to Hammons' pantyhose-clad headpiece sans eyeholes. The object that spins in Nengudi's hand finds a comfortable analogy in the flywhisks and other items often carried by African masqueraders. This feel or sensibility of West African performance is certainly intentional on Nengudi's part and again is in line with aesthetics of the Black Arts Movement, if perhaps belatedly.[85] In her mind she created an African environment:

> I really liked the space because there were little tiny palm trees and a lot of dirt. It wasn't as extreme as it is now, but even at that time there were a lot of transients who slept there; so there were little campfires and stuff. For me, it had the feel of what I imagined an African village to be. Because it was under the freeway it was kind of cloistered in a sense. You could have this rural atmosphere in the midst of an urban setting.[86]

As Kinshasha Conwill moved away from formal artmaking practices in the mid-1970s she became more involved with performative acts, particularly those connected with her husband's objects. She performed dances with elaborate costumes and makeup, sometimes singing, slicing a knife through the air in a cleansing ritual, or offering gifts to the audience.[87] But she also engaged in more quotidian actions linked to Black Arts Movement practice. Like so many others she changed the way she presented herself in everyday life, donning traditional African-style dress—with geles (head wraps) and long skirts; she made her own clothes. She adorned her hair with braids, beads, and feathers. Kinshasha has also described these activities as her own visceral reaction to California's multimedia sensibility.[88] Other artists saw personal adornment as a site of aesthetic play as well. Hammons was known to walk the streets with half his head or beard shaved (which also resulted in him being stopped often by police).[89] It was in California that Karen transformed into Kinshasha. Just as Sue Irons became Senga Nengudi in the moment that her work more openly embraced African modes. Just as Ron Everett became Ron Karenga and LeRoi Jones became Amiri Baraka. Or as Sonny Blount became Sun Ra or Yvette Richards became Chaka Khan. Or even earlier as Malcolm Little became Malcolm X, pointing to the Nation of Islam as a force in such naming and sartorial modes, the role of these practices as aspects of self-determination, and the organization's ideological impact on the Black Arts Movement. Yet we can point to a source for such actions a century before with newly liberated African Americans such as Frederick Douglass and Sojourner Truth choosing names *and* new identities for themselves.

Expanding simple notions of what "black art" could be, artists such as Hammons, the Conwills, Hassinger, and Nengudi took ideas such as affirmations of African American cultural identity, celebrations of African heritage, and notions of art's availability to audiences, to their endpoint. In moving away from figurative representations in two dimensions, through dematerialized practices and performance, ultimately and ironically, they were led back to the black body as form.

MIGRATION AND IMAGINATION

Most observers locate the ending of the Black Arts Movement in the mid-1970s. Kalamu ya Salaam, whose BLKARTSOUTH theater represented a southern branch of the movement, dates its demise to 1974, with the decimation of black activist groups such as the Black Panthers and US (through government-sponsored infiltration and assassination), the rejection of race-based organizing for that driven by Marxist philosophy, and the cooptation and commercialization of black aesthetics (in Blaxploitation films, for instance).[90]

Another endpoint is often seen in the outpouring of black women's writing and the growing prominence of figures like Toni Morrison and Alice Walker. One milestone in this regard is the opening of Ntozake Shange's *for colored girls who have considered suicide/when the rainbow is enuf* on Broadway in 1976. Called a "choreopoem" by its creator, *for colored girls* explored the lives of African American women through a combination of performance and spoken word. Yet the language, writing, and even Shange's name demonstrated roots in the Black Arts Movement. As Shange herself would later comment, "I am a daughter of the black arts movement (even though they didn't know they were going to have a girl!)."[91] To an extent, women's voices had been heard during the period, in the writings of Sonia Sanchez, and Nikki Giovanni, and anthologies like *The Black Woman* (1970), and *Soulscript* (1970), edited by Toni Cade Bambara and June Jordan, respectively, and in the political activities of Kathleen Cleaver, Elaine Brown, and Angela Davis, among many others.[92]

Yet even as the growing visibility of women became the flashpoint for disintegration of the Black Arts Movement, male voices of the time, some of them located, interestingly, in California, such as Ismael Reed and Quincy Troupe, rebelled against its "prescriptive and narrowly political nature."[93] In a sense, the movement imploded with the weight of it own "masculine bias, homophobia, anti-Semitism, violent imagery, [and] simplistic racial dichotomies. . . ."[94] But the lessons about the profound beauty *and* complexity of black culture were never lost, and moved forward into the future.

In a sense, African American artists working in Los Angeles also provided an alternative to the standard formulas of the Black Arts Movement. Their take on black heroes, affirmations of cultural identity, and links with the African past followed different routes. Their visions were not particularly two-dimensional or graphic, colorful or solely representational. This multimedia aesthetic also emerged from a California tradition that embraced the materiality of craft, and its notions of functionality may have issued to an extent from this trajectory as well as Black Arts Movement tenets. It also remains to be seen what kind of influence the work of Chestyn Everett, and his involvement with Art West Associated and other art-driven activities, may have had on his brother Ron Karenga in the 1950s and 1960s.

By the late 1970s, Hammons, Hassinger, Edwards, and the Conwills had all departed Los Angeles for New York. Nengudi had also developed her mature aesthetic there in the early 1970s. Indeed, another important aspect to consider in the work of these Southern California-based artists is what role migration might have played in the development of visual aesthetics. Many of the practitioners featured here migrated from the South or the Midwest or were children of others who had relocated to the area. As mentioned earlier, during and following WWII an increasing number of African Americans moved to California, drawn by the promise of work in the growing war and aeronautics industries. While many artists made their way to the state during these decades (Bruce Nauman, Edward Kienholz, and Edward Ruscha among them), migration holds a special place in the African American cultural imagination.

Scholar Farah Jasmine Griffin sees migration as *the* key text of modern African American life.[95] The majority of black people lived in the South until well into the twentieth century, their travel restricted by Jim Crow laws even as late as the 1950s. The "Great Migration" between the two World Wars radically altered the African American demographics of the United States. More importantly, migration held a significant place in the black creative mind, and was a major theme in a variety of cultural forms from literature to music and painting. Were these same themes discernable in the production of African American artists working more abstractly in Los Angeles during the 1960s and 1970s? How might we see migration reenacted in notions of place and space that came to be signified by the "dematerialization" of the art object?

This brings us back to Kwon's notion of the discursive role of site, one not necessarily tied to a fixed or physical locale; a sense of site being generated in and through a variety of places, tangible and intangible. In the context of 1960s and 1970s African America, we can discern site's relationship to notions of claim, land, territory, culture, spirituality, and imagination, particularly in the Los Angeles example of Watts. If the migration narrative is the voice of modern African America, and above all explores issues of urbanism, is its endpoint found in the deindustrialized landscape that then produces postmodern culture? And can that postmodern phase be defined in the trajectory that runs from assemblage to hip hop? We should also consider how the changing realities of material and lived experience of African Americans, vernacular, popular culture, *and* fine art contribute to our understanding of major art movements such as assemblage or pop. Indeed, what impact did these artists based in Los Angeles and their wide-ranging use of media have on the vitality of the post-minimalist landscape of the 1970s? And later how *did* their presence on the East Coast affect the expanding discourse of multiculturalism in the 1980s art scene?

While these questions remain largely unanswered here, we know that African American culture has played a major role worldwide in the late twentieth century. And many of its routes lead us back to the Black Arts.

"Black West, Thoughts on Art in Los Angeles" is in celebration of E. J. Montgomery and in memory of Ruth Waddy.

ACKNOWLEDGEMENTS

Thanks for research assistance goes to Regina Woods, Donna Mungen, and The Studio Museum in Harlem. I am also grateful for support from the Morse Junior Faculty Fellowship, and the Griswold Fund, Yale University, and University of California, Los Angeles, Chicano Studies Research Center. This article would have remained a passing thought without Yale University Art and Architecture Library, and all the librarians there, particularly Beverly Lett; University of California, Los Angeles, Robert Young Research Library, Special Collections, and particularly the librarians Jeffrey Rankin and Octavio Olvera; the Getty Research Institute, Research Library, Special Collections and Visual Resources; New York University, Bobst Library and The Fales Library & Special Collections.

NOTES

1. Hoyt Fuller, "Towards a Black Aesthetic," *The Black Aesthetic*, ed. Addison Gayle, Jr. (New York: Anchor Books, 1972; originally 1971), 8 (first published in *The Critic*, 1968).

2. Kalamu ya Salaam, "The Black Arts Movement," Elizabeth J. West, "Black Nationalism," in *The Oxford Companion to African American Literature*, ed. William L. Andrews, Frances Smith Foster, and Trudier Harris (New York: Oxford University Press, 1997), 71.

3. David Lionel Smith, "The Black Arts Movement and its Critics," *American Literary History* 3: 1 (Spring 1991): 99.

4. Ibid.

5. AFRI-COBRA (African Commune of Bad Relevant Artists) grew out of the multidisciplinary artists collective OBAC (Organization of Black American Culture) which was responsible for the well-known public mural *Wall of Respect*, 1967. Early members of AFRI-COBRA were Jeff Donaldson, Jae Jarrell, Wadsworth Jarrell, Barbara J. Jones, Gerald Williams, Napoleon Henderson, Nelson Stevens, Sherman Beck, Omar Lama, Howard Mallory, Jr., and Carolyn Lawrence. See Jeff Donaldson, "Ten in Search of a Nation," *Black World* 19: 12 (October 1970): 80–89. Mary Schmidt Campbell, *Tradition and Conflict: Images of a Turbulent Decade, 1963–1973* (New York: Studio Museum in Harlem, 1988), provides a wonderful overview of visual art and Black Arts Movement practice. However, her study focuses mostly on the East Coast. For a more profound discussion of West Coast aesthetics and the Black Arts Movement, see Lizzetta LeFalle Collins, *19Sixties* (Los Angeles: California Afro-American Museum, 1989).

6. Although numerous sources have written that US stood for "United Slaves" new scholarship by Scot Brown has confirmed that the name signifies "us Blacks as opposed to 'them' whites." Scot Brown, "The US Organization, Black Power Vanguard Politics, and the United Front Ideal: Los Angeles and Beyond," *The Black Scholar* 31: 3–4 (Fall/Winter 2001): 21.

7. Robin D. G. Kelley, *Freedom Dreams, The Black Radical Imagination* (Boston: Beacon Press, 2002), 74–75. US scholar Scot Brown dates Everett/Karenga's involvement with the Afro-American Association to 1963; Brown, "The US Organization," 23.

8. Emory Douglas, "On Revolutionary Art," *Black Panther*, January 24, 1970, 5, quoted in Erika Doss, "'Revolutionary Art is a Tool for Liberation,' Emory Douglas and Protest Aesthetics at the *Black Panther*," in Kathleen Cleaver and George Katsiaficas, eds., *Liberation, Imagination, and the Black Panther Party, A New Look at the Panthers and Their Legacy* (New York: Routledge, 2001), 175 (originally published in *New Political Science* 21: 2 (June 1999).

9. Ron Karenga, "Black Cultural Nationalism," *The Black Aesthetic*, 32 (first published in *Black World* (January 1968).

10. Ibid. David Lionel Smith has pointed out these views really reveal Marxist-Leninist roots on both accounts. David Lionel Smith, "Black Arts Movement," ed. Jack Salzman, David Lionel Smith, and Cornel West, *Encyclopedia of African American Culture and History*, 5 (1996): 327.

11. See Salaam, and Larry Neal, "The Black Arts Movement," *The Black Aesthetic*, ed. Addison Gayle, Jr. (New York: Anchor Books, 1972; originally 1971) (first published in *The Drama Review* 12: 4 [Summer 1968]).

12. Elijah Muhammad's Chicago-based Nation of Islam provided another strong philosophical cornerstone, as did the Revolutionary Action Movement out of Cleveland. See Salaam and Kelley, chapter 3.

13. Miwon Kwon, "One Place After Another: Notes on Site Specificity," *October* 80 (Spring 1997): 85–110.

14. Kwon, "One Place After Another," 95.

15. Henri Lefebvre, *The Production of Space*, trans. Donald Nicholson-Smith (Oxford, UK: Blackwell, 1995 [originally 1974]), 11.

16. For an illuminating discussion of Foucault's concept of heterotopia, see Edward Soja, "History: Geography: Modernity," in *The Cultural Studies Reader*, ed. Simon During (New York: Routledge, 1993), 143.

17. See Edward Soja, Rebecca Morales, and Goetz Wolff, "Urban Restructuring: An Analysis of Social and Spatial Change in Los Angeles, *Economic Geography* 59: 2 (April 1983): 195–230, and Mike Davis, *City of Quartz* (London: Verso, 1990).

18. Saskia Sassen, "Whose City is It? Globalization and the Formation of New Claims," in *Trade Routes: History and Geography*, 2nd Johannesburg Biennale, ed. Okwui Enwezor, 1997, 61 (originally *Public Culture* 8: 2 (Spring 1996).

19. At mid-century there was a meteoric increase in African American residents as migrants came to Los Angeles lured by the employment opportunities of the war industry. By 1943 about 10,000 African Americans per month were arriving in the city; in 1940 the African American population of Los Angeles was 124,306; by 1950 it was 462,172. Statistics taken from Lawrence B. de Graff and Quintard Taylor, "Introduction: African American in California History, California in African American History"; Lawrence B. de Graff, Kevin Mulroy, and Quintard Taylor, *Seeking El Dorado: African Americans in California History* (Seattle: University of Washington Press, 2001), 27–28.

20. White's students during this period included David Hammons, Suzanne Jackson, Alonzo Davis, Dan Concholar, and Timothy Washington. For more on African American artists in Los Angeles during the 1950s, see William Pajaud, *African American Artists of Los Angeles: William Pajaud* (Los Angeles: The Oral History Program of the

University of California, 1993); Curtis Tann, *African American Artists of Los Angeles: Curtis Tann* (Los Angeles: The Oral History Program of the University of California, 1995); Betye Saar, *African American Artists of Los Angeles: Betye Saar* (Los Angeles: The Oral History Program of the University of California, 1996); and Andrea Barnwell, *Charles White* (Petaluma, CA: Pomegranate, 2002).

21. Brown, "The US Organization," 22. See also John Riddle, *African American Artists of Los Angeles: John Riddle* (Los Angeles: The Oral History Program of the University of California, 2000), 15, and Ruth Waddy, *African American Artists of Los Angeles: Ruth Waddy* (Los Angeles: The Oral History Program of the University of California, 1993).

22. See Lucinda H. Gedeon, ed., *Melvin Edwards Sculpture: A Thirty Year Retrospective, 1963–1993* (Purchase, NY: Neuberger Museum of Art, State University of New York at Purchase, 1993), and Jayne Cortez, "Jayne Cortez, In Her Own Words," in *Watts, Art and Social Change in Los Angeles, 1965–2002*, (Milwaukee, WI: Haggerty Museum of Art, Marquette University), 2003.

23. Budd Schulberg, ed., *From the Ashes: Voices of Watts* (New York: New American Library, 1967). This volume was preceded by a special issue of the *Antioch Review*; Budd Schulberg, "Watts Writers Workshop," *Antioch Review* 27: 3 (1967): 274–416.

24. Troupe's poems appeared in *Paris Match* in 1964. Horace Coleman, "Quincy Thomas Troupe, Jr.," in *Afro-American Poets Since 1955*, ed. Trudier Harris and Thadious M. Davis (Detroit: Gale Research, 1985), 335.

25. Quincy Troupe, ed., *Watts Poets: A New Book of Poetry and Essays* (Los Angeles: House of Respect, 1968).

26. The word "ark" was employed by Tapscott for its biblical connotations, to suggest the gathering together and preserving of the world's black musics. Sun Ra—who was the first to form an "Arkestra" dedicated to avant-garde black music in 1953—was also a positive example. The founding members of the Pan-Afrikan People's Arkestra included Linda Hill, Lester Robertson, David Bryant, Alan Hines, Jimmy Woods, and Guido Sinclair along with Tapscott. A list of many of the members of the Arkestra and the larger organization, Union of God's Musicians and Artists Ascension (UGMAA), appears in Horace Tapscott, *Songs of the Unsung*, ed. Steven Isoardi (Durham: Duke University Press, 2001), 217–220.

27. Bruce M. Tyler, "The Rise and Decline of the Watts Summer Festival, 1965 to 1986," *American Studies* 31: 2 (Fall 1990): 63.

28. Brown, "The US Organization," 21.

29. Victor W. Turner, *The Ritual Process; Structure and Anti-Structure* (Chicago: 1969), 167; quoted in Tyler, "The Rise and Decline of the Watts Summer Festival," 63.

30. At the time, Malcolm X was still seen as a traitor by Nation of Islam and thus this commemoration was seen as a challenge to the older organization. Brown, "The US Organization," 24.

31. Despite their opposition, both the Los Angeles Police Department and the Fire Department had recruitment booths at the festival as did many government agencies. Tyler, "The Rise and Decline of the Watts Summer Festival," 62, 64–65.

32. *www.wattstowers.net* and www.epilef.com/0401/watts-towers/.

33. Part of Purifoy's interest as well was how art related to the life of the mind. Inspired by his readings in psychology and philosophy, as well as his earlier profession as a social worker, Purifoy saw art as a tool of psychotherapy, as a way to reintegrate the mind and body. It is interesting how Purifoy's practice mirrors that of Lygia Clark

of Brazil whose object making led her to a psychotherapy practice during roughly the same period. See Lygia Clark and Yves-Alain Bois, "Nostalgia of the Body," *October* 69 (Summer 1994): 85–109.

34. Noah Purifoy, *African American Artists of Los Angeles: Noah Purifoy* (Los Angeles: The Oral History Program of the University of California, 1992), 42.

35. Noah Purifoy as told to Ted Michel, "The Art of Communication as Creative Act," *Junk Art: "66 Signs of Neon"* (Los Angeles: 66 Signs of Neon, c. 1966), unpaginated.

36. Ibid. As evidenced by the catalogue, the artists involved in the project were a multiracial group including: Frank Anthony, Debby Brewer, David Mann, Max Neufeldt, Judson Powell, Noah Purifoy, Leon Saulter, Arthur Secunda, Ruth Saturensky, and Gordon Wagner. There were additional collaborators on the catalogue. Purifoy mentions that the show toured until 1969. The pieces (and artists) were substituted when something was sold or fell apart so the exhibition was always changing. Purifoy, *African American Artists of Los Angeles*, 1992, 90–92. Although not noted in the catalogue or in Purifoy's recollection in his oral history, John Riddle claims he took part in the exhibition as well. Riddle, *African American Artists of Los Angeles*, 117.

37. Samella Lewis, *African American Art and Artists* (Berkeley: University of California Press, 1990) (expanded edition 2003), 198.

38. Riddle, *African American Artists of Los Angeles*, 123.

39. Ibid.,124.

40. Elaine Woo, "Obituaries—John Riddle, Jr.: Artist and Curator," *Los Angeles Times*, March 9, 2002: B17.

41. Outterbridge quoted in Curtis L. Carter, "'Watts: The Hub of the Universe.' Art and Social Change," in *Watts, Art and Social Change in Los Angeles, 1965–2002*, 10.

42. John Outterbridge, *African American Artists of Los Angeles: John Outterbridge* (Los Angeles: The Oral History Program of the University of California, 1993), 362.

43. Outterbridge, *African American Artists of Los Angeles*, 1993, 243.

44. See John Szwed, *Space is the Place: The Life and Times of Sun Ra* (New York: DA Capo Press, 1977), cited in Jane H. Carpenter with Betye Saar, *Betye Saar*, (Petaluma, CA: Pomegranate, 2003), 18.

45. Although she had focused on interior design in college, this growing tendency towards the theatrical in Saar's art can be linked to her employment as a costume designer for theater productions at the Inner City Cultural Center in Los Angeles. Carpenter and Saar, *Betye Saar*, 33.

46. Ibid., 25.

47. Ibid., 43.

48. Gerald Horne, "Black Fire: 'Riot' and 'Revolt' in Los Angeles, 1965 and 1992," in de Graff, Mulroy, and Taylor, *Seeking El Dorado*, 382. Horne cites Eldridge Cleaver, *Soul on Ice* (New York: McGraw Hill, 1968).

49. Other African American artists groups that formed during this period include: Kamoinge Workshop (1961), Spiral (1963), Weusi (1967), Women Students and Artists for Black Liberation (1970), Where We At (1971) all in New York; and Organization of Black American Culture (1967) in Chicago.

50. Cecil Fergerson, *African American Artists of Los Angeles: Cecil Fergerson* (Los Angeles: The Oral History Program of the University of California, 1996), 140.

51. In an interesting parallel, protests by the Black Emergency Cultural Coalition in New York resulted in a number of solo exhibitions as well as a group show by African

Americans at the Whitney Museum of American Art in New York during this same period.

52. Curated by Ebria Feinblatt, head of the department of prints and drawings and the departmental assistant Joseph E. Young, this was the only one of the shows that relied on in-house curators; it later traveled to the Santa Barbara Museum of Art.

53. Suzanne Jackson, *African American Artists of Los Angeles: Suzanne Jackson* (Los Angeles: The Oral History Program of the University of California, 1998), 253–254.

54. Alonzo Davis, *African American Artists of Los Angeles: Alonzo Davis* (Los Angeles: The Oral History Program of the University of California, 1994), 133.

55. At the time Brockman Gallery opened in 1966 Alonzo was a teacher at Crenshaw High School. After leaving that position in 1970 and before being able to work full-time at Brockman in 1976 he taught as an adjunct at various colleges and universities, including Mount Saint Antonio College, Pasadena City College, UCLA, California State University at Northridge, and Otis Art Institute.

56. The gallery took its name from the apartment suite number 32; Jackson was inspired by the precedent of Alfred Stieglitz's modernist gallery 291. Jackson, *African American Artists of Los Angeles*, 253.

57. Jackson, *African American Artists of Los Angeles*, 256–57.

58. She was harassed on tax issues and even jailed for parking violations. Ibid., 150–53, 134.

59. E. J. Montgomery, who had been active in Los Angeles art networks in the 1950s and early 1960s, moved to the Bay Area in 1965. By 1967 she had founded an African American artists advocacy group there after Waddy's example, calling it Art West Associated North. Paralleling Lewis' hire at LACMA, Montgomery joined the staff of the Oakland Museum in 1968, as an "ethnic art consultant," a position she held through 1974 and under the guise of which she curated eight exhibitions. Samella Lewis, *Image and Belief,* interviewed by Richard Candida Smith (Los Angeles: Getty Research Institute for the Arts and Humanities, 1999), 199–201, and E. J. Montgomery, interview with the author, May 18, 2003, hereafter referred to as Montgomery May 2003.

60. Lewis states that upon moving to Pico Boulevard, The Gallery changed its name to Gallery Tanner. However, Kinshasha Conwill recalls the name as The Gallery even on Pico Boulevard. Kinshasha Conwill, *African American Artists of Los Angeles: Kinshasha Conwill* (Los Angeles: The Oral History Program of the University of California, 1996), 62. Further archival research will uncover more detailed information about these galleries and the exhibitions and other activities that took place there.

61. A significant early gift was a collection of more than fifty works by early modernist painter Palmer Hayden, donated by his widow. After a decade, Lewis and Hewitt relinquished all control of the museum.

62. *Art: African American* was first published in 1978 by Harcourt, Brace and Jovanovich. A second edition was published by the University of California Press in 1990 under the title *African American Art and Artists;* this version was updated in 2003. Interestingly, though Lewis provided the field with its major contemporary text, she has never taught African American art. Instead her teaching has focused on Asian, Native American, and African art. Lewis, "Image and Belief," 1999, 204.

63. John Chandler and Lucy R. Lippard, "The Dematerialization of Art," *Art International* 12: 2 (February 20, 1968): 34–35.

64. Judith Wilson, "In Memory of the News of Ourselves: The Art of Adrian Piper," *Third Text* 16/17 (Autumn/Winter 1991): 39.

65. See Kristine Stiles, "Between Water and Stone, Fluxus Performance: A Metaphysics of Acts," in *In the Spirit of Fluxus*, ed. Elizabeth Armstrong and Joan Rothfuss (Minneapolis: Walker Art Center, 1993), 92.

66. Rita Eder, "Razón y sin razón del arte efímero: algunos ejemplares latinoamericanos" *Plural* 8: 90 (second epoch) (March 1979): 28 [translation mine].

67. Joseph E. Young, "Three Graphic Artists," in *Three Graphic Artists: Charles White, David Hammons, Timothy Washington* (Los Angeles: Los Angeles County Museum of Art, 1971), 7.

68. Hammons learned this technique at Chouinard Art Institute. He never actually took this class but witnessed the demonstration as he passed by the room. David Hammons, personal communication, December 10, 1996, hereafter referred to as Hammons, December 1996.

69. Hammons, December 1996.

70. See "David Hammons" interviewed by Kellie Jones, *Real Life Magazine* 16 (Autumn 1986): 4.

71. Houston received his M.F.A in 1976. Kinshasha received an M.B.A. in arts management in 1980.

72. Judith Wilson, "Creating a Necessary Space: The Art of Houston Conwill, 1975–1983," *International Review of African American Art* 6: 1 (1984): 50.

73. Ceremonial stools are part of every aspect of traditional life among Akan peoples, including ceremonies marking puberty, death, birth, and marriage. They become objects through which ancestors are venerated. Most visibly the stool is a symbol of state power; political leaders' rise and fall are marked by the terms "enstooled" and "destooled," respectively. See Herbert M. Cole and Doran H. Ross, *The Arts of Ghana* (Los Angeles: Museum of Cultural History, University of California and Regents of the University of California, 1977).

74. Linda Goode Bryant and Marcy S. Philips, *Contextures* (New York: Just Above Midtown, Inc., 1978), 64.

75. Senga Nengudi, telephone interview with the author, June 3, 1996; hereafter referred to as Nengudi June 1996. Maren Hassinger, telephone interview with the author, May 29, 1996; hereafter referred to as Hassinger May 1996. Bill T. Jones touches on this issue in "You Don't Have to Be Thin to Dance," *New York Times* July 19, 1997: A19.

76. Maren Hassinger quoted in "Maren Hassinger," *International Review of African American Art* 6: 1 (1984): 40. This sense of process work as an initiatory practice is raised by Sandy Ballatore, "Hassinger and Mahan: Works in Transition," *Artweek* 7: 29 (September 4, 1976): 4.

77. Hassinger May 1996.

78. Hassinger, "Maren Hassinger," 1984, 40.

79. In the upper right hand corner of a photograph documenting the action, we see a work from Hammons' series called "Greasy Bags and Barbecue Bones," which were "collages" composed of oil-stained brown paper bags with spareribs (licked clean), hair and glitter. Hanging from the wall on the upper left is a Persian carpet, clearly the seeds of his *Flying Carpet* (1990) planted years before. Thanks to Maren Hassinger for point-

ing these works out to me. See the catalogue *Maren Hassinger, 1972–1991* (Brookville, NY: Hillwood Art Museum, Long Island University/C.W. Post Campus, 1991).

80. Nengudi completed both her B.A. and M.A. at California State University, Los Angeles, finishing in 1971.

81. Hammons in Jones, *Real Life Magazine*, 2.

82. Goode-Bryant and Philips, *Contextures*, 45.

83. Nengudi June 1996. Maren Hassinger has pointed out that a version of Studio Z performed together until 1986. Between 1982 and 1983 the group met at the studio of Ulysses Jenkins on Vermont Avenue and included Rudy Perez and May Sun. Though the initial place where Studio Z gathered was David Hammons' studio, during that period he was back and forth between New York and Los Angeles and performed with the group rarely; Hassinger May 1996. This was also confirmed by David Hammons; Hammons December 1996.

84. CETA stood for the Comprehensive Employment and Training Act. In effect 1974–1983, this job-training program used federal block grants for locally targeted programs, which were often aimed at underemployed populations (such as artists). Most programs with creative sections focused on utilizing their artist-employees as "resources," taping their painting, graphic, writing and theatrical skills for a broad range of publicly directed activities. Suzanne Jackson—artist and former proprietor of Gallery 32—coordinated Brockman's CETA projects for a while. "Professional Artist Employment Program Gets Underway at Brockman Gallery Productions," *Black Art* 2: 1 (1977): 68. On CETA see, Grace A. Franklin and Randall B. Ripley, *C.E.T.A. Politics and Policy 1973–1982* (Knoxville: University of Tennessee Press, 1984). Steven C. Dubin, "Artistic Production and Social Control," *Social Forces* 64: 3 (March 1986): 667–88.

The term "Fets" was short for Fetishes. Fetish is a word that comes with a lot of baggage, especially when applied to the African context. Within a colonial framework it was used in a disparaging manner to identify African religious articles. Certainly, the confluence with psychoanalytic meaning—as an object that elicits erotic desire—is not simply fortuitous.

85. Henry Drewal and Margaret Thompson Drewal, *Gelede, Art and Female Power the Yoruba* (Bloomington: Indiana University Press, 1990), and Robert Farris Thompson, *Flash of the Spirit* (New York: Random House, 1983).

86. Nengudi June 1996.

87. Kinshasha Conwill, *African American Artists of Los Angeles*, 62–65; Melinda Wortz, "Meditations on Death," *ArtNews* (November 1978): 154, 159; Suzanne Muchnic, "JuJu Ritual—Cycles of Life" *Artweek* 9 (February 25, 1978): 4. Even though Kinshasha speaks of winding down her own artmaking practice during this time, she is interviewed about it in Barbara McCullough's film, *Shopping Bag Spirits*, which was released in 1979. The couple also collaborated on a mural for St. Augustine Church in Houston's hometown of Louisville, Kentucky in 1974.

88. Kinshasha Conwill, *African American Artists of Los Angeles*, 75–77.

89. Jackson, *African American Artists of Los Angeles*, 153.

90. Salaam, "The Black Arts Movement," 74.

91. Ntozake Shange cited in Alan Read, ed., *The Fact of Blackness, Frantz Fanon and Visual Representation* (Seattle and London: Bay Press, Institute of Contemporary Arts, and Institute of International Visual Arts, 1996), 159.

92. Elizabeth Alexander has brilliantly argued this same point. She demonstrates that many of the black female literary figures that supposedly "emerge" after 1970 were, in fact, writing and publishing in the 1950s and 1960s, including Paule Marshall, Audre Lorde, Adrienne Kennedy, Lucille Clifton, and Alice Walker. Elizabeth Alexander, *The Black Interior* (St. Paul, MN: Graywolf Press, 2004), 61–65.

93. William J. Harris, "Black Aesthetic," *The Oxford Companion to African American Literature*, 69.

94. Harryette Mullen, "The Black Arts Movement," *African American Writers*, vol. 1, 2nd ed., ed. Valerie Smith (New York: Charles Scribner's Sons, 2001), 57.

95. Farah Jasmine Griffin, *"Who Set You Flowin'?" The African American Migration Narrative* (New York: Oxford University Press, 1995).

3
The Black Arts Movement and Historically Black Colleges and Universities

James Smethurst

Discussions of the Black Arts Movement of the 1960s and 1970s rarely give much consideration to black cultural activity in the South. This lack of interest is not only a feature of our own time. At the height of the movement, southern black artists and intellectuals complained about how difficult it was to attract the attention of their counterparts in the Northeast, the Midwest, and the West, even with the tremendous symbolic significance that the region retained in African American history and culture.[1] Yet despite this past and present scholarly inattention, Black Arts organizations, institutions, and events in the South were among the most successful grassroots black cultural efforts. These efforts made a powerful, and in many ways lasting, local impression in the South. At the same time, they were also central in promoting Black Arts as a truly national movement—national in the sense of bringing together activists from across the United States (and beyond) as well as in that of broadly embodying and articulating the concerns and the existence of a black nation.

Many of the political and cultural institutions of Reconstruction in the South had been destroyed by the disenfranchisement of most black southerners and the establishment of Jim Crow, but one legacy of Reconstruction and what might be thought of as the Reconstruction spirit still thrived in the 1950s and early 1960s: the historically black colleges and universities. The vast majority of these were located below the Mason-Dixon Line—though some important schools, notably Lincoln University, Cheney Training School for Teachers, and Central State University, were up North, and others, such as Howard University and Morgan State University, were to be found in such regionally ambiguous cities as Washington, D.C. and Baltimore. Since de jure segregation still operated in the South (and beyond) and de facto segregation or token integration was in effect at many colleges and universities elsewhere, a huge proportion of black college students (and black faculty) were concentrated at the African American schools in the South and the so-called Border States.

These concentrations of black schools and African American college students along with the national focus of the Civil Rights Movement on voting rights and the segregation of public facilities in the region left a deep imprint on the Black Arts Movement there. Of course, if we take Black Arts to be essentially the cultural wing of the Black Power Movement, the distinction between it and the Civil Rights Movement is difficult to draw precisely—perhaps more difficult than in any other region of the United States. To generalize broadly, the Civil Rights Movement of the late 1950s and early 1960s aimed in the first place at dismantling the segregation of public institutions and public accommodations and at the enfranchisement of African Americans across the South. Black Power was a contentious political formation, but generally speaking nearly all its manifestations involved a concept of liberation and self-determination, whether in a separate republic (e.g., the "Black Belt" of the South), some sort of federated state, black-run city (Detroit, for example), or some smaller community unit (say, Harlem, East Los Angeles, or the Central Ward of Newark). Black Power also generally entailed some notion of the development or recovery of a politically engaged "national" culture, often linked to an already existing folk or popular culture—in short, Black Arts. Yet this account oversimplifies things since it suggests that Black Arts simply issued from Black Power when both movements arose more or less simultaneously. Early Black Arts and proto-Black Arts institutions, such as the Umbra Poets Workshop, Black Arts/West, the Black Arts Repertory Theater/School (BARTS), the Free Southern Theater, and the Organization of Black American Culture (OBAC), played crucial roles in the development of important Black Power organizations and institutions in their regions. In fact, many of the best known Black Arts activists, such as Amiri Baraka, Haki Madhubuti, Askia Touré, and Larry Neal, were among the most important Black Power leaders. Similarly, if, as Amiri Baraka notes, the movement included many artists with an interest in politics, such as poet Sonia Sanchez, Neal, Touré, and Baraka himself, it also contained many political leaders with backgrounds in the arts, such as the Revolutionary Action Movement leader Muhammad Ahmad and Black Panther Party for Self-Defense founder Bobby Seale.[2]

Given the concentration of African Americans in the Deep South, Civil Rights efforts, particularly around voting rights, were always concerned with the issues of black political self-determination, black power if you will, that would come to be the hallmark of Black Power in its various manifestations. Thus, it is not surprising that Civil Rights organizations, most famously the Student Non-Violent Coordinating Committee (SNCC), played a central role in the development of the notion of Black Power and the Black Power Movement in the mid-1960s. Similarly, the considerable lag between legislation, federal policy decisions, and Supreme Court cases in Washington and the actual dismantling of old-style Jim Crow in the South during the late 1960s and early 1970s caused militant Black Power organizations on southern black campuses and in southern African American communities to concern themselves with issues of essentially de jure segregation that are more usually associated with the earlier Civil Rights Movement. Also, as writer Kalamu ya Salaam points out, the focus on electing black officials that emerged from the landmark 1972 National Black Political Convention in Gary, Indiana, necessitated a new Black Power orientation toward the South since the demographics of the region presented the greatest black electoral possibilities.[3] Again, this often meant that the resulting campaigns took on the tenor, the tactics, and often the goals of the Civil Rights Movement in order to have a chance of success. In fact, they *were* both civil rights and Black Power efforts, aiming at the final end of legal or quasi-legal Jim Crow and black self-determination at the same time—though, of course, one might argue that this had always been the case, especially in areas, such as many of the counties of the Mississippi Delta, where African Americans formed the overwhelming majority of the population.

Even the line between Civil Rights and Black Arts cultural institutions in the South is often quite fuzzy. Such institutions as the SNCC Freedom Singers and the Free Southern Theater were not, as northern black cultural institutions generally were, simply supportive of the southern Civil Rights Movement, they were actually prominent features of the movement. Though racked by personal and political contradictions throughout its existence, the Free Southern Theater (FST), founded in 1963 on the campus of historically black Tougaloo College in Mississippi, was the most important progenitor of community-based Black Arts activity in the South. As will be noted later, ironically, given the place of the theater's origin, the community-oriented southern cities in which the FST sparked the most successful regional manifestation of Black Arts, such as New Orleans (where the FST moved in 1965), Houston, Miami, and Memphis, remained relatively detached from the more prominent black campuses.

There was a symbiotic relationship between the educational institutions and Civil Rights—a relationship that significantly molded the movement and changed the institutions. Though the administrations, and often the faculties, were initially cautious or indifferent in their public relationship to the movement, the students of these institutions formed much of the core leadership and rank and file of the movement in the South. Students from southern black schools were instrumental in local sit-ins, picket lines, boycotts, and demonstrations, particularly in the 1960 sit-in movement that swept the South (and much of the North), coalescing into SNCC. Sometimes these young people organized under the auspices of established groups, such as the NAACP Youth Council or the Southern Christian Leadership Council (SCLC), and sometimes they created their own local organizations. As leading Black Arts activists Amiri Baraka, Kalamu ya Salaam, and Askia Touré have noted, these students inspired young black activists, artists, and intellectuals elsewhere in the United States (often themselves, like Baraka, poet and critic A. B. Spellman, poet, playwright, critic, and scholar Larry Neal, and Muhammad Ahmad, alumni of historically black schools) through their boldness, their militancy, and their refusal to wait for established leaders.[4]

A tremendous number of Black Arts activists, including many from outside the South, were politicized and introduced to a distinctly African American cultural tradition while at historically African American colleges and universities as students or faculty members (or both). Similarly, numerous younger black artists and intellectuals in San Francisco, Oakland, Los Angeles, Chicago, Detroit, Cleveland, New York, New Orleans, Washington, D.C. and so on, such as the writers Jayne Cortez, Tom Dent, David Llorens, Dingane Joe Goncalves (editor of the vital Black Arts magazine, *Journal of Black Poetry*), Sonia Sanchez, Kalamu ya Salaam, Ed Spriggs, Michael Thelwell, Askia Touré, Ebon Dooley, Haki Madhubuti, and Sterling Plumpp were active participants in SNCC, CORE, and other militant direct action civil rights groups that drew heavily on students from historically black campuses. Even those of this cohort of activist artists and intellectuals who never worked in the South or attended historically black schools, belonging instead to northern affiliates of the major Civil Rights groups or local organizations, generally saw themselves as both supporting the southern student movement and bringing that movement North to confront racism in their own regions. At the same time that they were energized by the southern movement, many future Black Arts activists who did go South (or were already in the South), tried to further radicalize the southern movement, introducing or reinforcing radical and/or nationalist thinking within SNCC and other civil rights organizations. Thus, while the Black Arts institutions and activities of the South had difficulty attracting attention beyond the region, the South was, nonetheless, far more crucial symbolically and practically to the development of the national movement than has sometimes been acknowledged.[5] At the same time, within the South itself, there was a distinction in style and orientation among cities such as Houston, New Orleans, and Miami where the Black Arts Movement was rooted largely in communities and other cities, such as Atlanta, Washington, D.C., Baton Rouge, and Nashville, where the movement was based more on the campus.[6]

The administrations of the historically African American schools in the South and in Washington, D.C., especially those dependent on public funding, were politically cautious and even conservative during the period immediately before and during the Cold War. A notorious example of such caution, if not cowardice, in the face of the emerging red scare was the firing of W.E.B. Du Bois from the faculty of Atlanta University in 1944. On a less public level, another sign of institutional conservatism was the exodus of many progressive and Left faculty members from historically black schools in the South during the late 1940s and the 1950s.[7] While administrators often sympathized with the sentiments and goals of the student movement that erupted in their institutions in 1960, under explicit or implicit pressure from the local and state power structure they frequently tried to rein in student protest, in some cases threatening to discipline or actually disciplining demonstrators—as when the Southern University expelled seven students (including the senior class president Marvin Robinson) arrested at a 1960 sit-in in Baton Rouge. And, however sympathetic these administrators might be, they often had a far different vision of appropriate tactics and even what goals were feasible than had the young demonstrators.[8] Even Martin Luther King, Jr. was unable to realize his long-held desire of being appointed to the Board of Trustees of his alma mater, Morehouse College, due largely to his perceived radicalism—particularly after King came out publicly against the United States' involvement in the Vietnam War.[9] As novelist John O. Killens noted while describing his experience as a writer-in-residence at Fisk, not only did early Black Power and Black Arts supporters have to contend with conservative (and often white) trustees and nervous (often black) administrators, but also conservative and liberal faculty members who saw "Fisk as a finishing school to train black boys and girls how to be nice little young white ladies and gentlemen in black skins" (63). These faculty members were notably hostile to Black Power and Black Arts, though often they attacked those movements passively or covertly. Killens recalls that when he organized the Black Writers' Conferences at Fisk, which were, as will be discussed below, landmarks in defining the existence and the shape of the emerging Black Arts movement and featured many leading older and younger black writers and scholars, the heads of the Fisk English, Speech, and Drama Departments did not attend.[10]

The administrations of many historically black schools took an extremely paternalistic and condescending stance toward their students, even at such elite schools as Howard.[11] Ironically, as was the case on many predominantly white campuses, such as the University of California at Berkeley, this sort of heavy-handed paternalism actually strengthened, and, in the case of Central State University in Ohio, inspired student activism by stoking general student dissatisfaction and creating broad support for relatively radical organizations, such as the earliest formation of the Revolutionary Action Movement at Central State in 1962.[12]

Nonetheless, such schools were often willing to hire (or retain) intellectuals, such as John O. Killens (Fisk University), poet and novelist Margaret Walker (Jackson State University), poet Melvin Tolson (Wiley College and Langston University), poet and scholar Sterling Brown (Howard University), critic and scholar Mercer Cook (Howard), poet, playwright, and director Owen Dodson (Howard), and poet Lance Jeffers (Howard), who had been part of the Popular Front subculture of the 1930s and 1940s, supporting organizations and events initiated by the Communist Party—and sometimes, like Walker, actually belonging to the Party. In some cases (as in Killens'), these faculty members still retained live connections to what remained of the cultural and political institutions of the Communist Left. Others were more distant from public support of Left initiatives and organizations in the 1950s and the early 1960s, but remained essentially unrepentant as to their political activities during the 1930s and 1940s—as did Walker, Brown, and Tolson. And quite a few of these veterans of 1930s and 1940s radicalism supported the journal *Freedomways*, conceived and founded by such prominent African American leftists as Louis Burnham, W.E.B. Du Bois, Shirley Graham Du Bois, Esther Cooper Jackson, and Margaret Burroughs, when it appeared in 1961, joining the editorial board and/or contributing stories, essays, poems, art work, and so on.

Not only did black colleges sometimes hire faculty with radical pasts (and presents), they also supported large-scale literary events initiated by intellectuals with some past or present connection to the Left. For example, Rosey Pool was a leftwing Dutch journalist and scholar living in Britain during the late 1950s and early 1960s. Her 1962 anthology, *Beyond the Blues*, the first serious anthology of contemporary African American poetry in more than a decade, highlighted politically and formally radical black writing.[13] Pool organized a festival of African American poetry at Alabama A & M in 1964 and again in 1966—though the featured participants were drawn from Pool's connections in the Midwest (e.g., Margaret Burroughs, Dudley Randall, Margaret Danner, and Mari Evans) where she spent much time while assembling her anthology rather than in the South. Pool also lectured on African American poetry at dozens of historically black campuses in 1959–1960. These festivals as well as Pool's lectures did much to create a sense of the emergence of a new black poetry that was both formally and politically radical. And, again, it needs to be noted that because the historically black schools drew on a national (and international) network of students and alumni, these sorts of events had an impact far beyond the South.

It is true that some schools, as was the case with Howard apparently, protected their faculty from various Red hunters with the understanding that they would not engage in high profile radical politics. Still, despite this limited and limiting resistance to McCarthyism, there were not many historically white universities where a professor who had been engaged in the activities of the Popular Front as publicly as had Sterling Brown could have survived without repenting of his or her political past (and sometimes even a public repentance would not save the former leftist). While many of the scholars and artists teaching in historically black schools had willingly, or under institutional duress, retreated from political activism, many became energized by the revived Civil Rights Movement, especially the Black Student Movement that in 1960 exploded after four North Carolina A & T freshmen sat-in at a downtown Greensboro, North Carolina Woolworth's lunch counter. This older generation of radicals helped open political and cultural spaces that were crucial to the development of what might be thought of as a Black Arts/Black Power cadre, especially in conjunction with the domestic and international currents of civil rights, nationalism, and national liberation that flowed together on historically black campuses in a distinctive way.

Interestingly, with the exception of peripheral Black Arts participant Julian Bond, few of those who would spearhead the Black Arts Movement participated directly in the early Black Student Movement in the South—though many would join CORE, SNCC, and other civil rights organizations in the North and the West. However, as noted earlier, a number such as Tom Dent, poet Calvin Hernton, Amiri Baraka, Larry Neal, A. B. Spellman, and poet and critic Sarah Webster Fabio attended historically black universities in the decade before 1960. Many of these writers found what they considered to be the generally cautious and accommodationist atmosphere of most historically black schools alienating. However, they also often discovered a sense of African American folk and popular culture and history as subjects that could be approached in an engaged and intellectually serious manner—though often this education took place outside the formal circuits of the institution. For example, Amiri Baraka recalls Howard as being "an employment agency at best, at worst a kind of church . . . for a small accommodationist black middle class."[14] Yet he also cites Sterling Brown's classes on African American music, also attended by A. B. Spellman, as "opening us to the fact that the music could be studied and, by implication, that black people had a history. He was raising the music as an art, a thing for scholarship and research as well as deep enjoyment."[15] Baraka and Spellman, in turn, would become leading Black Arts proponents of the notion of a black cultural continuum that included folk, popular, and avant-garde elements. Similarly, Tom Dent remembered that watching historian Benjamin Quarles working in the library of Dillard University gave him a sense that a serious intellectual life was possible.[16]

There was also a long tradition of civil rights activism at some historically black schools, particularly Howard and Fisk. Howard students, for example, had been instrumental in launching the campaign against Jim Crow in public facilities and accommodations during the 1940s, using many of the tactics of later activists, including sitting-in at lunch counters, and suffering much the same resistance from the Howard administration.[17] Given the inevitable turnover of students and the disinterest of college administrations in publicly acknowledging such past militancy, radical faculty often served as unofficial historians. In addition to introducing African American culture as a subject of serious study, Sterling Brown revealed to members of the Non-Violent Action Group (NAG), the SNCC affiliate on campus during the early 1960s, Howard's considerable history as a center of black political activism and radical thought as well as the sort of roadblocks previous administrations had presented to that radicalism— much like the resistance that NAG encountered in their own time.[18]

Also, the historically black schools drew a large international student body, especially from Africa and the Caribbean. A number of these students were radicals, sometimes Marxists or influenced by Marxism, and engaged with the liberation movements in their home countries and throughout Asia, Africa, the Caribbean, and Latin America. These international students were limited in their ability to participate directly in U.S. political movements by their legal status. However, through them native-born African Americans more closely encountered Post-Bandung Conference liberation movements and various strains of radicalism, Pan-Africanism, different sorts of communism and socialism, and militant anti-imperialism, than was the case on most U.S. campuses in the late 1950s and early 1960s.[19]

In turn, the students from the United States who became active in campus politics often had some experience in black nationalist organizations, particularly the Nation of Islam, and/or the Civil Rights Movement. Some at Central State, Howard, and other schools outside of the Deep South, such as Ed Brown at Howard, had been expelled from southern historically black schools for their civil rights activism. Others brought some background in various sorts of Left organizations with them. For example, Kwame Ture (Stokely Carmichael) came to Howard from New York City in 1960 with much exposure to Marxism. In part through his close friendship with fellow Bronx Science High School student Gene Dennis (son of the Communist Party national chairman Eugene Dennis), and through his membership in a progressive Bronx science student group, Ture met a number of leading black Communists, including Benjamin Davis (the well-known former City Councilperson from Harlem), and had participated in a range of Communist and Socialist activities and institutions.[20] Tom Kahn, a gay white Howard student and a leader of the Young People's Socialist League affiliated with the Socialist Party, worked closely with Ture in NAG. Kahn eventually became the head of the League for Industrial Democracy, the original parent organization of Students for a Democratic Society (SDS). Kahn brought not only his radical politics with him, but also a close friendship with the older gay African American Socialist Bayard Rustin who became a key adviser of NAG and, later, SNCC—though Kahn, like Rustin, later moved to the right end of the socialist political spectrum.

This encounter between the international independence movements and various strains of U.S. radicalism and activism was particularly intense at Howard University where the mix of black students from all the regions of the United States, Africa, and the English-speaking Caribbean was more diverse than at any other American college or university. As newly self-governing African, Asian, and Caribbean nations opened embassies in Washington, D.C., especially after the independence of Ghana in 1957, Howard students, many of whom were citizens of the newly independent nations, were invited to parties, lectures, receptions, and so on, at these embassies. This direct connection of Howard students to independence leaders of the often revolutionary new governments energized politically minded Howard students and, again, expanded their political horizons in a manner that was unique. In addition to the direct impact on political thought on campus, the international students and, at Howard, the direct links to the new states of the former colonial world also provided students at historically black schools a sophistication with respect to the possibilities of black culture and models of politically engaged art that were hard to come by on what might be thought of as historically white campuses in the later 1950s and early 1960s.[21] Not surprisingly, Howard became a particular locus of Left nationalist influence within SNCC and the Black Student Movement.

As mentioned earlier, a number of important black writers worked as teachers at the black colleges and universities in the South during the late 1950s and early 1960s. A very high percentage had radical pasts. Some like Robert Hayden had moved considerably from their earlier Left politics—though Hayden's continuing engagement with history in his work showed a link to his earlier Left poetry of *Heart-Shape in the Dust* (1940). Others, as previously noted, such as Margaret Walker, Sterling Brown, and John O. Killens, stayed much closer to their earlier Left commitments. Killens' writers' workshop at Fisk University was a particularly significant catalyst of the early Black Arts Movement during the middle 1960s. A number of important Black Arts writers, most notably Nikki Giovanni, were members of the workshop. Like other older radical writers, including Margaret Walker at Jackson State University and Sterling Brown at Howard University, Killens saw one of his main tasks in mentoring young black writers and political activists as reminding them of their artistic and political ancestors, especially those associated with the Popular Front era.[22] When Killens returned to New York in the late 1960s, the workshop continued under Donald Lee Graham (Le Graham) until Graham's death in 1971.

Fisk, of course, was the home of other important black poets, most notably Hayden and Arna Bontemps. Nonetheless, it was Killens and his workshop that figured most prominently in initiating the writers' conferences at Fisk in 1966 and 1967. These conferences were watershed events marking the emergence of the Black Arts Movement as the ascendant force in African American letters. Such older artists and scholars as Ossie Davis, Saunders Redding, Bontemps, Hayden, Margaret Walker, Loften Mitchell, and Melvin Tolson dominated the first conference. Virtually the only younger writer to appear on the program of the conference was the novelist Melvin Kelley—apparently Baraka was invited, but did not attend. However, the new militant nationalist writing made itself felt everywhere at the conference as participants obsessively mentioned Baraka and other younger writers, either disapprovingly or as the wave of the future (or often both). Some older writers took up the banner of the new militants, as did Walker in her reading of a poem to Malcolm X, and as did Tolson during his famous debate with Robert Hayden in which he asserted, "I'm a black poet, an African-American poet, a Negro poet," in response to Hayden's claim that "he was a poet who happens to be Negro." It was also at this conference that a chance meeting between Walker, Dudley Randall, and Margaret Burroughs resulted in Broadside Press's first book project, the seminal anthology *For Malcolm* (1969).[23]

Younger writers, particularly Baraka and Detroit playwright Ron Milner, one of the most important Black Arts theater workers, dominated the 1967 Fisk conference. Older writers, including Killens, Brooks, Danner, and scholar John Henrik Clarke, actively took part in the conference. However, these literary elders were among the most enthusiastic supporters of the new black writing. A number of those older artists not previously identified with the new cultural and political militancy, most famously Gwendolyn Brooks, publicly embraced

Black Power and Black Arts at the conference. In fact, these conversions, particularly that of Brooks, gave the conference much of its charge as an event marking a new day in African American letters. Those artists who had seemed to oppose or express doubts about the emerging national political/artistic movements at the earlier conference were for the most part absent or far less prominent. For example, Hayden did not participate directly in the conference—though he was a featured artist during the week of cultural events at Fisk. Despite the fact that the older writers were among the most sympathetic to the new militant literary nationalism, the younger members of the audience frequently took them to task. Though these attacks might have been unfair, reflecting in the view of a *Negro Digest* correspondent the ignorance of the attackers as to the work of those they attacked, nonetheless they demonstrated a much changed atmosphere from the previous year when the Black Arts Movement was more like a haunting presence.[24]

At Howard, Sterling Brown played much the same mentoring role as did Killens at Fisk—though with his own distinct style. One of his students from the early 1960s, the fiction writer and NAG member Mike Thelwell (author of the novel *The Harder They Come* [1980]), recalled that Brown's formal classes were extremely competent, but more or less standard literature courses of the day—though not entirely so since it was not unheard of for someone like pianist Willie "The Lion" Smith to show up at Brown's classes. However, as noted earlier, Brown's unofficial seminars and discussion sessions (with bourbon) on African American culture, history, music, literature, and politics, nurtured and inspired many Black Arts and Black Power activists (and also pre- and post-Black Arts writers) including Amiri Baraka, A. B. Spellman, Toni Morrison, and Thelwell. Brown also served as a mentor to the largely avant-gardist literary grouping around the student journal *Dasein*, including Percy Johnston, Oswald Govan, Walter De Legall, and Leroy Stone, as well as to the political activists in NAG, including Thelwell, Kwame Ture, Cleveland Sellers, Ed Brown, Rap Brown, Charlie Cobb, and Courtland Cox, who would play a key role in the leadership of SNCC and the emergence of Black Power.[25] While the *Dasein* group did not participate directly in the political activities of NAG and SNCC (and while the NAG activists considered the Howard Poets to be bohemians a little too concerned with their images as artists), the active existence of both groups contributed to a sense of a dynamic political and cultural environment on campus. At the same time, the fact that neither NAG nor *Dasein* were ever officially recognized by Howard highlights some of the contradictions of political and cultural life on historically black campuses in the early 1960s.[26]

The relatively modest campus venues for formally and politically radical black art and Left and/or nationalist politics took on a new significance as a mass constituency for the Black Power Movement and the Black Arts Movement grew in the general population of African Americans in the South as well as among black intellectuals and students. As young African Americans (as well as older African Americans) in the South became frustrated with the unwillingness or the open resistance of the white southern power structure to go beyond the desegregation of public facilities and to allow the black community full access to economic, educational, and political opportunities, militant Black Power groups emerged in neighborhoods and especially on the college campuses of such black schools as Southern University, North Carolina A & T, South Carolina State, and Jackson State. This led to the creation of important Black Power/Black Arts institutions, such as Malcolm X University (established in Durham, North Carolina, in 1969 and moving to Greensboro in 1970) and Student Organization for Black Unity (SOBU) (the most important national Black Power student organization, founded in Greensboro in 1969). The activities of these militant campus groups, especially at more working-class campuses, such as North Carolina A & T and South Carolina State, often revolved around neighborhood concerns, such as housing and school systems, as well as general concerns about the persistence of blatant Jim Crow practices, especially by white merchants. There was an extremely negative and often violent response to these activities by local authorities, leading to the death of students at Southern University, South Carolina State, and Jackson State at the hands of National Guardsmen or law enforcement agents. The extreme responses of the police and the local and state political establishments further radicalized students and faculty at the historically black schools.[27]

As a result of this new constituency for radical nationalist ideas, institutions, and activities on campus and in the broader black community, the historically black schools were increasingly willing to provide institutional support for Black Arts or Black Arts-influenced activities and institutions. In part, this was because the increased political engagement (or the willingness to make open their political engagement) of the faculty propelled this institutional support. After the Fisk conferences and the Alabama A & T conferences, the historically black colleges frequently hosted conferences and festivals of African American art and literature, including the annual Black Poetry Festivals at Southern University beginning in 1972 and the Phillis Wheatley Bicentennial Festival at Jackson State in 1973.[28]

In addition to this willingness to host Black Arts or Black Arts-influenced events, many historically African American schools hired Black Arts writers, artists, and scholars as permanent or visiting faculty. A very incomplete list would include poets Haki Madhubuti and Amos Zu-Bolton, OBAC painters Jeff Donaldson and Wadsworth Jarrell, and critic Stephen Henderson at Howard, poets Calvin Hernton and Jay Wright at Talladega, poet (and African National Congress activist in exile) Keorapetse Kgositsile, poets Jay Wright and Audre Lorde at Tougaloo, poet and critic A. B. Spellman and Henderson (before his departure to Howard) at Morehouse, poet and literary historian Eugene Redmond at Southern, and poet Donald Lee Graham at Fisk (taking over John Killens' Black Writers Workshop). In a number of cases, such as those of Henderson and Donaldson at Howard, these faculty members were hired essentially to remake departments in a Black Arts or Black Power mode.

Atlanta with its neighboring Spelman, Morehouse, Clark, Atlanta University, and Morris Brown College became an especially important locus of Black Arts and Black Power artists and intellectuals. The concentration of schools and, increasingly, artists and intellectuals, who participated in the Black Arts Movement and the Black Power Movement and were often on the faculty of one of the schools, led to the establishment of such institutions as the Center for Black Art and the Institute of the Black World. These institutions were not connected to particular schools, but were made possible by the sheer density of historically black colleges and universities and the new level of acceptance of Black Arts and Black Power by the faculty and administrations of the schools.

The Institute of the Black World was at first affiliated with the Martin Luther King, Jr. Memorial Center rather than one of the black colleges or universities. Though the Institute eventually developed a focus on education and the social sciences, it was imagined initially as a research-oriented hub of the emerging Black Studies movement in academia with a strong interest in furthering the Black Arts Movement. The Institute was largely the brainchild of historian Vincent Harding, chair of the History Department at Spelman, and Stephen Henderson, chair of the English Department at Morehouse. Henderson's *Understanding the New Black Poetry* (1972), an "Institute of the Black World Book," was the most prominent academic Black Arts statement on African American poetics as well as an extremely influential anthology.

In fact, when listing the central concerns of the field of Black Studies in the Institute's Statement of Purpose and Program, the second item of a list of ten points concerned nationalist art:

> The encouragement of those creative artists who are searching for the meaning of a black aesthetic, who are now trying to define and build the basic ground on which black creativity may flow in the arts. Encounter among these artists on the one hand, and scholars, activists, and students on the other, must be constant in both formal and informal settings.[29]

Again, though the Institute of the Black World was associated with the King Center, it would not have been possible without the black schools of University Center—a fact that is acknowledged in the statement.[30]

Even more grassroots-oriented initiatives, such as the Center for Black Art and the journal *Rhythm*, both largely organized by poet and critic A. B. Spellman (whose 1966 *Four Lives in the Bebop Business* remains a classic of jazz criticism) after his move to Atlanta, were largely based among the radicalized black university community and were aimed at an audience significantly outside the South. In fact, one finds a certain alienation or distance from the local communities, at least initially, by those, such as Spellman, who migrated South to work in the black schools of Atlanta. In a report on the Atlanta scene in *The Cricket*, a black arts music journal based in Newark and edited by Spellman, Amiri Baraka, and Larry Neal, Spellman clearly considers the music and arts scene in Atlanta to be backward—though he also found a rootedness in the black community of Atlanta that he felt New York lacked.[31]

Perhaps the greatest example of the strengths and weaknesses of the Black Arts Movement in Atlanta can be seen in the attempt of former *Black World* editor Hoyt Fuller and others to create a Black Power/Black Arts journal to replace *Black World*. With a readership in the tens of thousands, *Black World* had been the most important intellectual journal of the Black Arts and Black Power movements. Its parent company, Johnson Publications shut down *Black World* in 1976 after a heated debate over the alleged anti-semitism of the journal. Anti-semitism was only the ostensible issue in the debate. What was really in question was whether Johnson Publishing, which issued such popular magazines as *Ebony* and *Jet*, wanted to continue publishing a radical, though widely circulating, intellectual journal that did not make money. Of course, this had been an issue between Fuller and Johnson Publishing for years. However, the decline in the Black Power Movement, in part precipitated and certainly hastened by the internal battle in such key organizations as the Congress of African People (CAP), diminished and divided the audience of *Black World* (which was generally inclined toward the cultural nationalist side of the movement's internal struggles). As a result the considerable attempts to save the journal were not sufficiently unified and broad to successfully pressure Johnson Publishing into maintaining it.

The idea then was to create a new journal, *First World*, completely controlled by the movement that could carry on the work of *Black World* without depending on the financial support of an essentially unsympathetic owner. Atlanta, Fuller's birthplace, seemed like an ideal location given its concentration of African American colleges and universities and radicalized black faculty, including Stephen Henderson and Fuller's close friend (and, later, literary executor) Richard Long, and its prominence as a national center of the Civil Rights Movement and Black Studies as embodied in the King Center and the Institute of the Black World. However, after a promising start in 1977, *First World* failed, publishing its last issue in 1980. Fuller's premature death in 1981 foreclosed hope that it might be revived.

In part, *First World* suffered from the divisions that caused the movement as a whole to decline nationally. After all, *First World* was hardly the only important black intellectual or cultural journal to disappear in that era. Much of the early impetus to initiate a journal to replace *Black World* took place outside Atlanta.[32] Still, part of *First World*'s failure was due not only to the decline of Black Power and Black Arts nationally, but due also to an inability to build a local support network in Atlanta much beyond University Center that replicated the sort of network in Chicago that was crucial to the success of *Black World*. This is a failure that characterized the cultural movement as a whole in Atlanta. For example, despite Atlanta's reputation as a premier center of black artistic activity in the South, no viable African American theater group developed outside the confines of University Center during the Black Arts era.[33]

As a result, Atlanta became an increasingly important national center of nationalist thought and activity without a concomitant growth of local grass-roots institutions that reached much beyond University Center. It hosted the first Congress of African Peoples (CAP) convention in 1970, a landmark in what historian Komozi Woodard has termed the "Modern Black Convention Movement." It was at the Atlanta Congress that the CAP was established as an ongoing umbrella group of a wide ideological range of black political and cultural groups—though radical nationalism dominated CAP until its effective demise as a result of factional battles between Marxists and cultural nationalists in the mid-1970s.[34] However, the Black Arts Movement in Atlanta seems to have been relatively unconnected to the less academically centered movements in the South. For example, Henderson's *Understanding the New Black Poetry* did not contain any work by the writers associated with BLKARTSOUTH in New Orleans, Sudan-Southwest in Houston, or the Afro Arts Theater in Miami. The poets living in the South that Henderson did include, such as A. B. Spellman, Donald L. Graham, Keorapetse Kgositsile, and Laedele X, were almost all based in the relatively elite historically black colleges and universities of Nashville, Atlanta, and Washington, D.C.—and the more academically oriented institutions connected to those schools. Similarly, Black Arts theater and cultural groups from Atlanta seem to have been relatively uninvolved in the Southern Black Cultural Alliance, a dynamic regional Black Arts umbrella organization that included Black Arts groups and theaters from Texas to Florida.

However, to dwell solely on the shortcomings and failures of the academically (and nationally) oriented focus of the Black Power and Black Arts Movements in Atlanta, Nashville, and other southern black academic centers is to miss the important role that these centers played. Conferences at such schools as Jackson State, Fisk, Alabama A & T, Tougaloo, and Southern early on gave visibility to new black writing and aired the national debates that had been largely restricted to study groups, workshops, and little magazines. In the late 1960s and the 1970s similar conferences at Howard and the University Center schools of Atlanta, notably the 1968 Toward a Black University conference, brought together leading radical black cultural and political leaders (who were often one and the same), again providing a sense of national (and even international coherence) to now intersecting spheres of black politics, education, and art.

Atlanta today is a national African American cultural and intellectual center that shows a major nationalist and activist influence in ways that would have seemed incredible before 1960. And if, as political scientist Adolph Reed suggests, radical black organizations were unable to offer alternatives to the "black regime" of Maynard Jackson in the 1970s and the 1980s that attracted broad support within the black community, artists who had been leading Black Arts activists spearheaded cultural initiatives that *did* reach a mass audience. The advocacy of poet Ebon Dooley, a veteran of Chicago's Organization of Black American Culture (OBAC), played a major role in extending Jackson's desire to be known as the "culture mayor" to cover grassroots arts activities in black neighborhoods.[35] One of these activities was the establishment of a black art museum, Hammonds House, in the 1980s by poet and visual artist Ed Spriggs, who had been a leader in a wide range of Black Arts institutions in New York (including the founding of The Studio Museum in Harlem), in a then declining West End neighborhood rather than downtown. It also led to Atlanta's regionally and nationally known Black Arts Festival.

It is in no small part due to the Black Arts Movement and its impact on the students, faculties, and even administrations of the historically black schools there that Atlanta has gained a prominence in national African American intellectual and cultural discussions that is often quite at odds with the tradition of pragmatism and conciliation often associated with its African American politicians. Similarly, while the cities of Nashville and Washington, D.C. lacked the same density of black educational institutions, the traditional prestige, large number of African and Caribbean students, and longstanding, if uneven, traditions of political activism of Fisk and Howard allowed them to make major contributions to the growth of Black Arts as a national movement with international ties. As a result of the concentration of black students, intellectuals, and artists politicized by the Civil Rights Movement, Black Power, and Black Arts in Atlanta, Nashville, Washington, and other southern African American educational centers, radical African American political and cultural activities in these cities inspired black artists inside and outside the region, promoting a sense of Black Arts as a coherent national movement.

NOTES

1. Kalamu ya Salaam, "Enriching the Paper Trail: An Interview with Tom Dent" *African American Review* 27: 2 (Summer 1993): 339; Kalamu ya Salaam, autobiographical statement (unpublished); author's interview with Kalamu ya Salaam, April 23, 2000, New Orleans, Louisiana.

2. Author's interview with Amiri Baraka, July 15, 2000, Newark, New Jersey.

3. Author's interview with Kalamu ya Salaam.

4. Amiri Baraka, *The Black Arts Movement* (Newark: self-published mimeograph, 1994), 1; author's interview with Amiri Baraka; author's interview with Askia Touré, December 2, 2000, Cambridge, Massachusetts; Kalamu ya Salaam, *The Magic of Juju: An Appreciation of the Black Arts Movement* (Chicago: Third World Press, forthcoming), 5.

5. For a discussion of the difficulty in reaching an audience beyond the region due to the parochialism of northern Black Arts activists and institutions, see Salaam, "Enriching the Paper Trail," 338–39.

6. This is not to say that educational institutions such as Dillard University (where Tom Dent's father, Albert Dent, was president) and Southern University-New Orleans, did not figure prominently in the Black Power and Black Arts movements of Houston, Miami, and New Orleans. Nonetheless, the community oriented BLKARTSOUTH in New Orleans and the groups it inspired, such as Sudan Arts Southwest in Houston

and the Theatre of Afro Arts in Miami, were far more important in those cities than any institutions linked to a campus or group of campuses. These community-based groups formed the backbone of the Southern Black Cultural Alliance, the most successful regional Black Arts organization.

7. For example, Tom Dent notes the departure of progressive faculty members, such as L. D. Reddick and St. Clair Drake, and Left teachers, such as the visual artist Elizabeth Catlett, from Dillard University during the period. Tom Dent, "Marcus B. Christian: An Appreciation," *Black American Literature Forum* 18: 1 (Spring 1984): 25. Interestingly, historically black schools in the North, such as Central State University, Howard University, and Lincoln University, were often havens for progressive or Left faculty.

8. August Meier and Elliott Rudwick, *CORE: A Study in the Civil Rights Movement, 1942–1968* (New York: Oxford University Press, 1973), 107–108; David Harmon, *Beneath the Image of the Civil Rights Movement and Race Relations: Atlanta, Georgia, 1946–1981* (New York: Garland, 1996), 127–46; Jack Walker, "Sit-Ins in Atlanta: A Study in the Negro Revolt," in *Atlanta, Georgia, 1960–1961: Sit-Ins and Student Activism*, ed. David J. Garrow (Brooklyn: Carlson Publishing, 1989), 64–76.

9. Michael Eric Dyson, *I May Not Get There With You: The True Martin Luther King, Jr.* (New York: Free Press, 2000), 255–56.

10. John O. Killens, "The Artist and the Black University," *The Black Scholar* 1: 1 (November 1969): 63.

11. Author's interview with Michael Thelwell, February 20, 2003, Pelham, Massachusetts; author's telephone interview with Muhammad Ahmad, August 20, 2002.

12. Author's interview with Muhammad Ahmad.

13. Pool, a frequent writer for the journal, *Soviet Woman*, was clearly active in the international Communist movement—though on what level it is hard to say precisely. Pool's correspondence with such poets as Sam Allen, Chuck Anderson, Mari Evans, and Sarah Wright are fascinating documents of Cold War political circumspection. In these letters, the correspondents cautiously come out of their political closets through the mention of various names in common (e.g., W.E.B. Du Bois, Shirley Graham, David Du Bois, Walter Lowenfels) proclaiming Left political sympathies in ways that did not reveal too much at once either to the letters' recipients—or any third party who might be reading the mail (Rosey Pool Papers, Moorland-Springarn Research Center, Howard University, Box 82-1 Folders 6, 8, and 48, and Box 83-3, Folder 165).

14. Baraka, *The Autobiography of LeRoi Jones* (New York: Lawrence Hill, 1997), 134.

15. Baraka, *Autobiography*, 109–10.

16. Salaam, "Enriching the Paper Trail," 329.

17. Pauli Murray, "A Blueprint for First Class Citizenship," in *Reporting Civil Rights, Part One: American Journalism 1941–1963* (New York: Library Classics of America, 2003), 62–67.

18. Ekwueme Michael Thelwell, "The Professor and the Activists: A Memoir of Sterling Brown," *Massachusetts Review* 40: 4 (Winter 1999–2000): 617–38.

19. Author's interview with Muhammad Ahmad; author's interview with Michael Thelwell.

20. Kwame Ture (Stokely Carmichael) and Ekwueme Michael Thelwell, *Ready for Revolution: The Life and Struggles of Stokely Carmichael* (New York: Scribner, 2003), 86–95; Clayborne Carson, *In Struggle: SNCC and the Black Awakening of the 1960s* (Cambridge: Harvard University Press, 1981), 162.

21. Author's interview with Muhammad Ahmad; author's interview with Michael Thelwell.

22. For an example of this linking of the new and the old radicalisms written a little after the high-water mark of Black Arts/Black Power, see Killens, "The Artist and the Black University," 61–65.

23. For an account of the 1966 Fisk conference, see David Llorens, "Writers Converge on Fisk University," *Negro Digest* 15: 8 (June 1966): 54–68. For a brief description of the Hayden-Tolson debate at the conference, see Robert M. Farnsworth, Robert M. *Melvin B. Tolson, 1896–1966: Plain Talk and Poetic Prophecy* (Columbia: University of Missouri Press, 1984), 297–98.

24. For a short description of the 1967 Fisk conference, see "On the Conference Beat," *Negro Digest* 16: 9 (July 1967): 90–93.

25. Author's interview with Amiri Baraka; author's interview with Michael Thelwell; Thelwell, "The Professor and the Activists," 626–27. For the best account of the *Dasein* group and their work, see Aldon Nielsen, *Black Chant: Languages of African American Post-Modernism* (New York: Cambridge University Press, 1997), 59–77.

26. Author's interview with Michael Thelwell.

27. For accounts of Civil Rights and Black Power movements (and the difficulty of drawing a clear line between the two movements) in a number of small southern cities, often in the words of participants in those struggles, see Tom Dent, *Southern Journey* (New York: William Morrow & Company, 1996).

28. Eugene B. Redmond, *Drumvoices: The Mission of Afro-American Poetry: A Critical History* (Garden City: Anchor, 1976), 375–81.

29. Institute of the Black World, "Statement of Purpose and Program," in *New Black Voices: An Anthology of Contemporary Afro-American Literature*, ed. Abraham Chapman (New York: New American Library, 1972), 575–78.

30. For a short history of the inception and early days of the Institute of the Black World, see Stephen Ward, "'Scholarship in the Context of Struggle': Activist Intellectuals, the Institute of the Black World (IBW), and the Contours of the Black Power Radicalism," *Black Scholar* 31: 3–4 (Fall-Winter 2001): 42–53.

31. A. B. Spellman, "Letter from Atlanta," *Cricket* 3 (1969): 1–7; author's interview with A. B. Spellman, December 28, 2000, Washington, D.C.

32. Historian Robert Harris, Jr. recalls attending a meeting in John Henrik Clarke's apartment in New York City to discuss the creation of a new journal to replace *Black World* that helped lead to the founding of First World (Robert Harris, Jr., Comments, Modern Cultural Politics panel, Organization of American Historians annual meeting, Memphis, Tennessee, April 3, 2003).

33. For an account the black theater scene and its limitations in Atlanta during the Black Arts period, see Barbara Molette, "Atlanta," *Black World* 22: 6 (April 1973): 88–92.

34. For an account of the forces leading to the formation and the decline of CAP and its role in establishing this Modern Black Convention Movement, see Komozi Woodard, *A Nation within a Nation: Amiri Baraka and Black Power Politics* (Chapel Hill: University of North Carolina Press, 1999), 219–54.

35. Author's interview with Ebon Dooley, August 16, 2001, Atlanta, Georgia; Adolph Reed, *Stirrings in the Jug: Black Politics in the Post-Segregation Era* (Minneapolis: University of Minnesota Press, 1999), 1–52.

4

A Question of Relevancy

New York Museums and the Black Arts Movement, 1968–1971

Mary Ellen Lennon

Where has the Black Artist in America
been all this time?
He's been in the streets in Watts,
in Roxbury and Chicago.
He's been in his body. In hard times.
He's been in the eyes of people who love him
and in the eyes of people who hate him.
And he's been putting it all down.
On canvas. In stone. Out of wood.
—ABA: A JOURNAL OF AFFAIRS OF BLACK ARTISTS, 1972

The doors of a large metropolitan museum of art serve as a significant threshold, resonant with expectations. Inside wait carefully preserved masterpieces mounted on canvas and pedestal. These doors both promise and confirm the excellence of the works of art inside. Excellence substantiated further by the vaulted ceilings, marble staircases and uniformed guards charged with regulating voices (not too loud!) and bodies (not too close!). The ornate frames, the managed temperature, the skillful lighting . . . all these elements herald the importance of what is waiting to be viewed. Such rooms of hushed reverence impose their own expectations on the part of the visitors as well. In such a grand and sacred space, viewers are obliged not simply to look, but to *appreciate*.

The doors' power to command expectations derives from the power of exclusion. The works of art found inside are of "museum quality." By implication, those that remain outside are not. As arbiter of taste and authority on the singularly special, the art museum makes fundamental decisions over which pieces of art should be presented to and appreciated by the public as "genius."

If this particular visualization of the art museum gives the slightest pause, if perhaps the feeling persists that a museum *can be more, should be more* than the "temple of muses" its Greek etymology implies, an important but largely unacknowledged achievement of the Black Arts Movement in the United States is revealed. In the late 1960s and early 1970s, African American visual artists led an attack on the *de facto* segregation of the art world in all its institutionalized forms: the omission of historical and contemporary African American artists from the pages of art survey texts, racially biased art criticism, the absence of art education in urban ghettos, the dearth of teaching positions, scholarships, and grants for younger artists, and, most urgently, the absence of work by black artists on gallery walls throughout the country. But this challenge to the traditionally white art establishment went well beyond an "add-and-stir" strategy of inclusion. Instead, by asserting the African American community's identity both as creators and consumers of art, black visual artists offered nothing short of a revolutionary reappraisal of the meaning and function of the art museum in the United States.

In 1969, a thirty-four-year-old poet and painter named Edward Spriggs surveyed the "art Establishment" of the United States (his shorthand for the largest and most powerful fine art museums and galleries, their boards of trustees and their contributors) and wrote, "The thrust of the traditional museum's programs remains unchanged: they continue to be created by one small group for the benefit of another small group and still to be overwhelmingly oriented to white middle-class values and interests."[1] He described a "radical" new kind of art museum that both introduced the general public to gifted black artists long rendered invisible by the "institutional imperialism and racism" of traditional museums and, most importantly, embraced "a comprehensive and integral interrelationship with its community" by mounting exhibitions "with an eye to their *relevance* to black people."[2]

In the late 1960s and early 1970s, groups of artists in cities across the country echoed Spriggs' demand that art museums respond to the interests and needs of the black community. This critique drew its power from a language of self-determination articulated by the Black Power and Black Arts Movements. Calling for "relevance" rested on a critical understanding of culture's important role in the production of society's structures of domination as well as an optimistic assertion of its potential to alter these same oppressive power relations. In other words, art *mattered* dearly. Museums were instruments of power no less than political and economic institutions. While the protest efforts to combat the entrenched racism of the American art museum encompassed a spectrum of goals and strategies ranging from reformist to radical, the artist-activists involved all believed that their art was inextricably connected to the lives and struggles of the larger African American community.

As the newly crowned "center" of the Western art world, New York became the central target of the artists' dissent.[3] Yet no adequate account of the black artists' mobilization against the city's art museums exists.[4] But such an omission only lessens our appreciation for the complexity of debate, scope of achievements, and diversity of participation in the Black Arts Movement. The campaign to radically transform New York City's art scene was one of great breadth and variety, one of conflict as much as consensus. Yet connected by their shared aim of facilitating full recognition and development of the African American artist, visual artists forced curators and trustees to rethink the *function* of the art museum and made imperative a substantial and significant discussion on the role of art in the larger battle for black freedom.

BACKGROUND: THE BLACK AESTHETIC

The visual artists' mobilization against the art museum took place amid the mass struggle against racial injustice in America by both moderate civil rights organizations and militant Black Power groups.[5] The picketing, mass marches, and nonviolent protest of the older organizations and the more militant expressions of dissent by younger activists centered in inner cities drew attention to the racism prevalent in *all* aspects of American society, not simply its Southern voting booths. Dismantling Jim Crow was simply the *beginning* of the fight for African American liberation. For Black Power adherents, legal equality may have served as a starting point, but real freedom involved reaching beyond exclusively political goals to questions of economics and culture.

Black culture as an essential tool of liberation was anything but a new concept in the late 1960s. The culture created by enslaved Africans had nourished and sustained efforts to survive and ultimately win their freedom from bondage. Nationalists like Marcus Garvey celebrated the distinctive beauty and power of the clothing, music, and art of people of African descent. The Civil Rights Movement, although essentially about constitutional guarantees, drew its strength from the networks, philosophy, and music of the African American Christian church.[6] But in the late 1960s, the Black Power Movement elevated culture to the heartbeat of its quest for emancipation and power.

Disillusioned by the slow implementation of the goals and ideals supposedly achieved by the Civil Rights Movement, new groups advocated a radical restructuring of American society to achieve true economic, political, and social justice. These groups, including the Black Panthers, the Black Liberation Front, the Black Liberation Army, and Maulana Ron Karenga's US Organization among others, held diverse, and even contradictory, strategic views on how to win the war on white oppression. Importantly, however, all rested their political and economic programs on an independent black cultural base.[7] In the wake of centuries of white stereotypes of black inferiority, Black Power turned the racists' claim of racial distinctiveness on its head: Black Power asserted the remarkable beauty and strength of a black culture thriving and separate from that of white America.

Thus, "Black is Beautiful" was far from a mechanical or simpleminded rallying cry. Within these three deceptively simple words, the slogan held both a devastating critique of the psychic cost of racism and a cogent blueprint for personal and group self-definition. Black Power advocates urged the effort necessary to uncover and bear witness to the distinctive history and culture of people of African ancestry too long denied and/or disparaged by America's dominant white culture. Embracing and celebrating "blackness" was the essential first step to self-determination. Racial pride, advocates believed, could and would replace the crippling sense of inferiority and self-hate inculcated by white racism. In a 1964 speech, Malcolm X told the crowd that "the cultural revolution" was necessary to "unbrainwash an entire people."[8] Hoyt Fuller, the Black Arts writer and philosopher, explained: "Part of the struggle of Africans in America has been the affirmation of our special beauty in a land where everything about ourselves—our heritage, our physiognomy, our determination to survive—has been degraded and ridiculed."[9] When self-hate was excised, *only then* could political and economic power become possible.

The creative arts were a necessary element of this revolutionary black culture. "Black art is the aesthetic and spiritual sister of the black power concept," explained writer and scholar Larry Neal in theorizing the distinctive, empowering expression of black creativity known as the Black Arts Movement.[10] Cultural nationalists suggested that the aesthetic standards used to judge "great art" long assumed "natural" and "universal"—*everyone knows Shakespeare was a genius*—were fundamentally *subjective* and racist at their core. There was no "raceless" or "universal" experience in America, they argued. There was a black experience and there was a white one, only the black experience had not yet received its due on paper, stage, or canvas. "The white aesthetic would tell the Black Artists that all men have the same problems, that they all try to find their dignity and identity, that we are all brothers and blah blah blah. Is the grief of a black mother whose 14-year old son was killed by a racist the same as the grief of a WASP mother whose son was killed in a Saturday afternoon football game?" asked the poet Etheridge Knight.[11] Far from being a simple byproduct of white oppression, art and the Euro-American aesthetics used to police the boundaries of "great art" were instead "major tools of black oppression" and indispensable bulwarks for the white American power structure. This "Euro-Western sensibility" denied the black experience.[12]

Set free from assumptions of white superiority, unshackled from standards delineated by the white American experience and no longer "content to be a pale imitation of white middle class society," cultural nationalists explored a "black aesthetic" that was distinctive, meaningful, and authentically representative of the unique history, experience, and culture of people of African descent. But what did it look like? Black Art in all its forms, counseled the poet Eugene Perkins, must express "the total black experience." He discussed poetry as an example: "Black Poets should be concerned with creating authentic images of black people and dealing with the realities of black life as they actually exist, and not as some distraught illusion. They must be committed to describing the total feelings/emotions/attitudes and values of black people so that black people can better understand themselves within a black frame of reference."[13] In opposition to the dominant culture's effect of "negating" the black experience or distorting it to simplified caricature, he argued, Black Art should "awaken" in the black community "an awareness and appreciation of their own blackness." Such an awareness had profound political implications: it would "help enable black people to emerge from the depths of oppression and rise to self-determination, control of their destiny, and finally, complete liberation."[14]

Thus, fundamental to the black aesthetic was the creative artist's *responsibility* and *connection* to the black community. Instead of accepting Western culture's false assertion that art was "impartial" or apolitical, the black aesthetic asserted the liberatory impulse of the artist's craft: the black artist must realize, in the words of a Black Arts workshop director in Chicago, that "his primary responsibility is to black people and their plight."[15] Larry Neal announced the Black Arts Movement as "radically opposed to any concept of the artist that alienates him from his community" and Eugene Perkins described artists as "missionaries."[16] If an artist shirked this core responsibility, if his or her art did not "consciously support the revolutionary struggle" of the black community, the artwork "becomes irrelevant," warned Perkins.[17] In this "period of sustained militancy" and "revolutionary warfare" against white violence and power, artists were no mere observers on the sidelines; instead, they were the vanguard of change.[18]

The urgent enthusiasm with which Black Power advocates heralded the arrival of a cultural renaissance was hotly contested within the larger African American art and intellectual community. Martin Kilson, a Harvard political science professor and critic of black separatism, found the concept of the "black aesthetic" "excessively political" without any "elements of form, style and sensibility."[19] The Black Arts Movement's attempt to "make the creative process subservient to the new Black ideologies" was a "Frankensteinian travesty" that denied the "universal quality of humanity," he declared in a speech delivered at Lincoln University, a historically black college in Chicago.[20] Kilson outlined the fundamental divide in the black artist community over the very existence of a "black art": most artists, Kilson suggested, believed that art provided a fundamentally equal and apolitical meeting place for all cultures and races to contemplate the "nature of the human condition." *Great* art achieved a "universal statement" and *great* work by black creative artists was not determined solely by how well it served the black community but by how well it served the whole of humanity: "In other words, through Negro Jazz, men of profoundly diverse cultural, historical, religious, and racial backgrounds can discover something of their own fate on earth, something of their own persisting strivings to make life a more humanistically meaningful experience."[21]

Critiques of the black aesthetic elicited zealous responses from cultural nationalists insistent on the intrinsically political nature of art, the existence of a discrete and meaningful black culture, and the uselessness of the moderate civil rights agenda. Real emotion accompanied the studious arguments and heightened the intensity of the debates. Neal dismissed the criticisms of his detractors as "bullcrapping" and Addison Gayle, Jr., editor of *The Black Aesthetic*, called

Black Arts antagonists "Fridays": a literary reference to a loyal black servant similar to "Uncle Tom." [22]

But the heated rhetoric between the most prominent spokesmen of the two camps notwithstanding, the debate within the black art community over the intersection of aesthetics and politics was much more searching, ambiguous, and fluid. Despite their detractors' insistence that they were "telling other writers how to write," in truth, Black Arts theorists shied away from a reductive blueprint. [23] So while the purpose of Black Art—liberation—was clearly defined, what the art would look like remained unspecified. The debate over form and function raised crucial questions for artists: What constituted the black aesthetic? Was it one particular style or subject matter? If so, did that delegitimize other styles identified with Western aesthetic conventions even if interpreted by an artist of African descent? What did an "integral" relationship with the black community mean for the individual artist?

Sharing a sense of urgency if not a fixed definition of the black aesthetic, creative artists during the Black Power era attempted to realize their relevance to the larger black community and its freedom agenda through wide-ranging experimentation. Far from evidence of the movement's weakness, the diversity, complexity, and contradictions of "black culture" as lived, interpreted, and practiced by black Americans was for many participants the source of its vitality and strength. In responding to the charges of imprecision lodged against the "cultural spokesmen" as to the "content and character of Afro-American culture," the Marxist sociologist Robert Blauner answered, "These questions are being hammered out in the black communities, and the culture-builders are not interested in satisfying the curiosities and the academic criteria of white intellectuals. . . . Most importantly, Negro culture is in process: it is a dynamic, open-ended phenomenon, and that is why it is becoming such a central concern of the protest movement." [24] Dynamic experimentation was particularly true in the case of visual artists who were less apt to write manifestoes or articles than their literary brethren. While a complete chronicle of the vigorous popular movement to transform the "art Establishment" in New York City during the Black Power era is not possible here, dramatic highlights are recounted and assessed to provide an introduction to the artists' groundbreaking ideas and audacious creativity.

THE NEW YORK ART SCENE

"We are here to discuss some of the problems of the Black artist in America," the painter and collage artist Romare Bearden announced as moderator of a symposium held at the Metropolitan Museum of Art in the fall of 1968. Attended by six other black artists the discussion highlighted the shared concerns of visual artists surveying the history and future of the black artist in America, as well as their conflicting interpretations of what should be done.

All agreed with the kinetic artist Tom Lloyd's somber pronouncement: "The Black artist's existence has been denied for so long that people don't know him—even in the black community." [25] They discussed the unequal playing field of the art world: art by African Americans was both underrepresented in history books and on contemporary gallery walls. Children in the ghettos of the city received little if any art education or exposure. The very future of art by African Americans was in dire jeopardy; with little institutional support from the major art institutions and few teaching positions, young black artists had little chance of making a living by their craft. The reason for the inequity of the art world was never under dispute: the prejudice that limited the professional success of visual artists was symptomatic of the pervasive racism of American society. Explained Jacob Lawrence, "You take a man like Bill Robinson, who never attains the same kind of recognition as Gene Kelly. They say we're supposed to be good cooks, but we've never been made chefs in the Waldorf-Astoria, we've never been asked to give cooking lessons on television. Why? Because this calls for a certain recognition on the part of the white community that you have an intellectual capacity that either they don't want to accept or are so brainwashed they can't accept." The white community and the white-controlled art world "refuse to see and refuse to recognize what we can do," he continued. "You take a man like Horace Pippin, who I'm sure was a greater 'primitive' than Grandma Moses. But compare the amount of recognition the two have received."[26]

Lawrence's remarks were especially striking since he, as the young Lloyd admiringly commented, had "made it" along with Romare Bearden and Hale Woodruff. Indeed, the four younger men had also exhibited their work at prestigious museums or galleries and seemed well situated for continued success. But the frustration the group had with any suggestion that prejudice was no longer a factor for artists was similar to the impatience with which the larger African American community greeted the conservative responses of white Americans certain that the existence of a black judge or business executive proved "race" was no longer a problem in America.[27] Lawrence bitterly contested the white art critics' attempts to point to his fame as proof that equality of opportunity existed: "None of us wants to be selected as 'the one and only' or 'one of the few'. . . . None of us appreciates the idea of 'We'll accept you and this is it.'"[28] Lawrence defined the dilemma of the black artist in America in terms of access: prejudice rendered traditional art institutions and the white art critics who guarded them unwilling or unable to appreciate the work of African American artists, both past and present.

But if the discussion began in harmony, it quickly hit a discordant note over "the question of identity."[29] Tom Lloyd grew frustrated at the other participants' reluctance to call their work "Black Art" and their vociferous denials of a "black aesthetic." To him, Black Art was real, incontrovertible, and necessary. When Richard Hunt (a very successful fellow sculptor whose abstract metal sculptures were widely praised by critics) argued that his art was separable "from my life as a Black man in America," and further explained, "I see myself as a sculptor as being a person making things," Lloyd exploded, accusing Hunt of being a "conditioned Black man." Lloyd criticized, "To me you don't seem like a man concerned with Black people, with Black kids, with Black culture.

I don't think that enters into your feelings. And that bothers me, that bothers the hell out of me. You know, when I think of an artist, I think of a Black artist, not a Black white artist or someone who has given in to this kind of conditioning that the white people have put us in." [30]

But Lloyd proved unable to clearly articulate to the others' satisfaction his meaning of "Black Art." Lawrence, William Williams, and Hunt tried to pin down a detailed answer from him: Was it a particular style or medium? Did it need to deal with a particular theme or subject? Was it art by any black artist? No, no, no answered Lloyd. Black Art could not be reduced to a blueprint like that; it was something so much more: "We're talking about communication. I don't know why we are talking about forms necessarily. It's like how you feel and what you are doing." What was Black Art? It was art "relevant to the Black community." [31] The other symposium participants were hardly satisfied with his inexact and seemingly oblique reasoning. They pushed him to define "relevance," arguing that it was a "sociological" not an "aesthetic" term. Jacob Lawrence thought the term "Black Art" "sentimental slush," and argued that Lloyd's own abstract light sculptures in and of themselves refuted the idea of a uniquely black aesthetic: "From what I've seen of your work—although you may be a terrific artist—there's no possible way that I can see anyone in the Black community *relating* to your work. They may respond to it aesthetically, they may feel it is a terrific piece—but I can't see how anyone would *relate* to it, and I don't see why they should." But Lloyd was certain that it did: "It's related because I'm Black and I know where my feelings lie." [32]

Lloyd was much clearer in explaining the role of the black artist in society. "I think he has a compact, a relationship with the people that the ordinary person doesn't have. I think he can bring about changes." And the changes he envisioned went well beyond the canvas or gallery wall: "I'm with a group called Black Visual Environments, and we're a big group of professional artists who hope to bring a big, big change about in New York through various means—putting pressure on people if we have to, but mainly by working in the Black communities. We're not going to teach art, we're going to be involved in the whole political structure." [33] Williams was not impressed: "(T)he nationalism you're talking about is a very dangerous thing." [34]

When reading the transcript of the symposium, it is difficult not to be struck by how much the group agreed upon: the necessity of black-penned critical scholarship, more art education for children and scholarships and gallery space for young black artists, even future roundtable discussions to "sit down and beef like we're doing today." All expressed concern over the desperate conditions of an impoverished Harlem and all agreed with Woodruff's comment that the problems hindering the development of the black artist could only be solved through a "united front": "When we try to fight this battle singlehandedly we're lost." [35]

But in terms of how that battle should be fought, the differences were meaningful. The majority of the group viewed the preferred strategy as one of increased access and inclusion: for Hunt it meant getting "more integrated in the larger scene," for Bearden it meant getting "completely involved in the mainstream."[36] Both these phrases referred to places of power in the art world that Hunt and Bearden believed denied access to black artists due to white prejudice. Buyers, critics, and curators "don't always consider him" due to the black artist's skin color.[37] What they were asking for was a fair appreciation of the black artist's work and a chance to fully participate on equal footing with white artists. "We're always in *Negro* shows, not just shows," objected Lawrence.[38] African American artists were creating great works of art; the issue was that the white art community was willfully ignoring them.

But Sam Gilliam and Tom Lloyd spoke of "power" instead of "inclusion." When Lawrence advocated an infusion of federal government funds to support black artists, Lloyd scoffed at the suggestion and Gilliam suggested "Black-owned art galleries."[39] But there were important differences between the two as well. Gilliam objected to Lloyd's judgment of Hunt ("It's erroneous to presuppose that a person who doesn't follow a certain philosophy all the way doesn't care about his race or his kids") and believed that social concerns, while important and not necessarily antithetical to art, should never obscure the question of "quality."[40] The black community ought to have better access to great art by artists of every color, he argued. And to this end, Gilliam saw an essential role for the city's art museums: "It's easy to see that we could easily hustle up to Harlem . . . and put up alot of structures that would be meaningful. But instead . . . why can't museums really emphasize the kind of programs that will bring a person from where he is to where the better facility is? And when he's there why can't you make him actually welcome?"[41]

For Lloyd, however, there was no reason to go "downtown." It made all the difference if the artist worked in a predominantly black neighborhood; it made all the difference if the art was created above 110th Street.[42] "I feel that the Metropolitan is a museum for white people, not for Black people," he said, and didn't see it changing. But at the moment, Lloyd did not share Gilliam's desire to change the institution either: "I still maintain that Black art should be separate. I feel that is the only way for us to make it."[43]

The symposium threw into sharp relief the two major points of dispute within the black aesthetic debate. First, was there a distinctive form, style, or sensibility that made "Black Art" a discrete and unique category of art? And secondly, what was the specific responsibility of the visual artist to the black community? The questions were fundamentally intertwined: did the liberatory function of art dictate its form? Lloyd had answered no but he also argued art to be ultimately "secondary" to the freedom fight.[44] He implied that there might be a point where "relevancy" required the suspension of art for other kinds of protest: "I think we should be marching. I think we should do anything."[45]

Lloyd imagined a kind of submersion of the artist into the protesting masses of the larger black community: "I'm talking about unity, I'm not talking about one artist going that way and doing his thing."[46] It was a revolutionary stance that came into direct conflict with the traditional icon of the fiercely independent artist directed by inner muses, not outside social conditions. Sam Gilliam believed his move from figurative paintings depicting life in the black community to abstract canvases to be one of maturation: "But later on, you're a mature artist, maybe a great one, if you can personalize yourself, move from identification with something outside yourself to your own thing."[47] The ideal artistic "self" was apolitical and non-racial. As Hale Woodruff described, "It has nothing to do with race; it is that real spark, unfathomable, and unidentifiable, that is unassailable. . . it isn't black, white, green, or blue, but it is great art."[48]

Thus, the subjugation of artistic freedom to "the Cause"—no matter how worthy—was a peril to avoid. Where Lloyd called for "unity," most artists continued to see their art as separate from social movements, and themselves as separate from society. "As for the civil rights struggle it's very hard to distinguish what you, on a personal level, can do. My feeling is 'different strokes for different folks.' I kind of take it as it comes and hope I'm doing the proper thing at the proper time," William Williams concluded during the Met symposium.[49] "Political and social aspects should not be the primary concern; esthetic ideas should have preference," Norman Lewis, the artist and co-founder of the New York-based black artist circle, Spiral, definitively argued in a 1966 interview. He expressed the view of most of the group's membership. Earlier, in 1964, a proposal to create a Spiral exhibit entitled "Mississippi 1964" was voted down as "too pointedly 'social protest.'"[50]

But Lloyd's cultural and political nationalism ("I think there's going to be Black art, I think there's going to be a separate Black community") suggested the growing militancy of visual artists who questioned the conventional separation of art and politics.[51] This impassioned, persistent debate among the visual art community initiated a wide range of activist agitation that left the city's art museums forever transformed.

ALTERNATIVE ART SPACES

An important extension of separatist politics was the idea of the independent black art institution. "For those of you who are willing to support the oppressive tradition of art institutions, I hope for you a recent and tragic death, as the reciprocal injustices reveal the grave that is your own rational fabrication," began the artist Randy Williams' fiery 1973 article celebrating the four-year anniversary of The Studio Museum in Harlem. In this article and others for the journal *Black Creation*, Williams discussed both the failings of the white-controlled museums ("museums of royal servitude") and the revolutionary importance of black art institutions.[52] While at their most basic, black art museums and galleries provided prized *space* for black artists shut out of the "impenetrable museums and galleries of the white art world" to exhibit, the pioneers of the community workshop and gallery movement in the late 1960s articulated a much more revolutionary vision: "An art institution is not the measurement of an artist's individual success, but rather is the measure of the achievements of a dialogue between the artist, the art institution and the community."[53]

In the late 1960s in New York City, small storefront galleries financed by private sources, artist contributions, and city grants sprung up in all the city's boroughs. Such community workshops and galleries included Harlem's Studio Museum and Weusi Nyumba ya Sanaa ("House of Art" in Swahili), Greenwich Village's Acts of Art Gallery, Brooklyn's MUSE, Studio O and Operation Discovery, Inc., and Queens' Storefront Museum. This latter museum/community center averaged a weekly attendance of 300 people in its first two years of existence, many who were first-time museum visitors.[54]

These alternative art galleries sought nothing less than a reinterpretation of the very nature of art museum. They did not want to be "a tiny satelite of the white world" or "downtown art brought uptown" explained Edward Spriggs, the second director of The Studio Museum.[55] To achieve "relevance" they sought "a comprehensive and integral relationship" with the black community. They offered free instruction in black art history, art workshops, free workspace, day care, school outreach programs, and mobile exhibitions. Organizations provided art instruction to upstate prisons.[56] Finally, the city offered the African American community spaces to acknowledge their "rich cultural and historical heritage" in the visual arts.

Such diverse programs challenged the traditional concept of an art museum as articulated by the professional organ, the American Association of Museums. "A museum of art is primarily an institution of culture and only second a seat of learning," wrote the secretary of the Boston Museum of Fine Arts in 1917.[57] More than fifty years later, the chief art critic of the *New York Times* voiced a similar opinion on the role of the art museum: it was "to act as a disinterested custodian of the artistic achievements of both the near and the distant past."[58] Artist-activists rejected this "art for art's sake" philosophy and embraced a new vision of what a museum could do to empower a people. Black art institutions were not to be the "second choice" for black artists denied access to the white art world. They would be the *only choice* for artists committed to their community: "But why try for the Met, when black artists can show here?" Fred Lewis, the assistant director of The Studio Museum asked in 1973.[59] If Black Power's goal was the complete liberation of the African American community, black art institutions were understood as an essential vehicle towards this end.

But if the black galleries and museums celebrated their revolutionary distinctiveness from the traditional art museum and were united in their commitment to the black community, the question of quality proved meaningfully divisive. During the Met symposium, Tom Lloyd had bristled at William Williams' assertion that "art by nature is an aristocratic thing" and Randy Williams staunchly believed that black institutions were ideologically opposed to the white art world's "delirium of elitism."[60] Yet, "quality" was not a construct the cultural nationalists wanted to fully dispose of. They shared the integrationists' conviction that the underrepresentation of black arts on the walls of traditional art museums was due to institutional racism. In creating their own institutions, they articulated an unwillingness to accept white critical assessment of their creative work as well as their politics. Implicit in the community workshop directors' and museum curators' discussions of their institutions was a confidence in the fineness of the works.[61] In other words, even as they expanded the notion of "great art" to require a commitment and connection to the experience of the black community, cultural nationalists spoke of the technical proficiency of the artwork in terms shared with mainstream aesthetic theory. The authority of the city's large art museums and their critical custodians remained ever present even above 110th Street.

One of the most illustrative statements concerning this ambiguous separatism was Fred Lewis' articulation of his ambition for the future of The Studio Museum: "We'd like to see the day when black artists show down there because they can't show up here."[62] While the independence of the black art institution was underscored, there still remained a desire for black art to receive critical acknowledgment from "downtown." Despite (or, in a very real way, due to) the vibrancy of the community workshops and galleries, artists continued to question why traditional museums stayed closed to them. Organized, artist groups attempted to democratize the New York City art museum.

OPENING THE DOORS

One of the first skirmishes between artist and museum materialized thirty-five blocks south of Harlem on the corner of 75th Street and Madison Avenue. In the fall of 1968 the Whitney Museum of American Art opened its exhibition, "Painting and Sculpture in America: The 1930s." As organized by white curator William Agee, no black artist was included. The exhibit served to mobilize a small segment of the black artist population. Henri Ghent, the director of the Brooklyn Museum's Community Gallery, acted quickly and organized his own survey of art in the 1930s, titled: "Invisible Americans: Black Artists of the '30s." It opened on November 19, 1968 at The Studio Museum in Harlem. As Ghent explained in the preface to the catalogue, "Our title of course refers to Ralph Ellison's superb image of the exclusion of blacks from consciousness by the white art establishment. They refuse to see us. Small wonder our artists have not been taken seriously."[63] To further fight invisibility, a small band of black artists picketed outside the museum, chanting, "Ignored in the thirties, ignored in the sixties."[64]

In response, Whitney Museum director John I. H. Baur offered no apology, instead vociferously defending the Whitney's show. Any black artist, he asserted, "was to be judged on the same basis as any other artist—on the quality of his work."[65] Quality was Baur's gatekeeper, the allocator of access into his museum. Of course, defining what "quality" meant greatly differed for those on both sides of the Whitney's front door. For curators and critics confronted with the black artists' demands, quality was an objective, neutral standard of evaluation; an excellence defined not as opinion, but as fact. For members of the African American community, however, the authority of the white "art Establishment" and it's definition of "quality" was a social construct; a biased standard that served to narrow the canon of venerated "masterpieces," to reinforce the institutional barriers against African American artists, and to suggest the inferior aptitude of black creative expression.

The critical reception of the show at The Studio Museum continued to dwell on this question of quality as well. Hilton Kramer, art critic for the *New York Times*, judged the show "extremely feeble." Although he did acknowledge a few black artists who "would not have been out of place in the Whitney Show," he denied racially motivated exclusion. In fact, he accused Mr. Ghent of a "double standard": "Mr. Ghent is inviting us to judge black artists by standards greatly inferior to those we bring to the appreciation of—the term is absurd but unavoidable—white artists." Mr. Ghent, he continued, had committed the worst sin of subordinating "art" to the "political ideal." And on this, Kramer was extremely clear: while the plight of the African American might be regretted, "in matters of artistic standards, there is no justice in the social sense." "Quality" could not be ignored to fulfill quotas.[66]

Ghent's response defiantly critiqued the logic of Kramer's review. The white reception of black art was completely informed by politics rather than "untouched," Ghent argued. Kramer, he pointed out, never offered a reason why those artists he deemed "acceptable" by Whitney standards were excluded. The word "quality" was simply a defense for racially motivated exclusion.[67]

The conflict intensified in the next few months, moving uptown five blocks to the Metropolitan Museum of Art. There the new director, Thomas Hoving, was making preparations for the exhibit, "Harlem on My Mind," to open in January 1969. During the fall, the African American visual art community watched with measured anticipation. Thriving in the spotlight, Hoving gave interviews asserting that "Harlem on My Mind" would serve as a "turning point" for the Met and a rallying call to the museum world to become more responsive to the era's social and political events. ("To get into the swim," he quipped).[68] As he asserted in one press release: "(The Met's) charter, which is almost a hundred years old, enjoined this museum to apply itself vigorously to not only the study of fine arts but to relate them to practical life as well. Practical life in this day can mean nothing less than involvement and active participation in the events of our time. . . . "Harlem on My Mind" signals the turning point."[69]

Hoving saw "Harlem on My Mind" as the realization of the Metropolitan Museum of Art's founding mission. Artists warmed to this interpretation. His progressive rhetoric seemed to signal a metaphorical housecleaning of sorts for the Met: windows flung wide open with outside air and sunshine pouring in. His calls for "responsibility" seemed to echo the black aesthetic's call for "relevancy."

The black art community's enthusiasm for the project, however, soon soured. No African American artist, scholar, or critic was consulted. The Harlem Cultural Council, led by the African American artist Ed Taylor, withdrew its support when it was clear that it would not be given any input into the project. The community's anger spread with the unveiling of the exhibit in January 1969.

As conceived by Allon Schoener, visual arts director of the New York State Council on the Arts, "Harlem on My Mind" was a "multimedia event" taking up the whole second floor of the Met and all thirteen of its special event galleries. There were no paintings or sculptures, but several hundred photographs by the Harlem photographer James VanDerZee, taped interviews, slides, recordings, and even a TV monitor hooked up to a Harlem street corner. Its catalogue asserted its purpose to be a "a sincere attempt to increase the knowledge and understanding of the cultural history of Harlem by the public." The show was organized as a pictorial record of the different decades of Harlem's development. For example, the show opened with floor to ceiling photo enlargements of the Harlem tenement meetings at the turn of the century. In one gallery, the walls were placed close together so as to allow only movement by single file, thus invoking the constrained atmosphere of the Depression. Photos of black poets, musicians, and ministers filled more gallery walls, songs by Aretha Franklin and Billie Holiday played over the loudspeakers. The last gallery, titled "Militancy and Identity, 1960–68," held poster-sized photos of Malcolm X.[70]

While Hoving found the exhibit "powerful . . . and unforgettable," the Harlem community took great offense.[71] Where were the African American visual artists? Why *photographs*? Benny Andrews, a Harlem artist, described his reaction at a preview reception for the exhibit in this way: "I remember how helpless I felt as an artist and as an individual. The episode was to enable me to sustain a sense of indignation that will stay with me as long as I live."[72] In response, under the leadership of Andrews and Romare Bearden, Harlem artists organized themselves as the Black Emergency Cultural Coalition (BECC) and picketed the press preview of the exhibition on January 12, 1969. Holding signs reading, "Visit the Metropolitan Museum of Photography" and "That's White of Hoving!," they handed out leaflets urging blacks to boycott the show. Titled "Soul's been sold again!!!," the leaflets expressed outrage at the absence of work by black painters and demanded that the museum "seek a more viable relationship with the total black community."[73]

The responses elicited by the exhibit "Harlem on My Mind" made clear the problematic relationship between the museum and the black visual art community. Although the majority of white art critics panned the exhibit, very few even questioned why Schoener and Hoving did not use paintings. "There were excellent reasons for not having any works of art, of course, and, in fact, they would have crippled the impact of 'Harlem,'" Hoving wrote in his autobiography, without further explanation of what these reasons were. For his part, Allon Schoener bitterly criticized the protestors: "I'm accused of having stepped out of line in trying to do something significant about blacks."[74]

The exhibit, as orchestrated by Schoener and Hoving, offered an interpretation of Harlem that was palatable and easily digestible for quick, uncomplicated consumption. One outraged critic of the show described seeing a white couple dancing to James Brown just outside the "Militancy and Identity" gallery.[75] In the age of Black Power, here was a packaged image that was acceptable to a white audience and even danceable. For many artists, "Harlem On My Mind" proved the unbridgeable distance between the "guilded halls" of culture and the city's African American community. Others, however, continued to pound away at the gates.

For artists who sought to reform the New York City's art museums, there were two main organizational bodies to join. The Black Emergency Cultural Coalition (BECC) was an all-black organization. Members argued that prejudice blinded the "art Establishment" to the quality and diverse talent of African American artists. With approximately 150, members it concentrated its efforts on the Whitney Museum of American Art, demanding more positions for black curators, more one-man exhibits featuring black artists, and more black artists featured in the Whitney Annual.[76] But as articulated by Benny Andrews, one of the co-founders, the BECC had a comprehensive view of power that reached beyond the museum: "We're certainly not in this thing just to make sure black artists get their paintings sold. Social truths, injustices that are being committed need to be exposed *on a very deep level.* The black artist can do this. The organization needs to move in a political direction, to link up to all other human rights movements."[77] Their efforts continued into the 1970s.

Many younger artists found a niche within the ranks of the loosely organized interracial militant art group called the Art Workers' Coalition. Encompassing an eclectic group of artists—feminist, gay, black, white—they were united in their desire to radically change both the relationship between the artist and the museum, although the group splintered often over priorities and tactics. They viewed their art as fundamentally political and shared a mission of larger social change beyond the gallery walls. Meetings were held every Monday night at the MUSEUM, an artists' cooperative subsisting on contributions.

In January 1969, the Art Workers' Coalition submitted thirteen points to the Museum of Modern Art (MOMA). The five resolutions most emphasized demanded: (1) a separate wing for black artists, (2) that museum activities be extended into the neighborhoods, (3) night hours once a week, (4) free admission at all times, and (5) more artist control over the decisions of the museum. In reaction to MOMA's vague response, artist and spokesman for the black artist subgroup of the Art Workers' Coalition, Tom Lloyd, issued a press release in March, reading, "The number of artists aware of their rights, duties and responsibilities is growing. They will resort to whatever action they deem necessary."[78] On March 22, the Art Workers' Coalition staged a small demonstration outside the museum. In response, MOMA's director issued a statement rejecting the possibility of a black artists' wing. Artists, he claimed, were chosen because "the curators believed in the quality of their works without regard to race, political creed or national origin of the artist. . . ." The young artists accused the museum of using the argument for quality to mask their racist agenda.

A much larger demonstration occurred on March 30. Three hundred demonstrators gathered in MOMA's garden. There, amidst signs like "Bury the Mausoleum of Art" young artists read the thirteen points and made countless speeches, repeatedly demanding a "Martin Luther King Jr. Wing for Black and Puerto Rican Art." A little over a week later, the Art Workers' Coalition held another "Speak Out" at the School of Visual Arts on East 23rd Street. Over 350 artists "mostly under thirty" assembled.[79]

The snowball of protest grew, exploding into numerous graphic demonstrations. The Guerrilla Art Action group, a subcommittee of the Art Workers' Coalition, staged a "performance art" protest in the lobby of the Guggenheim Museum. Placing large packets of ketchup under their shirts, protestors "clawed" each other to release the red stain. Lying on the floor of the museum lobby, bloodied by ketchup, their bodies symbolized the "murder" of the artist by the Art Establishment. The Guerrillas also threw washable paint all over the museum's lobby.[80]

Within the larger all-encompassing goals of the Art Workers' Coalition, the specific demands for fuller institutional support and recognition of the black artist could get lost. During the alternative "People's Show," organized by the Art Workers' Coalition in November 1970 at Judson Memorial Church in Greenwich Village, visual artists shared the stage with poets, and Black Panthers shared the stage with Abbie Hoffman, the white feminist scholar and activist Kate Millett and members of the Gay Liberation Front. Yet, just as the Black Panthers promoted alliances with multiracial anticapitalist groups like the Brown Berets, Young Lords, Red Guards, the Young Patriots, and antiwar peace activists, many young visual artists did not see a fundamental conflict between their Black nationalism and their solidarity with other artists seeking to change the status quo.[81]

The most furious protests with the most sweeping agendas occurred in 1970. On May 18, 1970, two thousand artists gathered at the New York University's Loeb Student Center for a "tumultuous" meeting to raise the art agitation to a more grandiose condemnation of the Vietnam War and to make plans for a citywide "Art Strike." It was conceptualized as a complete shutdown of the city's museums to protest "racism, repression, sexism and war." Here, was a highly revolutionary attempt to redefine the role of the museum. Perhaps Thomas Hoving had challenged the art world to become more "relevant" to practical life, but these youthful agitators pushed the challenge even further: the museum as cultural institution must join in the protest of social injustice. The artists chose May 22, 1970 for the Art Strike to take place and began to dismantle their shows in preparation. As he pulled down his sculpture from the Jewish Museum, Robert Morris, a well-known white sculptor, told the press that the point of the strike was "to underscore the need I and others feel to shift priorities at this time from *art making and viewing* to unified action within the art community against the intensifying conditions of repression, war and racism in this country."[82] While most artists complied and dismantled their shows, the four-day notice and the "dictatorial" tone of the protestors angered New York

City's museum directors. (One Met official likened them to "Nazis.") They also feared to take such an overtly political act.

The museums were plagued by an identity crisis. Was the role of the museum to be a "repository of treasures" or a "social instrument"? Was it the role of the art museum to criticize U.S. foreign policy? Despite the protests of many museum trustees, the Jewish and the Whitney closed down, the Guggenheim took down its art, and MOMA suspended admission and showed war photos and films. In solitary resistance, the Metropolitan Museum of Art stayed open five extra hours. In response, Art Strikers staged an orderly sit-in on the Met's steps.

Evaluating the success of the Art Strike proved elusive. The protestors celebrated their power and the transformation of the art museum (at least for a day). Feeling invincible, a delegation of young artists traveled to Washington to personally inform Senators Jacob Javits and Claiborne Pell of the New York City art community's condemnation of the Vietnam War. The Senators "expressed puzzlement, condescension and perhaps contempt, and implied that the disapproval of artists—unlike, they suggested, that of doctors or air traffic controllers—would hardly constitute grounds for change."[83] The focus abruptly shifted back to museum reform.

Back in New York, artists continued their protests. The first day of the 1970 Association of American Museums' (AAM) annual convention began quite differently than any other year. Before the first meeting could be called to order by president William Steere, members of the Art Strike entered the ballroom and positioned themselves along the walls and the doors. They wore stenciled signs reading, "Art Strike Against Racism, Sexism, Repression and War." One protestor walked up to the podium and announced that the convention had this new theme. Thirty joined him on the stage and demanded that their speaker, Ralph Ortiz, director of the community museum El Museo del Barrio be allowed to address the audience at once. Ortiz angrily denounced museums for refusing to take a stand on the "vital issues of the day." Although President Steere adjourned the meeting for that day, most delegates remained to listen and, in some instances, to confront the protestors. Many delegates were sincerely interested in the artists' grievances and participated in ad hoc committee meetings—they, too, were rethinking the role of the museum. In these smaller groups, the demands of the artists were debated and revised before being presented to the general meeting for a vote at the end of the week. The discussions tempered the original "demands" of the artists into more moderate "resolutions" agreeable to the attendant members of the AAM. For example, where originally the Art Strike demanded that: "All urban museums are to devote 15% of their total funds the first year, 20% the second year, increasing to 40% of their total funds toward decentralizing museum facilities and services, e.g. inner city museums, community art programs, establishment of intern programs for Blacks, Mexicans, American Indians, Puerto Ricans, and other oppressed people," the final proposal simply agreed to "give high priority" to decentralization efforts. In another original demand, Art Strike called for the AAM to "declare as inseparable from the freedoms under which the arts flourish, the immediate release of the Black Panthers and all political prisoners in this country." Instead the final resolution read that AAM agreed to "oppose" "political arrests and persecution as that of the Black Panthers." [84]

Even with such changes in tone and specificity, only the first resolution (a bland proposal for a conference to discuss the role of the community in museum activities) even reached debate. Thomas Hoving introduced the resolution, emphasizing that "although the protestors were using harsh language, the goals they sought were essentially the same as being discussed at the conference—how to make museums more germane to the issues of our time." [85] But debate stalled on the wording of the resolutions and it took an hour for a weak and toothless version of the first resolution to be passed. AAM members walked out to lunch and the Art Strikers' attempted revolution ended. The week did draw attention to the art museum's internal attempts at self-examination. As one observer put it, "The demonstrators served as a catalytic agent, speeding up a process already underway." [86]

Nevertheless, the "process" crept along too slowly for the Art Strikers and they sustained their protests into the 1970s. The militant tone remained, but fissures in the movement were evident. As we have seen, the specific concerns of the black community motivated much of the Art Workers' Coalition and Art Strike agitation. This was due in large part to the leadership of Tom Lloyd. Yet there were times when the black artist subcommittee was at odds with the larger group of Art Workers' Coalition. One example involved the Metropolitan Museum's sixty million dollar master plan to expand its present structure into Central Park. The Art Strike and the Art Workers' Coalition, as well as many other smaller black community groups, were opposed to this plan believing that the money would be better used to decentralize the museum and expand its community-oriented activities. They believed that the traditional art museum was a relic, irrelevant to the lives of their communities. Tom Lloyd, however, was deeply involved in talks with the Met to create a black art study center with a library, slides, concerts, and films. Despite his continued support for community art institutions, specifically The Studio Museum, Lloyd became vocal in support of the extension plan, securing the resentment of many of his fellow artists. [87]

There were other cracks in the united front of black artists as well. With more and more museums mounting all-black exhibits in response to the artist-militant agitation, female artists (organized as WAR: Women Artists in Revolution) questioned the lack of art by African American female artists. The artist Dindga McCannon, who supplemented her canvases of black subjects and themes with multiple murals in Harlem and a children's center, described how racial and sexual caste systems interfaced in black female artists' lives: "First of all there's the problem for any Black artist in this racist society. The Art world is nothing but a huge Bigot . . . . Now as a woman you've got a double problem. First of all, most people don't take you serious . . . .(Black institutions) . . . some will accept your work but they will not do the same things that they'll do for men; like heavy advertising."[88] But their efforts to get male artists to boycott in solidarity the shows that marginalized them were often unsuccessful. The lure of being shown in an art museum was simply too strong.[89]

Finally, the theoretical debate over the meaning of the black aesthetic proved divisive, playing itself out in passionate angry rhetoric. In the Art Workers' Coalition's factious meetings in preparation for the Art Strike, artists hotly debated what black art looked like. Could artists agree on the stylistic manifestation of the black aesthetic? Most defined it by the art's *usefulness* to the project of black liberation. As phrased by artist Dana Chandler, "Black artists should devote their time to expressing the needs, aspirations, philosophy, and life style of their people. They should deal with the social problems that black people are having in this racist society, so that there will be an accurate record of our progress from an oppressed to a free people."[90]

But what this record should look like divided the art community. Many artists explored African culture in their work and celebrated the African heritage. During this period, Benjamin Jones worked with plaster masks, painting each in bright colors inspired by the tribal rituals of Africa. Others took their inspiration from the city neighborhoods around them and painted scenes of the urban ghetto. Portraits celebrated historical figures and heroes in the African American community: Martin Luther King, Bessie Smith, Jack Johnson. Elizabeth Catlett's *Sharecropper* (1970) is a powerful, highly stylized woodcutting of the upper torso of an anonymous black sharecropper. All these works took for their inspiration subjects that were absent from the walls of the traditional art museum.

Confrontational canvases documented the racism of American life. The American flag, for example, served as a frequent subject of black art in the 1960s and 1970s. Philip Lindsay Mason's *The Deathmakers* (1968) depicts two skeletons in police uniforms pointing to the slain body of Malcolm X. The stars and stripes of the American flag function as backdrop to the death scene. In Faith Ringgold's *Flag for the Moon: Die Nigger (1967–69)*, the stripes of the flag spell "NIGGER." In another canvas, the stripes drip as if made of blood. Such paintings provided powerful indictments of American society. "Art should be inseparable from the reality of the black community," explained Edward Spriggs (director of The Studio Museum in Harlem) in describing the black aesthetic.[91]

In promoting the black aesthetic, many of the cultural nationalists condemned African American artists who continued to create art in the Western tradition. Tom Lloyd harshly condemned "brown art" by African American artists that he judged not "black" enough. What did that mean? As Amiri Baraka explained, they were "whiteartists in Black face," artists who were "brainwashed."[92] But others criticized Lloyd's light sculptures as not "black" enough either. Such accusations were ultimately vague and undermined the artists' solidarity. In turn, other black artists criticized the work of the more militant protestors. Henri Ghent, the original organizer of the counter exhibit to the Whitney Museum's all-white show on the 1930s, claimed that "nationalist" artists were "too preoccupied with *what* they have to say rather than how *well* it should be said." Other young artists denied the concept of "black art" altogether: "I have mixed feelings about anyone being cubby holed in a show of 'black' art," complained one young artist who preferred to describe his art as "mainstream" rather than "black."[93]

Such emphasis on form by the agitators limited the success of the visual artists' agitation and the museum protests. Such contentious wrangling over formalistic categories tore at the organizational strength and unity of the protestors. Even today, this emphasis on form continues to limit understanding of the Black Arts Movement itself. For purposes of analysis, art historians quite reasonably classify the artists of this period into categories according to style and medium: one artist's work might be "mainstream" and another's "black." But this type of grouping obfuscates the vitality and vibrancy of the visual artists' contribution to the Black Arts Movement. For example, in a show mounted as a rebuttal to the 1971 Whitney Annual, the works by African American artist Betty Blayton were reviewed very favorably by a *New York Times* critic who suggested that she cannot "be called a black artist except by race." The critic goes on to wonder why she is involved in the boycott and "interested in what an artist happens to be."[94] It is true that her abstract oil collages, formless and nonrepresentational, deviates stylistically from some theorists' formalistic criteria for "Black Art." Yet as director of the Children's Art Carnival in Harlem, and advocate of art as a vehicle of self-actualization and black pride, she was an essential member of the Black Power and Black Arts Movements. Ironically, even Tom Lloyd, militant cultural nationalist and Art Worker, is usually defined as "mainstream" in art textbooks. His sculptures are considered abstract and therefore incapable of making a social or political statement. But to distinguish Lloyd from the Black Arts and Black Power Movements is both ahistorical and absurd.

If attempts to define a revolutionary aesthetics undermined the solidarity of African American artists determined to topple the seemingly "impenetrable" walls of New York City's art museums, it still must be emphasized that a dialogue was produced that redefined the relationship between politics and culture. Black artists pointed out that "aesthetic merit" as defined by the New York "art world" was not objectively determined, nor universally accepted. Instead, cries of "quality" often masked deep-rooted cultural and racial prejudices that served to strengthen the maintenance of an unequal society. The Black Arts Movement opened the artistic canon. Although the quieting of the New York art world in the 1970s corresponded with the decline of the Black Power Movement, the legacy is one of revolution. Even if it would never become the political animal envisioned by the Art Workers' Coalition, the art museum continued to wrestle with its new identity as a social instrument in its community.

NOTES

1. Edward Spriggs, "The Studio Museum in Harlem," *Black Shades* 2 (November 1971): 46–47.

2. Ibid., 47–48; emphasis mine.

3. Serge Guilbaut, *How New York Stole the Idea of Modern Art: Abstract Expressionism, Freedom and the Cold War*, trans. Arthur Goldhammer (Chicago: University of Chicago Press, 1983). Also, the artist Randy Williams' 1974 comment, "New York City is most likely the world center of chaos, as well as the heart of the art world." Randy Williams, "The Black Art Institution," *Black Creation* (1974–1975): 6.

4. While there are brilliant and comprehensive scholarly studies of African American art, they do not chronicle the social history of black art activism in New York City, which instead is found by examining contemporary newspaper and journal coverage. But for excellent overviews of the work of African Americans from the eighteenth century to the twenty-first, it is imperative to begin with Samella Lewis, *African American Art and Artists* (Berkeley: University of California Press, 2003) and Richard Powell, *Black Art: A Cultural History* (London: Thames and Hudson, 2003).

5. As will be discussed in the essay, African American artists' efforts to combat the entrenched racism of the American art museum encompassed a spectrum of goals and strategies ranging from reformist to radical. Furthermore, it will be argued that many of the artists themselves simultaneously embraced goals that appeared contradictory: supporting separate black art institutions while at the same time continuing to seek more representation of African American artists in the larger museums, for example. It is the task of this essay to define the ideological differences among the coalition of activist artists while at the same time recognizing that the line between "moderate" and "militant" was often a fluid one (frequently dependent upon "the eye of the beholder"). In this regard, I am indebted to William Van Deburg's brilliant and nuanced portrayal of the Black Power Movement. In addition to scrupulously painting a multifaceted movement of ideological variance, he carefully acknowledges how the "empowering spirit of blackness" that animated the Black Power and Black Arts Movements were "evident, in embryo" in earlier, "moderate" Civil Rights programs and creative artists. "Nevertheless, the ultimate concerns of the two movements were more compatible than contradictory. The latter would not have existed but for the former while the former was an incomplete formulation of the latter." William L. Van Deburg, *New Day in Babylon* (Chicago: University of Chicago Press, 1992), 24. Larry Neal, one of the most significant philosophers of the Black Arts Movement and, in his own words, "never an admirer of Rev. King," wrote of the importance of the Civil Rights Movement to the Black Power Movement: "In spite of the short term goals of these organizations, they have contributed significantly to the growth of black consciousness. The freedom rides, the sit-ins, bus boycotts, Selma March, Meredith March, Harlem rebellion, Watts rebellion, Newark rebellion, school take-overs, and the explosion of black culture all grow out of a conglomerate will towards black liberation." Larry Neal, "New Space/The Growth of Black Consciousness in the Sixties," in *The Black Seventies*, ed. Floyd B. Barbour (Boston: Porter Sargent Publisher, 1970), 10.

6. Literature on the role of culture in the centuries old African American freedom struggle prior to the Black Power Movement is rich and extensive. The following is a small sample of the exceptional historical work available: Eugene D. Genovese, *Roll, Jordan, Roll: The World the Slaves Made* (New York: Vintage Books, 1976); Maria

Diedrich, Henry Louis Gates, Jr., and Carl Pedersen, eds., *Black Imagination and the Middle Passage* (New York: Oxford University Press, 1999); Dexter B. Gordon, *Black Identity: Rhetoric, Ideology and Nineteenth-Century Black Nationalism* (Carbondale: South Illinois University Press, 2003); Tera Hunter, *To 'Joy My Freedom: Southern Black Women's Lives and Labors After the Civil War* (Cambridge: Harvard University Press, 1997); Stanley Nelson, prod., *Marcus Garvey: Look for Me in the Whirlwind* (Boston: Firelight/ Half Nelson Productions for American Experience/WGBH Educational Foundation, 2001); Wilson Jeremiah Moses, ed., *Classical Black Nationalism: From the American Revolution to Marcus Garvey* (New York: New York University Press, 1996); Robin D. G. Kelley, *Hammer and Hoe: Alabama Communists During the Great Depression* (Chapel Hill: University of North Carolina Press, 1990); Aldon Morris, "The Black Church in the Civil Rights Movement," in *Disruptive Religion: the Force of Faith in Social-Movement Activism*, ed. Christian Smith (New York: Routledge, 1996).

7. Van Deburg, *New Day*, 165; Scot Brown, *Fighting for US: Maulana Karenga, the US Organization, and Black Cultural Nationalism* (New York: New York University Press, 2003). Larry Neal described precisely the multiple manifestations of "black self-determination" including the actions of people who never officially joined political groups: "For example, take the concept of 'Black Consciousness.' When the thing got really going, black people in different places developed unique and often contradictory attitudes toward it; they operated out of the principle along a variety of different styles. Some people joined the Muslims. Some people stopped eating certain foods. Other people, just as sincere as the first group, began to relish those very same tabooed foods. Some people put on African clothing. Most wore naturals. Some wore brighter colors. Some raised hell in school. Some left their white wives and black husbands. Some joined RAM or the Black Panther Party. Some dug B. B. King, and some dug Coltrane. But shit. *It was all good and on time.* It was collective energy that could be harnessed and organized." Neal, "New Space," 11–12.

8. George Breitman, ed., *By Any Means Necessary: Speeches, Interviews and a Letter by Malcolm X* (New York: Pathfinder, 1970) reprinted in Van Deburg, *New Day*, 5.

9. Hoyt Fuller, "The Question of Aesthetics," *Black World* 24: 2 (1974): 50.

10. Larry Neal, "The Black Arts Movement," in *The Black Aesthetic*, ed. Addison Gayle, Jr. (New York: Doubleday and Company, Inc., 1971), 257.

11. Etheridge Knight, as quoted in James Cunningham, "Getting On with the Get On," *Arts in Society* 6: 3 (1969): 390.

12. Elsa Honig Fine, "The Afro-American Artist: A Search for Identity," *Art Journal* 29: 1 (1969): 32; Robert Chrisman, "The Formation of a Revolutionary Black Struggle," *Black Scholar* 1: 8 (1970): 2; Fuller, "Aesthetics," 49.

13. Eugene Perkins, "The Black Arts Movement: Its Challenge and Responsibility," *The Black Seventies*, ed. Floyd B. Barbour (Boston: Porter Sargent Publisher, 1970), 88–89.

14. Ibid., 88.

15. Francis and Val Gray Ward, "The Black Artist—His Role in the Struggle," *Black Scholar* 2: 5 (1971): 23.

16. ". . . missionaries who are dedicated to helping black people move from a negative state of existence to a positive state of survival." Perkins, "Black Arts Movement," 94.

17. "The art can remain legitimate only to the extent that it is relevant in helping liberate black people." Perkins, "The Black Arts Movement," 94.

18. Francis and Val Gray Ward, "The Black Artist," 23.

19. Martin Kilson, "What is a Black Aesthetic?" (speech delivered at Lincoln University in Chicago on March 21, 1974) reprinted in *Black World* 24: 2 (1974): 30, 44–48. Quote may be found on p. 44.

20. Ibid.,46.

21. Ibid., 47.

22. Larry Neal, "Black Art and Black Liberation," in *"Takin' It to the Streets": A Sixties Reader*, ed. Alexander Bloom and Wini Breines (New York: Oxford University Press, 1995), 163; Addison Gayle, Jr., "What is a Black Aesthetic?" *Black World* 24: 2 (1974): 31–43.

23. Gayle, Jr., "What is a Black Aesthetic?," 39; in his contribution to Addison Gayle's volume on the Black Aesthetic, theorist and poet Don L. Lee wrote, "a blk/aesthetic does exist, but how does one define it? . . . or is it necessary to define it? I suggest, at this time, that we not try." Don L. Lee, "Toward a Definition: Black Poetry of the Sixties (After LeRoi Jones)" quoted in William L. Van Deburg, *New Day*, 182. For an excellent discussion of the various manifestations of cultural nationalism during the Black Power Movement, see chapter 5 of *New Day:* "Black Power in Afro-American Culture: Folk Expressions."

24. Robert Blauner, "The Question of Black Culture," in *Black America*, ed. John F. Szwed (New York: Basic Books, Inc., 1970), 119.

25. "The Black Artist in America: A Symposium," *The Metropolitan Museum of Art Bulletin* 27: 5 (1969): 245.

26. Ibid., 246.

27. For an excellent discussion of the white emphasis on "moderation" as a key tactic in delaying social change, see William Henry Chafe, *Civilities and Civil Rights* (New York: Oxford University Press, 1981).

28. "A Symposium," 246.

29. Ibid., 256.

30. Ibid., 258–59.

31. Ibid., 249.

32. Ibid., 256, 253, 251, 249.

33. Ibid., 248, 249.

34. Ibid., 252.

35. Ibid., 260.

36. Ibid., 253.

37. Ibid.

38. Ibid., 246.

39. Ibid., 250, 254.

40. Ibid., 259, 251–52.

41. Ibid., 251.

42. "Black artists should be working in Black communities." Ibid., 248.

43. Ibid., 254.

44. "I'm not only concerned with art. With me art is a secondary thing." Ibid., 251.

45. Ibid., 260.

46. Ibid.

47. Ibid., 256.

47

48. Ibid., 253.

49. Ibid., 260.

50. Jeanne Siegel, "Why Spiral?" *ARTnews* 65: 5 (1966): 49.

51. "A Symposium," 248.

52. Randy Williams, "The Studio Museum in Harlem," *Black Creation* (Winter 1973): 50; Williams, "The Black Art Institution," 60–62.

53. Williams, "The Black Art Institution," 62.

54. "Community Galleries," *ARTGallery* 12: 4 (1969): 48–50; Jean Bergantino Grillo, "Studio Museum in Harlem: A Home for the Evolving Black Esthetic," *ARTnews* 72: 8 (1973): 47–49; Elsa Honig Fine, *The Afro-American Artist: A Search for Identity* (New York: Holt, Rinehart and Winston, 1973), 185–90.

55. Grillo, "A Home," 48.

56. *New York Times*, 16 November 1971; Richard Weiner, "Artists in Prison," *American Artist* 36: 354 (1972): 8.

57. Benjamin Gilman, *Museum Ideals of Purpose and Method* (Cambridge: Harvard University, 1923), xi.

58. Hilton Kramer, "Artists and the Problem of 'Relevance,'" *New York Times*, May 4, 1969, 23.

59. Grillo, "A Home," 49.

60. "A Symposium," 259; Williams, "The Studio Museum," 50.

61. As will be discussed more directly in the next section, black museum curators defiantly responded to white critics' charges that their museums were "overly inner-directed" or "often exhibiting work of poor quality." But rather than abandoning the word "quality" as immaterial perhaps to their project of "relevance" they often justified their choices and the artists' work by appealing to dominant aesthetic values.

62. Grillo, "A Home," 49.

63. Henri Ghent, "White is Not Superior," *New York Times*, December 8, 1968, 39.

64. *New York Times*, January 15, 1969, 41.

65. *New York Times*, November 18, 1968; Ghent, "White is Not Superior,"43.

66. Hilton Kramer, "Differences in Quality," *New York Times*, November 24, 1968, 27.

67. Ghent, "White is Not Superior," 43.

68. Thomas Hoving, *Making the Mummies Dance* (New York: Simon and Schuster, 1993), 165.

69. Benny Andrews, "The BECC," *Arts Magazine* 44: 8 (1970): 18.

70. Amy Goldin, "Harlem Out of Mind," *Art News* 68: 1 (1969): 52.

71. Hoving, *Making the Mummies Dance*, 169.

72. Andrews, "The BECC," 18.

73. *New York Times*, January 15, 1969, 41.

74. Hoving, *Making the Mummies Dance*, 167.

75. Jervis Anderson, "On the Edge of Hell," *New York Times*, January 26, 1969, 31.

76. Fine, "The Afro-American Artist," 193.

77. JoAnn Whatley, "Meeting the Black Emergency Cultural Coalition," *ABA: A Journal of Affairs of Black Artists* 1: 1 (1972): 5.

78. Therese Schwartz, "The Politicalization of the Avant-Garde, III," *Art in America* 61(1973): 67–71; *New York Times*, March 31, 969.

79. Schwartz, "The Politicalization of the Avant-Garde," 70.

80. Corinne Robins, "New York Art Strike," *Arts Magazine* 45: 1 (1970): 27–28; *New York Times*, January 5, 1970, 25.

81. "In attempting to achieve revolutionary solidarity, the (Black Panther) Party walked an ideological tightrope between the popular demand for Black Power and the communal ideal of 'people power' devoid of racial exclusivity." Van Deburg, *New Day*, 162–64.

82. Elizabeth C. Baker, "Pickets on Parnassus," *ARTnews* 69: 5 (1970): 32.

83. Ibid., 32.

84. David Katzive, "Up Against the Waldorf-Astoria," *Museum News* 49: 1 (1970): 14.

85. Ibid., 15.

86. Ibid., 16; for a complete list of the 1970 AAM proposals, see Katzive, "Up Against the Waldorf-Astoria," 17.

87. Baker, "Pickets on Parnassus," 33.

88. Pat Davis, "Dindga McCannon," *Black Creation* (Winter 1973): 53.

89. *Feminist Art Journal* 1:1, 6.

90. Tom Lloyd, *Black Art Notes* (n.p. 1971), quote taken from inside back cover.

91. Grillo, "A Home,"48.

92. Imamu Amiri Baraka, "Counter Statement to Whitney Ritz Bros," in Lloyd, *Black Art Notes*, 11.

93. *New York Times*, January 31, 1971.

94. *New York Times*, April 7, 1971.

5

Blackness in Present
Future Tense

Broadside Press, Motown
Records, and Detroit Techno

Wendy S. Walters

Writing about Detroit is not just writing about the past. It is also writing about the future because the issues have not yet been resolved.
  —GRACE LEE BOGGS

Political ideology uses nostalgia in much the same way as architecture, ironically enough. It builds the unremembered.
  —NORMAN KLEIN

Cities or places that don't have so much tend to create opportunities. People tend to use their imaginations to compensate.
  —DERRICK MAY

DETROIT SUMMER 1967: THE GREAT REBELLION

In early June 1967, at Detroit's Second Annual Black Arts Convention (dedicated to the memory of Malcolm X), H. Rap Brown spoke what turned out to be prophetic words, "Motown . . . we are going to burn you down," in response to a climate of mistreatment of blacks by the predominantly white Detroit Police Department.[1] Just a few weeks later, on July 23, 1967, an undercover police raid on the Blind Pig on Twelfth Street incited a massive rebellion. At least 7,231 people were arrested, 700 injured, and forty-three killed (thirty-three blacks and ten whites) over the next three days of fires, looting, and violence. Property damage in the city was estimated at over $50 million.[2] Joe Von Battle, a longtime supporter of local black music production, was dismayed to find his record store completely looted in the ensuing uprising. Edward Vaughn's Afrocentric Forum 66 bookstore was firebombed and vandalized by several Detroit Police officers.[3] The Chit Chat Club, an after-hours retreat for many of Motown's musicians, was scorched beyond repair, but the first home of Motown Records only a few blocks up the street remained untouched. Another noteworthy survivor of the Detroit uprising was Dudley Randall's Broadside Press, which at the time was the largest publisher of new voices in African American poetry. At the time, Motown and Broadside Press were easily the best-known producers of overtly black cultural products within and beyond the city proper.

Ever since that fiery summer, Detroit has been obsessed with promoting a vision of the future that elides the complicated racial history that brought about racial violence and rioting in 1967. This vision of the future focuses on the culture of industrial manufacturing that continues to dictate many of the city's political, economic, and social interests.[4] For the next ten years, out of smoldering ash Detroit attempted to reinvent its image as a destination city with a "New Center" of industrial manufacturing at the commercial center of the city named just that. And down on the riverfront, a hotel/office complex called the Renaissance Center was erected at a cost of $350 million. Its construction was a major attempt to reshape the city's skyline. Conceived "when the 1967 race riots were still fresh in people's memories," writes photographer and urban studies scholar Camilo José Vergara, "the Center stands like a fortress high above the streets, separated from the rest of downtown by a broad boulevard, East Jefferson."[5] The Renaissance Center's physical separation from the rest of downtown revealed the discrepancy between the modern vision of Detroit many wanted to project and the fact that its streets were growing blacker, older, and poorer.

Twenty-four years later, the Renaissance Center still stands alone as the primary fixture of the Detroit skyline. It was renamed the GM Building in 2001 after it was purchased for the automaker's new corporate headquarters, and has undergone a major restoration, including the addition of a public Wintergarden and the removal of the exterior shopping area and fortress-like facade. This renovation, like the initial construction of the building, has been noted as a sign of the city's next renaissance. More recent commercial developments such as Comerica Park, Ford Field, the new Detroit Opera house, and MGM Grand and Greektown casinos create the illusion of a thriving downtown entertainment district and are slowly improving the quality of housing, shopping, and transportation in its surrounding areas, but visible gaps in the landscape, most notably abandoned houses, storefronts, and factories continue to remind residents and visitors that a deliverance from a history of racial turbulence has not yet come to Detroit. These decrepit buildings are the unrelenting historical memory of the city's recent hardscrabble past, a lingering, phantom presence of racial turmoil, economic chaos, and domestic discord.

ACTION AS MOVEMENT

It is well documented that the Black Arts Movement (BAM) emphasized the need for action over contemplation, and "process" was an inherent element of the political discourse whether exercised through theatrical performance, protest, or ritual. Black art and black artists became both the means and ends to a revolution that was rooted in movement, politically, artistically, ideologically, and physically. The central question was often around the issue of identity—what was "black," how was it "seen" and also made invisible? While a variety of artists committed to developing a unique aesthetic that demonstrated a preference for "transformation rather than conservation, on spirit, rather than object" with regard to the representation of the self within the black community, there became a growing need to see the movement exercised in ways that could measure change.[6]

Antipathy for and mistrust of fixed forms such as text accounts for the pro-performance trends of the BAM. The invisibility of black authors and their work in most major publishing houses was at the root of the BAM's antipathy for text. There was also frustration over the inconsistency with which the way that laws were written and enforced. But the successful development of black literary publishers such as Broadside Press and independent music studios like Motown means that we must consider how the performance of identity affected the production of fixed forms such as the book or record and revaluate the ways in which the enactment of blackness in non-theatrical spaces shapes how blackness is defined.

Literary critic Biodun Jeyifo argues that drama "deals more obsessively than the other literary forms with man and his destiny" perhaps because "drama does not merely subsume conflict as its organizing structural motif; beyond this, drama also axiomatically attempts a resolution of sorts, a provisional synthesis in the conflicting pulls within its constitutive action, thereby approaching the limit of the dialectical image potentially realizable in art."[7] In retrospect, the daily drama of the BAM provided a "provisional synthesis" for black identity where the racial signification of "black" stood in contrast not only to "white" identities but also those previously acknowledged as "Negro" or "colored." This space between black and Negro or colored indicated a split between generations of thinking about blackness and allowed for the articulation of a new vision of black identity that refuted an idea of innate inferiority. This articulation of identity engaged a revised dialectic of racial conflict, one in which being black was a privileged state. In this context, experiences associated with racial identification could be translated into assertions of African American humanity in literature and history. Because prior to the BAM much of black life represented in theater, television, film, literature, and advertising reflected practices of segregation, coercion, and dehumanization as being more effective in confining the black experience than they actually were, it is not surprising that performative practices of "blackness" enacted across a broad stage served as counterpoint.

The period of 1964–1974 was a time when "the category of blackness served as the dominant sign of African American cultural activity."[8] While the category of blackness noted a locus of cultural activity, the term "diaspora" emerged in reference to the intangible bond between black people dispersed through the non-African world. While the original use of diaspora referred specifically to

Jews exiled from Israel from the sixth century B.C. to the present time, the word also came to refer to other communities of people who had been dismissed or removed from their original homeland. The concept of diaspora is critical to the study of Black nationalism prior to and during the BAM, and it provides a framework for thinking about the self-conscious process of knowledge and/or information production as political action.

Cultural historian Brent Edwards's discussion of the use of the word "diaspora" in Africanist discourse and the possibilities it affords force "us to consider discourses of cultural and political linkage only through and across difference."[9] This means that diaspora is a site for multiple points of signification, each of which reflects on, complements, and contrasts others. Where diaspora may have once presumed essentialist physical similarities and/or an economic or geographical connection to link people of African descent, Edwards's reevaluation of the term allows us to consider how the political ideology of the BAM becomes "an epistemological challenge explicitly stated out through a politics of diaspora that rejects Western assumptions about a link between knowledge production and the nation" when in cultural institutions.[10] Thus, we might infer that the process of knowledge production through cultural institutions such as Broadside and Motown helped to formulate a historical connection between a people without defining them solely in a context of a particular geography or set of repressive experiences. With this, blackness becomes "not an inevitable object, but rather a motivated, constructed, corrosive and productive process" enacted within the commitment to envisioning the future. At Broadside Press and Motown Records, the broad reach the concept of diaspora provided allowed for the expression of new articulations of black identity in the future.

BLACK CULTURAL PRODUCTION AS PERFORMANCE

In 1960, Detroit was home to the fourth largest African American population in the United States. It was a significant site of political and religious activity and was gaining notice for the quality of life it could provide its black residents. Black Detroiters were very politically active; however, there were not yet many elected officials. But the air of change in the southern states was slowly blowing north. Rosa Parks had migrated in 1957 from Alabama to the city, the same year William Patrick was elected to the Detroit City Council. Charles Diggs had been elected to Congress in 1954 and John Conyers followed him there in 1964. The early 1960s looked to be the beginning of a long period of prosperity. A number of black-owned businesses were sprouting up throughout the city and finding support from a new and growing black middle class comprised primarily of automobile workers. By 1966, the *Michigan Chronicle*, the newspaper of the black middle class, had a distribution of 48,000.[11] Artistic communities were also thriving. Ron Milner, Woodie King, Jr. and David Rambeau founded the Concept East Theater, one of the first black community theater projects. Poet Margaret Danner, originally from Chicago, developed the Detroit Artist's

Workshop to support emerging jazz musicians and other artists. She also established Boone House, where local poets were able to share political writings and organize happenings. As recording technology was becoming more affordable, independent record studios became popular for producing local talent. Each week Joe Von Battle taped and sold recordings of Reverend C. L. Franklin's (Aretha Franklin's father) sermon from his record store. Edward Vaughn supported African American writers and small black presses from around the country through his bookstore. Traditional civil rights organizations, including the NAACP, CORE, National Urban League, SCLC, and SNCC, engaged in a variety of meetings, marches, and demonstrations around the city. Black nationalist groups such as the Nation of Islam, Republic of New Africa, the Pan-African Congress, Freedom Now Party, Detroit League of Revolutionary Workers, and Black Christian Nationalists were also gaining a prominent voice in local politics.[12]

While Detroit could claim a sizeable black population, it was never seen as one of the thriving centers of black American culture. Places like New York, Washington, D.C., Los Angeles, and Chicago held higher profiles. Julius E. Thompson, author of *Dudley Randall, Broadside Press, and the Black Arts Movement in Detroit*, notes that these other cities were:

> the nerve centers for black college and university graduates and professionals, and even writers (with older black writer's workshops, black newspapers, magazines and publishers). Such factors served to remind Detroiters that they had to carefully nurture and cherish the black arts in Detroit—for other black artistic centers including Newark, New Orleans, Philadelphia and Cleveland, among others, stood ready to claim the honor of being a "national" center of black artistic endeavors.[13]

Broadside Press's humble beginnings reflected Detroit's lack of preeminence. From 1965 to 1966, Dudley Randall worked out of a single room in his home. He produced inexpensive, high quality broadsides, pamphlets, and cassette tapes of poetry. Randall's first broadside was of his poem "Dressed All in Pink" and was followed shortly thereafter by other broadsides featuring the work of Langston Hughes, Margaret Walker, Gwendolyn Brooks, Melvin B. Tolson, Amiri Baraka, and Robert Hayden. Randall paid for the production of all of the broadsides out of his librarian's salary. Many writers who published early with Broadside became major shapers of the cultural and intellectual movements of the BAM. Perhaps this was because, from the inception of the press, "Randall viewed Broadside Press' role as that of an active participant in the Black Arts Movement and the ongoing struggles of the Civil Rights Movement."[14] His vision would help to make Broadside Press the major black press in America from 1965 to 1975. Eventually the press produced books of poetry in pamphlet form by Haki R. Madhubuti (Don L. Lee), Margaret Walker, Etheridge

Knight, Sonia Sanchez, James A. Emmanuel, Audre Lorde, Clarence Major, Nikki Giovanni, Marvin X, Johari Amini, Sterling D. Plumpp, May Jackson, Alvin Aubert, Melba Boyd, and Lance Jeffers.

Significant challenges faced Randall in his development of the press including the high costs of entering the field; competition from other publishers; poetry's limited market; the lack of a good national distribution system; discrimination in breaking into the information market; a small staff; lack of ownership of a printing press; and the government surveillance of black presses.[15] Despite these obstacles, Randall was remarkably successful in developing Broadside Press into the most significant black press in the country from the mid-1960s to the mid-1970s. Part of the appeal may have been that the broadside form allowed for a strong visual presentation. Another way in which Broadside distinguished itself was in its connection to developing a specifically "black" discourse. In his study on Dudley Randall and Broadside Press, Julius Thompson notes: "The titles selected by Broadside authors and editors during the sixties reveal a clear linkage between the Africa [sic] past, present and future; and an emphasis on 'Black' issues of identity, historical consciousness, struggle and uplift."[16] Some of the topics addressed by Broadside Press included African heritage and Black Americans, criticism of American racism, black life in Chicago, black art, the complexity of the black experience, the struggle to maintain racial pride, the Civil Rights Movement, triumphs and setbacks for black women, war and peace, prison experiences, fostering consciousness and culture, the nature of the urban experience, the South, and Islamic faith in black life. "Broadside published a broader variety and a larger number of broadsides, anthologies, books, and tapes of poetry than did any other black publisher in the United States during the sixties," notes Thompson.[17] The business was built around mail orders taken in from all around the world. The cultural production of blackness at Broadside Press was, obviously, manifest through poetry. But Broadside offered more than just reproductions of text and illustration, it offered a vision of what black poetry could be.

Broadside Press exemplified how the self-conscious process of knowledge and/or information production was a kind of political action that set the stage to broaden what was perceived as the black experience. Broadside artists embellished the historical connection between African Americans without defining them solely in a context of a particular geography or against a set of repressive experiences. They also created a literary aesthetic to represent blackness, translated to the page. And it was Randall's careful selection of the poems, less so the individual poets, that created this performance of identity, as Randall chose work that came to be regarded as the standard for the press and by association black poetry at large. Through the publications from Broadside, Randall created a performance of blackness that, ultimately, brought attention to the significance of the process of articulating identity—both speaking it and writing it down for mass consumption. In this day when works by African Americans and other writers of color are readily available, such a feat might seem slight. But it is important to keep in mind that the general public did not have widespread access to work by black artists when Randall began publishing. And the idea of the black writer Broadside fostered was essential in asserting a perceptible connection between black art and blackness, where the performance of blackness became an achievement in the struggle between overt and implicit discourses of black inferiority/white superiority.

Perhaps much more obviously so than Broadside Press, the name of Motown is at once synonymous with and deeply distant from the reality of Detroit today. Even though Motown Industries left Detroit in 1971 for sunnier prospects in Hollywood, California, the original recording studio still stands at 2648 West Grand Boulevard. Now called the Motown Historical Museum, the original Hitsville U.S.A. studio showcases original recording and production equipment. As cultural historian Suzanne E. Smith has pointed out in her chronicle of Motown's early days in Detroit, *Dancing in the Street: Motown and the Cultural Politics of Detroit*, it is important to remember that Motown evolved out of the particular context of the city of Detroit as an effect of innovations in black art, politics, and business that were taking place there. Excising early Motown from the context that is Detroit fails to address the synergy between factory work and other modes of production.[18] "Using the technologies of automobile manufacturing to produce and market its music and applying industrial methods to record production, Hitsville, U.S.A. was able to reach the largest audiences in the history of black cultural production in Detroit," Smith explains.[19] These large audiences attested to Motown founder Berry Gordy's broad impact in reshaping performative black identities.

But unlike Broadside Press, Motown was not committed to delivering a political message through the careful design of their artists and music. Instead its songs celebrated traditional themes in popular music of the time such as: romantic love, dancing, and parties. While many of Motown's artists were well aware of the political debates raging around the city at the time, few were eager to represent these conversations in their music. Smith writes: "Many artists and writers felt compelled to address the 'Negro Revolt' in their work, but some producers were cautious about such subject matter since it might have limited marketability."[20] One notable exception to this was *Poets of the Revolution*, a recording by Langston Hughes and Margaret Danner. This album was supported by Motown, but they did not produce or promote it.[21] In October 1963, Danner flew to New York City to make a recording with Hughes of "Freedom's Plow" and "Sweet Words from Liberals on Race" and Danner's "To a Cold Caucasian on a Bus."[22] Motown did not pay for Danner's flight and the two handled the recording session on their own. Hughes arranged for photos to be taken by his friend Louis Draper, but Motown was embarrassingly slow in paying him.

While Motown did not identify as a member of the BAM or take an overtly political stance with regard to social issues of the time, owner Berry Gordy did have a broad vision for the company's future audiences including politicized black youth engaged in the Civil Rights and Black Power Movements, as well as suburban white youth. The music was designed for mass distribution and the widest possible range of listening audience. Records were engineered to sound better over new car speakers in order to gain the favor of younger, more prosperous audiences. Even though the songs were overwhelmingly by African American artists, Motown did not position itself as a "race record" label and encouraged "crossing over" onto white radio stations play-lists and television programs as a means of asserting a more integrated vision of popular culture. As cultural historian Gerald Early has explained:

> crossing over for many blacks meant a new kind of activism, a keen sense of nationalistic community embedded, in an ironic yet typically American way, in the idea of integration not through simple if noble endurance of degradation but through a persistent acknowledgement of claims—from court cases like *Shelley vs. Kramer* in 1948, to the Brown decisions (ruling and implementation) in 1954, to marches in the street, to the resurgence of Pan-Africanism.[23]

While part of the appeal of "crossing over" was obviously economic, Early's insight into its political implications cannot be ignored. He attributes four key factors to Motown's ability to cross over: a rise in interest in postwar Rhythm and Blues music; the growing popularity of the electric bass; the popularity of white artist's covers of black rhythm and blues songs; and the decline of the music industry due to the influence of television and Hollywood film production companies. "Gordy's objective was always to reconfigure what was meant by pop music, reiterate in his approach that pop was as black as it was white," writes Early.[24] Thus, if pop was black, then what was black could be pop.

While early Motown albums featured illustrations on the covers instead of photographs of the artists, to lightly veil that this music was created and performed by black artists, the popularity of Motown artists such as the Supremes and Martha and the Vandellas on programs such as the *Ed Sullivan Show* and *American Bandstand* quickly eliminated the need to disguise that fact.[25] Suddenly, black artists could represent both the social rebellion and deviance of Rock and Roll without suffering the kind of physical or economic redress that typically accompanied such transgressions of race, class, and gender. Conversely, white teenage girls could dance suggestively to Marvin Gaye or the Temptations without any appearance of impropriety. The materiality of the cultural product had other long-reaching implications. It created white audiences who supported the company by purchasing a lot of records. And young Motown fans offered better prospects for a long-term relationship with the company.

As has already been mentioned, the visibility of the Motown artists also introduced a new performance of blackness into the mass media. While it is true that in some very profound ways, Gordy's conceived ideal portrait of masculine and feminine black identity was limited by his own conceptions of marketability, he was successful in inserting an image into mainstream media that had not, heretofore, existed. And though he may not have been able to predict the ways in which this new image of doo-wop would eventually be co-opted (Lou Reed and Little Shop of Horrors) by white artists who needed a delimited conception of "blackness" as a backdrop to their "othering" of themselves within their own race, evidence suggests that Gordy was able to foresee the power in meticulously engineering the performance of black identity—from the wigs on their heads, to choreographer Cholly Atkins' signature dance steps, to their characterless voices.

In fact, one of the long-reaching legacies of the early Motown recordings was the perceived "automation" of the singing voice. Philosopher Roland Barthes describes "the grain of the voice" as "the body in the voice as it sings, the hand as it writes, the limb as it performs."[26] This embodiment of corporeality is precisely what Gordy avoided in choosing his singers to allow for the most effective technological shaping of the voice by production equipment. Some accounts of production at Motown suggest that artists were not always singing their own tracks and that there was a certain degree of interchangeability amongst them. For example in 1967, the Supremes' Florence Ballard was replaced by Cindy Birdsong, who shared a striking physical likeness to Ballard and an amazing ability to imitate her voice.

Gordy also required the standardization of the "Motown Sound." Only a few producers were allowed into the studios and most songs were under the guise of legendary songwriters and producers Holland/Dozier/Holland. Most Motown artists, notes Alexander Weheliye, "collaborated with Dozier/Holland/Dozier [sic] [and] Norman Whitfield who shaped the sonic provenances of the Temptations' early 1970s work . . . which ensured that the technological mediation and creation of soul became part and parcel of the musical performance."[27] Gordy's vision of performative blackness at Motown, with all of its "generic" characteristics seemed to suggest that if blackness then could not be "overcome" it could, at least, represent a state of cultural interchangeability. It should be made clear that Motown's objective was not to "pass" its artists as white, but to "pass" them as black, or, at the least, create an image that could not be refuted for its implausibility.

Motown pursued a supplanting of black "invisibility" with performed portraits suggesting possibilities for evolution, shape-shifting, and a disconnection with history. Retrospectively, we can now see where the existing narratives of history and modernity could not account for limitless possibilities for black identity, what one could make and what one could be. Thus, the vision of blackness performed by Motown's recording artists supplanted these perceived limitations. It was not lost on all black people that Motown was fabricating a fissure in history, a disassociation with the R&B past that had, not only, predicated its own existence, but laid the foundations of its audience. However, nowhere else were Motown's objectives so clearly in concert with the BAM than in this careful invention of cultural visibility.

Motown and Broadside Press were concerned with the production of conditions of possibility with regard to black identity; however, Motown was concerned with orchestrating its consumption as well. Of this, Gerald Early writes:

> Motown as a mode of both consumption and production, indeed, as stylization—as discipline forged from both art and politics—of both, probably held blacks together better than virtually anything else in the black national community, other than the demand for equal rights. That is what the words "Hitsville" and "Motown" signify, finally: a modern black urban community built on technology, on the American bourgeois principles of consumption and production, and on the Washingtonian principles of casting down one's buckets where one is.[28]

This practice of "casting down one's buckets" would only be effective in an environment in which consumption and production were stages in a performance of identity. These buckets hit the ground hard and rooted in the terra firma of Detroit. There they remained long after the cultural institutions that had cast them down had ceased production in the city. For decades to come, there would be some intense imagining that those buckets were half-full.

DETROIT IN PRESENT FUTURE TENSE

Every January, Detroit opens the annual North American Auto Show with the hope that talk about the future of automobiles will wipe away any obvious signs of the city's troubled past. Like a shimmering new engine orbiting on a raised stage, Detroit characterizes itself as a prototype of the city to come, the heart of a larger vehicle that will comfortably accommodate even the most particular of travelers. Detroit wants to be an international destination city, not just a pit stop for weary manufacturing executives. But the Auto Show's cars of the future visibly outpace the city's commitment to redesign as vestiges of the Great Rebellion of 1967 can still be found within walking distance from downtown's Cobo Center, where the Auto Show is held.

There is a tension between the kind of future the Auto Show represents and the past of the city that surrounds it. What is remembered is what is coming next, what is soon to be made—if not in Detroit, then in the name of Detroit, down snaking assembly lines in Canada and Mexico. But this is not the only vision. Throughout the city, there are touchstones for a future of possibility that have origins outside of manufacturing. For more than seventeen years, installation artist Tyree Guyton's Heidelberg Project, a public art project of found-object collage, car-hood paintings, tree and house sculptures, has provided a vision of the future of Detroit. Public art on buildings around the city also reveals a cultural history about the perception of the future and acts as a catalyst for recalling the conditions of possibility Broadside and Motown created, which once brought positive international attention to the Motor City. But Guyton's sculptural articulations of the future also serve as reminders of the recent past, almost as if to conjure the practice of envisioning a break with history for the sake of evoking possibility. Los Angeles cultural historian Norman Klein's words provide a helpful framework here:

> According to the ancients and many of the moderns, the only hope for retaining short-term memory in particular (number, names, dates, nonsense syllables)—to protect against distraction—is through mnemonic systems, where cues like place, sound, or contiguity are assembled mentally in order to bring the picture back ("Where did I park that car again?"). But even here, memory is a distracted imaginary, essentially a filing system where information disappears or reforms itself whenever you touch it. [29]

Like Klein's picture, the Heidelberg Project works to bring back cornerstones of the BAM: "'Black' issues of identity, historical consciousness, struggle and uplift"; however, what constitutes "black" is not defined in an agonistic context. [30]

Another example of a grassroots attempt to visualize the future can be found in *Blacktronic Science*, a mural found along a storefront wall on Mack Avenue on the city's east side (fig. 5.1). In its vision of the future, a master scientist sits at the center of an equation where science, culture, and funk are equal and quantifiable elements of future-production. In the image, energy radiates in from an anonymous central source. In the background, planets spin and volcanoes erupt. The combination of computer technology with Egyptian icons signals that Afro-centricity is both a source and effect of this generation of energy, along with 1970s funk/soul music, namely Funkadelic and Parliament's George Clinton and William "Bootsy" Collins. A hot orange earth is relatively tiny in the forefront and partly occluded by a skull that seems to suggest a kind of death, if not apocalypse. A Daliesque clock hangs by a noose but only one hand is visible on its face. From this we might assume that time is omni-directional and that the past, present, and future will convene on this single landscape of information, evoked as a vision. Conceptually, the future materializes as information in a mnemonic system stretched across a landscape that does not allow blindness to occlude the future or the past.

The landscape of information *Blacktronic Science* provides reminds us, as new media theorists Elaine Svenonius, Friedrich Kittler, and Paul Virilio have shown, that as the industrial product becomes less valuable, information gains in significance. In Svenonius's studies of structures for organizing information, she defines the word "information" broadly: "Informing is done through the mechanisms of sending a message or communication; thus information is 'the content of a message' or something that is communicated," she explains. [31] The content of a message is inevitably shaped by its relationship to history, and our perception of a moment is deeply affected by our ability to perceive how time passes in a given space; history becomes the form through which we are able to recall information and translate experience into record. Painter Ben Shahn reminds us that "form is formulation—the turning of content into a material entity, rendering a content accessible to others, giving it permanence, willing it to the

race."[32] Thus if history is form, or a shape of information, then the relationship between time and history does not necessarily have to be linear/chronological, although that is the primary way in which we experience time. If we can imagine the relationship between history and time to be manifest as layers in the way that the *Blacktronic Science* mural depicts history, then the future might also be perceived as a composite of past and present moments rather than a destination. Studies in cinema and digital media have shown that "digital compositing, in which different spaces are combined into a single seamless virtual space, is a good example of the alternative aesthetics of continuity."[33]

Where performances of blackness at Broadside and Motown during the BAM might be conceived of as montage, or a juxtaposition of successive events in almost a cinematic technique, a re-examination of the Detroit artists' present relationship to the future tense allows us to consider alternative representations of *time in space*. While Broadside and Motown focused on emphasizing rifts in history, fracturing predictability with assertions of possibility, Detroit Techno artists manifest possibility by fusing history. The past, present, and future exist simultaneously as in a layered effect of a software graphics program—these layers of space and time provide the opportunity for vision again. Thus, as Peggy Phelan suggests, history affords the privilege of seeing, whereby seeing is to observe that disorder "which does not fit into a narrative—either the movement narrative or the narrative of a sentence."[34] In this reading of time and space, Detroit's cultural history becomes a landscape of information and Detroit Techno is a composite resulting from a fusing of these influences. "Detroit Techno is aerial. It transmits along routes through space, is not grounded by the roots of any tree," notes Kodwo Eshun.[35] While Eshun offers an evocative portrait of how Techno occupies conceptual space, his argument for groundlessness elides the history of performing blackness in the city of Detroit.

It is well known that early Detroit Techno was led by the initiative of high school classmates Juan Atkins, Derrick May, and Kevin Saunderson, also known as the Belleville Three. Their early compositions were strongly influenced by the Funkadelic incantations of fellow Detroiter George Clinton and the German band, Kraftwerk. In the early 1980s, FM DJ Charles Johnson, a.k.a "The Electrifying Mojo" (1977–1982), played a copy of Kraftwerk's *Computer World* (1981) that he had discovered in a discard bin at a previous record station almost every night. The record left a distinct impression on Atkins who eventually founded the group Cybotron with May, Saunderson, and veteran Rick Davis. Eshun explains the group's meaning: "Cybo[rg] + [Elec]tron[ic] = Cybotron. The Cybotron is the electronic cyborg, the alien at home in dislocation, excentered by tradition, happily estranged in the gaps across which electronic current jumps."[36] In 1981, Cybotron released "Alley of Your Mind" on their own Deep Space Records. Mojo played it regularly. Their 1982 follow up, "Cosmic Cars," sold ten to fifteen thousand copies in Detroit alone. Early Detroit Techno production was homespun, like Joe Von Battle and Berry Gordy's early labels. In his essay, "Techno: Days of Future Past," Mike Rubin writes: "Like a black version of punk rock, techno musicians around Detroit suddenly started their own labels—most notably, Saunderson's KMS and May's Transmat—and began releasing their own records, a case of brothers doing it for themselves."[37] Eventually, Cybotron signed a contract with California-based Fantasy Records (Berkeley) and the album "Enter" followed. "Clear" soon after became a hit on Billboard's black singles chart.

Kodwo Eshun argues that Cybotron's "Techno City is a futuropolis of the present, planned, sectioned and elevated from station to studio, transmitting from a Detroit in transition from the industrial to the information age."[38] We might consider Cybotron's futuropolis as an aural simulation of vision, in which materiality is delivered through the performative gesture, again in Phelan's terms, of producing or reproducing visibility. But unlike Broadside Press or Motown, Detroit Techno exercised a vision that was not contingent on performative practices of black cultural production. This is, in part, because blackness no longer needed to be defined in the specific context of Detroit. Demographic and political changes in the past twenty years had rendered the city overwhelmingly African American. Blackness was now pervasive in a way it had not been during the BAM. For this reason or others, Detroit Techno artists did not emphasize black identity politics as part of the music. Perhaps the association seemed implicit, or insignificant.

One unfortunate result of this lack of attention to articulating and performing black identity, however, was an eventual disassociation of Detroit Techno from black audiences. Mike Rubin writes:

> More disturbing to the Motor City posse is that techno has been portrayed as "white" music. As techno's digitized signals crisscrossed Planet Rock, most of the producers and consumers who tuned in were white and the identity of the music's forefather's often got lost in the transmission. Meanwhile, black audiences and musicians ceased to see techno as their own art form, leaving the electronic pioneers of Detroit not only feeling spurned by indifferent white-owned record companies, but estranged from their own community as well.[39]

Although Dudley Randall and Berry Gordy might have predicted and warned against such break with black audiences, not all Detroit Techno lacks a connection to performances of identity that reflect either a discourse of differentiation or an epistemological challenge explicitly stated out through a politics of diaspora. Producer Mad Mike Banks continues to produce black nationalist techno through his label Underground Resistance. And James Stinson, who died suddenly at the age of 32 in 2002, led the visionary group Drexciya for nearly eleven years. Of which, Rubin claims:

> Drexciya—the mysterious collective who propose a scenario in which pregnant African women thrown overboard during the Middle Passage might not have drowned but instead gave birth to a race of water-breathing Afronauts, who any day now, are coming back to the surface to deliver whitey a beatdown.[40]

While Drexciya extends the concept of the Black Atlantic below the surface of those sea routes that defined the Middle Passage, it also evidences a kind of composite history where, once again, the opportunity of vision is created. Through these assertions of history, the Drexciyans counter the idea of Detroit's transformation from a space of industry to a space of information by asserting that, in the diaspora, virtuality already has been manifest in the envisioning of survivability beyond the dictates of historical teleology. In other words, where all historical evidence points to death as the ending point for those Africans lost in the voyage across the Atlantic, death is, ultimately, unable to cease the regenerative, performative practices of black cultural production.

Although Motown relocated to Los Angeles in 1977 and Broadside Press is no longer in regular production, during the 1960s their performative practices of black cultural production challenged the ideological tensions between the racial categories of "black" and "white," and produced a discourse of differentiation through which the cultural product of blackness became an achievement in the struggle between overt and implicit discourses of black inferiority/white superiority enacted to subvert existing social relations. As we reconsider the importance of the BAM, it is essential that we continue to investigate newer modes of cultural production that, overtly or subversively, address these residual discourses. The case of Detroit Techno provides an opportunity to reconsider the site-specific significance of performative practice and to better understand how preceding performative practices of black cultural production make possible the kind of cultural production that is not primarily based on representations of identity. There is a synergistic relationship between the performative practices of cultural production in Detroit during the 1960s and 1970s and its persistent reputation as a "city of ruins." Retrospectively, one might argue that it was the overt demonstration of blackness, perceived metaphorically, that lit Detroit on fire in 1967; a controlled brushfire burn that, in the end, could not be contained. Thus in Detroit, one legacy of the BAM is the regenerative practice of black cultural production in electronic music. Critic Mike Rubin claims:

> Detroit's post-apocalyptic mystique is crucial to the mythology of Detroit Techno. It's from this blighted backdrop that techno comes forth, like the city motto, "'Resurget Cineribus'—It will rise from the ashes." The contradictions in imagining a future while both the past and present sit in shambles all around you are rich indeed, as are those of having a high-tech movement hail from a burnt out urban shell or sophisticated art music flourishing amidst such a stubbornly close-minded, culturally intolerant, blue-collar town such as Detroit.[41]

The legacy of the BAM is a performative blackness that now manifests as possibility through a disassociation from the kind of identity politics that led practices of black cultural production during the late 1960s. Performative blackness manifests in demonstrations of technological innovation and black futurism in electronic music and extends the legacy of the BAM beyond its predictable outcome.

NOTES

1. Suzanne E. Smith, *Dancing in the Street: Motown and the Cultural Politics of Detroit* (Cambridge: Harvard University Press, 1999), 189.

2. Ibid., 188–89.

3. Ibid., 197.

4. In the riot of 1943, thirty-four people were killed, twenty-five of them black. More than 1,800 people were arrested in the 36 hours of rioting. In 1925, "The home of black physician Ossian Sweet became the site of a racial incident that resulted in a nationally publicized murder trial. Dr. Sweet, a graduate of Howard University Medical School, bought this two-story brick house in an all-white Detroit neighborhood in 1925. On July 14, the neighborhood's residents protested his plans to move in and stated that they intended to retain what they called "the present high standards of the neighborhood." On September 8, Dr. Sweet, his wife, and nine gun-carrying associates moved into the house under police escort. The next night a large crowd of whites began pelting the house with rocks and bottles; they then rushed the house. A volley of gunshots issued forth from the second story windows, killing one man and seriously wounding another. The Detroit police arrested Dr. Sweet and his companions and charged them with first-degree murder." http://www.cr.nps.gov/nr/travel/detroit/d4.htm.

5. Camilo José Vergara, *The New American Ghetto* (New Brunswick, NJ: Rutgers University Press, 1995), 209.

6. Mike Sell, "The Black Arts Movement: Performance, Neo-Orality, and the Destruction of the 'White Thing'," in *African American Performance and Theatre History: A Critical Reader*, eds. Harry J. Elam, Jr. and David Krasner (New York: Oxford University Press, 2001), 60.

7. Biodun Jeyifo, *The Truthful Lie: Essays in a Sociology of African Drama* (London: New Beacon Books, 1985), 7, 59.

8. Kimberly Benston, *Performing Blackness: Enactments of African-American Modernism* (New York: Routledge, 2000), 3.

9. Brent Hayes Edwards, "The Uses of Diaspora," *Social Text* 19: 1 (Spring 2001): 56.

10. Ibid.

11. Julius E. Thompson, *Dudley Randall, Broadside Press, and the Black Arts Movement in Detroit, 1960–1995* (Jefferson, NC: McFarland and Company, 1999), 23.

12. Lorenzo Thomas, *Extraordinary Measures: Afrocentric Modernism and Twentieth-Century American Poetry* (Tuscaloosa: University of Alabama Press, 2000), 140. The Nation of Islam was founded by W. D. Fard "a Detroit junk man and door-to-door peddler, but along with his curios he disseminated the Muslim doctrine."

13. Thompson, *Dudley Randall, Broadside Press, and the Black Arts Movement in Detroit*, 30.

14. Ibid., 29.

15. Ibid., 46.

16. Ibid., 38.

17. Ibid., 47.

18. Smith, *Dancing in the Street*, 13.

19. Ibid., 116.

20. Ibid., 98.

21. Ibid.

22. Ibid., 107.

23. Gerald Early, *One Nation Under a Groove* (Hopewell, NJ: Ecco Press, 1995), 95.

24. Ibid., 84.

25. The Supremes first appeared on the *Ed Sullivan Show* in 1964 and *American Bandstand* in 1967.

26. Roland Barthes, *Image-Music-Text* (New York: Hill and Wang, 1977), 188.

27. Alexander G. Weheliye, "'Feenin': Posthuman Voices in Contemporary Black Popular Music," *Social Text* 20: 2 (Summer 2002): 30–31.

28. Early, *One Nation Under a Groove*, 114.

29. Norman Klein, *The History of Forgetting: Los Angeles and the Erasure of Memory* (London: Verso Press, 1997), 15.

30. Thompson, *Dudley Randall, Broadside Press, and the Black Arts Movement in Detroit*, 38.

31. Elaine Svenonius, *The Intellectual Foundation of Information Organization* (Cambridge: MIT Press, 2000), 7.

32. Ben Shahn, *The Shape of Content* (Cambridge: Harvard University Press, 1957), 53.

33. Lev Manovich, *The Language of New Media* (Cambridge: MIT Press, 2001), 144.

34. Peggy Phelan, "Feminist Theory, Poststructuralism and Performance," in *A Sourcebook of Feminist Theatre and Performance*, ed. Carol Martin (London: Routledge, 1996), 159.

35. Kodwo Eshun, *More Brilliant Than the Sun: Adventures in Sonic Fiction* (London: Quartet Books, 1999), 101.

36. Ibid.

37. Mike Rubin, "Techno: Days of Future Past," in *Modulations: A History of Electronic Music*, ed. Peter Schapiro (New York: Caipirinha Productions, 2000), 116.

38. Eshun, *More Brilliant Than the Sun*, 102.

39. Rubin, "Techno," 112.

40. Ibid., 120.

41. Ibid., 113–14.

II.
GENRES AND IDEOLOGIES

6

A Black Mass
as Black Gothic

Myth and Bioscience in
Black Cultural Nationalism

Alondra Nelson

BLACK FRANKENSTEIN

In "The Black Arts Movement," the defining and definitive manifesto of the radical current of African American arts and letters that flourished in the 1960s and 1970s, Larry Neal famously described the era's cultural activism as the "aesthetic and spiritual sister" of black power political insurgency.[1] United in the shared goal of black liberation, the twinned movements differed in emphasis: black power activism centered on the "art *of* politics," while the performers, poets, playwrights, and novelists of the Black Arts Movement were dedicated to forging the "relationship between art *and* politics."[2] Neal declared the task facing the latter group as nothing less than "a radical reordering of the western cultural aesthetic," a creative revolution aimed at redirecting the impetus of African American art, raising political consciousness, and rousing racial pride.[3]

Neal's essay identified Amiri Baraka's play, *A Black Mass*, as one of a small number of works that exemplified the ideal form of Black Arts Movement cultural praxis and politico-aesthetic philosophy. *A Black Mass* is a moral narrative that, in Neal's words, dramatizes the costs of "the aesthetic impulse gone astray" and puts forth a black creative demiurge as salvation and substitute.[4] Gathering influences from African American folklore, religious cosmology, and popular culture together,[5] Baraka portrayed scientific and artistic experimentation as analogous generative principles that emerge from opposite political imperatives—the former stemming from ambition unmoored from social sanction and racial purpose, the latter organically rooted and crafted solely for the good of the black nation.

First performed in the spring of 1966, with accompaniment from experimental jazz musician Sun Ra and his Myth-Science Arkestra, and subsequently presented at community centers throughout the United States, *A Black Mass* staged the story of Jacoub, a black mad scientist who, in a moment of transgression and hubris, disregards the warnings of his fellow scientists and creates a white Beast (metonymically white people) that wreaks havoc on the prelapsarian black world. The play was a dramaturgical adaptation of the story of Yakub, a central mythology of the Nation of Islam (NOI) that had circulated since the 1930s, and which by the late 1960s was beginning to find broader circulation in the writings of Malcolm X and Eldridge Cleaver, among others.[6] The transformation of this NOI cosmology into a theatrical performance served to dramatize what was believed by some to be the inherent incommensurability of black and white experience, a theme that was present in a good deal of Baraka's work during this period and in much of black power ideology also.

For the most part, *A Black Mass* has been overshadowed by analyses of Baraka's better-known plays, especially *Dutchman* and *The Slave*. Among those scholars who have commented on the play, many have noted its deep roots in African diasporic religious traditions, reading Jacoub[7] as a twentieth-century derivation of an ancient African priest, while others have highlighted allusions to black magic and witchcraft.[8] While acknowledging these thematic currents, I interpret *A Black Mass* primarily as a narrative about bioscience and race.[9]

In this general sense, the play was mostly in keeping with the cultural nationalist legend that inspired it. Early NOI cosmology and ideology evidenced a strong and positive engagement with the biosciences, including anthropology, genetics, and molecular biology, as well as a current of "scientism"—the application of the analytical approaches of the sciences to other spheres of life. For example, most probably extrapolating from developments in physical anthropology and archeology, the NOI famously asserted that blacks were the Earth's first men. Black Muslim belief further held that these "original men"—a cohort that included Yakub—were also the world's first scientists. The Yakub story, therefore, is less a disavowal of scientific experimentation run amok than a warning about how the noble pursuit of science, left in the wrong hands, can produce deleterious social aftereffects.

A Black Mass shares key character and narrative elements with the Yakub myth. This Black Muslim inheritance has been well rehearsed by critics.[10] However, little has been made of the key point on which Baraka departed from the NOI's origin story: the racial stakes of bioscientific experimentation. Contra the somewhat cautionary, but ultimately pro-science, tone of the NOI mythology, Baraka's play is a thoroughgoing critique of the biosciences. While scientific experimentation is characterized as an inherently black practice in the Nation's genesis story, in Baraka's drama, it is depicted as anathema to authentic black creative expression. Indeed, in Baraka's re-telling, alchemists are substituted for the scientist protagonists of Nation of Islam cosmology; African-derived (black) magic is posited as the ethical substitute to the biosciences. To what factors might we attribute this dramatic shift in the moral register of the Yakub story? In the pages that follow, I trace the emergence of *A Black Mass* from the Nation of Islam's Yakub story, and place both in a larger context of derivations of Mary Shelley's Frankenstein story, which is in a sense the primal scene of artistic meditations on the consequences of science.

A Black Mass is a particularly rich cogitation on race and bioscience because it depicts a moment when "race" (in the form of a population of white beings) is literally created by the mad scientist Jacoub. In this way, Baraka alludes to (and reverses) the centuries-old processes through which medical and scientific practice have scrutinized, codified, classified, and otherwise constructed black bodies.[11] Ultimately, the playwright not only upends the laboratory power relations that typify the history of racial science, but, as befitting Black Arts Movement cultural politics, he also critiques the epistemological underpinnings of bioscience. Importantly, Baraka's play also foreshadowed the uneasy nexus of racial politics and bioscience that would take center stage in the late 1960s and early 1970s. *A Black Mass* dramatically depicted African American skepticism about biomedicine and scientific experimentation, a sentiment that would find wide-ranging assent in black communities following the revelation, in the early 1970s, of state-implicated scientific and medical research abuses. In this way, the play provides insight into how some African Americans perceived bioscience on the eve of these developments.

While it was an exemplar of Black Arts Movement aesthetic politics, *A Black Mass* is also in keeping with a long tradition of artistic reflections on the intersections of bioscience and society. Jacoub could easily take a place in the literary pantheon of mad scientists such as Dr. Faust and Dr. Frankenstein. Considered from this perspective, Baraka's play could be said to have appended an explicit racial politic onto Shelley's nineteenth-century gothic tale. I propose that by understanding *A Black Mass* (and the Yakub myth that preceded it) in a continuum of iterations of the Frankenstein myth, we might come to better understand its larger symbolic importance.

It has become commonplace among science studies scholars to look to cultural narratives as a way of understanding popular attitudes about science and its applications.[12] Such representations shape and inform public perception of scientists and scientific and medical research practices. The mad scientist, or reckless originator of anomalous inventions, the social impact of which is not fully known prior to conception, remains a central metaphor for the power of science and medicine within and beyond the laboratory.[13] And the misbegotten monster, made at the hands of a transgressive researcher, is an enduring icon of the potentially disastrous outcomes of scientific experimentation. Though this allegory has roots in older Western myths, including those of Prometheus and Faust, its most well-known source is Mary Shelley's *Frankenstein*, first published in 1818.[14]

The tragic tale of Victor Frankenstein has been depicted in many cultural forms since the publication of Shelley's novel, including drama and film, but it has always been interpreted as a social mirror. Its precise meaning, at any given historical moment, has been closely linked to developments in science and technology. Historian of medicine Susan Lederer explains that the novel was initially received as "a moral lesson illustrating the punishment for ambitious scientists who seek to usurp the place of God by creating life."[15] Yet, beginning in the early twentieth century, as versions of the story proliferated in mass culture, the "Frankenstein story [became] a powerful metaphor for addressing the ways in which American society responds to the rapid pace of discoveries in biology and medicine, discoveries that challenged traditional understandings of what it means to be human."[16] According to Lederer, in the current moment, the metaphor of Frankenstein retains "continuing power" to "articulate concerns raised by new developments in biomedicine such as cloning and xenografting (the use of animal organs in human bodies), and the role responsible scientists and citizens play in the ongoing dialogue to determine the acceptable limits of scientific and medical advances."[17] What has remained consistent across the many permutations of the Frankenstein myth is an underlying unease with biomedical research and an acute awareness of the potential costs of pushing the envelope of experimental science.

"YAKUB'S HISTORY"

Although the finer details of *Frankenstein* are often lost in the diverse re-tellings it has received since its initial publication many decades ago, the novel's popular re-imaginings are typically faithful to the broad contours of the original narrative. One case in point is the portion of the Nation of Islam's cosmogenesis myth known as "Yakub's story" or "Yakub's history" from which *A Black Mass* is adapted.[18] The myth tells of a disaffected black "god-scientist" named Yakub who, millennia prior to the research of Gregor Mendel, deploys his knowledge of the mechanics of dominant and recessive genes to eliminate black humanity by inventing and propagating a conquering tribe of white people.[19] As with Mary Shelley's novel, this myth portrays a transgressive scientist whose unrestrained curiosity results in the murder of members of the scientist's kin. However, in this NOI narrative, the mad scientist is also a traitor to his race whose unbridled experimentation causes the decimation of a large segment of a population and sets the stage for the impending racial oppression of the survivors.

Emerging in the crucible of the Great Migration and the Great Depression, the Black Muslim community afforded safe haven to recent arrivals to urban centers, while the NOI's belief system—in which the Yakub myth figured prominently—explained blacks' position in the social hierarchy vis-à-vis white Americans, "rationalized the predicament of the black race," and forecast the imminent upending of the pecking order.[20] Described by sociologist C. Eric Lincoln as "the central myth of the Black Muslim movement," the Yakub story has been in circulation since the establishment of the Nation of Islam in 1930.[21] According to the legend, in the beginning of human history, many types of black people inhabited the moon. A black god-scientist, unhappy that all the moon's inhabitants did not speak the same language, exploded the planet, one piece of which became the Earth. The Earth was inhabited by a surviving community of inherently righteous black people, many of whom settled in

Mecca.[22] Yakub, who was born twenty miles outside of Mecca, was among the thirty percent of citizens of this all-black, utopian society who were dissatisfied with their lives.

As a child, Yakub was nicknamed "big head," a tag that was reputedly both literal and figurative, and referred to the unusually large size of his skull as well as his extreme arrogance and intelligence.[23] A formative experience in his youth would inspire Yakub's life's work. Playing with iron bars one day, he discovered the properties of magnetism. He observed that similarly charged magnetic poles repel one another while opposite poles attract. From this physical law, Yakub hypothesized a social one: if he could create a race of beings diametrically opposite to black people, he could reign over them. Blacks would be attracted to this opposite race and would thus be blinded to the "tricknology" used to rule over them.

Yakub carried this idea with him into adulthood. He excelled at school and quickly outgrew the education available to him at the local university. He subsequently turned his complete attention to the task of developing a technique to "breed races scientifically."[24] At the same time, Yakub began to spread his mutinous racial philosophy and drew a large following among other dissatisfied Meccans. Alarmed authorities were fearful of Yakub's dangerous ideas and his hubris; they attempted to contain the scientist's ambitions by banishing him and his 59,999 disaffected followers to a distant island.

On this island, Yakub set up a laboratory and continued his efforts to create the white race. Yakub discovered that black men contained two "germs," a dominant black one and a recessive brown one. As Malcolm X explained, the scientist "conceived the idea of employing what we today know as the recessive genes structure, to separate from each other the two germs, black and brown, and then grafting the brown germ to progressively lighter, weaker stages."[25] Although his precise methods are not elaborated, Yakub purportedly used genetic science to mutate and cross-breed the black race into the white race—creating the "red, yellow and brown" races along the way.[26] He also instituted a eugenics policy in which infanticide was practiced (black babies were killed and brown ones were allowed to live) and established "selective birth control" by encouraging lighter-skinned people to mate with each other and outlawing marriages between darker-hued residents.[27]

Although Yakub died before the human "bleaching" process was complete, many centuries after his death the island was exclusively populated by a white race. This group migrated back to the mainland. Because they did not possess the inherent righteousness of the original black man, the white race became corrupt, immoral, and atavistic—more animal-like, covered with body hair, and impervious to frigid climes. This devolution was accompanied by the initiation of a master plan to oppress and eliminate black people.[28]

As with Shelley's *Frankenstein*, "Yakub's history" is an origin story in which unfettered scientific experimentation serves as the engine of epic creation and cataclysm. Perhaps owing to its science fictional elements, the Yakub myth is regarded, in the words of historian Claude Clegg, as the "most peculiar part of the [Black] Muslim's theology."[29] Yet, however unusual it might appear at first glance, the myth clearly draws on more familiar and conventional cosmologies. Religious studies scholar Michael Lieb characterizes the NOI's creation story as a "reinscription of the Genesis narrative" of the Old Testament.[30] Extending Lieb's argument, Clegg maintains that the Yakub myth is "at least partially anchored in both Judeo-Christian and Islamic theology."[31]

Yakub's story is also redolent of recurring themes in African American folklore, most notably narratives that invert conventional accounts of racial origins. Lawrence W. Levine has observed that during slavery oral legends circulated which were based on "the assumption of a black creation [and] allowed slaves to stand the white creation myths on their heads."[32] For example, the conceit that all creation stemmed from the black race was also found in the famous Uncle Remus tales that were popular among African Americans in the South.[33] In one witty story, "Origin of the Races," Uncle Remus tells of a time when all of humanity was black, until a pond was discovered that turned black people who were submerged in it white.[34]

While aspects of the Yakub story draw on ancient and folkloric mythologies, its scientific themes and modern temporality make it distinct from them. The myth evinces an engagement with contemporary research developments. Black Muslim leaders were known to be widely read in genetic science and probably "interpreted" the writings of Gregor Mendel as proof of the Yakub myth.[35] As the references to coercive birth restrictions reveal, the architects of the Yakub story were most certainly aware of eugenic science. This theme additionally anticipated fears of race genocide that would permeate black power discourse some years later. NOI leaders have also acknowledged that the theories of early twentieth-century archeologists and anthropologists, particularly the "out of Africa" thesis, figure centrally in their worldview. Most recently, the NOI has claimed that advances in medical genetics supply a new basis of evidence to bolster its beliefs.[36]

In addition to these scientific influences and borrowings, the NOI injected scientism into its beliefs. In the strict sense of the word, scientism refers to the application of the analytical approaches of the sciences to other spheres of life. This practice was best exemplified in the numerological bent of the NOI's biblical exegesis and cosmology.[37] A form of scientism was also apparent in the appropriation of science-like terms as tropes and metaphors. For example, the word "tricknology" allocated a measure of rigorous calculation to what Black Muslims believed to be age-old cunning on the part of whites, while the frequently used term "science" referred to any and all exacting knowledge about Islam and the experiences of black people. A similar strategy was employed in the Yakub story: Michael Lieb has described the myth as a cosmogony that "anchors its narrative in the language of scientific discourse . . . distinguished by an emphasis on racial difference."[38] The NOI's leaders, Clegg adds, also used a "façade" of science and other "modern trappings"—including mention of "genetic experimentation"—to confer "a rational, calculated veneer" and twentieth-century credibility to the Yakub story.[39] Both forms of scientism provided a semblance of scientific epistemological authority to NOI ideology in general and to its creation narrative in particular.

As an African American Frankenstein story, the Yakub myth is a paradoxical statement on race, science, and society. The Yakub story evidences skepticism about the use of knowledge to alter the "natural order" (that is, the "racial" order) of things and depicts a scientist's act of misconduct as the principle catalyst of the epic dispersal of black people and the central cause of their generations-long subjugated status. While the myth clearly conveys some uncertainty about bioscience, it is less of a critique of scientific experimentation per se and more a cautionary tale of the possible consequences of it should the aspirations of ambitious researchers go unchecked. "Yakub's history" would become the blueprint for Amiri Baraka's Black Arts Movement-era play, *A Black Mass*. But the play would offer an even more dour assessment of biomedical research; it would declare the risks that science posed for black people even more directly.

BARAKA'S EXPERIMENT

Amiri Baraka penned *A Black Mass* at a critical juncture in his development as an artist. According to literary theorist William J. Harris' timeline, the play was composed at the beginning of Baraka's "black nationalist" phase—after the playwright had left his life as a Beat poet and New York City bohemian and at the beginning of his ascension as a leader of the Black Arts Movement.[40] The transition from bohemian to black cultural nationalist began with a visit to Cuba in 1960, which Baraka described in retrospect as "a turning point" in his life.[41] Baraka traveled to Cuba with a delegation of artists, activists, and writers assembled by the Fair Play for Cuba Committee—the group included critic Harold Cruse, historian John Henrik Clarke, and radical Robert F. Williams—at the invitation of Fidel Castro. The trip was sponsored by the Castro government in the hope that first-person accounts of Cuba from members of this influential group upon their return would serve as a counterbalance to Cold War red-baiting.

Recalling the impact of his trip on his political evolution Baraka wrote, "I carried so much back with me [from Cuba] that I never was the same again. The dynamic revolution had touched me . . . . The growing kernel of social consciousness I had was mightily fertilized by the visit . . . . It was not enough just to write, to feel, to think, one must act! One *could* act."[42] The production of *A Black Mass* and other dramatic works in the mid-1960s reflected Baraka's radicalization as well as his aesthetic strategy of linking artistic form with political content. He recalled, "[T]he dramatic form began to interest me because I wanted to go 'beyond' poetry. I wanted some kind of action literature . . . [Drama] is an *action* form . . . . It reaches more people."[43] Just as Baraka had been stirred by the Cuba trip to act for social change, with his creative work, he aspired to produce action in art and to provoke his audiences to act politically.[44] Writing for the stage, Baraka realized, served both these agendas.[45]

Baraka learned of the Yakub myth—the seedbed for "A Black Mass"—from Malcolm X, whom he greatly admired.[46] Not surprisingly, the assassination of the former NOI leader on February 21, 1965, marked another defining moment in the playwright's life.[47] According to Baraka, the death of Malcolm X stirred him to sever all ties with his downtown Manhattan life and to solidify his total commitment to black cultural nationalism.[48] Within a month of the assassination, Baraka left his family and Greenwich Village, and took up residence in Harlem.[49] There, he and other African American activist-artists formed the Black Arts Repertory Theater/School (BARTS), an arts center that, among other programming, held studio art classes and organized public performances including street theater and music.[50] At BARTS, Baraka worked collaboratively with musicians—including Sun Ra, who has been described by John Szwed as Baraka's "silent partner"—on cultural nationalist projects to entertain and mobilize the local black community.[51]

A Black Mass was first staged on a spring evening in May 1966 at the RKO Proctor's Theater in Newark, New Jersey. Performed by the Spirit House Movers—the in-house acting troupe of Spirit House, Baraka's recently established cultural institution—the play presented his reinterpretation of the Yakub myth.[52] The partly improvised drama was fittingly accompanied by the experimental jazz of Sun Ra and the Myth-Science Arkestra, which created aural vertigo—a sense of the world spinning out of control—with music that simultaneously banged, screeched, and undulated.[53] With this performance, Sun Ra and Baraka married their distinctive styles of avant-garde cultural politics to striking effect.[54]

As the play opens, the audience encounters three "black magicians" working in the darkness of "some fantastical chemical laboratory . . . with weird mixtures bubbling, [and] colored solutions."[55] The shadowy space is furnished with Arabic and Swahili signage, "strange drawings, diagrams of weird machines" (22), signifying the lab's African and scientific inheritance. Two of the alchemists, Nasafi and Tanzil, are working at a "leisurely, casual" pace, humming to Sun Ra's gentle musical accompaniment (21).[56] Jacoub, the third experimenter, is laboring more feverishly and more deliberately.

Nasafi announces his successful creation of a potion that will render "time, that white madness" meaningless (22). Expressing pleasure with the news of Nasafi's invention, Tanzil complains that time "drives brothers across the Earth" and anticipates the day when the potion will have eliminated "time" and "the animals who bring it into the world" (23). Alluding to the NOI myth's claim that a black god-scientist had first fashioned the whites from the "germ" of the black race, Nasafi reminds Tanzil that "the animals" to which he refers, "are ourselves . . . . We thought them up. We have deserved whatever world we find ourselves in. If we have mad animals full of time to haunt us, to haunt *us*, who are in possession of all knowledge, then we have done something to make them exist" (21).

It is then revealed that "time" was the result of one of Jacoub's experiments:

> NASAFI: You deal in a strange logic, brother Jacoub. You spoke once of time
> and we forgot about it. Now there are animals who hiss time madness in the air,
> and into our lives. I had forgotten but now I'm sure it was you, Jacoub. (23)

The mad scientist Jacoub has a track record of composing inventions that
have not served black people well. Nasafi has crafted an antidote to Jacoub's
prior handiwork. Jacoub disagrees that his prior act of creation was a negative
affair. He asks, "Can knowledge be evil?" and proclaims "we must find out
everything" (24).

Turning to Jacoub, Nasafi asks what presently holds his attention so intently. Jacoub responds that he is engrossed in the task of "Creating a new
organism . . . . A man like ourselves, yet separate from us. A neutral being . . . .
Neutral because I have created him. And can fill him up as I will. From beyond
the powers of natural creation, I can make a super-natural being" (27). An
alarmed Tanzil warns Jacoub that "[i]t's a fool's game to invent what does not
need to be invented" (24). Nasafi concurs, "Jacoub, you speak of a magic that
is without human sanction" (25). Jacoub boldly counters, "Let us be fools. For
creation is its own end" (24). (In the midst of this debate, three women enter
the lab, and are reproached for encroaching on male space but are permitted
to stay.) Tanzil and Nasafi try to persuade Jacoub of another understanding
of creation that derives from the inherent intellectual and spiritual wisdom of
black people:

> NASAFI: We already know everything.
> JACOUB: That is not possible. (24)

And later,

> NASAFI: We know what is evil and what is perfection . . . . We know beyond
> knowing, knowing there is nothing to know. And knowledge is repetition, and the
> bringing forth again of things that were so anyway. Everything already exists. You
> cannot really create. (25)

Jacoub continues his experimentation.

Sun Ra's musical accompaniment grows louder and more violent, and suddenly a "new organism" is born from a cacophony of sparks, light, smoke, and
music. We are told that the being is "absolutely cold white" in color, with the
awkward gait of an "animal robot" (33). Incapable of developed speech, he gur-
gles, slobbers, and repeatedly howls: "White. White. Me. White." The white
beast lashes out at those around him, including Jacoub, and succeeds in attack-
ing a nearby black woman, who is transformed into a beast after losing her

pigment (she is turned white); her grace (she begins to walk clumsily); and her humanity (she is now an animal, too). Whiteness, here, is contagious, a meme. Jacoub says, "The whiteness spreads itself without effort. For the thing is sexless. It cannot breed" (34).

Distressed by the destructive power of the monster, Jacoub's fellow scientists rebuke him. Nasafi declares, "Jacoub, your error . . . the substitution of thought for feeling. A heart full of numbers and cold formulae" (34). Tanzil reprimands the mad scientist for "Asking God's questions, and giving animal answers!" (34). Nasafi and Tanzil demand that the beast and his "bride" be sent away to the "cold north"; but Jacoub, convinced that he can teach them language and imbue them with humanity, demands that they be allowed to remain. After the beasts kill all but him, Jacoub realizes that his fellow scientists were right. As the performance concludes, he expels the beast to "the evil diseased caves of the cold" and then dies from wounds inflicted by it (39).[57]

Several textual parallels support a reading of *A Black Mass* as an African American Frankenstein story. Like Shelley's novel, the play centers on the actions of a compulsive scientist set on the goal of fashioning life. Both Jacoub and Victor Frankenstein carry out their experiments with little forethought of, and utter disregard for, the potential consequences. In both instances, the power of creation was harnessed by men (and specifically precluded the contribution of women).[58] Although Victor Frankenstein immediately rejects the Being he creates, and Jacoub hopes to nurture and educate his creation, both eventually come to confront the fatal consequences of their incautious creative deeds. More troubling still, both narratives leave the question of the respective Beings' prospects unanswered; each concludes with an opening up of an uncertain future in which the actions of the Creatures can only be imagined, anticipated, and dreaded by the audience.[59] It is this speculative opening, this lacunae, I would argue, that has caused *Frankenstein* and its many iterations to be so easily taken up as both reflections on, and forecasts of, the societal effects of biomedical science.

A few scholarly observers have read the Jacoub character as a transgressive scientific investigator not unlike Victor Frankenstein. Commenting upon the gothic elements of *A Black Mass*, Kimberly Benston suggests that Jacoub alludes to "the 'mad scientist' of Romantic and post-Romantic 'horror' stories."[60] And critic Werner Sollors observes that "Jacoub's mistake is the flaw of countless scientists in science fiction."[61] Certainly, Jacoub deserves a place among the pantheon of characters whom Theodore Roszak has called "titans who create monsters," a group in which he includes Victor Frankenstein, Dr. Moreau and Dr. Faustus, among others.[62] Created through hubris and blind ambition, and in keeping with the dystopian genres of Enlightenment commentary, these monsters become the very *betes noires* of the protagonists—the cause of their makers' annihilation and of unknowable future social damage as well.

Yet, in *A Black Mass*, Jacoub's "new organism" is also his *bete blanc*, for it is implied that in conceiving the white Beast and in failing to destroy it when he had the opportunity to do so, he has created the source of black people's oppression and sown the seeds of anti-black racism. In keeping with the original Yakub myth, the mad scientist falls victim to white "tricknology," attracted as he was to the very thing that, in the logic of the NOI's black nationalist ideology, was most opposite him. And because the Beast can turn black people white with its mere touch, Jacoub's transgression additionally poses the threat of annihilation by means of assimilation and miscegenation.[63] Unlike the NOI's origin story, which is in many ways an uncritical embrace of racialized experimental science, including eugenics, Baraka's play is an unambiguous indictment of scientific experimentation without limits and "without human sanction." With the play's treatment of "time," Baraka explicitly critiques the relentless rationalization of life that is metaphorical for a way of living that is antithetical to "traditional" black forms. Tanzil's statements imply that a Western orientation to "time" was one factor that set the Middle Passage and the African diaspora in motion.

Perhaps the most consequential moral of *A Black Mass*, in striking dissimilarity to the NOI cosmology, is its suggestion that black people are right to be suspicious and mistrustful of scientific experimentation, given the negative consequences it has held for them. Through the characters of Nasafi and Tanzil, Baraka criticizes the valuing of scientific discovery for its own sake. Yet he also articulates an alternate ideology of invention and experimentation. He puts forth another definition of the creative process that is more akin to magic or intuition than medical or scientific research. Baraka counterposes artistic creation against Jacoub's self-interested, scientific, and ultimately destructive experimentation.

CONCLUSION

The broad critique of a "Western" mode of thinking presented in *A Black Mass* made it an iconic piece of Black Arts Movement ideology. The play characterized scientific and medical experimentation as the epitome of the Western "aesthetic impulse gone astray," in Larry Neal's words, against which Black Arts Movement advocates defined their craft (Neal argued that the Beast was "created merely for the sake of creation," and was in this respect similar to the non-functional nature of Western art). Yet its focus directly on the sciences, rather than the arts, also made it unique. In *A Black Mass*, the biosciences and the pursuit of scientific knowledge are considered superfluous and dangerous. The audience is confronted with the philosophical possibility that all that is necessary to know about the world is presently known and the blame for many of the problems of black life is laid at the feet of scientific research.

The power of the admittedly far-fetched *A Black Mass* lay not in its literal truth but in the fact that African Americans who saw or read the play might perceive resonances with their lived experiences. Perhaps unconsciously, *A Black Mass* harked back to African American communities' historically based anxieties about biomedical malpractice; the play was in keeping with a rich mythology that encoded blacks' lived experiences of medical maltreatment into folklore and oral tradition. For example, Gladys-Marie Fry's study of the black oral tradition that originated in slavery around crimes that occurred at night asserts that tales of "night doctors" were exploited by southern whites to control black behavior, to discourage slaves from running away at night out of fear of the supernatural evils and, following Reconstruction, to discourage blacks from migrating to the North. Fry explains that the phrase was "applie[d] to both students of medicine who supposedly stole cadavers from which to learn about body processes, and professional thieves, who sold stolen bodies—living and dead—to physicians for medical research."[64]

Similarly, Spencie Love has argued that historical atrocities linking race and biomedical research have sedimented in the collective memory of African American communities. She cites the 1950 death of Charles Drew, a noted African American surgeon and contributor to the construction of the U.S blood bank system during WWII, after sustaining serious injuries in a car accident. When blacks in rural North Carolina learned of the incident, many believed that Drew had been denied services at the nearby "whites only" emergency room, despite his standing in the medical community; rumors to this effect spread within hours.[65] Love discovered that white doctors had in fact attempted to save Drew. However, months prior to his death, a black GI had been denied access to another nearby segregated hospital and died as a result. Love concludes that it was not the veracity of the rumors about Drew that mattered, but that they could have been true.

While *A Black Mass* was of a different order of myth from the tales described by Fry and Love, taken together they reveal that Baraka's play tapped into a deep vein of community memory and collective consciousness with regard to African American experiences with bioscientific research. In that sense, *A Black Mass* could be described as crystallizing African American attitudes about scientific experimentation into a potent, condensed series of images that, while obviously not literally factual, did feed off larger truths about the historical relationship between African Americans and biomedicine. It also fed into more immediate historical developments. In the summer of 1972, the *New York Times* disclosed that hundreds of black men in Macon County, Georgia had been left with untreated syphilis for four decades. In a recent anthology on the topic of the Tuskegee syphilis experiment, historian of medicine Susan Reverby describes the unfolding of the study from its origins in 1932 to its final denouement as "[p]laying out with all the drama of a southern gothic tale."[66] A gothic tale in its own right, *A Black Mass* re-inscribed a longstanding tradition of skepticism about scientific experimentation into the radical context of its times, and presaged (and perhaps preconditioned) the explosion of mistrust and anxiety that would develop in African American communities following the revelation of Tuskegee.

NOTES

Many thanks to Lisa Gail Collins, Margo Natalie Crawford, Howard Rambsy II, Andrew Ross, Alexander G. Weheliye, Ben Williams, and Christopher Winks for being generous with their feedback and frank in their criticism. I am grateful to each of them for their helpful responses to ideas presented here.

1. Larry Neal, "The Black Arts Movement," *The Black Aesthetic*, ed. Addison Gayle, Jr. (Garden City, NY: Doubleday, 1971), 272.

2. Ibid., 272; emphasis added.

3. Ibid., 272.

4. Ibid., 284.

5. Werner Sollors, *Amiri Baraka/LeRoi Jones: The Quest for a 'Populist Modernism'* (New York: Columbia University Press, 1978), 37, 52–57, and Harry Elam, Jr. *Taking It to the Streets: The Social Protest Theater of Luis Valdez and Amiri Baraka.* (Ann Arbor: University of Michigan Press, 1997), 56–57.

6. Both Malcolm X and Eldridge Cleaver make reference to the Nation of Islam's Yakub myth; see Malcolm X (with Alex Haley), *The Autobiography of Malcolm X* (New York: Random House, 1965), 164–76, and Eldridge Cleaver, *Soul on Ice* (New York: Dell, 1968), 101.

7. "Jacoub" is the spelling Baraka uses in the play. Throughout this essay, I use this spelling to refer to the antagonist of "A Black Mass"; when invoking the mad scientist of the Nation of Islam creation myth, I use "Yakub."

8. Nilgun Anadolu-Okur, *Contemporary African American Theater: Afrocentricity in the Works of Larry Neal, Amiri Baraka, and Charles Fuller* (New York: Garland, 1997), 101, 105; Kimberly Benston, *Baraka: The Renegade and the Mask* (New Haven, CT: Yale University Press, 1976), 238; Alain Ricard, *Theatre and Nationalism: Wole Soyinka and LeRoi Jones*, trans. Femi Osofisan (Ile-Ife, Nigeria: University of Ife Press, 1972), 136–46; and Sollors, *Amiri Baraka/LeRoi Jones*, 211.

9. The American Heritage Dictionary of the English Language defines bioscience as: "Any of several branches of science, such as biology, medicine, anthropology, or ecology, that deal with living organisms and their organization, life processes, and relationships to each other and their environment," January 28, 2004, http://dictionary.reference.com/search?q=bioscience.

10. See, for example, Sandra G. Shannon, "Manipulating Myth, Magic, and Legend: Amiri Baraka's Black Mass," *College Language Association Journal* 39 (1996): 357–68.

11. The construction of race and blackness in the biomedicine and the social sciences is detailed in: Lee Baker, *From Savage to Negro: Anthropology and the Construction of Race, 1896–1954* (Berkeley: University of California Press, 1998); Frantz Fanon, *Black Skin, White Masks*, trans. Constance Farrington (New York: Grove, 1991 [1952]); Stephen Jay Gould, *The Mismeasure of Man* (New York: W. W. Norton & Company, 1981); and William Stanton, *The Leopard's Spots: Scientific Attitudes Toward Race in America, 1815–59*, reprint edition (Chicago: University of Chicago Press, 1982).

12. Scholars working in this vein include, Gillian Beer, *Open Fields: Science in Cultural Encounter* (New York: Oxford University Press, 1999); Susan Lederer, *Frankenstein: Penetrating the Secrets of Nature* (New Brunswick, NJ: Rutgers University Press, 2002); Lisa Nakamura, *Cybertypes: Race, Ethnicity and Identity on the Internet* (New York: Routledge, 2002); and Dorothy Nelkin and Susan Lidee, *The DNA Mystique: The Gene as a Cultural Icon* (New York: Freeman, 1996).

13. See, for example, Peter H. Goodrich, "The Lineage of Mad Scientists: Anti-Types of Merlin," *Extrapolation* 27 (1986): 109–15; Roslyn Haynes, *From Faust to Strangelove: Representations of the Scientist in Western Literature* (Baltimore, MD: The Johns Hopkins

University Press, 1994); Lederer, *Frankenstein;* and Theodore Roszak, "The Monster and the Titan: Science, Knowledge and Gnosis," *Daedelus* 103 (1974): 17.

14. Mary Wollstonecraft Shelley, *Frankenstein: Or, the Modern Prometheus: The 1818 Text,* ed. Marilyn Butler (Oxford: Oxford University Press, 1998).

15. Lederer, *Frankenstein,* 1.

16. Ibid.

17. Ibid. Tellingly, the Frankenstein metaphor has also recently taken on new linguistic power in the context of new developments in biotechnology, as denoted by the recent use of the term "Frankenfoods" to refer to the dangers that might be inherent to genetically modified foods, and to their preternaturalness.

18. The Nation of Islam origin myth was frequently referred to as "Yakub's history"; for example, Malcolm X with Alex Haley, *Autobiography,* 190, 194, and Cleaver, *Soul on Ice,* 101. See also Warith Deen Muhammad, *As the Light Shineth from the East* (Chicago: WDM Publishing, 1980), 17.

The transformation of the Yakub myth into a play was not an unusual treatment of NOI philosophy, for as sociologist C. Eric Lincoln observed, the group frequently staged large-scale cosmological and moral dramas including "The Trial," in which whites were tried for crimes against black humanity. See C. Eric Lincoln, *The Black Muslims in America,* 3rd ed. (Trenton, NJ: Africa World Press, 1994 [1961]), 1–2.

19. Mattias Gardell, *In the Name of Elijah Muhammad: Louis Farrakhan and the Nation of Islam* (Durham: Duke University Press, 1996), 176; E. U. Essien-Udon, *Black Nationalism: The Search for an Identity* (Chicago: University of Chicago Press, 1993 [1962]), 133. While incarcerated, Malcolm X read Mendel's "Findings in Genetics," a book suggested to him by Elijah Muhammad, Malcolm X with Alex Haley, *Autobiography,* 202.

20. Claude Andrew Clegg III, *An Original Man: The Life and Times of Elijah Muhammad* (New York: St. Martin's Press); Essien-Udom, *Black Nationalism,* 7–8. Essien-Udom explains: "The ostensible enemy of the Nation of Islam is, of course, the Caucasian race and specifically the American white man, who is responsible for the moral and material conditions of the Negro. The enemy is not simply the white race. It is their claim to cultural, moral, and spiritual superiority . . . ," 124.

21. Lincoln, *Black Muslims,* 72.

22. My synopsis of the Yakub myth is drawn from W. Muhammad, *As the Light Shineth,* 13–14, 17, 149–51; Elijah Muhammad, *Message to the Blackman in America* (Chicago: Muhammad Mosque of Islam, No. 2, 1965), 103–22; Essien-Udom, *Black Nationalism,* 128, 133–34; Lincoln, *Black Muslims,* 72–73; and Malcolm X with Alex Haley, *Autobiography,* 164–76.

23. Malcolm X with Alex Haley, *Autobiography,* 165.

24. Ibid.

25. Ibid. Also, Elijah Muhammad quoted in Lincoln, *Black Muslims,* 72.

26. Lincoln, *Black Muslims,* 72. Obviously, these procedures for obtaining racial purity through "breeding" and birth control regulations are similar to racist eugenics of the early twentieth century.

27. Clegg, *An Original Man,* 50.

28. Elijah Muhammad, *Message to the Blackman,* 68.

29. Clegg, *An Original Man,* 50.

30. Michael Lieb, *Children of Ezekiel: Aliens, UFOs, the Crisis of Race and the Advent of the End Time* (Durham: Duke University Press, 1998), 140.

31. Clegg, *An Original Man*, 50. Lieb concurs: "Yakub the black scientist is thereby ultimately the figure the Bible refers to as Adam," 141.

32. Lawrence W. Levine, *Black Culture and Black Consciousness. Afro-American Folk Thought from Slavery to Freedom* (New York: Oxford University Press, 1977), 85.

33. Harold Courlander, ed., *A Treasury of Afro-American Folklore: The Oral Literature, Traditions, Recollections, Legends, Tales, Songs, Religious Beliefs, Customs, Sayings and Humor of Peoples of African Descent in the Americas* (New York: Crown Publishers, 1976). Also, see Henry Louis Gates, Jr. *The Signifying Monkey: A Theory of African-American Literary Criticism* (New York: Oxford University Press, 1988).

34. Courlander, "Origin of the Races, According to Uncle Remus," 497. Similar tales of blacks who become white are present in later African American fiction, most famously, George Schuyler's *Black No More* (New York: Modern Library, 1999).

35. Gardell, *In the Name of*, 176.

36. Ibid. NOI leader Louis Farrakhan has said that his favorite anthropologist is "Dr. [Louis] Leakey [who] discovered that the root and the origin of man was in Africa," quoted in Gardell, *In the Name of*, 175.

37. Gardell, *In the Name of*, 174–85.

38. Lieb, *Children of Ezekiel*, 139.

39. Clegg, *An Original Man*, 46, 50.

40. William J. Harris, "Introduction," *The LeRoi Jones/Amiri Baraka Reader*, ed. W. J. Harris (New York: Thunder's Mouth Press, 1991), xvii–xxviii.

41. Amiri Baraka, *The Autobiography of LeRoi Jones* (Chicago: Lawrence Hill Books, 1997 [1984]), 243, also 241–46.

42. Baraka, *Autobiography*, 246 (emphasis in original).

43. Baraka, *Autobiography*, 275. (emphasis added).

44. Amiri Baraka, "The Revolutionary Theatre," *Home: Social Essays* (New York: Ecco, 1998 [1966]), 210–15.

45. Ibid.

46. Baraka, *Autobiography*, 306.

47. Baraka, *Autobiography*, 306; also mentioned in Sollors, *Amiri Baraka/LeRoi Jones*, 210. Baraka's time in Harlem was short-lived. Difficult internecine politics compelled Baraka to move away. Coming full circle, he returned to his birthplace of Newark, New Jersey, where he established another cultural institution, the Spirit House.

48. Amiri Baraka, "The Legacy of Malcolm X, and the Coming of the Black Nation," *Home: Social Essays*, 238–50. Baraka offers other reflections on Malcolm X in "November 1966: One Year Eight Months Later," in *Raise Race Rays Raze: Essays Since 1965* (New York: Random House, 1969).

49. Baraka, *Autobiography*, 293–94. Several years prior, Baraka had written of the significance Harlem held for him and black Americans more generally; see "City of Harlem" in *Home: Social Essays*, 87–93.

50. Baraka, *Autobiography*, 294–97. For additional details about the founding of the BARTS, see Komozi Woodard, *A Nation within a Nation: Amiri Baraka (LeRoi Jones) and Black Power Politics* (Chapel Hill: University of North Carolina, 1999), 63–68.

51. John Szwed, *Space is the Place: The Lives and Times of Sun Ra* (New York: De Capo Press, 1998), 209. On the relationship between Sun Ra and Baraka, see also Baraka, *Autobiography*, 298–299. As a critic, Baraka wrote about Sun-Ra's music in articles reprinted from columns in *Down Beat* magazine, LeRoi Jones, *Black Music*

(New York: William Morrow & Company, 1968) 128–30, 134–37, 173–76, 193–95, 198–200.

52. Amiri Baraka, "A Black Mass by Amiri Baraka: The Black Arts, Spirit House, Sun Ra, Creating What Needs to Be Created!" Liner notes. Amiri Baraka (LeRoi Jones) with Sun Ra and the Myth Science Arkestra, *A Black Mass* CD, Son Boy Records, 1998.

53. A recording of this performance was recently re-released: Amiri Baraka (LeRoi Jones) with Sun Ra and the Myth Science Arkestra, *A Black Mass* CD, Son Boy Records, 1998. It was previously released in 1968 on Baraka's Jihad Records.

54. Baraka used music in his dramas because he felt it provided "an added dramatic dimension." He collaborated with Sun Ra precisely because the musician's compositions provided "the feeling of some kind of otherworldly wisdom or dimension, which changes sometimes to fear, terror, contemplation of the laboratory, contemplation of what wisdom and knowledge really are." Quoted from Sandra G. Shannon, "Amiri Baraka on Directing," *Conversations with Amiri Baraka*, ed. Charly Reilly (Jackson: University Press of Mississippi, 1994), 232.

55. LeRoi Jones, "A Black Mass," *Four Black Revolutionary Plays: All Praises to the Black Man* (New York: Bobbs-Merrill, 1969), 21. Page numbers will be cited in text for the remaining discussion of the play. This discussion also relies on a recently re-released recording of the 1966 performance and its accompanying liner notes written by Amiri Baraka.

56. Amiri Baraka (LeRoi Jones) with Sun Ra and the Myth Science Arkestra, *A Black Mass*.

57. Note the similarity here to Victor Frankenstein's self-imposed Artic exile with his Creature. In Shelley's text, the Creature was described as being impassive to the cold.

58. Notably, what is not altered in this inverted Frankenstein story is the fact that reproduction remains solidly in the hands of men. There is an extensive body of scholarship that deals with the way reproduction is gendered in Shelley's narrative and specifically excludes women from the creative process. On gender and creation in Frankenstein, see Margaret Homans, "Bearing Demons: Frankenstein's Circumvention of the Maternal," in *Bearing the Word: Language and Female Experience in Nineteenth-Century Women's Writing* (Chicago: University of Chicago Press, 1986); Barbara Johnson, "My Monster/My Self," in J. Paul Hunter, ed., *Frankenstein*, by Mary Wollstonecraft Shelley (New York: W. W. Norton & Company, 1996), 241–51; Anne K. Mellor, "Possessing Nature: The Female in Frankenstein," in Hunter, *Frankenstein*, 274–86; and Marc Rubenstein, "'My Accursed Origin': The Search for the Mother in Frankenstein," *Studies in Romanticism* 15 (Fall 1976): 165–94.

59. Sollors observed that the majority-black audiences of "A Black Mass" are frequently more outraged by and disapproving of mad scientist Jacoub's acts than by the Creature he created. In performance call-and-response, "verbal criticism [was] launched only a Jacoub." Sollors interpreted this as more of an "indictment of blacks who create" white beasts than of the beasts themselves. In this way, Baraka's play might be said to be less effective as black power agitprop than it was as a challenge to unchecked experimental science. Sollors, *Amiri Baraka/LeRoi Jones*, 214 and 296, fn. 22, fn. 26.

60. Kimberly Benston. *Baraka: The Renegade and the Mask*, 239.

61. Sollors, *Amiri Baraka/LeRoi Jones*, 213.

62. Roszak, "The Monster," 31; Sollors, *Amiri Baraka/LeRoi Jones*, 214.

63. Benston, *Baraka*, 240.

64. Gladys-Marie Fry, *Night Riders in Black Folk History* (Knoxville: University of Tennessee Press, 1975), 171.

65. "Johannas," a Black Arts Movement-era play by Bill Gunn parses similar territory. The play's eponymous lead character is a child prodigy born to a mother, Hilly, whose other children had died from untreated illness after a white physician insisted that they be taken to a "colored" doctor for treatment. Bill Gunn, "Johannas," *The Drama Review* 12—Special Issue on "Black Theatre" (1968): 131–32.

66. Susan Reverby, *Tuskegee's Truths: Rethinking the Tuskegee Syphilis Study* (Chapel Hill: University of North Carolina Press, 2000), 3.

7

Natural Black Beauty and Black Drag

Margo Natalie Crawford

As some male writers and visual artists in the Black Arts Movement attempted to castrate white power and render it feminine, black women were often objectified as the embodiments of black beauty ("African Queens" and "natural black beauty"). The male gaze of some Black Arts poets and photographers objectified black women even as it engaged in the laudable attempt to remove black women from the dominant visual culture that continues to define quintessential femininity through the sign of the white woman's body. The body of the black woman was often imagined as the motherland, the receptacle for the black (male-dominated) nation, and this black motherland became the ambiguously gendered space between the black phallus (the male position in the Black Arts ethos) and feminized whiteness.

In "Natural Black Beauty" (1969), an essay in *Black Arts: An Anthology of Black Creations*, poet Joe Goncalves explains the "Black is Beautiful" ideology of the 1960s in the following manner: "As for our natural beauty: Our lips complement our noses, our noses 'go with' our eyes and they all bless our skin, which is black. If your face does not complement itself, you are in a degree of trouble. . . . The real geometry of our faces, the natural geometry in terms of art is found, among other places, in African sculpture. Our natural architecture, our natural rhythm."[1] The idea of natural black beauty was a key part of the body politics of the Black Arts Movement. Black Arts participants often imagined that the black body was the most local site of the black nation that needed to be protected from dominant beauty standards. The new physical beauty standards privileged looking "natural" and looking "African." "Africa" signified nature, roots, authenticity, and purity within this Black Arts imagination. Clothing and hairstyles that were deemed "African" became signs of this natural black beauty. The short "afro" hairstyle began to be named the "natural." The cover story of a 1967 issue of

Ebony magazine celebrates the "afro" as the "natural" hairstyle.[2] In addition to "natural" hair, dark-skinned blackness was embraced, in the Black Arts gaze, as the epitome of natural beauty. In a 1969 issue of *Ebony* magazine, Black Arts leader Larry Neal crystallizes the body politics of the Black Arts Movement when he proclaims, "The new references of clothing and hair are essentially visions of ourselves perfected; they are sign posts on the road to eventual Self-Determination. For a Sister to wear her hair natural asserts the sacred and essentially holy nature of her body. The natural, in its most positive sense, symbolizes the Sister's willingness to determine her own destiny. It is an act of love for herself and her people. The natural helps to psychologically liberate the Sister. It prepares her for the message of a Rap Brown, a Robert Williams, a Huey Newton, a Maulana Karenga."[3] Unfortunately, Neal does not imagine that the "Sister with the Natural" might be more drawn to Audre Lorde's poem "Naturally" (1970). This poem fully unveils the male gaze that often shaped Black Arts Movement formulations of "natural black beauty" and the Black Arts Movement equation of "natural" beauty and dark-skinned blackness. The speaker in this poem proclaims skeptically, "Since Naturally Black is Naturally Beautiful / I must be proud / And, naturally, / Black and /Beautiful / Who always was a trifle / Yellow / And plain though proud / Before."[4] Lorde muses on yellow skin, light-skinned blackness, becoming a badge of shame in the "Black is Beautiful" lens that fought against the fetishism of light-skinned blackness in the advertising industry of bleaching creams and hair straightening products.[5] The "Black is Beautiful" fetishism of the "natural" was incredibly subversive and incredibly reactionary.

When studying the 1960s and 1970s Black Arts Movement from a contemporary vantage point, we must remember the aesthetic overhaul that the "Black is Beautiful" sensibility represented. In "Big Bushy Afros" (1998), a post-Black Arts Movement tribute to the movement, poet and critic A. B. Spellman explains, "It is hard to teach today the power of Black is Beautiful. The sensuality of a collective consciousness that declared itself on sight."[6] Black Arts Movement photography illuminates how this "collective consciousness" was visualized. In *In Our Terribleness* (1970), as Amiri Baraka responds to the photography of Fundi (Billy Abernathy), a Chicago Black Arts Movement photographer, he announces, "I can take off these clothes and wear some others."[7] Like *In Our Terribleness*, the photography of Bob Crawford, another Chicago Black Arts Movement photographer, presents the "clothing" of black cultural nationalism.[8] In his photograph entitled "The Middle Passage" (fig. 7.1), the lack of clothing, the bare chest of the young boy, is overcompensated for by the expanse of water that recalls the middle passage although it is, in actuality, the shores of Lake Michigan in Chicago. The title of the photograph emphasizes the huge signifying power that "Africa" has in the African American imagination. The bare chest of the photographed subject makes the title "The Middle Passage" even more intriguing. Crawford's photographic lens imagines an undressing of the African American body in order to locate the lost origin, Africa.

Fig. 7.1. Bob Crawford, *The Middle Passage*, 1968. Courtesy of the artist.

In Crawford's photograph entitled "Beauty Culture" (fig. 7.2), the beauty salon, the "College of Beauty Culture" that straightens "natural" black hair, is figured as the background against which signs of Black nationalism (the clothing of the Nation of Islam) emerges. The rage in the face of the gesticulating woman is imagined, within this photographer's frame, as rage against the "College of Beauty Culture." The erectness of the young man wearing the Fruit of Islam uniform represents the bold efforts of the newly emergent black aesthetic to combat this dominant white "beauty culture." In *In Our Terribleness*, Baraka explains the body politics of the Black Arts Movement in the following manner:

So we are parts of a body. And this is what you see. The energy revealed. Its slow parts for you baby. And what is the changing same for us, the reality beneath illusion that binds us, as the body is bound by its motion its intent. From the kids the simbas to the old folks, sweet sisters in between, what will hold us in motion, with the content of the black chemist the black magician, the changers of what is to what must be, what but our selves. (133)

Fig. 7.2. Bob Crawford, *Beauty Culture,* 1967. Courtesy of the artist.

The words "changing same" place such a transcendent emphasis on the simultaneous evanescence and durability of "blackness." The notion of "sweet sisters in between" reveals that the black woman's body is objectified as a medium through which black male nationalism is articulated. The words "we are parts of a body" recall Baraka's insistence, earlier in *In Our Terribleness,* that "we are trying literally to get our selves back together" (43).

As opposed to Baraka's sense that African Americans are "parts of a body," theorist Judith Butler argues that "one does one's body" in the sense that gender is a performance, a "stylized repetition of acts." [9] Baraka's understanding of culture and the body is not entirely different from Butler's understanding of gender and the body. Baraka theorizes about the performance of African American culture even as he lapses into racial essentialism. His focus on the "changing same," as Houston Baker has shown, is a dazzling definition of African American modernism. [10] The assertion "we are parts of a body" and the idea that "faces collect the change" demonstrate that Baraka is attempting to visualize the elusive "changing same." [11] The "collection" of change belies the evanescence of the "changing same." This attempt to capture the elusive essence of blackness was a core component of the Black Arts ethos.

Fig. 7.3. Bob Crawford,
Culture, 1969.
Courtesy of the artist.

As Baraka responds, in *In Our Terribleness*, to Abernathy's photographs, he insists, "not represents, but *is*" (114). Crawford's photograph *Culture* (1969) (fig. 7.3) is an explicit rendering of how the Black Arts ethos often imagined representations of blackness as more than representations. The subject in this photograph holds two texts in a manner of exhibition as if she is either posing for the camera or selling these texts on the city street, her own body becoming the display shelf. One of the texts she holds is entitled "American Negro in Bible Prophecy." The word "negro" in this title is one of the signifiers that the photographer's Black Arts gaze is aiming to subvert. The camera focuses on the features of the woman's face that is framed by the texts. As we read her body through the Black Arts lens, she is the "American Negro" in the process of being transformed into the Black Arts "prophecy"; the "negroness" of her body and the texts she holds are transformed into the "blackness" celebrated in Crawford's photographic gaze. The title of the second text announces, "Return to Africa Her Stolen Children." The woman displaying these books is positioned, in this photograph, as the "motherland" through which this "return to Africa" might occur.

What if the woman in this photograph displayed James Baldwin's *Tell Me How Long the Train's Been Gone*, a novel published in 1968, the heyday of the Black Arts Movement? How does *Tell Me* complicate a quick and easy packaging and display of the Black Arts ethos? In *Tell Me*, James Baldwin connects the Black Power Movement and gay black male identity. In the documentary *James Baldwin: The Price of the Ticket* (1989), Baraka asserts, "Jimmy Baldwin was neither in the closet about his homosexuality nor was he running around proclaiming homosexuality."[12] In *Tell Me*, he "proclaims" homosexuality as he "proclaims" that "Black is Beautiful." Baldwin insists that there is no rift between "Black is Beautiful" and "black is gay." Theorist Eve Sedgwick remembers, in *The Epistemology of the Closet*, a National Public Radio discussion of the 1960s as "the decade when Black people came out of the closet."[13] Baldwin makes "coming out of the closet" much more than a trope for the Black Power Movement when he explores, in *Tell Me*, the inseparability of the "racial closet" and the "sexual closet."

Early in the novel, Baldwin presents the "long career of blackmail" of the central character, Leo Proudhammer—a "blackmail" rendered explicitly as the "blackmail" of his "imperious bit of flesh," his penis.[14] Black Christopher, Leo's lover, emerges as the black phallus, the "black male" as opposed to Leo's affliction by "blackmail" (6). Baldwin imagines the emergence of the black phallus in the scene when Leo and his brother, Caleb, become physically intimate. Leo wrestles with the "god of the flesh" (210), as Baldwin invokes the biblical image of Jacob wrestling with the angel. As Leo curses "God," he proclaims his love of the blackness of his brother. The phallus, "God," is resisted as a black phallus is imagined. Gaining sexual access to the brother's body enables Leo to discover "black power." When his love affair with Black Christopher begins, he fully realizes the erotic nature of "Black Power." The darkness of Black Christopher's skin reminds Leo of "Africa" (107). Leo connects his brother, Caleb, and Christopher to "undiluted blackness." In the scene when Leo and Caleb become physically intimate, the celebration of "undiluted blackness" adds a new twist to the infamous comparison of incest and miscegenation in *Absalom, Absalom!* (1936): "So it's the miscegenation, not the incest, which you [Henry] can't bear."[15] When Leo curses "God," he embraces black incest and curses the white phallus. As he refers to the black "balls" (210), he reclaims the "undiluted blackness" of his brother as the phallus.[16]

Baldwin places the Black Power Movement and the sexual revolution of the 1960s in close proximity. In the penultimate scene of the novel, immediately prior to Black Christopher's succinct explanation of his understanding of black power—"We need guns" (482), Baldwin describes a dance party that reflects the sexual revolution of the 1960s. Leo thinks, "It was a rite that I was witnessing—witnessing, not sharing. . .The music drove and drove, into the past—into the future. It sounded like an attempt to make a great hole in the world, and bring up what was buried. And the dancers seemed, nearly, in the flickering, violent light, with their beads flashing, their long hair flying, their robes whirling—or their tight skirts, tight pants signifying—and with the music assaulting them like the last, last trumpet, to be dancing in their grave-clothes, raised from the dead" (368–9). Black Christopher takes Leo Proudhammer to this dance party. Christopher is the embodiment, for Leo, of Black Power

Natural Black Beauty and Black Drag   159

and "Black is Beautiful." As if rewriting the heterosexist, homophobic images produced by some of the key black male leaders of the Black Power and Black Arts Movement, Baldwin presents Black Christopher as "macho" and gay. Leo Proudhammer falls in love with the seemingly authentic, unadulterated blackness of Black Christopher. The older Leo is also enchanted with the fearlessness of Black Christopher's generation; he marvels at the young gay men's ability to "dar[e] to embrace another in the sight of all the world" (368). At the height of the "Black is Beautiful" and Black Power movement, Baldwin presents the subversive image of Black Christopher.

Leo admires the aesthetic of Black Christopher and his friends: "[T]heir beautiful black kinky hair spinning around their heads like fire and prophecy—this hair putting me in mind, somehow, of the extravagant beauty of rainforests—and with Camus or Fanon or Mao on their person, or with *Muhammad Speaks* under their arms" (454). Leo, the central character in the novel, is a consummate performer who believes that the "dressing room [is his] only home" (11). The novel is an intense meditation on the relation between performance and identity. Leo understands that identity is performative, but he also views acting as an "impossibility" given the way that people are trapped by the ideologies written on their bodies (82). When he decides to become an actor, Leo "commit[s] [himself] to this impossibility" (82). The interracial love affair between Leo and Barbara and the homosexual love affair between Leo and Black Christopher does not fit in the politics of the Black Power movement. Baldwin's position in the Black Power and Black Arts Movement was tenuous due to his depictions of homosexuality and bisexuality. Eldridge Cleaver, in *Soul on Ice* (1968), published the same year as *Tell Me*, attributes Baldwin's homosexuality to "self-hatred." When Cleaver articulates his own dilution anxiety, fear of loss of "authentic" blackness, it is clear that Cleaver views black homosexuality as a dilution of "blackness" and erasure of black power.[17] Baldwin subverts this dominant discourse of the Black Power Movement when he writes unflinchingly about the urgency for black power and a "Black is Beautiful" gaze even as he places homosexuality and interracial love in the center of the text. We often quickly define the Black Arts Movement as the artistic counterpart of the Black Power Movement. When we think about the significance of the publication of *Tell Me* in 1968 and Baldwin's insider/outsider status in the Black Power Movement compared to his key presence in the Civil Rights Movement, *Tell Me* complicates a quick definition of Black Arts Movement literature. If we place *Tell Me* in a canon of Black Arts Movement literature, we need to define the Black Arts Movement as the artistic complication of the Black Power movement, as opposed to the artistic counterpart or bedfellow.

Like *Tell Me*, Bob Crawford's photographs of a black crossdressing Halloween ball in 1969, in Chicago, complicate a quick and easy definition of the Black Arts ethos. When Crawford photographed the crossdressing ball, he departed from his usual imaging of street life in black Chicago.[18] In contrast to the celebration of dark skin blackness, afro hair styles, black power fists, Nation of Islam cloth-

Fig. 7.4. Bob Crawford, Halloween Ball in Chicago, 1969. Courtesy of the artist.

ing, and Black Panther images in Crawford's typical Black Arts photography, the photographs of the gay crossdressing ball place new subjects within his "Black is Beautiful" gaze. Crawford remembers being amused by the outlandishness of the crossdressers. The representation of crossdressing as a spectacle is overshadowed, however, by the "Black is Beautiful" sensibility that overdetermines his photographic gaze. In the photographs of the crossdressers, blond wigs, straight hair wigs, and skin lightened with makeup become part of the performance of "Black is Beautiful." Typical Black Arts photography inveighs against these signs of "whiteness." Like *Tell Me*, the photographs of the crossdressers present new signs of "Black is Beautiful." The photographer's memories of his amused spectatorship at the ball naturalize the conflict of signs between "Black is Beautiful" and black drag. The photographs themselves, however, might reveal that black drag, for the crossdressers, is black power (fig. 7.4).

Crawford's camera captures the sense of empowerment the men achieve through the crossdressing. The crossdressers' wigs beg to be compared to Crawford's photograph entitled "Wigs," which confronts mammy and Aunt Jemima stereotypes (fig. 7.5). The wigs on the maternal black women, domesticated in the photograph by the background of the rural-looking home in Chicago's South Side, may be read as signs of racial-self-hatred and a desire for white femininity, however, upon comparison with the crossdressers' wigs, they can also be read as signs of empowerment, a bold sense of style. In the pho-

Fig. 7.5. Bob Crawford, *Wigs,* 1970. Courtesy of the artist.

tograph *Batman* (fig. 7.6), we see Crawford's explicit attempt to subversively objectify the white crossdressers at the ball. The batman suit can be interpreted as the racialized "darkness of sexuality" worn by the white man. The "Black is Beautiful" photographer laughs at the ridiculousness of this "dark suit of sexuality." The photograph can be read as a response to Frantz Fanon's recognition that the black man has become "the genital" in the white imagination.[19] The white phallus is demystified in this photograph. The white male is reduced to a body part. The psychoanalytic understanding of the fetish as the covering or masking of lack gains real meaning in this photograph. The dark batman suit makes the white male performer feel connected to the potent sexuality attributed to black men.

How does this subversive fetishism of the white male body compare to the imaging of the women in the photograph entitled *Wigs*? The wigs do not match the "Black is Beautiful" aesthetic of unstraightened hair. In *In Our Terribleness*, Baraka writes, "So the blood with the Agbada (robe) and the sisters with the natural must also represent the consciousness that change symbolizes."[20] The very word "natural" as a reference to the afro hairstyle fully displays the way that the "Black is Beautiful" ideology often led to a belief in the embodiment of abstraction—seemingly, the "natural," the hairstyle, embodies a blessed state of "nature." The fetishism of the afro as "natural" during the Black Arts Movement was comparable to the fetishism of dark-skinned blackness as "naturally" beautiful. In the photograph *Wigs* and the photographs of the black male crossdressers wearing wigs, Crawford's normal fetishism of the "natural" is forced to confront the fetishism of the "unnatural"—the blond wigs, the make-up, the

Fig. 7.6. Bob Crawford, *Batman*, 1969. Courtesy of the artist.

female clothing on male bodies. The juxtaposition of these photographs and Crawford's "Black is Beautiful" images reveals connections between black drag and the cultural nationalism of the Black Arts Movement. As we look at these photographs, we hear Baraka's insistence that "I can take off these clothes and wear some others" (fig. 7.7).[21]

In *Tell Me*, Leo Proudhammer often feels that his acting career becomes black drag whereas Black Christopher is figured as the embodiment of "Black is Beautiful." Leo becomes a consummate racial crossdresser as he plays roles that have been imagined as "white" roles. He "commit[s] [himself] to [the] impossibility" of acting because genuine acting, as opposed to the body of the actor being read through the lens of racial stereotypes, seems impossible to Leo.[22] He becomes painfully aware that any performance that does not cater to stereotypical, racist notions of blackness is liable to be interpreted as black drag. Once he becomes a famous actor, he yearns to take off the mask that may be the real cause of the heart attack described in the opening scene. Black Christopher is potentially the antidote for the pain of the black drag. Leo's love affair with "Black is Beautiful" begins at the end of a "long career" of black drag.[23] The beauty of Black Christopher is described as "black in color, black in pride, black in rage" (73). Leo tells Christopher that "he [is] certainly black enough to be an African, and even . . . that the structure of his face reminded [him] of faces [he] had seen in Dakar" (107). In the Black Arts Movement, the words "Black is Beautiful" and "African" often became synonymous. The recurring references to Africa in *Tell Me* reveal Baldwin's interest in the meaning of "Africa" in the African American imagination.[24]

Natural Black Beauty and Black Drag   1 6 3

Fig. 7.7. Bob Crawford, Halloween Ball in Chicago, 1969. Courtesy of the artist.

There is a rift between Leo's black drag and Black Christopher's "African essence." Even as Baldwin thinks deeply, through the representations of Leo and Barbara, about identity itself as performative, he removes Black Christopher from the realm of the performative. In a key scene in the first of the three sections of the novel, Baldwin muses on the difficult, but necessary task of making sure that public expressions of black power do not become cathartic performances. In this scene, it becomes abundantly clear that Leo Proudhammer, the famous actor, has much in common with James Baldwin, the famous novelist. Like Baldwin, once Leo gains fame, he is invited to speak in public forums and rallies. In this scene of the novel, Leo is waiting to deliver his speech at a rally. As he waits and listens to a little girl singing, he wonders if he can deliver an uplifting speech without reducing black power to a cathartic performance. He wonders about the "price of the song": "No song could possibly be worth the trap in which so many thousands, undelivered, perished every day. No song could be worth what this singing little girl had already paid for it, and was paying, and would continue to pay. And yet—without a song?" (111). Baldwin refuses to give his reader any cathartic moment in the scene when Leo and his brother, Caleb, become physically intimate and Leo curses a white God as he imagines a black God. In a manner comparable to his way of seeing Black Christopher, as Leo becomes physically intimate with Caleb, he imagines Caleb as the embodiment of black power. This scene is an explicit rendering of how the equation of the phallus and the penis is transmuted into the phallus as God, the phallus as cultural power.

The black crossdressers, in Crawford's photographs, fight against the white phallus by putting on that which is interpreted, through the Black Arts lens, as signs of white femininity, described by Baraka in "Black Art" (1968) as "girdlemamma mulatto bitches whose brains are red jelly stuck between 'lizabeth taylor's toes."[25] The social construct "white woman" is the clothing that the black male crossdressers put on. Barbara, in *Tell Me*, argues that white women have been conditioned to believe that they can be transformed through sexual intimacy with black men. According to Barbara, "everybody wants to be changed" (278). In Crawford's photographs of the black crossdressers wearing blond wigs, signs of white femininity are the means through which black men "change."

In *Soul on Ice*, Cleaver feminizes Baldwin. Baldwin expresses, in a metanarrative moment in *Tell Me*, his own awareness of the homophobia that led to mixed opinions of his work: "Some people considered me a fagot, for some I was a hero, for some I was a whore, for some I was a devious cocks-man, for some I was an Uncle Tom. My eminence hurt me sometimes . . . , but I tried not to think too much about it. I certainly couldn't blame the people if they didn't trust me—why should they?" (454). Baldwin was aware that he was viewed by some as "Martin Luther Queen."[26] Huey Newton explains, in "On Eldridge Cleaver: He is No James Baldwin," that Baldwin did not respond publicly to Cleaver's accusations. When Newton recounts a kiss exchanged between Cleaver and Baldwin, Cleaver's homophobia emerges as a form of drag, a disguising of his real feelings toward Baldwin: "When we arrived, Cleaver and Baldwin walked into each other, and the giant, six-foot-three-inch Cleaver bent down and engaged in a long, passionate french kiss with the tiny (barely five feet) Baldwin . . . . I later expressed my surprise to Cleaver, who pleaded that I not relay this incident to anyone."[27] The release of tension and overcoming of boundaries, described in this anecdote, is comparable to the merging, in Crawford's photographs of the Halloween ball, of the signs of "Black is Beautiful" and black drag.

A post-Black Arts Movement novel, Toni Morrison's *Tar Baby* (1981), illuminates the imagined tension between a "Black is Beautiful" "essence" and the celebration of black drag. In *Tar Baby*, Morrison meditates on the ability of a red wig against midnight skin to cause profound disorientation in the black nationalist sensibility. Son, who consciously attaches himself to a "Black is Beautiful" gaze, feels great anxiety when he sees Alma Estée wearing a red wig. The red wig on Alma's head makes Son think her "midnight skin" is a sign of authenticity that he cannot relinquish.[28] The sight of the red wig against Alma's midnight skin greatly saddens him because he believes her skin is a literal picture of authenticity, home, and kinship. The red wig is a sign of artifice attached to the midnight skin, which Son believes is Alma's essence. Son desires to remove it from Alma's head, so that her midnight skin can continue to "speak" authenticity. Without the wig, Son would no longer see the surreal picture that disturbs him to such a great extent. Seemingly, instead of seeing a "bougainvillea in a girdle," a "baby jaguar with lipstick on," and an "avocado with earrings" (299), he would be able to see Alma as she "really was" (299).

The irony of Son's need to remove the wig and control the image of Alma is that Jadine, the light-skinned black model with whom he falls in love, supposedly has rid him of the need to imagine icons of authenticity. When he reacts so vehemently to the sight of Alma wearing the wig, he realizes that he still believes in icons of authenticity. The text reads, "So he had changed, given up fraternity, or believed he had, until he saw Alma Estée in a wig the color of dried blood. Her sweet face, her midnight skin mocked and destroyed by the pile of synthetic dried blood on her head. It was all mixed up. But he could have sorted it out if she had just stood there like a bougainvillea in a girdle, like a baby jaguar with lipstick on, like an avocado with earrings, and let him remove it" (299). Can the red wig against the "midnight skin" of Alma Estée, in *Tar Baby*, become an image of "Black is Beautiful"? Can we heal the imagined conflict between signs of "Black is Beautiful" and black drag? In her essay "Imitation and Gender Insubordination," Judith Butler presents drag as that which proves that gender itself is always drag, so that drag itself must not be understood as the "putting on of a gender that belongs properly to some other group."[29] As opposed to Butler's sense that "gender is a kind of imitation for which there is no original," Son, in *Tar Baby*, views Alma Estée's "midnight skin" as "authentic" and "original."[30] This imagined originality and purity is the precise reason why Son cannot fathom the red wig against the "midnight skin" of Alma Estée. In the 1993 afterword to *The Bluest Eye* (1970), Toni Morrison explains that a "Black is Beautiful" point of view was the impetus of her first novel. A "very dark" friend expresses her desire for blue eyes, and this confession compels Morrison to know beauty for the "first time" and to contemplate its "shock" and "force."[31] She writes, "[T]hat moment was so racially infused (my revulsion at what my school friend wanted: very blue eyes in a very black skin; the harm she was doing to *my* concept of the beautiful), the struggle was for writing that was indisputably black" (211). Morrison wrote *The Bluest Eye* during the 1960s "Black is Beautiful" movement. In this afterword, written from the vantage point of the 1990s, Morrison remembers the "concept of the beautiful" that undergirded the 1960s "Black is Beautiful" movement. Alma's red wig, within this "Black is Beautiful" gaze, is comparable to the "very blue eyes in a very dark skin" (211).

In order to understand how this idea of the dark-skinned original becomes so tied to the "Black is Beautiful" gaze, we must think about the meaning of the "black primitive" in the African American imagination. In the poem "Black People: This is Our Destiny" (1966), Baraka celebrates the "black primitive" when he insists on a "rhythm a playing re-understood now by one of the 1st race / the primitives the first men who evolve again to civilize the world."[32] In this poem, Baraka reclaims the very word "primitive" (countering its use, in antiblack racism, to describe the supposed backwardness of black people). Baraka's spoken word poetry is included in "Phrenology" (2002), the Hip Hop compilation by "The Roots," that includes the lyrics, "You savages are primitive. I'm the true primitive."[33] In contrast to Butler's sense that "gender is a kind of imitation for which there is no original," these performances of the "black primitive" revel in an imagined original state of blackness.[34] Leo Proudhammer, in *Tell Me*, surmises that, if his family did not live in a psychological state of exile, [they] "would have known less about vanished African kingdoms and more about each other. Or, not at all impossibly, more about both" (23). Leo thinks critically about African American belief in a purity and authenticity that becomes coded as "African." Leo, while an aspiring actor, poses as a model for white artists who render him a "noble savage." Baldwin, in *Tell Me*, thinks deeply about the meaning of the "black primitive" in both the African American and the white imagination.

In *The Ideologies of African American Literature* (2002), Robert Washington presents black primitivism as African American participation in the modernist lens that viewed African Americans as exotic primitives and "Africa" as the "purest embodiment of emotional and sexual freedom" (32). Washington defines the Harlem Renaissance as the "Primitivist School" and the Black Arts Movement as a fundamentally different school, the "Cultural Nationalist School." He argues that Baldwin is part of the "moral suasion school," the black literary faction in the 1950s and early 1960s, that aimed to appeal to the moral conscience of a white audience. *Tell Me*, however, is a text that cannot be easily placed inside or outside the "Cultural Nationalist School." In a 1985 interview, Baldwin explains, "I am not a black nationalist but some of my best friends are."[35] And theorist Stuart Hall, in a review in the *New Statesman*, surmises that *Tell Me* was a "meditation by a middle-aged black revolutionary on a revolution he has witnessed—but cannot, finally, share."[36] Washington argues that there are "no major novels" produced during the Black Arts Movement.[37] *Tell Me* is Baldwin's "Black is Beautiful" novel. Baldwin's intense love affair with "blackness" is the heart of this novel that adds new layers to the canon of Black Arts Movement literature.

Washington focuses on the "black primitivist writers" of the Harlem Renaissance, however, Black Arts Movement poetry such as Haki Madhubuti's "The Primitive" (1968) represents primitivism as explicitly as some Harlem Renaissance texts. In "The Primitive," the white enslavers of Africans are proclaimed as the "real savages": "taken from the / shores of Mother Africa / the savages they thought / we were / they being the real savages."[38] When Michelle Cliff in a post-Black Arts movement novel, *Free Enterprise* (1993), describes the embodiment of "Africa" as the hair that is "going back to Africa," when it is not straightened, we see that the "natural black beauty" reified during the Black Arts Movement is a prelapsarian state of blackness.[39] In this innocence, blackness is imagined not as a societal sign nor a performance but a birthmark, a corporeal enactment of "home," an idea that is exemplified when Baraka, in *In Our Terribleness*, insists, "not represents, but *is*" (114). The "Black is Beautiful" ideology of the Black Arts Movement wrote "Africa" on African American bodies. This imagined embodiment of "Africa" is at the core of the reasons why there is an imagined tension between the "Black is Beautiful" and black drag images. Through the "Black is

Beautiful" lens that imagines that "Africa" is embodied, black drag emerges as the grotesque black imitation of whiteness. When the 1968 publication of *Tell Me* is juxtaposed with the 1969 Chicago Black Arts Movement images of black crossdressers, and then filtered through the lens of Morrison's post-Black Arts Movement novel, *Tar Baby*, we see that the 1960s "Black is Beautiful" sensibility was a transformative consciousness-raising experience that ironically often defined blackness as non-transformative.

In order to historicize the recovery of black beauty through an emphasis on the non-transformative nature of blackness, we must remember the discussion of "Negro transformation" in Harlem Renaissance texts.[40] In the opening essay of *The New Negro* (1925), the philosopher and cultural theorist Alain Locke asserts that "[i]n the very process of being transplanted, the Negro is becoming transformed."[41] Bodily transformation is imagined when different temporal meanings are often written on light skin and dark skin black bodies—the imagined newness of light skin blackness (the "altered" state of blackness) and the imagined oldness of dark skin blackness (the "original" state of blackness). The very title of Joel Williamson's study of interracialness, *New People* (1995), underscores this trap. In "Vestiges," one of the short stories in *The New Negro*, written by Rudolph Fisher, the "New Negro" body is transformed through a cosmetic product named "Egyptian rouge." The text reads, "Her vanity-case mirror revealed how exactly the long pendant earrings matched her red coral beads and how perfectly becoming the new close bob was, and assured her for the tenth time that Egyptian rouge made her skin look lighter" (79). As opposed to Harlem Renaissance visual artists' use of Egyptian art to signal the "rebirth" and deformation of racist minstrel images, Fisher's short story presents "Egyptianism" as the exoticism fueling racial self-hatred, the desire for the lighter skin. Fisher continues to represent this racial self-hatred when he describes Harlem as the "modern desert" that makes the character, Jutie, "paint her face and straighten her hair, instead of leaving it as God intended" (80). In the short story, "Fog," John Maltheus also thinks about this "new negro" body when he describes the "Egyptian-faced girl with the straightened African hair" (91). These short stories of the Harlem Renaissance era illuminate the Harlem Renaissance interest in and critique of the "transformed" negro body.

Like Son, in *Tar Baby*, who cannot bear the red wig's transformation of Alma Estée, the "Black is Beautiful" ideology of the Black Arts Movement inveighed against the transformed black body. Haki Madhubuti provides a prime example of this protest in the poem "On Seeing Diana Go Maddddddddd" (1970). As the speaker in this poem begs Diana Ross to resist being co-opted by a white power structure, to "stop! in the name of love before [she] break[s] [black] heart[s]," he highlights her position as "the wearer of other people's hair" as one prime example of her co-option.[42] In Madhubuti's "Black is Beautiful" gaze, a black woman wearing a straight hair wig is wearing something that does not conform to her "nature"—she is in drag. In the poem, "To Those of My Sisters Who Kept Their Naturals" (1969), Gwendolyn Brooks reveals that signs of "Black is

Beautiful" were imagined, during the Black Arts Movement, as transcendence of black imitation of whiteness. The speaker in this poem asserts, "Farrah's hair is hers."[43] The images of the empowerment of the black crossdressers, in the Halloween ball Crawford photographed in 1969, deliver the message "Farrah's hair is ours." The speaker in "To Those of My Sisters" pays homage to the black women wearing "naturals" who "never worshipped Marilyn Monroe."[44] Through the character, Leo Proudhammer, who views the "dressing room as his only home" and his "natural" hair as a "vile plantation," Baldwin imagines that performance and crossdressing may be a way of changing the script that has constructed kinky black hair as a "vile plantation."[45] Baldwin's use of these words underscores that black bodies themselves have become the most local site of post-slavery trauma.

When Baraka, in *In Our Terribleness*, insists that African Americans must wear "new clothes," we see that the "Black is Beautiful" ideology of the Black Arts Movement often took the shape of revolutionary crossdressing.[46] The vitriolic images of transgendering in *Black Fire* demonstrate why it is so important that 1969 Black Arts photographs of a crossdressing ball be included in the archive of the Black Arts Movement. The striking images of this transgendering include the poet Welton Smith's rage against the "nigga," an unenlightened black person, who has "made [his] women / to grow huge dicks."[47] The black male crossdressers, in Crawford's photographs, put on signs of femininity even as the legacies of American slavery continued to defeminize black womanhood. The many references to "black queens" in *Black Fire* can be viewed as black male nationalists' huge objectification of black women as well as their strident attempt to counter the lie that beauty and femininity are the natural properties of white womanhood. In "Special Section for the Niggas on the Lower Eastside or: Invert the Divisor and Multiply," one of the poems in *Black Fire*, Welton Smith presents another recurrent image of crossdressing in Black Arts Movement literature, the black "sell-out" wearing the clothing of the black revolutionary. Smith attacks this type of crossdressing by accusing the "sell-out" who wears the "wire-rim glasses" (a visual sign of the black male nationalist) of desiring to be a white woman: "you don't just want a white woman / you want to be a white woman / you are concubines of a beast / you want to be lois lane, audrey hepburn, ma perkins, lana turner."[48] Can the performance of the black male crossdressers, photographed through the Black Arts lens, defy this claim "you want to be a white woman"? Considering that the afro and "natural" are not hairstyles that are coded as exclusively female, if the black male crossdressers were consciously performing black femininity as opposed to white femininity, what type of hair would they wear, if straight hair wigs are signs of white femininity?

The short "natural," the short version of the "afro" hairstyle, within contemporary black lesbian culture, is both embraced and contested as a sign of "black butch" identity. When the short "natural" is read as a sign of the "black butch," are we witnessing the transformation of "natural black beauty" into a particular gender identity, the gender identity of black women who have no desire to be the "earth" of the particular black male nationalism exemplified in "Earth," one of Rolland Snellings' poems in *Black Fire*? After reiterating the classic nationalist images of the male soldier and the feminized territory that needs protection, Snellings pays homage to "Mother of the World! / Fecund, Beating Heart! / Enduring Earth!"[49] Snellings differentiates between the castration of the black male soldier by the white "snow queen" and the home the black woman's "Womb" provides. Like this image of the black male appropriation of the womb, Baraka's reference, in *In Our Terribleness*, to the black "male tits" (as opposed to the images of the penis which abound in *Black Fire*) may be the real sign of the black phallus imagined during the Black Arts Movement. Baraka refers to the "male tits," in *In Our Terribleness*, as he presents the black male body as the black mind. He writes, "The two male tits and navel and the penis are a big face."[50] In a manner that is comparable to drag, the masculinist discourse of the Black Arts Movement often gained "male tits" as it used images of black women as a means to express black male fraternity (brotherly love). This latent black male homoeroticism in the cultural nationalism of the Black Arts Movement is brought to the surface in *Tell Me How Long the Train's Been Gone*, Baldwin's liminal, long-lost Black Arts novel.

NOTES

1. Ahmed Alhamisi and Harun Kofi Wangara, eds., *Black Arts: An Anthology of Black Creations* (Detroit: Black Arts Publications, 1969), 19–20.

2. This 1967 issue of *Ebony*, Davis Llorens, "Natural Hair—New Symbol of Race Pride," *Ebony* 23: 2 (December 1967): 139–44, includes a cover story on natural black hair. The cover image is framed by the words "Natural Hair—New Symbol of Race Pride."

3. Larry Neal, "Any Day Now: Black Art and Black Liberation," *Ebony* 24:10 (August 1969): 58.

4. Toni Cade Bambara, ed., *The Black Woman: An Anthology* (New York: Penguin, 1970), 18.

5. In *Report from Part One* (1972), Gwendolyn Brooks remembers how Black Arts Movement devotees chastised *Ebony* magazine for its inclusion of bleaching cream advertisements and light-skinned models.

6. A. B. Spellman, "Big Bushy Afros," in *The International Review of African American Art: The Art of Political Struggle and Cultural Revolution of the 1960s and 70s* 15:1 (1998): 53.

7. Imamu Amiri Baraka and Fundi (Billy Abernathy), *In Our Terribleness* (Indianapolis and New York: The Bobbs-Merrill Company, Inc., 1970), 122. In this "long image story in motion . . . papermotion," no page numbers are included. Page numbers would arrest the steady flow of images.

8. Bob Crawford began photographing "Black life in America, mainly Chicago" in 1964. Crawford defines his work in this manner in the biography accompanying

the photographs shown in the "41st Annual Arts Festival—The Arts in a Changing Society," held in April 1970 at Fisk University.

9. Judith Butler, "Performative Acts and Gender Constitution: An Essay in Phenomenology and Feminist Theory," in *Performing Feminisms*, ed. Sue-Ellen Case (Baltimore, MD: John Hopkins University, 1990), 272.

10. Houston A. Baker, Jr., *Modernism and the Harlem Renaissance* (Chicago and London: University of Chicago Press, 1987), 15.

11. Baraka and Abernathy, *In Our Terribleness*, 100.

12. *James Baldwin: The Price of the Ticket*, directed by Karen Thorsen, Nobody Knows Productions, 1989.

13. Eve Sedgwick, *Epistemology of the Closet* (Berkeley: University of California Press, 1990), 72.

14. James Baldwin, *Tell Me How Long the Train's Been Gone* (New York: Vintage International, 1968), 6.

15. William Faulkner, *Absalom, Absalom!* (New York: Vintage, 1986 [1936]), 285.

16. In contrast to the incestuous male rage of this scene, when the "miscegenation" between Leo and Barbara, a white actress, occurs, a "black woman moaning" becomes the background music (361). The "black woman moaning," inside the white woman's body, is a disturbing example of the overcompensation for lack that shapes fetishism. The "black woman moaning" overcompensates for the supposed lack attached to the white woman. The white woman's body covers and masks the lack attributed to the black body that produces this moan. This "black woman moaning" is heard in the moment of orgasm Leo and Barbara experience; the black phallus literally secretes black womanhood. The "black woman moaning" becomes the background music during the sexual intimacy of the black man and white woman (361).

17. Cleaver's dilution anxiety emerges as he explains African American racial self-hatred: "Quite simply, many Negroes believe, as the principle of assimilation into white America implies, that the race problem in America cannot be settled until all traces of the black race are eliminated. Toward this end, many Negroes loathe the idea of two very dark Negroes mating. The children, they say, will come out ugly. What they mean is that the children are sure to be black, and this is not desirable." Eldridge Cleaver, *Soul on Ice* (New York: Delta, 1968), 127.

18. The crossdressing ball was held at the "Old Coliseum." It was located at 18th and Wabash in Chicago.

19. In Charles Markmann's translation of the French original (1952) of *Black Skin, White Masks*, Fanon writes, "The Negro is the genital" (180). Frantz Fanon, *Black Skin, White Masks*, trans. Charles Markmann (New York: Grove Press, 1967), 180.

20. Baraka and Abernathy, *In Our Terribleness*, 152.

21. Ibid., 122.

22. Baldwin, *Tell Me*, 82.

23. The "long career" of black drag stems from the "long career of blackmail," his understanding of what it means to have the "imperious bit of flesh," the black penis, in an anti-black world (6).

24. Leo muses about the possibility that if he and his family, and, by extension, all African Americans, did not bear the history of being uprooted from "home," "[they] would have known less about vanished African kingdoms and more about each other. Or, not at all impossibly, more about both" (23). In this passage, Baldwin is thinking

about the self-alienation, the sense of loss that fueled some of the psychological journeys to "Africa" during the Black Arts and Black Power Movements.

25. LeRoi Jones and Larry Neal, eds., *Black Fire: An Anthology of Afro-American Writing* (New York: William Morrow & Company, 1968), 302–303.

26. William Spurlin, "Culture, Rhetoric, and Queer Identity," in *James Baldwin Now*, ed. Dwight McBride (New York & London: New York University Press, 1999), 109.

27. Kimberle Williams Crenshaw, *Black Men on Race, Gender, and Sexuality* (New York & London: New York University Press, 1999), 314.

28. Toni Morrison, *Tar Baby* (New York: Plume, 1981), 299.

29. Judith Butler, "Imitation and Gender Insubordination," *The Second Wave: A Reader in Feminist Theory*, ed. Linda Nicholson (New York: Routledge, 1997), 306.

30. Ibid., 306.

31. Toni Morrison, *The Bluest Eye* (New York: Plume/Penguin, 1970), 211.

32. LeRoi Jones, *Black Art* (Newark, NJ: Jihad Productions, 1966), 2.

33. "Phrenology," The Roots, MCA Records, 2002.

34. Butler, "Imitation," 306.

35. Fred Standley and Louis Pratt, eds. *Conversations with James Baldwin* (Jackson and London: University of Mississippi Press, 1989), 259.

36. David Leeming, *James Baldwin* (New York: Alfred A. Knopf, 1994), 282.

37. Robert Washington, *The Ideologies of African American Literature* (New York & Oxford: Rowman & Littlefield Publishers, Inc., 2001), 307. Washington argues that poetry and drama are the privileged genres of the "Cultural Nationalist" literary school because they "were accessible to the black American masses" (307).

38. Haki Madhubuti, *GroundWork: New and Selected Poems* (Chicago: Third World Press, 1996), 26.

39. Michelle Cliff, *Free Enterprise* (New York: Plume, 1993), 23.

40. Bakhtin's theory of the chronotope, the spatialization of time, illuminates the timeline aspect of the fetishism of shades of blackness, the way that skin color is imagined as a condensation of time. According to Bakhtin, "Time, as it were, thickens, takes on flesh" (84). The fetishism of dark-skinned and light-skinned blackness often functions as a chronotope. These skin color shades are often imagined as the embodiment of time, the thickening of time, the "flesh" of the old and the new. M. M. Bakhtin, *The Dialogic Imagination*, ed. Michael Holquist, trans. Caryl Emerson and Michael Holquist (Austin: University of Texas Press, 1981), 84.

41. Alain Locke, *The New Negro* (New York: Touchstone, 1997[1925]), 6.

42. Madhubuti, *GroundWork*, 84–85.

43. Brooks, *Blacks*, 460.

44. Ibid., 460.

45. Baldwin, *Tell Me*, 11, 53.

46. Baraka and Abernathy, *In Our Terribleness*, 122.

47. Jones and Neal, *Black Fire*, 286.

48. Ibid., 288.

49. Ibid., 327–28.

50. Baraka and Abernathy, *In Our Terribleness*, 99.

8

Sexual Subversions, Political Inversions

Women's Poetry and
the Politics of the
Black Arts Movement

Cherise A. Pollard

Feminized from the moment of its inception as the Black Power Movement's "spiritual sister," the Black Arts Movement was in no way feminine.[1] During the 1960s, the Black Power Movement's emphasis on Black nationalism informed the Black Arts Movement's political mission. From 1965 to 1976, the Black Arts Movement employed the theories of the black aesthetic to develop popular, yet political art forms such as music, theater, literature, and dance that tapped into America's black urban communities.[2] In the realm of literature, most of the theorists of the black aesthetic were men such as LeRoi Jones (Amiri Baraka), Larry Neal, Addison Gayle, Jr., and Don L. Lee who attempted to reach the black masses through art forms that advanced the Black Power Movement's militant message. Political and didactic, black aesthetic poetry contributed greatly to the Black Arts and Black Power Movements' popularity. As they articulated black manhood through the pen, the gun, the penis, and the microphone, male poets in the Black Arts Movement defined and reified revolutionary black male identity.

Black women poets occupied a curious position in this political, social, and artistic environment. Most critics assume that women poets such as Nikki Giovanni and Sonia Sanchez were silenced and objectified by their black male counterparts as they stood in the men's shadows. To the contrary, many of these women worked both within and against the men's assumptions about the relationships between race and gender and art and politics. This chapter is a comparative analysis of the ways that black women poets critiqued the complexities of America's racial, sexual, and gender politics in the late 1960s in such works as LeRoi Jones' and Larry Neal's anthology, *Black Fire: An Anthology of Afro-American Writing* (1968), Sonia Sanchez's collection of poems entitled *Home Coming* (1969), and Nikki Giovanni's book of poems, *Black Feeling, Black*

Talk, Black Judgement (1970). Published during "the apogee years" of the black aesthetic, 1968–1971, these texts are imbued with the artistic energy of a movement at the height of its powers.[3] *Black Fire* gives readers insight into the values that were crucial not only to the editors of the anthology, but also to the entire system of production and reception that drove the Black Arts Movement.[4] Even though they are published around the same time as *Black Fire*, many of the poems in Sanchez's and Giovanni's collections give voice to critical black female perspectives that are muffled in Jones' and Neal's anthology.

Black Fire was one of the first anthologies that presented the "black aesthetic." According to critic Addison Gayle, Jr., the volume met with "expected opposition" from white literary critics who argued that, "There is no Black aesthetic because there is no white aesthetic."[5] Edited by LeRoi Jones and Larry Neal, two poet-critics who were central to the development of the Black Arts Movement's goals, *Black Fire* has been cited as "a definitive movement anthology."[6] Under the control of black male editors, black women's poetry is overshadowed by black manhood in this anthology. However, black female poets published in *Black Fire* used highly coded language to open up revolutionary possibilities.

Attention to Sanchez's and Giovanni's shifting stances towards the black male revolutionary highlights many women poets' deeply ambiguous relationship to their male counterparts' political positions. Black women poets sometimes voiced their opinions quietly, through more reflective lines; other times, a brasher, more subversive stance is apparent. According to black feminist literary critic Erlene Stetson, editor of the anthology *Black Sister: Poetry by Black American Women, 1746–1980*, black women have consistently returned to the themes of ambiguity and subversion in their poetry. Stetson argues that there are several central threads in black women's poetic tradition: "a compelling quest for identity, a subversive perception of reality, and subterfuge and ambivalence of the works."[7]

My conceptualization of black women poets' subversive practice takes Stetson's categories of "subversiv[ity] . . . subterfuge, and ambivalence" into consideration as I explore the ways that these poets pressured male-centered discourse through creative works that critiqued this point of view from a "sisterly" perspective—one that supports the black communal family, but one that can be gently (or not so) corrective, or responsive to their "brothers'" political positions.[8] As "sisters," these women were defined as helpmates, but it is clear that as poets, black women who aligned themselves with the black aesthetic articulated a radical sense of identity that called many of their "brothers'" assumptions about gender roles and sexuality into question. I use these terms, "brother" and "sister" to invoke the familial rhetoric that played an important role in the popularization of both the Black Arts and Black Power Movements. Within the patriarchal structure of the Western family, "brothers" inherit the father's power and "sisters" the mother's disempowerment. Yet, despite these confines, it is possible to imagine a radical politics that enabled black women poets to invert this power dynamic. In the spirit of "sisterly" subversion, I have decided to put these words in quotation marks to indicate that these terms reflect the movement's sexist underpinnings as well as to suggest that one must continually maintain a critical stance even with the most commonplace, seemingly innocuous phrases.

Loosely defined as a set of principles that articulated the relationship between Black nationalism and black art, the black aesthetic celebrated the African origins of the Black community, championed black urban culture, critiqued Western aesthetics, and encouraged the production and reception of black arts by black people.[9] Despite its centrality to the Black Arts Movement, critics such as Neal, Jones, Addison Gayle, Stephen Henderson, and Don L. Lee never defined the black aesthetic in concrete terms. As literary critic David Lionel Smith argues, "[E]ven at the height of . . . [the Black Arts Movement], there was no real agreement about the meaning of this term."[10] However, theorists of the black aesthetic agreed that, due to its accessibility, art should be used to galvanize the black masses to revolt against their white capitalist oppressors. Black Arts Movement participants believed that creative works, especially poetry, gave voice to the social frustrations, cultural pride, and political aspirations of this struggle as it motivated black people to fight not just for social equality, but for palpable shifts in the American power structure.

In "The Black Arts Movement" (1966), Larry Neal defines the Movement as the "spiritual sister" of the Black Power Movement.[11] The reference to the "spiritual sister" is not inherently sexist but the Black Arts Movement was riddled with sexist assumptions. One of the most provocative examples of a critic's sexist stance is Don L. Lee's "Toward a Definition: Black Poetry of the Sixties (after LeRoi Jones)."[12] After describing the social and cultural politics that led to the emergence of the poets who championed the black aesthetic, Lee launches a role call:

> The *men* of the movement were: John Coltrane, LeRoi Jones, Cecil Taylor, James Baldwin, Charles White, Marion Brown, Ornette Coleman, Don Cherry, John A. Williams, Lerone Bennett, *Mari Evans*, William Melvin Kelley, John O. Killens, Grachun Manour III, Thelonius Monk, Sunny Murray, Ed Bullins, Ronald Milner, Calvin C. Hernton, Larry Neal, Dudley Randall, James Brown, A. B. Spellman, Lew Alcindor, Hoyt Fuller, Conrad Kent Rivers, Archie Shepp, Sun Ra, Pharaoh Sanders, *Gwendolyn Brooks*, Malcolm X, Frantz Fanon, Martin Luther King, and we can go on for days.[13]

One wonders whether Lee considered Evans' and Brooks' work to be so accomplished that it transcended the limitations of their female gender, or if this inclusion of women was an afterthought. Either way, this emphasis on black male talent is indicative of an even greater issue of aesthetic values that reflects a fusion of the categories of blackness and maleness within the critics' own analytical frameworks.

Black Power theorists argued that capitalism and racism deprived black men of their manhood. Within this dynamic, powerlessness became associated with femininity and homosexuality. Literary critic Phillip Brian Harper suggests that the Black Arts and Black Power Movements' insistence upon a repeated invocation of an idealized black manhood reflected deeply held ambivalences and "anxieties" in relation to issues of political power and sexual prowess.[14] According to Harper, in Black Arts rhetoric, the "fag" is the educated Negro who is distanced from the black urban community because of his intellectualism.[15] Representations of the black man as "fag" reflect the heterosexism of the movement. Literary critic Charles I. Nero contends that during the 1960s, "Images of pathetic homosexuals were often used to show what black manhood was not or to what it could degenerate."[16]

Often, Black Arts poetry functioned as a weapon of the idealized black warrior's revolutionary power and as a sign of his sexual prowess. The poets in *Black Fire* offer the reader various images of the black revolutionary male. Amiri Baraka (LeRoi Jones) reveals his sexist perspective in the "Foreword." What begins as his deft call towards nation building slips quickly into romanticized notions of maleness steeped in the rhetoric of war-like violence and misogyny. Women fall to the wayside as Baraka shifts toward a direct invocation of a masculinist perspective. Baraka informs his readers of the spiritual and cultural importance of this text: "This is the source . . . the black man's comfort and guide. Where we was we will be agin [*sic*]. Though the map be broke and thorny though the wimmens sell they men . . . . The black artist. The black man. The holy holy black man."[17] As he continues to elevate "the black man," he also accuses the "wimmens" of undermining them. The Foreword to *Black Fire* is a prose poem that frames the collection of political essays, poems, and short stories in ways that are disconcerting.

For many of the male poets in *Black Fire*, the black male body is the site of warrior strength and the phallus is its ultimate weapon. In "Jitterbugging in the Streets," Calvin Hernton's speaker exclaims, "America, why are you afraid of the phallus!"[18] In this poem, "the phallus" becomes symbolic of white fear of black social and sexual power: white men work to keep white women away from black men as they live in fear of the riotous violence spilling out of the ghetto and into their neighborhoods. For Hernton, "the phallus" is the ultimate weapon of social retribution.

In many of these poems, the penis is employed as a marker of territory. In James Stewart's "Announcement," the speaker expresses his prowess as he defines himself in the first lines of the poem as a weapon: "I am a hammer."[19] The speaker then proceeds to threaten white people: "I'll sandbag all you white motherfuckers, / and then I'll pee, / I'll pee wet patterns on granite walls."[20] Here, urination is not just a release of the speaker's pent-up urges, but an act of artful violation.

The Black Arts Movement's masculinist rhetoric was shaped by the discourses of revolutionary violence and Black nationalism. As a vehicle for the message of social change, this poetry often captured the revolutionary imagination through metaphors that championed male power. In much of this poetry, the penis and the testicles are signs of lack as well as strength: damaged balls symbolize disempowerment and ejaculation is a show of power.[21] In Keorapetse Kgositsile's poem, "The Awakening," the speaker describes the process of identity formation for black male revolutionaries as being akin to sexual maturation. He argues that Malcolm X "[taught] Black manhood in Harlem USA":

> Retrieving Black balls cowering in glib Uncle Tomism
> Forcing me to grow up ten feet tall and Black
> My crotch too high
> For the pedestal of Greco-Roman Anglo-Saxon
> adolescent Fascist myth.[22]

This speaker aligns sexual prowess with political power. Emboldened by his new, black perspective, he towers over European hegemonic structures; his genitalia become a palpable weapon against these oppressive forces. His body is overwhelmed by this rush of power that "enthrall[s] [him] like the cataract of a cosmic orgasm."[23] A show of inherent physical power and revolutionary release, his metaphorical orgasm disrupts the social hierarchy. Kgositsile's depiction of physical disruption of the social order through sexual action becomes the perfect merger of social thought and political poetics.

Poems by black women in *Black Fire* can be read as critiques of revolutionary black manhood. The poetry section includes work by fifty-six men and five women. Many of the women poets appear to position their speakers as powerless but they are not. They question the social and sexual power of this emergent black manhood. One of Sonia Sanchez's poems, entitled "to all sisters," is an example of this kind of gendered critique:

> to all sisters
> hurt.
>   u worried abt a
>   little hurting.
>   man
> hurt ain't the bag u
>   shd be in.
>   loving is
>   the bag. man.
>   there ain't
> no MAN like a
>   black man.
> he puts it where it is
> and makes u
>   turn in/side out.[24]

At first, the speaker seems to be admonishing her "sisters" for shying away from the responsibility to love and support the "black man." The speaker appears to be saying that her "sisters'" abandonment of black men is the women's loss because no other man loves like them. Yet, a careful consideration of the poem's line breaks, punctuation, and use of white space yields a contradictory interpretation. Line four suggests that the man is in some way powerless, "little" and "hurting." In lines five through eight, the speaker argues that the man should not be wallowing in his disempowerment.

Black female poets selected by Jones and Neal for inclusion in *Black Fire* work both with and against the masculinist rhetoric. One aspect of conventional arguments about black women poet's contribution to the movement is that these women wrote poetry that unquestionably supported their "brothers'" struggle for equality. It was often assumed that race took precedence over gender. Black women were, in many cases, expected to subsume their own gendered interests and silence their own voices. Literary critic Fahamisha Patricia Brown, author of *Performing the Word: African American Poetry as Vernacular Culture* (1999), argues that during the 1960s and 1970s, black women poets supported their "brothers'" efforts: "Although they did not hesitate to chastise them for their flaws, they also took it as their mission to give African American men 'back their manhood.'"[25] In order to put black men at social and political ease, black women were expected to assume a position of passivity.

There are poems in *Black Fire* that articulate this idealized passive position. A poem by Odaro presents the voice of a "sister" who is complicit with the conventional Black Arts ideology. The poem, entitled "Alafia," is somewhat epistolary. It appears to be addressed to the editors, but it speaks directly to the audience. The poem is a cover letter that indicates that several men of the movement, "Larry Neal, Ed Spriggs, and Harold Foster," have encouraged her to submit poems. At the end of the poem, the speaker defines herself using Black Power rhetoric:

I am 20 years Black, born in
Harlem
Poverty's little girl
Black Woman, Queen of the World [26]

It is clear that Odaro's speaker is trying to curry favor with the editors. In this context, her adaptation of their terms is strategic. The speaker's description of herself as a "little girl," then as "Black Woman, Queen" gives the reader the impression that she is trying to define herself as every idealized female figure. At the same time, one can also see in these strategic moves an effort to define herself on her own terms.

Although conventional critics see black women poets as being subsumed within the Black Arts Movement, these writers can be seen as adopting an oppositional stance. An example of this contestation is Lethonia Gee's "By Glistening, Dancing Seas." In this *Black Fire* piece, the poet writes:

By glistening, dancing seas
On ancient time-spun sands
Black woman bends her wooly head
And thinks about her man

In the ghost house of the ghetto
With folded, wrinkled hands
Black woman bends her tired head
And thinks about her man

On ugly, cement, city streets
Or quiet village-lands
Black woman has one heavy thought
And it's about her man.[27]

On the surface, the poem is aligned with the rhetoric of "sisterly" support. But, a closer look at the speaker's argument reveals some ambivalence towards the men. One wonders what this "heavy thought" is: it could be one of disgust towards his actions, or one that is steeped in love for him and fear for his prospects in a racist society.

In black women's poetry of the period, there is a sense of doubleness reminiscent of Du Bois' "two-ness." The duality that emerges is not between race and nation, but between race and gender. The women are pulled between their allegiances to their race (which has been politicized and defined in masculinist terms) and their own female identities. Given this conflict, how does one interpret black female poetic expression?[28] Black women's poetic expression works on multiple levels and is often critical of dominant conceptions of black manhood and revolution. In the process of addressing complicated social, racial, and political issues, many black women poets give voice to the ambivalent power dynamic that exists in the black community, envisioning new imaginative spaces for black women to occupy in relation to their "brothers." The focus of their poetry is primarily political such as race riots, poverty, and institutionalized racism, as well as traditional issues such as rearing children and romantic relationships between men and women.

Nikki Giovanni and Sonia Sanchez both published popular poetry collections concurrently with *Black Fire; Sanchez's Home Coming* was published in 1969, Giovanni's *Black Feeling, Black Talk, Black Judgement* in 1970. Both of these collections are brimming with poems that present their readers with the rage of a people in the midst of revolution. An examination of their use of voice and figurative language reveals how these women exposed the Black Arts

Movement's sexist limitations through their usurpation of male social power as well as their critique of sexual prowess.

Through their exploration of the role of the woman revolutionary in their poems, both Sanchez and Giovanni call their "brothers'" abuse of power into question. In the third poem of the series "Memorial," entitled "3. rev pimps," Sanchez's speaker tells her "sisters" to stop having sex with "so-called" black male revolutionaries. The language is confrontational: she tells them "git yr/ blk/asses/out of that/ rev/olution/ary's/ bed."[29] The line breaks as well as the use of the page reflect the speaker's anger in regard to this exploitative situation. The speaker interprets the situation with raw accuracy: "that aint no revolutionary / thing com / munal / fuck / ing / aint nothing political / bout fucking."[30] The speaker's appeal to her "sisters" is an open critique that is meant to be heard by the men who are the perpetrators of this crime. As the speaker continues her argument, she endorses this kind of action and calls the men's identity into question:

> and that so/
> called/brother there
> screwing u in tune to
> fanon
> and fanon
> and fanon
> aint no re
> vo/lution/
> ary
> the game he's running
> aint called no
> post/office
> cuz. U show me
> a revolutionary/fuck &
> i'll send my ass   C.O.D.
> to any Revolutionary,
> u dig? [31]

For this speaker, there are other, more politically necessary roles for women to assume within the Black Power Movement other than reifying black male sexual power through sex. Openly critical, this poem exemplifies the ways Sanchez addresses the social, sexual, and political inequalities that vexed many women in the movement.

Nikki Giovanni's "seduction" offers readers another depiction of the subversive "sister" who is working both within and against the Black Arts Movement. Throughout the poem, the speaker is undressing herself and her male partner who is obsessed with the revolution. As the poem continues, it is clear that Giovanni is riffing on the male-body-as-weapon theme that is a feature in much of the revolutionary poetry published by black men during this period. Toward the end of the poem, she imagines that her counterpart will consider her use of her body and the enactment of female sexual power as "counter-revolutionary":

> then you'll notice
> your state of undress
> and knowing you you'll just say
> "nikki,
> isn't this counterrevolutionary...?[32]

As the speaker inverts the political dynamic, and makes the male the object, not the agent of sexual conquest, she usurps the black male revolutionary's power by privileging her own sexual desire. Like Sanchez's call to her "sisters" in "rev pimps," Giovanni's "seduction" demonstrates how black male power is easily inverted by politically reflective women.

Sanchez and Giovanni also critique men's power through their use of heterosexist and homophobic language. Some male poets leveled the charge of "fag" at any man that they considered to be overly intellectual, too preoccupied with the West, or not connected with "the people." When a black woman accuses a black man associated with the Black Power Movement of being a "fag," this act of naming assumes other meanings. In Sanchez's poem, "to a jealous cat," the speaker accuses her boyfriend of being jealous:

> no one ever told
> you that jealousy's
> a form of homo
> sexuality?
>   in other
> words my man
> you faggot bound
> when you imagine
> me going in and
> out some other cat.
>   yeah.
>   my man.
> perhaps you ain't
> the man we thought.[33]

Here, the speaker voices what might be this man's deepest fear: that he is not man enough to keep "his woman." This female speaker undermines the authority of "my man" as she suggests that perhaps they have both been operating under false pretenses. In another poem, "for unborn malcolms," Sanchez also uses the word "fag" in relation to white men who are not "man enough" to repress the revolution. Overwhelmed with anger following the assassination of Malcolm X, the speaker suggests that white people were responsible for his death. This poem stands as both a threat and a promise of future retaliatory action:

the next time he kills one
of our
        blk/princes
        some of his faggots
gonna die
        a stone/cold/death.
it's time.
        an eye for an eye
        a tooth for a tooth
        don't worry bout his balls
they al
        ready gone. [34]

Referring to white men as "fags" undermines their power on multiple levels. This act of naming rewrites the previous poem: it de-racinates and neuters black manhood. Both Sanchez and Giovanni focus on the symbolism of male genitalia. In a rhetorical "kick below the waist," they take a different approach to traditional symbols of male potency than many of their "brothers." When they are mentioned in the work of Giovanni and Sanchez, "balls" are usually missing or they are on the verge of violation. For the male poets included in this essay, genitals are a source of regenerative political and sexual power. This is one of the reasons why Nikki Giovanni's multifaceted use of the term "dick" to refer not only to the penis, but also to President Richard Nixon is such a provocative move. In "A Short Essay of Affirmation Explaining Why (With Apologies to the Federal Bureau of Investigation)," Giovanni's speaker ruminates about the reasons why so many people in America think that black revolutionaries are unstable. She argues that:

but we can't be black
and not be crazy
how the hell would anyone
        feel
with a mechanical dick
in his ass
lightening the way
for   whitey
and we're supposed to jack off
behind it. [35]

Black frustration is compared to the anger felt by a man who has been anally violated. The speaker also uses male-oriented language of masturbation ("jack off") to describe the performance of sexual gratification that "whitey" imagines black revolutionary leaders experience in the aftermath of this rape. As Giovanni assumes a stereotypically male perspective through the adoption of violent language and highly sexualized tropes central to the black aesthetic, she is critiquing the stereotypes. What does she accomplish by adopting this male perspective? On the one hand, this move strategically connects the speaker to her male audience. On the other, the poet's use of this masculinist vocabulary demonstrates her awareness of the elasticity of language: these terms resonate on multiple levels.

During the Black Arts Movement, women poets pushed the boundaries of the black aesthetic. They gave voice to the frustration of the period. Black women poets should be seen as women who stood their ground in a male-dominated rhetorical landscape, as poets whose pens marked new territory for future women writers, and as artists who navigated the sexism of the Black Arts and Black Power Movements. Nikki Giovanni, Sonia Sanchez and their contemporaries paved the way for black feminist voices to be heard.

NOTES

1. Larry Neal defined the Black Arts Movement as the "aesthetic and spiritual sister of the Black Power concept" in an essay entitled, "The Black Arts Movement" (1968). Larry Neal, "The Black Arts Movement," in *Within the Circle: An Anthology of African American Literary Criticism from the Harlem Renaissance to the Present*, ed. Angelyn Mitchell (Durham: Duke University Press, 1994), 185.

2. The Black Arts Movement is considered by many critics to have occurred between 1965 and 1976. Critics of the period argue that the movement formed in reaction to crucial historical and cultural events. David Lionel Smith argues that, "In 1965, however, several events occurred that gave direct impetus to the movement: the assassination of Malcolm X . . . ; the conversion of the literary prodigy LeRoi Jones to Imamu Amiri Baraka . . . ; the formation of the musically revolutionary Association for the Advancement of Creative Musicians in Chicago . . . ; and the founding of Broadside Press, which became a leading publisher of BAM poets, in Detroit" (325). The movement ends primarily because of the Vietnam War and the rise of Black Feminism. For more information on the historical factors that affected the rise and fall of the Black Arts Movement, see Kalamu ya Salaam, "The Black Arts Movement," in *The Oxford Companion to African American Literature*, ed. William L. Andrews, Frances Smith Foster, and Trudier Harris, foreword by Henry Louis Gates, Jr. (New York: Oxford University Press, 1997), 70–74; David Lionel Smith, "The Black Arts Movement," *The Encyclopedia of African-American Culture and History*, Vol. 1, ed. Jack Salzman, David Lionel Smith, and Cornel West (New York: Macmillan, 1996), 325–32; Sylvia Wynter, "Black Aesthetic," *The Encyclopedia of Aesthetics*, Vol. 1, ed. Michael Kelly (New York: Oxford University Press, 1998): 273–81.

3. Sylvia Wynter argues that "the years from 1968 to 1971 . . . [were the movement's] apogee years." For more of Wynter's definitions of the "black aesthetic,"

see "Black Aesthetic," *The Encyclopedia of Aesthetics*, Vol. 1 (New York: Oxford University Press, 1998), 274.

4. Houston Baker, Jr.'s analysis of Baraka's introduction to *Black Fire*, as well as his interpretation of the text's cover art reveals much about the collection's importance as a text that articulated many black American's social frustrations and political anxieties. Baker's critique of Baraka, Neal, and Gayle's deployment of Black Power rhetoric is insightful. Houston Baker, Jr., *The Journey Back* (Chicago: University of Chicago Press, 1980), 132–43.

5. To read Addison Gayle, Jr.'s full rebuttal to these literary reviews, see his essay, "Cultural Strangulation: Black Literature and the White Aesthetic," *The Black Aesthetic*, ed. Addison Gayle, Jr. (New York: Doubleday and Company, 1971), 39. Gayle argues that there is a "white aesthetic" and that white critics of African American literature have had a long history of misinterpreting black writer's works.

6. ya Salaam, "Black Arts Movement," 73.

7. Erlene Stetson, "Introduction," *Black Sister: Poetry by Black American Women, 1746–1980* (Bloomington: Indiana University Press. 1981), xvii.

8. As the introduction continues, Stetson seems to abandon this bold definition of black women's poetics for a safer, more woman-centered definition of topics important to black women poets from Lucy Terry to Nikki Giovanni that focuses on the "home [as symbolic of] a woman's search for place" and the "insistent metaphor of the flower." While I do not take issue with the interesting possibilities for literary investigation that Stetson offers in this piece, I do wonder why she so quickly abandons an analysis that further supports her earlier definition of a black female poetic tradition. Ibid., xxii–xxiii.

9. There are several anthologies and essays that are particularly helpful to scholars interested in the Black Arts Movement; see LeRoi Jones and Larry Neal's *Black Fire: An Anthology of Afro-American Writing* (New York: William Morrow & Company, 1968); Addison Gayle, Jr.'s *The Black Aesthetic* (New York: Doubleday, 1971); Stephen Henderson's *Understanding the New Black Poetry* (New York: William Morrow & Company, 1973). The Black Arts Movement is well represented in recently published anthologies of African American literary criticism such as Angelyn Mitchell's *Within the Circle* (Durham: Duke University Press, 1994), and Winston Napier's *African American Literary Theory* (New York: New York University Press, 2000).

10. David Lionel Smith, "The Black Arts Movement and Its Critics," *American Literary History* 3: 1 (Spring 1991), 94.

11. Larry Neal, "The Black Arts Movement," 184. Neal continually uses the male pronoun when referring to the black writers and his critical approach also indicates his adherence to a sexist position when he argues that the black artist should not consider himself to be an individualist because he has been "breast-fed the poison of 'individual experience'" (185).

12. There are several rhetorical moments in the essay that reflect Lee's sexism. He continually analyzes the "sister's" works in terms that refer to the body and sexuality, while the men are cited for their effective use of language or politics. When he praises Mari Evans' poem, "I Am a Black Woman," he follows the title with this phrase "not just a woman" (217). Later, in reference to the same poem, he says, "The woman herein recreated is not fragmented, hysterical, doesn't have sexual problems with her mate, doesn't feel caught up in a 'liberated womanhood' complex/bag" (217). Don L. Lee,

"Toward a Definition: Black Poetry of the Sixties (after LeRoi Jones)," in *Within the Circle*, 213.

13. Lee, "Toward a Definition," 215–16.

14. For further analysis of the ways that black gay male identity threatened Black Arts conceptualizations of social and sexual power, see Phillip Brian Harper's *Are We Not Men?: Masculine Anxiety and the Problem of African American Identity* (New York: Oxford University Press, 1996) and Charles I. Nero's "Toward a Black Gay Aesthetic," in *African American Literary Theory*, ed. Winston Napier (New York: New York University Press, 2000).

15. Harper, *Are We Not Men?*, 50.

16. Nero, "Toward a Black Gay Aesthetic," 399.

17. Jones' use of misogynistic language in his anthologized poems such as "Black Art" and "The World is Full of Remarkable Things" reveal his strong sexist leanings. See the LeRoi Jones section in *Black Fire*, 292–303.

18. Calvin Hernton, "Jitterbugging in the Streets," in *Black Fire*, 209.

19. James T. Stewart, "Announcement," in *Black Fire*, 202.

20. Ibid., 202.

21. In his provocative critique of several of the stereotypes that limited the black aesthetic, entitled, "You Touch My Black Aesthetic and I'll Touch Yours," Julian Mayfield takes the myth of black male "supposed supersexuality" to task (26). He argues that both whites and blacks believe in the myth and that it has incited both affirmative (black male pride and prowess) and violent (the lynching of black men) responses. He suggests that for the myth is perhaps the most empowering for the impoverished: "And let us not rob the poor, for in this land of faggotry the poorest black man has always been able to wake up in the morning with one pitiable certainty, and that was that his thing was larger than any white man's and that he could manipulate it more skillfully and produce better results." Julian Mayfield, "You Touch My Black Aesthetic and I'll Touch Yours," *The Black Aesthetic*, ed. Addison Gayle, Jr. (New York: Doubleday and Company, 1971), 27.

22. K. William Kgositsile, "The Awakening," in *Black Fire*, 226.

23. Ibid., 226–27.

24. Sonia Sanchez, "to all sisters," in *Black Fire*, 255.

25. Fahamisha Patricia Brown, *Performing the Word: African American Poetry as Vernacular Culture* (New Brunswick, NJ: Rutgers University Press. 1999), 96.

26. Odaro (Barbara Jones, slave name), "Alafia," in *Black Fire*, 356.

27. Lethonia Gee, "By Glistening, Dancing Seas," in *Black Fire*, 221.

28. Brown, *Performing the Word*, 105. In her analysis of the tensions between race and gender in black women's poetry, Brown argues, "In the language of African American women poets we might find a kind of "double veiling, the encoding of both race and gender . . . . African American women poets demand that we read their works as statements of African American women. Gender and race are inseparable, parts of one integral whole." Brown's argument raises several questions: what does it mean to read the works of African American women poets? What are the features of a raced or gendered, or even American perspective? The problem has much to do with the structures of critical inquiry that influence our interpretation of these works.

29. Sonia Sanchez, "memorial: 3. rev. pimps," in *Home Coming* (Detroit: Broadside Press, 1969), 31.

30. Ibid.

31. Ibid.

32. Nikki Giovanni, "seduction," in *Black Feeling, Black Talk, Black Judgement* (New York: W. Morrow, 1970), 38.

33. Sonia Sanchez, "to a jealous cat," in *Home Coming*, 13.

34. Sonia Sanchez, "for unborn malcolms," in *Home Coming*, 28.

35. Nikki Giovanni, "A Short Essay of Affirmation Explaining Why (With Apologies to the Federal Bureau of Investigation)," in *Black Feeling, Black Talk, Black Judgement*, 22.

9

Transcending the
Fixity of Race

The Kamoinge Workshop and
the Question of a "Black
Aesthetic" in Photography

Erina Duganne

The African American photographer and filmmaker James Hinton first applied
the term "black aesthetic" to photography in 1969 when he singled out Roy
DeCarava as the "the first black man who chose by intent . . . to devote serious attention to the black aesthetic as it relates to photography and the black
experience in America."[1] In his statement, Hinton isolates DeCarava's photographs and defines them in relation to one predetermined value, DeCarava's
racial identity.[2] In a contemporary statement, DeCarava seems to corroborate
Hinton's reading of his photographs. He writes: "You should be able to look at
me and see my work. You should be able to look at my work and see me."[3] Here
DeCarava, like Hinton, appears to conflate his racial identity with the character of his work. However, upon closer inspection, one realizes that in evoking
the word "me," DeCarava actually spoke not from the fixed position of race
but from the multiple positions that he as a man of African descent inhabited
within the structure of language.[4]

Hinton's classification of DeCarava as the creator of a "black aesthetic" in
photography has by and large eclipsed DeCarava's interest in coming to terms
with himself as a subject who speaks from a particular point of view. Conversely, the prominence that DeCarava has himself given since the late 1960s to
the social purpose of his work has further exacerbated this problem. DeCarava
explained in 1972: "I don't see art as an individual function as much as a social
function."[5] In this statement, DeCarava appears to contradict his prior emphasis on photography as a vehicle of self-expression. His account of "A Photographer's Gallery," an alternative photography space that he and his wife ran out of
their home from 1955 to 1957 illuminates this discrepancy: "We are interested
in that area of photography which strives for the expression of self, which seeks
to extend the vision that which has heretofore been invisible and elusive."[6] In

this statement, DeCarava reveals his interest in photography's relationship to subjectivity, a concern that seems to stand in contrast to his 1972 statement about photography's social function as well as Hinton's categorization of him in terms of the "black aesthetic."

To DeCarava, however, his use of photography to express his individual *and* group identity is not contradictory. Although DeCarava supported Hinton's connection of his work with the "black aesthetic" and at times even used the term to position himself and his work as separate from Anglo culture, he never intended these associations to align his production with the exclusionary ideologies of the Black Arts Movement.[7] In fact, whereas activist Maulana Ron Karenga argued that "there is no such thing as individualism, we're all Black,"[8] DeCarava consistently used his photographs to speak about African American identity from *both* an individual and collective point of view.[9] A 1989 statement by DeCarava affirms this intent: "At the same time that we fight for our blackness, we also have to fight for our universal quality; we're human beings."[10]

In spite of DeCarava's interest in using the "black aesthetic" to evoke both his individual and group identity, the term's collective associations continue to provide a standard against which the images of numerous African American photographers are evaluated, including those made by members of the African American photography collective known as the Kamoinge Workshop, for which DeCarava served as director for several years. Founded in 1963, when two informal groups of African American photographers living and working in New York City merged into a single collective, the members named themselves "Kamoinge" after the Gikuyu word meaning "a group of people acting and working together."[11] Their African-inspired name and status as a collective notwithstanding, the members of Kamoinge never aligned their photographic practices with the ideologies or collective-based goals of Black Power or the Black Arts Movement. Rather, they came together as a community of friends who casually gathered in each other's homes—usually on Sundays—to eat, listen to music, and discuss photography, among other things.[12] Often disagreeing with one another about the purpose and intention of their work, the members had no set ideology to which they prescribed as a group, either artistically or politically. This nonalignment is reflected in the diversity of their individual styles and subject matter. While some members, like Louis Draper, photographed black subjects in the tradition of street photography, others, like Albert Fennar, turned to abstraction and "non-black" subjects. Additionally, as a group, the members of Kamoinge never attempted to make a collective-based art, instead, they frequently photographed alone, although occasionally in pairs.[13]

The group did agree, however, on the artistic nature of their work and its relationship to their lived experiences, including race. As a group, the members of Kamoinge aspired to make artistic images that would "reflect a concern for truth about the world, about the society, and about themselves."[14] To achieve this aim, the members rooted their work in their personal and collective experiences, believing that, as Draper explains in 1972: "Contact with self is the key . . . . We speak of our lives as only we can."[15] As a result of the emphasis on the self, both individually and collectively, a number of Kamoinge members photographed black subjects. However, unlike Black Arts Movement supporters such as writer Melvin Dixon, who argued, in 1971, "Black Art, by definition, exists primarily for Black people. It is an art which combines the social and political pulse of the Black community into an artistic reflection of that emotion, that spirit, that energy,"[16] the members of Kamoinge did not assume an unmediated continuity between themselves and this subject matter, nor did they intend their photographs to provide illustrations of their race or to instigate social change.

Rather than speak for African Americans as a group or act as a corrective lens, the Kamoinge members used their photographs to explore how the particularities of their individual circumstances—including their collective experience of racial difference—informed and complicated their art. This emphasis on the dialogic relationship between their individual and collective experiences also influenced the manner in which members of Kamoinge have retrospectively used the term "black aesthetic" in relation to their work. A 2001 interview with Kamoinge member Beuford Smith reiterates this intent: "I think the black aesthetic is different for everyone . . . I think it is based on how you live as a black person. Some people say Bryant Gumbel isn't black, just because he doesn't say them, those, and that, just because he wasn't born in the ghetto. I think that this will go on as black people have different life experiences."[17] Here Smith, like DeCarava, reflects his interest in the individual *and* collective associations of the "black aesthetic."

Nonetheless, scholars and critics, both during the 1960s, 1970s, and today, continue to rely solely on the collective associations of terms like "black aesthetic" and "Harlem" in their discussions of the Kamoinge members' photographs. For instance, in 1972, Ray Gibson described the formation of the Kamoinge Workshop as resulting from "a common need to form a Black esthetic,"[18] while in 1996, Peter Galassi characterized the Workshop as, "centered on community life: The Harlem neighborhood was both its essential subject and intended principle audience."[19] Despite such characterizations, there is no evidence that any of the members of Kamoinge used the term "black aesthetic" to describe their work during the 1960s or 1970s. Furthermore, while the members often photographed in Harlem and even briefly opened a gallery there, most of the members did not live there nor did they photograph exclusively for this community. Smith explains: "I don't recall any discussion of the black aesthetic or such . . . . I never lived in Harlem. I lived on the Lower East Side but I wasn't part of any art movement there either. I would just go to Harlem to photograph but I also took photographs of the Lower East Side."[20]

Even though the members of Kamoinge frequently used Harlem as a vehicle for expressing their individual experiences of racial difference, a conceptualization that many of them later expressed using the term "black aesthetic," the continued interpretation of their work based solely on an essentialized racial subject overlooks the complex and often contradictory relationships that existed between their individual and collective identities. To come to terms with this problem, I consider a number of images made by members of the Kamoinge Workshop during the 1960s both in terms of their production and reception. This methodology is critical to my analysis since the members of Kamoinge aspired to explore the representation of subjectivity in photography beyond generalized notions of African American identity implied by terms such as "black," "Harlem," and "insider" and as sustained by Black Arts Movement supporters like Karenga who argued, "We were Black before we were born."[21]

INSIDERS AND OUTSIDERS:
THE KAMOINGE WORKSHOP'S "HARLEM" PORTFOLIO

Besides the product of friendship, the formation of the Kamoinge Workshop also resulted from the alienation and isolation that many of the members felt with respect to established photographic institutions.[22] As a collective, the members attempted to nurture and protect one another in their efforts to secure access to the representation and reflection of their own experiences both individually and collectively. Despite these efforts to speak about African American identity on their own terms, more generalized conceptions of race frequently provided the standard for evaluating the Kamoinge members' images when they were exhibited or reproduced. The publication of a photographic portfolio by the Kamoinge Workshop entitled, "Harlem," in the July 1966 issue of the photography magazine *Camera* provides a case in point.[23] In the introductory statement to the magazine, *Camera* editor Allan Porter asserts that the Kamoinge portfolio resulted from the members' racial ties to their subjects: "In each case the camera observes not as a curious outsider peeping through keyholes and pointing a finger, but as an insider, as part of the life it observes."[24] Through his statement, Porter validates the photographs included in *Camera* based on the "insider" status of their makers.

Porter believed that the African American point of view offered by the members of Kamoinge resulted in more sympathetic and truthful representations of Harlem and served to counterbalance the "sensational" photographs of Harlem—depicting its "problems, desperation, and poverty"—circulated contemporaneously by the print media. However, when characterizing one as the product of "insiders" and the other of "outsiders," Porter never explains how these categories work visually or why the Kamoinge members' racial backgrounds predisposed them to represent Harlem more truthfully. To what extent did generalized conceptions of race essentialize the interpretation of the Kamoinge members' photographs, and, at the same time, how did their images resist such categorizations?

Comparing the cover image of *Camera* taken by Draper (fig. 9.1) with a photograph from *Time* (fig. 9.2) that appeared as part of a photo-essay for a cover story on Harlem published in the magazine's July 31, 1964 issue provides a means of addressing these questions. On the surface, these two images seem to support Porter's distinction between "insiders" and "outsiders." The closeness

camera

of Draper's subjects suggests intimacy, or that he is "part of the life he observes," while the distance of the subjects in the *Time* photograph implies detachment, or that "a curious outsider peeping through keyholes" took the picture. However, such an explanation does not account for the affectedness of Draper's subjects. According to Porter, Draper knew his subjects intimately; yet, their postures do not reflect familiarity. In fact, one could argue that the distance that the *Time* photographer Robert Cottrol establishes between himself and his subjects renders them more naturalistic than those depicted in Draper's image. In contrast to Cottrol who uses his anonymous distance to explore the ephemeral, everyday aspects of social life, aligning his image with a "snapshot" or "things as they are" aesthetic, Draper, wanting to move beyond merely documenting his subjects from the supposed impartiality of photojournalism or documentary photography, appears to pose his subjects. The woman in his image holds one arm up to her chin, the seated man slightly cocks his head while holding a cigarette in his clasped hands, and the standing man rests his hands on his lower back in anticipation of the shot. Except for the obscured woman in the lower left-hand corner of the *Time* photograph, the subjects in this image do not acknowledge having their picture taken nor do they appear to pose for the shot.

While the posed quality of Draper's subjects separates his photograph from the seeming neutrality and objectivity demanded of photojournalists like Cottrol, the formality of Draper's image shares certain commonalities with

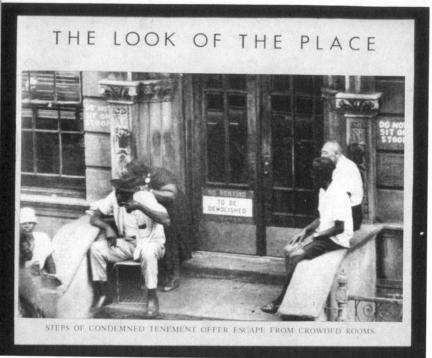

THE LOOK OF THE PLACE

STEPS OF CONDEMNED TENEMENT OFFER ESCAPE FROM CROWDED ROOMS.

Fig. 9.2. Robert W. Cottrol, "Steps of condemned tenement offer escape from crowded rooms," *Time* (July 31, 1964). Courtesy of the artist.

aesthetic strategies associated with 1930s documentary photography and the production of Walker Evans in particular. For his photograph of the Ricketts family, published in the 1960 edition of *Let Us Now Praise Famous Men* (1941) (fig. 9.3), Evans encouraged his subjects to arrange themselves before his camera.[25] By not telling his subjects how to pose for the shot, Evans believed that he could distinguish his work from the candid, "sensational" images of Southern tenant farmers featured in Margaret Bourke-White's and Erskine Caldwell's 1937 book *You Have Seen Their Faces*.[26] In adopting this seemingly detached approach, Evans acts like Cottrol who depicts his subjects using a "snapshot" or "as you are" aesthetic. However, unlike Cottrol, who uses his anonymous distance to document a moment of passing social life, Evans believed that his professional distance allowed him to transcend the material realities of his subjects' poverty-stricken lives and depict their beauty.[27] Cultural historian William Stott explains: "In documentary, the beauty, if any, is *in* the scene, though it takes an outsider's eye to behold it."[28] Here Stott implies that Evans' deliberate detachment from his subjects, essentially his "outsider" status, allows Evans to transform the members of the Ricketts family into art.

The posed appearance of Draper's subjects also encourages the viewer to appreciate his subjects aesthetically. At the same time, however, the image's "naturalistic" details such as the woman leaning against the railing, the man casually sitting on the stairs, and the second man standing with his back toward the camera disrupts the viewer from appreciating their formal beauty. Unlike the members of the Ricketts family who rigidly line up as a group portrait, essentially presenting themselves to the viewer for full aesthetic contemplation, the subjects in Draper's image both offer and conceal themselves from his camera

and by extension the viewer. This interplay between the affectedness and naturalness results in the simultaneous engagement and distancing of the viewer,
a strategy that calls attention to Draper's position as "insider" *and* "outsider."
Here, Draper, in contrast to Black Arts Movement "spiritual leader" Larry Neal
who argued that the primary duty of the black artist "is to speak to the spiritual
and cultural needs of Black people,"[29] suggests that his relationship with the
black subjects in his photograph is neither essential nor uncomplicated.

According to Porter, the Kamoinge members' photographs resulted from
their intimate involvement with their subjects. However, Draper did not personally know any of the subjects in his photograph, which he took close to his
home at 240 West 10th Street in New York City's Lower East Side. Draper
recalls feeling a sense of fear, not comfort when he took the photograph. He
explains that the man in the foreground "kind of scared me. I shot him with
his back turned. I hoped that the woman would not alert him to turn around
and holler at me for having made the picture."[30] Draper's anxiety with respect
to his subjects undermines Porter's assumption that the racial background of
the members of Kamoinge necessarily predisposed them to intimately knowing
the black subjects of their photographs. Unlike Evans, Draper neither spent
extended periods of time with his subjects nor waited for them to arrange
themselves in front of his camera; rather, he photographed them spontaneously
on the street. Yet what prevents Draper's "snapshot" approach from producing

overtly "candid" photographs like the one in *Time* is his interest in his subject's reactions to him and his camera.

To initiate a dialogue between himself and his subjects, Draper uses the formal device of the gaze. This approach stands in contrast to that of Evans who believed that photographers should not "touch" reality. Stott explains, "For Evans, documentary is actuality untouched; the recorder not only does not put anything in, he does his best not to disrupt or revise what is already there."[31] In other words, Evans attempts to approach his subjects with detachment, or as an "outsider." Yet in spite of Evans' efforts to distance himself from his subjects and transform them into art, his professional presence and intention still inform the meaning of his image. Like the caption, "Steps of condemned tenement offer escape from crowded rooms," accompanying the *Time* photograph (see fig. 9.2), which serves to influence the readers' perception of Harlem as a problem, it is impossible to separate Evans' image from the particularities of its maker or the circumstances of its making.

In Draper's photograph that context is central, as the contrast created between the gazes of the standing woman and the seated man suggests. For instance, the way that the man coolly gazes out at the viewer from behind his hat encourages a sense of openness in comparison to the woman whose tense gaze and raised hand distances her from the viewer. In balancing emotional investment and disinterest, Draper reinforces his discursive relationship to these black subjects and begins to break down the subject/object hierarchy embedded in most photographic approaches, including that used by members of the Black Arts Movement. Whereas Karenga called for art that would "remind us of our distaste for the enemy, our love for each other, and our commitment to the revolutionary struggle,"[32] Draper used his photographs to explore the complicated positions that photographers occupy in relation to their subjects.

A comparison between another photograph from *Camera* made by Kamoinge member Beuford Smith and one taken by his Anglo contemporary Bruce Davidson further clarifies this point. Smith's photograph of a young girl who coyly glances from behind a doll that she grasps with two mitten-covered hands (fig. 9.4) assimilates the tension found in Draper's image between the gazes of the man and the woman into a single subject.[33] The girl's firm hold of the doll denotes self-assurance; yet, at the same time, she partially hides her face behind the doll, suggesting her reluctance to have her photograph taken. Davidson's image also depicts a girl holding a doll (fig. 9.5).[34] Yet, unlike the subjects in the *Time* photograph (see fig. 9.2), her downward gaze does not result from her indifference to the camera. Her proximity to Davidson and the manner in which she holds the doll in between her legs and away from her face suggests affectedness not naturalness. The young girl may not look directly at Davidson, but, like Smith's subject, she is aware of his presence. In fact, whereas Smith's use of the gaze encourages the viewer to respond to his subject subjectively, Davidson's efforts to photograph the girl in a seemingly natural pose only heightens the affectedness of his image and leads to her objectification.

Fig. 9.4. Beuford Smith, *Girl with Doll*, 1965. © Beuford Smith/Césaire.

This comparison also appears to corroborate Porter's distinctions between "insiders" and "outsiders." The manner in which Smith photographs the girl suggests a personal relationship between photographer and subject, while Davidson's image implies emotional detachment, distance, and disinterestedness. But, is the racial makeup of the photographers what differentiates these approaches? Porter endorses such causality, believing that the racial background of the members of Kamoinge provided them with a greater sensitivity to photograph black subjects than someone like the Anglo "outsider" Davidson. Yet, by assuming that their respective positions as "insider" and "outsider" determined their involved or detached relationship with their subjects, Porter only reinforces the separation between art and life that the members of Kamoinge attempted to resolve in their works. As a collective, the members of Kamoinge aspired to make artistic images. However, in so doing, they rejected the assumption that photography required disinterestedness. Kamoinge member

Fig. 9.5. Bruce Davidson,
West Virginia, 1962.
© Bruce Davidson
and Magnum Photos.

Herbert Randall explains, "Photography is not an entity unto itself and cannot be disconnected from life."[35] Rather than separate their art from their lived experiences, the members of Kamoinge used their photographs to explore the ways in which they informed and complicated one another.

At the same time, the Kamoinge members' efforts to use their lived experiences to inform their art did not preclude them from adopting a detached or "outsider" perspective, as the following comparison reiterates. Unlike in Smith's and Davidson's images (see figs. 9.4 and 9.5), the racial identities of the photographers of these next two pictures are more difficult to discern. In one image (fig. 9.6), although the photographer depicts his subjects at a distance, the man-

Fig. 9.7. Herbert Randall, Virginia farm girl, 1961. Courtesy of the artist.

ner in which he photographs them caught in the act of laughing implies emotional investment on the part of the photographer. Conversely, in the second image (fig. 9.7), while the distance between the photographer and subject is reduced, the diverted gaze of the depicted girl suggests detachment. Accordingly, one could hypothesize that an "insider" took the first image, while an "outsider" photographed the second one. However, the opposite is true. Bruce Davidson and Kamoinge member Herbert Randall, respectively, authored these images.

In his photograph (see fig. 9.7), also included in *Camera*, Randall emphasizes the formal qualities of the girl as well as those of her rural surroundings. The texture of her checkered dress produces a strong visual contrast to the graininess of the wooden structure behind her, and, although she appears pregnant, her diverted gaze elicits an aesthetic as opposed to sentimental response on the part of the viewer. One could argue that Randall's image invites detached enjoyment or that an "outsider" took the photograph. In contrast, the subjects in Davidson's image (see fig. 9.6) interact with the viewer intimately. Davidson photographs the two women unposed—their left and right hands hold onto each other in anticipation or culmination of a friendly embrace—and, although they respond spontaneously to the camera, their wide grins suggest ease and not discomfort with being looked at. Unlike Davidson's previous image of the girl and her doll (see fig. 9.5), the candidness of this photograph complicates assumptions about the emotional disinterest of "outsiders."

This comparison reveals that the choices that Randall and Davidson made in terms of form and content influenced their pictures' meanings more so than their racial identities. Essentializing the photograph of Randall as the product of an "insider" and that of Davidson as an "outsider" obscures this important distinction, pigeonholing the images and filling them with predetermined values. This interpretative strategy is particularly problematic for African American photographers, since it posits the identification of African American photographers with black subjects as essential and uncomplicated. However, as the Kamoinge members repeatedly reveal in their photographs in *Camera*, the relationship between photography and race is not transparent. In photographing black subjects from the seemingly contradictory positions of "insiders" *and* "outsiders," the members of Kamoinge transform their photographs from "illustrations" of their race or as "evidence" of some social problem to multifaceted aesthetic statements that reflect conflicting experiences about African American identity.

THE KAMOINGE WORKSHOP AND HARLEM

Like his relegation of the Kamoinge members to "insiders," Porter's decision to subtitle the *Camera* portfolio, "A Photographic Report on Harlem," also served to isolate the Kamoinge members' images and define them in relation to generalized notions of racial identity. Rather than explore the Kamoinge members' interest in the dialogic relationship between their individual and collective identities, Porter uses generalized conceptions of Harlem to fix their images. The photographs included in the *Camera* portfolio underscore this discrepancy. While some of the images depict specific locations and people in Harlem, unlike the title suggests, many were taken in various cities throughout New York, New Jersey, Virginia, Mississippi, and Bermuda.[36] The article's "post scriptum," written by members of Kamoinge, attempts to justify this inconsistency: "The Kamoinge Workshop sees Harlem as a state of mind, whether it exists in Watts in California, the south side of Chicago, Alabama, or New York."[37] Through this disclaimer, the members challenged Porter's prescriptive categorization of their photographs, arguing that their images reflected a more complex and emotionally driven understanding of Harlem than the one offered by Porter.

A photograph (fig. 9.8) by Herbert Randall in *Camera* of a mother and child walking past a ravaged building provides a case in point. If read in terms of the description of Harlem offered by Porter in the accompanying essay, Randall's image seems to provide evidence of Harlem's particular poverty-stricken conditions and racial problems: "a disreputable scar on the New York landscape" where "people . . . live in extreme poverty and without any real faith in the future."[38] In making this allusion, Porter largely relies on ideas of Harlem

Fig. 9.8. Herbert
Randall, Mother and
child—demolished
building, 1963.
Courtesy of the artist.

disseminated during the 1960s by the print media. For instance, in an effort to move beyond merely "reporting" Harlem's racial troubles, the editors at *Time* strategically used photographs to influence their readers' perceptions of Harlem as a problem. The *Time* photograph (see fig. 9.2), discussed earlier, reiterates this intent. In adding the caption, "Steps of condemned tenement offer escape from crowded rooms," to this otherwise mundane picture depicting a group of individuals casually sitting on a stoop, the editors collapse the distinction between what the photograph depicts and what it signifies. Rather than describe the image, the caption directs readers to a meaning that the editors have already chosen in advance, namely providing visual support for their article on the unbreakable cycle of overcrowding and dilapidated living conditions existing in Harlem. The words "condemned" and "crowded" influence the image's meaning and encourage readers to interpret the people depicted in the picture in relation to these descriptions.

Porter's accompanying essay seems to serve the same purpose. However, what prevents Porter from overdetermining the meaning of Randall's photograph is the Kamoinge members' description of Harlem as a "state of mind." Through this statement, one realizes that rather than describe the specific social or economic aspects of Harlem, Randall actually attempted to explore its psychological impact. The fact that Randall's photograph depicts a site in New Jersey not Harlem further supports this intent. Although obviously an urban subject, Randall's image is not meant to describe Harlem literally. Instead, interested in the relationship between what his image depicts and signifies, Randall uses the associations evoked by the dilapidated building to question how the construction of Harlem as a "problem" influenced opinions about African American people and their artistic creations. Porter's reduction of Randall's image to an "insider's" view of Harlem obscures Randall's efforts to explore the complexity of that position.

The Kamoinge members' interest in Harlem did not occur only on the pages of *Camera*. Between 1964 and 1965, the members rented a gallery space, known as the Kamoinge Gallery, in a brownstone at 248 W. 139th Street where they met and held two exhibitions. However, as mentioned previously, despite the physical location of the gallery, most members did not live in Harlem nor did they photograph exclusively in this neighborhood. Also, unlike the objectives of the Black Arts Movement, the Harlem community did not make up the primary audience for the gallery. In fact, a number of individuals from the Anglo mainstream, including curator John Szarkowski and photojournalist Henri Cartier-Bresson, visited the gallery. Additionally, several members of the Harlem community who attended exhibitions at the gallery are said to have found certain photographs objectionable.[39] In sum, while many Kamoinge members felt an emotional affiliation toward Harlem and often photographed there, defining their production solely in terms of generalized understandings of this locale fixed their images as the product of a collective expression, not unlike the one prescribed by supporters of the Black Arts Movement.

A 1965 photograph (fig. 9.9) taken by Kamoinge member Beuford Smith offers additional insight into this problem. In *Camera*, Porter contrasts this image with the more "sensational" pictures of Harlem circulated by the print mass media, claiming that the Kamoinge members' intimate knowledge of Harlem gave them uncontested access to what Harlem is really like. Yet instead of substituting a positive image for a negative one or revealing his intimate knowledge of a place that he had never actually inhabited, Smith uses this image to explore how photographs constitute reality. A comparison between Smith's image and one taken by a UPI photographer in 1964 (fig. 9.10) and later included in the 1969 exhibition *Harlem on My Mind* at the Metropolitan Museum of Art clarifies this distinction.

Both Smith and the UPI photographer depict a well-known Harlem landmark, the National Memorial African Bookstore. However, unlike the UPI photograph, in which the bookstore's facade fills the entire frame, in Smith's image, the building's immediate legibility is obscured. As a result, Smith's image encourages the viewer to read the bookstore and the nationalistic posters and images lining its facade in relation to the elderly woman sitting alone in the darkened doorway to the left of the building. The horizontality of Smith's picture adds to this effect. In contrast to the verticality of the UPI photograph, a compositional device that serves to draw attention away from the figures in the foreground to the stacked blocks of nationalistic images and posters in the

background, the horizontality of Smith's image gives the elderly woman and the void in which she sits equal weight to that of the nationalistic imagery surrounding her. As a result, Smith's photograph creates a dialogue between the two. Leaning her head against the doorway with her glasses hanging around her neck and a closed book in her lap, the woman in Smith's image appears tired and unenthusiastic, a stark contrast to the energetic assortment of images and texts next to her.

The National Memorial African Bookstore, also known as the "House of Common Sense and Home of Proper Propaganda," served as a frequent meeting place for Malcolm X and other black nationalist leaders. Capitalizing on the bookstore's nationalistic connotations and particularly those evoked by the posters and images on its facade, Smith uses those associations to elicit meaning in his photograph.[40] Having begun his photographic career as a photojournalist for the *Amsterdam News*, Smith had firsthand experience with some of the limitations of photojournalism and its endorsement of photography's transparency in particular.[41] As a result, Smith considered how he might encourage the viewer to look *at* rather than *through* his photographs.[42] By slightly altering the view of the black nationalist bookstore, Smith modifies the viewer's assumptions about what she or he sees. Whereas an image like the UPI photograph seems to impartially illustrate the facade of the bookstore and by extension Black nationalism, Smith refocuses the viewer's attention on the discontinuity between the bookstore's collective nationalist agenda and the individuals who lived in the Harlem community. Through his juxtaposition of the woman and the bookstore, Smith encourages the viewer to reconsider African American identity as a set of relational rather than fixed associations.

Smith's exploration of the print mass media's use of photography to transparently convey information about Harlem is quite different from Black Arts Movement photographers like Robert Sengstacke who saw themselves "as graphic historians, conveyors of love, combating what we felt were negative photographic images of black in the major American press."[43] Instead of simply exchanging a positive image for a negative one or presenting Harlem, as Porter claims, from a "Negro's point of view," Smith uses his photograph to confront the narrow and frequently judgmental representations of Harlem and African Americans in general disseminated by the print media. Smith reiterates this point: "Part of the purpose of my work is to challenge the general public's understanding of black America then as well as currently."[44] By aligning Smith's image as the product of an "insider" whose relationship to Harlem is seamless, Porter overlooks this meaning and dismisses important connections that lie in between Smith's singular and collective identities.

Smith intended his retrospective use of the term "black aesthetic" to reflect this dialogue between his individual and collective identities. Smith explained in 1999: "The black aesthetic for me comes from my culture and background . . . I think the black aesthetic is different for everyone."[45] Here, Smith again posits the "black aesthetic" as an expression of *both* his individual and group identity. The use of the "black aesthetic" by members of the Black Arts Movement as well as its application to photography by Hinton overlooks this distinction. In defining the "black aesthetic" solely in terms of generalized conceptions of race, Hinton as well as Karenga, Neal, and other supporters of the Black Arts Movement essentially replace the "I" with the "we," an interpretative strategy that, like the collective-based terms "Harlem" and "insider," fixes African American identity instead of opening it up to the multiple positions from which a subject speaks, is spoken to, and is spoken about. As the Kamoinge members' images in *Camera* so astutely reveal, it is only in setting aside the question of whether or not an image is representative of an essential racial subject that a whole new set of issues and relational spaces begins to emerge in which one can more effectively explore the complicated relationship that race and by extension the "black aesthetic" brought and continues to bring to the representation of subjectivity in photography.

NOTES

An earlier version of this essay was presented at the conference, "Laying Claim: (Re)Considering Artists of African Descent in the Americas," held at Colgate University, Ithaca, New York, in 2001. I am grateful to Ann Reynolds, Heather Mathews, Lisa Gail Collins, and Margo Natalie Crawford for their criticism, advice, and encouragement as I reworked it. This essay is dedicated to the members of the Ka-moinge Workshop and particularly Louis Draper who died on February 18, 2002, after a short illness.

1. James Hinton, quoted in Roy DeCarava, *Thru Black Eyes* (New York: Studio Museum in Harlem, 1969). References to Hinton's statement are also found in Larry Neal, "To Harlem with Love," *New York Times*, October 5, 1969, sec. 2, 33–34; A. D. Coleman, "Roy DeCarava: Thru Black Eyes," *Popular Photography* 66 (April 1970): 68–70ff; James Alinder, *Roy DeCarava, Photographer* (Lincoln: University of Nebraska Press, 1970); and Maren Stange, "'Illusion Complete Within Itself': Roy DeCarava's Photography," *The Yale Journal of Criticism* 9 (1996): 63–92.

2. Hinton's statement also separates DeCarava's photographic production from the concerns of his Anglo contemporaries and overlooks his efforts to integrate his production within the mainstream. For instance, by 1969, DeCarava had received considerable mainstream institutional support, including a 1952 Guggenheim Fellowship, the inclusion of his work in exhibitions like the Museum of Modern Art's *The Family of Man* (1955) and *The Photographer's Eye* (1964), and a contractual job working for *Sports Illustrated*.

3. Roy DeCarava, *Thru Black Eyes*.

4. Here I mean that in asserting his selfhood, DeCarava constitutes himself through language, which unlike race relates to people on a singular not collective level. My argument relies on the linguistic model of the subject proposed by Emile Benveniste and particularly his supposition that it is through language that people constitute themselves as subjects. Accordingly, one can argue that while subjectivity concerns the persons "I" and "you," race, which often poses as the subjective "I-you" pair, actually corresponds to the non-subjective person, the "he/she." See Emile Benveniste, " Relationships of Person in the Verb," *Problems in General Linguistics*, trans. Mary Elizabeth Meek (Coral Gables, FL: University of Miami Press, 1971).
In making this distinction between subjectivity and race, I am not implying that race is irrelevant to considerations of subjectivity. Using Michel Foucault's discursive understanding of the subject as a model, one can also argue that when placed within the actual workings of culture, individual subjectivities differ according to their particular race, class, gender, and ethnicity. However, while cultural traditions such as race may inform one's experience of subjectivity, and by implication one's sense of self, they do not overdetermine one's selfhood, as Hinton's reading implies. Consequently, although race remained central to DeCarava's assertion of his selfhood, in defining his photographs solely in term of DeCarava's racial identity, Hinton fixes DeCarava's subjectivity instead of considering it as discursively constituted. See Michel Foucault, *The Archaeology of Knowledge and the Discourse on Language*, trans. A. M. Sheridan Smith (New York: Pantheon Books, 1972).

5. Roy DeCarava, quoted in Ray Gibson, "Roy DeCarava: Master Photographer," *Black Creation* 4: 1 (Fall 1972), 36.

6. Roy DeCarava, quoted in Peter Galassi, *Roy DeCarava: A Retrospective* (New York: The Museum of Modern Art, 1996), 23.

7. Steeped in the politics of Black Power, the Black Arts Movement represented the cultural wing of African American liberation struggles in the 1960s and 1970s. Attempting to situate themselves as separate from the universal values of the Anglo cultural mainstream, Black Arts Movement supporters like Larry Neal advocated the development of

a "black aesthetic," which consisted of art works judged for their social consideration, made for and of black people (community), and reflective and supportive of the Black Revolution. See Addison Gayle, Jr., ed., *The Black Aesthetic* (New York: Anchor Books, 1971) and LeRoi Jones and Larry Neal, eds., *Black Fire: An Anthology of Afro-American Writing* (New York: William Morrow & Company, 1968). Throughout this chapter I use these collective-based and separatist ideologies of the Black Art Movement as a foil to my larger argument about the production and reception of photographs made by members of the Kamoinge Workshop. I recognize that my characterization of the Black Arts Movement is necessarily reductive and leaves out many of its nuances; however, for the purposes of this essay, it represents some of the general assumptions underlying the movement.

8. Maulana Ron Karenga, *The Quotable Karenga* (Los Angeles: US Organization, 1967), 1.

9. James Cunningham offers a similar critique of Karenga's collective-based ideology in his "Hemlock for the Black Artist: Karenga Style," in *New Black Voices: An Anthology of Afro-American Literature*, ed. Abraham Chapman (New York: Penguin, 1972).

10. Roy DeCarava, interview by Sherry Turner DeCarava, *Artist and Influence*, vol. 8 (New York: Hatch-Billops Collection, Inc., 1989), 33.

11. Louis Draper and Albert Fennar are both said to have discovered the name "Kamoinge" in the glossary of Jomo Kenyatta's book *Facing Mt. Kenya*. The name "Kamoinge" was initially connected with an informal group of photographers to which both Draper and Fennar belonged. In 1963, this original Kamoinge group merged with another group of African American photographers known as Group 35, whom they had befriended at a meeting held at photographer Larry Stewart's studio to discuss some of the problems encountered by African American photographers, including their isolation and exclusion from mainstream institutions. This larger group subsequently adopted the name Kamoinge Workshop. See Louis Draper, interview by author, tape recording, New York, NY, March 24, 2001.

12. Louis Draper, Albert Fennar, Ray Francis, Herman Howard, Earl James, James Mannas, Calvin Mercer, and Herbert Randall belonged to these early informal groups. Other members of Kamoinge during the 1960s included Anthony Barboza, Bob Clark, David Carter, Roy DeCarava, Melvin Mills, Herbert Robinson, Beuford Smith, Ming Smith, Larry Stewart, Shawn Walker, and Calvin Wilson. These individuals came from a variety of photographic backgrounds; some, like Draper and Randall, studied with Harold Feinstein and W. Eugene Smith, while others, like Francis and Smith, were largely self-taught. None, however, had an established reputation within the photographic community. As a result, they asked Roy DeCarava, present at that first meeting but not belonging to either informal group, to serve as their first director. He resigned in 1965.

With many new members, the group, now known as Kamoinge Inc., continues to meet and exhibit together. Its current president is Beuford Smith. For more information on Kamoinge, see Louis Draper, "The Kamoinge Workshop," *Photo Newsletter* 1 (December 1972): 3–8; Shawn Walker, "Preserving Our History: The Kamoinge Workshop and Beyond," *Ten.8* 24 (1987): 20–25; Iris Schmeisser, "Liberating Views/Views of Liberation: Black Photographers of the Civil Rights Era" (Master's thesis, University of Munich, 1997); and Carrie Weems, "Personal Perspectives on the Evolution of American Black Photography: A Talk with Carrie Weems," *Obscura* 2 (1982): 9–17.

13. This circumstance again testifies to the difference between the Kamoinge Workshop and other African American collectives such as Spiral, Weusi, OBAC, and AFRI-COBRA.

14. Kamoinge Workshop, *Portfolio No. 1*, 1964.

15. Draper, "The Kamoinge Workshop," 3.

16. Melvin Dixon, "White Critic—Black Art???," in *Black Art Notes*, ed. Tom Lloyd (n.p., 1971), 1.

17. Beuford Smith, interview by author, tape recording, Brooklyn, NY, March 1, 2001.

18. Ray Gibson, "Roy DeCarava: Master Photographer," *Black Creation* 4: 2 (Fall 1972), 36.

19. Galassi, *Roy DeCarava*, 32.

20. Smith, interview by author.

21. Karenga, *The Quotable Karenga*, 3.

22. Many of the Kamoinge members had firsthand experience with the shortcomings of freelance photography both in terms of the limited number of available jobs and the compromises demanded by them. Wanting to work without the constraints of the print mass media or commercial photography, the members positioned their production in the realm of fine art, and they used their meetings as a forum for debating the aesthetic merits of each other's prints as well as the advantages of approaching their subject matter through such formal means such as realism and abstraction.

23. The Kamoinge Workshop's "Harlem" portfolio consists of twenty-eight images made by members Louis Draper, Ernest Dunkley, James Mannas, Herbert Randall, Beuford Smith, Shawn Walker, and Calvin Wilson. In addition to the Kamoinge portfolio, the issue also contains a portfolio by Pepi Merisio of the Italian rustic mountain village Valtellina, one by Jean Mohr on the Wisconsin Amish, and one by Leonard Freed on a celebration of Purim in Jerusalem.

24. Allan Porter, Introduction, *Camera* (July 1966): 3.

25. In August of 1936, writer James Agee and photographer Walker Evans, on assignment for *Fortune*, spent one month chronicling the lives of three families of impoverished, cotton-growing tenant farmers in Hale County, Alabama. Rejected by *Fortune* but eventually published in 1941 by Houghton Mifflin as a book titled *Let Us Now Praise Famous Men*, the first edition met limited success, selling only 1,025 copies. Reissued in 1960, with twice as many photographs, the second edition achieved instant critical acclaim and became one of the most read books of the Civil Rights Movement. For an additional discussion of the differences between these two editions, see William Stott, *Documentary Expression and Thirties America* (Chicago: University of Chicago Press, 1973), 278–89.

26. A discussion of the differences between Walker Evans' and Margaret Bourke-White's photographic approaches is found in Stott, *Documentary Expression*, 222–23 and 270–71.

27. For a discussion of the function of beauty in Walker Evans' photographs in *Let Us Now Praise Famous Men*, see Stott, *Documentary Expression*, 267–89 and Margaret Olin's discussion of the relationship between beauty and the gaze, in her "'It is not going to be easy to look into their eyes': Privilege of Perception in *Let Us Now Praise Famous Men*," *Art History* 14 (March 1991): 92–115.

28. Stott, *Documentary Expression*, 272.

29. Larry Neal, "The Black Arts Movement," in *The Black Aesthetic*, 273.

30. Louis Draper, telephone conversation with author, October 29, 2001. Draper later titled this photograph *John Henry* after the African American folk hero.

31. Stott, *Documentary Expression*, 269.

32. Ron Karenga, "Black Cultural Nationalism," in *The Black Aesthetic*, 32.

33. Although Smith did not know this girl personally, her white doll caught Smith's attention. Smith explains, "I would not have photographed the girl if she had not had the white doll. To this day I can count on one hand the little white girls that I've seen with black dolls" (Smith, email with author, August 12, 2002).

34. Davidson took this picture in 1962 on the porch of a company housing in a mining area of West Virginia as part of his "Negro American" or "Black American" photographic project. Supported in part by a John Simon Guggenheim Memorial Foundation fellowship to document "Youth in America," Davidson spent roughly four years producing images for this project, most of which depict aspects of the Civil Rights Movement, both those that attracted international attention as well as smaller ones otherwise overlooked by the media. The most comprehensive grouping of Davidson's "Negro American" photographs is found in Bruce Davidson, *Time of Change: Bruce Davidson Civil Rights Photographs 1961–1965* (Los Angeles: St. Ann's Press, 2002).

35. Herbert Randall, quoted in *The Black Photographers Annual 1973*, vol. 1 (New York: Black Photographers Annual Inc., 1972), 133.

36. Members of the Kamoinge Workshop do not agree on the circumstances behind the *Camera* magazine portfolio. For instance, Louis Draper claims that Romeo Martinez, the former editor of *Camera*, invited the Kamoinge members to participate after seeing photographs at one of their meetings. Beuford Smith remembers the invitation as resulting from Roy DeCarava's connections with Martinez. The relationship between Martinez and Allan Porter, who took over as editor of *Camera* in 1965, is also unclear, and there is some speculation that Henri Cartier-Bresson, who also visited the Kamoinge Workshop's Gallery in Harlem, convinced Martinez to publish the portfolio. See Draper, "The Kamoinge Workshop," 6; Kamoinge, Inc. The Photographers Group, "Kamoinge History," (Organizational Brochure, 1999–2000, photocopy), 2; and Smith, interview by author.

37. "Harlem: A State of Mind," *Camera* (July 1966): 25.

38. Porter, "Harlem," *Camera* (July 1966): 25.

39. The exhibitions included *Theme Black* (March 15-April 19, 1964) and *The Negro Woman* (June 6-July 4, 1965). Visitors to the gallery included a racially diverse group: South African photojournalist Peter Magubane, Student Nonviolent Coordinating Committee (SNCC) photojournalist Tamio Wakayama, playwright George Bass, curator John Szarkowski, poet and playwright Langston Hughes, photojournalist Henri Cartier-Bresson, and *Camera* magazine editor Romeo Martinez, among others. The gallery closed at the end of the second exhibition. The members do not agree on the circumstances surrounding the closure; however, a number of them have noted that several photographs exhibited in *The Negro Woman* generated controversy both within the group and the Harlem community. See Beuford Smith, "Beuford Smith: In the Humane Tradition," interview by Van Wilmer, *Ten.8*, 24 (1987): 26–33 and Smith, interview by author.

40. Smith took a number of photographs of the National Memorial African Bookstore, including ones inside the bookstore depicting Lewis Michaux, Malcolm X, Max Roach, and Adam Clayton Powell, Jr. See Beuford Smith, email with author.

41. Here I am referring to the manner in which the editors of magazines and newspapers assume that the relationship between photographs and their referents is transparent. For a discussion of this paradox, see Roland Barthes, "The Photographic Message," in *Image, Music, Text*, trans. Stephen Heath (New York: Farrar, Straus and Giroux, 1977).

42. Smith discusses his desire to involve the viewer implicitly in his work in Beuford Smith, interview by Lou Draper, in *Artist and Influence*, vol. 18, ed. James V. Hatch, Leo Hamilton, and Judy Blum (New York: Hatch-Billops Collection, Inc., 1999), 163–64.

43. Robert Sengstacke, quoted in Deborah Willis-Thomas, *An Illustrated Bio-Bibliography of Black Photographers, 1940–1988* (New York: Garland Publishing, 1989), 125.

44. Smith, interview by author.

45. Smith, interview by Lou Draper, in *Artist and Influence*, 164.

10

Moneta Sleet, Jr. as Active Participant

The Selma March and the Black Arts Movement

Cherise Smith

Taken by Moneta Sleet, Jr. on March 25, 1965, the image of Dr. and Mrs. King leading marchers in Montgomery, Alabama, on the cover of the May 1965 volume of *Ebony* documents the completion of the Selma to Montgomery March after two failed attempts.[1] At the front of the procession and the center of the image, Martin Luther King, Jr. is pictured mid-stride and mid-song, flanked by Coretta Scott King to his left and Ralph Bunche, under-secretary to the United Nations, to his right. Looking determined, Rosa Parks, and Ralph and Juanita Abernathy are positioned to the right of Bunche.[2] Although each of the leaders is dressed in a smart suit, their mud-covered casual shoes communicate the arduous fifty-four mile journey they had just completed. Sleet focused attention on King and company through the single point perspective created by the foreshortened asphalt in the foreground and the receding, directional lines formed by the buildings and signs along the street. With locked arms and hands, the leaders appear to be a single unit and larger than life in stature. The supporters in the background are out of focus and blurred, their expressionistic faces and diminished scale reading as a mass that extends backward indefinitely.

As the cover image of the magazine, Sleet's photograph functioned as a symbol of the triumphant nature of the march, and, along with the superimposed, bold-faced and capitalized footer reading, "50,000 March on Montgomery," it announced the twenty-one-page photographic essay inside the volume.[3] Moreover, the choice of the preposition "on," instead of "in" or "to," in the title is poignant and telling. It is a militant declaration: 50,000 supporters of the civil liberties of African Americans marched *on* Montgomery, the capital of Alabama which was understood by the magazine's readership to be "the cradle of the Confederacy" and "the land of the bomb and the bullet...where tiny children are not safe even when attending Sunday School."[4]

A historic relic of the Black Freedom struggle, the image also provides a useful entry point to discuss the photographer Moneta Sleet, Jr. Instead of assuming the "passive" position of objective observer, Sleet acted as an active participant. He fought for African American equality on several fronts simultaneously: he participated in demonstrations, created aesthetically and socially powerful photographs, and distributed them nationally through his employment with *Ebony* magazine. My goal is to give form to Sleet's artistic vision by interpreting his portrayal of the 1965 Selma March in his 1970 exhibition at the St. Louis Art Museum. I will discuss Sleet's complicated relationship to his employer, *Ebony* magazine, highlighting how differently the photographer and the editors depicted the same event.[5] Finally, I will suggest that it is valuable to compare Sleet's aversion to the complacency *Ebony* sponsored and his commitment to the tenets promoted by Black Arts Movement members. He, too, contributed to the artistic and historic milieu of the late 1960s and early 1970s by producing many powerful images that served as social catalysts and artistic precedents.

SLEET AND *EBONY*

In 1955, when Sleet became a staff photographer for the large-format feature and news picture magazine *Ebony*, he had been a journalist for a number of years, honing his political affiliations and photo-documentary sensibilities while working for the black publications *Our World* and *Amsterdam News*. *Ebony*, the flagship of the Johnson Publishing Company magazines, was different, however, because of its large national distribution. *Ebony* featured articles—on world and national events, race relations, and celebrities—that the editors deemed relevant and important to black Americans, and it continues to maintain a high circulation.[6] During the 1950s and 1960s, the magazine, along with its sister publications *Negro Digest* and *Jet*, played an important role in the Black Freedom struggle because it offered news and information at an affordable price and distributed it nationally.[7] The regularly circulated publications encouraged a broader sense of community by providing updates on events that may have seemed distant or isolated to many African Americans.

The images of the Civil Rights Movement that Moneta Sleet, Jr. took for *Ebony* garnered support from its readers and helped mobilize them to act. For instance, when the magazine covered the Montgomery Bus Boycott in 1956, Sleet's photographs put faces to the names Rosa Parks and Martin Luther King, Jr. It was Sleet's pictures from the March on Washington D.C. (1963) that conveyed most effectively the historic nature of the event and record-number of attendants. Similarly, the images that Sleet took at Martin Luther King, Jr.'s funeral, in 1968, have reached the status of icon, burned into the collective memory of Americans. Sleet's advocate-style photography provided evidence and support and allowed readers to see themselves as participating in a greater national, and even international, process of liberation.[8] Indeed, Sleet's photographs in *Ebony* articles dictated how African Americans understood the movement itself.

Sleet preferred to forward the cause of black Americans and the Black Freedom struggle through his photographs in an engaged, direct way. In 1992, he explained: "My basic feeling . . . was . . . [that] I was observing . . . and trying to record, but I also felt a part of it because I'm black, and it was one way I could pay my dues."[9] "My contribution," he continued, "was to record and pass on, to whoever might see, what was happening."[10] He felt that *Ebony* was a supportive vehicle through which he could communicate his commitment to African American equality and his own cultural heritage. The photographer also agreed with the magazine's mission statement: "In a world of despair we wanted to give hope. In a world of negative Black images, we wanted to provide positive Black images. In a world that said Blacks could do few things, we wanted to say they could do anything."[11]

In March of 1965, Sleet was sent, along with a staff writer and several photographers, to Alabama to cover the Selma voter registration drive and demonstration.[12] Sleet and the rest of the Johnson Publishing Company team recorded various aspects of the event from walking demonstrators to the setting-up of campsites and all activities in between.[13] Authored by Simeon Booker and edited by Herb Nipson, the resultant article, "50,000 March on Montgomery," followed the sequence of the protest with pictures. The story was illustrated largely with Sleet's photographs, with forty-two of the ninety-five images taken by the photographer, demonstrating that the editorial staff considered his images appropriate to their vision. Rather than functioning in an exclusively news-providing capacity, the lavishly illustrated, twenty-one-page essay seems to have been conceived as a memorial in nature and function.[14]

The sole article on the Selma March presented in *Ebony*, "50,000 March on Montgomery"[15] was published one month after the successful completion of the demonstration. The editorial staff told the entire history of the voter registration drive, including the two failed attempts at marching. The logistics of the demonstration were described, including the weather conditions, the military presence, and overnight and meal accommodations. Protestors were portrayed as model American citizens who maintained their cleanliness, remained fashionable, and upheld sexual propriety.[16] The economic, cultural, racial, and religious diversity of the demonstrators was also emphasized.

Overall, the march was characterized as victorious, but *Ebony* represented its ideological platform as ambivalent, swinging between militant and conformist. The editorial staff made a deliberate decision, for instance, to acknowledge but not sensationalize the deaths related to the march. In that way, the magazine provided the appearance of calm in a time of growing unrest and discontent. However, it did not succumb to mainstream publications'—*Newsweek* and *Life*, for example—tendency to characterize all demonstrations as chaotic. Furthermore, the magazine, as represented by "50,000 March on Montgomery," subverted the status quo by presenting views of masses of people who would not tolerate legalized segregation and disenfranchisement.

In spite of Sleet's commitment to the Black Freedom struggle and the magazine, he had no say in which of his of photographs were used in "50,000 March on Montgomery," nor in their manner of display. As a staff photographer based in New York, Sleet was miles away from Johnson Publishing Company headquarters in Chicago and from influencing the design of the photographic essay. He could not change the fact that the editors employed a considerable amount of text, in the form of paragraphs and captions, which functioned to control the reading of the images. Sleet could not break rank with the editors, telling them that they sacrificed aesthetic concerns for narrative flow by choosing photographs that, for the most part, were easily understood and not formally compelling.

SLEET'S REPRESENTATION OF THE SELMA MARCH

Taken four years after the Selma March was completed, Sleet's well-known photograph (fig. 10.1), featuring Bernice King leaning into the lap of her mother at the memorial service of Martin Luther King, Jr., made Sleet the first African American man to win the coveted Pulitzer Prize in Feature Photography in 1969. The image is compelling because Sleet framed the Kings with a tight focus, leaving the other funeral attendants slightly blurred. The framing, combined with the right-angled point of the pew arm, make Bernice and Coretta Scott King the focal point. By placing the widow and child close to the picture plane, the photographer directs the viewer's attention, demanding empathy with the King family's grief.

Mistakenly, the image of the two Kings was sent out on the Associated Press wire, instead of being sent to the Johnson Publishing Company headquarters, landing it on the front page of national newspapers and qualifying it for the Pulitzer Prize.[17] The twist of fate that made the photograph eligible for the award led to another. Sleet's winning the Pulitzer Prize encouraged the St. Louis chapter of Alpha Kappa Alpha sorority to pressure the St. Louis Art Museum to mount an exhibit of the photographer's work in 1970 (fig. 10.2). The resultant exhibition, *Moneta Sleet: Photographer*, afforded Sleet the unique opportunity to flex his artistic muscles and demonstrate his artistic vision, separate from Johnson Publishing Company and *Ebony* magazine. Sleet's selection of which Civil Rights Movement photographs to include in the St. Louis Art Museum exhibition begs to be studied through the lens of the Black Arts Movement.

When given the chance, Sleet revised the depiction of the demonstration by including images that he felt were both aesthetically and symbolically meaningful. On display from May 15 through June 21, 1970, the exhibit, *Moneta Sleet: Photographer*, featured more than one hundred photographs that were eventually donated to the museum.[18] Of that number, eighteen were dedicated to the Selma March, though other subjects, including portraits of politicians and celebrities, street photography, and African independence celebrations among others, were displayed. Sleet eliminated thirty-six images that appeared in the *Ebony* article, "50,000 March on Montgomery." In other words, Sleet chose only six out of

Fig. 10.1. Moneta Sleet, Jr., Coretta Scott King and daughter Bernice at the April 9, 1968 funeral of Martin Luther King, Jr. Courtesy AP/Wide World Photos.

the forty-two images published in the magazine to represent the Selma March in his mid-career retrospective. Clearly, his interpretation of the march differed dramatically from that of the magazine.

A significant expression of his artistic subjectivity, Sleet's mid-career retrospective allowed him to do what he normally could not: control the presentation of his work. Sleet acted as both featured artist and artistic director. He chose which of his photographs to display, managed the printing, and altered some of the images to ensure dramatic compositions. For example, though he shot the Selma March with both black-and-white and color film, he decided that the prints should be black-and-white, the print type most commonly associated with "art." Modeling his presentation on earlier precedents, Sleet enlarged the majority of the prints to sizes that were more like the dimensions of paintings than photographs.[19] Overall, the show demonstrated a significant aspect of his approach to photography. "I just work with it until I think it feels right. I just observe a situation and photograph it the moment it all comes together from my point of view. Bringing it together with my instinct and feeling and my own feeling of form."[20]

Fig. 10.2. Installation shot of *Moneta Sleet: Photographer* at the St. Louis Art Museum, 1970. Courtesy of the St. Louis Art Museum.

His claim that "the type of photography I do is one of advocacy" is also apparent in the exhibit.[21] In his close-up image of three protestors, for instance, Sleet portrayed a cross-section of the participants, emphasizing the fact that civil rights supporters included people of different ethnicities and economic circumstances (fig. 10.3). On the right is a striking white woman whose dress and manicured appearance indicate some measure of wealth. A white man with styled goatee and tailored clothes appears in the top of the frame. Occupying the left of the composition is a black man wearing a misshapen felt hat and the dungaree overalls that came to be regarded as the unofficial uniform of civil rights workers. The swollen joints of his wrinkled hand identify him as a laborer or farmer. The triangular composition of this image encourages the viewer to move from subject to subject rather than settling at a single point. In contrast, this compelling photograph is lost in a sea of images in the *Ebony* photo-essay. Sleet's decision to enlarge the picture and allow it to stand on its own submerges the individual identities of these protestors in such a way that they become representative types, surrogates for the many others who participated in the demonstration.

A striking image of "whiteface" in another work in this series presents a youth staring directly into the camera in an intense manner, while his companion looks back over his shoulder with a confrontational expression (fig. 10.4). Each of the young men wears heavy sunscreen with the word "vote" inscribed onto their foreheads, signaling the major goal of the demonstration. The contrast between the white zinc oxide and the darkness of their skin makes the youth appear ghostly. This imaging of "whiteface" dramatizes the racial politics of the march.

Fig. 10.3. Moneta Sleet, Jr., Three protestors, from *Moneta Sleet: Photographer* exhibition. Courtesy of the St. Louis Art Museum.

The photographer's picture of marchers with United States and United Nations flags was also included in both the photographic essay and the exhibition (fig. 10.5). The picture focuses on a middle-aged white woman walking with her right arm locked in the arm of a young African American man who carries the United States flag and wears a stern expression. Her left hand clutches the arm of another black youth, who carries the United Nations flag and holds his head low. A sense of motion is created by Sleet's use of a slow shutter speed, which freezes the marchers in the middle of their steps and blurs the asphalt beneath their feet. Symbolic in its depiction of forward-motion, this image communicates the artist's interest in racial equality and demonstrates his awareness of the international implications of the freedom struggle.

Sleet's photograph of a demonstrator's calloused and bandaged feet stands as a testament to the physical rigor of the March and the determination of the marchers (fig. 10.6). The hand and feet in the outer edges of the picture frame, along with the vertical lines of the man's pants, draw attention to the marcher who stands with his feet rolled outward, as if his soles hurt. In the *Ebony* layout, the same photograph was confined to function as mere illustration, but in Sleet's exhibition, it can be appreciated for its abstraction, demonstrated in the pattern effect of the asphalt and printed fabric and in the play of light and dark.

Separated from the constrictions of the magazine, Sleet was better able to display the support and gratitude of local black Alabama citizens in three

images (figs. 10.7, 10.8, 10.9) instead of the one that appears in *Ebony*. He pictured an elderly man standing on the side of a road, welcoming marchers who walk past on the left. The man occupies the foreground, while the supporters form a diagonal line that extends deep into the right of the frame. Intended to convey a sense of motion, sequential images, such as these, were generally employed to display violence against blacks.[22] Sleet's suite of images, however, produces a resounding crescendo by showing the man first with one arm raised, then both, and finally clapping.

The photographer's goal was not to show the details of the Selma March. Rather, Sleet felt he had "to communicate . . . tell stories."[23] "I have to do it in a way that the viewer looks at it and gets an emotional response."[24] In his portrayal of the Selma March, he did exactly that. Sleet made a visual narrative out of his subjective feelings and experiences of the demonstration, then he forced viewers to respond. When Sleet said, "I hope that empathy with my subjects comes across. That's what I strive for," we could respond with one of his overly humble expressions: he was "reasonably successful."[25]

SLEET AND THE BLACK ARTS MOVEMENT

Raised by college-educated parents in segregated, rural Kentucky, Moneta Sleet, Jr. was instilled with a high regard for education and a deep respect for his racial heritage. The man loved to take pictures: growing up he was his family's

Fig. 10.5. Moneta Sleet, Jr. Marchers with flags, from *Moneta Sleet: Photographer.* Courtesy of the St. Louis Art Museum.

photographer, he was the photographer of his college campus, and later he founded the photography department at Maryland State College. In 1947, Sleet decided that he wanted photography to be his career. He moved to New York where he enrolled at New York University and received a Master's degree in Journalism in 1950. Later that same year, Sleet renewed his commitment to black people by following in the footsteps of other African American photographers, such as Morgan and Marvin Smith and Gordon Parks, and taking his first journalistic job with New York's *Amsterdam News*, a black periodical. Then, Sleet joined the staff of the black-owned and operated large-format picture magazine *Our World*.[26] At *Our World*, the photographer began to understand the complexities and narrative possibilities of the picture essay, brainstorming with editors about possible shooting scenarios that would enable him to communicate emotions and events effectively through his images.

Learning to photograph during the height of the documentary genre, Moneta Sleet, Jr. was aware of the social and political commentary of images and photo-essays. In addition to working with seasoned editors, Sleet studied the work of other social documentary photographers, including Henri Cartier-Bresson, Gordon Parks, and W. Eugene Smith, in order to understand how to

blend social activism and formal elements successfully. Humble in regard to his work, Sleet considered himself a photojournalist rather than an artist.[27] His artistry,[28] however, is apparent not only in his talent for composing compelling photographs that blend content and emotion, but also in his frank admission of subjectivity: "The type of photography I do is one of showing from my point of view."[29] In his photographs, one sees a deep respect for all people, especially those of African descent. Though Sleet's photographs speak to a broad section of the population, the aesthetic is uniquely African American: "I'm dealing from a black experience. I make no apologies for that."[30]

Sleet's process of selecting images for the 1970 exhibition was conscious and deliberate, especially when viewed in the context of his commitment to the Black Freedom struggle. Though he considered himself a social documentarian and not an artist, the photographer created an aesthetic, subjective, and activist vision of the protest.[31] Sleet's selection of Selma March photographs is characterized by equal parts of activism, celebration, aestheticism, heroism, and the manifestation of an overt political affiliation with his blackness—attributes that were promoted by theoreticians of the black aesthetic.

The philosophy scaffolding the Black Arts Movement, the black aesthetic, was theorized as art by black people for black people; its function was to transform black audiences.[32] Occurring roughly from about 1960 to 1975, the Black Arts Movement, like the Harlem Renaissance, was a blossoming of art made by black people.[33] Parallel to the social and cultural activism of Black Power, the Black Arts Movement is characterized by a nationalistic interest in blackness.

Figs. 10.7, 10.8, 10.9.
Moneta Sleet, Jr.,
Elderly man, I-III, from
Moneta Sleet:
Photographer. Cour-
tesy of the St. Louis
Art Museum.

Larry Neal wrote that artists of the Black Arts Movement needed to "speak to the spiritual and cultural needs of Black people."[34] He explained that art and action are the same, saying, "the Black Arts Movement believes that your ethics and your aesthetics are one."[35] Other figures in the movement weighed in on the topic. Ron Karenga, the Black Arts activist and Kwanzaa-founder, asserted that "black art initiates, supports, and promotes change."[36] Cultural worker James Stewart claimed that "the artist is a man in society, and his social attitudes are just as relevant to his art as his aesthetic position."[37]

Moneta Sleet, Jr. was one of a large number of black visual artists working during this period. Though Sleet is not often recognized as a Black Arts Movement photographer, he was aware of both the notion of the black aesthetic and the nationalistic writings and attitudes of the movement, largely through the black press, particularly through the magazine *Negro Digest* (which was renamed *Black World* in 1970).[38] In the spirit of the Black Arts Movement, he, too, blended activism and aesthetics and sought to communicate on a mass scale to his audience.

Through his affiliation with *Ebony* and the Johnson Publishing Company, Sleet responded to the Black Arts Movement by tapping into mass distribution. As Houston Baker states in his introduction to the Black Arts Movement section of *The Norton Anthology of African American Literature*, "the Black Arts Movement was, indisputably, committed to a goal of black mass communication."[39] The magazine's circulation statistics demonstrate that his images enjoyed a large viewing audience. In fact, in 1965, the year of the Selma March, his photographs were seen by at least one million people.[40] Similarly, Sleet's photographs from the independence celebrations of Ghana (1957), Nigeria (1961), and Kenya (1963), among other significant international and national events he covered, appeared in Johnson Publishing Company magazines and informed viewers about the African struggle against domination.

One of the more than one million viewers that Sleet's photographs reached was Reginald Gammon, African American artist and member of the New York City-based Spiral group. Indeed, Gammon was so moved by the work that he modeled an expressionistic painting (fig. 10.10) after one of the photographer's pictures of a crowd at the March on Washington.[41] Painted in 1965, *Freedom Now* is a close-up representation of a cross-section of the crowd: all feet, signs, and disembodied faces. The grisaille painting references the original black and white of Sleet's photograph, but Gammon tweaked it. Like Andy Warhol, Roy Lichtenstein, and other Pop artists of the period, Gammon took a piece of popular culture and abstracted it. Unlike his Pop counterparts who appropriated images from the popular media as a way to critique American consumer culture and divest it of meaning, however, Gammon appropriated Sleet's photograph in order to invest more meaning in it and encourage viewers to act. No longer read as individual identities, the abstracted faces become surrogates for the masses of people who demonstrated for their rights.

Because of his political affiliations and aesthetic choices, Sleet's Selma March photographs should not be classified as merely narrative or documentary in nature. Formally compelling, the images communicate the essence of the event because they illustrate the commitment of both the supporters and the photographer to the cause of equality. They must be seen as an attempt, on the part of the photographer, to revise the manner of communication in which his

Fig. 10.10. Reginald Gammon, *Freedom Now,* 1965. Courtesy of the artist.

photos were employed and to establish himself in the artistic arena. Sleet did nothing less than reassign his personal ideology to his own images. His primary goal was to depict the strength, courage, and dignity of African American people. Sleet's photographs show that he was concerned with both creating the aesthetic value of the work and conveying his own emotional and spiritual response to the Selma March.

Moneta Sleet's representation of the Selma March stands in stark contrast to *Ebony*'s portrayal of the event. The ideological program put forth in the photo-essay "50,000 March on Montgomery" is characterized by ambivalence. The magazine sought to instill in readers a conservative and patriotic ideology, while also encouraging readers not to be content with the racist status quo and to support the Civil Rights Movement. Sleet, however, was informed by the black aesthetic and, in the spirit of the Black Arts Movement, advocated spiritual strength, civil equality, cultural expression, and independence for African Americans. He, like other artists, students, and activists of the time, was aware of the fact that ideology was functional: he could use it, or have it used against him. Sleet seized it, attempting to secure a visual space for African Americans in which they would not be subjected to the dominant ideology.

NOTES

1. I would like to thank my colleagues at the Research Institute for Comparative Studies in Race and Ethnicity (RICSRE) at Stanford University and the W.E.B. Du Bois Institute for Afro-American Research at Harvard University for their intellectual engagement of this project. I also appreciate the support of Amy Mooney, Gwendolyn DuBois Shaw, and Geoffrey Sorrick. The Johnson Publishing Company holds the copyright to the majority of images taken by Moneta Sleet, Jr., because he was a staff photographer. For this publication, I sought the right to reproduce eighteen photographs he took during the Selma March as well as several pages from *Ebony* magazine. Johnson Publishing Company denied permission. Due to those unfortunate circumstances, I refer readers to their book, *Special Moments in African-American History: 1955–1996. The Photographs of Moneta Sleet, Jr. Ebony Magazine's Pulitzer Prize Winner*, (Chicago: Johnson Publishing Company, 1998).

2. Ralph Abernathy was a civil rights leader and aide to Martin Luther King, Jr.

3. Simeon Booker, "50,000 March on Montgomery," *Ebony* 20 (May 1965): 46–86.

4. The first quote refers to the fact that the South called itself "the Confederacy" during the Civil War. The Confederate flag and the Confederacy remain symbols of Southern support of segregation, racism, and violence. Ibid., 85. The second refers, of course, to the tragic 1963 incident when four black girls were killed when a bomb exploded in their Birmingham, Alabama, church. "Backstage," *Ebony* 20: 7 (May 1965): 22.

5. The Johnson Publishing Company began publishing *Ebony* in 1945. Like *Our World*, *Ebony* was modeled after *Life*. Like *Life*, *Ebony* is no longer published in large format. The dimensions of both magazines are now those of the standard sheet of paper, 8 x 11 inches.

6. According to the Publisher's Statement reported to the Audit Bureau of Circulation, the total average paid circulation for the magazine from January 1 to June 29, 1995, was 1,985,558; the total circulation from June 30 through December 31, 1995, was 1,927,675.

7. *Negro Digest* began publication in 1942, and in 1970, it became *Black World*. Modeled after *Quick* and *Reader's Digest*, the magazine featured articles and creative writing and was a major venue for Black Arts Movement writing. It ceased publication in 1976. *Jet* began in 1951 and is a pocket-sized, newsmagazine that Johnson Publishing Company circulates weekly. *Tan/Black Stars*, *Copper Romance*, and *Hue* are other Johnson Publishing Company magazines that are no longer published. *Ebony* was the first African American magazine to be distributed nationally. From January 1 through June 30, 1965, the total paid circulation was 757,228, and from July 1 through December 31, 1965, the total paid circulation was 872,555. In 1965, the prices for *Ebony* and *Jet* were $.50 and $.20, respectively.

8. Sleet used the word "advocacy" to describe the type of photography he practiced. "World of Photography," Brockway Broadcasting Corporation (1986). The photographer was present at the independence celebrations of many newly liberated African nations, including Ghana (1957), Nigeria (1961), Kenya (1963), and South Africa (1994), among others.

9. Interview with Moneta Sleet, Jr., 1992.

10. Ibid.

11. John Johnson, *Ebony* 48 (November 1992): 31. That statement was made by owner and editor in chief, John Johnson and underlines his desire to allow African Americans to see themselves as participating in the American middle class. The statement also communicates his understanding of the print media as an important ideological force by which subjectivity is determined. His mission statement is inflected with the same rhetoric that publisher Henry Luce employed in his prospectus for *Life*: "To see life; to see the world; to eyewitness great events; to watch the faces of the poor and gestures of the proud; to see strange things—machines, armies, multitudes, shadows in the jungle and on the moon; to see man's work; to see things thousands of miles away, things hidden behind walls an within rooms, things dangerous to come to; the women that men love and many children; to see and take pleasure in seeing; to see and be amazed; to see and be instructed." From Phillip B. Kunhardt, ed., *Life: The First Fifty Years 1936–1986* (New York: Time-Life Books, 1986), 5.

12. In some instances, an *Ebony* team would be sent to an event with a pre-planned story, for which writers and photographers were expected to find support. In this case, the Selma March was documented as it unfolded due to the two earlier unsuccessful attempts at completion. Interview with Herb Nipson, 1996.

13. Interview with Moneta Sleet, Jr., 1992.

14. It is likely that other factors, including other news media, may have influenced the presentation of the *Ebony* essay. For instance, the Johnson editorial staff may have realized that, in addition to their own weekly publication, *Jet*, other magazines with weekly distribution schedules, such as *Life*, provided more timely presentations of the event. Furthermore, the demonstrations were televised on the broadcast news. In August of 1965, 92 percent of American households had television sets. It is safe to assume, then, that most of the population was informed of the news of the Selma March very soon after it took place. From *Statistical Abstract of the United States, 1967* (Washington, D.C.: U.S. Department of Commerce, 1967).

15. It is significant to note that short, weekly updates on the Selma March were published in *Jet* magazine. In a five-week period, from March 25 to May 1, 1965, Johnson Publishing Company printed twenty articles totaling seventy-seven pages on the demonstration in the sister magazines.

16. The captions that accompanied the photographs contain information that addressed these topics. For instance, one caption read, "Stepping spryly, young marchers dressed more for comfort than looks yet managed to look attractive," and another read " . . .At every night's stop, separate tents were erected for men and women." Booker, "50,000 March on Montgomery," 83.

17. Interview with Moneta Sleet, Jr., 1992.

18. Sleet and the Johnson Publishing Company donated the prints to the St. Louis Art Museum in 1991.

19. The prints range from 9 1/2 × 13 3/4 inches to 19 × 14 inches.

20. Interview with Moneta Sleet, Jr., 1992.

21. Ibid.

22. See "Selma: Beatings Start the Savage Season," *Life* 58 (March 19, 1965): 30–37.

23. Interview with Moneta Sleet, Jr., 1992.

24. Ibid.

25. Ibid.

26. *Our World* was fashioned after *Life* magazine, but is no longer published.

27. When asked what, in his opinion, made a strong photograph, Sleet answered, "when you look at it and the message is immediately conveyed . . . and they [viewers] are moved by it, for me as a photojournalist, I feel I am reasonably successful. As a photojournalist, I have to communicate. That's my job." Interview with Moneta Sleet, Jr., 1992.

28. Sleet's photographic work has been admired both journalistically and artistically, as exemplified in the number of exhibitions in which it has been featured. In 1960, Sleet's work was featured in the group exhibition, "Photography in the Fine Arts, II," at the Metropolitan Museum of Art. During the summer of 1970, the St. Louis Art Museum presented the exhibit, "Moneta Sleet, Jr.: Photographer," which focused on the Pulitzer Prize photograph. In 1974, he was featured in the group exhibit, "Black Photographers," at Chicago's Southside Community Arts Center, and later, his work was showcased in a one-man show prepared by the New York Pubic Library (1986), and in several other group exhibits, including "Tradition and Conflict: Images of a Turbulent Decade 1963–1973" at The Studio Museum in Harlem (1985); "The Black Photographer: An American View" at the Chicago Public Library (1985); "A Century of Black Photographers, 1840–1940" at the Rhode Island School of Design (1989); and "Black Photographers Bear Witness," at the Williams College Art Museum (1989). In addition, Sleet is represented in several publications including *An Illustrated Bio-Bibliography of Black Photographers, 1940–1988* (1988), *Moments: The Pulitzer Prize Photographs* (1978), and *Eyes of Time: Photojournalism in America* (1988); the latter two focus on the Pulitzer Prize image with little discussion of the photographer or any of his other work. More recently, his work was featured in the exhibitions, "My Point of View: Photographs by Moneta Sleet, Jr." at the St. Louis Art Museum (1993) and "Picturing the South" at the High Museum of Art (1996). Sleet continued to photograph for *Ebony* magazine until his death in October 1996.

29. Interview with Moneta Sleet, Jr., 1992.

30. Ibid.

31. Ibid.

32. See Addison Gayle, Jr., *The Black Aesthetic* (New York: Doubleday and Company, 1971).

33. The dates of the Black Arts Movement vary widely, depending on the source. Houston A. Baker provides the dates 1960–1970 in Henry Louis Gates, Jr. and Nellie Y. McKay, eds., *The Norton Anthology of African American Literature*, (New York: W.W. Norton and Company, 1997). Others link the dates to LeRoi Jones: his name change to Amiri Baraka in 1967 marking the beginning and his alienation from Black nationalism in 1974 marking the end. Notwithstanding Baraka's seminal role in the Black Arts Movement, I support a more inclusive and open-ended framework. For example, artists such as Jeff Donaldson and Joe Overstreet were making militant works before Baraka's name change, and many artists continue to adhere to the philosophy of the black aesthetic, decades after Baraka changed his position on Black nationalism.

34. Larry Neal, "The Black Arts Movement," in *The Norton Anthology of African American Literature*, 1960.

35. Ibid., 1962.

36. Ron Karenga, "On Black Art," in *Black Theater*, 9–10.

37. James Stewart, "The Development of the Black Revolutionary Artist," in *Black Fire: An Anthology of Afro-American Writings*, ed. LeRoi Jones and Larry Neal (New York: William Morrow & Company, 1968), 9.

38. Sleet had the opportunity to photograph fellow New Yorker Amiri Baraka (a.k.a. LeRoi Jones) on several occasions. In addition, the Johnson Publishing Company, for which Sleet worked, published the magazine *Negro Digest/Black World*, a major venue for Black Arts Movement texts. Because Sleet was a staff photographer for the Johnson Publishing Company, he most likely read *Negro Digest/Black World*. Therefore, he had to have been aware of Black Arts Movement ideology.

39. Houston A. Baker, "The Black Arts Movement," in *The Norton Anthology of African American Literature*, 1799.

40. From January 1 through June 30, 1965, the total paid circulation was 757,228, and from July 1 through December 31, 1965, the total paid circulation was 872,555. Many more people than that saw the magazines.

41. Sharon F. Patton, *African-American Art* (New York: Oxford University Press, 1998), 187, and conversation with the artist, March 2003.

11

"If Bessie Smith Had Killed Some White People"

Racial Legacies, the
Blues Revival, and the
Black Arts Movement

Adam Gussow

You've taken my blues and gone—
You sing 'em on Broadway
And you sing 'em in Hollywood Bowl,
And you mixed 'em up with symphonies
And you fixed 'em
So they don't sound like me.
Yep, you done taken my blues and gone...
— Langston Hughes, "Notes on Commercial Theatre," 1940

"Look like ah, what the Klan couldn't kill, look like we gonna let die for lack of love. Look like now we dont, we don't much listen to ourselves, you know what I mean. We don't really listen to ourselves any more, Mister Can't Sing Blues Black Man, be telling me the blues is 'bout submission, shuffling, and stuff too ugly to hang on yonder wall. But submission is silence, submission is *silence,* and silence is NOT my song!"
— Kalamu ya Salaam, "My Story, My Song," 1990

OUR STORY, OUR SONG

Jazz, not blues, is generally taken to be the soundtrack of the Black Arts Movement. Young jazz musicians of revolutionary temperament such as Archie Shepp, Sun Ra, and Albert Ayler—proponents of the so-called "New Thing"— played downtown fundraisers and uptown marches for Amiri Baraka's Black Arts Repertory Theater/School in the heady spring and summer of 1965, joining the newly established BARTS faculty as founding members. Black Arts poets reimagined John Coltrane as a secular saint, modeling their spoken-word performances on his keening, freedom-yearning, glossolalic saxophone style— what literary critic Kimberly Benston has termed "the Coltrane poem." This elegiac praise-song declaimed by griots as diverse as David Henderson, Haki Madhubuti, Sonia Sanchez, Jayne Cortez, A. B. Spellman, and Michael Harper stands as one of the movement's signal innovations and (*pace* Skip Gates) enduring achievements.[1] Yet blues, a politically more problematic but equally vital expressive legacy, turns out to have been a crucial instrument of racial and cultural self-definition for a surprisingly wide array of Black Arts writers and their academic fellow travelers, including Sanchez, Cortez, and Madhubuti, Amiri Baraka, Larry Neal, Ron Karenga, Stephen Henderson, Ben Caldwell, Eugene Redmond, Henry Dumas, Quincy Troupe, Al Young, Stanley Crouch, Nikki Giovanni, James Cone, Kalamu ya Salaam, Tom Dent, and a host of lesser-known writers published in *Negro Digest* and *Black World* and anthologies such as *Black Fire* (1968), *The New Black Poetry* (1969), and *The Black Aesthetic* (1971). To this list might be added writers and critics such as Toni Morrison, August Wilson, Sherley Anne Williams, Ishmael Reed, Sterling Plumpp, Alice Walker, Gayl Jones, Arthur Flowers, Angela Davis, Yusuf Komunyakaa, John Sinclair, Jon Michael Spencer, Kevin Young, Harryette Mullen, and Allison Joseph: contemporaries and inheritors of the Black Arts Movement whose work significantly engages with blues forms, blues themes, and the black ancestral "blues god" invoked by Larry Neal. Far from being the "shortest and least successful" movement in African American cultural history, as Henry Louis Gates, Jr. has provocatively claimed, the decade-long Black Arts Movement has had a broad and enduring impact on African American literature.[2] It has remade that literature as a blues-toned legacy—unabashedly invested in, and supremely conscious of, its own southern-born vernacular taproot, a jook-honed survivor's ethos of self-willed mobility, self-determined sexual personhood, and bittersweetly lyric self-inscription.

To the extent, however, that the Black Arts Movement envisioned a splitting-off of "Black Art" from white America and a purification of that separate sphere, it has proved to be a stunning failure—at least insofar as contemporary blues culture, a thoroughly whitened blues culture, is concerned. Although the so-called "chitlin' circuit" of juke joints, clubs, and concert venues lingers on in the modern South, supplying a small but loyal black audience with so-called "soul blues," the mainstream blues universe of festivals, nightclubs, bands, record labels, DJ's, blues societies, websites, and Internet discussion groups has grown in the past forty years from a coterie audience of folk blues fans into a multimillion dollar, worldwide enterprise: predominantly but not exclusively white-administered and white-attended except for a healthy salting of black blues musicians on the bandstands, a palpably non-African American thing. Blues are *white* culture these days: a way in which a certain kind of earthy, hip, antiracist whiteness (and a certain kind of geeky, volunteerist, middle-American whiteness) knows itself, and shares that knowledge with like-minded others—including, ideally, amenable black folk with certain specific musical inclinations. The irreversible onslaught of white blues fandom and musicianship is an incontrovertible fact, one that younger, politically conscious black blues performers such as Guy Davis and Corey Harris, paradoxically indebted to such audiences for their livelihoods, have noted with dismay.[3] In one branch of blues literature, too, the rising tide of blue-white integrationism is unmistakable. The 1990s saw a remarkable flowering of black blues autobiographies by Sammy Price, Mance Lipscomb, Willie Dixon, B. B. King, David Honeyboy Edwards, Yank Rachell, and Henry Townsend; in every case, black vernacular voices were shaped into print by white ghostwriters. The very existence of such autobiographies is partly a result of the long shadow cast by the folk-and-electric blues revival of the 1960s, which gave performers such as Lipscomb and King access to large new mainstream audiences, and partly a result of the traditionalist tenor of the contemporary scene, which venerates King, Edwards, and Townsend as "legends of the blues," sources of badly needed, Delta-born authenticity for a brave new blues world unsettled by its own uncannily overweening whiteness.

This world, grounded in the drama of cross-racial connoisseurship, had already become visible to black intellectuals as a cultural crisis in the early 1960s when Amiri Baraka, then LeRoi Jones, did his best to dynamite the rails down which the Down Home Blues Express was roaring into the hearts and minds of white America. "Old bald-headed four-eyed ofays popping their fingers," rages Clay in *Dutchman* (1964), tarring Lula by implication with the brush of white cluelessness to the inner life of black folk,

> and don't know yet what they're doing. They say, 'I love Bessie Smith.' And don't even understand that Bessie Smith is saying, 'Kiss my ass, kiss my black unruly ass.' Before love, suffering, desire, anything you can explain, she's saying, and very plainly, 'Kiss my black ass.' And if you don't know that, it's you that's doing the kissing .... If Bessie Smith had killed some white people she wouldn't have needed that music. She could have talked very straight and plain about the world. No metaphors.[4]

Where do we stand, forty years later? "Pack your bags & head to Memphis! for the Blues Foundation's BluesFirst," proclaimed the website for the nation's premier blues advocacy organization in the winter of 2002:

> The ONLY International Convention and Expo for Blues Societies, Fans, Musicians and Industry.... Learn Important Strategies for Successful

> Blues Retail
> Publicity
> Studio Recording
> Budget Preparation
> Newsletter Production
> Blues Radio
> Internet Marketing

Grant Writing
Blues in the Schools Programs
Plus a Special Information Panel by The BMA

Includes:
- 3 Days of Strategy-Packed Learning Opportunities to Make Your Blues Organization Succeed
- 3 Days of Fun, Friends and Blues Networking
- A VIP Pass to All the Clubs on Beale Street for the International Blues Challenge Competition

Plus admission to:
- Shake and Howdy Reception
- The Keeping the Blues Alive Awards Brunch
- Blues, Brews & BBQ Party
- The International Blues Challenge Competition.[5]

Bessie Smith would have to kill a whole mess of white people to make a dent in *this* particular blues world, and whether or not she "need[s] the music" has become a moot point: Marcia Ball, a redheaded Texas pianist and star on the contemporary circuit, is more than ready to cover the gig. Baraka's Lula has become a blues diva in the year 2003; Baraka's Clay still doesn't stand a chance against her—unless he picks up a guitar and starts moaning the blues, in which case the promoters will be happy to make him the headliner.

He'd better steer clear of hip hop, though. Young African American bluesman Chris Thomas King debuted songs such as "Welcome To Da Jungle" and "Mississippi KKKrossroads" during the 2001 "All Over Blues Tour" in support of his album, *Dirty South Hip-Hop Blues*, and found his almost entirely white audience fleeing in droves, booing. "I've found a lot of resistance in the United States," King told a reporter. "We've been banned from a lot of blues festivals."[6] What had attracted blues fans to King in the first place wasn't his sounding of the New, but his re-creation of the mojo-spooky—and safe—sound of 1930s Delta bluesman Tommy Johnson in the Coen brothers' unexpected hit, *O Brother, Where Art Thou* (2000). Raised with a Louisiana blues pedigree (his father, Tabby Thomas, was an Excello recording artist in the 1960s) but claiming the Sugar Hill Gang and Jimi Hendrix as his formative influences, the authenticity King brought to his film portrayal was in fact "authenticity," a simulacrum of the Real Blues signified by Tommy Johnson, Robert Johnson, and their devil-at-the-crossroads kin and a quality acutely hungered for by white blues aficionados. *Dirty South Hip-Hop Blues*, on the other hand, is the *real* Real Blues in all its unnerving, category-busting, down-home glory— although "blues" may not be quite the right word for this latest incarnation of the New Thing. Still, that audience antipathy raises a crucial question: If the white blues lovers don't cotton to King's one-man revolution, whom does he turn to? Whose griot *is* he at a time when older African Americans manifest much the same antipathy for the hip-hop nation as white blues fans, and when black radio and its youth market has long said goodbye to the blues?

BLACK POWER AND BLUES POWER

Ironies abound on the postmodern blues scene; one of the most poignant is evoked by Kalamu ya Salaam, Black Arts poet and historian, at the end of his pithy and provocative treatise, "the blues aesthetic" (1994). "[Why] and when," he laments, "did blues people stop liking the blues?"[7] Salaam's plaint about waning black interest in the quintessential black artform is not new; it is the "changing same" of *all* blues commentary, white and black, during the past four decades.[8] In its white incarnation it led to the founding of *Living Blues* magazine ("A Journal of the Black American Blues Tradition") by a group of white aficionados in 1970 and still animates white-run blues societies intent on "keeping the blues alive" by teaching "blues in the schools" to puzzled black children. In its black version the complaint echoed through the pages of *Ebony* in the integrationist late 1950s and early 1960s in articles with titles such as "Are Negroes Ashamed of the Blues?"[9] As the 1960s progressed and James Brown and Aretha became the rage, the complaint was picked up by black DJ's and blues musicians such as B. B. King, who watched helplessly as the black youth audience for blues melted away. "[O]n this particular night in this particular city," King remembered later of a soul show he'd played during the period, "the audience booed me bad. I cried. Never had been booed before. Didn't know what it felt like until the boos hit me in the face. Coming from my own people—especially coming from young people—made it worse."[10]

If by "liking the blues" one means "believing in the cultural value and political efficacy of the blues," then a significant number of Black Arts poets and theorists—the self-appointed intellectual vanguard of the blues people—stopped liking the blues around 1965, when LeRoi Jones broke faith with bohemian interracialism and took the A-Train from Greenwich Village up to Harlem. The Mississippi Freedom Summer and its Delta blues groundnote were swept out—integrationist! accommodationist!—as Black Power angrily swept in. Fanon's dismissal of the blues in *Towards the African Revolution* (1967)—a "black slave lament . . . offered up for the admiration of the oppressors"—undergirded the Black Arts revaluation; the song-form was guilty by association with the now intolerable social conditions that had produced it.[11] "[T]he blues are invalid," Maulana Ron Karenga declaimed in an oft-reprinted essay in *Negro Digest* (1968), "for they teach resignation, in a word acceptance of reality—and we have come to change reality."[12] For Karenga, Madhubuti ("Don't Cry, Scream" [1969]), Sanchez ("liberation / poem"[1970]), and others, blues were the embarrassing residue of an older generation's helpless passivity, no longer useful in a time of revolutionary transformation and expressive license.[13] "[W]e ain't blue, we are black," insisted Madhubuti, deploying blues repetitions only to reject the stance of black dejection he construed them as signifying. "[W]e ain't blue, we are black./ (all the blues did was/ make me cry)."[14] "no mo / blue / trains running on this track," agreed Sanchez. "[T]hey all be de / railed."[15] Soul and jazz were the sounds of the urban North: hip, inspiring freedom-songs. "Soul music is an expression of how we feel today," black DJ Reggie Lavong at New York's WWRL told Michael Haralambos in 1968, "blues was how we felt yesterday."[16] Blues *could* be the sounds of the urban North, and hip in their own fashion—white scholar Charles Keil helped clarify this in *Urban Blues* (1966)—but for an influential segment of Black Arts proponents, blues signified the benighted rural South: they were the cry of the slavery/sharecropping continuum, the sorrow-songs associated with what Baraka, in *Blues People*, had termed "the scene of the crime."[17]

Yet for another, considerably larger cohort of Black Arts writers led by Larry Neal, the blues were something quite different: a cherished ancestral rootstock, an inalienably black cultural inheritance that could be put to political as well as aesthetic good use. "The blues," countered Neal in "The Ethos of the Blues" (1972),

> with all of their contradictions, represent, for better or worse, the essential vector of the Afro-American sensibility and identity. Birthing themselves sometime between the end of formal slavery and the turn of the century, the blues represent the ex-slave's confrontation with a more secular evaluation of the world. They were shaped in the context of social and political oppression, but they do *not*, as Maulana Karenga said, *collectively* "teach resignation." To hear the blues in this manner is to totally misunderstand the essential function of the blues, because the blues are basically defiant in their attitude toward life. They are about survival on the meanest, most gut level of human existence. They are, therefore, lyric responses to the facts of life.[18]

These blues are not sorrow songs (or not *only* sorrow songs), but *survivor* songs: the soundtrack of a spiritual warriorship that refuses to die—and, not coincidentally, wrests far more than its share of swaggering lyric joy out of an evil world, inscribing personhood and sustaining the tribe in the process. "To write a blues song," wrote Etheridge Knight in "Haiku" (1968), "is to regiment riots / and pluck gems from graves."[19] Such are the blues defended and celebrated by Neal ("For Our Women," "Can You Dig It?"), Salaam ("The Blues [in two parts]"), Stanley Crouch ("The Big Feeling," "Howlin' Wolf: A Blues Lesson Book"), Jayne Cortez ("Lead," "Dinah's Back in Town," "You Know"), James Cone (*The Spirituals and the Blues*), Al Young ("A Dance for Ma Rainey"), Stephen Henderson ("Blues, Soul, and Black Identity: The Forms of Things Unknown"), Quincy Troupe ("Impressions / of Chicago; for Howlin Wolf"), Eugene Redmond ("Double Clutch Lover"), Nikki Giovanni ("Poem for Aretha," "Master Charge Blues"), Tom Dent ("For Walter Washington"), and Henry Dumas ("Keep the Faith Blues"), among others.[20]

"[B]lk people have done it to the english language," insisted the southern-born Salaam in *New Black Voices* (1972), making his case for the aesthetic revolution wrought by those blue-toned survivor songs. "[T]hey have niggerized it . . . we are finding that blk poetry has to do mostly with rhythm, images, & sound . . . most good images come from blues, blues singers were our 1st heavy poets."[21] "[T]he blues," proclaimed Crouch somewhat more grandiosely in "The Big Feeling" (1969),

> is the most important art form ever produced in America, ever, possibly in the West. Because it has the "big feeling," as John Lee Hooker says: It broke past the lie, became rudely vulgar in its exposition of truth, spit in the face of Venus de Milo (the armless bitch incapable of embrace), stumbled through the flung lye of loneliness, so often scalded walking barefoot in the glass-strewn alleys of anguish, maimed by memories, suffering the treason against the self which is called sentimentality, but, at the end with its tongue hanging out, in love: "Dun't you want to rock?" Or, "Got a good rocking mama and the way she rock is all right!" That, is the final specificity of feeling and, of life: The woman reached, or wished for—"And say, babe, don't you remember me?" That is, the Blues to me means: No one is crushed if he, or she, can summon the strength to understand what has happened, which is identity. Therefore, B. B. King need not be threatened by white musicians, he knows who he is and knows, as we all must: "As long as you've got Black People, you'll have the blues . . . "[22]

Theomusicologist James Cone, like Neal and Crouch, defended the blues in the name of black identity-formation; in *The Spirituals and the Blues* (1972) he had one eye on those white folklorists who claimed that the blues had no real "protest" content and another eye on Karenga, who argued essentially the same point from a Marxist perspective:

> The political significance of the blues is not very impressive to those who have not experienced black servitude. Neither is it impressive to persons who are fascinated by modern theories of political revolution. But for black people who live the blues, who experience and share that history with their black fathers and mothers, the blues are examples of Black Power and the courage to affirm black being.[23]

Blues Power is Black Power! Both the white folklorists and the black revolutionists, Cone argues by implication, miss the liberationist moment in blues: the way in which, as he puts it elsewhere in his study, the "ritual and drama" of blues performance "preserve the worth of black humanity" and "affirm the somebodiness of black people" in the face of oppression. At once functional, collective, and committed, the blues foster a continuing revolution of black spirit, excavating and purging despair—rather than surrendering to it—on a daily basis.[24]

Some Black Arts writers, most notably Baraka, articulated a multivalent vision of the blues' cultural and ideological function. *Blues People* (1963), *Dutchman* (1964), and "Black Music (The Changing Same)" (1966) together limn a capsule history of the Black Arts blues dialectic: from a relatively benign index of "the Negro's" changing attitudes towards America, to a register of political impotence and aestheticized black rage ("If Bessie Smith had killed some white people, she wouldn't have needed that music"), to a rich, enduring, and endlessly inspiring black ancestral wellspring ("Blues [Lyric] its song quality is, it seems, the deepest expression of memory . . . . It is the racial memory").[25] Even Don L. Lee (Haki Madhubuti), who rejected the blues in "Don't Cry, Scream" (1969) as an art that "exhibits illusions of manhood" and is "destroyed" by John Coltrane's freedom-yearning ascension into "scream-eeeeeeeeeeeeeee-ing," could seemingly reverse his revaluation, celebrating Delta bluesman Son House in an untitled but closely observed praise poem published in 1970:

> to himself he knew the answers
> & the answers were amplified
> by the sharpness of the broken bottle
> that gave accent to the muddy music as it screamed
> & scratched the unpure lines
> of our many faces,
> while our bodies jumped to the sounds of
> mississippi.[26]

House, a Delta blues recording star in the 1930s and early 1940s, had been tracked down in the summer of 1964 by young white blues enthusiasts Dick Waterman, Phil Spiro, and Nick Perls, who found House in Rochester, New York, after searching to no avail down in Mississippi. The trio put a guitar in House's hands, coaxed him out of retirement, and worked the levers of white power, so to speak, to get him onto the bill at the Newport Folk Festival by summer's end. With Waterman acting as his manager and booking agent, House played Carnegie Hall the following year, was featured in several documentaries, enjoyed an entirely unexpected second act as a performer and recording artist.[27] Without those efforts, it is safe to say, House would have died in obscurity and Lee would never have had the occasion to observe him in action, or write the poem that resulted.

If white blues aficionados and black poets could, on occasion, be secret sharers of the music they loved and admired, then the polarized racial climate of the period tended to preclude overt acknowledgment of that common bond. Virtually all Black Arts writers, in fact, saw white enactments of and claims on the blues as an insult and threat, one more invidious example of cultural theft rife with overtones of minstrelsy and false consciousness. "[I]t should come as a surprise to no one," critic Stephen Henderson told a black college audience in 1970,

> that white people have tried to usurp the concept of "Soul" and to dilute its meaning. That is a function of their historical relationship to us, and that relation-

ship has been parasitic, cannibalistic . . . . The history of our national music, i.e., so-called serious music, the history of popular music, the history of the American popular theatre, would be pallid indeed without the black energy and forms which were appropriated from us, and which we have foolishly called "contributions" to American culture. This is only now becoming clear, only now being publicly admitted . . . . [T]he Janis Joplins of this world, and the Mike Bloomfields, and the Laura Nyros, and the Tom Jones' are merely carrying on a time-honored tradition of swallowing the nigger whole. They are cultural cannibals. But how do you deal with the sickness?[28]

The sickness to which Henderson's polemic refers is, of course, the Blues Revival, which by 1970 had shifted into high gear and by 1971 had been officially certified in Bob Groom's slim monograph by that name.[29] Henderson's jeremiad, which was seconded in the writings of Don L. Lee, Ron Wellburn, Calvin C. Hernton, and others, makes clear the degree to which the Black Arts Movement's desire to reclaim and define the blues as a black cultural inheritance rather than a Negro "contribution" to American culture was being pressured by the truly daunting emergence of a mass white blues audience—an audience no less galvanized, it must be added, by established black performers such as B. B. King and Muddy Waters than by white *arrivistes* such as Joplin and Bloomfield. The white culture-industry seemed determined to overwhelm any Black Arts separation-and-purification scheme by capitalizing on white omnivorousness for all things blue, recasting black ancestral lines of descent in a way that seemed anathema to black aesthetic radicals.

"Paul Butterfield worships Muddy Waters," inveighed Ron Wellburn in his essay on black music in *The Black Aesthetic* (1971),

who has never had so much money in his life. In fact, a black fathers/white sons syndrome is developing. A Chess label album cover pictures a black god giving the life-touch, a la Michaelangelo, to a white neo-Greek hippie in shades. This is part of the Euro-American scheme. The black music impetus is only to be recognized as sire to the white world; a kind of wooden-Indian or buffalo-nickel wish. A vampirish situation indeed!

African-Americans should continue to move as far away from this madness as humanly possible, spiritually, psychologically, and in the immediate physical sense at least . . . . Black music should not be allowed to become popular outside the black community, which means that the black community must support the music.[30]

"Fathers and Sons" (1969) was the title of a highly successful double LP that paired Muddy and Otis Spann with Butterfield, Bloomfield, Sam Lay, Donald "Duck" Dunn, and Buddy Miles: four black guys and three white guys, but also three fathers (Muddy, Spann, and Lay) and four sons, which is to say a thread of black ancestral connection in the person of Miles, a point elided by the album's iconographic cover art. The "shoulds" and "musts" that mark Wellburn's irritable jeremiad, in any case, are a holding action in the face of a troubling and indisputable social fact: the young white audience for blues had swelled to fill a vacuum created by a vanishing young black audience. Even younger black intellectuals such as Henderson, enamored of the blues and angered at white borrowings, were forced to admit this. "About three years ago," he chided his black college audience in 1970, "I wrote a short article in which I lamented the seeming indifference of young black people to what I call the most characteristic feature of black cultural life—the blues."[31] Like Wellburn's jeremiad, Henderson's address at Southern University in New Orleans was an attempt to drum up black community support for an art form that suffered as many negative connotations within the race as it enjoyed positive (and profitable) ones out in the wider world. The black blues musicians themselves, as Wellburn is too honest not to note, followed the money trail. "Until the mid-1950s" observed *Time* magazine in 1971, "the music of Muddy [Waters] and his fellow bluesmen was marketed as 'race music' aimed almost exclusively at black communities. Today his new audience is largely young whites; Muddy now makes 20 to 30 college appearances a year, and he plays mostly in white clubs and theaters. For one thing, says Muddy, young whites are more responsive. 'The blacks are more interested in the jumpy stuff. The whites want to hear me for what I am.'"[32]

"Yes, the blues is alive and well, all you people," Hamilton Bims informed his *Ebony* readers in 1972,

> Indeed it is the subject of a worldwide craze. Blues performers are toasted in Europe and at open-air festivals from Monterey to Newport . . .
>
> Chicago bluesmen have had their crosses to bear. Many are respected, even idolized in Europe—yet the places that await them when they venture back home are often dungeons of violence and the paychecks are absurd. They have also been the victims of an intraracial snobbery—a legacy of the times when the blues was the property of contemptible old men hawking dimes on a street corner. Urbanized blacks have tended to deprecate the blues in favor, initially, of contemporary jazz and more recently that ethnic amalgam described as "soul." The blues is often seen as an Uncle Tom expression, a cowardly admission of impotence and despair; while the "positive" projections of the James Brown school are viewed as infinitely more consistent with the current black mood.[33]

Even as Black Arts poetry readings and theatrical troupes were flowering in urban centers and on college campuses across the country during the late 1960s, even as Crouch, Al Young, Tom Dent, and other young poets were crafting praise songs to blues performers such as Howling Wolf, Ma Rainey, and Walter "Wolfman" Washington, there remained a fundamental disconnect between the younger black generation and their blues-playing elders. Was this merely a black variation on the period theme, "Never trust anybody over thirty"? Yet "the burgeoning white youth audience for blues" not only trusted those elders, it venerated them in a way that most black kids—except that segment of the Black Arts vanguard—didn't begin to. As late as 1969, after his remarkable success at the Fillmore West had certified his star status in the eyes of young whites, B. B. King could tell an interviewer, "I've never been asked to appear at a black college."[34] Junior Parker, according to cultural historian Michael Hara-lambos, hungered for but never achieved the sort of crossover success King, Waters, and Albert King had enjoyed; "[t]he title of his last LP, 'You Don't Have To Be Black To Love The Blues,' shows he was still trying to break through to that audience."[35] If the title of Parker's 1974 album says little about Parker's real designs on the mainstream market and much about his record label's marketing strategy, then it makes painfully clear just what sort of pressures the Blues Revival was exerting on a black folk/popular form that Black Arts poets and theoreticians were intent on defining *away* from grasping whiteness and mainstream Americanness, away from capital-driven exoticism of the sort that Hernton lambasted in *Black Fire*: "Ray Charles, Mahalia Jackson, Lightning Hopkins, Little Richard—sex, soul, honkytonk!—it all represents something that will turn white folks on, something that will gratify their perversities."[36]

To complicate the ideological situation even more thoroughly, 1969 marked the birth of the Ann Arbor Blues Festival: the first major blues festival held in North America, featuring Muddy Waters, B. B. King, Lightnin' Hopkins, Junior Wells, Howlin' Wolf, Otis Rush, T-Bone Walker, Luther Allison, Magic Sam, and Son House. It also marked the emergence, in the festival's program notes, of what might be called the ideology of self-conscious white blues universalism. The spectre of "black rage," evident on both college campuses and in the urban riots inventoried by the Kerner Commission Report (1968), had clearly roused the anxieties of white blues aficionados about the possible bad faith attendant on so thoroughgoing a white embrace of a black art so closely identified with the oppression of blacks by whites. White anxiety compensated by insisting mightily on the black social provenance of the blues (no white boys at *these* origins!), even while elaborating a narrative of popular music's "roots" in the blues and naturalizing the ascendance of contemporary white blues performers to a position of respectful cofraternity alongside their black elders and peers. "[S]omewhere in this headlong rush of publicity and profit," a certain Habel Husock informed Ann Arbor festivalgoers,

> contemporary music has stumbled on its roots in a joyous reunion. What that means is a full-fledged revival of the blues, the unique music of the American black man that has infused popular music with its echoes of Africa, slavery, and rural and urban poverty . . .
>
> The blues evolved in the secret culture of black America; a pure, ethnic form of self-expression. (Blues was neither invented by a Columbia recording engineer nor by the Cream) . . . . The blues is alive and very well—it cannot be relegated to history for it continues to answer needs for man and has come to reach an audi-

ence much larger than a ghetto bar, a new audience which has recognized in itself the same passions and emotions that found their form in blues. The blues grows continually in the artistry of such men as James Cotton, Junior Wells and Buddy Guy. Many faithful white musicians refine the blues and mold the blues to suit the emotions of their backgrounds further, blues has been a launching pad for jazz riffs and improvisations.[37]

Husock is happy to grant Black Arts theoreticians their racial-ancestral claims—blues as "a pure ethnic form of self-expression" that evolved as "the secret culture of black America"—but only in order to clear a space for his universalist claims about "new audience[s]" outside the ghetto and "faithful white musicians" who "refine" and "mold" the blues. It was these latter sorts of sentiments, not merely antithetical to the ethnic-consolidationist project of the Black Arts Movement but an insult to black intelligence—was Janis Joplin really *refining* Big Mama Thornton's blues?—that justifiably infuriated Henderson, Wellburn, Hernton, and Lee. "Our music," wrote Lee in 1970,

is being stolen each and every day and passed off as another's creation—take Tom Jones and Janis Joplin, two white performers who try to sing black. They've not only become rich, while black musicians starve in their own creation, but those two whites, plus others—who are at best poor copies of what they consider black—will, after a short period of time become the *standard*. It will get to the point where when you speak of *soul* and black music, you will find people automatically thinking of white imitators.[38]

Whether or not Lee's prophecy about white imitators has, in fact, come true in our own day is debatable. The white blues audience's hunger for what the Europeans are fond of calling "real black blues" has, if anything, grown stronger in recent decades; B. B. King, Buddy Guy, Koko Taylor, and other headliners on the mainstream blues circuit command premium prices, and the European festivals (Burnley, Notodden, Blues Estafette) are notorious for preferring little-known black blues artists to rising white stars such as Jonny Lang and Kenny Wayne Shepard. On the other hand, it is possible to find blues festivals advertised in the pages of major American blues publications such as *Blues Revue* in which six of the eight acts are all-white or contain a single black member, making white blues the acceptable *de facto* norm, if not exactly the standard.[39] Often that token black member is a drummer or bassist, but not infrequently he is the Old School legend, the celebrated master—Pine Top Perkins, Robert Junior Lockwood—backed up by willing white apprentices. Black fathers and white sons all over again, staging rituals of fellowship and reconciliation.

Or are they symbolic transfers of cultural power in the service of profiteering white universalism? Once the fathers die, after all, the annointed sons take over; guitarist Bob Margolin makes a good living these days on the basis of having played behind Muddy Waters in the early 1970s, as does harmonicist Paul Oscher. The white blues audience today seems only too happy to embrace the actual children of deceased black blues legends—Shemekia Copeland, Bernard Allison, Big Bill Morganfield—as performers in their own right, but there was no way that Black Arts spokesmen could have anticipated this particular plot twist in the late 1960s. It was the white blues-kids, cultural interlopers and harbingers of the future, who bedeviled them. "For the 1970s and beyond," insisted Wellburn in *The Black Aesthetic*, "the success of political, economic, and educational thrusts by the black community will depend on both an aesthetic that black artists formulate and the extent to which we are able to control our culture, and specifically our music, from theft and exploitation by aliens."[40] At the height of the blues revival, black anxiety and annoyance at the displacement of black people from blues performance was an understandable response to a combination of factors: not just the swelling white audience and shrinking black audience for the music, not just the emergence of white blues stars such as Joplin and Butterfield, but also the historical parallel offered by the rock-n-roll "cover" phenomenon of the 1950s (Pat Boone and Bill Haley profiting off the songs of Fats Domino and Big Joe Turner), and the rapidly evolving ideology driving the revival—a putatively antiracist, universalist ideology based on "feeling the blues," an ideology that cleared space for white participation by either rejecting privileged black claims on the music or asserting them with a fervency that hoped to fend off black nationalist objections. In the former case the ideology might be summarized, "Now that we play the blues, we play them better than you"; in the latter case, "Now that we listen to your blues, we feel them as strongly as you." Exhibit A in the former case was journalist Albert Goldman, author of a *New York Times* article entitled, "Why Do Whites Sing Black?," that Henderson vigorously deconstructed before his college audience in 1970:

> [W]hen he waxes ecstatic about Stevie Winwood, whom he calls "Super-Whitey No. 1," who pretended that he was "Ray Charles crying in an illiterate voice out of the heart of darkness," we see finally what it is all about. White people really understand black people and black culture better than black people, so why shouldn't they get the credit. Thus Stevie Winwood, "Attaining a deeper shade of black than any dyed by Negro hands . . . became the Pied Piper of Soul." And Paul Butterfield has created "a new idiom," which is "half black and half white," and has "done for the blues what no black lad could do—he has breathed into the ancient form a powerful whiff of contemporary life." So there you have it. If that isn't plain enough, Goldman ends his article with the following statement, which really shows the extent of his perversion.

> Next Friday night at Madison Square Garden, Janis Joplin and Paul Butterfield will lock horns in what should be the greatest blues battle of recent years. The audience will be white, the musicians will be black and white, and the music

will be black, white and blue, the colors of a new nation—the Woodstock Nation—that no longer carries its soul in its genes.

> That is as plain as it has to be, for Goldman is sanctioning the use, the exploitation of black music for white nationalist purposes, without really owning that the music still belongs to us at all. And the technique of expropriation is plain—detach the music from its cultural context under the guise of liberalism and integration, then ZAP them niggers again.[41]

One may feel, as I do, that Paul Butterfield was a true innovator—one of the few white blues instrumentalists who extended the tradition rather than merely ventriloquizing his black influences—and at the same time share Henderson's assessment of Goldman's invidious fatuity here. That fatuity is, it must be said, a byproduct of Goldman's hyperbolic style: he burlesques Winwood in the original article even as he celebrates him ("a fey pixie, who looks as if he was reared under a mushroom"), and he characterizes Joplin as "this generation's campy little Mae West."[42]

Yet Goldman, precisely by virtue of his tactlessness, asks all the right questions about the "musical miscegenation" that marked the heated late sixties moment at which the Black Arts Movement and the Blues Revival came to loggerheads:

> Driven apart in every other area of national life by goads of hate and fear, black and white are attaining within the hot embrace of Soul music a harmony never dreamed of in earlier days. Yet one wonders if this identification is more than skin deep. What are the kids doing? Are they trying to pass? Are they color blind? Do they expect to attain a state of black grace? Let's put it bluntly: how can a pampered, milk-faced, middle-class kid who has never had a hole in his shoe sing the blues that belong to some beat-up old black who lived his life in poverty and misery?[43]

Goldman shrewdly frames the blues revival in the context of racial polarization—a polarization clearly abetted by (if not reducible to) the Black Arts Movement's dedication to, as Larry Neal put it, "the destruction of the white thing, the destruction of white ideas, and white ways of looking at the world."[44] It seems entirely plausible, in fact, that the passion which drove white blues fans into the "hot embrace" of musical blackness as the sixties progressed was in fact an anxious response to the hot, angry *rejection* of white patronage, white solicitude, and interracial fraternity by a politicized blackness manifesting variously as Black Power, the Black Panthers, the Black Aesthetic, the Black Arts Movement, and *Black Rage* (1968). In the black blues recordings with which they established private rituals of communion, in the black blues artists who were delighted by (if sometimes also puzzled and unnerved by) their adulatory attentions at clubs and festivals, white blues fans during the Black Power years found themselves able to make a separate peace with blackness of a sort that ideologically driven public tensions (not to mention the Kerner Commission's celebrated warning about the emergence of "two societies, one black, one white—separate and unequal") made almost impossible in any other civic setting. *Blues Power*, the title of albums by Albert King (1968) and Eric Clapton (1970), was, by this reading, a kind of anxiety-formation against Black Power. *The World of Blues Power!* and *Blues Power, Vol. 2*, bestselling Decca compilations in 1969 and 1970, were anthologizing integrationist responses to the anthologizing separatist calls made by *Black Fire* (1968) and *The Black Power Revolt* (1968).

For all his trash-talk about "the white thing," it was *Black Fire*'s co-editor Larry Neal, alone among his Black Arts peers, who was willing to entertain the idea that the Blues Revival's white audiences might testify to the glorious power and universal reach of black music. "Even though the blues were not addressed to white people and were not created by white artists," he told Charles Rowell in 1974, "when white people heard the blues they knew it was a formidable music."[45] But of course the blues were being *played*, if not precisely created, by a sizeable cohort of white performers by the time the sixties drew to a close: what had begun at the Newport Folk Festival in 1963 as a charmed encounter between superannuated, mildly exoticized black country bluesmen and an audience of white folkies had metastasized by 1968 into Eric Clapton and Cream transforming Robert Johnson's "Crossroads Blues" into sheets of sound at the Winter Garden in San Francisco with the help of banked Marshall amps and hallucinogens. It had also morphed into Jimi Hendrix's "Voodoo Child" version of the same New Thing. Musical miscegenation was a two-way street in the late 1960s; Black Arts sensibilities betrayed considerable unease about what seemed like treacherously shifting blues ground, a postmodern hall of mirrors in which blue-eyed blues people were determining the idiom's prevailing feeling-tone and those few younger blacks who had embraced the blues seemed to be losing contact with their essential blackness. James Thompson's poem, "Media Means," published in *Negro Digest* in 1969, clearly signifies on the media-driven "scene" that embraced both Clapton and Hendrix:

> speaking
> to Young Blacks
> whom MEDIA has made
> BELIEVE
> that a Black Blues Chord
> played by BLACKS
> is an
> ACID ROCK TUNE
> that White imitation
> of a very black feeling/
> I was forced to scream:

INTEGRATION IS DREADFUL
when you don't control
the media which makes
ZOMBIE/ISM a constant
condition.) IT SELLS IMAGES—
imitations of REAL
and REALITY imitates
          IT:
Black folks imitating
                    white folks
                    who
                    imitate
                    THEM!⁴⁶

"[B]lues done gone and got / Americanize," complained poet Mae Jackson in a
similar vein, also in *Negro Digest* (1969):

i says
blues ain't nothing like it use to be
. . . and the folks singing it
ain't singing for me
no more.⁴⁷

Both of these poems sing the Blues Revival blues, voicing in the first-person "I"
a collective black sense of outrage, enervation, and loss: loss of a familiar low
blues-home safe from the encroachment of whiteness. Jackson's vernacular voice
reconstructs that home as a complaint against blues-singing white interlopers
and their cooptive liberal platitudes—or, more precisely, against a comprehensive whiteness that manifests as *both* blues singing and platitude-mongering.
"The Black Arts Movement," Neal had famously declared a year earlier, "is
radically opposed to any concept of the artist that alienates him from his community."⁴⁸ Means and Jackson embody this creed—their own black community
orientation is evident—but the song they sing is a lament about their alienation
from a brave new "blues" world that no longer speaks to or for them.

CANNIBALS AND BLUES GODS

The year 1970 was a watershed year for both the Blues Revival and the Black
Arts Movement's engagement with blues, a liminal moment in which two very
different social formations seemed suddenly to come into uneasy alignment.
One index of this shift was *Living Blues*, a mimeographed newsletter featuring
lengthy interviews with black blues musicians founded that year in Chicago by
a group of seven young white journalists, oral historians, and French surrealist
fellow travelers. What made the magazine unusual and controversial was an editorial policy that hewed to a black aesthetic critique of white blues later summa-

rized by Paul Garon, one of the founders: "[F]or those interested in the support and study of African-American culture, blues as purveyed by whites appears unauthentic and deeply impoverished; further, it too often represents an appropriation of black culture of a type sadly familiar. Finally, it can be economically crippling to black artists through loss of jobs and critical attention."[49] Each of these statements was a half-truth. The flailing, gravel-voiced, minstrelsy-tinged excesses of Janis Joplin could and did coexist with the preternaturally wise—and black-mentored—blues stylings of Bonnie Raitt, who took pains to acknowledge and share stages with her mentors; although middling rock-blues boogiemen such as Canned Heat and Alvin Lee may indeed have made more money than they deserved off of black-authored blues songs, black bluesmen such as Muddy Waters and B. B. King found the loss of the black youth market far more economically crippling than any such white appropriations, and were relieved and highly gratified, if also a bit mystified, by their sudden ascension into the mainstream. What was significant, in any case, was the emergence of such consciously "black" aesthetic radicalism among young white blues fans. Larry Neal's call for the "destruction of the white thing" had drawn an unexpected response from his blue-eyed brothers.

Neal himself was hard at work on his blue-toned reconstructionist project: in the January 1970 issue of *Negro Digest*, he used his review of Phyl Garland's *The Sound of Soul* to celebrate B. B. King's achievement in terms that constituted an implicit rebuttal of Ron Karenga's dismissal of the blues in the magazine's pages two years earlier. "We are the continuation of Black memory," Neal insisted,

our songs are the emanations of that memory; our rhythms the force that drives that memory.

Bessie Smith sang: that the meanest folks in the whole wide world lives on Black Mountain. She was singin' 'bout niggers, evil and bad but surviving in spite of everything. Nigger/Black. Black music/niggers/the "nigger" in the music being its dominant force . . . . But it is nigger energy that will rule. B. B. King has more to tell me about the world that I can use than most poets and intellectuals. Here he is talking to Phyl Garland:

"*blues* is B. B. King. Yes, and I've been a crusader for it for 21 years. Without this, I don't think I could *live* very long—not that I think I'm goin' to live a long time anyway, but I don't think I could live even *that* long if I had to stop playin' or if I couldn't be with the people I love so, the people that have *helped* me so much . . . I couldn't live! I try to give them a message. I try hard."

How many of us are so dedicated to whatever it is that we do? How many of us commit ourselves so thoroughly to our work? How many of us link our work to the survival of both ourselves and our people? . . . . *We will write our own scriptures.* We will seek validation of the truths that we sense must exist in the holiest work of each one of us. From spirits like B. B. King, Jimmy Reed, Son House,

James Brown, Smokey Robinson, Moms Mabley . . . an ethnic [*sic*] will be fashioned whose fundamental truths can be denied by no one . . . . New scriptures are in order. New mythologies. New constructs: Black Music as the Model for the Black Nation . . . . We are a new species of Man, child. Liberation will come out of honky-tonk bars, gut-bucket blues, and the meanest niggers that have ever walked the planet. (Saw Bobby Blue Bland singing Uptown. He had on silver dashiki *and* his process.) The current Soul Music explosion illustrates the mass culture of Black America is still strong; and still dominated by the eternal spirit of the Blues God."[50]

Not only don't King's blues, according to Neal, "teach resignation," as Karenga had insisted, but they powerfully respond to Karenga's demand for revolutionary black art: they are functional, collective, and committed—as committed as soul music, which the blues underpin spiritually and aesthetically as "the eternal spirit of the Blues God." In the figure of soul-crooner Bobby Blue Bland, sporting Afrocentric clothes and a blues-identified hairstyle, Neal finds a way of dissolving the seeming contradiction between the ancestral African origins, the gut-bucket New World transformations, the freedom-demanding soul extensions, and the pan-African revolutionary consciousness that together constitute the black aesthetic in his eyes. "He was compelled by the evolving/changing critical discourse of his era to go through changes," Houston A. Baker, Jr., notes of Neal, "but in the synapses of all those connections made with Western thought were sounds of an African/Caribbean/New World/Afro-American/Funky-But-Downhome/Journeyed-Back/Gut-Bucket/Honky Tonk changing same called the blues . . . . [H]e was a pivotal figure in the evolution of a vernacular, blues theory of Afro-American expression in the United States."[51] Neal's Blues God was an emblem of black cultural survival—"the god that survived the middle passage," as he put it in a 1978 interview—but also a god of native lyricism, one inflected by the race's American oppressions. "[W]e are *an* African people, but we are not Africans," Neal insisted in "New Space: the Growth of Black Consciousness in the sixties" (1970): "We are slave ships, crammed together in putrid holds, the Mali dream, Dahomey magic transformed by the hougans of New Orleans. We are field hollering Buddy Bolden; the night's secret sermon; the memory of your own God and the transmutation of that God. You know cotton and lynching. You know cities of tenement cells."[52]

It is striking to compare Neal's 1970 statements with the program copy for the 1970 Ann Arbor Blues Festival and realize that the Blues Revival, too, was struggling to articulate a version of the Blues God: an ancestral source, indisputably black, yet one in which whites as well as blacks could be baptized. The 1970 program, Exhibit B in the evolving ideology of white blues universalism, relinquished Habel Husock's claims of the previous year that "faithful white musicians" could "refine the blues." This year the ideological core wasn't "Now that we play the blues, we play them better than you," but "Now that we listen to your blues, we feel them as intensely as you." What the festival organizers felt more than anything was a sense of mourning for the pantheon of black blues performers who had died since the previous year's festival and whose photographs and capsule biographies were featured in the program: Kokomo Arnold, Skip James, Magic Sam, Slim Harpo, Earl Hooker, and Otis Spann. "Their deaths," wrote the organizers, "have left a vacancy in our hearts that will never be filled."[53] One might, if one wanted to be irritable, dismiss such effusions as an updated version of the plantation sentimentalism that accompanied the death of a faithful black retainer: sadness for the passing of the Old Negroes imbued with nostalgia for an integrationist/paternalist idyll that had been exploded by black social assertiveness in the Black Power era. Or one might decide that real family feeling across racial lines is being evidenced: a beloved black-and-white blues community. Or both. One legacy of the Black Arts Movement in this postmodern age is that we are, most of us, conscious enough to entertain contradictory responses—both reflexive suspicion and progressive idealism—and dwell in the paradox. The roots of the modern "keeping the blues alive" movement, in any case, are visible in the 1970 Ann Arbor Blues Festival program, along with a surprisingly forceful statement of the black aesthetic:

> The Blues will never die. We of the Blues Festival Committee whole heartedly believe this, but we also accept that time changes everything, even the blues. The Ann Arbor Blues Festival is set up as a tribute to an American musical genre that has been part of black culture in this nation since slave days. It is from and of the black experience. Those who bemoan the passing of the so-called rural blues fail to realize that the same intensity and feeling is apparent in the blues that pour from the black urban community today. The blues are the same—only the problems are different . . . . We of the festival hope to achieve, as last year, a true rapport between the audience and the performing artist. This shouldn't be too difficult as this year's show contains some of the greatest blues acts around.[54]

"[T]he black experience," a linguistic marker deployed in the Black Power era for the anti-assimilationist assertion of black singularity, is bent to different ideological purposes here. A critique is being leveled, for one thing, at folk blues "purists" such as Alan Lomax and Samuel Charters who had famously denigrated urban blues artists such as B. B. King as too commercial—and whom Charles Keil had skewered so effectively in *Urban Blues* (1966). Hip white blues aficionados, these program notes suggest, fall into Larry Neal's camp: they groove to the Blues God's unities rather than engaging in silly cultism. But wait a minute: Neal's claim about the Black Arts Movement's being "radically opposed to any concept of the artist that alienates him from his community" has been stealthily reworked here: what had been a description of the black performer's organic relationship with his *black* public has been transformed into a prophecy about the black performer's relationship with what would turn out to be an almost entirely *white* festival audience. What guarantees the "true rapport" between black performer and white audience is a seemingly effortless marriage between black artistry and the emotional response such artistry compels. The social solvent here is white blues feeling, understood as the evoked and adequate correlate to (black) Blues Power. Such feeling celebrates a pantheon of black blues gods only to explode the idea of a black nation: an integrationist rather than ethnic-consolidationist ethos. It is counterrevolutionary to the core—if by revolutionary you mean intent on forging a close bond between black performer and black community of a sort that discourages or precludes white participation.

It was perhaps inevitable, amid so much ideological struggle, that black blues promoters with sensibilities shaped by the Black Arts Movement would stage their own Blues Revival event. "The Washington [D.C.] Blues Festival held in November 1970," according to Michael Haralambos, "was the first blues festival produced by blacks for blacks. According to the press handout it was "an attempt to return blues to the black community given that many white interests have exploited the music at the expense of many of the black musicians who will be performing."[55] The lineup was a treasure-trove of black cultural riches: Muddy Waters, B. B. King, Richie Havens, Libba Cotton, Rev. Robert Wilkins, Furry Lewis, J. B. Hutto, Luther Allison, Fred McDowell, Howlin' Wolf, Sleepy John Estes, John Jackson, Buddy Guy & Junior Wells, and Mance Lipscomb. The multi-day event announced its departure from mainstream festival practice by kicking off, on Thursday evening, with what *Jazz Journal*'s correspondent characterized as "the volatile and exciting African Heritage Dancers and Drummers [who] began by taking us back to the African motherland in the highly skilled and rigorous performance of ceremonial dances of West Africa."[56] This deliberate, prideful framing of the blues as a New World extension of African musical practice was new—a logical extension, perhaps, of the Pan African Cultural Festival in Algiers the previous summer, which had been attended by at least one blues-loving Black Panther, Stokely Carmichael.[57] New, too, was the venue: Howard University, which made the festival, according to *Jazz Journal*, the first such event to be held on a black college campus. What was *also* new, and at the same time uncannily familiar for black blues advocates during the Blues Revival, was the spectacle of Black Art overrun by white blues fans. "Topper Carew," reported the *Jazz Journal*,

(Director of The New Thing Art and Architecture Center which sponsored the event) had hoped to instill pride and interest in the cultural heritage of a 76% black community of Washington by presenting the blues—the raw-boned music which so essentially encompasses the experience of the black man in America.

Sadly, only a small percentage of blacks were in attendance, sprinkled amongst a predominantly white, hippy crowd who came to listen to the blues and dig the overall scene. The blues are created by blacks but are apparently supported by whites! The magnetic grip of the soul genre, tawdry in comparison with the rugged purity intrinsic to the blues idiom perhaps has its slick hooks in the young generation of blacks. Or maybe with the growing black pride, the blues are all too unpleasant reminders of a wishfully forgotten past; and understandably so.[58]

What to make of such a flagrant sociological paradox? If such an event, carefully framed to enable the unembarrassed participation of a politicized young black audience, had failed to draw such an audience, or much of any black audience, it would seem hard to continue to rail, as Stephen Henderson had railed a few months earlier on a different black college campus, against white "cultural cannibalism." In this case, the culture cannibals shored up *somebody's* profit margins, and not a white man's.

THE BLUES IS ALRIGHT
What is the shared legacy, finally, of the vexed and unacknowledged partnership between the Blues Revival and the Black Arts Movement? One might argue that the disco craze of the mid-1970s helped undo both social formations, dissolving the dirty realism of the former and the ethnocentric political engagement of the latter in a multiracial, gender-crossing bath of depoliticized techno-beats. The truth, somewhat more complex, allows for a pair of striking generalizations about the past thirty years:

1. White blues fans and musicians have taken blues music—including a significant helping of black blues elders—and run with it, letting (blackened) white blues feeling blossom into blues societies, blues festivals, blues magazines, blues instructional videos, and the like.

2. Black blues writers and cultural custodians, unable to prevent these proliferating appropriations, have taken their stand on the printed page; black literature has become the locus of a fresh, wide-ranging, and profound re-engagement with ancestral blues, a cultural legacy that white writers can't begin to appropriate with anything like the cultural ease that marks a surprising proportion of contemporary white blues performance.

White folk came away from the sixties with the music, in short; black folk came away with the talking books. (White folks also came away with the ghostwriting credits for a series of black blues autobiographies—a genre that requires them selflessly to suppress their own voices so that the voices of their black subjects may emerge.) The result in our own day is a curiously bifurcated blues culture in which white blues aficionados who can easily list Robert Johnson's recorded sides (including unreleased alternate takes) and various rumored burial sites draw a blank when literary works such as "The Weary Blues" and *Train Whistle Guitar* are mentioned; a culture in which younger black poets who can name you a dozen poems by Langston Hughes, know enough about Albert Murray to reject his cultural politics, and are hip to Kevin Young and Harryette Mullen, will draw a similar blank when two of blues music's brightest young black stars, Shemekia Copeland and Alvin Youngblood Hart, are mentioned.

Such sweeping generalizations, true as they may be, obscure significant and fascinating local exceptions. One of these exceptions is poet and former White Panther John Sinclair, whose new volume, *Fattening Frogs for Snakes: Delta Sound*

Suite (2002), takes a series of interviews with black blues musicians gathered by white journalists over the years and transforms them into a kind of documentary free verse, so that Sinclair's own poetic voice essentially disappears for long stretches into the voices of Howlin' Wolf, Sonny Boy Williamson, Robert Junior Lockwood, Bukka White. "The book," insists Amiri Baraka in his foreword, a helpful authenticating document in this post-Black Arts era, "is not a Homage to the Blues, it is a long long long blues full of other blues and blues inside of them. John all the way inside, and he got the blues."[59] A white man has written a literary blues beyond color, it would seem, but also a blues securely anchored in a griotic ambition to sing the black ancestors—Sinclair's, Baraka's, ours.

Another exception—in this case, to the hoary truism that blues is no longer a black popular music—can be found in the contemporary soul blues scene in Jackson, Mississippi. In the fall of 2002, I attended a heavily advertised show in Canton, a northern suburb of the state capitol. By my count, I was one of four whites in a crowd of perhaps three thousand blacks, all of whom had come to spread lawn chairs on the dirt infield of an indoor rodeo facility and groove to heavy-rotation soul blues stars Sir Charles Jones ("Love Machine"), Marvin Sease ("Women Would Rather Be Licked"), Peggy Scott-Adams ("Hot and Sassy"), and Willie Clayton ("Call Me Mr. C"). The endless round of Chicago shuffles and revivalist acoustic fingerpicking that mark the post-Blues Revival mainstream were conspicuously absent, but *blues*—as a timbral and microtonal vocabulary, a harmonic home, a familiar place that an otherwise conventional soul composition could suddenly "go"—was very much in evidence. "Do you mind if I sing you some *blues*?" Clayton demanded of the crowd midway through his exhilarating set. "Do you mind if I throw a *hurtin'* on you?" The deafening roar, the hands raised in willing testimony, the brisk CD and t-shirt sales I noticed later at Clayton's merchandizing table: all suggest—as *Living Blues*, to its credit, has been insisting for some time—that blues music for certain sectors of the black community is alive and well, albeit in a form that the self-policing mainstream can't quite bring itself to acknowledge *as* blues.

A final paradox, and a heartening one, begs to be considered. The revitalized black market for blues that I've just described, roughly twenty years in duration, can be traced to two releases, Z. Z. Hill's "Down Home Blues" (1982) and Little Milton's "The Blues is Alright" (1984). Both songs, twelve-bar shuffles of the sort that white blues audiences and musicians had been keeping alive through several decades of black popular neglect, were also, with their roots-and-pride ethos, the answer to a prayer sung by Black Arts spokesmen such as Larry Neal, Stephen Henderson, Ron Wellburn, and even Ron Karenga: black art for the black community. Both songs were functional, collective, committed to self-respect and spiritual uplift, and—surprise!—profitable. They were and are popular with whites, too: Little Milton works the mainstream as well as the soul blues circuit these days, and makes a good living doing it. The title of his song, in fact, is the official motto in this congressionally certified "Year of the Blues" (2003). *The blues is alright*: not quite the revolution we thought we were having, way back when, but no mean feat either. The Blues Revival and the Black Arts Movement, unacknowledged co-conspirators, did indeed transform our world.

NOTES

1. See "Renovating Blackness: Remembrance and Revolution in the Coltrane Poem," in Kimberly Benston, *Performing Blackness: Enactments of African-American Modernism* (New York: Routledge, 2000), 145–186.

2. Henry Louis Gates, "Black Creativity: On the Cutting Edge," *Time* (10 October 1994): 74–75.

3. For Guy Davis, see Frank Matheis, "Favored Son," *Blues Access* 45 (Spring 2001). For Corey Harris, see Art Frede, "Words Sound Power: The Blues Vision of Corey Harris," *Living Blues* 126 (March/April 1996): 22–33. "You know," Harris told *LB*, "one time this guy took my picture after I told him not to. I was on the street. He had one of those little disposable cameras. I said, 'Why'd you take my picture?' He said, 'Well, my son said, 'I just want a picture of this big fucking black guy playing a guitar.' He was talking about me. I said, 'You're a real idiot, you know that. You sit here and say that to me, how do you think I'm going to react.' I said, 'Give me your camera.' I took his camera and I threw it in the sewer'" (31).

4. Amiri Baraka (LeRoi Jones), *Dutchman* (1964), in *The Norton Anthology of African American Literature*, ed. Henry Louis Gates, Jr., and Nellie Y. McKay (New York: W. W. Norton & Company, 1997), 1897.

5. <http://www.blues.org/bluesfirst>.

6. Ryan Whirty, "Chris Thomas King Wants to Bring the Blues into the 21st Century," *IDS Weekend* (October 31, 2001) <http://idsnews.com/story.php?id=6777>.

7. Kalamu ya Salaam, "the blues aesthetic," in *What is Life?: Reclaiming the Black Blues Self* (Chicago: Third World Press, 1994), 19.

8. I take the phrase, which I am redeploying with ironic intent, from LeRoi Jones's essay, "The Changing Same (R&B and the New Black Music)," in *Black Music* (1967; Da Capo, 1980), 180–211.

9. Berta Wood, "Are Negroes Ashamed of the Blues? (White critic says they scorn tradition that produced jazz, prefer white culture)," *Ebony* (May 1957): 64. See also "Why I'll Always Sing the Blues" ("Singing since he was five, B. B. King feels that old songs serve social purpose.") *Ebony* 17: 6 (April 1962): 94–96, 98. "Although B. B. considers the type of songs he plays and sings America's greatest contribution to the music world, he realizes 'a lot of people don't like to be associated with the blues because the songs embarrass them . . . . It's a drag. You know why? Because it is Negro music and they are afraid of anything Negro while we're going through this integration business.' . . . B. B. realizes that the blues are still going through their period of disgrace as did ragtime, jazz and swing."

10. B. B. King, *Blues All Around Me* (1996: New York: Avon Books, 1997), 213.

11. Frantz Fanon, *Toward the African Revolution* (New York: Grove Press, 1967), 37.

12. Ron Karenga, "Black Art: A Rhythmic Reality of Revolution," *Negro Digest* 17: 3 (January 1968): 9. Karenga's germinal essay was retitled and reprinted several times during the period: as "Black Cultural Nationalism," in *The Black Aesthetic*, ed. Addison

Gayle, Jr. (New York: Doubleday, 1971), 32–38; and as "Black Art: Mute Matter Given Form and Function," in *New Black Voices: An Anthology of Contemporary Afro-American Literature*, ed. Abraham Chapman (New York: New American Library, 1972), 477–482.

13. The volume entitled *Don't Cry, Scream* in which the titular poem appears was published in 1969. The volume *We a BaddDDD People*, in which the cited poem appears, was published in 1970.

14. Haki Madhubuti (Don L. Lee), "Don't Cry, Scream," in *Don't Cry, Scream* (Detroit: Broadside Press, 1969), 27.

15. Sonia Sanchez, "liberation / poem," in We a *BaddDDD People* (Detroit: Broadside Press, 1970), 54.

16. Michael Haralambos, *Soul Music: The Birth of a Sound in Black America* (1974; New York: Da Capo, 1985), 118.

17. Charles Keil, *Urban Blues* (1966; rev. ed., Chicago: University of Chicago Press, 1991); LeRoi Jones (Amiri Baraka), *Blues People: The Negro Experience in White America and the Music That Developed from It* (New York: William Morrow & Company, 1963), 95.

18. Larry Neal, "The Ethos of the Blues," *The Black Scholar* (Summer 1972), 42.

19. Etheridge Knight, "Haiku" (1968), in *The Black Poets*, ed. Dudley Randall (New York: Bantam Books, 1971), 203.

20. Larry Neal, "For Our Women" and "Can You Dig It," in *Hoodoo Hollerin' Bebop Ghosts* (Washington, D.C.: Howard University. Press, 1974), 55, 71–72; Kalamu ya Salaam, "The Blues (in two parts)," in *New Black Voices*, 375–77; Stanley Crouch, "The Big Feeling," *Negro Digest* (July 1969): 45–48; Stanley Crouch, "Howlin' Wolf: A Blues Lesson Book," in *Ain't No Ambulances For No Nigguhs Tonight* (New York, R.W. Baron Publishing Co., 1972), 25; Jayne Cortez, "Lead," *Negro Digest* (September 1969): 60; "Dinah's Back in Town," in *Pisstained Stairs and the Monkey Man's Wares* (New York: Phrase Text, 1969), 17; Jayne Cortez, "You Know," in *Coagulations: New and Selected Poems* (New York: Thunder's Mouth Press, 1984), 41–43; James Cone, *The Spirituals and the Blues* (1972; rpt. Maryknoll, NY: Orbis Books, 1992); Al Young, "A Dance for Ma Rainey," in Abraham Chapman, *New Black Voices*, 366; Stephen A. Henderson, "Blues, Soul, and Black Identity: The Forms of Things Unknown," *Black Books Bulletin* 1: 1 (Fall 1971): 11–15, 36–38; Quincy Troupe, "Impressions / of Chicago; for Howlin Wolf" (1972), in Chapman, *New Black Voices*, 348; Eugene Redmond, "Double Clutch Lover," in *The Eye in the Ceiling* (New York: Harlem River Press, 1991), 171–73; Nikki Giovanni, "Poem for Aretha" (1970), *The Selected Poems of Nikki Giovanni* (New York: William Morrow & Company, 1996), 75–78; Giovanni, "Master Charge Blues" (1970), *Selected Poems*, 87; Tom Dent, "For Walter Washington," in Chapman, *New Black Voices*, 372–73; Henry Dumas, "Keep the Faith Blues," in Stephen Henderson, *Understanding the New Black Poetry: Black Speech and Music as Poetic References* (1972; New York: William Morrow & Company, 1973), 370.

21. Val Ferdinand (Kalamu ya Salaam), "Food for Thought," in Chapman, *New Black Voices*, 378–79.

22. Stanley Crouch, "The Big Feeling," *Negro Digest* (July 1969): 45.

23. James H. Cone, *The Spirituals and the Blues*, 122.

24. Ibid., 105.

25. LeRoi Jones (Amiri Baraka), "The Changing Same (R&B and New Black Music)" (1966), *Black Music* (1967; New York: Quill, 1980), 180.

26. Don L. Lee (Haki Madhubuti), *We Walk the Way of the New World* (Detroit: Broadside Press, 1970), 5.

27. See <http://bluesnet.hub.org/son.house/interview.html>and <http://www.hickorytech.net/~tlkremer/pages/lookingforblues.html>.

28. Henderson, "Blues, Soul, and Black Identity," 36.

29. Bob Groom, *The Blues Revival* (London: Studio Vista, 1971).

30. Ron Wellburn, "The Black Aesthetic Imperative," in Gayle, *The Black Aesthetic*, 147.

31. Henderson, "Blues, Soul, and Black Identity," 14.

32. "Down Home and Dirty" [sidebar about Muddy Waters], *Time*, August 9, 1971: 46.

33. Hamilton Bims, "Blues City," *Ebony* (March 1972): 76.

34. Quoted in Haralambos, *Soul Music*, 91.

35. Ibid., 91.

36. Calvin C. Hernton, "Dynamite Growing Out of Their Skulls," in *Black Fire: An Anthology of Afro-American Writing*, ed. LeRoi Jones (Amiri Baraka) and Larry Neal (1968; New York: William Morrow & Company, 1969), 81.

37. Habel Husock, essay in "The Ann Arbor Blues Festival" [program for 1969], n.p. (From the Blues Archive, University of Mississippi).

38. Don L. Lee (Haki Madhubuti), *We Walk the Way of the New World*, 19.

39. An advertisement for the 1999 Santa Cruz (CA) Blues Festival featured headliners Jimmie Vaughan (Saturday) and Gregg Allman (Sunday), with John Mayall and the Bluesbreakers, Rod Piazza and the Mighty Flyers, BoneShakers, Nina Storey, Ronnie Earl, and W. C. Clark. The BoneShakers are a "mixed" band; W. C. Clark is African American. *Blues Revue* 47 (May 1999): 61.

40. Wellburn, "The Black Aesthetic Imperative," in Gayle, *The Black Aesthetic*, 132.

41. Henderson, "Blues, Soul, and Black Identity," 38.

42. Albert Goldman, "Why Do Whites Sing Black?," *New York Times*, December 14, 1969: 25, 46. Quoted online at Blues World 2000 <http://www.geocities.com/bluesworld2000/history56.htm>.

43. Ibid.

44. Larry Neal, "The Black Arts Movement" (1968), in *The Norton Anthology of African American Literature*, 1997.

45. Charles H. Rowell, "An Interview with Larry Neal" [Taped 1974], *Callaloo* 23 (Larry Neal: A Special Issue) (Winter 1985): 29.

46. James Thompson, "Media Means," *Negro Digest* (September 1969): 86–87.

47. Johari Amini, "Books Noted" (review of Sister Mae Jackson, *Can I Poet With You*), *Negro Digest* (September 1969): 51.

48. Neal, "The Black Arts Movement," in *The Norton Anthology of African American Literature*, 1960.

49. Paul Garon, "White Blues" <http://www.bluesworld.com/WHITEBLUES.html>.

50. Larry Neal, "The Sound of Soul" (a review of Phyl Garland, *The Sound of Soul*), *Negro Digest* (January 1970): 43–47.

51. Houston A. Baker, Jr., "Critical Change and Blues Continuity: An Essay on the Criticism of Larry Neal," *Callaloo* 23: 82.

52. Larry Neal, "New Space/The Growth of Black Consciousness in the Sixties" (1970), quoted in Paul Carter Harrison, "Larry Neal: The Genesis of Vision," *Callaloo* 23: 173.

53. "Ann Arbor Blues Festival Program 1970," n.p. From the Blues Archive, University of Mississippi.

54. Ibid.

55. Haralambos, *Soul Music*, 169.

56. Martha Sanders Gilmore, "Washington Blues Festival '70: A Benefit for Blacks in Blues," *Jazz Journal* (February 1971): 18–29, online at <http://www.blues.co.nz/dig-this/page5.html>.

57. Don Lee interviews Stokely Carmichael at the Pan-African Cultural Festival in Algiers.

58. Gilmore, "Washington Blues Festival "70."

59. Amiri Baraka, foreword to John Sinclair, *Fattening Frogs for Snakes: Delta Sound Suite* (New Orleans: Surregional Press, 2002), 9.

III.
PREDECESSORS, PEERS, AND LEGACIES

12
A Familiar Strangeness
The Spectre of Whiteness
in the Harlem Renaissance
and the Black Arts Movement

Emily Bernard

We younger Negro artists who create now intend to express our individual dark-skinned selves without fear or shame. If white people are pleased we are glad. If they are not, it doesn't matter. We know we are beautiful. And ugly too. The tom-tom cries and the tom-tom laughs. If colored people are pleased we are glad. If they are not, their displeasure doesn't matter either. We build our temples for tomorrow, strong as we know how, and we stand on top of the mountain, free within ourselves.
—Langston Hughes, "The Negro Artist and the Racial Mountain," 1926

"I would like to be white." This phrase ends the first sentence of Langston Hughes' formidable 1926 essay, "The Negro Artist and the Racial Mountain." This statement is not autobiographical. Rather the sentiment is Hughes' translation of a declaration made by an unnamed poet—Countee Cullen—about his preferred professional identity.[1] Cullen told Hughes that he wanted to be known as "a poet—not a Negro poet" and Hughes heard behind Cullen's words a lamentable self-loathing, a pitiable hankering for whiteness. The path from Cullen's sentiment to Hughes' interpretation is circuitous at best, however, and there are, finally, multiple ways in which Cullen's desire could be understood. Surely, Hughes, in his long acquaintanceship with Cullen, perceived myriad subtleties inherent in Cullen's resistance to the label "Negro poet," and experienced his own ambivalence about such labels. But Hughes' interest in Cullen's words here is not philosophical but polemical. Only in this reduced and distorted version does Cullen's language serve a significant role in Hughes' essay. It provides an occasion for the exposure and condemnation of the black middle class, reviled here as the most eminently insidious agent of white supremacy. But while Hughes' essay pretends to curse Cullen and his kind—black imitators of pernicious whiteness—his explicit objective is belied by the essay itself, which depends on Cullen's putative self-loathing for its own declarations of self-love.

Whiteness and black agents of white supremacy are similarly "condemned" all over the rhetorical landscape of the Black Arts Movement. In *Are We Not Men? Masculine Anxiety and the Problem of African American Identity* (1996), literary critic Phillip Brian Harper identifies intraracial conflict as having a central function in the rhetoric of Black Arts nationalism, and the same mechanism works in the idiom of the Harlem Renaissance. In addition, Harper's analysis applies to interracial conflict in both the Black Arts and New Negro Movements. In other words, just as social divisions within the black community as perceived by Black Arts intellectuals were never meant to be resolved but instead actually served, in Harper's words, to "solidify the meaning of the Black Aesthetic," black struggles with white power were similarly meaningful to both Black Arts and Harlem Renaissance ideology.[2] Both movements built their foundations upon a common belief that authentic black art could only be produced when black artists liberated themselves from white influence. Anxieties about white control were often figured in sexual terms, and the racial discourses historically linked to both the Harlem Renaissance and the Black Arts Movement brim with heteronormative directives. Finally, black creativity in both movements depended upon white influence in various guises—both material and non-material—to enable *and* to handicap it. Ultimately, an examination of the Harlem Renaissance and the Black Arts Movement reveals that intimate relationships—whether generative or repressive—with whiteness are not extraneous or even peripheral to authentic black experience, they are defining aspects *of* that experience.[3]

* * *

The resounding lines that serve as this chapter's epigraph have often been quoted to represent not only the spirit of "The Negro Artist and the Racial Mountain," but the essence of Harlem Renaissance ideology, as well. Langston Hughes composed "The Negro Artist" as a response to "The Negro Art-Hokum" (1926), an essay by George Schuyler that lampoons the idea that a distinct black art could ever exist in a context in which "the Aframerican is subject to the same economic and social forces that mold the actions and thoughts of the white American."[4] Among its other accomplishments, Schuyler's essay effectively provided a platform for Hughes to codify his own aesthetic politics in what biographer Arnold Rampersad describes as "the finest essay of Hughes' life."[5] "The Negro Artist" reverberates with Hughes' triumphant convictions that authentic black art not only existed but thrived and would be essential to the cultural salvation of the race.

The rhetoric of liberation that runs through "The Negro Artist," however, as well as through much of the language of the New Negro movement, depends upon a constant invocation of all that inhibits and compromises fearless and shameless artistic expression from actually being realized, namely the black middle class. Countee Cullen serves "The Negro Artist" as a perfect—and perfectly despicable—representative of the black bourgeoisie, who are, in Hughes' definition, "people who are by no means rich yet never uncomfortable or hungry—smug, contented, respectable folk, members of the Baptist church."[6] In Hughes' formulation, the black middle class not only fails to fulfill the promise of black progress, it is also the most sinister impediment to "younger Negro artists" and to positive African American group identity, in general. With their "Nordic manners, Nordic faces, Nordic hair, Nordic art (if any)" they present "a very high mountain indeed for the would-be racial artist to climb in order to discover himself and his people."[7]

Cullen and his bourgeois milieu are not the only enemies to black progress that Hughes castigates. Another foil is his "Negro clubwoman in Philadelphia" who disdains spirituals in favor of the "drab melodies in white folks' hymnbooks."[8] Together, Cullen and the Negro clubwoman function in "The Negro Artist" as personifications of the ideological hurdles that stand between the black artist and the "serious racial art" that he would produce. Formidable enemies though they may be, all is not lost, Hughes informs us. Real, unmitigated, unspoiled blackness flourishes: "But then there are the low-down folks, the so-called common element, and they are the majority—may the Lord be praised!"[9] Once the dead layer of faux whiteness is rhetorically vanquished, authentic blackness is revealed and celebrated, only to be buried again under more references to its black oppressors. Obviously, the real adversary to black progress here and everywhere is white supremacy, but I'd like to explore the particular threats that its black ambassadors are understood to offer to the integrity of black identity.

A potent current of disgust for the black middle-class runs energetically through the discourse of Harlem Renaissance, the Black Arts Movement, and beyond.[10] In their aping of "white" ways and values, the black middle class is figured as more pernicious, more insidious than whiteness itself. Why? As Zora Neale Hurston described the ambivalent response of Eatonville's modest citizens to Mayor Jody Starks' middle-class ways in *Their Eyes Were Watching God* (1937): "It was bad enough for white people, but when one of your own color could be so different it put you on a wonder. It was like seeing your sister turn into a 'gator. A familiar strangeness. You keep seeing your sister in the 'gator and the 'gator in your sister, and you'd rather not."[11] What this suggests is chilling and obvious: if your sister could so easily turn into a 'gator, then maybe your sister and the 'gator weren't so different in the first place. The "familiar strangeness" that alienates Eatonville from Starks created a hysteria during both the Harlem Renaissance and the Black Arts Movement that fed on itself and informed both movements with meaning; it revealed the true proximity to whiteness that blackness could never actually escape, even though attempts to do so have always been central to black experience. Distinguishing the "'gator" from your sister was a fixation in both movements, and it demanded a constant vigilance.

What is finally most important here is not the actual disunion of sister from "'gator," but the ritual inherent in the attempt. In other words, these black foils were effectively not *obstacles to* but *essential to* the ideological constructions of black identity in both the Harlem Renaissance and the Black Arts Movement. The threats they posed were necessary and productive. The "The Negro Artist and the Racial Mountain" is theoretically a paean to Hughes' "low-down folks," but word-for-word, Hughes spends much more time in his essay focused on the self-hating elitists he claims to pity and despise. After his first reference to his celebrated authentic black folk, he returns again to his Philadelphia clubwoman, ostensibly to bemoan her shame for jazz. "Years of study under white teachers, a lifetime of white books, pictures, and papers, and white manners, morals, and Puritan standards made her dislike the spirituals. And now she turns up her nose at jazz and all its manifestations—likewise almost everything else distinctly racial." Hughes sees it as a duty of the "younger Negro artist, if he accepts any duties at all from outsiders, to change through the force of his art that old whispering 'I want to be white,' hidden in the aspirations of his people, to 'Why should I want to be white? I am a Negro—and beautiful!'" [12] But the energy of his essay is provided by the conflict itself, not by the promise of its resolution.

In *Are We Not Men?*, Phillip Brian Harper reveals that similar contradictions were inherent features of the black nationalist project, and argues that "the response of Black Arts nationalism to social division within the black populace is not to strive to overcome it, but rather to articulate it in the name of black consciousness." [13] Putatively nationalist, the Black Arts Movement based its very existence upon the idea that there were those who could never be incorporated into the fold. As Amiri Baraka announced in *Raise Race Rays Raze* (1969): "There are people who might cry BlackPower, who are representatives, extensions of white culture. So-called BlackPower advocates who are mozartfreaks or Rolling Stones, or hypnotized by Joyce or Hemingway or Frank Sinatra, are representatives, extensions of white culture, and can never therefore signify black power." [14] Addison Gayle, Jr., editor of *The Black Aesthetic* (1971), believed there was a cure: "The Black Aesthetic then, as conceived by this writer, is a corrective—a means of helping black people out of the polluted mainstream of Americanism, and offering logical, reasoned arguments as to why he should not desire to join the ranks of a Norman Mailer or a William Styron." [15] The continuous need to weed out the righteous from the fallen, the "blacks" from the "Negroes," was not really a necessary, recuperative step on the way to group solidarity, however; finally it served as the essence of the project of Black nationalism itself.

An ambiguity and ambivalence inherent in the objectives of the movement itself accounts for the intraracial tensions invoked so commonly by Black Arts artists. Harper's analysis of Amiri Baraka's poem "SOS"(1969) makes plain that "the threatening unpredictability of exactly what will issue from the essentially contradictory nationalist urge accounts for Baraka's decision not to project beyond the call manifested in "SOS": "Calling black people." [16] Group solidarity could not be achieved because the practical purpose of this solidarity was never clear. The urgent, relentless effort to ferret out those blacks who were potentially hurtful to black progress was finally a ruse that served to distract even Black Arts leaders themselves from the contradictions that threatened the ostensible cohesion and focus of the black nationalist project.

A very similar strategy was at work in the New Negro Movement, whose complications began with the term "New Negro" itself. As Henry Louis Gates, Jr. reminds us in "The Trope of a New Negro and the Reconstruction of the Image of the Black" (1988), the term "New Negro" was not invented in the 1920s but had, in fact, been circulating in African American public discourse since the 1700s. This figure was composed, in part, by blacks attempting to correct the negative stereotypes about them that were already in play by the time they arrived in the New World. "Almost as soon as blacks could write, it seems," Gates explains, "they set out to redefine—against already received racist stereotypes—who and what a black person was, and how unlike the racist stereotype the black original indeed actually could be."[17] Black people attempted to convert popular stereotypes about blacks from those based upon absence (of morality, intelligence, and other basic features of humanity) to presence. Those who participated in the circulation of this figure, "the New Negro," believed that this semantic strategy would have serious political and cultural ramifications in the lives of black Americans. A preoccupation with this term, and the liberation it represented, became a near-obsession for Harlem Renaissance intellectuals. In fact, Gates suggests that the Negro Renaissance was finally nothing more than a vehicle created to contain the "culturally willed myth of the New Negro."[18]

But the term "New Negro" does not make sense without its counterpart—"Old Negro." In fact, the terms are hardly in opposition at all. Instead, they are in dialectical harmony and fundamentally necessary to each other; a definition of one term is only possible in light of the other. In other words, the New Negro is finally only what the Old Negro is not, and vice versa. Gates discusses the contradictions built into the terms "Old Negro" and "New Negro":

> The paradox of this claim is inherent in the trope itself, combining as it does a concern with time, antecedents, and heritage, on the one hand, with a concern for cleared space, the public face of the race, on the other. The figure, moreover, combines implicitly both an eighteenth-century vision of utopia with a nineteenth-century idea of progress to form a black end-of-the-century dream of an unbroken, unhabituated, neological self—signified by the upper case in "Negro" and the belated adjective "New." A paradox of this sort of self-willed beginning is that its "success" depends fundamentally upon self-negation, a turning away from the "Old Negro" and the labyrinthine memory of black enslavement and toward the register of a "New Negro," an irresistible, spontaneously generated black and sufficient self.[19]

The inextricability of the terms "Old Negro" and "New Negro" presented a problem for black intellectuals intent upon severing the relationship between the two types, embracing the latter while turning the collective racial back on the former, thereby obliterating forever the ugly history of shame and servility that the Old Negro represented. But the progress promised by the New Negro Movement could be evident only in relation to this agonizing history. Continuous comparisons were necessary, and that meant that the figure of the Old Negro had to be kept alive and in the center of discussions about racial progress. It was finally impossible for Harlem Renaissance intellectuals to leave the Old Negro behind; they needed to maintain a concentrated focus on this symbol in order to remind themselves exactly what they were shedding, and conversely, what precisely it was that they were becoming. The necessity of keeping close at hand the very image that they were so desperate to cast off created an acute anxiety among Harlem Renaissance intellectuals whose relief was attempted by a seemingly continuous celebration of the symbolic death of the Old Negro. The compulsion to create distinctions between an Old Negro ideology—imbedded in white expectations—and a New Negro framework—free from preoccupations with white standards—was a compulsion that necessitated and effectively created its own antagonists.

Harlem Renaissance writers were eminently aware of their status as members of a cultural vanguard, yet they lacked clear, physical evidence of the progress that their art was supposed to have achieved. The acute self-reflexivity of this moment in African American literary history apparently left its black writers with few alternatives but to look inside the movement itself for the source of their problems.[20] By the middle of the 1920s, when the Harlem Renaissance was in full swing, those black writers casting about frantically to identify the outdated features of black cultural identity that were preventing them from self-actualization found useful targets in each other, as Hughes exemplifies in his treatment of Countee Cullen in "The Negro Artist and the Racial Mountain." The Harlem Renaissance, then, can be characterized by mechanics of exclusion that are similar to those that travel through the rhetoric of the Black Arts Movement.

"Negro life is not only establishing new contacts and founding new centers, it is finding a new soul," Alain Locke proclaimed in the opening pages of *The New Negro* (1925).[21] African American arts of the 1920s was intoxicated with the idea that it had invented itself, not only in terms of its creative ambitions, but as a locus of a new black identity. A version of the same fantasy characterizes the Black Arts Movement. "We advocate a cultural revolution in art and ideas," Larry Neal echoed in 1966.[22] In his introduction to *The Black Aesthetic*, Addison Gayle, Jr. summarized the objectives of the Black Arts Movement: "Speaking honestly is a fundamental principle of today's black artist. He has given up the futile practice of speaking to whites, and has begun to speak to his brothers."[23] Gayle posits the Black Arts strategy as historically unique, but his gesture itself is actually redundant, Alain Locke and Langston Hughes being among those Harlem Renaissance artists and intellectuals who preceded him. Like the Harlem Renaissance, the Black Arts Movement articulated its objectives in powerful but pointedly abstract language that was finally more confusing than illuminating. How a black artist "could speak to his brothers" without any white mediation proved more confounding than Black Arts leaders were willing to concede. But if the Black Arts Movement wasn't clear on how it would get where it was going, it was very clear on where it was *not* going, and that was in the direction taken by the movement against which it continuously measured itself: the Harlem Renaissance.

A central project of the Black Arts Movement was to correct the mistakes made by the Harlem Renaissance. As Larry Neal concluded about the Harlem Renaissance: "The Black Arts Movement represents the flowering of a cultural nationalism that has been suppressed since the 1920s. I mean the 'Harlem Renaissance'—which was essentially a failure." It failed, Neal explains, because it did not "address itself to the mythology and the life-styles of the black community." [24] In the first chapter of *The Crisis of the Negro Intellectual* (1967), Harold Cruse sees white patronage as having played a significant role in the failure of the New Negro Movement. In his view, "the Harlem Renaissance became partially smothered in the guilty, idealistic, or egotistical interventions of cultural paternalism." [25] Like Addison Gayle, Jr., Harold Cruse felt that the Black Arts Movement should serve as an "ideological tonic that cures misguided assimilationist tendencies." [26]

In opposition to the Harlem Renaissance, the Black Arts Movement strived to succeed without white influence. In *Blues People* (1963), LeRoi Jones sized up the role whiteness played in the New Negro Movement:

> The rising middle class-spawned intelligentsia invented the term New Negro and the idea of the Negro Renaissance to convey *to the white world* that there had been a change of tactics as to how to climb onto the bandwagon of mainstream American life. The point here is that this was to be conveyed to white America; it was another conscious reaction to that white America and another adaptation of the middle-class Negro's self-conscious performance to his ever appreciative white audience. [27]

Like other Black Arts Movement spokesmen, Jones often used the term "Negro" to refer to, in his own words, "white-oriented schizophrenic freaks of a dying society," [28] African Americans he considers less progressive, less revolutionary than his own cohort. Elsewhere in Jones' writing, "Negro" is simply a synonym for "black." [29] African Americans have been debating nomenclature as long as they have been struggling with the burden of representation, which is to say, since the inception of African presence in this country. But whether or not terminology has material or symbolic impact on the African American condition, the debate itself, in all of its variations, is consistently front and center in all of the major historical shifts in African American experience, and always represents an evolving interpretation *of* that experience. More than simply a semantic shift, the mythological distance between "Negro" and "black" was as necessary, meaningful, and mysterious to the Black Arts

Movement as was the stretch between "Old Negro" and "New Negro" for the Harlem Renaissance.

The safest way to ensure one's status as "black" during the Black Arts Movement was to snitch on the Negroes. "The colored people, negroes, who are Americans, and there are plenty, are only colored on their skin. They are white murderers of colored people," proclaimed Baraka in *Raise Race Rays Raze*.[30] The essays in *Raise* are peppered with distinctions between "Negro artists" and "Black Artists" (98); references to deluded "hip negroes" (139) and the potential for "negro politics" to result only in "negro egos aggrandized at the expense of the ultimate development of the Black nation." Baraka warns: "We cannot lose our values and become negroized" (160). To become negroized would have been a fate worse than death—but reversible.

In *New Day in Babylon* (1992), cultural historian William Van Deburg describes the elaborate process by which Negroes could become black.[31] Whether or not you were worthy of the moniker "black" depended on how far at bay you held "whiteness." Conversely, an immediacy to "whiteness" compromised the authenticity of your "blackness." The same equations were in effect during the Harlem Renaissance, but just as Harold Cruse points out, so much of the Harlem Renaissance was connected to white support that it was—and is—impossible to determine where it ended and unalloyed black art actually began. Langston Hughes describes the significance of the title of the 1926 vanguard journal *Fire!!* in his 1940 autobiography, *The Big Sea*: "the idea being that it would burn up a lot of the old, dead conventional Negro-white ideas of the past, *épater le bourgeois* into a realization of the existence of the younger Negro writers and artists."[32] Countee Cullen worked as a personalization of these "dead conventional Negro-white ideas" in "The Negro Artist," and as such, had to be rhetorically cast from the Edenic racial landscape of Hughes' manifesto. But even *Fire!!*, as a realization of an authentic racial dream, could not have existed without white financial support. Wallace Thurman, the magazine's editor, lamented the fact that *Fire!!* could not burn "without Nordic fuel," even as he sought help from his current lover, who was white, and Carl Van Vechten.[33] This type of dependence played a crucial role in the eviscerating assessments made by Black Arts Movement intellectuals about the Harlem Renaissance.

Just as some Harlem Renaissance intellectuals needed to distinguish themselves from peers whom they considered to be too focused on the expectations of whites, Black Arts Movement spokesmen clarified the racial purity of their own objectives and beliefs by juxtaposing them against the "interracialism," as Harold Cruse characterized it, practiced by the Harlem Renaissance. "Learn to kill niggers/Learn to be Black men," commands Nikki Giovanni's 1968 poem, "The True Import of the Present Dialogue: Black vs. Negro."[34] Hughes' "The Negro Artist and the Racial Mountain" never advocates murder, but the brutality inherent in the language he uses to dismiss Countee Cullen ensures that readers will not associate him with the "old, dead conventional Negro-white ideas" that Cullen is charged to represent.

This rhetoric of purification is central to the ritual of separation that preoccupies both Harlem Renaissance and Black Arts Movement spokesmen. Upon Malcom X's assassination, LeRoi Jones famously left his white wife and family to move uptown, to Harlem, the "black Mecca." In his autobiography, Jones describes how his birth into blackness, Black Power-style, took a predictable course:

> The middle-class native intellectual, having outintegrated the most integrated, now plunges headlong into what he perceives as blackest, native-est. Having dug, finally, how white he has become, now, classically, comes back to his countrymen charged up with the desire to be black, uphold black, & c . . . a fanatical patriot![35]

But even in this moment of total immersion in blackness, a full rejection of whiteness, though proclaimed, is ultimately impossible. As Phillip Brian Harper argues, even though Black Arts poetry derives much of its power through its presentation as a black-only product, "it achieves its maximum impact in a context in which it is understood as being heard directly by whites, and overheard by blacks." [36] The constant iterations of murderous fantasies about whites that are staples in Black Arts poetry are finally most effective if they are directed at white people, Harper explains. To speak these fantasies *to* a white listener effects a symbolic annihilation, which is immeasurably important considering the great improbability that its physical counterpart would ever actually take place. According to Harper's argument, Black Arts poetry was meant to be only *overheard* by blacks, who were then meant to experience envy and awe for the racial righteousness being espoused. So, even within this decidedly black-only movement, white influence was inescapable. Indeed, efforts to elaborate on the meaning of blackness depended on invocations of whiteness. Literary critic David Lionel Smith points out that Hoyt Fuller, in the lead essay in *Black Aesthetic*, must quote at length from a white writer, George Frazier, in order to effectively illustrate the enigmatic superiority of black style. Ironically, Fuller excuses Frazier for being "a white writer who is not in the least sympathetic with the likes of LeRoi Jones." [37] These sorts of contradictions, I believe, impelled Black Arts Movement thinkers to use strategies that became more and more desperate in order to purge the whiteness without and within.

In another instance of this ritual of separation, Black Arts Movement prolocutor Eldridge Cleaver used James Baldwin as a handy target in his own rhetoric of purification, utilizing him in the same manner that Hughes employed the symbolic figure of Countee Cullen in "The Negro Artist." In *Soul on Ice* (1968), Eldridge Cleaver warned his readers about the wolves in sheep's clothing—"'gators" disguised as sisters—with a fanatic intensity. "Those truly concerned with the resurrection of black Americans have had eternally to deal with black intellectuals who have become their own opposites, taking on all the behavior patterns of their enemy, vices and virtues, in an effort to aspire to alien standards in all respects," Cleaver railed.[38] To Cleaver, Baldwin represented the quintessential "intellectual sycophant . . . a white man in a black body. A self-willed automated slave, he becomes the white man's most valuable tool in oppressing other blacks."[39] Cleaver was not alone in his judgments of Baldwin. According to Amiri Baraka, Baldwin was "Joan of Arc of the cocktail party" with a "spavined whine and plea" that was "sickening beyond belief."[40] Ishmael Reed described him as "a hustler who comes on like Job."[41] While it is important to note here that several of these Baldwin-haters have since revised their positions on the man, and now understand the stances they took then as a function of the times, it is meaningful to recognize how central these denunciations of James Baldwin were to the establishment of a kind of racial authenticity for those who perpetuated them. "A new generation, so it seemed, was determined to define itself by everything Baldwin was *not*," concludes Henry Louis Gates. "By the late sixties, Baldwin-bashing was almost a rite of initiation."[42]

Cleaver's disdain for Baldwin's counterfeit whiteness was inextricably bound up in his anxieties about Baldwin's sexual orientation. Cleaver's racial objections to Baldwin were always sexualized, and he believed homosexuality to be a white man's plague. He wrote in *Soul on Ice*, "Many Negro homosexuals, acquiescing in this racial death-wish, are outraged and frustrated because in their sickness they are unable to have a baby by a white man."[43] According to Cleaver, if the middle-class black was dangerous, then the black homosexual was deadly: "The white man has deprived him of his masculinity, castrated him in the center of his burning skull."[44] Thus zombie-fied, the black gay man, in Cleaver's fantasy, had the potential to undermine all of African American progress. The ugliness of Cleaver's distortions of Baldwin had more to do with anxieties around black masculinity than it did with any authentic hatred of James Baldwin as an individual. The stridency in Cleaver's language finally only represents the weaknesses in the movement's message about manhood. But as Phillip Brian Harper maintains, this is a "masculine anxiety that is rendered no less potentially oppressive by the sense of vulnerability it clearly conveys."[45]

Virtually all crises in African American culture have been historically portrayed as crises in black heterosexual male authority. Heterosexism is by no means unique to African American culture, of course, but the historical intersection of heterosexual masculinity with the discourse of authenticity in African American identity is central to this discussion.[46] Figured as perennially at risk, African American ideologues have privileged the recuperation of black heterosexual masculinity as primarily important, and then exhibited its recuperation as a "best foot forward" gesture in the continuous struggle for race uplift. Historically, homosexuality has been implicitly understood to be simply incommensurate with the ideal of the black male hero. At worst it has been considered detrimental to racial progress. This latter assumption, of course, reached a volcanic intensity during the Black Arts Movement, and it found an individual target in James Baldwin. The sexualization of Black nationalism is inherently connected, of course, to its proponents' portraits of the Harlem Renaissance as an effeminate movement. Harold Cruse wrote, tellingly, that the failures of the New Negro movement left it, not only whitened, but "emasculated."[47]

When it comes to the legacy of the Harlem Renaissance (and beyond), the intersection of anxieties about black male heroism and homosexuality finds an important expression in the controversy surrounding one black cultural icon: Langston Hughes. Commonly idealized by black communities with histories of competing interests, Hughes' status as a cultural hero, historically and presently, depends upon a public "whitewashing" of two features of his life that would otherwise tarnish his image as the ultimate race man: his presumed homosexuality, and the degree and quality of his involvement with whites.

There is an implicit imperative at work that demands that all discussions about Hughes' possible homosexuality be swiftly repressed in order for Hughes to maintain his central place in the annals of African American cultural history. The most remarkable instance of this repression occurred around the release of the 1989 film, *Looking for Langston*. The film, directed by Isaac Julien, is a meditation on gay male culture during the Harlem Renaissance through the vehicle of the enigmatic sexual identity of Langston Hughes. When Julien and other members of the black British film collective, Sankofa, showed the film to the Hughes estate, officials there refused to grant permission unless every direct visual and textual reference to Hughes' sexuality was removed from the film. The panic generated by even this speculation about Hughes' homosexuality itself testifies to the centrality of heterosexuality to the discourse of black male heroism. Ada Griffin, then director of the New York City-based Third World Newsreel, the distributor for *Looking for Langston*, bolstered this argument when she suggested that many of those involved in the production and distribution of the film were simply unaware of the degree of resistance they would encounter from the members of the "black bourgeoisie" who consider Hughes "a racial icon."[48] Clearly, Hughes' status as an icon has consistently been implicitly contingent upon the assertion of his heterosexuality. And conversely, the repression of discussions about the possibility of his homosexuality has been necessary to the conservation of this status.

Equally threatening to Hughes' status as a "race man" are specific representations of his relationships with whites. I have discussed elsewhere how crucial the figure of white promoter Carl Van Vechten was to the younger generation of New Negro writers who manipulated Van Vechten's symbolic presence to differentiate themselves from their older, more conservative counterparts.[49] Van Vechten has always been considered to pose a particular threat to Langston Hughes, both as a mentor and as a friend.[50] That Carl Van Vechten, who was married for more than forty years to Russian actress, Fania Marinoff, also enjoyed erotic relationships with men only increases the level of danger associated with him. The determination with which contemporary historians and scholars consistently attempt to sever or downplay relations between Van Vechten and Hughes results from the intersection of Van Vechten's public identity as a homosexual and a discourse about Hughes that prevents even the speculation that he might have had an intimate affiliation with gay male culture during his lifetime. But Langston Hughes enjoyed a textured, long-term relationship with Carl Van Vechten and many other white people, gay and straight, both formally and informally.[51] The possibility of a legitimate, mutual beneficial relationship between Hughes and Van Vechten jeopardizes Hughes' status as a racial icon, a status that demands black male heterosexuality and forbids close, positive associations with whites.

The demonization of homosexuality, as an agent of white power, was central to Black Arts Movement discourse. According to the philosophy of the Black Arts Movement, the central lesson of the Harlem Renaissance was that white power, in all of its forms, was perilous, even lethal. "We hated white people so publicly, for one reason, because we had been so publicly tied up with them before," Baraka explains provocatively in *The Autobiography of LeRoi Jones/Amiri Baraka* (1984). Baraka's "before" refers directly to his own life, and it also speaks to the generational congruities of interracialism in African American cultural history. The final, incontrovertible purging of whiteness from black lives was, both collectively and individually, the central objective of the Black Arts Movement, and its constituents pursued this mission with convert-like fervor. But all projects hatched toward this end were almost always necessarily distributed through white-controlled institutions.[52] "What's needed now for 'the arts' is to get them away from white people," Amiri Baraka announced in "What the Arts Need Now," and this tenet is echoed in other essays in his 1969 collection *Raise Race Rays Raze*. Does Baraka contradict himself by publishing these words with Random House?[53] The note to the first paperback edition of *Black Fire: An Anthology of Afro-American Writing* (1968), edited by LeRoi Jones and Larry Neal, apologized for the omission of work by several authors, and then explained:

> We hoped it wd be in the paperback, but these devils claim it costs too much to reprint. Hopefully, the 2nd edition of the paperback will have all the people we cd think of. The frustration of working thru these bullshit white people shd be obvious.[54]

In its candid language and innovate syntax, the above note emblematizes the passion and purpose of the Black Arts Movement. But finally, the "bullshit white people" called out by the editors are the same "bullshit white people" that make such a calling out possible in the first place. In other words, it was only by the grace of the white "devils" at William Morrow that, in this case, the flames of black fire were able to blaze.[55] Did the editors of *Black Fire* see the ironic connection between their own inconsistencies and that of the conundrum in which the editors of the 1926 journal *Fire!!* found themselves? The implicitly revisionist intentions of *Black Fire* serve as a microcosm for the equally ambitious, equally contradictory imperatives that kindled the Black Arts Movement as a whole. In both movements, the spectre of whiteness that hovered ambiguously over black art generated multiple crises whose resolutions were never as important as the fertile heat they ignited.

The crisis mentality that characterizes African American cultural history is responsible for the anxieties occasioned by the personas of Hughes and Baldwin, among others. African American culture has been continuously represented as a culture in crisis; witness the obvious significance of the appellation of one of the most important African American periodicals to date, *The Crisis*. The hysteria created by this crisis mentality accounts for the insistence upon nomenclature revisions, as well as the paranoid, short-sighted fantasies about weeding out internal enemies. In an essay about contemporary feminist discourse, literary critic Carla Kaplan argues that a parallel phenomenon impacts the language of contemporary feminism. According to Kaplan, the ubiquitous "language of crisis does not so much *represent* the current state of affairs as *construct* it in particular—and particularly disadvantageous—ways."[56] Kaplan's argument provides a provocative lens through which we might understand something fundamental about African American culture. African American culture has been historically figured by ideologues as troubled, fragmented, and in need of re-unification. The imperative to re-name and root out internal enemies are common strategies employed to resolve these perpetual crises; resolutions are proclaimed in declarations of the birth of another "renaissance."[57] Obscured in these rituals are not only the substantial problems that continue to drain black communities, but also the fact that the language of crisis serves mainly to produce more crises, among them the perpetuation of heterosexism within the black community, which itself only serves to represent, yet again, how useful this divisiveness is within the black community in the continuing drama of the pursuit of racial authenticity. In other words, those who identify homosexuality as aberrant, a threat to black male heterosexuality, only further underscore how crucial homosexuality is to the articulation of heterosexual masculine identity—as essential as whiteness is to blackness.

* * *

I'm looking for a house
In the world
Where the white shadows
Will not fall.

There is no such house,
Dark brothers,
No such house
At all.
—LANGSTON HUGHES, "HOUSE IN THE WORLD" (1931)[58]

I have conceived this essay, in part, as a response to Toni Morrison's *Playing in the Dark: Whiteness and the Literary Imagination* (1992), in which she discusses the "dark, abiding, signing Africanist presence" that hovers like a shadow over American literature.[59] My purpose here is not to propose that the shadow of whiteness performs an identical function in African American literature, mainly because the relationship between white and black power is not, and has never been, equitable. What I have attempted to explore here is the degree to which the spectre of whiteness—and black embodiments of that spectre—has informed two important episodes in African American cultural formation: the Harlem Renaissance and the Black Arts Movement. The examples upon which I base my argument are not meant to epitomize the totality of either movement, but are rather only intended to suggest something meaningful about the nature of this feature common to both episodes in African American cultural history. In its indirect, ambiguous, non-material forms, white influence has impacted black culture powerfully, and engendered equally powerful, even desperate, attempts by black people to finally extinguish it. Those attempts involve efforts to purge the whiteness from within—to wrest the noble sister from the pernicious "'gator." Such attempts are meaningful but futile: your sister and the "'gator" were always intertwined.

"House in the World" sighs resignedly at the impossibility of ever separating the righteous from the reptilian, therefore evoking a very different spirit than Hughes' 1926 essay, "The Negro Artist and the Racial Mountain." If his 1926 essay celebrated black freedom from white (and black) expectations, this 1931 poem wearily cedes the impossibility of ever extricating black identity from the constancy of the white normative gaze. The mood of the poem more closely resembles Hughes' tone in his 1940 autobiography, *The Big Sea*, when he writes about the Harlem Renaissance: "As for all those white folks in the speakeasies and night clubs of Harlem—well, maybe a colored man could find some place to have a drink that the tourists hadn't yet discovered."[60] Hughes' metaphor of the house represents the conviction devotedly espoused during the Black Arts Movement that institution-building would be the key to black political, cultural, and ideological liberation from white power. The poem also portends the futility of such an enterprise to do the work with which it is *really* charged, which is to protect blackness from white influence not only materially but symbolically, as well. The linguistic distinction—"white shadows" and "dark brothers"—is about as close as you can get. But if "House in the World" is a lament on the unrelenting power of whiteness—a whiteness so powerful it can permeate physical structures—then it is also an honest reckoning with it, a meditation on the inevitability of white presence as a constant—and significant—feature of black life.

Truly, the white normative gaze has always been at work in African American culture. It has played a fundamental role in structuring black cultural forms at every significant moment in African American cultural production. Because white support *and* corruption have been central to every episode in the evolution of African American creativity, we can safely name it as a crucial part of what makes African American art exactly what it is. In other words, there would be no black creativity without white influence.

Even more than artistic expression, the centrality of whiteness to black cultural *identity*, along with attendant anxieties about that centrality, are fundamental features of black American experience. Efforts to denounce and extinguish white presence from black life are important dynamics in the evolution of African American identity. The contradictions I assert here are deliberate; they resonate absolutely with the essentially contradictory nature of black American experience. The patron saint of Black nationalism during the Black Arts Movement, Amiri Baraka, himself explains: "The paradox of the Negro experience in America is that it is a separate experience, but inseparable from the complete fabric of American life."[61] Intimate struggles with whiteness are perhaps the only continuous—*essential*, if you will—aspects of black identity. White shadows make blackness, as we know it, visible.

NOTES

1. "If I am going to be a poet at all," Countee Cullen told a *Brooklyn Daily Eagle* reporter in 1924, "I am going to be a POET and not a NEGRO POET." Quoted in Stephen Watson, *The Harlem Renaissance: Hub of African-American Culture, 1920–1930* (New York: Pantheon, 1995), 78.

2. Phillip Brian Harper, *Are We Not Men? Masculine Anxiety and the Problem of African-American Identity* (New York: Oxford University Press, 1996), 45.

3. My essay borrows from the groundbreaking work done by generations of scholars on the inherently and "incontestably mulatto"—to use the phrase made famous by Albert Murray—nature of American culture.

4. George S. Schuyler, "The Negro-Art Hokum," *The Nation* 121 (June 16, 1926): 3180, reprinted in *The Portable Harlem Renaissance Reader*, ed. David Levering Lewis (New York: Penguin, 1994), 97–98. In *Authentic Blackness: The Folk in the New Negro Renaissance*, J. Martin Favor's thoughtful interpretation of Schuyler's position expands upon and enlivens traditional scholarly discussions that have dismissed "The Negro-Art Hokum" as accommodationist and counterproductive to the race uplift ideology spearheaded during the Harlem Renaissance and beyond. See J. Martin Favor, *Authentic Blackness: The Folk in the New Negro Renaissance* (Durham: Duke University Press, 1999), 120–26.

5. Arnold Rampersad, *The Life of Langston Hughes*, Vol. I (New York: Oxford University Press, 1986), 130.

6. Ibid., 175.

7. Ibid., 176.

8. Ibid., 178.

9. Ibid., 176.

10. In *Authentic Blackness*, Favor identifies the equation of "folk" identity with authentic black experience as a fundamental feature in African American cultural discourse. Hazel Carby makes similar arguments in the essays that make up "Fictions of the Folk," a section of her essay collection, *Cultures in Babylon: Black Britain and African America* (London: Verso, 1999).

11. Zora Neale Hurston, *Their Eyes Were Watching God* (New York: HarperCollins, 1998), 48.

12. Langston Hughes, "The Negro Artist and the Racial Mountain," *The Nation* 122 (23 June 1926): 3181, reprinted in *The Black Aesthetic*, ed. Addison Gayle, Jr. (Garden City, NY: Doubleday, 1971), 180.

13. Harper, *Are We Not Men?*, 44.

14. Amiri Baraka, *Raise Race Rays Raze: Essays Since 1965* (New York: Random House, 1969), 43.

15. Addison Gayle, Jr., *The Black Aesthetic*, xxiii.

16. Harper, *Are We Not Men?*, 52.

17. Henry Louis Gates, "The Trope of a New Negro and the Reconstruction of the Image of the Black," *Representations* 24 (Fall 1988): 131.

18. Ibid., 132.

19. Ibid.

20. In "What He Did for the Race: Carl Van Vechten and the Harlem Renaissance," I argue that, by 1926, one of the most successful strategies by which the "younger Negro artists" Hughes champions in "The Negro Artist and the Racial Mountain" distinguish themselves from their more conservative peers and mentors, was to claim public support for Carl Van Vechten and his 1926 novel, *Nigger Heaven*. I discuss the 1926 magazine *Fire!!* in its primary significance as a vehicle for the deployment of this strategy.

21. Alain Locke, ed., *The New Negro* (New York: Atheneum, 1968), xxvii.

22. Larry Neal, *Visions of a Liberated Future: Black Arts Movement Writings* (New York: Thunder's Mouth Press, 1989), 63.

23. Addison Gayle, Jr., "Introduction" to *The Black Aesthetic*, xxi.

24. Neal, *Visions of a Liberated Future*, 78.

25. Harold Cruse, *The Crisis of the Negro Intellectual* (New York: William Morrow & Company, 1967), 38.

26. David Lionel Smith, "The Black Arts Movement and Its Critics," *American Literary History* 3: 1 (Spring 1991): 95.

27. LeRoi Jones, *Blues People* (New York: William Morrow & Company, 1963), 134.

28. Imamu Amiri Baraka, "The Need for a Cultural Base to Civil Rites & Bpower Mooments," in *Raise Race Rays Raze*, 46.

29. In his 1963 study, *Blues People*, Jones' use of the term "Negro" does not contain the politically charged meaning that it takes on in his writing after 1965, the year Malcom X was assassinated and Jones moved uptown to begin his journey into blackness.

30. Baraka, *Raise Race Rays Raze*, 39.

31. William L. Van Deburg, *New Day in Babylon: The Black Power Movement and American Culture, 1965–1975* (Chicago: University of Chicago Press, 1992). See pages 53–55.

32. Langston Hughes, *The Big Sea* (New York: Alfred A. Knopf, 1940), 235.

33. Quoted in Arnold Rampersad, *The Life of Langston Hughes*, Vol. I, 137.

34. Quoted in Harper, *Are We Not Men?*,195.

35. Amiri Baraka, *The Autobiography of LeRoi Jones/Amiri Baraka* (New York: Freundlich Books, 1984), 202.

36. Harper, *Are We Not Men?*, 46.

37. Smith, "The Black Arts Movement," 95.

38. Eldridge Cleaver, *Soul on Ice* (New York: Dell, 1968), 100.

39. Ibid., 101.

40. LeRoi Jones, "brief reflections on two hot shots," in *Home: Social Essays* (New York: William Morrow & Company, 1966), 116.

41. Quoted in *Thirteen Ways of Looking at a Black Man* (New York: Random House, 1997), 12.

42. Ibid., 12.

43. Cleaver, *Soul on Ice*, 100.

44. Ibid., 101.

45. Harper, *Are We Not Men?*, 73.

46. Recent scholarship by Cathy J. Cohen, Phillip Brian Harper, J. Martin Favor, Dwight McBride, and Mason Stokes, among others, explores this topic in fascinating depth. See Cathy J. Cohen, *The Boundaries of Blackness: AIDS and the Breakdown of Black Politics* (Chicago: University of Chicago Press, 1999); Dwight McBride, "Can the Queen Speak? Racial Essentialism, Sexuality, and the Problem of Authority," in *The Greatest Taboo: Homosexuailty in Black Communities* (Los Angeles: Alyson Books, 2001): 24–43; and Mason Stokes, *The Color of Sex: Whiteness, Heterosexuality & the Fictions of White Supremacy* (Durham: Duke University Press, 2001).

47. Cruse, *The Crisis*, 37. The equation of the progression of black identity with the recuperation with manhood stays with us even today. Phillip Brian Harper argues that inherent in the "cultural-political reclamation supposedly represented by the widespread adoption of the term African-American" is the equation of the term with "the achievement of manhood, a good twenty-five years after the similarly significant advent of *black*." (Harper, *Are We Not Men?*, 68).

48. Douglas Sadownick, "Protest from Poet's Estate Keeps Film Out of Gay Festival" *Los Angeles Times*, July 12, 1989, part 6, p.2.

49. Emily Bernard, "What He Did for the Race: Carl Van Vechten and the Harlem Rcnaissance, *Soundings* 80: 4 (Winter 1997): 531–42.

50. Faith Berry provides an excellent example of this current of suspicion that circulates in discussions about the relationship between Van Vechten and Hughes in her 1976 essay, "Did Van Vechten Make or Take Hughes' Blues?" In this essay, Berry attempts to reaffirm Hughes' status as an authentic literary forefather by belittling Van Vechten's importance to his career. *Black World* (February 1976): 22–28.

51. See Arnold Rampersad, *The Life of Langston Hughes*, Vols. I and II (New York: Oxford University Press, 1986, 1988).

52. I do not mean to suggest here that black-run institutions, like Broadside Books, for instance, did not meet with success during the Black Arts Movement. For a thorough discussion of the accomplishments of Broadside Books, see Julius E. Thompson, *Dudley Randall, Broadside Press, and the Black Arts Movement in Detroit, 1960–1995* (Jefferson, NC: McFarland & Co, 1999).

53. To his credit, Baraka (Jones) owns up to the contradictions he veritably embodied in his autobiography, *The Autobiography of LeRoi Jones/Amiri Baraka*.

54. LeRoi Jones and Larry Neal, eds., *Black Fire: An Anthology of Afro-American Writing* (New York: William Morrow & Company, 1968), xvi.

55. For a description of the Ford Foundation's role as a source of support for the Black Arts Movement, as well as a larger discussion of the continuing tensions between black art and white money, see Henry Louis Gates, Jr., "The Chitlin Circuit," *The New Yorker* (February 3, 1997): 44–55.

56. Carla Kaplan, "The Language of Crisis in Feminist Theory," *Bucknell Review* 36: 2 (1992): 68–89.

57. For examples of this continuing phenomenon, see Trey Ellis, "The New Black Aesthetic," *Callaloo* 12 (Winter 1989): 233–50. The October 10, 1994 cover of *Time* magazine featured a photograph of Bill T. Jones with the caption: "Black Renaissance: African American artists are truly free at last."

58. Langston Hughes, "House in the World," in *The Collected Poems of Langston Hughes,* ed. Arnold Rampersad and David Roessel (New York: Alfred A. Knopf, 1998), 138.

59. Toni Morrison, *Playing in the Dark: Whiteness and the Literary Imagination* (Cambridge, MA: Harvard University Press, 1992), 5.

60. Hughes, *The Big Sea*, 128.

61. Amiri Baraka, *Home: Social Essays* (New York: William Morrow & Company, 1966), 111.

13

The Art of
Transformation

Parallels in the Black Arts and
Feminist Art Movements

Lisa Gail Collins

What we got to do is to dig into this thing that tugs at our souls—this blue yearning to make a way of our own. *Black people you are Black art.*
—LARRY NEAL, "ANY DAY NOW: BLACK ART AND BLACK LIBERATION," 1969

I wanted to wed my skills to my real ideas and to aspire to the making of art that could clearly reveal my values and point of view as a woman.
—JUDY CHICAGO, *THROUGH THE FLOWER: MY STRUGGLE AS A WOMAN ARTIST*, 1975

BLACK POWER/WOMAN'S LIBERATION

Similar utopian visions linked the Black Power and Women's Liberation Movements of the 1960s and 1970s. Passionate participants in both struggles ardently imagined a world where they would thrive, be safe, and feel connected, authentic, and whole. Holding these honest aspirations close, activist-participants worked tirelessly to realize them by transforming the dominant social order. Both Black Power and Women's Liberation agitators struggled to unite and mobilize the people they saw as their allies and kin in order to dismantle oppressive power relations, redistribute wealth and other resources, gain value and legitimacy, and design a new and just destiny. While Black Power advocates saw their primary goal as defeating white supremacy and feminist advocates saw their primary goal as overthrowing patriarchy, or male supremacy, activists in both struggles shared a common goal for their imagined allies and kin—social and psychological liberation and freedom from oppression.

The Black Power and Women's Liberation Movements, as well as their cultural corollaries the Black Arts and Feminist Art Movements, closely resembled each other; both movements shared similar traits, tendencies, tactics, and goals.

Yet these were truly parallel struggles, for only a vital handful of courageous visionaries such as Frances Beal, Toni Cade Bambara, Audre Lorde, Alice Walker, Faith Ringgold, June Jordan, Betye Saar, Angela Davis, and Ntozake Shange drew from and shaped both movements. From the late 1960s through the late 1970s, the two movements' striking similarities went mainly unseen and almost wholly unutilized, as participants in both struggles drew insight and energy, precisely, from imagining their collective histories, identities, and struggles as exquisitely unique.

NATIONALISM/FEMINISM

Black Power and Women's Liberation activists drew explanatory power from two different sources, for underlying the movements were the ideologies of nationalism—specifically Black nationalism—and feminism, respectively. Though often seen as rival forces and opposing worldviews, Black nationalists and feminists frequently employed these two ideologies in quite similar ways. Drawing from their respective theoretical reserves, both advocates for Black nationalism and advocates for feminism sought to construct a potent collective identity and a strong communal voice for their imagined allies and kin in order to best mobilize them to pursue, gain, and consolidate power and other group resources. Appeals to shared experiences, distinct and distinctive identities, proud (but shrouded) histories, and righteous futures characterized both Black nationalist and feminist rallying cries. Larry Neal, for example, the quintessential theorist and advocate for the Black Arts Movement, approached fellow African Americans during this period as latent nationalists, and considered the spirited activation of this dormant energy a crucial early goal in the struggle for Black Power. In this way, Neal, who saw the Black Arts Movement as the cultural wing of the struggle for black nationhood, sought to tap the "group ethos" that he believed, "tugs at all black people" for the prideful purposes of empowering, uniting, and mobilizing.[1]

Feminist writer Jane O'Reilly in the preview issue of *Ms.* magazine, a key organ of the Women's Liberation Movement, demonstrated a similar intimate approach to her imagined allies and kin. By coining the concept "Click!," she revealed a sanguine belief that a latent feminism—one that was just waiting to be actively engaged—resided in women. In her pivotal essay on housewives, O'Reilly supported her activist belief that everyday interactions could unveil the truth of women's subordination and how, in turn, this "shock of recognition" could serve to complete "the puzzle of reality in women's minds" and prompt the heady declaration that "the revolution has begun."[2]

MALCOLM X/SIMONE DE BEAUVOIR

In their attempts to empower, unite, and mobilize their oppressed and suppressed allies and kin, Black Power and Women's Liberation activists deployed their respective theoretical reserves in similar ways. Yet in drawing explanatory power from two different ideologies, Black nationalism and feminism, movement activists claimed different intellectual histories and trajectories, as well as different patron saints. The towering, fiery, uncompromising figure of Malcolm X and his militant call for self-definition, self-determination, self-respect, and self-defense for African America served as a principal referent and a prime inspiration for the Black Power Movement and its corollary Black Arts.

Malcolm X's harrowing assassination on February 21, 1965, typically marks the official beginning of the Black Arts Movement as within weeks of Malcolm X's murder writer LeRoi Jones, in response, dramatically (and traumatically) fled the Village and relocated to Harlem to start the Black Arts Repertory Theater/School (BARTS), an alternative community center, school, and performance space based on the evolving principles of Black Power and Black Consciousness.[3] For establishing this short-lived (1965–66) but highly influential cultural institution—BARTS spawned around 800 black theaters and cultural centers in the United States—and simultaneously coining the term "Black Arts," LeRoi Jones is often credited with founding the Black Arts Movement.[4]

Yet while the prominent writer and emerging activist certainly performed the dashingly symbolic and concrete acts that launched Black Arts in the wake of Malcolm X's assassination, it was the living Malcolm who truly sparked the cultural movement that outlived him. Eight months before his death, Malcolm X had called for a black cultural revolution. On June 28, 1964, at a Harlem rally devoted to announcing the aims and objectives of his Organization of Afro-American Unity (OAAU), the Black nationalist leader had stressed the necessity of culture in revolutionary struggles for social and political change. Drawing from the words and deeds of Négritude advocates such as Aimé Césaire and Léopold Senghor, Malcolm X declared from the stage of the Audubon Ballroom: "Culture is an indispensable weapon in the freedom struggle. We must take hold of it and forge the future with the past."[5]

Sparking and shaping the contours of a black cultural revolution, Malcolm X in his OAAU speech called for the recovery, dissemination, and embrace of a shared African past, as a creative way to psychologically empower black Americans and to knit them more tightly to both African peoples and their own local black communities. He explained:

> We come from Africa, a great continent and a proud and varied people, a land which is the new world and was the cradle of civilization. Our culture and our history are as old as man himself and yet we know almost nothing of it. We must recapture our heritage and our identity if we are ever to liberate ourselves from the bonds of white supremacy. We must launch a cultural revolution to unbrainwash an entire people. Our cultural revolution must be the means of bringing us closer to our African brothers and sisters. It must begin in the community and be based on community participation.[6]

Black Power activists and adherents to Black Arts overwhelmingly claimed Malcolm X as their patron saint. Yet it was Los Angeles-based scholar and grassroots organizer Maulana Ron Karenga (a chosen name meaning "Master Teacher" [Maulana] and "Keeper of Tradition" [Karenga]) who drew most immediately and decisively from Malcolm X's declaration that a black cultural revolution was essential to the revolutionary struggle for Black Power. Ignited by Malcolm X's message, incensed by his brutal murder, and informed by his own work as a community leader directly following the August rebellions in Watts, Karenga formed US (meaning "us" as opposed to "them"), a cultural nationalist organization in Los Angeles in the fall of 1965.[7] Profoundly influenced by Malcolm X's theory that African Americans were both politically and psychologically disempowered, Karenga, a scholar of African political affairs and African languages, devoted his organization to his deceased mentor's assertion that cultural revolution was crucial to black liberation.[8] "You must have a cultural revolution before the violent revolution," the US leader insisted in *The Quotable Karenga*, a distillation of his cultural nationalist views on revolution modeled after the widely read *Quotations from Chairman Mao Tse-Tung* (popularly known as the "Little Red Book").[9]

By locating, shaping, and sharing alternative histories, values, rituals, and myths, Karenga hoped to heal and transform African America. "The culture provides the bases for revolution and recovery," he promised.[10] The Los Angeles-based leader believed that the development of a strong, healthy, culturally cohesive black nation would provide a firm foundation for revolutionary struggle. "We stress culture because it gives identity, purpose, and direction. It tells you who you are, what you must do, and how you can do it," he explained.[11]

While Black Power activists such as Larry Neal, LeRoi Jones, and Maulana Ron Karenga fiercely turned to Malcolm X and his legacy for courage, clarity, and insight, Women's Liberation activists avidly turned to Simone de Beauvoir and her enormously influential 1949 book *Le deuxième sexe*—translated into English four years later as *The Second Sex*, for intellectual guidance and political direction. Widely available in the United States in 1953, the French intellectual's ambitious, learned, and unprecedented book on the construction of womanhood and the oppression and suppression of women served as a clarion call for Women's Liberationists in the following decades. A multidisciplinary examination of the stifling subordination of women throughout time and place—and in relation to biology, psychology, economics, anthropology, folklore, religion, philosophy, literature, and the arts—Beauvoir's book lay bare the predicaments of women due to the entangled forces of culture and biology. And though her findings were quite depressing, she concluded her tome with a treatise entitled "Toward Liberation." Here in the final pages of *The Second Sex*, the existential philosopher and not-yet-feminist explained that up until her book's publication, women had not been able to excel in the arts and humanities due to the heavy restrictions that engulfed them. This tragic loss of creativity and insight, however, was soon to end as, she presciently proffered, "the free woman is just being born."[12] This emergent woman, Beauvoir continued, would finally have the freedom to create vital work that would lend meaning to the world. Firmly believing that freedom from entrenched restrictions would expand women's worldview and, in this way, enrich their work, Beauvoir wrote:

> Art, literature, philosophy, are attempts to found the world anew on a human liberty: that of the individual creator; to entertain such a pretension, one must first unequivocally assume the status of a being who has liberty. The restrictions that education and custom impose on woman now limit her grasp on the universe; when the struggle to find one's place in this world is too arduous, there can be no question of getting away from it. Now, one must first emerge from it into a sovereign solitude if one wants to try to regain a grasp upon it: what woman needs first of all is to undertake, in anguish and pride, her apprenticeship in abandonment and transcendence; that is, in liberty.[13]

Lamenting the muffling and loss of women's past thoughts and creations—and refraining from theorizing if women's future thoughts and creations would be any different from men's—Simone de Beauvoir closed her book with a dire assessment of the past coupled with a hopeful assertion for the future: "What is certain is that hitherto woman's possibilities have been suppressed and lost to humanity, and that it is high time she be permitted to take her chances in her own interest and in the interest of all."[14]

The force of Beauvoir's findings, the brilliance of her writing, and the originality of her life all served as critical inspiration for the Women's Liberation Movement. Feminist writers, in particular, frequently paid tribute to her exemplary work through their dedications, epigraphs, and citations, as well as through the scope, method, direction, and even the existence, of their own writings. Yet it was Los Angeles-based artist and emerging activist Judy Chicago who most intently wrestled with the French intellectual's findings on the problems of women creators throughout Western history in relation to the struggles of contemporary women artists. Before wrestling with this history, however, Chicago publicly declared herself "free" and thus—in line with Beauvoir's insights—capable of vital work and worthy of note. In the fall of 1970, Judy Chicago, who had been born Judy Cohen and had become Judy Gerowitz upon her first marriage, boldly announced via the entry wall to her solo show at California State College in Fullerton, a change in her last name to reflect the city of her birth and to signal her "emerging position as a feminist."[15] Her name change sign read: "Judy Gerowitz hereby divests herself of all names imposed upon her through male social dominance and freely chooses her own name Judy Chicago."

In conjunction with this assertive act of self-definition and feminist solidarity which strongly echoes numerous acts of self-naming and bonding within the Black Power Movement, Judy Chicago also launched the Feminist Art Program at Fresno State College (now California State University, Fresno) in the fall of 1970. Like LeRoi Jones's establishment of the Black Arts Repertory

Theater/School five years earlier, this first experiment in feminist art education was short-lived but highly influential. Fifteen students joined the Fresno program during the year of its existence under Chicago to devote themselves to its alternative curriculum which included: consciousness-raising sessions, performance workshops, radical artistic experimentation, and extensive research into women's history, literature, and art.[16] Directly responding to Simone de Beauvoir's claims that women in the past had not been able to excel in the arts and humanities and that their thoughts and creations had been stifled and lost, Chicago made historical research central to the Feminist Art Program's curriculum.[17] Driven by the desire to personally understand—and perhaps refute—Beauvoir's findings, program participants eagerly visited libraries; gathered, studied, and shared the work of their artistic female predecessors; made slides; and built the first archive of women's art on the West Coast.[18]

Yet only a few short years after Judy Chicago and her feminist art students at Fresno State (1970–71) and, later, at the California Institute of the Arts (1971–73) began exploring art created by women, and a full quarter of a century after the publication of *The Second Sex*, Chicago reiterated much of Beauvoir's dismal assessment of women's historical inability to excel in the arts due to the stifling restrictions that entrapped them. In a 1974 interview with feminist art critic Lucy Lippard, the artist and teacher explained:

> My investigation of women's art has led me to conclude that what has prevented women from being really great artists is the fact that we have been unable so far to transform our circumstances into our subject matter. That is the process of transformation men have been able to make while we have been embedded in our circumstances, unable to step out of them and use them to reveal the whole nature of the human condition.[19]

In a striking departure from Beauvoir, however, who sought to solve the "problem" of female greatness by freeing women from gendered restrictions so they could inhabit the highly desirable status of "sovereign solitude" and begin an "apprenticeship in abandonment and transcendence," Chicago believed the "problem" could best be solved if women, freed from restrictions, could draw strength, insight, form, and content, precisely, from fully grasping their former "circumstances."

SOUL-SEARCHING/CONSCIOUSNESS-RAISING

Studying the past, confronting the present, and envisioning a new future were central to the Black Power and Women's Liberation Movements. Although Black Power advocates and Women's Liberation activists drew from different intellectual histories and trajectories, their shared common goal for their imagined allies and kin—social and psychological liberation and freedom from oppression—led them both to place a high premium on new ways of seeing, particularly new ways of seeing the self and the collective in relation to society. Activists in both movements believed that increased self-awareness accompanied by ideological awakening would benefit oppressed and suppressed individuals by healing psychic wounds, curbing feelings of alienation and despair, and turning individuals outward so they could more fully unite with their now more visible allies. Underlying their calls for self-examination, reflection, and scrutiny was the belief that increased knowledge of the self and the collective in society, past and present, would lead to a strong communal consciousness which, in turn, would lead to an empowered and unified activist community ready to transform the dominant social order. Concerning the necessity of this trajectory, Larry Neal professed: "It is impossible for a people to struggle and win without a sense of collective consciousness."[20] Likewise, Kathie Sarachild, an early member of New York Radical Women (1967–69), the first NYC-based Women's Liberation group, evoked the need for a similar trajectory when she expressed the activist group's priorities in 1968: "The first job now was to raise awareness and understanding, our own and others—awareness that would prompt people to organize and to act on a mass scale."[21]

Closely connected to their emphasis on individual awareness, both movements also encouraged explorations of communal identity—of blackness and femaleness, respectively. LeRoi Jones voiced the necessity of this form of collective awareness work most succinctly when he declared: "There is no black power without blackness conscious of itself."[22] Larry Neal, who along with Jones had been central to the workings of BARTS in Harlem in 1965–66, and who had co-edited *Black Fire*, the essential anthology of the Black Arts Movement, with LeRoi Jones in 1968, was one of the first to publicly laud the palpable impact of awareness work—the emerging change in mass consciousness—and to explain its meaning and direction. Within the pages of the August 1969 special issue of *Ebony* devoted to "The Black Revolution," Neal testified:

> We bear witness to a profound change in the way we now see ourselves and the world. And this has been an ongoing change. A steady, certain march toward a collective sense of who we are, and what we must now be about to liberate ourselves. Liberation is impossible if we fail to see ourselves in more positive terms. For without a change of vision, we are slaves to the oppressor's ideas and values—ideas and values that finally attack the very core of our existence. Therefore, we must see the world in terms of our own realities.[23]

Women's Liberationists also viewed new ways of seeing the self and the collective in relation to society as crucial to the struggle to overthrow male supremacy. Revealing this shared trait, Gloria Steinem, a founding editor of *Ms.* magazine, wrote in 1972: "If it weren't for the Women's Movement, I might still be dissembling away. But the ideas of this great sea-change in women's view of ourselves are contagious and irresistible. They hit women like a revelation, as if we had left a small dark room and walked into the sun."[24] Central to the Women's Liberation Movement was the practice of consciousness-raising.

Kathie Sarachild, a prime architect of the practice and its principles, drew from her memories of rap sessions as a Civil Rights Movement organizer in the early 1960s to further develop this powerful agent of personal and social change as a member of both New York Radical Women (1967–69) and Redstockings (1969–70).[25] Consciousness-raising, or informed and attentive life-sharing and analysis, quickly became integral to the growing Women's Movement and lent palpable meaning to its prime rallying cry: "The personal is political." Concerning the initial purpose of this critical method of self-awareness and social change, Kathie Sarachild later explained: "Our idea in the beginning was that consciousness-raising—through both C-R groups and public actions—would waken more and more women to an understanding of what their problems were and that they would begin to take action, both individual and collective."[26] Many early Women's Liberationists saw both homes and streets as important sites for consciousness-raising. Private analysis and public actions were both viewed as essential to the overthrow of patriarchy. Clarifying this interconnectedness of theory and practice, Sarachild explained:

> In consciousness-raising, through shared experience, one learns that uncovering the truth, that naming what's really going on, is necessary but insufficient for making changes. With greater understanding, one discovers new necessity for action—and new possibilities for it. Finding the solution to a problem takes place through theory and action both. Each leads to the other but both are necessary or the problem is never really solved.[27]

Consciousness-raising was integral to the Feminist Art Program's curriculum at Fresno State College in 1970–71. With Judy Chicago's encouragement, the women art students used this vital tool of increased awareness and inspired transformation to heal, bond, and create authentic new work. In line with Women's Liberation Movement objectives, program participants studied the past through their historical research on women artists, and by courageously and attentively sharing their life experiences, they confronted the present and saw the necessity for future action—the necessity to create anew. Faith Wilding, one of the first students to enroll in the program—and who was leading a feminist readings course called "The Second Sex" when Chicago was hired—explained how she and her peers conducted intensive consciousness-raising sessions:

> The procedure was to "go around the room" and hear women speak from her personal experience about a key topic such as work, money, ambition, sexuality, parents, power, clothing, body image, or violence. As each woman spoke it became apparent that what had seemed to be purely "personal" experiences were actually shared by all the other women; we were discovering a common oppression based on our gender, which was defining our roles and identities as women. In subsequent group discussions, we analyzed the social and political mechanisms

of this oppression, thus placing our personal histories into a larger cultural perspective. This was a direct application of *the* slogan of 1970s feminism: "The personal is the political."[28]

Using the insight and courage they gained from these difficult sessions, the fifteen women students of the Feminist Art Program created the first raw and eloquent work of what would soon be called the Feminist Art Movement.

BLACK ARTS MOVEMENT/FEMINIST ART MOVEMENT

The Black Arts and Feminist Art Movements were cultural corollaries, or wings, of the larger Black Power and Women's Liberation Movements. Participants in both arts movements shared the same utopian visions, drew from the same theoretical reserves, turned to the same patron saints, and placed the same premium on awareness and consciousness as advocates and adherents of their respective larger social movements. Yet members of the Black Arts and Feminist Art Movements were also artists who firmly believed in the necessity of cultural work in the struggle for social and political change and, due to this, they were more apt to advocate for cultural nationalism and cultural feminism—ideologies that embrace the creative construction of alternative and/or oppositional cultures of resistance—than their peers who were not committed to the arts.[29] LeRoi Jones, for example, embraced Maulana Karenga's theoretical principles in 1967, precisely for their explicit focus on culture. He explained: "Because Karenga's whole premise was of cultural revolution, I was pulled closer. Being a cultural worker, an artist, the emphasis on culture played to my own biases. And no doubt in a society where the advanced forces too often put no stress on culture and the arts at all, I thought his philosophy eminently correct."[30]

From 1967 to October 7, 1974 (when he officially rejected nationalism for Third World-based Marxism), LeRoi Jones worked closely with Karenga's cultural nationalist philosophy Kawaida (a Swahili term translated as "tradition and reason") which served, for the writer and activist, as a blueprint for the creation of a revolutionary black culture in the United States.[31] Along with this embrace of Kawaida, LeRoi Jones also changed his name. In 1967, Jones was honored with the Arabic name Ameer Barakat ("Blessed Prince") by Hajj Heesham Jaaber, a Sunni Muslim priest closely affiliated with Malcolm X during his last months. Yet soon after, and with Karenga's counsel and interest in "Bantuizing or Swahilizing" words, Jones changed the spelling and pronunciation of his name slightly to Amiri Baraka. Reflecting on the replacement of his birth name, Amiri Baraka recalled feeling liberated from his "slave name," honored by his mighty new one, and enthused by the embrace of "blackness" that this name change represented.[32]

If LeRoi Jones/Amiri Baraka served as founder of the Black Arts Movement, Larry Neal served as its top theorist and advocate, for he penned many of the movement's most engaged and engaging position papers. A poet, dramatist, essayist, and activist, Neal saw the arts, like his frequent collaborator, as ripe terrain on which to graft lofty ideals—ideals that would enable black people to envision and propel change. And like other adherents to Black Arts, he saw cultural work as central to the struggle for social and psychological liberation and freedom from oppression. Revealing the inherent intimacy between Black Power and Black Arts, Neal wrote:

> Now along with the Black Power movement, there has been developing a movement among Black artists. This movement we call the Black Arts. This movement, in many ways, is older than the current Black Power movement. It is primarily concerned with the cultural and spiritual liberation of Black America. It takes upon itself the task of expressing, through various art forms, the Soul of the Black Nation. And like the Black Power Movement, it seeks to define the world of art and culture in its own terms. The Black Arts movement seeks to link, in a highly conscious manner, art and politics in order to assist in the liberation of Black people.[33]

In a similar manner to how LeRoi Jones served as founder of the Black Arts Movement, Judy Chicago served as founder of the Feminist Art Movement. Like Jones, Chicago performed the dashingly symbolic and concrete acts that both directly responded to the tactics and tendencies of the larger liberation struggle and worked to birth and shape its cultural wing. Seven years after Jones established BARTS in an old brownstone at 109 W. 130th Street in Harlem and six years after Jones launched Spirit House, a second Black Arts cultural center and Black Power political hub on 33 Stirling Street in Newark, Judy Chicago, Miriam Schapiro, and their twenty-one art students transformed a condemned mansion at 533 Mariposa Avenue in Hollywood into the quintessential Feminist Art project. Participants in the second incarnation of the Feminist Art Program, which was now housed at the California Institute of the Arts (CalArts) and led by both Chicago and Schapiro, these art students employed newly acquired house-renovating skills to create a feminist treatise on home-making.

Called *Womanhouse*, this collaborative project tackled the subject of the suppression (and depression) of post-World War II suburban housewives trapped in limited and limiting gender roles. Through room-specific installations and performances, each of the seventeen rooms of the house as well as the five living room-based performances grappled with the restricting gender roles and social expectations that the students had explored as part of their group consciousness-raising sessions. Extensively covered by the press, and experienced firsthand by about 10,000 people during the only month of its existence (January 30-February 28, 1972), this large-scale watershed work powerfully introduced the emerging Feminist Art Movement to the interested public in a way similar to how BARTS had introduced the Black Arts Movement to attentive America.[34]

If Judy Chicago served as founder of the Feminist Art Movement, Lucy Lippard served as its principal critic and preeminent advocate. Holding a role similar to Larry Neal, she penned many of the evolving movement's most engaged and engaging position papers. Lippard, like her activist predecessors and peers, saw art and politics as linked for, she believed, they both held "the power to envision, move, and change."[35] Like others committed to the goal of social and psychological liberation and freedom from oppression for their imagined allies and kin, she, too, placed a high premium on new ways of seeing, particularly new ways of seeing the self and the collective in relation to society. Lippard saw "a developed feminist consciousness" as leading to a new kind of art, a new way to experience art, and a new role for it—one with crucial links to feminist activism. She explained:

> A developed feminist consciousness brings with it an altered concept of reality and morality that is crucial to the art being made and to the lives lived with that art. We take for granted that making art is not simply "expressing oneself" but is a far broader and more important task—expressing oneself as a member of a larger unity, or comm./unity, so that in speaking for oneself one is also speaking for those who cannot speak.[36]

Like Larry Neal, Lucy Lippard championed a new art that expressed an alternative and liberatory consciousness, and touted its creators for articulating the yearnings of a larger and less heard community.

THE ROLE OF THE ARTIST

Proclaiming pivotal roles for creators and their creations within social and political struggle was crucial to both the Black Arts and Feminist Art Movements. Both movements avidly touted the ideal of activist artists who could prompt change through their inspired and committed work. "The artist and the political activist are one. They are both shapers of the future reality," Larry Neal pronounced in 1968.[37] Underlying this spirited vision and charge lay a critique of the controlling ideal of the artist in the West—the isolated, typically white male individual whose genius lies far outside the grasp and relevancy of local communities. In direct response to this dominant modernist myth, participants in the Black Arts and Feminist Art Movements envisioned the perfect artist as one who, immersed in his or her community, created vital work that honored and empowered his or her new and non-elite audience for art through validation and consciousness-raising. Proposing a politically potent and intimate role for creators and their creations within the Black Arts Movement, Larry Neal proffered: "The Black Arts Movement is radically opposed to any concept of the artist that alienates him from his community. Black Art is the aesthetic and spiritual sister of the Black Power concept. As such, it envisions an art that speaks directly to the needs and aspirations of Black America."[38]

The Feminist Art Movement also sought to overthrow the modernist myth of the combative and elusive artist. Critiquing this dominant standard, Lucy Lippard asserted: "The history of the male avant-garde has been one of reverse (or perverse) response to society, with the artist seen as the opposition or as out-of-touch idealist."[39] Championing an equitable relationship based on honesty and accountability, not aloofness and combativeness, Lippard theorized that a reciprocal stance would enhance the creation and reception of art. "I do not think it is possible to make important or even communicable art without some strong sense of source and self on one hand and some strong sense of audience and communication on the other," she explained.[40]

In the spring of 1974, Lucy Lippard was one of seventy-one women to respond to a short letter from the seventeen women art students currently enrolled in the Feminist Art Program at CalArts. Dated March 6, 1974, the students' letter explained that they along with their teacher Miriam Schapiro, the sole director of the Feminist Art Program at the time, were planning a seven-day Women's Art Festival as a forum to share their work and celebrate the emergence of their own "new spirit of visibility and vitality in the arts."[41] As part of this event, the students explained, they were soliciting letters they could publish in *Anonymous Was a Woman*, the accompanying catalog. They wrote: "We plan to document this event with the publication of a catalog which will have a section called "Letter to a Young Woman Artist." We would be deeply honored to include such a letter from you about your experiences, or advice, or whatever feelings you might wish to express. Your letter would be an invaluable contribution in our efforts to build a strong identity for women."[42]

Inspired by Czech poet Rainer Maria Rilke's gracious and heartfelt words of advice to an aspiring young writer collected in *Letters to a Young Poet*, the students asked their respected elders—women in the arts—for words of wisdom to guide their journey as emergent women artists.[43] Echoing the intimacy and urgency of Rilke's letters to the young poet, Lippard promptly responded to the students of the Feminist Art Program with the following note:

> To a Young Woman Artist,
> I'm sorry this has be so short, because I have a lot I'd like to talk about with you, but try to read between the lines. I hope you're angry but get it over with fast and *use* it while you've got it. I hope you don't stop being angry now and then until things are better for all women, not just artists; I hope you're working from yourself and know how to fuck the art world pressures when you get out there; and I hope you're working for everybody else too; I hope you'll be the one to figure out a way to keep art from being used the wrong way and for the wrong things in this society; I hope you make your art accessible to more people, to all women and to everybody; I hope you think about that now and aren't waiting till you make it, because that's likely to be too late. I hope you remember that being a feminist carries with it a real responsibility to be a human. I hope and I hope and I hope . . . love, Lucy Lippard.[44]

In her frank and intimate response, Lippard voiced what she saw as the role of the artist within the Women's Liberation Movement. After affirming the students' rage at the imposed social order and pressing them to see themselves as participants in a larger struggle, she encouraged them to create honest and heartfelt work and to resist the mainstream art world's pressures to conform. And, finally, she asked them to make their work "accessible to more people, to all women and to everybody."

For activists who yearned for art that transforms, the issue of accessibility was central. Maulana Karenga put it most bluntly when he claimed: "There is no art in the world you should have to go to school to appreciate."[45] Participants in both the Black Arts and Feminist Art Movements yearned for the creation of art that could communicate directly with their imagined allies and kin. Beneath this desire to intimately and authentically communicate with new and non-elite audiences for art was the belief that art, because it dealt in images, was a particularly rich site for the creation of liberatory visions. Articulating the ideal of an art that could target allies and kin for the purposes of validation, consciousness-raising, and the revelation of a "liberated future," Larry Neal pressed artists to create:

> An art that addresses itself directly to Black people; an art that speaks to us in terms of our feelings and ideas about the world; an art that validates the positive aspects of our life style. Dig: An art that opens us up to the beauty and ugliness within us; that makes us understand our condition and each other in a more profound manner; that unites us, exposing us to our painful weaknesses and strengths; and finally, an art that posits for us the Vision of a Liberated Future. So the function of artistic technique and a Black esthetic is to make the goal of communication and liberation more possible.[46]

Participants in the Feminist Art Movement similarly yearned for artists who could make art that spoke honestly and directly to their imagined allies and kin, and like their Black Arts Movement peers, they too criticized modernist values for creating the hostile gap between artists and non-elite viewers they avidly sought to overhaul. Judy Chicago understood the problem as two-fold—involving both art making and art viewing. Concerning this two-pronged barrier to authentic communication, she explained: "It's not only the making of art but the perception of art that is too formalized in our tradition, and has to be opened up to a new human dimension."[47] Pledging to serve as a "bridge between artists and community," Chicago saw her goal as an artist as "introducing art into the life of the community in a way that allows people to see images they can relate to."[48]

A similar desire to dismantle the barriers that isolated art from people and life, infused the creation of the New York City-based Heresies Collective and their "idea-oriented" journal, *Heresies: A Feminist Publication on Art and Politics*. Committed to "the broadening of the definition and function of art," the Heresies Collective included the following mission statement in every issue of their journal beginning with the first in January 1977: "As women, we are aware that historically the connections between our lives, our arts, and our ideas have been suppressed. Once these connections are clarified they can function as a means to dissolve the alienation between artist and audience, and to understand the relationship between art and politics, work and workers . . . . Our view of feminism is one of process and change, and we feel that in the process of this dialogue we can foster a change in the meaning of art."[49]

THE PURPOSE OF ART

Activists in both movements were aligned in their desire to expand the purpose and meaning of art. They worked to replace the imposed modernist ideal of "art for art's sake" with a chosen activist ideal of "art for people's sake." In essence, they sought to counter the dominant ideal, which they viewed as decadent and immoral, with a more responsible and life-enhancing one. Karenga put it boldly when he stated: "Black Art must be for the people, by the people, and from the people. That is to say, it must be functional, collective and committing."[50] Similarly, Jeff Donaldson, a founder of Chicago's Organization of Black American Culture (OBAC) and a painter on the *Wall of Respect*, expressed the critical consciousness-raising role he envisioned for artists and their art in the quest for Black Power. In his 1969 article titled "The Role We Want for Black Art," Donaldson wrote: "Black image makers are creating forms that define, glorify, and direct black people—an art for the people's sake. Those of us who call ourselves artists realize that we can no longer afford the luxury of 'art for art's sake.'"[51]

A similar critique of modernist artistic values and embrace of an emerging counter-culture was made by feminist activist Robin Morgan when she reported: "Beneath the expansion of presses and magazines is an explosion of women's culture so energetic and widespread that it is not only giving voice to women as a people but shows signs of rescuing art itself from the necrophiliac modernism of the establishment, making poetry and music and drama and visual art and dance once again relevant, passionate, accessible; something to be integrated into all of our daily lives."[52]

Disgruntled—horrified even—with the role of the artist and the purpose of art as dictated by mainstream modernism, both Larry Neal and Lucy Lippard, the principal critics and preeminent advocates of the two parallel movements, advocated the reclamation of, what they saw as, the primal purposes of art. Stressing what he envisioned as the ancient link between art, ritual, and religion and encouraging its renewal, Neal offered the following vital vision for Black art:

> The Black Arts movement is rooted in a spiritual ethic. In saying that the function of art is to liberate Man, we propose a function for art which is now dead in the West and which is in keeping with our most ancient traditions and with our needs. Because, at base, art is religious and ritualistic; and ritual moves to liberate Man and to connect him to the Greater Forces. Thus Man becomes stronger psychically,

and is thus more able to create a world that is an extension of his spirituality—his positive humanity. We say that the function of art is to liberate Man.[53]

Tendering a vision of artists working collectively and responsibly, and of an art deeply embedded in community life, Lippard offered this vitalizing vision for feminist art:

> The feminist (and socialist) value system insists upon cultural workers supporting and responding to their constituencies. The three models of such interaction are: (1) group and/or public ritual; (2) public consciousness-raising and interaction through visual images, environments, and performances; and (3) cooperative/collaborative/collective or anonymous artmaking. . . . All these structures are in the most fundamental sense collective, like feminism itself. And these three models are all characterized by an element of outreach, a need for connections beyond process or product, an element of *inclusiveness* which also takes the form of responsiveness and responsibility for one's own ideas and images—the outward and inward facets of the same impulse."[54]

Rejecting what they saw as the unprincipled dictates of mainstream modernism, Larry Neal and Lucy Lippard championed a world where art was embedded in both the awesome and mundane rituals of everyday life, and where ethics and aesthetics were one.

BLACK AESTHETIC/FEMALE IMAGERY

Participants in the Black Arts and Feminist Art Movements not only critiqued the role of the artist and the purpose of art within mainstream modernism, they also critiqued the dominant art world's exclusion of them, especially when they chose to openly express their distinctive experiences and identities in their art. While some artists actively struggled for inclusion into a transformed art world, others devoted themselves to the creation of alternative structures for the making and experiencing of art. The Chicago-based Organization of Black American Culture (OBAC) made plain its lack of faith in mainstream art institutions and criticism and its full support of new autonomous structures for black artists and their art. Its statement of purpose read: "Because the Black artist and the creative portrayal of the Black Experience have been consciously excluded from the total spectrum of American arts, we want to provide a new context for the Black artist in which he can work out his problems and pursue his aims unhampered and uninhibited by the prejudices and dictates of the mainstream."[55] Seeking independence from the dictates of the dominant art world, OBAC visual artists created the heroic *Wall of Respect* and, through this autonomous act, launched an urban outdoor mural movement.

Feminist artists also devoted themselves to a range of struggles, including rallying for inclusion into a transformed mainstream, building alternative women-centered sites and structures, and struggling simultaneously on both fronts. Judy Chicago voiced the anger of many feminist artists who had attended art schools and fully envisioned participating in the mainstream art world, when she shared her life-shaking realization that her dream for herself was not possible. Around 1969, the fairly prominent young artist realized that her access to formal training and professional development had been dependent on her refraining from exploring her own personal and collective experiences as a woman in her art. Explaining the effect of this form of entrenched misogyny, she wrote: "I learned that if I wanted my work to be taken seriously, the work should not reveal its having been made by a woman. One of the best compliments a woman artist could receive then was that 'her work looked like it was made by a man.'"[56]

Lucy Lippard voiced a similar critique when she explained her short-term support for a separate women's art world due to women's inability to fully thrive in the male-dominated and exclusionary art world. In her introduction to *From the Center: Feminist Essays on Women's Art*, she asked:

> Why are we all still so afraid of being *other* than men? Women are still in hiding. We still find it difficult, even the young ones, to express ourselves freely in large groups of men. Since the art world is still dominated by men, this attitude pervades the art that is being made. In the process, feelings and forms are neutralized. For this reason, I am all in favor of a separatist art world for the time being—separate women's schools, galleries, museums—until we reach the point when women are as at home in the world as men are.[57]

While Lippard considered inclusion into a transformed art world and "real" world the appropriate long-term goal for feminist artists, she also felt that due to the current mainstream art world's exclusion and suppression of women artists and their work, a temporary separatist respite was an important step to the creation and recognition of art that confidently expressed the female gender of its maker.[58]

Infused with cultural feminist and cultural nationalist ideologies which, by definition, privilege cultural terrain while championing the unique histories, separate experiences, and distinct and distinctive identities of its imagined allies and kin, artists from both struggles went on creative separatist quests. Some Feminist Art Movement participants went searching for shared imagery, while some Black Arts Movement activists pursued a collective aesthetic. Based in femaleness or blackness, respectively, artists in both movements searched for a set of shared characteristics or principles that would guide the creation of a generative art—an art that would induce feelings of connection, authenticity, and wholeness among its community. Initially, adherents to both movements looked to earlier art for the bases of their quests. In a special issue of *Everywoman* devoted to the Feminist Art Program at Fresno State College, Faith Wilding explained that while conducting historical research on women artists in 1970–71, program participants sought to discover a body of work created by women that intimately and courageously reveled in its femaleness:

> One of our major tasks then, in this research project, is to find, carefully isolate and then document "female art," that is, art that deals directly with the experience, sensations, and emotions of women. We are not indiscriminately interested in just any art made by women, for a lot of women have emotionally and psychically internalized the male world, and have learned to produce images which will please men and win their recognition. No, rather, we are interested in very particular images and forms, those which are honest, direct, exposed, tender and emotionally evocative in terms of experience. We have begun to discover that there is a common body of imagery in female art, that there is, in fact, a world of values and experience and sensation that is quite different from that of men.[59]

Based on this archival and conceptual research, Judy Chicago and Miriam Schapiro lectured widely on the topic of "female imagery" in 1971–72 while co-directing the Feminist Art Program at CalArts.[60] After intently studying the works of women artists of the past and visiting the studios and other workspaces of contemporary women artists, the two feminist artists and art educators began to see a common imagery in some of the art created by women, particularly those who worked abstractly. Recurrent in the work of these artists, they posited— while showing work by Georgia O'Keeffe, Louise Nevelson, Barbara Hepworth, Lee Bontecou, and themselves—was the use of a "central image." Frequently echoing a flower or vagina, this "central core imagery," they theorized, symbolized the female body and though often hidden or disguised "behind the façade of formalized art concerns," this core imagery served as a proud assertion of femaleness.[61] In her autobiography *Through the Flower: My Struggle as a Woman Artist*, Judy Chicago explained that this hidden sexualized imagery was a path of our female predecessors. Knowing that access to training and professional opportunities was dependent on downplaying overt expressions of their femaleness, some prior women artists, she argued, had created a coded imagery informed by an awareness of, and pride in, their female bodies. Detailing her discovery of this coded and recurrent female imagery with Miriam Schapiro, Chicago wrote:

> Mimi and I looked at work together, examining paintings and sculptures of women known and unknown, concentrating on those who had worked abstractly. From our own experiences as artists, we both had an understanding of how to look for the hidden content in women's work. What we discovered in our studies and later, in our studio visits overwhelmed me; and reinforced my own early perceptions. We found a frequent use of the central image, often a flower, or abstracted flower form, sometimes surrounded by folds or undulations, as in the structure of the vagina. We saw an abundance of sexual forms—breasts, buttocks, female organs. We felt sure that what we were seeing was a reflection of each woman's need to explore her own identity, to assert her sense of her own sexuality, as we had both done.[62]

Underlying Chicago's and Schapiro's theory of "female imagery," which was hotly controversial upon its first articulation in 1971, was the ardent desire for a world where women artists, could break free from the misogynist injunction for "coded art" and fully revel both symbolically and concretely in their distinct and unique identities as women. Believing that women's different lived experiences from men had led to the creation of a female consciousness or sensibility, Judy Chicago and Miriam Schapiro encouraged women artists to draw from this shared resource for the material to make honest work without apology.

Paralleling the quest for "female imagery" was the search for a "black aesthetic." Black Arts adherents searched for a set of principles that could birth an art that addressed black realities, affirmed black history and culture, spoke to the masses of black people, and aligned itself with liberation struggles throughout the world. No group of people worked more intently on this mighty project than AFRI-COBRA, a Chicago-based group that grew out of the Organization of Black American Culture's Visual Art Workshop. After the creation of their legendary mural the *Wall of Respect* on Chicago's South Side during the summer of 1967, OBAC's Visual Art Workshop largely disbanded; however, individual members including Jeff Donaldson, Barbara Jones Hogu, and Wadsworth Jarrell continued meeting to discuss how to give further visual expression to the goals of Black Power.[63] Along with other local artists, they pondered a question Jeff Donaldson had asked Wadsworth Jarrell at an outdoor art fair in 1962, a year before the March on Washington. Partially daydreaming, Donaldson had asked his fellow painter: Would it be possible "to start a 'Negro' art movement based on a common aesthetic creed?"[64] Six years later, in 1968, after the assassination of Martin Luther King, Jr. and the riots and rebellions that followed, five of the Chicago-based artists took the name COBRA (Coalition of Black Revolutionary Artists), poised to answer Donaldson's prescient question affirmatively.[65] The next year, in 1969, wanting to express their black diasporic consciousness and allegiances spurred by the late Malcolm X's teachings, the now seven artists changed their name to AFRI-COBRA (African Commune of Bad Relevant Artists).[66] By July 1970, when their traveling exhibition, "Ten in Search of a Nation," opened at The Studio Museum in Harlem, they were ten artists committed to a shared black aesthetic. As part of their Studio Museum show, founder Jeff Donaldson explained AFRI-COBRA's history and mission to the larger public:

We are a family—COBRA. The Coalition of Black Revolutionary Artists, is now AFRICOBRA—African Commune of Bad Relevant Artists. It's NATION TIME and we are searching. Our guidelines are our people—the whole family of African people, the African family tree. And in this spirit of familyhood, we have carefully examined our roots and searched our branches for those visual qualities that are most expressive of our people/art. Our people are our standard for excellence. We strive for images inspired by African people/experience and images which African people can relate to directly without formal art training and/or experience. Art for people and not for critics whose peopleness is questionable. We try to create images that appeal to the senses—not to the intellect. The images you see in an AFRICOBRA exhibition may be placed in three categories:

1. Definition—images that deal with the past.
2. Identification—images that relate to the present.
3. Direction—images that look into the future.

It is our hope that intelligent definition of the past, and perceptive identification in the present, will project nationfull direction in the future—look for us there, because that's where we're at."[67]

AFRI-COBRA artists sought to create a new art that confidently drew sustenance from the past, engaged the present, and envisioned a new future. To create this new activist art, members collectively defined their political goals, philosophical concepts, and aesthetic principles. Black Power was their political goal and their philosophical interest, one member explained, "was a school of thought that would heighten consciousness and delve into cultural sensibilities in an effort to promote a strong sense of pride in black people."[68] To further these political and psychological goals, the artists of AFRI-COBRA searched for a shared black aesthetic. Founding member Wadsworth Jarrell stated that members looked for "a collective concept that would say 'black art' at a glance."[69] After studying their own work as well as the work of other black artists, however, the activist artists decided to construct their own set of aesthetic principles for the creation of their own Black Arts art. Drawing from "their inheritable art forms as an African people," members developed five guiding aesthetic principles which founding member Barbara Jones Hogu outlined in 1973:

A. FREE SYMMETRY, the use of syncopated rhythmic repetition which constantly changes in color, texture, shapes, form, pattern, movement, feature, etc.
B. MIMESIS AT MID POINT, design which marks the spot where the real and the unreal, the objective and the non-objective, the plus and the minus meet. A point exactly between absolute abstractions and absolute naturalism.
C. VISIBILITY, clarity of form and line based on the interesting irregularity one senses in a freely drawn circle or organic object, the feeling for movement, growth, changes and human touch.
D. LUMINOSITY, "Shine," literal and figurative, as seen in the dress and personal grooming of shoes, hair (process or Afro), laminated furniture, face, knees or skin.
E. COLOR, Cool-ade color, bright colors with sensibility and harmony.[70]

With their dynamic, hip, high-key, and shimmering offerings of figurative abstraction, AFRI-COBRA artists sought to make accessible and affordable art reflective of the realities, experiences, and dreams of African Americans. Drawing from the "roots and branches" of the Black Diaspora, and committed to shared goals, philosophical concepts, and aesthetic principles, the individual members of this "family of imagemakers" brilliantly gave visual expression to Larry Neal's tender declaration: *"Black people you are Black art."* [71]

SECOND RECONSTRUCTION/SECOND WAVE

The protracted efforts on the part of Black Power and Women's Liberation activists in the 1960s and 1970s to unite and mobilize the people they saw as their allies and kin in order to dismantle oppressive power relations, redistribute wealth and other resources, gain value and legitimacy, and design a new and just destiny were intensifications of longstanding struggles for social and psychological liberation and freedom from oppression. And in a similar dynamic to the earlier struggles for abolition and women's rights during the nineteenth century, the perceived competition between the two postwar movements created a unique predicament for African American women. The Black Power and Women's Liberation Movements as well as their cultural corollaries the Black Arts and Feminist Art Movements shared strikingly similar traits, tendencies, and goals. Activists in both struggles sought to create a politically and psychologically viable collective consciousness for their imagined allies and kin in order to overthrow white supremacy and male supremacy, respectively, and to heal from its dire effects. Yet the tone of unity and tenor of urgency in both movements made it difficult for women of African descent to articulate their own distinct histories, identities, experiences, and dreams to strong, calm, and attentive ears. Additionally, the easy equation of fulfilled manhood, brotherhood, and liberation in the Black Power Movement, as well as the high premium placed on shared experiences and safe sisterhood in the Women's Liberation Movement made it a supreme challenge for African American women to assert the validity of their uniqueness to their resistant peers.

Despite these difficulties, however, a handful of courageous and visionary women were able to draw from the fruits of both movements, and perhaps no one was better able to do this than Ntozake Shange (a self-chosen Zulu-derived name meaning "she who comes with her own things" [Ntozake] and "she who walks like a lion" [Shange]). In December 1974, the twenty-six-year-old poet, dancer, and teacher first performed her choreopoem *for colored girls who have considered suicide/when the rainbow is enuf* with four others at a women's bar outside Berkeley, California. Infused with the spirit of her daily life in the early 1970s—teaching courses in Women's Studies at Sonoma State College and then commuting back to the San Francisco to study dance of the African diaspora—this raw and eloquent merging of poetry, music, and dance explored the struggles of seven African American women and revealed how they drew sustenance from each other as well as from themselves. [72] Drawing insight and energy from the previously parallel cultural movements, this dynamic work reveled in the movements' shared tendencies and unique histories. Exposing how her work, her body, and her being had flourished from her embrace of the rich resources of both movements, Shange explained:

> Knowing a woman's mind & spirit had been allowed me, with dance I discovered my body more intimately than I had imagined possible. With the acceptance of the ethnicity of my thighs & backside, came a clearer understanding of my voice as a women & as a poet. The freedom to move in space, to demand of my own sweat a perfection that could continually be approached, though never known, waz poem to me, my body & mind ellipsing, probably for the first time in my life. Just as Women's Studies had rooted me to an articulated female heritage & imperative, so dance as explicated by Raymond Sawyer & Ed Mock insisted that everything African, everything halfway colloquial, a grimace, a strut, an arched back over a yawn, waz mine. I moved what waz my unconscious knowledge of being in a colored woman's body to my known everydayness.[73]

Committed to expressing the histories, identities, and struggles of women of African descent, Ntozake Shange, with *for colored girls*, joined advocates for the Black Arts and Feminist Art Movements as well as activists for Black Power and Women's Liberation in daring to imagine a world where they would thrive, be safe, and feel connected, authentic, and whole, and in devoting themselves to creating that world by all possible means.

NOTES

1. Larry Neal, "New Space/The Growth of Black Consciousness in the Sixties," in *The Black Seventies*, ed. Floyd B. Barbour (Boston: Porter Sargent, 1970), 15.

2. Jane O'Reilly, "The Housewife's Moment of Truth," *Ms.* Preview Issue (Spring 1972): 54.

3. Amiri Baraka, *The Autobiography of LeRoi Jones* (New York: Freundlich Books, 1984), 200–201.

4. Kalamu ya Salaam, "The Last Movement, "*Mosaic* 13 (Spring 2002): 23. See also Komozi Woodard, *A Nation within a Nation: Amiri Baraka (LeRoi Jones) and Black Power Politics* (Chapel Hill: University of North Carolina Press, 1999), 66.

5. Malcolm X, "Statement of Basic Aims and Objectives of the Organization of Afro-American Unity," in *New Black Voices: An Anthology of Contemporary Afro-American Literature*, ed. Abraham Chapman (New York: Penguin, 1972), 563.

6. Ibid.

7. Scot Brown, "The US Organization, Black Power Vanguard Politics, and the United Front Ideal: Los Angeles and Beyond," *The Black Scholar* 31: 3–4 (Fall-Winter 2001): 21.

8. Scot Ngozi-Brown, "The US Organization, Maulana Karenga, and Conflict with the Black Panther Party: A Critique of Sectarian Influences on Historical Discourse," *Journal of Black Studies* 28: 2 (November 1997): 157.

9. Maulana Ron Karenga, *The Quotable Karenga*, ed. Clyde Halisi and James Mtume (Los Angeles: US Organization, 1967), 11. Mao Tse-Tung, *Quotations from Chairman Mao Tse-Tung* (Peking: Foreign Languages Press, 1966; reprint, New York: Bantam, 1967).

10. Karenga, *The Quotable Karenga*, 7.

11. Ibid., 6.

12. Simone de Beauvoir, *The Second Sex*, trans. H. M. Parshley (New York: Alfred A. Knopf, 1953), 715. Simone de Beauvoir discussed her 1971 entry into the Women's Liberation movement in France in an interview published in the first issue of *Ms* magazine. See Alice Schwartzer, "The Radicalization of Simone de Beauvoir," *Ms.* 1: 1 (July 1972): 60–63, 134.

13. Beauvoir, *The Second Sex*, 711.

14. Ibid., 715.

15. Judy Chicago, *Through the Flower: My Struggle as a Woman Artist* (Garden City, NY: Doubleday, 1975; reprint, New York: Penguin, 1993), 62–63. See also "Judy Chicago, Talking to Lucy R. Lippard," *Artforum* 13: 1 (September 1974): 60–65; reprinted in Lucy Lippard, *From the Center: Feminist Essays on Women's Art* (New York: E. P. Dutton, 1976), 217.

16. Laura Meyer, "A Feminist Chronology, 1945–95," in *Sexual Politics: Judy Chicago's "Dinner Party" in Feminist Art History*, ed. Amelia Jones (Berkeley: University of California Press, 1996), 239.

17. Simone de Beauvoir's claim that women in the past had not been able to excel in the arts and humanities also energized art historian Linda Nochlin in her field-shaking essay of 1971. See Linda Nochlin, "Why Have There Been No Great Women Artists?" *Art News* 69: 9 (January 1971): 22–39, 67–71.

18. Chicago, *Through the Flower*, 86.

19. Chicago, "Talking to Lucy R. Lippard," in *From the Center*, 230.

20. Neal, "New Space/The Growth of Black Consciousness in the Sixties," 12.

21. Kathie Sarachild, "Consciousness-Raising: A Radical Weapon," in *Feminist Revolution*, ed. Redstockings of the Women's Liberation Movement (New Paltz, NY: Redstockings, 1975; revised reprint, New York: Random House, 1978), 145.

22. LeRoi Jones, "The Need For a Cultural Base to Civil Rites & Bpower Mooments," in *The Black Power Revolt*, ed. Floyd B. Barbour (Boston: Porter Sargent, 1968), 124.

23. Larry Neal, "Any Day Now: Black Art and Black Liberation," *Ebony* 24:10 (August 1969): 54.

24. Gloria Steinem, "Sisterhood," *Ms.* Preview Issue (Spring 1972): 48.

25. Sarachild, "Consciousness-Raising," 145. See also Alice Echols, *Daring to Be Bad: Radical Feminism in America, 1967–1975* (Minneapolis: University of Minnesota Press, 1989), 83–90.

26. Sarachild, "Consciousness Raising," 149.

27. Ibid., 148.

28. Faith Wilding, "The Feminist Art Programs at Fresno and CalArts, 1970–75," in *The Power of Feminist Art: The American Movement of the 1970s, History and Impact*, ed. Norma Broude and Mary D. Garrard (New York: Harry N. Abrams, 1994), 32, 35.

29. For a discussion of the competing wings of feminism within the Women's Liberation movement, see Echols, *Daring to Be Bad*, 3–11. For a discussion of the various forms of Black nationalism during the Black Power Movement, see William L. Van Deburg, *New*

Day in Babylon: The Black Power Movement and American Culture, 1965–1975 (Chicago: University of Chicago Press, 1992), 129–91.

30. Baraka, *The Autobiography of LeRoi Jones*, 254.

31. Ibid., 253, 312.

32. Ibid., 266–67.

33. Neal, "Any Day Now," 54.

34. Arlene Raven, "Womanhouse," in *The Power of Feminist Art: The American Movement of the 1970s, History and Impact*, ed. Norma Broude and Mary D. Garrard (New York: Harry N. Abrams, 1994), 48, 61.

35. Lucy R. Lippard, "Moving Targets/Concentric Circles: Notes from the Radical Whirlwind," in *The Pink Glass Swan: Selected Feminist Essays on Art* (New York: New Press, 1995), 10.

36. Lucy R. Lippard, "Sweeping Exchanges: The Contribution of Feminism to the Art of the 1970s," *Art Journal* 40: 1–2 (Winter 1980): 363.

37. Larry Neal, "And Shine Swam On," in *Black Fire: An Anthology of Afro-American Writing*, ed. LeRoi Jones and Larry Neal (New York: William Morrow & Company, 1968), 656.

38. Larry Neal, "The Black Arts Movement," *The Drama Review* 12: 4 (1968): 29–39; reprinted in *The Black Aesthetic*, ed. Addison Gayle, Jr. (Garden City, NY: Doubleday, 1971), 257.

39. Lippard, "Sweeping Exchanges," 364.

40. Lucy R. Lippard, "The Women Artists' Movement—What Next?" in *From the Center*, 148.

41. Feminist Art Program, *Anonymous Was a Woman: A Documentation of the Women's Art Festival; A Collection of Letters to Young Women Artists* (Valencia: California Institute of the Arts, 1974), 53.

42. Ibid.

43. Rainer Maria Rilke, *Letters to a Young Poet*, trans. Stephen Mitchell (New York: Random House, 1984).

44. *Anonymous Was a Woman*, 102–103. For another insight into the dialogue on the role of the artist, see Judy Chicago's and Arlene Raven's joint letter to the Feminist Art Program students at CalArts from their vantage point as founders of LA's Feminist Studio Workshop in 1973, the first entirely independent alternative structure for women in the arts-related professions, 67–68.

45. Karenga, *The Quotable Karenga*, 23.

46. Neal, "Any Day Now," 56.

47. Chicago, "Talking to Lucy R. Lippard," in *From the Center*, 227.

48. Chicago, *Through the Flower*, viii.

49. Statement of Purpose, *Heresies: A Feminist Publication on Art and Politics* 1 (January 1977), inside cover.

50. Karenga, *The Quotable Karenga*, 22. See also Maulana Ron Karenga, "Ron Karenga and Black Cultural Nationalism," *Negro Digest* 17 (January 1968): 5–9; reprinted as "Black Art: Mutter Matter Given Force and Function," in *New Black Voices: An Anthology of Contemporary Afro-American Literature*, ed. Abraham Chapman (New York: Penguin, 1972), 476–82.

51. Jeff Donaldson, "The Role We Want for Black Art," *College Board Review* 71 (Spring 1969): 17.

52. Robin Morgan, "Forum: Rights of Passage," *Ms.* 4: 3 (September 1975): 78.

53. Neal, "Any Day Now," 56.

54. Lippard, "Sweeping Exchanges," 364.

55. Quoted in "Wall of Respect," *Ebony* 23: 2 (December 1967): 49.

56. Chicago, *Through the Flower*, 36.

57. Lippard, "Introduction: Changing Since *Changing*," in *From the Center*, 11.

58. Ibid., 8.

59. Faith Wilding, "Women Artists and Female Imagery," *Everywoman* 2: 7 (May 7, 1971): 18–19.

60. See Miriam Schapiro and Judy Chicago, "Female Imagery," *Womanspace Journal* 1: 3 (Summer 1973): 11–14.

61. Chicago, *Through the Flower*, 144.

62. Ibid., 143.

63. OBAC artist Carolyn Lawrence also joined the group later in 1970.

64. Jeff Donaldson, "Africobra 1 (African Commune of Bad Relevant Artists): 10 in Search of a Nation," *Black World* 19 (October 1970): 80.

65. Ibid., 82.

66. Robert L. Douglas, *Wadsworth Jarrell: The Artist as Revolutionary* (San Francisco: Pomegranate Artbooks, 1996), 30.

67. Donaldson, "Africobra 1," 82–83.

68. Wadsworth A. Jarrell, "Heading for a Black Aesthetic," *Art Papers* 9: 6 (November-December 1985): 17.

69. Quoted in Douglas, *Wadsworth Jarrell: The Artist as Revolutionary*, 26.

70. Barbara Jones Hogu, "The History, Philosophy and Aesthetics of AFRI-COBRA," in *AFRI-COBRA III* Exhibition catalog (Amherst: University of Massachusetts Art Gallery, 1973), unpaginated.

71. Donaldson, "Africobra 1," 86. Neal, "Any Day Now," 58.

72. Ntozake Shange, *for colored girls who have considered suicide/when the rainbow is enuf* (New York: Macmillan, 1977; reprint, New York: Collier, 1989), x–xi.

73. Ibid., xi.

14

Prison Writers and the Black Arts Movement

Lee Bernstein

The period of the Black Arts Movement—roughly 1965 to the late 1970s—saw a dramatic turn in the cultural life of American prisons. Many people were incarcerated for crimes that were driven by their anti-war, anti-colonial, and anti-racist positions and activities. In addition, the very definition of "political prisoner" underwent radical transformation by those who argued that African Americans, Native Americans, and Latinos were unfairly targeted by the criminal justice system regardless of the nature of their crime. Finally, the literary, visual, and performing arts were explicitly politicized by the Black Power Movement inside and outside prison walls just as prison authorities, universities, and government and nongovernment funding agencies began experimenting with ambitious arts and education programs in major U.S. correctional facilities. This convergence of political, cultural, and penological influences created a legacy that might fruitfully be called the "Prison Arts Movement" of the 1960s and 1970s. This movement introduced artists and writers of all races and cultures who would achieve widespread attention, impressive sales, and continuing influence: Jack Henry Abbott, Jimmy Santiago Baca, Carolyn Baxter, Claude Brown, Edward Bunker, Eldridge Cleaver, Ericka Huggins, George Jackson, Etheridge Knight, Miguel Piñero, Assata Shakur, Iceberg Slim, and Piri Thomas, to name a few.

Furthermore, artists from the Black Arts Movement took an active role in fostering the artistic and literary ambitions of incarcerated people while including the plight of prisoners as subject matter in their work. Faith Ringgold painted a mural and worked with women prisoners at New York's Riker's Island. Benny Andrews curated a show of prisoner artwork at The Studio Museum in Harlem. Poet Gwendolyn Brooks mentored Etheridge Knight when he was still writing from a prison cell. Similarly, arts organizations provided funding and vision for numerous prison projects. Throughout the country, an impressive array of artists and writers ran workshops, published chapbooks at their own expense, taught music classes, and did the daily work of fostering the Prison Arts Movement.

Much of this legacy has been obscured or forgotten. Incarcerated people—and particularly artists—had strong links to the Black Arts Movement. These links were forged by individual and institutional commitments inside and outside of correctional facilities. What impact did the institutional context have on this key arts movement? What was the significance of the image and idea of "the prisoner" to the Black Arts Movement? What did incarcerated writers contribute to the Black Arts Movement? By remembering the institutions, images, and inmates that influenced the Prison Arts Movement, we gain new insight into the politics and aesthetics of the Black Arts Movement. While those who created these programs hoped that access to the arts and education would aid in the reformation of the convict, the incarcerated artists themselves believed that they were artists in service to a revolution. Incarcerated people were central to the revolutionary aims of the Black Arts Movement both in the works they wrote and in the symbol they provided of "imprisonment" in a racially oppressive society.

PSYCHOLOGICAL WARFARE OR RACIAL AWARENESS?: INSTITUTIONAL CONTEXTS

Federal and state governments, along with major non-profit funding agencies, provided key backing for prison arts and education programs throughout the 1960s and 1970s. Between 1965 and 1973 the number of college-level programs in U.S. prisons increased over fifteen-fold, to 182. As of 1982 there were 350 programs in forty-five states, with roughly 10 percent of all inmates attending a prison college. Perhaps the biggest boost to post-secondary education in prisons came with the Pell Grant program in 1965. It provided funding to eligible prisoners for post-secondary study until 1991.[1] In addition, the National Endowment for the Arts funded the publication of prisoner works, while other organizations began major initiatives to create freestanding programs behind prison walls.[2] The California Arts Council, under the leadership of Eloise Smith, included California's prisons in its Artists in Social Institutions Program, established in 1976. This would eventually grow into the Arts-in-Corrections program in 1981.[3] In many cases, these programs were attempts to provide nonviolent outlets for the increasingly radical ideologies circulating in American prisons. In the aftermath of a prison riot in 1968, the Oregon State Penitentiary began a creative writing program.[4] The Arizona State Department of Corrections joined forces with the state's Commission on the Arts and Humanities to form the Writer's Workshop at the Arizona State Prison in 1973.[5] In that same year, the PEN American Center held its first literary competition for prisoners, which would become an annual event.[6] The University of California at Berkeley's Prison College at San Quentin, funded by the Ford

Foundation in 1968, was among the most ambitious of a growing number of degree-granting programs in U.S. prisons.[7]

Spurred by personal convictions, a career goal, or merely a rare economic opportunity for a young artist or teacher, the people who worked in these programs described going into prisons as an experience that transformed them politically and personally. Young men and women entered prison classrooms and studies hoping to bring about individual or social change. Sociology instructor Paul Goodman, then a doctoral candidate at the University of California at Berkeley and an instructor at San Francisco State College, empathized with the students in their courses. Of his course in the late 1960s in San Quentin, Goodman wrote, "Not *less* than for the teacher as an outsider, their experience is frightening to themselves. Ignore that and you ignore the student. Deal with it and, interestingly enough, you find their greatest strength toward learning: they want out."[8] Without question, many teachers viewed themselves as "on the side" of the inmates based on political, emotional, or aesthetic sensibilities. Furthermore, some white teachers became more sympathetic to the rhetoric of black liberation as it took on added force behind prison walls. As perhaps the most dramatic remnants of slavery, southern prison farms were frequently on former plantations, wardens in women's prisons demanded that they be called "Mistresses," and African American people made up 40 percent of the people in chains in the United States in 1973.[9]

While the correctional authorities greatly expanded the arts and educational offerings, access was not distributed evenly across race and gender lines. For example, Chicano poet Jimmy Santiago Baca wrote of his thwarted attempts to enter a G.E.D. program during the 1970s. After authorities denied his request to enter the program at the penitentiary in Florence, Arizona, he refused to work his assigned kitchen job. Because of this resistance, he was "confined to deadlock maximum security in a subterranean dungeon" for twenty-three hours per day.[10] Despite the presence of a literacy program in his jail, Baca was forced to practice his reading and writing skills by transcribing passages from a free pamphlet sent to him by a Christian Scientist.[11]

This was not an isolated example. While prisons contained much higher proportions of the poor and people of color when compared to the rest of the United States, during the 1960s and 1970s prison classrooms did not maintain this proportion. For example, while San Quentin was 54 percent white in 1968, its college program was 70 percent white. The figures for African Americans were 20.2 percent in program vs. 30 percent in the general population, for Chicanos, 9.2 percent vs. 15 percent.[12] One explanation for this discrepancy is that they determined eligibility for the program based on an evaluation of mental status and I.Q. scores, which had long been notoriously racist measurements inside and outside prison walls. Similarly, there is a long history of excluding African Americans and the foreign-born from reformatory-based incarceration. When New York's Bedford Hills Reformatory for Women opened in 1901, judges continued to sentence the vast majority of African American and foreign-born women to the punitive incarceration of the prison in Auburn. Most judges seemed to see only native-born white women as good candidates for reform.[13] In the late 1960s, reform-based programs within prisons echoed this history.

Even when they were eligible for the courses, this legacy left some African American prisoners critical of the content in the new classes and writing workshops that emerged during the 1960s and 1970s. They viewed the teachers as too compromised by the system in which they worked to teach anything that would help them achieve personal transformation or the political and economic goals of the various liberation movements of the time. Juno Bakali Tshombe, an inmate in Massachusetts, believed that the programs not only lacked a useful political perspective, he saw them as methods of ideological control and psychological warfare: "Clearly the administration is thinking in terms of 'let them niggers put on some plays describing their condition to each other or write poetry that no one gives a damn about, but under no circumstances whatsoever let them produce anything with political overtones.'"[14]

Confirming at least part of this critique, prison educators often spoke of "rehabilitation" rather than the liberation sought by many movement activists. These well-intentioned reformers were instead influenced by an earlier period of prison reform, the 1930s, when one administrator wrote that, "in the penal institution, 'education' is the process or the means of achieving the reformation, correction, or rehabilitation of inmates in correctional institutions. It comprehends all of the experiences that such an institution can bring into the lives of inmates. It goes beyond the programs of academic and vocational instruction commonly found at the present time and includes the activities of every department or division of the institution with which inmates have contact. It makes prisons and reformatories basically educational institutions."[15]

But not all programs could be swept aside with Tshombe's critique. He made an exception for the Elma Lewis Technical Theater Training Program at the Massachusetts Correctional Institution, Norfolk. Elma Lewis was a central figure in the Boston-based National Center of Afro-American Artists, an organization with firm ties to the Black Arts Movement. When Lewis entered the prison to teach her class, she discovered that inmates were already familiar with the political rhetoric and aesthetic sensibilities of the Black Arts Movement. She described her entry into the prison as a learning experience: "the men . . . are my brothers, they are my sons, they are my students, and in a very real sense, they are also my teachers."[16] The prisoners in the Norfolk program hoped to teach not only Lewis, but also African American communities outside of prisons. According to Lewis, "They would like their children, their brothers, their sisters, their mothers and fathers to sidestep the trap before it's sprung. They teach the development of alternatives. They no longer see through a glass darkly. They would like to see their communities move toward ownership and control. They hope to pass along the revelation to blacks in all black communities."[17]

The unique purpose of Lewis' program made a difference to the inmates. At the time, Norfolk contained programs in everything from oil burner repair to G.E.D. and college-level courses. Tshombe, a participant in the Norfolk theater program, made an exception because of the political and aesthetic sensibilities of Lewis' course: "There is no program other than Elma Lewis's here that is working towards attaining some degree of thinking and a positive direction that will relate to the confined black prisoner and offer him a productive analysis needed for self-awareness and racial awareness."[18] The artists and writers in the program called themselves "the Norfolk Prison Brothers," linking them not only to each other but also to the then famous "Soledad Brothers" in California. Many of them changed their names to Swahili or Islamic names and some were active in the Nation of Islam. Decades earlier, Malcolm X had himself been incarcerated in Norfolk and credited its debating program as his "baptism into public speaking."[19] The politicized brothers recalled his legacy by hanging pictures of Elijah Muhammad, Angela Davis, or Muhammad Ali in their cells.

The Black Arts Movement and the institutions it formed provided other important contexts for prisoner art in the 1970s. The Studio Museum in Harlem was one venue where prisoner arts could be shown during the 1970s. In the autumn of 1977, the artist Benny Andrews curated a show called "Echoes: Prisons, U.S.A." at the innovative museum located in the heart of the nation's most famous African American neighborhood. Like Elma Lewis, Andrews argued that "the accomplishments of these men, women, and children serve to educate us all."[20] In contrast to the Norfolk program—which did not seek to make an immediate intervention into mainstream art institutions—Andrews emphasized the effect he hoped the works would have on what viewers considered "art": "Along with losing many of their basic rights, it seems that prison artists have also lost their right to be considered fine artists, regardless of their artistic accomplishment. The public has been reluctant to be open minded in its approach to art created behind prison walls."[21] This hope for inclusion grew out of Andrews' efforts to open up the art world's most visible institutions to the products of African American creativity. Andrews was active in the Black Emergency Cultural Coalition, an organization formed in 1969 in response to the Metropolitan Museum of Art's controversial "Harlem On My Mind" exhibit. The BECC found offensive the lack of African American participation in the design of the show and the curator's decision to show few works by African American painters and sculptors.[22] The BECC soon formed its Prison Art Program as an extension of its merging of political and aesthetic agendas, working with incarcerated artists in New York. The Studio Museum show, like the Museum itself, created opportunities for artists who would not otherwise have access to the general public.

Incarcerated artists and writers gained access to talented and experienced teachers because of a growing momentum for change within the system. While uniquely situated in Black Arts Movement organizations, the Norfolk Program and the BECC Prison Art Program were two of many new initiatives throughout the 1960s and 1970s. Even the teachers and artists without the political motivations of Lewis and Andrews contributed to the aesthetic and political sensibilities of prisoners. At times, the institutional context made it difficult to pursue their more militant goals through the arts. Because of the widespread use of indeterminate sentencing, many inmates carried long sentences with parole determined by state officials who did not look kindly on political activities.[23] The Black Arts Movement, however, often provided an energizing visual and literary rhetoric to pursue shared goals. For some prisoners, the Black Arts Movement helped them determine whether a program was a tool of psychological warfare meant to "tame" them or a route to individual or collective liberation. In turn, prisoners would become a central symbol for a growing number of African American artists outside of prisons.

"AMERICA IS THE PRISON": PRISONS AND THE BLACK ARTS MOVEMENT

Theorist Ron Karenga wrote in 1968 that "black art must expose the enemy, praise the people, and support the revolution."[24] Prisoners would become important symbols and contributors to the formation of this new aesthetic. The political and aesthetic sensibilities of the audience—particularly the movement that had recently transformed from the "Civil Rights Movement" to the "Black Liberation Movement"—saw an iconic significance in the plight of incarcerated African American men and women. Rather than outcasts from African American communities, incarcerated people provided evidence of the ongoing oppression of all African American people throughout U.S. history. Inspired at times by their own experiences with the justice system or by the writings of Malcolm X, Angela Davis, George Jackson, and Eldridge Cleaver, these artists would use police officers as metaphors for white oppression. In poetry and drama, convicts became potential revolutionaries; in sharp contrast, guards and police became storm troopers for the white power structure.

To be sure, prisons have often served as catalysts for social change. The prison experiences of Henry David Thoreau gave rise to his inspirational "Civil Disobedience" in the mid-nineteenth century. Eugene Debs, Kate Richards O'Hare, Jimmy Hoffa, and Martin Luther King, Jr. are just a few of the many Americans who used their prison experiences as evidence of their oppression and as opportunities to inspire their movements. This tradition became more pronounced with the events of the late 1960s and early 1970s. While many people knew that Malcolm X had done time in a Massachusetts prison, publication of his autobiography made clear that his time in Norfolk was the catalyst in his religious and political transformation. Malcolm X would be joined by Huey P. Newton, George Jackson, Ericka Huggins, and Angela Davis in the belief that incarcerated people could play a central role in the liberation not only of themselves, but also of all black people. On the East Coast, Attica became the most well known of the approximately 300 prison riots in the United States between the late 1960s and early 1980s. Forty-eight of these were concentrated between 1968 and 1971.[25] Rather than being dismissed as the evil deeds of the worst among us, these uprisings—called a "war behind walls" by convict Edward Bunker writing in *Harper's Magazine* in 1972—became emblematic of the increasingly volatile racial politics in the United States as a whole.[26]

Activists—artists and otherwise—increasingly saw little if any distinction between political and non-political crimes. Zayd Shakur, the Deputy Minister of Information for the New York State chapter of the Black Panther Party, drew on Malcolm X when he titled his 1970 essay "America is the Prison." In it, Shakur argued that life behind bars was merely an "extension of our communities": "The penitentiaries, as they call them, and the communities are plagued with the same thing: dope, disease, police brutality, murder, and rats running over the places that you dwell in. We recognize that most of the militant-dissatisfied youth are off in the penitentiaries. Eighty percent of the prison population [298,000 in 1967] is black, brown, and yellow people. You look around and say, 'what happened to my man. I haven't seen him for along time,' then you get busted, go to jail, and there he is.'"[27]

This link led scholar Roberta Ann Johnson to argue that prisons gave rise to the Black Power Movement itself.[28] According to Johnson, danger of physical conflict, experience of confinement, poor health and educational services, and few job opportunities existed in correctional facilities and in African American communities. As African Americans saw the common experiences and contexts between lives lived on both sides of the wall, the rhetoric and goals of social justice movements shifted from dismantling segregation to demanding power. At this point, the liberation of all black prisoners became a central component in the freedom struggle. As Huey P. Newton—the founder of the Black Panther Party whose incarceration became a focus of Panther efforts—said at the eulogy for Jonathan Jackson and William Christmas, "THERE ARE NO LAWS THAT THE OPPRESSOR MAKES THAT THE OPPRESSED ARE BOUND TO RESPECT."[29] Jonathan Jackson's older brother George would soon be well known for *Soledad Brother*, in which he observed that "There are still some blacks here who consider themselves criminals, but not many."[30] These writers saw the experience of "free" African Americans reflected in the lives of prisoners. In this way, the liberation of African American prisoners and the elimination of white supremacy went hand in hand.

For some Black Arts Movement writers, prisoners were more than symbols of black oppression. Several Black Arts Movement figures had been incarcerated. LeRoi Jones, for example, was arrested as early as 1961 on obscenity charges.[31] Later, after he changed his name to Amiri Baraka and increased his participation in cultural nationalist organizations, he became subject to persistent surveillance and harassment by the FBI and other criminal justice organizations.[32] He would be arrested twice in 1967, first during the first night of the Newark Riot and later for weapons' possession.[33] During the trial on the gun charge, Baraka was sentenced to thirty days in the Morristown, New Jersey jail for contempt of court because of his refusal to be judged by an all-white jury.[34] At his sentencing for the initial gun charge, the judge read from Baraka's infamous poem, "Black People" (1967): "Up against the wall, motherfucker, this is a stickup!" While the judge omitted the profanity, he felt that the line justified an especially harsh three-year sentence with no parole. Convicted, as Baraka put it, "of possession of two guns and a poem," he would be sent to the Trenton State Penitentiary, where he reconnected with old acquaintances from high school and met "some real warriors and even a few scholars."[35] Baraka quickly appealed his sentence and was released on bail after little more than a week in prison. He won the appeal, but the prison experience made him see that prisons' "real function is as institutions of oppression for the poor and the minorities."[36]

Baraka would draw on these experiences in several works. He wrote portions of *Raise Race Rays Raze* (1971) in the Essex Country Prison and would dramatize his sharp criticism of African American police officers in "Police," written in 1967 and first published in 1968.[37] In it, a character named "Black Cop" murders a character named "Black Man." While "Black Man" is mourned as a brother and husband, "Black Cop" is reviled by the surviving "Black Woman": "he ain't no kin to me . . . the lousyass murderer . . . for the white folks too." The one-act play ends when "Black Cop" kills himself under orders of "Black Woman." The "White Cops" are seen "slobbering on his flesh, a few are even eating chunks of flesh they tear off in their weird banquet."[38] While inspired from his experiences with African American police officers, Baraka transformed his arrests into an archetypal encounter that showed both the mechanics of oppression and a route to liberation. Two black men—one a police officer, the other his victim—are both dead; one is killed in the service of oppression, the second to achieve a temporary retribution. That the white officers do nothing to stop either death underscores Baraka's opinion of an African American police officer he met during the violence that followed Martin Luther King's 1968 assassination: "Someone or something had created him and what I was hearing was obviously tapes running through his brain track."[39]

In addition to Baraka, other artists and writers would be incarcerated for their political views. For example, the San Francisco playwright and founder of Black House, the Black Arts/West Theater, and the Recovery Theater, Marvin X, was incarcerated for his resistance to the draft. These experiences gave rise to "Take Care of Business," a 1968 play set in a jail cell.[40] Incarcerated on a trumped-up marijuana charge, Wes, described as a "do-rag nationalist" and Joe Simmons, "a typical college student" meet the devil. Joe's father does not believe his declaration of innocence and refuses to get him out of jail. While Wes gives the guard the finger and responds to racism with snide comments, Joe discovers that his polite demeanor and college enrollment mean nothing. Class differences melt as the two young men learn that their black skin defines how they will be treated.

Just as the Black Power Movement saw the role of prisons in maintaining white supremacy—and the role of prisoners in dismantling it—many artists of the Black Arts Movement worked with prisoners and created works that featured prisoners in roles of heroes and liberators of black people. Moreover, these works manifested the belief that, as Larry Neal wrote in 1968, the Black Arts Movement was the "aesthetic and spiritual sister of the Black Power concept."[41] Neal mined the African American folklore and blues traditions in his "Shine" poems. These traditions had long highlighted struggles against the criminal justice system and many texts had been written and sustained in the prison farms of the Reconstruction South.[42] In "Shine Goes to Jail" (1974), we see the mundane indignities of life in jail transformed into a story about collective experience and kinship ties:

> There was no toilet to speak of. And they gave us old newspapers to wipe our asses with. There was only this rut running through the cell. It was flushed three times a day with water from a special pump. The water was mixed with pine oil disinfectant. There is this cell. It's supposed to accommodate three men, but there are four of us here right now. Woody Neal from Georgia, down around Atlanta; Silas T. Washington, over here, he's near Titusville, Alabama; I know his folks. Blind Jack, sitting yonder with his guitar; well he from Florence, Tennessee, same as Handy. And me? I'm from everywhere . . . [43]

In contrast to the tendency to see incarcerated people as pariahs, Neal drew on a tradition that saw prisoners as connected to one another and to their communities outside prison walls.

In addition to documenting the connections between African American communities on both sides of prison walls, Baraka and Neal believed the same violence and exploitation convicts used for personal gain while on the streets could be constructively channeled toward their political aims. In "Black Art," (1969) Baraka saw poems as phallic:

> Fuck poems
> and they are useful, they shoot
> come at you, love what you are,
> breathe like wrestlers, or shudder
> strangely after pissing.[44]

The "shooting" of semen signals both virility and violence, as in "Police" when the paper gun that "Black Cop" holds in his hand is cut in the shape of a penis.[45] Similarly, Larry Neal argued that poetry "is a concrete function, an action. No more abstractions." While action is not always associated with masculinity, for Neal the concrete action was a violent and phallic masculinity in service of revolution. Poems, he wrote, were: "fists, daggers, airplane poems, and poems that shoot guns."[46] While sexualized violence would prove to be an important theme in the Black Arts Movement, Neal was careful to denounce same-sex intimacy as a "rejection of the body"[47] when practiced by women or as simply "sick" when practiced by men.[48] In the homosocial culture of prisons, this hostility would take on increased significance.

Rather than focus on the potential for same-sex intimacy as a route to building political alliances, Neal felt that pimps were better suited to serving as symbols of the potential for revolution among the criminals. In order to do so, however, pimps would need to undergo a political transformation. Without this transformation, they would be intermediaries in white exploitation. In "Brother Pimp" (1966), Neal wrote,

> You help the beast make whores out of black women,
> only you yourself are a whore.
> you and your brother pimps kill each other
> for the right to destroy our women.
> would-be heroes. would-be black men.
>
> JOIN THE STRUGGLE
> FOR REAL MANHOOD
> LINK YOUR NATURAL LIFE-SENSE
> TO THE REAL SOUL-THING[49]

In what capacity would "Brother Pimp" join the struggle? Neal hoped that he would

> become a new kind of pimp. yeah, brother, pimp for the
> revolution. I say pimp for the revolution,
>   not pimp on the revolution.

Neal dedicated this poem to Iceberg Slim, a former pimp whose *Pimp: The Story of My Life* would be released the following year.[50] Neal's dedication of this poem—and his numerous poems about Malcolm X—indicate that he sought to create role models for the transformation of outlaws into revolutionaries. This image of the pimp—alongside other criminals and convicts—provided a hyper-masculine, sexualized image that could be used (once transformed) to serve the revolution.

"PIMPS FOR THE REVOLUTION": PRISON WRITERS OF THE BLACK ARTS MOVEMENT

In his introduction to the 1969 anthology, *The New Black Poetry*, Clarence Major argued that poetry could be an important tool in transforming pimps into revolutionaries. Just as Larry Neal hoped that incarcerated African Americans would become "pimps for the revolution," Major argued that the new poetry signaled "death cries to the pimp par excellence of the recent capitalistic stages of the world."[51] Juno Bakali Tshombe plumbed this theme in a dialogue he imagined between two Los Angeles pimps. The first pimp asks the second pimp, "have you dug this new black awareness thing going around?" They contemplate the effect of cultural nationalism on their careers after the first pimp is confronted by someone who threatens to rip him off if he "didn't quit that counter-revolutionary stuff." He then explains that earlier that same week, the nationalists castrated and killed three pimps and put a sign around their heads with a warning that "there ain't going to be any more pimping, shooting dope, and other counter-revolutionary activity in the nationalist community." As he laments the increasing difficulty of hiring new prostitutes, the first pimp vows to put his mother out on the street as a prostitute.[52]

As counter-revolutionaries, Tshombe explains, pimps needed to be eliminated from black communities. However, Tshombe also felt that the lawlessness that brought him to Norfolk Prison was a key step in his political transformation. In his autobiographical poem "discovering myself," (1972) he notes:

> in order
> to become a black man
> instead of a nigga,
> I would first
> have to be a nigga.
> in order to become that black man.[53]

Although Tshombe recognizes that his lawlessness and incarceration would not be a permanent solution, he also feels that it would be a necessary step toward becoming a strong patriarch. James A. Lang, a Muslim poet in Norfolk, asks in a 1972 poem to his son if his incarceration is a

> disservice
> To the struggle? Or, have I contributed to
> The intensification of the struggle
> By breaking the genealogical
> Progression of paternal submission
> To the oppressor's blueprint
> For eternal enslavement?[54]

Answering his own question, he acknowledges his prison conversion to Islam as a necessary step in restoring "Harmony and tranquility / To our be-deviled planet." Rather than pariahs or parasites, their previous criminal activities showed that prisoners were committed to resistance. This, they argued, would be an important characteristic for future revolutionaries.

Lang creates a character, in the short story "The (Un?)Making of a Revolutionary," who undergoes a religious and political transformation in prison.[55] Unsatisfied with the options of being unemployed, under-employed, or deployed to Vietnam, Eddie turns to robbing banks. Once in prison, "the total liberation of black people" became his "only concern." Prison gives him "the opportunity to examine the plight of black people in America from a much broader viewpoint."[56] His dedication to this cause leads him to conclude that the elimination of drug-dealers and pimps "in whatever manner necessary" would be his first priority. However, upon his release he is tempted by his brother—a pimp driving a new Cadillac Eldorado and dressed in a "white long-haired-beaver hat with a six-inch brim and a blue band"—with heroin and two prostitutes.[57] The story ends with the reader left wondering if Eddie will give in to temptation or follow through on his violent solution. Will he shoot heroin or his brother? Will this be the "unmaking" of a revolutionary or a fulfillment of his mission?[58]

If former pimps and bank robbers could become soldiers in the revolution, what role would women play? Carolyn Baxter would eventually achieve some public notice for her 1979 collection of prison poems, *Prison Solitary and Other Free Government Services*.[59] Black Panther Ericka Huggins published numerous poems from her time in Connecticut's Niantic State Prison.[60] Her work was included in Angela Davis' collection—written and edited while Davis was incarcerated in the Marin County Jail—*If They Come in the Morning*.[61] Huggins' works reflect her commitment to social change. She saw the prison as merely one of many walls facing African Americans:

> if only all barriers could be removed
> and we could walk/talk/sing
> be . . .
> free of all psychological, spiritual
> political, economic
> boundaries
> all of us all the freedom lovers of
> the world but especially
> right now—prisoners.[62]

She wanted all barriers removed, but also knew that they needed to get past the walls of steel and concrete before tackling the political and economic boundaries.

Some poetry by women writers did emerge during the Prison Arts Movement. Women also played important symbolic roles in the poems by incarcerated men. Despite their incarceration, some prison writers felt that they could serve as protectors of African American women. In "Stride, Strut Lady," Imani Kujichagulia, a convict in the Florida State Prison, tells a prostitute to "Come in out the cold, lady / give me your hand . . . tell me / your problems . . . lady, / i'll be your man."[63] Kujichagulia offered more than a warm room and a kind ear; in his name he indicated a devotion to the seven principles of Maulana Karenga's US organization. "Imani" signified faith: "To believe with all our heart in our parents, our teachers, our leaders, our people and the righteousness and victory of our struggle." "Kujichagulia" stood for the principle of self-determination: "to define ourselves, name ourselves, and speak for ourselves, instead of being defined, and spoken for by others."[64] Instead of the objectification, commodification, and exploitation of her body as a prostitute, the poet offered his faith and self-determination as an alternative value system based on spiritual and cultural nationalism of the Black Arts and Black Power Movements. Other poets displayed more ambivalence about the role they could play in protecting Black women. Etheridge Knight, perhaps the best known poet to emerge from prison during this period, explores the sexual exploitation of black women by white men in "The Violent Space (or when your sister sleeps around for money)":

> O Mary don't you weep don't you moan
> O Mary shake your butt to the violent juke,
> Absorb the demon puke and watch the white eyes pop.[65]

While men defile his seventeen-year-old sister—cast in the role of the Virgin—the narrator can only watch and descend into drug addiction.

With encouragement from Gwendolyn Brooks, Sonia Sanchez, Dudley Randall, and Haki Madhubuti, Knight published *Poems from Prison* in 1968. Like Neal and Baraka, Knight also believed that poetry should serve to represent and transform black communities, but here he reveals that he cannot protect his sister with a poem:

> I sit counting syllables like Midas gold.
> I am not bold. I can not yet take hold of the demon
> And lift his weight from your black belly,
> So I grab the air and sing my song.
> (But the air can not stand my singing long).[66]

Perhaps because he has not conquered his own addiction or simply because "counting syllables" is too self-centered, Knight implies that his song would only provide a temporary comfort that will not transform the circumstances of his sister's exploitation. Who, Knight asks, is the real criminal? Is it the seventeen-year-old prostitute or the "demon" on top of her? Is it her incarcerated, drug-addicted brother or those who imprison him? Elsewhere, Knight showed that his crimes pale in comparison to the larger crimes that plague African American communities: "When a people set out, with a gun in one hand and a Bible in the other, to exploit and enslave and imprison all the other peoples of the world (and succeed), and then the exploited and enslaved are called the criminals—it is time to redefine terms. It is time to put the proper shoe on the proper foot."[67]

Prostitutes represented both the willingness of some African American men to exploit African American women and the impotency of others to protect them. At the same time, virtually all prison collections from the Prison Arts Movement contain homages to "Black Queens." These idealized figures represented the ongoing oppression of all black people. At the same time, some writers could draw on literary traditions that used women as allegories for nations and freedom struggles. This could be used to describe a public figure, as in Michael Thomas, Sr.'s "Poem to Angela":

> Tomorrows Black Queen who guerrilla Sisters today
> from yesterdays unidentified image.
> Spread the words of Revolution
> via pain & suffering
> us all b/chanting.[68]

Here, the "Black Queen" is Angela Davis—an actual revolutionary who appears in the works of many prison writers during the Black Arts Movement—but she bears characteristics of the more common usage of the "Black Queen" as an archetypal figure of black suffering.[69] Where the pimp stood in for the potential revolutionary inside all prisoners, the Black Queen was the suffering "voice of humanity" who could also be the harbinger of revolution.

In contrast to the actual Angela Davis, literary Black Queens were usually placed on pedestals far from the front lines. She served to inspire black men to lead and fight; but more than anything, she served as a source of love that fueled, as Willi X wrote in California's Folsom Prison in 1975, "the soul of our people": "I write these lines for love, out of love, my love for your love. Love for your being, and love that reflects the soul of our people, love that saved our lives and kept our vision intact through four hundred years of long struggle, the love that gives us the will to survive with the hope that our love will carry us to the promised land."[70] Contained in a collection called *Captive Voices*, Willi X's work merges the struggle to survive his incarceration with the collective struggles of black men and women. In his invocation of "the promised land," he connects the modern struggle for liberation and power to the longer struggles against slavery, Jim Crow laws, and ongoing oppression. Black women, of course, were central to all of these struggles. The Black Queen, however, provided food for a hungry soul and an ideal for a lonely man. In an almost entirely male environment, it would be difficult for the Black Queen to be much more than this.

In fact, the "Black Queen" provides insight into the relationship between masculinity and Black nationalism through its elision of femininity and the "motherland." Like many Black Arts Movement writers in and out of prison, James Lang invokes the image of the Black Queen in the opening of "For My Ex-Wife" (1972):

> To the most heavenly mother
> In all of creation
> The beautiful black queen
> Of our glorious black nation.

Lang's nationalism had clear gender lines: women served as mothers of the black nation. It is unclear in this poem if the nation Lang hopes to possess will be patriarchal. In replacing the familiar Christian invocation of "the heavenly father" with a mother, Lang nods to the variety of kinship, religious, and national structures that would be possible in the "black nation." As little more than an object, however, the "Black Queen" becomes the personification of the "motherland" he hopes to possess.

As he indicates in his title, the symbolic Queen of Lang's opening is also his ex-wife. Lang reminds his readers that his incarceration made it impossible for this couple to maintain their relationship:

> Like a fool I have allowed myself
> To be taken away from you,
> And now all that we once had is gone—
> Our dreams may never come true.[71]

Lang understands that his incarceration is a product of his own actions and the larger social context. He was "taken away" by an oppressive system, but he also acted in some foolish way to allow this to take place. The central point of this poem is similar to Etheridge Knight's "The Violent Space." Lang makes note of the helplessness he surely felt while behind bars. While images of the Black Queen appear throughout the writings of the Black Arts Movement, incarcerated writers were clearly anguished that these Black Queens were left to fend for themselves while they served their time. But these writers also make clear that incarcerated people could—and did—serve as catalysts for change. Knight hoped his poems—along with his efforts to bring the works of other incarcerated people before the larger public—would assist in the transformation of consciousness that would ultimately liberate black people from "the larger prison outside."[72] As literary critic Patricia Liggins Hill notes, "Knight means for his prison experiences to serve as a microcosm of the freedomless void that his people are experiencing."[73]

Prison writers made important contributions to the Black Arts Movement. Their presence in prisons served as a key metaphor for "free" writers who hoped that art would aid in the transformation of black consciousness and conditions. In addition, incarcerated writers and artists participated in the movement by fostering connections with writers and artists like Elma Lewis, Benny Andrews, and Gwendolyn Brooks. Incarcerated artists frequently echoed the theme that prisons could be fruitfully seen as a symbol of white oppression. They supplemented this theme by arguing that prisons could be sites of transformation and that convicts would be key participants in the revolution that followed the shift in consciousness.

* * *

The Prison Arts and Black Arts Movements converged historically, aesthetically, and ideologically. A strong argument could be made that the two movements were the same: first, key figures of the Black Arts Movement either did time or worked closely with incarcerated artists and writers; second, the aesthetic sensibility and ideological convictions of prison artists and writers often drew on and closely resembled their more mobile contemporaries; third, real and folk prisoners proved popular as subjects of the Black Arts Movement. Perhaps most powerfully, writers inside and outside prisons agreed with Malcolm X's contention that "America is the prison" and that African American convicts could accurately be called residents of "prisons within prisons." In short, the late 1960s and early 1970s were unprecedented in the way prisoners inspired and participated in a major cultural movement. Many intellectuals and artists struggled to show the consistency between lives lived in poor African American communities and behind prison walls: limited control, consistent physical and ideological oppression, and the daily experience of racism.

While a handful of the key figures from the Prison Arts Movement continue to create extraordinary work, the movement that fostered them has fallen on hard times. In practical terms, the artists and teachers who continue to go into American prisons are little more than a skeleton crew, applying for grants to provide sorely needed and much appreciated programming. Outside of prison walls, a handful of activists, scholars, and aficionados know of the Prison Arts Movement. But walk into a classroom inside of a prison and you will find a community of artists and writers who nurture that legacy by creating new works, participating in the few programs that remain, and reminding anyone who will listen of the little-known writers who fostered a movement. They are still behind bars, but the links they add provide personal relief and a legacy for future writers who will surely follow.

NOTES

1. The Pell Grant program stopped providing money for prison programs in 1991, due largely to the efforts of North Carolina Senator Jesse Helms. John Marc Taylor, "Pell Grants for Prisons," in *Doing Time: 25 Years of Prison Writing—A PEN American Center Prize Anthology*, ed. Bell Gale Chevigny (New York: Arcade Publishing, 1999), 111. It is important to note that many of these programs were correspondence courses through the extension service of major universities. At the primary and secondary levels, other inmates routinely provided the instruction. Etheridge Knight describes how this worked in the Indiana State Prison in "Inside These Walls," Etheridge Knight and other inmates of Indiana State Prison, *Black Voices from Prison* (New York: Pathfinder Press, 1970), 135.

2. See, for example, Folsom Creative Writers Workshop, *Captive Voices: Echoes Off the Walls III, An Anthology of Works by Folsom Writers* (Paradise, CA: Dustbooks, 1975); Michael Hogan, ed. *Do Not Go Gentle: Poetry and Prose from Behind the Walls*, (Tuscon, AZ: Blue Moon Press, 1977); Frank Graziano, ed., *A Season in the Hour: Poems from the Prisons of South Carolina*, (Columbia: South Carolina Arts Commission, 1978). They were funded by the National Endowment for the Arts.

3. Liz Lerman, "Arts-in-Corrections: Art from California Prisons," in *Art in Other Places: Artists at Work in America's Community and Social Institutions* (Center for the Study of Art and Community, 2000). Available on-line at http://www.artandcommunity.com/aopcorrex.html.

4. Faith G. Norris, "Preface," in *Men in Exile: An Anthology of Creative Writing by Inmates of the Oregon State Penitentiary*, ed. Faith G. Norris and Sharon J. Springer (Corvallis: Oregon State University Press, 1973), 8.

5. Richard Shelton, "Preface," in *Do Not Go Gentle: Poetry and Prose from Behind the Walls*, iii.

6. Bell Gale Chevigny, "Introduction," *Doing Time: 25 Years of Prison Writing—A PEN American Center Prize Anthology*, ed. Bell Gale Chevigny (New York: Arcade Publishing, 1999), xx.

7. Stuart Adams, *The San Quentin Prison College Project*, Final Report, Phase 1 (Berkeley: School of Criminology, University of California, April 1968), 1. Copy located in the Bancroft Library, University of California at Berkeley. According to John Marc Taylor, there were already twelve post-secondary programs in U.S. prisons in 1965. The University of Southern Illinois began its program in Stateville Prison in 1953. John Marc Taylor, "Pell Grants for Prisons," in *Doing Time*, 107. A fascinating account of how Nathan Leopold and Richard Loeb—the infamous, highly educated, upper-class convicted murderers—began a high school in Stateville in 1932 is in Nathan F. Leopold, *Life Plus 99 Years* (Garden City, NY: Doubleday, 1958), 222–37. Prior to the founding of the University of Southern Illinois' program, prisoners—including Leopold—could take correspondence courses through many universities.

8. Paul Goodman quoted in Adams, *The San Quentin Prison College Project*, 24. On the other extreme, W. Reason Campbell wrote in the mid-1970s that he saw virtually every inmate as manipulative. His open hostility was evident when a student lit a wastebasket on fire. Pushing the wastebasket into the center of the room and leaving, Campbell recalled that he said to the inmates—many of whom were from Los Angeles, "I know how homesick you all are for a little smog. Breathe it in and be happy." W. Reason Campbell, *Dead Man Walking: Teaching in a Maximum Security Prison* (New York: Richard Marek Publishers, 1978), 30.

9. National Advisory Commission on Criminal Justice Standards and Goals, *Report on Corrections* (Washington, D.C.: U.S. Government Printing Office, 1973), 474.

10. Jimmy Santiago Baca, *Working in the Dark: Reflections of a Poet of the Barrio* (Santa Fe: Red Crane Books, 1992), 8. This story is told more completely in Jimmy Santiago Baca, *A Place to Stand: The Making of a Poet* (New York: Grove Press, 2001), 162.

11. Ibid., 8.

12. Adams, *The San Quentin Prison College Project*, 27.

13. Jean Harris, *"They Always Call Us Ladies": Stories from Prison* (New York: Scribner's, 1988), 53–55; Estelle B. Freedman, *Their Sisters' Keepers: Women's Prison Reform in America, 1830–1930* (Ann Arbor: University of Michigan Press, 1981), 116–18. Bedford Hills would become an important site for extensive IQ and psychological testing on women inmates in the 1910s. See Scott Christianson, *With Liberty for Some: 500 Years of Imprisonment in America* (Boston: Northeastern University Press, 1998), 197–98.

14. Juno Bakali Tshombe (previously known as Craig Dee Anderson), "Psychological Warfare at Norfolk Prison Camp," in Norfolk Prison Brothers, *Who Took the Weight?: Black Voices from Norfolk Prison* (Boston: Little, Brown and Company, 1972), 95.

15. D. Ross Pugmire, *The Administration of Personnel in Correctional Institutions* (New York: Bureau of Publications, Teachers College, 1937), 14–15. By World War II, R. L. Mosely noted, prisons became "more livable." In addition to education programs, the forty-three-year veteran of the Indiana State Prison noted in 1970 that in 1942 he was

finally allowed to "put up a few family pictures, secure a table, have pencils, pens, ink, paints, drafting equipment and hobby crafts." R. L. Mosely, "An Old-Timer Looks at 42 Years Behind Prison Walls," in *Black Voices from Prison*, 71–72,

16. Elma Lewis, "Foreword," in *Who Took the Weight?*, xiv. The Elma Lewis Technical Theater Training Program of the Massachusetts Correctional Institution, Norfolk was a project of the Boston-based National Center of Afro-American Artists.

17. Ibid., xv.

18. Tshombe, "Psychological Warfare at Norfolk Prison Camp," in *Who Took the Weight?*, 95.

19. Malcolm X, *The Autobiography of Malcolm X* (New York: Balantine, 1964), 182. Malcolm X converted to Islam in 1947 while in prison. The Nation of Islam had a profound influence on the creative and intellectual development of incarcerated African Americans. In addition to Malcolm's term in Norfolk, Elijah Muhammad served a four-year prison term for draft resistance during World War II. Muhammad's time in prison led him to believe that spiritual conversion to the Nation of Islam could transform black felons. After his release, Muhammad devoted substantial time and money to converting incarcerated people to the Nation of Islam. During the 1970s, Malcolm X became an icon of the Black Arts Movement. Richard Brent Turner, *Islam in the African American Experience* (Bloomington: Indiana University Press, 1997), 182. These efforts continued to bear fruit. According to Asma Gull Hasnan, 90 percent of the estimated 300,000 to 350,000 American Muslim inmates in 1985 were African American. Asma Gull Hasnan, *American Mulims: The New Generation* (New York: Contiuum, 2000), 75. The Nation of Islam's emphasis on economic independence, individual self-worth, and collective identity formation would jibe well with both the ethics of the Black Arts Movement and the needs of incarcerated African Americans. On the cultural significance of the Nation of Islam, see Lawrence H. Mamiya and C. Eric Lincoln, "Nation of Islam," in *Encyclopedia of African-American Culture and History* (New York: Macmillan, 1996), 1966–69, and C. Eric Lincoln, *The Black Muslims in America* (Boston: Beacon Press, 1961).

20. Benny Andrews, *Echoes: Prisons, U.S.A.* (New York: The Studio Museum in Harlem, n.d. [1977]), n.p.

21. Ibid.

22. Doloris Holmes, "Interview with Cliff Joseph, 1972," Smithsonian Archives of American Art. Available on-line at: http://artarchives.si.edu/oralhist/joseph72.htm. See also Stephen C. Dubin, *Displays of Power: Memory and Amnesia in the American Museum* (New York: New York University Press, 1999).

23. Etheridge Knight, "Inside These Walls," 137.

24. David Lionel Smith, "Black Arts Movement," in *Encyclopedia of African-American Culture and History*, 327.

25. Christianson, *With Liberty for Some*, 268; see also Bert Useem and Peter Kimball, *States of Siege: U.S. Prison Riots, 1971–1986* (New York: Oxford University Press, 1989).

26. Edward Bunker, "War Behind Walls," *Harper's Magazine* (February 1972): 39–47. Reprinted in Burtono M. Atkins and Henry R. Glick, *Prisons, Protest, and Politics* (Englewood Cliffs, NJ: Prentice-Hall, 1972), 60–76.

27. Zayd Shakur, "America is the Prison," in *Off the Pigs! The History and Literature of the Black Panther Party*, ed. G. Louis Heath (Metuchen, NJ: The Scarecrow Press, 1976), 247–80. Author was "Deputy Minister of Information" Black Panther Party,

State of New York, 1370 Boston Road, Bronx, New York. This was a mimeographed article collected in NYC on October 17, 1970.

28. Roberta Ann Johnson, "The Prison Birth of Black Power," *Journal of Black Studies* 5: 4 (June 1975): 395–414.

29. Huey P. Newton. "Eulogy for Jonathan Jackson and William Christmas." Delivered at St. Augustine's Church, Twenty-Seventh and West Streets, Oakland, California, August 15, 1970. Reprinted in *Off the Pigs!*, 322–23. Emphasis in original.

30. George Jackson, *Soledad Brother: The Prison Letters of George Jackson* (New York: Bantam, 1970), quoted in Johnson, "Prison Birth," 36.

31. Hettie Jones, *How I Became Hettie Jones* (New York: E. P. Dutton, 1990), 143–44.

32. Amiri Baraka, *The Autobiography of LeRoi Jones* (New York: Freundlich Books, 1984), 280.

33. Ibid., 263.

34. Ibid., 269.

35. Ibid., 270–71.

36. Ibid., 271.

37. Amiri Baraka, *Raise Race Rays Raze: Essays Since 1965* (New York: Random House, 1971). See especially "Newark Courthouse—'66 Wreck (Nigger Rec Room)," 3–9, and "From: The Book of Life," 49–55.

38. Amiri Baraka, "Police," *The Drama Review* 12: 4 (1968): 3–12.

39. Baraka, *Autobiography*, 273.

40. Marvin X, "Take Care of Business," *The Drama Review* 12: 4 (1968): 29–124.

41. Larry Neal, "The Black Arts Movement." in *Visions of a Liberated Future: Black Arts Movement Writings* (New York: Thunder's Mouth Press, 1989), 62.

42. H. Bruce Franklin, "Songs of an Imprisoned People," *MELUS* 6: 1 (Spring 1979): 6–22.

43. Larry Neal, "Shine Goes to Jail" in *Visions of a Liberated Future*, 175.

44. LeRoi Jones, "Black Art." Reprinted in Larry Neal, "Black Arts Movement," in *Visions of a Liberated Future*, 65

45. Baraka, "Police," 1.

46. Neal, "Black Arts Movement," 66.

47. Ibid., 75.

48. Ibid., 68.

49. Larry Neal, "Brother Pimp," in *Visions of a Liberated Future*, 216–17.

50. H. Bruce Franklin, *Prison Writing in 20th Century America* (New York: Penguin, 1998), 167.

51. Clarence Major, "Introduction," *The New Black Poetry* (New York: International Publishers, 1969), 11; quoted in Patricia Liggins Hill, " 'The Violent Space': The Function of the New Black Aesthetic in Etheridge Knight's Prison Poetry," *Black American Literature Forum* 14: 3 (Fall 1980): 115. Amiri Baraka explicitly contrasted "pimp art" with Black nationalism in a 1969 *New York Times* essay. See Imamu Amiri Baraka, Nationalism vs. PimpArt" [*sic*], in *Black Writers of America: A Comprehensive Anthology*, ed. Richard Barksdale and Keneth Kinnamon (New York: Macmillan, 1972), 759–61.

52. Juno Bakali Tshombe/Craig Dee Anderson, "The Only for Real People (Two Pimps' View of Black People and the National Liberation Movement," in *Who Took the Weight?*, 8–13.

53. Juno Bakali Tshombe/Craig Dee Anderson, "discovering myself," in *Who Took the Weight?*, 27.

54. James A. Lang, "A Letter for James Andrew Lang, Jr. (Age Six)," in *Who Took the Weight?*, 61–62.

55. James A. Lang, "The (Un?)Making of a Revolutionary," in *Who Took the Weight?*, 133–37.

56. Ibid., 134.

57. Ibid., 137.

58. Pancho Aguila, a poet in the Creative Writers' Workshop in California's Folsom Prison visually noted the four steps it took to go from a convict to a revolutionary in "Boomerang":

Convict
    Ex-convict
        Fugitive
            Criminal
                Revolutionary

Pancho Aguila, "Boomerang," in *Captive Voices: Echoes Off the Walls III, An Anthology of Works by Folsom Writers* (Paradise, CA: Dustbooks, 1975), 9.

59. Carolyn Baxter, *Prison Solitary and Other Free Government Services*, (Greenfield Center, NY: The Greenfield Review Press, 1979).

60. Huey Newton and Ericka Huggins, *Insights & Poems* (San Francisco: City Lights Books, 1975); her work from this period is also in *Wall Tappings: An Anthology of Writings by Women Prisoners*, ed. Judith A. Scheffler (Boston: Northeastern University Press, 1986), 292–300.

61. Angela Davis and Other Political Prisoners, *If They Come in the Morning: Voices of Resistance* (New Rochelle, NY: Tshird Press Publishers, 1971), 97–105.

62. Ericka Huggins, Untitled, in *If They Come in the Morning*, 99.

63. Imani Kujichagulia, "Stride, Strut Lady," in *Bound and Free: The Poetry of Warriors Behind Bars* (Washington, D.C.: King Publications, 1976), 18. Copy in the Bancroft Library, The University of California, Berkeley.

64. Amiri Baraka, "7 Principles of US Maulana Karenga & the Need for a Black Value System," in *Raise Race Rays Raze: Essays Since 1965*, 133–34.

65. Etheridge Knight, "The Violent Space (or when your sister sleeps around for money)," in *Poems from Prison* (Detroit: Broadside Press, 1968), 23.

66. Ibid., 23.

67. Etheridge Knight, "Preface" in *Black Voices from Prison*, 6.

68. Michael Thomas, Sr., "Poem to Angela from Black Political Prisoners," *The Black Scholar* 2: 8–9 (April/May 1971), 50.

69. Gomvi Malik invoked both Assata Shakur and Angela Davis in a poem that critiqued the idea that African American women should be put on a pedestal at all. Gomvi Malik, "Funky Nigger/Nigger Funky," in *Bound and Free*, 14.

70. Willi X, "To My Beautiful Woman," in *Captive Voices*, 203.

71. James A. Lang, "For My Ex-Wife," in *Who Took the Weight?*, 59.

72. Ibid., 9.

73. Patricia Liggins Hill, "The Violent Space," 120.

15

"To Make a Poet Black"

Canonizing Puerto Rican Poets in the Black Arts Movement

Michelle Joan Wilkinson

Yet do I marvel at this curious thing:
To make a poet black, and bid him sing!
  —COUNTEE CULLEN, "YET DO I MARVEL," 1925

The reflective tone with which Countee Cullen ends his 1925 poem "Yet Do I Marvel" stands in relief to the urgent pleas in poems from the height of the Black Arts Movement. Cullen's speaker, a Harlem Renaissance era double for the author, marvels, almost from a distance, at the conundrum God has made of him: a black man and a poet in early twentieth-century America.[1] In his efforts to share his verses, the black bard fares no better than Sisyphus, the mythological figure who, Cullen reminds us, was doomed to "struggle up a never-ending stair."[2] During the 1920s, the obstacle that doomed Negro artists assumed form as the "racial mountain"—to borrow Langston Hughes' terminology.[3] Particularly for those who preferred to be called poet, instead of "Negro poet" or "black poet"—characterizations they imagined as limited and limiting—the "racial mountain" could prove insurmountable.

Unlike the poet in Cullen's verse who is made "black" by God, the 1960s generation of Black Arts poets imagined themselves as black magicians making black poems in and for a black world. As Amiri Baraka (then LeRoi Jones) expressed in his 1965 "State/meant": "We are black magicians, black art / s we make in black labs of the heart."[4] Baraka's poetic "State/meant" stages a reversal in which blackness is a license, not a limit. With its definitive title and declarative sentences, "State/meant" signaled an aesthetic turn and epitomized the direction that other writers would move toward as the decade progressed.

While a full range of voices informed both the Harlem Renaissance and the Black Arts Movement, much of the later poetry, composed in an era of Civil

Rights and Black Power struggles, dispels with distanced contemplation to employ the directed speech codes of the contemporaneous social movements. The self-proclaimed "black poet" of the 1960s acted as an orator, activist, entertainer, and aesthetician of a Black Arts Movement. Here blackness functioned as a legitimating factor, and "black" served as a qualifying adjective conveying authenticity and authority. Working alongside black activists, black poets expressed their revolutionary commitments by creating art that doubled as ammunition. This position is best characterized in Larry Neal's 1968 essay, "The Black Arts Movement," which called black art "the aesthetic and spiritual sister of the Black Power concept."[5] Identifying with art of social and political interest—as opposed to disinterested expressions—black artists wrested the meaning of "the aesthetic" away from its Kantian stronghold. With the same vigor that the Ancients and the eighteenth-century philosophers had debated their ideas, the leading theorists of the Black Arts era—the black aestheticians—proposed alternatives to the "art for art's sake" version of aesthetics. The new slogans included "art for the people's sake," "art for survival," and even "art for the revolution."

Similarly, by honing and crafting a socio-aesthetic in their position papers, black aestheticians rejected the term "anti-aesthetic," which seemed to connote propaganda, polemics, or protest. As art critic Hal Foster notes in his edited volume on the subject, the term "anti-aesthetic" signals not only "forms that deny the idea of a privileged aesthetic realm," as a black aesthetic position might suggest, but also, and too often, an "assertion of the negation of art."[6] The latter definition discounts the affirmative value of envisioning a "black aesthetic"—that is, an aesthetic that finds coherence with the ethics and experiences that inform black life. Though much-debated (and much-derided), the concept of "black aesthetics" offered a counternarrative to the falsely universal or objective interpretations of "the aesthetic."[7] As scholar Carolyn Fowler writes in *Black Art and Black Aesthetics* (1976), the 1960s black aesthetic affirmed black life, positing that "a specific world view, an ethos, a sensitivity" could be found in the works of black artists.[8] If such is the case, how, then, do we account for the inclusion of works by Puerto Ricans in the now-canonical volumes of the Black Arts Movement? To what extent did "black," in its late 1960s usage, define aesthetic criteria compatible with the expressive range of Puerto Rican poets such as Victor Hernández Cruz and Felipe Luciano, poets whom literary scholar and fellow poet Louis Reyes Rivera refers to as "spanning between African American and Puerto Rican literature"?[9]

Despite the rhetorics of blackness they invoked, black aestheticians initiated theoretical discussions that would prove viable for other ethnic groups. In *The Mask of Art: Breaking the Aesthetic Contract—Film and Literature* (1998), cultural critic Clyde Taylor posits that an increase of scholarly interest in aesthetic pluralism was a "largely unacknowledged response to the impact of the Black Aesthetic."[10] Although Taylor challenges the use of "the aesthetic" as a constructive category in and of itself, he contends that the discourse on "ethno-aesthetics" owes a debt to the black aestheticians who forged a revolution in language by "unnaming the 'the aesthetic' as 'the White aesthetic.'"[11] Without recovering the narrow nationalisms or the exclusionary posturing within the black aesthetic movement, Taylor provides a way for contemporary scholars to read the cultural borrowings that emerged. For Chicano and Puerto Rican poets especially, the precedent set by the Black Arts Movement proved instructive.

The affirmation of a "black aesthetic" encouraged assertions of a "Nuyorican aesthetic"—a New York Puerto Rican aesthetic as defined by Miguel Algarín, the enterprising founder and director of the Nuyorican Poets Café since 1975.[12] Yet, prior to the 1970s Nuyorican poetry movement, Puerto Rican poets were participating and collaborating in the development of the Black Arts Movement. In New York City, where blacks and Puerto Ricans often lived adjacent to each other, the connection was particularly strong. In his study of the relationships between blacks and Puerto Ricans in New York, political economist Andres Torres claims, "it would be futile to define the African American-Puerto Rican experience within the terminology of race relations, for in reality, both groups occupy an ambiguous space, somewhere between melting pot and mosaic."[13] Torres's analysis supports the claims that a substantial number of Puerto Ricans and African Americans publicly promoted each other's agendas, providing the intergroup alliances that lent support to both social movements. For example, African Americans participated in the predominantly Puerto Rican Young Lords Party and Puerto Ricans participated in the Black Panther Party.[14] Attempts at political coalition and artistic collaboration were not always successful, however, but Torres explains that despite specific instances of conflict or competition, blacks and Puerto Ricans in New York "created movements, organizations and institutions—often with shared participation—many of which survive to this day and continue to work together."[15]

Though short-lived, the Umbra Poets Workshop and the Last Poets groups were such institutions in New York City. Beginning in 1962, the Umbra Poets Workshop grew out of informal gatherings at the Lower East Side apartment of writer and activist Tom Dent. In the lively downtown sessions, poets originally hailing from as far as down South and the Caribbean, or as close as uptown and the Bronx, spent hours encouraging and challenging each other. The 1968 founding of the Last Poets in Harlem's Mount Morris Park was more spontaneous, with differing accounts of the group's origin coming from different members. For example, the name "Original Last Poets" refers to a subset of the group that was active between 1968 and 1970, preceding the later, and larger, incarnations of the performance poetry troupe. Predominantly African American in membership, both the Umbra Poets Workshop and the Original Last Poets included Puerto Rican poets who had been listening to and musing on the same array of urban rhythms as their black American peers. Stirred by the sounds of sirens, saxophones, and subway trains, the black and Puerto Rican poets in these groups shared mutually resonant languages of expression as they explored similar terrains of experience.

"WHAT WAS PUERTO RICAN ALL ABOUT": VICTOR HERNÁNDEZ CRUZ AND FELIPE LUCIANO

In the late 1960s, "new black poetry" emerged as a major genre of Black Arts Movement writings. The new poets were channeled into the Black Arts canon through volumes titled *Black Fire* (1968), *The New Black Poetry* (1969), *New Black Voices* (1972), and *Black Spirits* (1972).[16] Literary critic Stephen Henderson, in his appropriately titled compilation, *Understanding the New Black Poetry: Black Speech and Black Music as Poetic References* (1973), charts how the two referents—speech and music—inform the new black poetic praxis.[17] Henderson asserts that "the techniques and timbres of the sermon and other forms of oratory, the dozens, the rap, the signifying, and the oral folktale" contribute to poetic voice.[18] Likewise, in identifying "jazz as a model and inspiration" for the new black poets, Henderson examines the structural challenges of composing word music on the page.[19] Henderson posits that by listening to the poets, not merely by reading their works, we witness the interplay of the two references.

Where Henderson focuses on speech and music in the new black poetry, Martin Espada, a poet and cultural activist, also names two primary strains in U.S. Puerto Rican poetry of the same period. In his seminal essay, "Documentaries and Declamadores: Puerto Rican Poetry in the United States," published in 1987, Espada writes that poems "document, and protest, incidents which would otherwise be left undocumented," and draw on traditions of oral recitation to reach the community represented in the work.[20] Although Espada acknowledges that the orality of the new black poetry encouraged a similar trend in Puerto Rican poetry in the United States, he notes that there is a rich Puerto Rican oral tradition that antedates the poets' experiences of interaction with black American communities. As the title "Documentaries and Declamadores" suggests, Espada argues that Puerto Rican poets in the United States descend from the "*declamador*, a dramatic public performer of memorized verse," who, in Spain and then in the Spanish colonies of Latin America and the Caribbean, addressed audiences in plazas and town squares.[21] The poetry of the declamador is a public announcement, a popular response to current events and everyday life. In this way, the declamador is not unlike the African griot or djali—the oral archivist who is perhaps a more distant ancestor for Puerto Rican poets.

Acknowledging that traditions of Puerto Rican oral history on the island informs the mainland poetry; scholars such as Juan Flores and Geneviève Fabre point also to the shared "affinities" of black and Puerto Rican writers in the United States.[22] In a detailed summary, Felix Cortés, Angel Falcón, and Flores address the shared aesthetic and political values in poetry:

> There are many elements characteristic of the new Puerto Rican poetry which were clearly drawn from the Afro-American poetry of the period of "Black Power" and the democratic, nationalist organizations in the Black community. Such elements include the militant tone of anger and struggle, the declamatory and musical quality of the presentation, the street imagery of Black youth and

culture, the basically democratic themes in the condemnation of the ruling "white establishment" and its repressive, chauvinist institutions, the call to fight back and to mold national unity and pride, the denunciation of exploiters and opportunists within the ranks of the Black community.[23]

Mainland poetry displays these traits, not simply as literary influence but more so as a result of a similarity in the experiences and perspectives of the authors. While tracing a "clearly drawn" line from African American political and aesthetic expression to "the new Puerto Rican poetry," Cortés, Falcón, and Flores are equally instructive about the "Spanish origins" of the declamatory style that allowed Puerto Rican peasants a public voice.[24] Documenting and protesting—a joint primary function suggested by Espada—U.S.-based Puerto Rican poetry builds on its own traditions as it engages stylistic features gleaned from African American models.

The works of Puerto Rican poets Victor Hernández Cruz and Felipe Luciano reveal the overlapping and intersecting expressions of a Black Arts aesthetic and a Puerto Rican cultural consciousness. Victor Hernández Cruz was a member of the Umbra Poet's Workshop, a literary group that began on New York's Lower East Side. The group included founder Tom Dent, Calvin Hernton, David Henderson, Askia Muhammad Touré, and Ishmael Reed, the personal friend who first brought Hernández Cruz to Umbra. Hernández Cruz was associated with Umbra and contributed to the *Umbra* literary journal during the period of its move from East to West Coast in the late 1960s. Felipe Luciano was a member of the Last Poets—a group that epitomized the performance style of Black Arts poetics. Fittingly, Baraka describes Luciano as an "old friend" in his *Autobiography of LeRoi Jones* (1984).[25] Luciano, who self-identifies as black Puerto Rican, and Hernández Cruz, who embraces his mixed racial ancestry, were both regularly included in anthologies of "blackpoetry," to use Haki Madhubuti's terminology from "Blk Poetics."[26] Madhubuti differentiates between black poetry (any poetry by black people) and "blackpoetry," which he defines as poetry focused on "the idea" and committed to the expression of social and racial consciousness, and disconnected from the aesthetic expectations of a "white literary mainstream."[27] In myriad ways, however, the poems of Luciano and Hernández Cruz challenge Madhubuti's consciousness quota for "blackpoetry" by introducing Puerto Rican expression as a matrix of aesthetic, cultural, linguistic, and geographic cadences that go beyond specific responses to racial or social codes. Nevertheless, the poetry of Luciano, while never collected in a single volume, appears in anthologies and recordings that can be categorized as "blackpoetry." And Hernández Cruz, whose poetry was championed and published by the mainstream literati, sparked his career with contributions to now-canonical Black Arts Movement texts.

With his 1966 chapbook *Papo Got His Gun* and his first collection with a major publisher, 1969s *Snaps*, Hernández Cruz carved out a literary space full of fractured images, abstracted language, and incantatory states. Sounding new vocabularies and sampling new musics, the early poetry of Hernández Cruz provides a transcript of the years in which the first full generation of Puerto Ricans raised in the United States came of age. Espada calls the poetry of Hernández Cruz "surreal, insistently musical, and bilingual."[28] Indeed, Hernández Cruz's insistence on music predominates with invocations to congas, trombones, *descarga* (a jam session), and *ritmo* (rhythm). In addition to calling out urban funkmasters Pucho & the Latin Soul Brothers in "Cities," Hernández Cruz dedicates poems to musicians Ray Barretto ("Free Spirit"), Joe Bataan ("latin & soul"), and Eddie Palmieri ("/MOVING/").[29]

In Hernández Cruz's poems, music carries Puerto Rican nationalist sentiment but also bridges the cultural gaps between Puerto Ricans and other Americans. A number of pieces specifically refer to (Latin) boogaloo music, a hybrid form fusing Latin and funk rhythms, often with English lyrics and call-and-response patterns. Predated by a black dance called the boogaloo, the mid- to late 1960s Latin boogaloo was a wildly popular music that brought Latinos and blacks together on the same dance floor and often in the same bands. Writing about the Latin boogaloo period, Juan Flores explains: "the defining theme and musical feature of boogaloo is precisely this intercultural togetherness, the solidarity engendered by living and loving in unison beyond obvious differences."[30] At its height, Latin boogaloo music increased the social interaction among the two groups in a way only foreshadowed by the Latin jazz and mambo crazes of previous decades.

Of Hernández Cruz's poems using boogaloo as a recurring trope, "The Eye / Uptown & Downtown / (three days)" introduces the music as a structural and thematic element. In two of the poem's thirty-two numbered stanzas, boogaloo song titles or lyrics appear in capitals as the only text. Stanza thirteen sings:

CURA CURA CURA
BAILA BOOGALOO.[31]

And stanza twenty-five, again in all capitals, chants the title and refrain of Joe Cuba's famous 1966 boogaloo:

BANG BANG.

These two insertions, roughly centered throughout the poem's thirty-two stanzas, provide doses of musicality in a poem not specifically about music. Indeed, the "eye" of the poem roams uptown and downtown observing the scene. For example, stanza eighteen reports, "the lexington train broke down"; and stanza twenty-three warns, "the stairs are full of holes." In a color-by-number style, the poem's composite parts unify to create a surreal portrait of the city. However, in choosing to use only capital letters in the sections invoking boogaloo lyrics, Hernández Cruz highlights the role of Latin music as the soundtrack in the communities his poetic eye surveys. The boogaloo is the background rhythm that Hernández Cruz grants solo status for two of his thirty-two bars of verse.

Appearing in a host of anthologies including *Black Fire*, the landmark "anthology of Afro-American writing," edited by Baraka and Larry Neal, poems by Hernández Cruz also reflect the militant posture of 1960s works. For example, Hernández Cruz's poem "O.K.," with its images of "brains chewed like juicy fruit" and "teeth full / of blood" recalls the violence of Baraka's "Black Art," which called for poems teeming with teeth, flesh, hearts, and brains.[32] The power of poetry itself, a power "Black Art" envisions, is most directly treated in another poem by Hernández Cruz, "today is a day of great joy":

> when they stop poems
> in the mail & clap
> their hands & dance to
> them
>
> .   .   .   .   .   .
>
> when poems start to
> knock down walls to
> choke politicians
> when poems scream &
> begin to break the air
>
> that is the time of
> true poets that is
> the time of greatness
>
> a true poet aiming
> poems & watching things
> fall to the ground.[33]

Frequently anthologized, "today is a day of great joy," captures the fun and function of poetry—it is both entertainment and armament. Positioning the poet as assassin, Hernández Cruz gives new meaning to the words "BANG BANG" in "The Eye"; they now evoke the lines of a popular song as well as the line of fire. In "today," Hernández Cruz combines the present moment with the immediate future ("when poems start to . . . "), thereby creating a poetic reality that demands fulfillment of the present's potential. Each new day and each new poem is an opportunity for transformation.

Hernández Cruz's inclusion in journals and anthologies of black writing continued through the 1970s, with poems published in *Dices or Black Bones: Black Voices of the Seventies* (1970), edited by Adam David Miller, *3000 Years of Black Poetry* (1970), edited by Alan Lomax and Raoul Abdul, and *New Black Voices: An Anthology of Afro-American Literature* (1972), edited by Abraham Chapman.[34] In *3000 Years of Black Poetry*, "today" is the final contribution. The anthology's 3000 year trajectory, beginning with the praise songs of the Gabon Pygmy and ending with the poem of a New York Puerto Rican, attempts to record the stylistic elements unifying the "varied poetry of the African peoples."[35] Hernández Cruz's inclusion in the volume speaks to the fluidity of the poet's work as well as the aesthetic flexibility in the editors' vision of "black poetry."

While Hernández Cruz's poetic style reflected aesthetic criteria that defined the new black sensibility, the content of some poems doubly sealed his place within a black literary tradition. The poem "african things" is such an example. Published in *Negro Digest* in 1969, the poem communicates Puerto Rico's ambivalence about its African heritage as well as the speaker's appreciation for the influences that inform his New World identity. At first, directing his thoughts to an unknown auditor, the speaker reflects, "what was Puerto Rican all about. / all about the / indios & you better believe it the african things."[36] But as he gains assurance, he redirects the question, and insists:

grandmother speak to me & tell me of african things
                      how do latin
boo-ga-loo sound   like you
             conga drums in the islands you know
  • • • • • • • • • • • • •
                 dance & tell me black african things
i know you know.

By referencing the grandmother as the guardian of things African, Hernández Cruz both defines a singular familial relationship to a revered elder and comments on a Puerto Rican national identification of blackness as residing within the figure of a hidden *abuela*, as in the saying: "¿y tú abuela, dónde está?" (and your grandmother, where is she?).[37] But unlike the banished black grandmother implicit in the question, the grandmother in "african things" is called out and called on. In his attention to the blackness evinced in the Puerto Rican national imaginary, and to the blackness evoked through U.S. Puerto Rican cultural expression—in the lines "how do latin / boo-ga-loo sound like you," for example—Hernández Cruz locates Africa not only in memories of the past, but also in the musics and movements of the present.

With his references to conga drums, Latin boogaloo, and Puerto Rico, Hernández Cruz crafted a Puerto Rican literary identity within the pages of a canonical blackness. But having been included in multiple anthologies of black poetry, was Hernández Cruz hovering in the shadows of blackness, perhaps the umbra effect of his early association with African American poets? During a time in which there were few anthologies featuring Puerto Ricans writing in English, being published as a "black poet" provided exposure and the entrée to other publishing ventures, some unsolicited and unauthorized. Hernández Cruz explains that once Random House owned the rights to his poems from *Snaps*, they submitted various poems to anthologies without his knowledge (although this was not the case with *Black Fire*).[38] Therefore, Hernández Cruz's inclusion in anthologies of black writing was not always a reflection of his desire to be in these anthologies or the desire of the editors to seek out his work, as did Larry Neal. Instead, Hernández Cruz's "black poetry" was part authorial tone, part social kinship, and part publisher's ploy.

Nevertheless, if not for the Afro-Latino sensibility and the continuities between his work and that of his African American peers, Hernández Cruz would have been an unlikely candidate for *Black Fire*. Integrating tropical referents and urban accents, Hernández Cruz constructs a poetics of cultural identity that is at once informed by Puerto Rican and U.S. literary traditions, as well as a "deformation" of these master narratives.[39] In this respect, Hernández Cruz's experiments are reminiscent of the linguistic permutations of William Carlos Williams, Hernández Cruz's literary ancestor whose own Puerto Rican heritage influenced his vision of a New World poetics.[40] Disrupting the standardized grammars of English and Spanish, Hernández Cruz opts instead for soundings that correspond to the Black English and Spanglish cadences of the city. Reforming, more than deforming American literary history, Hernández Cruz writes himself into being by writing a poetry that passes through and contests racially segregated canons.

For Felipe Luciano, rhetorical tenor, perhaps more than his poetic diction, scaled his place in the Black Arts canon. As a member of the Last Poets, Luciano, along with Gylan Kain and David Nelson, read his work in *Right On! The Original Last Poets*—a film featuring the African American and Afro-Puerto Rican trio.[41] In the film, each poet recites his own verse while the others provide background harmonies, chants, or provocations. Sometimes singing, sometimes dancing, the poets orchestrate stylized gestures that may culminate in freeze-frame poses at the end of a performance. The recordings pair highly repetitive rhymed or unrhymed speech with rhythmic drumming. Accompanied by a conga player, the performed poems link musicality and orality, sound and sense.

While popularizing a brand of rap poetry that engaged issues of racism, drugs, and poverty, the Last Poets also championed the cultural resources of their communities, suggesting the need for pride in the face of prejudice. For example, Luciano's "Jíbaro/My Pretty Nigger" celebrates the *jíbaro*, the Spanish-descended Puerto Rican peasant who was formerly a subject of ridicule and later a popular icon of national identity on the island. Other poems by Luciano from the film soundtrack include "Puerto Rican Rhythms" and "Jazz," pieces that identify his Puerto Rican heritage and make clear his connection to both black and Latino artistic communities. "Puerto Rican Rhythms" pays homage to Nuyorican native sons Eddie Palmieri and Tito Puente, as well as to Cuban-born musicians Chano Pozo, Mongo Santamaria, and Machito. Likewise, "Jazz" conjures up the sounds of African American musicians Charlie "Bird" Parker, Dizzy Gillespie, John Coltrane, and Miles Davis.[42]

Luciano's tenure with the Last Poets lasted less than one year, from 1968 to 1969, but leads into his more directly political work as co-founder and deputy chairman of New York's Young Lords Party, the Puerto Rican revolutionary nationalist organization modeled after the Black Panther Party. The tone and themes of Luciano's work consistently exhibited his commitment to black and brown liberation. In "You're Nothing but a Spanish Colored Kid," Luciano suggests parallels in the lives of Puerto Ricans and blacks in the United States. Published in *Black Spirits: A Festival of New Black Poets in America*, the poem is a telling historical portrait. Puerto Ricans in New York City are depicted as a displaced group, similar to the Africans who suffered a forced migration to the New World. Luciano begins:

> I see them
> Puerto Ricans/Spanish niggers
> Bronzed farmers look silly being doormen
> Their fingers are more honest than their eyes.
> Earth hands turned metallic gray
> The plow rots, the mule dies, the hands rust
> And the elders sit with ashes on their crowns
> making fools of themselves in bars.
> Those fingertips will never touch the soil again.[43]

The poem imagines the jíbaro transplanted to the island of Manhattan from the island of Puerto Rico. Although the speaker recognizes the "honesty" in the rusting hands of the Puerto Rican men he describes, he turns dispassionate toward them—these men who he can no longer admire, whose integrity he seems to question. As if depicting the ridiculous, Luciano continues: "Brown people look so funny in the snow." Contrasting the farmers' sun-bronzed bodies to their pale gray surroundings, Luciano suggests that migration has caused a physical and visual incongruity. Moreover, psychic disruption ensues when, having "lost their land," the migrants begin "losing their minds." Luciano's poem works in contrasts to illustrate the juxtaposition of the migrated subject to his/her new context.

Luciano ends "You're Nothing but a Spanish Colored Kid" by issuing an ultimatum and challenging the title's presumption of second-class citizenship for Puerto Ricans:

> C'mon spic.
> Learn to tell time.
> Your daddy was a peasant
> And you're nothing but a Spanish colored kid
> unless you
> Get real nigger
> And stop making gestures.

The lines "Learn to tell time" and "stop making gestures" directed internally at the Puerto Rican audience whom Luciano wants to motivate, recall the internal address of poems by Baraka and other Black Arts poets. Akin, also, to poems that ridicule the empty gestures of black revolutionaries, Luciano's missive finds fault with the current generation of "Spanish niggers," demanding that they "get real." In his contrast between the archetypal construction of the elders ("your daddy was a peasant") and the stereotypical construction of the youth ("c'mon spic"), only the words "unless you / get real" offer a way out for the addressed persona, who has been "nothing but a Spanish colored kid" since the beginning of the poem. At the very end, the way out leads into an atypical, self-defined identity that has yet to be named.

In "You're Nothing but a Spanish Colored Kid" and other poems such as "Jíbaro/My Pretty Nigger," Luciano uses the word "nigger" as a symbolic code. Although pejorative and hateful when used by those not identified as "in-group," terms such as "nigger" have been and continue to be used by those who share a racially or socially constructed identity to denote intimacy between speaker and listener, author and audience. Elaborating on Luciano's use of the word, literary critic William Luis writes:

> the word *nigger* points to the intermingling of Latino and African American cultures, already reflected in the political cooperation between the Young Lords and the Black Panthers and other African American organizations. It also represents the common ground shared by the Last Poets. The articulation of the word *nigger* by Puerto Ricans and Latinos suggests that even though this and other words particular to African American speech had a specific historical origin, the use of such words also became an acceptable method of expression when sharing a common inner-city experience.[44] (Italics in original)

As a dark-skinned Puerto Rican, Luciano's poetic license with the term might also be inspired by his lived experiences of racial discrimination. In either case, the title of Luciano's signature poem, "Jíbaro/My Pretty Nigger," exemplifies Luis's point about shared ground. Using "jíbaro" and "nigger" as alternating terms—one a reclaimed term of national identity for Puerto Ricans and the other a term in the process of reclamation by African Americans—Luciano establishes the power of words to demean as well as the power of the community to transform and restore meaning. Moreover, as a result of Luciano's possessive usage, "*my* pretty nigger," the sting of the word "nigger" is offset by his personalization of the impersonal term. The otherwise ugly, anonymous term "nigger" is placed in a personal ("my") and approving ("pretty") context. Similarly, the juxtaposition of the English words "my pretty nigger" with the Spanish word "jíbaro" obviates linguistic or cultural tension to foster the integration of black and Puerto Rican perspectives.

Often composed in a dialogic form, Luciano's poems use direct address to initiate a conversation with others in the Puerto Rican community. In "Hot Blood/Bad Blood" Luciano reviews the cultural history of his addressee: "You a machete and a pyramid / A nigger gone wild / An Indian madman and a Congo rhythm."[45] These lines reference the dual African and Amerindian ancestry, intimating a set of parallel influences on the contemporary culture of Puerto Ricans. "Hot" Latin blood and "Bad" African or black blood flood the body of the "you" Luciano addresses, a collective entity that we learn comprise "the everyday people." As in "You're Nothing But a Spanish Colored Kid" where Luciano uses the line "c'mon spic" to mark a shift from descriptive discourse to the demanding directive of "learn to tell time," Luciano's "Hot Blood/Bad Blood" uses the near final line "c'mere stuff" to mark the shift from descriptive images to the poem's affirmative finale: "We, the sometimes artists, salute you / the everyday people." Here again the endurance of the "everyday people" and a quotidian way of life are recognized by "the sometimes artists"—poets who rise to the occasional needs for celebratory or documentary verses. In keeping with the volume's title of *Black Spirits*, both "Hot Blood/Bad Blood" and "You're Nothing But a Spanish Colored Kid" pay homage to Puerto Rican blackness.

If black speech and black music informed the creation and recitation of much of the new black poetry, poetry by Puerto Ricans like Luciano embodied the declamatory and polyrhythmic styles of Latino Caribbean expressive culture. Yet, like other poets of the Black Arts Movement, Luciano relied on the oratorical qualities of speechmaking to generate an imperative tone and to call listeners to action. By combining Spanish words with black vernacular expressions, rhetorical intonations with rhythmic drumming, Luciano's chant-like performances signaled a kind of boogaloo poetics. His linguistic play and verbal dexterity aptly reflected the musical fusions orchestrated by the era's black and Latino ensembles.

Each appearance by Hernández Cruz and Felipe Luciano in black anthologies and journals prepared readers for the swell of mainland Puerto Rican poets writing in English. In 1972, Hernández Cruz and Luciano were both included in *The Puerto Rican Poets*, a bilingual anthology edited by Alfredo Matilla and Iván Sílen and published in a Bantam series of poetry anthologies.[46] *The Puerto Rican Poets* contextualizes Hernández Cruz and Luciano with other New York writers, showing the seeds of the movement in that city. In the mid-1970s, a full-fledged Nuyorican Poetry Movement bloomed with the voices of Pedro Pietri, Miguel Algarín, Miguel Piñero, Jesus Papoleto Melendez, José Angel Figueroa, Sandra Maria Esteves, and Tato Laviera. Curiously, neither Hernández Cruz nor Luciano appeared in the 1975 volume *Nuyorican Poetry*, edited by Algarín and Piñero.[47] Hernández Cruz had moved to the Bay Area and Luciano, then a radio host and disc jockey, was rarely represented in the later anthologies of black or Nuyorican writing.[48] But readers will find contributions by Hernández Cruz and Luciano in the 1974 "Latin Soul" issue of *Umbra*, for which Hernández Cruz was a contributing editor. Although the editorial clarifies that the term "Latin Soul" has currency in areas of New York where blacks and Puerto Ricans "jam to the same music" and may participate in "progressive coalition politics," the California-based issue reaches beyond a black-Puerto Rican connection toward the merger of all Third World peoples, especially those in the Latin and African Americas.[49]

As suggested by their inclusion in the "Latin Soul" issue, Hernández Cruz and Luciano represent a "spanning" between African American and Latino American literary diasporas. While both poets stand at the vanguard of mainland Puerto Rican cultural expression in the 1960s, analyses of their foundational roles must also take into account their contributions to the Black Arts Movement.

Writing in a climate of cross-cultural literary influences and daily intercultural exchanges, black and Puerto Rican poets in New York City during the late 1960s shared an aesthetic sensibility, albeit one that has been canonized as Black Arts, without due attention to the intrinsic Afro-Latin or Latin Soul elements of that era's (and that city's) blackness. Indeed, to re-think the Black Arts Movement is to reconsider any historical record that identifies the period with a one-dimensional blackness. Instead, as the poetry of Victor Hernández Cruz and Felipe Luciano suggests, writing within the grain of Black Arts poetry did not mean editing out the specificity of, and their sensitivity to, mainland Puerto Rican experiences. For both poets, then, their places within the annals of the Black Arts Movement should serve less to conceal cultural nuances, but work more to convey a cultural milieu in which poetry by African Americans and Puerto Ricans shared a communal resonance.

NOTES

1. Countee Cullen, "Yet Do I Marvel," in *The Black Poets*, ed. Dudley Randall (New York: Bantam Books, 1971), 100.

2. Ibid.

3. Langston Hughes, "The Negro Artist and the Racial Mountain," *The Nation* (23 June 1926): 692–94.

4. LeRoi Jones, "State/meant," *Home: Social Essays* (New York: William Morrow & Company, 1966), 251–52.

5. Larry Neal, "The Black Arts Movement," in *The Black Aesthetic*, ed. Addison Gayle, Jr. (Garden City, NY: Doubleday, 1971), 272.

6. Hal Foster, ed., *The Anti-Aesthetic: Essays on Postmodern Culture* (Port Townsend, WA: Bay Press, 1983), xv.

7. See Addison Gayle, Jr., ed., *The Black Aesthetic* (Garden City, NY: Doubleday, 1971).

8. Carolyn Fowler, *Black Arts and Black Aesthetics: A Bibliography*, 2nd ed. (Atlanta: First World, 1981), xi.

9. Louis Reyes Rivera, "Inside the River of Poetry," in *ChickenBones: A Journal* [electronic bulletin board] (cited 6 February 2003); available from http://www.nathanielturner.com/insidetheriverofpoetry.htm.

10. Clyde R. Taylor, *The Mask of Art: Breaking the Aesthetic Contract—Film and Literature* (Bloomington: Indiana University Press, 1998), 7.

11. Ibid., 62.

12. See Miguel Algarín, "Nuyorican Aesthetics," in *Images and Identities: The Puerto Rican in Two World Contexts*, ed. Asela Rodríguez de Laguna (New Brunswick, NJ:

Transaction Publishers, 1987), 161–63. See also Algarín, "Nuyorican Language," introduction to *Nuyorican Poetry: An Anthology of Puerto Rican Words and Feelings*, ed. Miguel Algarín and Miguel Piñero (New York: William Morrow & Company, 1975), 9–20; Algarín, "Nuyorican Literature," *MELUS* 8: 2 (Summer 1981): 89–92. The "Café" grew out of a literary salon Algarín started in his living room around 1973.

13. Andrés Torres, *Between Melting Pot and Mosaic: African Americans and Puerto Ricans in the New York Political Economy* (Philadelphia: Temple University Press, 1995), 4.

14. One example is Denise Oliver, an African American woman who was the Minister of Finance (later Economic Development) of the Young Lords Party and a major influence on the feminist consciousness of the group. Oliver left the New York Lords in 1971 to join the group of Black Panthers led by Eldridge Cleaver. On Oliver, see Young Lords Party and Michael Abramson, *Palante: Young Lords Party* (New York: McGraw Hill, 1971).

15. Torres, *Between Melting Pot and Mosaic*, 166.

16. See LeRoi Jones and Larry Neal, eds., *Black Fire: An Anthology of Afro-American Writing* (New York: William Morrow & Company, 1968); Clarence Major, ed., *The New Black Poetry* (New York: International Publishers, 1969); Abraham Chapman, ed., *New Black Voices: An Anthology of Contemporary Afro-American Literature* (New York: Mentor, 1972); Woodie King, ed., *Black Spirits: A Festival of New Black Poets in America* (New York: Random House, 1972).

17. Stephen E. Henderson, *Understanding the New Black Poetry: Black Speech and Black Music as Poetic References* (New York: William Morrow & Company, 1973).

18. Ibid., 31.

19. Ibid., 30.

20. Martin Espada, "Documentaries and Declamadores: Puerto Rican Poetry in the United States," in *A Gift of Tongues: Critical Challenges in Contemporary American Poetry*, ed. Marie Harris and Kathleen Aguero (Athens: University of Georgia Press, 1987), 262.

21. Ibid., 260.

22. See Juan Flores, *Divided Borders: Essays on Puerto Rican Identity* (Houston, TX: Arte Público Press, 1993). See Geneviève Fabre, "Introduction: Blueprints in the Development of a New Poetics," in *European Perspectives on Hispanic Literature of the United States*, ed. Geneviève Fabre (Houston, TX: Arte Público Press, 1988), 5–21.

23. Felix Cortés, Angel Falcón, and Juan Flores, "The Cultural Expression of Puerto Ricans in New York: A Theoretical Perspective and Critical Review," *Latin American Perspectives* 3: 3 (Summer 1976): 144.

24. Ibid., 141.

25. Amiri Baraka, *Autobiography of LeRoi Jones*, restored ed. (Chicago: Lawrence Hill Books, 1997), 393.

26. Madhubuti was then known as Don L. Lee. See Don L. Lee, "Blk Poetics," *Don't Cry, Scream* (Detroit: Broadside Press, 1969), 15.

27. Ibid.

28. Espada, "Documentaries and Declamadores," 258.

29. See Hernández Cruz, *Snaps* (New York: Random House, 1969), 63, 71, 67, 127.

30. Juan Flores, *From Bomba to Hip-Hop: Puerto Rican Culture and Latino Identity* (New York: Columbia University Press, 2000), 82.

31. Cruz, "The Eye," *Snaps*, 109–13. When quoting from poems, I will provide the bibliographic reference and inclusive page numbers in a note following the first citation only, as is given here.

32. Hernández Cruz, "O.K.," in *Black Fire: An Anthology of Afro-American Writing*, ed. LeRoi Jones and Larry Neal (New York: William Morrow & Company, 1968), 436. Cf. Jones, "Black Art," in *Black Fire*, op cit. As in some poems by black poets during this period, some poems by Puerto Rican writers also exhibited elements of homophobia.

33. Hernández Cruz, "today is a day of great joy," *Snaps*, 29.

34. See Adam David Miller, ed., *DICES or Black Bones: Black Voices of the Seventies* (Boston: Houghton Mifflin, 1970); Alan Lomax and Raoul Abdul, eds., *3000 Years of Black Poetry* (New York: Dodd, Mead, 1970); Abraham Chapman, *New Black Voices*.

35. Lomax, introduction to *3000 Years of Black Poetry*, xx. It is worth mentioning that in the introductory comments to the volume's "U.S.A." section, the editors quote Victor Hernández Cruz's poem "today," but incorrectly attribute it to "Juan Hernández Cruz, a young Puerto Rican." Although the error is not repeated in a biographical note preceding the poem later in the volume, the misnaming captures the element of misrecognition that at times accompanies Hernández Cruz's position adjacent to his fellow contributors. Lomax and Abdul, *3000 Years of Black Poetry*, 195.

36. Hernández Cruz, "african things," *Negro Digest* (November 1969): 48.

37. The saying "*¿Y tú abuela, dónde está?*" originates in Fortunato Vizcarrondo's 1942 poem, colloquially titled "*¿Y tu agüela a'onde ejtá?*. The Puerto Rican poet's verses were performed by *declamadores*—such as Juan Boria—who recited poetry throughout Puerto Rico. Later, singer Ruth Fernández further popularized the expression by recording Vizcarrondo's poem as a song.

38. When asked by interviewer Victor Rosa in 1974 how his poems got into the *Black Fire* anthology, Hernández Cruz cites the dearth of Anglophone Latino poets in 1966–1967 before responding that: "Larry Neal asked me for a poem and I gave it to him. I believe in illuminating the string that unites all peoples of this earth." Hernández Cruz, Interview with Victor Rosa, *The Bilingual Review/ La Revista Bilingue* 2: 3 (September/December 1975): 282–83. Hernández Cruz's comments about Random House are from a personal interview. See Victor Hernández Cruz, interview by author, tape recording, New York, NY, February 13, 1998.

39. On "mastery of form" and "deformation of mastery," see Houston Baker, *Modernism and the Harlem Renaissance* (Chicago: University of Chicago Press, 1987), 49–52.

40. But, unlike the pairing of Hernández Cruz with African American poets, William Carlos Williams is most often canonized as a (white Anglo) American poet, a fact that similarly mitigates Williams's Puerto Rican heritage. On Williams as an influence, see Hernández Cruz, *Red Beans* (Minneapolis: Coffee House Press, 1991), 52.

41. Since the founding of The Last Poets on May 19, 1968 in Harlem's Mount Morris Park, and through its many reincarnations, the group has included several different members: David Nelson, Gylan Kain, Felipe Luciano, Abiodun Oyewole, Umar Bin Hassan, Nilija (drummer), Suliaman El Hadi, and Jalal Nuriddin. See Abiodun Oyewole and Umar Bin Hassan, with Kim Green, *On a Mission: The Last Poets* (New York: Henry Holt, 1996).

42. The poems "Jíbaro/My Pretty Nigger," "Puerto Rican Rhythms," and "Jazz" appear on the compact disc soundtrack for *Right On!: The Original Last Poets*. See, Last Poets, *Right On! The Original Last Poets*, soundtrack, (Juggernaut, 1969; Collectables Records, 1994) COL-CD-6500, compact disc. The motion picture was released in 1971.

43. Felipe Luciano, "You're Nothing But a Spanish Colored Kid," in *Black Spirits: A Festival of New Black Poets in America*, ed. Woodie King (New York: Random House, 1972), 122–23. King is the African American dramatist who produced the motion picture *Right On!: The Original Last Poets*, based on a theater piece he directed for the group. King's *Black Spirits* anthology also includes selections by Gylan Kain and David Nelson, Luciano's fellow Last Poets.

44. William Luis, *Dance Between Two Cultures: Latino Caribbean Literature Written in the United States* (Nashville: Vanderbilt University Press, 1997), 56.

45. Luciano, "Hot Blood/Bad Blood," in *Black Spirits*, 124.

46. Alfredo Matilla and Iván Sílen, eds., *The Puerto Rican Poets/Los Poetas Puertorriqueños* (New York: Bantam, 1972). Dudley Randall's now classic paperback *The Black Poets* appeared a year earlier in the same Bantam Poetry series.

47. Miguel Algarín and Miguel Piñero, eds., *Nuyorican Poetry*.

48. In a 1974 interview, Hernández Cruz does mention, however, his founding role in a New York-based group called Boricua Artists Guild (BAG). The group included Felipe Luciano, Pedro Pietri, José Angel Figueroa, all poets, as well as musicians, architects, actors, filmmakers, and visual artists. See Hernández Cruz, Interview with Victor Rosa, 285–86.

49. *Umbra: Latin Soul* 5 (1974), 3.

16

Latin Soul

Cross-Cultural Connections
between the Black Arts
Movement and Pocho-Che

Rod Hernandez

In 1974, *Umbra* magazine, the journal of the Umbra literary group and one of the most influential publications of the Black Arts Movement, relocated from its birthplace on the Lower East Side of New York City to its new home base in the East Bay city of Berkeley, California. The move wasn't merely geographical. An anthology marked the occasion, and it was significant not least because of its theme and subtitle: Latin Soul. What this term meant to the editors of *Umbra*—who at that time were David Henderson, Barbara T. Christian, and contributors such as Victor Hernández Cruz—is mentioned in the opening sentence of their brief introduction to the anthology. "'LATIN-SOUL,'" they write, "has been in use for a while, mainly in the Black and Puerto-Rican areas of New York where both groups often jam to the same music: Latin and Soul."[1] They go on to identify this term not only with the various minority communities inside the United States (the Mission District of San Francisco, in particular) but also with poets who represent disenfranchised peoples throughout the Americas.

The anthology itself contains tributes to Nicolás Guillén and César Vallejo (which include translations of their poems); a section on the "Guerrilla Poetry of South America" (with works by Otto Rene Castillo, Roque Dalton, Violeta Parra, Ernesto Cardenal, and Fernando Alegría); selected poems by a range of writers from Latin America as well as the United States (among them Luis Pales Matos, Pedro Pietri, Roberto Vargas, Ishmael Reed, Pablo Neruda, Alejandro Murguía, Carmen Alegría, Victor Hernández Cruz, Thulani Davis, David Henderson, Langston Hughes, and Avotcja); and graphic art contributed by Rupert García, Isabel Alegría, Joe Overstreet, Arthur Monroe, Alejandro Stuart, and Adal.

Published in the waning days of what is normally considered the period of the Black Arts Movement (1965–1975), the Latin Soul edition of *Umbra* maga-

zine serves today as an example of diasporic consciousness and cross-cultural poetics, even if these concepts are never explicitly addressed as such by the editors or by the contributors. This seems somewhat at odds with the image of an era known for the widespread proliferation of cultural nationalism. Of course movements like Black Arts were never monolithically nationalist or separatist. In fact, with regard to precursors such as Umbra, we see that they have origins in organizations like On Guard for Freedom, which actively opposed the U.S. Bay of Pigs invasion in Cuba while actively supporting liberation in the Congo.[2] The Latin Soul *Umbra*, however, is a more substantial embrace of internationalism because it resonates strongly with similar developments elsewhere.

One hotbed of internationalism in the 1970s was undoubtedly the Bay Area. When *Umbra* magazine set up shop there back then it joined some like-minded publishers such as Pocho-Che and Third World Communications (the latter was helpful in the production of the Latin Soul anthology). Pocho-Che was a multiethnic though mostly Latino/a collective of writers based in the Mission District. In 1971, Pocho-Che began Third World Communications (TWC), a multicultural coalition of artists and writers dedicated to putting out works by people of color. Both organizations sought in their own ways to bridge cultural and geopolitical distances. Pocho-Che rhetorically fused the figure of an Americanized Mexican, the pocho, with the image of Latin American revolutionary Che Guevara. TWC gathered together African Americans, Asian Americans, American Indians, and Latinos under the rubric Third World (a now unfashionable term).

While Latin Soul is yet another of these constructs, it remains unique for the specific attention devoted to cross-cultural connections between blacks and Latinos. Moreover, by focusing on shared musical sensibilities, Latin Soul taps into deep currents that run through the history of each group. To the Latino/a writers who appear in the Latin Soul edition of *Umbra*, for example, the varied musical traditions of the African diaspora were instrumental in bringing about greater awareness of the blackness of brownness.

Among the writers most involved in the cross-cultural exchange was U.S. Puerto Rican poet Victor Hernández Cruz. Born in Aguas Buenas, Puerto Rico, in 1949, Hernández Cruz migrated as a child with his family to New York City, growing up on the Lower East Side (pronounced "Loisaida" by the locals). He began writing early in his life, developing a poetics of fruitful tensions between Spanish/English, rural/urban, and vernacular/literary cultures. He was a part of Umbra when it was still in New York, and preceded the magazine's move to the Bay Area just after Random House published his first book of poetry when he was twenty. He has described his own work as the history of his migrations.[3]

This migrant sensibility fit in well with the transnational consciousness of Pocho-Che/TWC. Hernández Cruz penned a quarterly column, "El Rinconsito Sabrosito" (the delicious little corner), for the Pocho-Che magazine *Tin-Tan*.[4] As a contributor, he used this venue to comment upon trends in contemporary art and popular culture. Most of the time he reviewed and recommended new books; told jokes or made other humorous remarks; and editorialized upon cultural events taking place around the Bay Area and throughout the country. For example, he critically documents in the following passage from the summer of 1975 the emergent local salsa scene, providing important historical and ethnographic context:

> A recent wave of Salsa music has been pouring over San Francisco and the Bay Area. The term Salsa is of recent origin, though the music that it describes goes back a few decades into the folk music of Cuba, Puerto Rico, Santo Domingo and all those hispanic countries that touch the Caribbean; they all have their good sprinkling of African culture. It is in Africa that we find the origin of Rumba, Guaganco, Bomba, Plena. It's an old story and everyone knows it, Africans brought their music to the Americas. African and indigenous indio music have mixed, el guiro is an Indian instrument that can keep time within an African rhythm. Hector La Voe, Willie Colons original singer jumping out of Bronx Rican streets has the high pitch of el jibaro Aguinaldo, which in turn was the tone of the indian song, El Areyto. The Areytos were a form of teaching history and worshiping god, it was oral literature it was poetry . . . . What is amazing about well groomed Salsa musicians is their ability to play all styles of music, rock and roll, classical, jazz and what have-you. Ask Lawrence Welk to keep up with a Son Montuno. (12)

In noting the popularity of salsa, Hernández Cruz makes a very deliberate effort to situate this music historically. During the mid-1970s many musicians and fans (including Hernández Cruz) resisted "salsa" as an umbrella term, preferring to think of the music it labeled with respect to the traditions of certain ethnic and national cultures. Hence, Hernández Cruz discusses the music with specificity and detail. At the same time, however, he sees it as a diasporic and hybrid form: the product of cultures with a history of slavery and colonization. He concludes all of this by underscoring the versatility of subaltern musicians, who often know more about the dominant culture than it knows about them.

Certainly, this has been true of African American jazz musicians and their ability to quote from dominant forms in improvisational performances. Having grown up within earshot of the jazz clubs in Greenwich Village during the 1950s, Hernández Cruz has been greatly influenced by jazz music. This interest in jazz developed from the concrete interactions between black and U.S. Puerto Rican communities living side-by-side and responding to similar material conditions within the ghettos and barrios of New York City. Cultural critic Juan Flores has shown how such relations in daily life have made New York Puerto Ricans, or Nuyoricans, generally more conscious of and affirmative toward their blackness.[5] The intercultural process that Flores refers to as "branching out"— the complex negotiations done daily by Nuyoricans and other urban communities—bears a striking resemblance to Ralph Ellison's description of improvising as a liminal experience in which identity is lost and found simultaneously.[6]

From Latin music and jazz Hernández Cruz adopts as a formal feature of his poetry the call-and-response structure characteristic of black cultures in the Caribbean and United States, which derive from West Africa. Call-and-response, or antiphony, is intertextual as well as intercultural. Cultural critic Paul Gilroy observes that it "has come to be seen as a bridge from [Black] music into other modes of cultural expression."[7] Yet it also serves a socially symbolic function. Critics of salsa music have argued, for example, that antiphony is liberating to the extent it remains an open-ended structure for improvising performances and combining diverse voices in a single text.[8] These readings—grounded in the material history of Afro-Caribbean cultures— establish a genealogical connection between the oppositional practices of salsa and the subversive rhythms of slaves. Organized into religious and mutual aid societies during the colonial period, slaves used drumming and singing as ways of maintaining cultural memory.[9]

We can hear a similar process at play in the writing of Hernández Cruz. The rhythms and textures of Afro-Caribbean music serve a mnemonic purpose for him, presenting the possibility of using cultural memory to transform urban spaces symbolically into tropical homelands. To a transnational subject coming from a community deracinated by the mechanisms of U.S. colonial governance and industrial capitalism, the significance of such a metaphorical transformation cannot be underestimated by regarding it simply as the product of fantasy or of nostalgia. Instead, it should be treated as the outcome of a political act in which specific sounds and images are strategically deployed by the subaltern poet for the goal of self-representation.

The act occurs, for example, in "Los New Yorks," a poem that appears in Hernández Cruz's second book *Mainland* (1973). Although New York remains the subject or setting of a number of the poems in the book, many of them were composed while Hernández Cruz was residing in the Bay Area. The antiphonal structure of this interlingual poem echoes what is known as the soneo section of a salsa song. A chorus in Spanish, "Suena" (the word sound, per the command "make that sound"), alternates with an improvisational solo voice in English as the speaker tropicalizes New York City, which is already pluralized and Latinized in the poem's interlingual title by the Spanish article "Los":[10]

Suena

I present you the tall skyscrapers
as merely huge palm tress with lights

Suena

The roaring of the trains is a fast
guaguanco
dance of the ages

Suena

Snow falls
Coconut chips galore
Take the train to Caguas
and the bus is only ten cents
to Aguas Buenas

Suena. (10–11)

Here salsa serves as catalyst in the reconfiguration of New York according to the speaker's memories of his tropical homeland, making buildings into palm trees, the sound of subways into Afro-Caribbean rhythms, and snowfall into nothing more than coconut shavings. City transportation systems are even re-routed in order to collapse the distance between New York and rural towns in Puerto Rico.

Hernández Cruz once again eschews a strictly geographical view of reality in "BronxOmania":

snake horse stops at bronx clouds
end of lines and tall windowed cement
comes to unpaved roads and wilderness
where the city is far

and spanish bakeries sell hot bread
the roar of the iron snake
plunges at closing doorways
down fifty blocks
is the island of Puerto Rico.[11]

Flores calls this the "transposition of the cultural background" or the "atmospheric, visionary presence of the homeland."[12] He says, "Looking at New York, the Nuyorican sees Puerto Rico, or at least the glimmering imprint of another world to which vital connections have been struck" (189). Hernández Cruz discusses the matter in more aggressive language: "When I was younger I felt that I had to get the city, the actual pavement, out of the way because I felt the physical setting of the city was hiding the mountains that I knew as a child, hiding the palm trees and the pineapple fields. I was reacting with deep hostility to the urban environment around me" (see note 3, Moyers, *The Language of Life*, 100). Such hostility stirs in him the desire to see what else the city is hiding.

Beholding the visionary presence of another world in the midst of modern New York City, the speaker of the generically entitled "Poem" excavates the built environment and illuminates its shadow history:

The greater cities are
surrounded by woods
Jungles secretly
of America

Behind lights
the green
Green eyes of Tree gods
Rhythm we would call it Puerto Rico
But it doesn't begin to be as real.[13]

These opening stanzas recall the last paragraphs of F. Scott Fitgerald's Jazz Age novel, *The Great Gatsby* (1925), wherein Nick Carraway, sitting on the beach of Long Island in the almost preternatural glow of the moon, imagines that he can discern "the old island here that flowered once for Dutch sailors' eyes—a fresh, green breast of the new world."[14] But unlike Carraway, who sees it as the "old, unknown world," the virginal yet vacant wilderness upon which will be built "the last and greatest of all human dreams," the speaker of "Poem" views in the modern landscape the abiding material and spiritual presence of the first residents, the island's native population ("Green eyes of Tree gods"). A link is thus established between the island of Puerto Rico and an island in New York, especially between the memories of their respective indigenous cultures (Taíno and Algonquian). The repetition of the word "secret" in the subsequent stanza emphasizes the fact that knowledge of these native cultures has been suppressed within the metropolis, within canonical narratives, and within the larger text of American history itself. [15]

Nevertheless, secrets about race and ethnicity pervade Latino/a cultures as well. Hernández Cruz discloses one such secret in "african things," a poem that deals with the speaker's own family:

> ...african spirits
> dance & sing in my mother's house. in my cousin's house.
> black as night can be/ what was Puerto Rican all about.
> all about the
> indios & you better believe it the african things
> black & shiny
> grandmother speak to me & tell me of african things
> how do latin
> boo-ga-loo sound   like you
> conga drums in the islands you know
> the traveling through many moons
> dance & tell me black african things
> i know you know. [16]

Again, music uncovers the African heritage that some Latino families are at pains to conceal with silence—even in the face of incontrovertible evidence that they are in fact black. The reference to Latin Bugalu implies a precedent for this sort of recovery. Ethnic music scholar George Lipsitz argues that the mid-1960s cross between the mambo and rhythm and blues, Latin Bugalu, highlighted repressed African elements in U.S. Puerto Rican culture and thus anticipated subsequent crossings. [17]

It would be a mistake, though, to see this racial recovery by Puerto Ricans or their "deliberate self-insertion into the urban landscape" (see note 5, Flores, *Divided Borders*, 189) as a phenomenon exclusive to New York City. The second half of *Mainland* reads as a travelogue, with poetry about other cities like Detroit, Chicago, Salt Lake City, Las Vegas, Fresno, and of course Berkeley and San Francisco. Hernández Cruz covers terrain previously mapped by Beat generation writers Jack Kerouac and Allen Ginsberg. And his bicoastal and transnational migrations are significant, given that most of his early work was written and published while he lived in the Bay Area and traveled (both literally and imaginatively) to New York City, Puerto Rico, and beyond.

Tropicalization (1976) picks up where *Mainland* leaves off, but does so in more abstract and experimental fashion. Latin music informs the thirty-three sides of the first part, New York Potpourri, and lends to the poems about urban life during the 1950s a polyphonic texture reminiscent of the jazz beat in Langston

Hughes's poetic suite for Harlem, *Montage of a Dream Deferred* (1951).[18] The second part, Electricity, continues recounting memories of Puerto Rico and New York City through Latin music, which plays a central role in the fantastic narrative poem, "A Tale of Bananas." Montuno, the protagonist of the poem, is named after the improvisational call and response section of the Cuban son.[19] Like his namesake, Montuno embodies a sense of freedom and possibility.

His extraordinary tale can be read as a humorous allegory of the conflict between hegemonic and subaltern cultures in the metropolis. Montuno, asleep at the start of the poem, wakes up to a dream in which green bananas fall from the sky, five-foot avocados lie on the ground, and a big fish in a checkered suit swims aboard the subway. Indebted to fictive strategies of the Latin American novel, particularly magical realism, or *lo real maravilloso*, and in defiance of an oppressively rationalist epistemology, the story displays the playful though oppositional attitudes of a historically marginalized urban group. A festive yet subversive ethos of collectivity—a utopian or carnivalesque longing for social change—disrupts the normalized conditions of injustice and the institutionalized state-of-emergency.[20] While green bananas continue to fall and civil unrest ensues, the military has orders to shoot looters if required; the public phones don't work in this particular part of town; the ambulance is delayed for two hours; and the local supermarket overcharges for tropical fruit that now can be obtained easily if you have an upturned hat or an empty baby carriage to take outdoors.

The precipitation of green bananas represents, on one hand, the arrival of Montuno's displaced and transplanted subjectivity in the greater metropolitan regions of the United States—the symbolic transformation of New York City or San Francisco into a tropical island. On the other hand, it parodies xenophobic fears harbored by U.S. citizens that a deluge of immigrants from the Caribbean, Mexico, Central and South America will wrought cataclysmic changes on their cities. Ultimately, the rain is a subversive rhythm ("Takatakatakatakat akataka") born of cultures usually ignored or else perceived as a threat by U.S. society, the "different sense of time" that, according to the narrator of Ellison's jazz-infused novel *Invisible Man*, comes from being socially invisible.[21]

A different sense of time is precisely what we hear in the voice of Avotcja, who also came from New York City and who took part in Latin Soul as well as Third World Communications. Immersed from an early age in the music of the African diaspora (bomba, plena, boleros, blues, jazz, soul), Avotcja is a writer, a musician, and a composer. She has explored the links between these forms not only as an artist but also as a DJ at Bay Area community radio stations since the 1970s.[22] In addition to writing for theater and performing for festival audiences, she hosts La Verdad Musical, a program of pan-African music on KPOO 89.5 FM in San Francisco. The poems she published in two multicultural anthologies from TWC, *Third World Women* (1972) and *Time to Greez!* (1975), stand among the best examples of the relationship between diasporic music and poetry, between black and Latino/a cultures of resistance as well.[23]

In "The Black Latin and the Mexican Indian" (1972), identification and solidarity are structured around the juxtaposition of these racial, national, geographic and socioeconomic categories: African/Indian, Puerto Rican/Mexican, east/west, urban/rural, industrial/agricultural. A line of communication then opens up between these social positions. The speaker compares the personal experiences of a streetwise Nuyorican to those of a seasoned Mexican farm worker from the fields of California:

> While you picked tomatoes
> I picked pockets
> And we both learned how to lie and steal and fight
> Some call it survival
> I call it loneliness.[24]

Solitude, a theme of the poem and a fact of life for every disenfranchised subject, binds each person through the mutual recognition of shared vulnerability. This connection also provides at least one way of overcoming such loneliness. Once more, Latin music supplies the main trope:

> The Mariachi met the Mambo
> And so did we . . .
> I will praise the Gods for your existence
> I will dance to your rhythms
> Even as the sun grows cold
> And I'm not lonely anymore. (133)

The allusion to plural deities evokes the pre-Christian religions of both Africans and Indians, particularly the musical practices—singing, drumming, dancing—through which they have held on to their spiritual beliefs and values in the face of cultural erasure.

Solidarity based upon race, class, and gender lies at the center of Avotcja's "Canción de la Negrita." This brief poem combines call and response with code-switching in a rhetorical strategy that crosses linguistic borders and relates the experiences of black women "from Dar Es Salaam to San Juan" (135). It consists of a chorus called out in Spanish, "Yo soy negrita!" (I am a black woman!), and improvisational soneo-like stanzas answered in English:

> I am the beauty
> that Helena Rubenstein
> has tried for a hundred years
> to find in one of her plastic bottles. (135)

The interplay of these declarative voices demonstrates the multi-accentual nature of female blackness—alternately ignored, denigrated, and fetishized as a sign by racist and patriarchal ideologies around the world. Nowhere is this complex identity more defiantly proclaimed than in the last lines, which mix expressions of resistance in Spanish with similar sentiments in African American vernacular English:

> Sí, yo soy negrita!
> Y nosotros venceremos muthafuckas!
> Yo soy negrita!
> Yo soy negrita!
> Now let somebody beat that! (135)

The challenge issued at the conclusion of "Canción" does more than continue the call and response form. It enacts a rhetorical practice that Henry Louis Gates, Jr. refers to as "calling out"—a way of expressing defiance but also of demystifying and reconstituting subjects.[25] Thus, Avotcja deftly ends the poem not simply with another call but with an emphatic recapitulation of the central motif: the construction of black female identity.

Another short poem entitled "A Soulful Sister" expands upon this project by representing black female subjectivity with respect to the various geographic, cultural, linguistic, and ideological spaces it traverses:

> I am all the chants of Africa
> I am the black light of Harlem
> I am chitterlin's and corn bread, arroz amarillo y cuchifritos
> I am a star, a queen from Mississippi
> I am that big mouthed bitch next door
> THAT'S RIGHT!!

The poem signifies upon collectivity and the diversity of roles occupied by black women. Such roles range from the ethereal and exalted to the quotidian and despised. The catalogue of opposing metonyms speaks to the internal divisions and contradictory discourses.

Religious and secular impulses converge again in "Cuando Baila Ramón," a rapturous celebration of a black Puerto Rican salsa dancer who bursts on the scene with "Africa screaming in his feet."[26] He is both described and urged on by the female speaker in the following passage:

> Baila mi Borinqueño Negro
> Sweat runs shiny rivers down his face
> He drops, turns, jumps, screams
> Vaya Papi—vaya—vaya
> Women hold their stomachs & sigh
> While the colored spanish boys intellectualize their non-existence

And even Ochun smiles
Cuando baila Ramon. (178)

This is what it might look like if James Brown danced to a mambo. Indeed, like James Brown, Ramón "comes sliding sideways across the floor" with a sense of personal and cultural freedom that can't be felt by the "nappy headed would be spanish boys" who "[s]tand up against the walls in yanqui sophistication" (178). In spite of the boys' racially marked bodies and in contrast with Ramón (whose bodily functions, motions, and utterances go unrestrained), these black Latinos refrain from using their bodies in the dance because they subscribe to the mind/body dichotomy associating whiteness with intellect. Ramón, on the other hand, freely embodies the sound of the African diaspora, answering "an invitation to Afro-Latino hearts" (178) with uninhibited movements performed at the very center of cultural space. Thus, his dance constitutes a social encounter in which the body and the dance floor become sites of momentary emancipation from the racial repressions normalized daily.[27]

The poem makes us aware of this, but also of the fact that women of color approach the dance floor from a different political and social position than men. Speaking specifically about the gender politics of salsa, Frances Aparicio writes that: "While going dancing has been defined as a cultural space where freedom and pleasure are enjoyed beyond the social dictates of everyday life, Latino men enjoy a higher degree of freedom in publicly expressing sexual desire and erotic behavior than that accorded to women."[28] Ramón's flirtations with the musical instruments certainly demonstrate this point; he is described in one line as a "one man orgy" (178). But he is also the object of the female gaze and a source of erotic pleasure for the women in the poem, including the speaker, the dancers on the floor, and Ochun, the Yoruba goddess of sensual love. Together these women enact a subversive role-reversal. Instead of remaining objectified and restraining themselves, they all express sexual desire: "And all the women hold their breath / (Some hold other things) / Cuando baila Ramón" (178). As a result, they briefly disrupt the predominant gender ideology of the dance floor. Cultural critic Leslie Gotfrit notes: "There is disruption of the dance floor scene when women take pleasure for themselves and with each other."[29] For the women who disrupt the dance floor in the poem, theirs is a significant though transient appropriation of racialized and gendered social space.

Even writers who didn't contribute to the Latin Soul issue or who were not black or Puerto Rican addressed the cross-cultural relationship between Latinos and African Americans with music. Chicana writer Dorinda Moreno, a longtime resident of the Mission District until 1990 and an active member of TWC, writes passionately about the healing power of music in "Stations/of the Cross Roads/ Never-For-Gotten Paths." This long pastiche-style poem about the struggles of interracial love is a cross between the narrative ritual that depicts the crucifixion of Jesus Christ and a women's blues tradition in which a singer usually decries social inequities, relieves suffering, and gathers strength by naming or "quoting" important music. Moreno uses the occasion of the poem to revisit the scenes of her own life's passions (12 rather than 14). She mixes her memories of growing up in a racist society with the lyrics of popular songs by black composers from Mexico, the Caribbean, and the United States. Moreno dedicates this poem to her son Andre, a child of African American and Mexican descent she lovingly calls a "Blaxican"; to Afro-Caribbean singer Toña la Negra as well as Black Arts poet Nikki Giovanni; to "the writers of those songs which helped ease the color hurt of being dark in a society saturated with false racial superiority. And to the Black magic that has prevailed."[30]

Conscious since childhood of her social difference as a person of color in a racist society, she reflects upon her empathy with black communities throughout the Americas—an intercultural connection strengthened by the healing effects of music and language (English verse/Spanish lyrics):

> how those adolescent images formed
> the attitudes which carried me into adulthood;
> These sensitivities created my identification
>   with black hurt.
>
>   "Negra, negra consentida
>   Negra, de mi vida, Quien te
>   quiere, a ti." (169–170)[31]

She recalls feeling alienated ("outcast") because of her racial identity and poverty (symbolized by Salvation Army shoes) and because of racist attitudes confronted in her own family: "I tearfully sang the song at family parties . . . / while everyone laughed" (170). Painful experiences such as this one have conditioned a hope for racial reconciliation. She remembers:

> Gentle was I—wanting to be a curandera. Inspired
> by healer San Martín de Porres, Patron saint of Latin
> America (the only saint *real* enough for me). (171)[32]

The invocation of San Martín de Porres of Lima, Peru, the very first mulatto to be canonized and the patron saint of social justice, suggests a critique of historically institutionalized racism encountered inside the church. Lyrics of the theme song from the Mexican film *Angelitos negros* put a finer point on this suggestion:

> Pintor, de santos y alcobas,
>   si tienes alma en el cuerpo
>   por qué al pintar esos cuadros
>   te olvidaste de los negros? (171)[33]

As she goes on to tell of her son's birth and to counsel him about growing up the "child of two cultures" (172), pieces of popular songs that have been chosen for allegorical significance (Billie Holiday's "God Bless the Child," Hugh Masakela's "The Zulu and the Mexican," "Bye, Bye Blackbird," "The Lion Sleeps Tonight," "La feria de las flores," "De colores,") fade in-and-out constantly.

Although different types of black music are included in it, the prevailing structure of feeling has to be the blues.[34] Some scholars have argued that the blues supplanted religious music as a vehicle for spiritual expression among African Americans in the decades after slavery.[35] In her illuminating discussion of the proto-feminist consciousness inscribed within the blues, Angela Y. Davis informs us that the great blues women, Ma Rainey and Bessie Smith, were largely responsible for this secularization of spirituality (1998). Their reappropriation of "previously religious channels of expression," Davis points out, threatened church control, which had been consolidated under patriarchal leadership.[36] Given that the Roman Catholic Church is no less patriarchal, imbuing one of its sacred ritual ceremonies with the spirituality of the blues enacts a cross-cultural critique of ecclesiastical sexism.

Protesting these social maladies through the blues contributes to healing. In this respect Moreno's poem echoes a blues tradition that, according to Davis, relieves pain and gathers strength by conjuring the sound and the spirit of the blues:

> Blues music performs a magical—or aesthetic—exorcism of the blues, those things that lead to unhappiness and despair. Ritually invoking the names of blues songs serves the purpose of preparing the blues woman for the process of conferring aesthetic form on her emotional troubles. By creating out of them a work of art, she is giving herself aesthetic control over the forces that threaten to overwhelm her. (129)

Davis cites "Countin' the Blues," a song composed by Ma Rainey, as an example of this sort of invocation. She traces the origins of this ritual to the West African practice of "naming" or "nommo" (128). "Stations/of the Cross Roads," though naming songs by lyrics rather than by titles, draws upon the power of the blues in the manner described by Davis. But it also names the pain itself, fashioning what Davis calls "magical (or, in the case of the blues, aesthetic) control over the object of the naming process" (33). Naming the source of the pain and a remedy for it enables the blues woman to be an agent of her own healing. The fact that this healing is shared in the poem makes it a tribute to the blues as a product of concrete social relations.

Looking back at Latino/a poets who examined their own relationship to blackness during the Black Arts Movement, we see how much the music of the African diaspora played a mediating role. The most recent "explosion" of Latin music in American pop culture, by contrast, has obscured the African presence not only in what is deemed Latin music but also in Latino/a cultures generally.

It has become commonplace to hear commentators herald the rapid demographic growth of Latinos as some sort of "browning" of American culture. Regardless of the numbers, this conversation ignores the past of the communities that will continue to sustain and adapt the traditions of Latin music in the future, just as the notion overlooks the internal complexities of brownness itself.

The writers and editors who contributed to the Latin Soul issue of *Umbra* and to the publications of Pocho-Che/TWC compelled their readers to question the black-white binarism that has historically dominated discussions about race in the United States. In doing so, they anticipated some of our present concerns with multiculturalism and transnationalism. By no means did they resolve any of these matters through the concept of Latin Soul. If anything, it demonstrates the difficulty of accomplishing politically what we are sometimes only able to achieve rhetorically. But in exploring the cross-cultural and transnational links between blacks and Latinos, by developing a language with which to talk over differences and commonalities, the people who worked within this framework built a foundation for the creation of social alliances. At a time when relations are strained by economic hardships, when politicians and the press exacerbate tensions by sensationalizing demographic figures, it is critical that we carry on with the kind of work epitomized by Latin Soul.

NOTES

1. Society of Umbra. *Umbra: Latin Soul* 5 (1974): 3.

2. See Kaluma ya Salaam, "Black Arts Movement," in *The Oxford Companion to African American Literature*, ed. William Andrews, Frances Smith Foster, and Trudier Harris (New York: Oxford University Press, 1997), 70–71.

3. Bill Moyers, *The Language of Life: A Festival of Poets*, ed. James Haba (New York: Doubleday, 1995), 99; Victor Hernández Cruz, *Mainland* (New York: Random House, 1973).

4. Victor Hernández Cruz, "El Rinconsito Sabrosito: Notes of a Night Owl," *Tin-Tan: Revista Cosmica* 1: 2 (September 1975).

5. Juan Flores, *Divided Borders: Essays on Puerto Rican Identity* (Houston, TX: Arte Público Press, 1993), 188.

6. Ralph Ellison, *Shadow and Act* (New York: Random House, 1964), 234.

7. Paul Gilroy, *The Black Atlantic: Modernity and Double Consciousness*. (Cambridge, MA: Harvard University Press, 1993), 78.

8. Roberta L. Singer, "Tradition and Innovation in Contemporary Latin Popular Music in New York City," *Latin American Music Review* 4 (Fall-Winter 1983): 194. Angel Quintero Rivera, *Music, Social Classes, and the National Question in Puerto Rico* (Rio Piedras: University of Puerto Rico, Centro de Investigaciones Sociales), 1987. Frances R. Aparicio, *Listening to Salsa: Gender, Latin Popular Music, and Puerto Rican Cultures* (Hanover and London: University Press of New England, 1998).

9. See Frances R. Aparicio, "Salsa, Maracas, and Baile: Latin Popular Music in the Poetry of Victor Hernández Cruz," *MELUS* 16: 1 (Spring 1989–90): 43–58.

10. Frances R. Aparicio and Susana Chávez-Silverman, ed. *Tropicalizations: Transcultural Representations of Latinidad* (Hanover and London: University Press of New England, 1997).

11. Ibid., 12.

12. Flores, *Divided Borders*, 189, 190.

13. Aparicio and Chávez-Silverman, *Tropicalizations*, 55.

14. F. Scott Fitzgerald, *The Great Gatsby* (New York: Scribner's, 1925), 182.

15. See John F. Callahan, *The Illusions of a Nation* (Urbana: University of Illinois Press, 1972), for one of the few historical and political readings of Fitzgerald and *The Great Gatsby*. Callahan asks, "to what extent are Carraway's analyses, judgments, and predictions contingent on his own background—his particular, psychological, social, economic, and cultural context, that total configuration of his history and personality?" (45).

16. Aparicio and Chávez-Silverman, *Tropicalizations*, 64.

17. George Lipsitz, *Dangerous Crossroads: Popular Music, Postmodernism, and the Poetics of Place* (New York: Verso, 1994), 78.

18. Langston Hughes, *Montage of a Dream Deferred* (New York: Henry Holt, 1951).

19. John Storm Roberts, *The Latin Tinge: The Impact of Latin American Music on the United States* (Oxford: Oxford University Press, 1999 [1979]), 265.

20. Mikhail M. Bakhtin, *Rabelais and His World*, trans. Helene Iswolsky (Bloomington: University of Indiana Press, 1984); Robert Stam, "Mikhail Bakhtin and Left Cultural Critique," *Postmodernism and Its Discontents: Theories, Practices*, ed. E. Ann Kaplan (London: Verso, 1988), 116–45; Walter Benjamin, *Illuminations: Essays and Reflections*, trans. Harry Zohn, ed. Hannah Arendt (New York: Harcourt, Brace & World, 1968), 257.

21. Ralph Ellison, *Invisible Man* (New York: Vintage Books, 1952), 8.

22. Laura Post, *Backstage Pass: Interviews with Women in Music* (Norwich, VT: New Victoria Publishers, 1997), 19.

23. Third World Communications, *Third World Women* (San Francisco: Third World Communications, 1972); Third World Communications, *Time to Greez!: Incantations from the Third World* (San Francisco: Third World Communications and Glide Publications, 1975).

24. Avotcja (Jiltonilro), "The Black Latin and the Mexican Indian" (Third World Communications, 1972), 133.

25. Henry Louis Gates, Jr., *The Signifying Monkey: A Theory of Afro-American Literary Criticism* (New York: Oxford University Press, 1988), 54–55.

26. Avotcja (Jiltonilro). "Cuando Baila Ramón" (Third World Communications, 1975), 178.

27. Iain Chambers, *Popular Culture: The Metropolitan Experience* (London: Methuen, 1986), 135.

28. Aparicio, *Listening to Salsa*, 96–97.

29. Leslie Gotfrit, "Women Dancing Back: Disruption and the Politics of Pleasure," *Postmodernism, Feminism, and Cultural Politics: Redrawing Educational Boundaries*, ed. Henry A. Giroux (Albany: State University of New York Press, 1991), 186.

30. Dorinda Moreno, "Stations/of the Cross Roads/Never-For-Gotten Paths" (Third World Communications, 1975), 169.

31. The following is my own translation of the lyrics: "Black woman, black woman, apple of my eye/Black woman of my life, who/loves you."

32. "Curandera" in Spanish means folk healer. Initially, San Martin de Porres was prohibited from entering the Dominican order as a member because of racism. See entry by Carlos Parra in *Africana: Encyclopedia of the African and African American Experience*, ed. Kwame Anthony Appiah and Henry Louis Gates, Jr. (New York: Basic Civitas Books, 1999), 1540.

33. Once again, this is my own translation: "Painter of saints and altars/if you have a soul in your body/why, in painting those portraits, /did you forget the black ones?" See *Angelitos negros*, Joselito Rodríguez, dir. (1948).

34. Raymond Williams, *Marxism and Literature* (New York: Oxford University Press, 1977), 128–35.

35. James H. Cone, *The Spirituals and the Blues: An Interpretation* (New York: Seabury, 1972); Lawrence Levine, *Black Culture and Black Consciousness: Afro-American Thought from Slavery to Freedom* (New York: Oxford University Press, 1975); Houston A. Baker, Jr., *Blues, Ideology, and Afro-American Literature* (Chicago: University of Chicago Press, 1984).

36. Angela Y. Davis, *Blues Legacies and Black Feminism: Gertrude "Ma" Rainey, Bessie Smith, and Billie Holliday* (New York: Pantheon Books, 1998), 9.

17

Black Arts to Def Jam

Performing Black "Spirit Work" across Generations

Lorrie Smith

The Arts Are Black (and coming back!)
—Charlie Braxton

An emblematic moment in the emergence of the Black Arts Movement occurred at a writers' conference at Fisk University in 1967 when Gwendolyn Brooks—up to that point a genteel integrationist anointed by the Pulitzer Prize-awarding literary establishment—had a conversion experience that gave birth to "new consciousness." The catalyst for her transformation from "Negro" to "Black" poet, as she describes it in her 1972 autobiography, *Report from Part One*, was the charismatic performance of revolutionary young poets like Amiri Baraka, Hoyt Fuller, and Ron Milner. The fruitful response to this awakening—Brooks' rebirth into "surprised queenhood in the new black sun," her switch from Harper and Row to Dudley Randall's Broadside Press, her transition from formalism to free verse and the idioms of black consciousness, and her mentoring of young poets, including The Blackstone Rangers and Don L. Lee / Haki Madhubuti, in Chicago's OBAC (Organization of Black American Culture) workshops—are now engraved in the history of the Black Arts Movement.[1] Other poets of Brooks' generation, including Margaret Walker, Margaret Danner, Dudley Randall, and Samuel Allen, while perhaps equally disoriented and surprised by the Black Arts explosion at first, would also forge alliances with radical young poets. Whatever tensions and anxieties of influence might have existed between older and younger African American poets who subscribed to the principles of a black aesthetic were obscured by the imperatives of racial unity. If some young Black Arts writers sometimes polemically renounced all earlier African American writing as not authentically or sufficiently "black," their personal relationships with older writers forced acknowledgment of shared terrain.

We are currently witnessing a similarly high-profile display of intergenerational affiliation in the black poetry community. Now, however, it is not so much older poets who are being awakened by young radicals, but younger poets who are discovering and revising a legacy of black aesthetic writing. The older generation, meanwhile, seems to be acknowledging more publicly that "the weight is still on us as a generation" to preserve tradition and guide younger poets.[2] As in the earlier era, alliances between generations are ideologically strategic rather than serendipitous. The bond, now as then, is an articulation of "blackness" as a sign of solidarity, spiritual oneness, cultural unity, and political struggle—though this sign is constantly being interrogated and complicated by poets of the hip hop generation.[3] Often, bonds of kinship are a defining feature of publications and literary events, proclaiming continuity between the ancestral spirits of Brooks' generation, the embodied spirits of Black Arts Movement poets esteemed as elders and griots, and the rap and hip-hop-inflected spirit of young poet-performers just coming into their prime. Thus, we find Amiri Baraka sharing the stage with DJ Spooky and other rappers, Sonia Sanchez in a high profile photo shoot in *Black Issues Book Review* (March/April 2000) embracing Mos Def like a proud mama, with a headline asserting (lest any skeptics are still holding out) that "Rap IS Poetry!" and Nikki Giovanni offering a hagiographic introduction to Tupac Shakur's posthumous volume of lyrics, *The Rose That Grew from Concrete* (2000). Numerous literary gatherings make a point of including intergenerational readings and panels that articulate a unifying black aesthetic. At a conference honoring the centenary of Langston Hughes' birth in his home town of Lawrence, Kansas, creative cross-currents flowed between a number of venerable Black Arts-era poets (Mari Evans, Amiri Baraka, Sonia Sanchez, Eugene Redmond, Kalamu ya Salaam, Ishmael Reed) and younger black poets, most of whom gained reputations as performance and slam poets before developing literary careers (Kevin Powell, Kevin Young, Willie Perdomo, Tony Medina, Jessica Care Moore). On a panel exploring continuities between blues, bop, and hip hop aesthetics, Kevin Powell claimed Grand Master Flash's "The Message" (1982) was his generation's "Montage of a Dream Deferred" (1951) and Tupac Shakur was a direct descendant of Langston Hughes.

In part, such expressions of intergenerational affiliation may simply reflect demographic cycles and social decorum. Black Arts-era poets are growing older, and several (Larry Neal, Etheridge Knight, Audre Lorde, June Jordan) have already passed on, so there may be a sense that surviving writers of this period are precious cultural resources as well as canonical literary figures. Poets born during the 1960s and 1970s are now coming into maturity as writers and are naturally aligning themselves with older mentors. But there is a deeper impulse behind these alliances, one informed by literary critic Craig Hansen Werner's recognition that "it seems vital that those sharing a serious interest in

African American culture join in constructing a usable tradition, one capable of providing theoretical insights adequate to the needs of particular struggles."[4] Both the frequency and the urgency surrounding recent intergenerational affiliations suggest that "particular struggles" on cultural, social, and political fronts have propelled the "constructing of a usable tradition" which plays changes on the fundamental principles of the black aesthetic articulated in the 1960s. The emergence of what poets Kevin Powell and Ras Baraka call "a new Black Consciousness Movement" signals a "generational shift," but it does not constitute a revolutionary "new object of study" such as the one Houston A. Baker, Jr. graphed in describing the radical expressions of the Black Arts Movement in reaction to integrationist politics and poetics.[5] Nor is it a movement with a cohesive and discernable program rooted in the kind of "profound reorientation of energy and vision" literary critic Kimberly Benston associates with the Black Arts Movement.[6] Poet and journalist Jabari Asim asserts that recent developments in black poetry, for all their "def" energy, cannot be called "a new movement, new renaissance, or new poetry, because the only thing truly new about it is us, newly born into poetic awareness." Emerging poets, according to Asim, "don't herald a brave new world unless they result in the creation and maintenance of significant institutions and bodies of work."[7]

We need to recognize that such creation is, in fact, underway; intergenerational activity in the black poetry community marks an important moment of literary-political consolidation, a new growth of "significant institutions and bodies of work" fed by the roots of the Black Arts Movement. Examining what Powell and Baraka call "a continuum of artistic, political, spiritual and psychological struggle" offers one approach to questions posed by Kimberly Benston in his masterful re-reading of the Black Arts Movement: "What is the continuing meaning of the Black Arts Movement? On what terms shall we calculate its aims, achievement, and legacy?"[8] The cross-pollination of Black Arts and hip hop sensibilities makes for a particularly fruitful moment in the evolution of black poetry in America, opens new spaces for the imagination, both literary and political, in which the unfinished (or abrogated, depending on your interpretation of its history) business of the Black Arts Movement might be adapted to the exigencies of "the color line" in the twenty-first century. My intent is thus not simply to show how the earlier movement influenced the later one or to show how younger poets pay homage to older poets, but to chart a more dynamic, reciprocal call and response interplay between generations which extends, renews, and recreates what Houston A. Baker, Jr. calls the "eternally transformative impulse" of black poetic "spirit work."[9] The wellsprings of this profoundly visionary impulse reside in what Robin D. G. Kelley calls reciprocity between political engagement and poetic imagination. Flipping the cliché that "the personal is political," Kelley suggests that the political is, in fact, deeply poetic: "Progressive social movements . . . do what great poetry always does: transport us to another place, compel us to relive horrors and, more importantly, enable us to imagine a new society. We must remember that the conditions and the very existence of social movements enable participants to imagine something different, to realize that things need not always be this way. It is that imagination, that effort to see the future in the present, that I shall call "poetry" or "poetic knowledge."[10] It is this visionary impulse—diffuse rather than centralized in a social movement or ideological position—that constitutes the continuum of black "spirit work" across poetic generations.

Any genealogy of contemporary black poetry must begin with the recognition that many Black Arts poets continue to extend black aesthetic principles into the present through living precept and practice. That the revolutionary writers of the 1960s have continued to grow and change through long and productive careers should be obvious, though all too often they have been viewed, within mainstream literary culture, as aberrations and eruptions safely locked in the past. Central to these careers has been one of the cardinal principles of the Black Arts Movement: the commitment to foster black expressivity within grassroots communities and within a political context of black liberation, self-determination, and resistance to white supremacy. Examples of such literary activism are plentiful: June Jordan's People's Poetry workshops in Berkeley and Oakland, Kalamu ya Salaam's Nommo collective and Runagate Press activities in New Orleans, Steve Cannon's Gathering of the Tribes on the Lower East Side, Eugene Redmond's Writers Club in East St. Louis, Amiri Baraka's Spirit House theater and home salon activities in Newark, Haki Madhubuti's continuation of Gwendolyn Brooks' legacy and OBAC activities in Chicago and his dedicated leadership of Third World Press, Sonia Sanchez's work with younger poets in Philadelphia. When younger writers like Powell and Baraka claim direct lineage with radical black activist writers of the past, they are attesting to an experience that is often personal and emotional as well as literary.

The construction of a tradition of "social and political black literature and art" (as a 2002 intergenerational anthology, *Role Call*, is sub-titled) is always a *re*-construction, always a process of discovery and negotiation, of a "changing same" relation to the past. But the reclamation of a usable Black Arts past is fraught with challenges particular to our age: (1) a vacuum caused by the critical neglect, disparagement, and suppression of Black Arts writing since the late 1970s until very recently in African American as well as mainstream literary criticism; (2) the fear that black identity is being melted down in the kettle of a bland multiculturalism, globalized monoculture, and disingenuous color-blindness; (3) the concomitant and paradoxical "high visibility" commodification of "blackness" and the commercialization of hyper-black modes of rap and hip hop; (4) postmodern and new black aesthetic forms of pastiche and parody that undercut a visionary political tradition; (5) a generation gap within the larger black community that, according to journalist Bakari Kitwana, divides the hip hop generation from the Civil Rights/Black Power generation; and (6) economic and political conditions that fuel rage and nihilism in black urban communities. Theories of vernacular transmission inform the re-construction of tradition, and recent collaborations between Black Arts and hip hop poets retrieve black aesthetic writing from erasure and engage in what Amiri Baraka calls the "advanced work" of building institutions that sustain its political and literary force.[11] My argument concurs with Werner's affirmation of "the continuing relevance of the most politically committed and intellectually adventurous writing of the Black Arts Movement to our contemporary struggles."[12]

"WHERE IS YOUR FIRE?"—SONIA SANCHEZ

It would be comforting, in our age of postmodern dislocation and diasporic upheaval, to think of literary kinship as an unbroken umbilical cord, a natural evolution, a seamless inheritance of soulful vernacular purity, a mystical rite of spiritual oneness, a solemn passing of the torch, a deep river nourishing a fragmented African self and nation, a drum beat reverberating from Yorubaland to the South Bronx. Such metaphors are, in fact, often invoked, and they serve as potent expressions of the "wholeness," "continuity," and unified "soul field" literary critic Stephen Henderson claimed, in his seminal study of the black aesthetic, "The Forms of Things Unknown," as the defining features of the black poetic tradition.[13] But real history is more tangled and complicated than such mythologizing metaphors, marked by "animating tensions," as Benston claims, that are both "contradictory" and "productive."[14] The relation between tradition and individual talent may have more to do with the idea that it is achieved with great labor rather than imbibed like mother's milk. At the same time, however, it is important to recognize that "tradition," "spirit," "soul," and "roots" are what Henderson describes as "mascon" ideas in black literary culture—symbols grounded in a "massive concentration of Black experiential energy" which powerfully affects the meaning of "Black speech, Black song, and Black poetry."[15] Like kinship, they have undeniable power and significance in people's lives, and they cannot be easily dismissed with poststructuralist abstractions about roving signifiers, nor can they be eulogized along with the disappearing author, reader, and text. "Mascon" ideas like "tradition" operate in a web of intertextual relations that accrue meaning, revision, and resonance over time. Indeed, the vitality of such relations may be one of the defining features of African American literature.[16]

To illustrate this mechanism with reference to the current discussion, we can look at the titles of several anthologies of black writing that use the "mascon" image of fire. Invoking connotations that yoke apocalyptic biblical destruction with revolutionary fervor (as in James Baldwin's play on Old Testament iconography in *The Fire Next Time* [1963]), this image has come to signify the spirited and righteously angry emergence of new generations speaking in new idioms but accountable to the past. Wallace Thurman's *Fire!!* gave voice, in 1926, to "the younger Negro artists" inspired by Langston Hughes' 1926 manifesto, "The Negro Artist and the Racial Mountain." In 1968, LeRoi Jones and Larry Neal edited the classic Black Arts collection, *Black Fire: An Anthology of Afro-American Writing*. Keith Gilyard plays a slight variation in his 1997 anthology, *Spirit and Flame: An Anthology of Contemporary African American Poetry*. In 1998,

Derrick I. M. Gilbert (a.k.a. D-Knowledge) compiled *Catch the Fire!!!: A Cross-Generational Anthology of Contemporary African-American Poetry.* The last section of Third World Press' 2002 compendium, *Role Call: A Generational Anthology of Social and Political Black Art and Literature,*" is entitled simply "Black Fire," paying direct homage to its 1968 predecessor, while its title invokes parallels with earlier "Black Art."[17] The image, of course, evolves in shifting historical contexts. Thus, Thurman might associate fire with lynching and public burning; Jones and Neal attest to the fulfillment of Baldwin's 1963 prophecy with evocations of Newark, Detroit, and Watts in flames, and evoke the Black Panther rallying cry, "Burn, Baby, Burn"; recent volumes call up riots in L.A. and Miami, the MOVE bombing in Philadelphia, and burning churches in the South; all synthesize the accumulated association of personal passion with political rage and revolt, as well as the paradoxical symbolic associations of fire with love and with the imperative to shoot. When Sonia Sanchez preaches "CATCH YOUR FIRE . . . HOLD YOUR FIRE . . . LEARN YOUR FIRE . . . BE THE FIRE" in her recent poem called "Catch the Fire" she invokes a whole tradition of apocalyptic activism, and when poet Derrick I. M. Gilbert responds to her call, he riffs on the "chills," "frozen lives," and "frozen souls" of political quietism and invokes the names of black leaders of the past to re-ignite "THE FIRE VISION."[18] Modulating over time and across generations, the image gathers force and signifies the continuity of the black liberation struggle. It becomes a thread of living tradition, what Houston Baker calls a "unifying myth" nourished by "black spirit work."

A theory of literary transference (like theories of identity formation) must thus account for both the constructed nature of literary tradition and the emotional power of family and community connections rooted in history. As with theories of racial identity, what seems natural, immanent, authentic, and self-evident (the birthright of a fiery torch passed from generation to generation) must be deconstructed even while the experiential and political contingencies of such identity (the need to continually re-ignite the torch in the darkness) are acknowledged. Working out of Amiri Baraka's classic model of the "changing same" of black music, Houston Baker emphasizes the improvisational and dynamic nature of African American "spirit work" as a model for the construction of tradition: "The spirit evoked by the Afro-American modernists is an eternally transformative impulse that converts desire not only into resonant and frequently courageous sound but also into ceaseless motion . . . the process and product of a felicitous (surprising) transformation of racial soul sounds into a report from black vernacular valleys."[19] While Baker's invocation of "racial soul sounds," "black cultural geography" and "black vernacular valleys" may come dangerously close to a static and essentialized blackness, he is, in fact, describing a dynamic literary tradition highly attuned to the social and political contexts that form the ground for the "vernacular valleys" of ordinary black folks. This is the same wellspring of black expression tapped by Langston Hughes and re-invented by Black Arts writers and theorists as a central tenet of a black aesthetic.

In discussing the continuity of "black spirit work," Baker allows us to see how black aesthetic writing of the 1960s was both a "reclamation" of earlier work and a new "invention."[20] One of the primary inventions of Black Arts writing was to give political force to the vernacular celebrated by Langston Hughes, Sterling Brown, Zora Neale Hurston, and others, adding the extra jolt that art should above all communicate with ordinary black people and inspire them to black pride and militancy. In a recent interview, Sonia Sanchez comments on this significant aspect of Black Arts writing:

I took the whole idea of using black English and dealing with it in an urban setting, incorporating the hipness that was in that black urban setting, which means that the English is going to change, right? Langston Hughes did a similar thing via the jazz idiom that he employed. This urban thing is a smart, take-no-prisoners kind of language, right? It has its own cadence and rhythm. It has its own way of looking at the world. It goes out and says simply that "I am here. Deal with me." The interesting thing that I learned from this was that it also said: "I come as an equal. And I appreciate the language that I speak here in this urban setting." We made this poetic, which is fascinating to me, still, today.[21]

The terms of this stylistic legacy are currently being renegotiated and reinvented by the hip hop generation—for whom the "ordeal of integration" has vexed racial identity, for whom a coherent revolutionary program is a distant dream of their parents' day, for whom Black Arts terms like "the people," "the streets," "urban," and especially "blackness" itself are troubled, and for whom the animating tension in black art between what literary critic Aldon Nielsen calls oral "voicings" and written "scriptings" has new dimensions and complications in an age of digital reproduction.[22] DJ Renegade's well-broadcast claim that rap is the CNN of the black community is elaborated by poet-editor Louis Reyes Rivera: "The news of the day, testament and affirmation, current and advanced, informs [spoken-word] poetry that outlines the immediate and understudied aspirations of African and Latino Americans caught in the crossfire between skin game caste and an ever-shrinking planet of high tech advances."[23]

Extending Baker's model to the Black Arts Movement's legacies, Kimberly Benston calls us to see "the Black Arts Movement not as a creed or even as method, but rather as a continuously shifting field of struggle and revision in which the relations among politics, representation, history, and revolution are productively revalued."[24] Benston builds upon Baker's notions of tradition as fluid and dynamic in theorizing how a "performative ethos" across a range of genres during the Black Arts Movement serves to resist fixed, essentialist notions of racial identity and cultural uniformity. His model contrasts a notion of "blackness as essence" he associates with Amiri Baraka against an Ellisonian (proto-postmodernist) sense of the "polymorphic movements of blackness." For Benston, "Blackness is not an inevitable object, but rather a motivated, constructed, corrosive, and productive process."[25] Building on the vernacular theories of Gates, Baker, and Benston, it is reasonable to refine our conception of a continuum of "struggle" and "black spirit work" that refuses a monolithic view of either the history of the Black Arts Movement or the theory and practice of a black aesthetic, that takes place within a constantly "shifting field of struggle and revision." The rediscovery and invention of cross-generational ties are a strategic construction serving specific literary, cultural, and political needs at the turn of the twenty-first century, rather than a natural inheritance of essential and immanent blackness, as it is often represented. This constructedness in no way diminishes the intensity of the "fire" of tradition or its social and political efficacy. A bridge that has been repaired may, in fact, be stronger than the original.

"IN THE TRADITION, TOO"—RAS BARAKA

The strategic assertion of ties between Black Arts and hip hop sensibilities (and between older and younger poets themselves) indicates a mutual need to recover a usable history of the Black Arts Movement that has been repressed, disparaged, erased, constricted, and distorted. The emotional force that attends affiliations between Black Arts Movement and emergent black poetry can be understood as a sign of recovery on two fronts: the realm of cultural production, criticism, and canon formation, and a social and political milieu that rendered the Black Power and Black Arts Movements nearly invisible and that created feelings of anger, abandonment, and political impotence among those born in the wake of the 1960s.

The critical reception and understanding of Black Arts Movement poetry is complex. Partly, it has been the victim of a more generalized neglect of poetry in the field of African American literature. As literary critic Fahamisha Patricia Brown says in her introduction to *Performing the Word*, "a search for critical discussions of African American poetry reveals sparse treatment compared to that for prose narrative" and "there has been little sustained critical inquiry into African American poetry as a body of literature."[26] More specifically, as recently as 1991, David Lionel Smith found that "the silence regarding the Black Arts Movement is deafening," and he details the critical and cultural forces that have contributed to this neglect.[27] What attention the critical establishment had paid to Black Arts writers ranges from mildly dismissive to viciously castigating, often rehashing old debates about art and propaganda, universality and cultural specificity, that continue to plague black literary theory. Craig Hansen Werner tracks the ways Black Arts writing fell victim to theoretical rifts that resulted in "the breakdown in the dialogue between the sixties and the eighties."[28] For Baraka, still characteristically combative, backlash against a Black Arts agenda is part of a larger political climate of conservatism and accommodation: "The continuous stream of distorted anti-democratic and anti-Black and counter revolutionary images in all media have been used to try to 'reverse correct verdicts' reached through struggle, to character assassinate the Black Liberation Movement and its chief combatants."[29]

By the late 1970s, most of the poetry, essays, and manifestos from the period had gone out of print, including the seminal *Black Fire*. As Kalamu ya Salaam points out, many black-controlled publishing venues like *Negro Digest/Black World*, *The Journal of Black Poetry*, *Black Dialogue*, *Black Books Bulletin*, *Black Scholar*, and *Soul Book* disappeared, taking with them the chance that "people-oriented poetry was heard, read, widely disseminated and broadly discussed throughout the Black community."[30] Keith Gilyard talks about "the lean years, that is, the period (1975 or so until now?) when corporate publishers pulled the plug on the Electric Black Poetic."[31] While local activity and small press publishing continued to flourish among those who wished, according to Gilyard, "to maintain an aesthetic fervor to help propel progressive political struggle," the general result of these combined forces was a "vacuum" (Baraka) and a "void" (ya Salaam) that made access to the full range of Black Arts thought and creativity difficult for aspiring young writers, not to mention the community at large.[32] In terms of the larger canon of contemporary poetry, all but a few token and decontextualized Black Arts poems disappeared.

Only recently has the critical establishment reconciled some of these tensions and responded to David Lionel Smith's call for a more nuanced and rigorous "black pluralist historiography" of the Black Arts Movement.[33] Most notable and welcome have been the book-length studies already cited (Benston, Nielsen, Werner), as well as Lorenzo Thomas' *Extraordinary Measures: Afrocentric Modernism and Twentieth-Century American Poetry*.[34] Nielsen and Thomas examine extensive new archival material that greatly enlarges our understanding of the scope of the Black Arts Movement and that places it in a richly diverse cultural milieu leading up to and simultaneous with the 1960s. Benston constructs an important new interdisciplinary paradigm that connects the "performance" of blackness in poetry, drama, jazz, the "chant-sermon," and "autocritography." Each of these books makes use of poststructuralist theory to launch an attack on totalizing views of black poetry, black vernacular culture, and the racial sign of blackness, without relinquishing "a love supreme" for black expressive culture—a rapprochement that is enormously important for the progress of African American literary criticism hobbled by the reductive polarity of universalism and identity politics.

Recent books like Robin D. G. Kelley's *Yo' Mama's Disfunktional!* (1997), Kevin Powell's *Keepin' It Real* (1992), Bakari Kitwana's *The Hip Hop Generation: Young Blacks and the Crisis in African American Culture* (2002), and Todd Boyd's *The New H.N.I.C.: The Death of Civil Rights and the Reign of Hip Hop* (2003) testify to a painful sense of abandonment and a sometimes divisive generation gap, accusing elders in the black community of promoting obsolete models of social change and dismissing the idioms and political potential of hip hop and rap.[35] Kitwana argues that "the old paradigms" of Civil Rights and Black Power still dominate racial conversations but "no longer apply" to the dire and paradoxical crises facing young blacks in America today. Kevin Powell and Ras Baraka voice the hip hop generation's sense of being let down by history, the unfinished business of their parents' struggles: "We are children of the post-integration (nightmare!), post-Civil Rights era, abandoned to find our way in a pot bent on melting our culture into mainstream oblivion."[36]

However, while these generational rifts (as well as more long-standing class tensions in the black community) might be operating in the culture at large, poets (perhaps, after all, the true "antennae of the race" as Pound claimed) are vigorously mending bridges and forging alliances. Two phenomena—one in the realm of cultural production and the other grounded in political and economic realities—fuel the effort to re-construct a black aesthetic tradition. The first (voiced by Powell and Baraka above) is anxiety over the shifting sign of blackness in "post-integration" society where racial complexities have been channeled into multicultural platitudes. The second impetus is rage about what Kitwana calls "America's unfulfilled promise of equality and inclusion": "Ignored [in contemporary popular discussion, media reports, and public policy] is the grim reality that concrete progress within the civil rights arena has been almost nil for nearly four decades. Neither acknowledged are the ways persisting institutionalized racism has intensified for hip-hop generationers despite 1950s and 1960s civil rights legislation."[37]

The current manifestation of racial crisis in the United States is nothing less than a pernicious new nadir for those most vulnerable in the economic system and trapped in blighted inner cities and cycles of poverty. On the economic front, the effects of deregulated, post-industrial free market policies, the loss of jobs in urban areas, and cutbacks in social programs have been devastating to black communities and to members of the hip hop generation raised in America's urban ghettoes. The secession of many middle-class blacks from poor and working-class black communities and widespread white flight and white liberal retreat from racial struggle have assured the continuation of *de facto* hyper-segregation. Politically, the alliance of the Republican Party, the Christian Right, and black conservatives, with their concerted attack on civil rights and affirmative action programs, the systematically disproportionate incarceration of young black men, and the absence of unifying black leadership have confounded progress towards social justice. Clearly, these are forces that have fed the rise of rap and hip hop. But while black cultural production may be more popular and commercially successful than ever, the ideological entanglements of the culture wars, identity politics, class tensions, the canon debates, and the rise of black public intellectuals have complicated both black cultural unity and interracial alliance. Any view of black poetry after the 1960s must take into account the ways these economic social, ideological, and cultural contexts have complicated the evolution of a black aesthetic.

In his 1984 retrospective essay, "The Black Arts Movement," Amiri Baraka historicizes the decline of the Black Arts Movement but refuses to eulogize it. He emphasizes three foundational principles that he claims still have efficacy for black poetry today: the establishment of an art that is "identifiably Afro American," the establishment of a "mass art" that speaks to ordinary black people in the idioms of black vernacular, and the establishment of an art that is "revolutionary."[38] He asserts that the Black Arts Movement was a radical, visionary wedge, "the largest cultural upsurge that our people have had in this century," but that there is a continuing need to engage in the "advanced work" of keeping black cultural traditions alive.[39] Rather than seeing the black aesthetic as a programmatic set of precepts doomed to fail or as a cement "straitjacket" limiting freedom of expression, it is important to see it as multiple, rhizomatic, enabling practices that redirected the course of black poetry and that continue to be enacted in enormously diverse and diffuse ways.[40] Thus, we can talk fruitfully about the legacy of the Black Arts Movement in general terms, as what Baraka calls a "broad spearhead of Blackness."[41] Most importantly, the affirmation of black pride and self-definition and the broad defeat of double consciousness was a fundamental and enduring paradigm shift. As Haki Madhubuti recently wrote, "In the United States, others have always defined us. The poets, writers, artists and musicians of the sixties, i.e., the Black Arts Movement, changed all of that forever!"[42] No one even questions now the visibility of black vernacular culture. Manifestations of black pride such as ritual return trips to West Africa, dashikis and kente cloth graduation sashes, cowrie shell jewelry, the artistry of cornrows and dreadlocks, black-owned book stores, the widespread use of Islamic and African names in the black community would be unimaginable without the instigations and celebrations of the Black Arts Movement. In the poetry community, a lively debate paralleling debates about black-ownership of hip hop production has given rise to important new publications, most notably the work of BlackWords and Runagate Press that resulted in a cross-generational anthology, *360 Degrees: A Revolution of Black Poets*, and a gigantic compendium of radical black writing and art, *Role Call*, published by Haki Madhubuti's Third World Press. Such ventures start to address Baraka's charge that "we still have not built organizations and institutions to struggle for Self Determination, Self Respect, Self Defense."[43] The triumph of Russell Simmons' Def Poetry Jam on cable television and on Broadway can be taken either as a sell-out or a successful achievement of black self-determination in the mainstream; in either case, it has been enormously influential in spotlighting hip hop and spoken-word poetry.

While it may be true, as cultural critic bell hooks claims, that Black Power ultimately "did not deliver the goods" ideologically and that black nationalism and separatism were doomed to failure, there is no question that in the cultural realm, as Baraka writes, "a torrent of inspiration . . . lifted Black artistic communities across the country, and the evidence is coming in."[44] We might even say that the Black Arts Movement was a victim of its own success, unleashing a heterogeneous, polyglot, multiplicitous "torrent" of "Black Art" that could never be contained or measured by a singular racial identity or political ideology. Indeed, the first anthologies to reconfigure the shape-shifting canon of black writing in the wake of the Black Arts Movement—Clarence Major's *The New Black Poetry* (1969), Abraham Chapman's *New Black Voices* (1972), June Jordan's

Soulscript (1970), Dudley Randall's *Black Poets* (1971), Arnold Adoff's *The Poetry of Black America* (1973), and Stephen Henderson's *Understanding the New Black Poetry* (1973), as well as the dozens of anthologies emerging out of local poetry communities—articulate this pluralism within a general framework of black aesthetic principles. By 1976, in his important "critical history," *Drumvoices: The Mission of Afro-American Poetry*, Eugene Redmond documented and affirmed the diversity of black poetry as one of its glories.[45] That contemporary young writers as different as Harryette Mullen, Trey Ellis, Tracie Morris, Mos Def, Chuck D, and Willie Perdomo can claim legitimate lineage from the Black Arts Movement speaks to this pluralism.[46] Quiet as it's sometimes kept, black poetry has always been hugely diverse and black experience has never been unitary. Such a fact has always caused tensions between the pull towards heterogeneity, hybridity, and "polymorphous performances of blackness" and the need to assert a strategic black identity in a racist culture. The current manifestation of intergenerational alliances coalescing around the principles of the black aesthetic suggests that despite the popular culture construction of "postethnic" and "transracial" America, there is still a need, as Larry Neal put it in 1968, for "an art that speaks directly to the needs and aspirations of black America, still a "necessity for black people to define the world in their own terms."[47]

"THIS IS NOT A SMALL VOICE"—SONIA SANCHEZ

The crux of this tension and the point of contact between Black Arts and hip hop generations turns out to be in part the age-old debate in African American literary theory between orature and writing, the "speakerly text" and the "writerly text," the stage and the page. The most visible and audible "performance of blackness" in poetry today takes place quite literally as performance. The younger generation has taken the possibilities unlocked by the public performance of poetry in the 1960s and adapted them to the conditions of the new nadir, new technologies undreamed of in their parents' day, and new audiences now hungrily seeking the live, spoken word. Gil Scott Heron and The Last Poets have been adopted as honorary griots, and younger poets have learned much from older poets well known for their distinctive performance styles. The vernacular speech patterns and rhythms evident in Baraka's jumpy improvisations and scats, Sonia Sanchez's keening moans and stutters, Kalamu ya Salaam's melodic riffs and meditative interludes, and Madhubuti's understated ironies are easily traceable through bebop, blues, sorrow songs, and African beats. There is no question, as Baraka asserted in his seminal Black Arts era essay, "The Changing Same" (1966), that one of the main sources of what Houston Baker called the "eternally transformative" power of "black spirit work" resides in black music and other forms of vernacular expression; Baraka writes, "Indeed, to go back in any historical (or emotional) line of ascent in Black music leads us inevitably to religion, i.e., spirit worship. This phenomenon is always at the root in Black art, the worship of spirit—or at least the summoning of or by such force."[48] Not least of the possibilities passed on in this tradition of spiritual receptivity are visionary, oppositional political speech and community-building call and response.

Nothing has been more energizing to poetry in general than this black-saturated orality, sparked and energized by the power surges of rap and hip hop. Recently, however, there have been charges leveled against the perceived excess and flaccidity of some spoken-word poetry, with a concomitant re-affirmation of the political principles of the Black Arts Movement. The problem is not performance per se, but performance for the sake of showmanship, cut off from vital community connections and aesthetic force. Tony Medina says in *bum rush the page:* "Too often in this [slam] arena, poetry is not what matters, but performance—how well one can recite a line or two, no matter how backward or banal . . . here, poetry is cheap, is cheapened."[49] Harryette Mullen complicates what she sees as constructions of racial authenticity that rest on the presumed di-chotomy between spoken and written language, and she warns that "any theory of African American literature that privileges a speech-based poetics, or the trope of orality, to the exclusion of more writerly texts will cost us some impoverish-ment of the tradition."[50] Jabari Asim measures the impoverishment that attends both the publishing of less than excellent spoken-word poetry and the facile privileging of orality: "As we attempt to study and understand this new thing, we must also examine the changing and challenged role of the printed page. So far, books have not held their own against compact discs and music videos, the popularity of which encourages sound-bite poetry and devalues complex literary explorations."[51] One result of this devaluation, Medina claims, is that "serious poets who also happen to perform well on stage are constantly being called spo-ken-word artists and are not taken seriously as writers."[52] His volume seeks to maintain "the integrity of the page, of the written word" even as it celebrates the resurgence of poetry in performance, and he and Louis Reyes Rivera have re-cruited Sonia Sanchez to support "the craft of writing, the discipline of writing" energized by "the pace of sound, the swiftness of sound, the blackness of sound, the color of sound, the beat of sound."[53] In the past ten years, a growing number of younger poets like Medina have gone to the woodshed, with the guidance of their elders, to study history and the African American poetic tradition, and the result is a diverse group of poets serious about their craft and committed to ex-tending both the black aesthetic and black presses and cultural institutions into our time. Medina echoes the spokespeople of the Black Arts Movement when he aims to rescue poetry from the "mindless circus show of slam sluts" and the criti-cal dismissals of "socially responsible poetry" by bringing "poetry—relevant, meaningful, provocative poetry—back to the people."[54]

The record of this return can be found in a number of recent anthologies that represent themselves as inheritors of the entwined aesthetic and politi-cal ideas of the Black Arts Movement. Like all anthologies, they also serve as strategic and polemical consolidations of aesthetic and cultural theories, and they provide a useful graph of the rapidly changing evolution of recent black poetry as the younger generation comes of age and begins to define itself with more precision. As such, they perform the "advanced work" of continuing to articulate the connections between politics and poetry for a new era, building institutions for the perpetuation and dissemination of black art (black-run presses, journals, bookstores, and recording labels, community-based writing workshops and theaters, anthologies), and engaging in rigorous self-criticism, craft, revision, and discipline in their writing. As in the earlier movement, these anthologies resist monolithic conceptions of blackness and testify to the vitality of individual voices and local poetry communities.

Several titles of recent anthologies establish overt connections with the Black Arts/Black Power Movements: *In the Tradition* (1992), edited by Kevin Powell and Ras Baraka, is a "fat" volume of poetry and fiction with a nationalistic black, red, and green cover design. Its title pays homage to the elder Baraka's well-known tribute to black music, "In the Tradition." The younger Baraka's "In the Tradition, Too," dedicated to his parents, signifies with great respect on his father's original poem, and places his own hip hop generation's poetry in a "changing same" continuum of "an / African war song. / A spiritual slave song. / A radical Public Enemy song . . . the expressions of what is / and what will be."[55] Alan Spears' *Fast Talk/Full Volume: An Anthology of Contemporary African American Poetry* (1993) claims in its introduction to say "good riddance to the African-American hegemony" and "Death to the 'Black monolith'"—distancing itself from any residual 1960s-style ideological constrictions. But it also positions itself as ringing changes on the "activism and commitment" of sixties poetry, in an era "in which a new conservatism coincided with an increase in homelessness, drugs and crime across America."[56] Keith Gilyard's *Spirit and Flame: An Anthology of Contemporary African American Poetry* (1997) is a highly inclusive volume that not only breaks down boundaries between generations, but also those often erected between older poets from different poetic communities simplistically rendered "academic" and "vernacular." *Catch the Fire!!!: A Cross-Generational Anthology of Contemporary African-American Poetry* (1998), edited by Derrick I. M. Gilbert (a.k.a. D-Knowledge), is organized thematically and is structured as a call and response between Black Arts writers—June Jordan, Amiri Baraka, Ntozake Shange, Abiodun Oyewole, Quincy Troupe, and Sonia Sanchez are interviewed by the editor—and younger poets associated with rap, hip hop, and spoken-word communities.

Recent volumes assert an even more militant iconography and ideology. Kalamu ya Salaam (Black Arts) and Kwame Alexander (hip hop) suggest in their title, *360 Degrees—A Revolution of Black Poets* (1998), that the Black Power/ Black Arts revolution begun in the 1960s has come full circle in the 1990s. The book's cover image of a closed black fist around a pointed pen announces that this is the weapon of choice in the current struggle. *bum rush the page: a def poetry jam* (2001), another intergenerational collaboration, between Tony Medina and Louis Reyes Rivera, comes out of the Afro-Latin-bohemian cultural melange of the Nuyorican Poets Café on the Lower East Side. The book opens with a spiritual "Invocation" in the form of poems by elders Margaret Walker, Dudley Randall, Zizwe Ngafua, Raymond R. Patterson, Safiya Henderson-Holmes, Gwendolyn Brooks, and Rivera, and the book is significant for offering (as did earlier spoken-word collections) an ethnically diverse representation of poets who can be said to work within a black aesthetic. And finally, a volume that appeared with much ceremonial fanfare constructs the strongest ties yet between older and younger poets, Black Arts Movement and hip hop aesthetics and politics. *Role Call: A Generational Anthology of Social and Political Black Art and Literature* (2002), edited by Tony Medina, Samiya A. Bashir, and Quraysh Ali Lansana, including a foreword by Haki Madhubuti and published by Third World Press, attempts to synthesize black consciousness and a black aesthetic for the twenty-first century. Enacting Kimberly Benston's idea that the Black Arts Movement is "a continuously shifting field of struggle and revision in which the relations among politics, representation, history, and revolution are productively revalued," the section headings of *Role Call* send out calls and provocations demanding response from both generations.

> What is the role of today's emerging young artists in the current struggle for equality and justice?
> How do the voices of the next generation define the issues and politics of today?
> A litmus test of—and a call to arms to—a generation grown fat on the limited freedoms won by the Civil Rights Struggle.
> Takes on race, sexuality, education, nationalism, spirituality, AIDS, globalization, hip hop and the Prison Industrial Complex.
> Journey through the tropics of black rage, black love, and black fire.

These subtitles starkly indicate the complexity of challenges facing contemporary poets accountable to the Black Arts legacy and responsive to the conditions of postmodern black life.

A poem like devorah major's "nommo: how we come to speak" pays homage to past poets while cleansing and renewing poetic language for her "third word" generation, which she calls to task, as Medina does, for some of its moral and linguistic failings:

> . . . .
> but before a generation
> passed we children
> of the third word
> knew how to take
> this gift of language
> contort it crimson
> and sew it to our teeth

how to mangle
this tongue that needs
constant translation
reiteration
clarification
purification
release.[57]

While "it seems clear that any effective progressive agenda for the nine-ties, whether cultural or political, will require increased cooperation between races, genders, and classes," for many writers a strategic consolidation of black tradition, black identity, and black political struggle is a pre-condition to cross-cultural alliance.[58] The creation of a world where, in the words of Toni Morrison, "racial specificity minus racist hierarchy" is possible, "a place where race both matters and is rendered impotent," will depend not on the erasure of the sign of blackness, but on the full appreciation that "our Black Aesthetic is influential on and relevant to all of humanity."[59] Thus, we cannot afford to suppress or squander the rich literary heritage of poetry from the Black Arts Movement, with its "eternally transformative impulse" that converts "racial soul sounds into a report from black vernacular valleys."[60] At this important juncture, older poets have taken on the task of passing on their tradition, while a vanguard of young black poets recognizes the need to reclaim the past in order to invent the future.

NOTES

1. Gwendolyn Brooks, *Report from Part One* (Detroit: Broadside Press, 1972), 86.

2. Amiri Baraka, in conversation with Askia Touré, quoted in Joanne V. Gabbin, *The Furious Flowering of African American Poetry* (Charlottesville: University Press of Virginia, 1999), 150.

3. For a full and thoughtful treatment of these aesthetic and political connections, see Marvin J. Gladney, "The Black Arts Movement and Hip Hop," *African American Review* 29: 2 (1995): 291–301.

4. Craig Hansen Werner, *Playing the Changes: From Afro-Modernism to the Jazz Impulse* (Chicago: University of Chicago Press, 1994), 106.

5. Kevin Powell and Ras Baraka, eds., Introduction, *In the Tradition: An Anthology of Young Black Writers* (New York: Harlem River Press, 1992), n.p. Houston A. Baker, Jr., "Generational Shifts in Recent Criticism of Afro-American Literature," *Black American Literature Forum* (1981), rpt. in Angelyn Mitchell, ed., *Within the Circle: An Anthology of African American Literary Criticism from the Harlem Renaissance to the Present* (Durham, NC: Duke University Press, 1994), 282.

6. Kimberly W. Benston, *Performing Blackness: Enactments of African-American Modernism* (London: Routledge, 2000), 3.

7. Jabari Asim, "What is This New Thing?" in Gabbin, *The Furious Flowering*, 311.

8. Powell and Baraka, Introduction, *In the Tradition*; Benston, *Performing Blackness*, 6.

9. Houston A. Baker, Jr., *Afro-American Poetics: Revisions of Harlem and the Black Aesthetic* (Madison: University of Wisconsin Press, 1988), 5.

10. Robin D. G. Kelley, *Freedom Dreams: The Black Radical Imagination* (Boston: Beacon Press, 2002), 9.

11. Baraka asserts the importance of the black literary community's engagement in "advanced work" of institution-building in a number of places. See, for instance, his interview with Askia Touré on the *Furious Flower* video (Vol. 3: "Warriors"), and "The Black Arts Movement" (1994) in *The LeRoi Jones/Amiri Baraka Reader*, ed. William J. Harris (New York: Thunder's Mouth Press, 1999), 495–506.

12. Werner, *Playing the Changes*, 107.

13. Stephen Henderson, "The Forms of Things Unknown," Introduction to *Understanding the New Black Poetry: Black Speech and Black Music as Poetic References* (New York: William Morrow & Company, 1973).

14. Benston, *Performing Blackness*, 4.

15. Henderson, "The Forms of Things Unknown," 44.

16. The fullest articulation of this theory of black literary tradition as an intertextual play of differences is presented in Henry Louis Gates, Jr.'s influential work, *The Signifying Monkey: A Theory of African-American Literary Criticism* (New York: Oxford University Press, 1988).

17. Wallace Thurman, ed., *Fire!!: A Quarterly Devoted to the Younger Negro Artists* 1926), rpt. by Thomas H. Wirth, (The Fire!! Press, 1982); LeRoi Jones and Larry Neal, eds., *Black Fire: An Anthology of Afro-American Writing* (New York: William Morrow & Company, 1968); Keith Gilyard, ed., *Spirit and Flame: An Anthology of Contemporary African American Poetry* (Syracuse, NY: Syracuse University Press, 1997); Derrick I. M. Gilbert, ed., *Catch the Fire!!!: A Cross-Generational Anthology of Contemporary African American Poetry* (New York: Riverhead Books, 1998); Tony Medina, Samiya A. Bashir, and Quraysh Ali Lansana, eds., *Role Call: A Generational Anthology of Social and Political Black Art and Literature* (Chicago: Third World Press, 2002).

18. Sonia Sanchez, "Catch the Fire," (n.d.) in Gilbert, *Catch the Fire!!!*, 226, 243.

19. Baker, *Afro-American Poetics*, 5.

20. Ibid., 6.

21. Susan Kelly, "Discipline and Craft: An Interview with Sonia Sanchez, *African American Review* 34: 4 (2000), 682.

22. Orlando Patterson, *The Ordeal of Integration* (New York: Basic Civitas, 1997). Aldon Lynn Nielsen, *Black Chant: Languages of African-American Postmodernism* (Cambridge: Cambridge University Press, 1997), 22.

23. Louis Reyes Rivera, "Inside the River of Poetry," posted on E-Drum@topica.com, April 22, 2002.

24. Benston, *Performing Blackness*, 3.

25. Ibid., 6.

26. Fahamisha Patricia Brown, *Performing the Word: African American Poetry as Vernacular Culture* (New Brunswick, NJ: Rutgers University Press, 1999), 1.

27. David Lionel Smith, "The Black Arts Movement and Its Critics," *American Literary History* 3: 1 (Spring 1991), 95.

28. Werner, *Playing the Changes*, 106.

29. Amiri Baraka, "The Black Arts Movement," 595.

30. Kalamu ya Salaam, Afterword to *360 Degrees: A Revolution of Black Poets* (New Orleans: Runagate Press, 1998), 203.

31. Gilyard, "Introduction" to *Spirit and Flame*, xix.

32. Ibid.

33. Smith, "Black Arts Movement and Its Critics,"97.

34. Nielsen, *Black Chant*; Lorenzo Thomas' *Extraordinary Measures: Afrocentric Modernism and Twentieth-Century Modernism* (Tuscaloosa: University of Alabama Press, 2000); Werner, *Playing Changes*; Benston, *Performing Blackness*.

35. Robin D. G. Kelley, *Yo Mama's Disfunktional!: Fighting the Culture Wars in Urban America* (Boston: Beacon Press, 1997); Kevin Powell, *Keepin' it Real* (New York: One World Press, 1997); Bakari Kitwana, *The Hip Hop Generation: Young Blacks and the Crisis in African American Culture* (New York: Basic Civitas, 2002); Todd Boyd, *The New H.N.I.C.: The Death of Civil Rights and the Reign of Hip Hop* (New York: New York University Press, 2003).

36. Powell and Baraka, Introduction, *In the Tradition*.

37. Kitwana, *The Hip Hop Generation*, xxi.

38. Baraka, "The Black Arts Movement," 502.

39. Quoted in Gabbin, *The Furious Flowering*, 152.

40. Horace Coleman, "The Black Aesthetic Straitjacket," *Confrontation* 2: 2 (1976).

41. Baraka, "The Black Arts Movement, 503.

42. Haki Madhubuti, "The Generation Now," Introduction to *Role Call*, xv.

43. Baraka, "The Black Arts Movement, 505.

44. Quoted in Werner, *Playing the Changes*, 104; Baraka, "The Black Arts Movement," in Harris, *Jones/Amiri Baraka Reader*, 503.

45. Clarence Major, *The New Black Poetry* (New York: International Publishers, 1969); Abraham Chapman, *New Black Voices* (New York: Penguin, 1972); June Jordan, *Soulscript: Afro-American Poetry* (Garden City, NY: Doubleday, 1970); Dudley Randall, *Black Poets* (New York: Bantam Books, 1971); Arnold Adoff, *The Poetry of Black America* (Newark, NJ: Afroarts Anthology, 1973); Henderson, *Understanding the New Black Poetry*; Eugene B. Redmond, ed., *Drumvoices: The Mission of Afro-American Poetry, A Critical History* (New York: Anchor Books, 1976). Redmond's bibliography gives a good sense of how many anthologies have gone out of print since the mid-1970s.

46. The Marjorie Cook Poetry Festival and Conference at Miami University of Ohio (September 2003), entitled "The Diversity of Contemporary African American Poetry," gave ample evidence of this pluralism in both creative practices and critical approaches.

47. David A. Hollinger, *Postethnic America: Beyond Multiculturalism* (New York: Basic Books, 1995); Leon E. Wynter, *American Skin: Pop Culture, Big Business and the End of White America* (New York: Crown Publishers, 2003). Larry Neal, "The Black Arts Movement" (1968), rpt. in Larry Neal, *Visions of a Liberated Future: Black Arts Movement Writings* (New York: Thunder's Mouth Press, 1989), 62.

48. Amiri Baraka, "The Changing Same (R&B and the New Black Music)" in Harris, *Jones/Amiri Baraka Reader*.

49. Tony Medina, Introduction to Tony Medina and Louis Reyes Rivera, eds., *bum rush the page: a def poetry jam* (New York: Three Rivers Press, 2001), xix.

50. Harryette Mullen, "African Signs and Spirit Writing," *Callaloo* 19: 3 (1996): 671.

51. Asim, "What is This New Thing," 311.

52. Medina, *bum rush*, xx.

53. Sonia Sanchez, foreword to Medina and Rivera, *bum rush*, xv.

54. Medina, *bum rush*, xx.

55. Ras Baraka, "In the Tradition, Too," in Powell and Baraka, *In the Tradition*, 85.

56. Alan Spears, ed., *Fast Talk, Full Volume* (Cabin John, MD: Gut Punch Press, 1993), n.p.

57. devorah major, "nommo: how we come to speak," Medina and Rivera, *bum rush*, 227–29.

58. Werner, *Playing the Changes*, 106.

59. Toni Morrison, "Home," in Wahneema Lubiano, ed., *The House That Race Built: Black Americans, U.S. Terrain* (New York: Pantheon Books, 1997), 8–9; ya Salaam, Afterword to *360 Degrees*, 208.

60. Baker, *Afro-American Poetics*, 11.

Afterword
This Bridge Called
"Our Tradition"

Notes on Blueblack,
'Round'midnight,
Blacklight "Connection"

Houston A. Baker, Jr.

> That night I dreamed I was at a circus with [my grandfather] and that he refused to laugh at the
> clowns no matter what they did. Then later he told me to open my brief case and read what was
> inside and I did, finding an official envelope stamped with the state seal; and inside the envelope
> I found another and another, endlessly, and I thought I would fall of weariness. "Them's years,"
> he said.
> —RALPH ELLISON, *INVISIBLE MAN*, 1952

Editors Lisa Gail Collins and Margo Natalie Crawford, under the title *New Thoughts on the Black Arts Movement*, have done a wonderful scholarly service, producing an outstanding work designed to connect fallen leaves and furiously new flowerings of black insight and talent. The recent Furious Flower Black Poetry Conference convened in the fall of 2004 at James Madison University. It debuted a brilliant documentary film in remembrance of the much heralded 1994 Furious Flower Conference, whose lively artistic and critical interchange led to books, striking video series, poetry collections, and legendary first meetings. In bold colors, the documentary film captures black poets philosophizing, preaching, signifying, hugging, chanting, patting their feet, clapping their hands in righteous harmony to the positive vibrations of the occasion. There was Amiri Baraka trying to out-theorize Askia Touré, Gwendolyn Brooks working her crowd magic in wise and lyrical vibrato, Sonia Sanchez caught in the welcoming smile of Raymond Patterson. Then, without seam or flicker, the documentary segued into a black-and-white "in memoriam" to our "fallen leaves." A hush fell over the audience as gorgeous filmic portraits of Gwendolyn Brooks, June Jordan, Raymond Patterson, Margaret Walker, and others appeared with the dates of their living and death scripted for our witness. One could hear soft breathing from far away rows, and, the gentle sound of weeping.

As the lights came back up, a casual survey of the audience revealed the presence of Eugene Redmond, Askia Touré, Lucille Clifton, Kalamu ya Salaam, and other poets of the Black Arts generation. Clearly energized and on board for this moment, they were ready to enliven and bring venerability to the proceedings. In the same brief survey, it was apparent that literally scores of young and beautiful students were in attendance—some sponsored by savvy mentors like Trudier Harris. An impressive cadre of young black writers sprinkled the audience, a number of whom eagerly responded when the moderator asked for a show of hands from the "young people in the audience who are writers."

The conference organizer Joanne Gabbin had once again worked her magic in Virginia. The lineup of younger poets included: Tony Medina, jessica care moore, Kevin Young, Major Jackson, Thomas Sayers Ellis, and many, many others—some already celebrated, others yet to make their mark. All who viewed the documentary shared a profound, reverential sense of loss. But in the "now" of the conference, and especially in the glad presence of the younger generation, there was a heartening sense that the best of the black arts is, quite astonishingly, yet to come. Leaves have fallen, but a continuation of brilliant black artistry will exist for generations to come. And Lisa Gail Collins and Margo Natalie Crawford have given us with *New Thoughts on the Black Arts Movement* a vital scholarly bridge toward a productive future.

Born in the 1960s and 1970s, our new creative and critical generation is exuberant, talented—and certainly: *rock-the-house amazing!* Even the kinesthetics of their ordinary conversation is poetic. What is most encouraging and striking, however, is their indisputable allegiance to black forebears, some of whom have been lost to them forever. It is, I think, the same sense of "generational connectedness" manifested by the young writers and scholars at the Furious Flower Conference that serves as catalyst and motive force for the outstanding collection of essays presented to us by *New Thoughts on the Black Arts Movement*.

The Black Arts Movement spanned slightly more than a decade from the founding of the Black Arts Repertory Theater/School in Harlem (1965) to the demise of *First World Magazine* in Atlanta (1980). A number of essays in *New Thoughts on the Black Arts Movement* persuasively make clear that the movement has been critically neglected, deliberately ignored, and, at times, cynically dismissed by subsequent generations. The editors mean to: redress the neglect, rebut the cynicism, and complicate our scholarly understanding of the movement. They mean to suture the unfortunate wound of ignorance that has deprived us of a fit understanding of our black artistic past.

The Black Arts Movement emerged in conjunction with a radical shift in strategy and protocols of the black liberation struggle in America. When in the mid-1960s, non-violent, direct action protest yielded to the rhetoric and agenda of Black Power, there seemed to arise a felt need for a "cultural wing," as it were, of the Black Power Movement. What would a "black nation"—one gained through revolutionary action—be without arts, artists, theorists, theories, and aesthetics of a new national (read: "black") culture? Such cultural nationalism was not, of course, new to black America. After all, the Harlem Renaissance of the 1920s, in its own creative engagements with Western modernity, issued many of the same claims for and upon the "black (read: 'Negro') artist" as the Black Arts Movement of the 1960s. What was new about the Black Arts Movement, however, were: its avowed political and revolutionary intentionality, in combination with its ubiquitous national presence. Also unique were the sometimes stunning posts at America's foremost universities occupied by several of the movement's most "revolutionary" members. (One recalls Amiri Baraka furiously lecturing at Yale, and Haki Madhubuti dynamically changing the Negro Mind at Howard University.) The arts were either drawn headlong into the politics of Black Power, or, in the hands and voices of some of their foremost theoreticians and practitioners, they were shaped to contours of what came to be known as the "Black Aesthetic." They willed themselves, in short, to an extreme revolutionary makeover. They unabashedly became propagandistic, fiercely form re-defining, and sometimes sycophantically collaborative with the "baddest kid on the block"—Black Power. In the words of Margo Natalie Crawford, coeditor of *New Thoughts on the Black Arts Movement*: "The black aesthetic of this period was a bold re-visioning of life itself as a work of art dedicated to the advancement of black people . . . . Blackness emerged as a veritable liberation theology: to be free one had to love blackness" (Introduction).

Two of the most problematic issues in the creativity and criticism of the Black Arts Movement were: Can art truly possess a distinctive racial uniqueness? And, should an artist who is phenotypically "black" be compelled to devote herself to an instrumentally revolutionary black cultural production—a "functional" art of the people, as it were? Should, in brief, a person who is merely "young gifted and black" be required to take on the task of changing (revolutionarily) the world through art?

Yet, artists of the Black Arts Movement found reinforcement for their idealism of "change" and their certainty that there was an unequivocal "racial" distinctiveness and energy at work in their culture. They inferred such propositions from witnessing American cities in flame, black urban rebellions proliferating, and the black masses (with utter dignity of pride and person) everywhere proclaiming: "Black is beautiful! And *I'm* black and *I'm* proud!" Surely, such mass black energy—buttressed by canny oratory and stirring political rhetoric of charismatic men like Malcolm X, Stokely Carmichael (Kwame Ture), H. Rap Brown, and others—foretold ineluctable, culturally informed revolution.

After all, Black Power and Black Arts advocates were not alone in their rebellion and revolutionary intent. Progressive revolutionary coalitions and collaborations with anti-war and feminist protesters, Puerto Rican activists and artists, white radical students on campuses across the nation were distinctive features of the times. All seemed involved; all seemed consumed. So, there could be no turning back the black revolution, or, the black aesthetic that would guide, celebrate, map, and artistically record its victories.

Like Black Power, the Black Arts Movement was marked and moved by a productive, often naïve, frequently misogynistic, bold, and sometimes quite fantastical *black idealism*. In fact, such idealism (often, one now knows, a feigned idealism actually in service to almighty white dollars from the Great Society's treasure troves) constituted the unifying force of black political and black artistic energies. But, the relevant, twice-told tale here is of the repressive political regimes of presidents Ronald Reagan, Richard Nixon, George Herbert Walker Bush, and George W. Bush that violently capped all revolutionary idealism in the United States. They capped it as fiercely and decisively as Enron Corporation now imperialistically caps oil wells in militarily occupied deserts, and "caps" as well, secular dissent in the homeland in the name of "national security," or even worse, "patriotism." Some of us feel we live in parlous times—that we inhabit not an age of "national security," but rather one of anti-secularist intolerance for any dissent, much less revolutionary mass protest against social injustice. At first blush, then, one might think it is a very bad era for both the Black Arts and black critical thought in general. And just as we do so, along comes *New Thoughts on the Black Arts Movement* to renew our faith in the creative possibilities of the human spirit.

The collection is committed to documenting and celebrating, in fact, the critical and historical continuities of black thought in America. Idealism is its engine. The book reflects all that is best in the enduring "spirit work" of black life on these American shores. (Bear in mind, in this regard, that *90 percent of black voters in 2004* did not cast their ballots for a repressive regime.)

So much that was complex and heartening and energizing and productive about the Black Arts Movement has never been critically addressed or carefully remembered. (As the famous reggae puts it: "Half the story has never been told!") But, *New Thoughts* means to correct such forgetfulness. Writing of the younger generation of artists and critics like those present at the Furious Flower Conference, one contributor asserts: "The rediscovery and invention of cross-generational ties are a strategic construction serving specific literary, cultural, and political needs at the turn of the twenty-first century, rather than a natural inheritance of essential and immanent blackness, as it is often presented. This constructedness in no way diminishes the intensity of the 'fire' of tradition or its social and political efficacy. A bridge that has been repaired may in fact be stronger than the original" (Lorrie Smith, chap.17).

This seems precisely what is most compelling about *New Thoughts*. It seeks to give back to us from the rude dismissals of interested denigrators, a strong bridge to the past and a "usable tradition." The collection is vital scholarly work, endorsing a Blues God, scripting in handily distributable form so much that so many of us have not known about the Black Arts Movement. For example, the essays devoted to the "Prison Arts Movement" and the "Blues Revival" suggest a greatly enriched context for understanding the allied liberation and rhythmic motions that accompanied the work of such celebrated arts institutions as the Organization of Black American Culture in Chicago, the Black Arts Repertory Theater/School, and the Free Southern Theater. The role of southern black colleges and universities as sites of Black Power and the Black Arts is encyclopedically engaged in nuanced and extraordinary mnemonic ways.

The connections—the bridges and intergenerational energy between Calvin Hernton, Amiri Baraka, A. B. Spellman and an "old school," "Popular Front" black genius like Sterling Brown at Howard University—remind us that the "work" has always been ongoing. As a teenager, Tom Dent watched Benjamin Quarles carving out black history in the basement of the Dillard University library where Tom was shelving books. This was the "intergenerational" making of a black/bluesman/poet, which is precisely what Tom became. (Over bourbon at *Snug Harbor* in "*N'awlings*," he was quick to call to mind and share the shaping influence not only of Quarles, but also of Delta bluesmen and jazz greats a'plenty.)

Photography, color fetishism, and gender complexities that marked the Black Arts Movement are expertly analyzed in the quite stunning efforts of co-editor Margo Natalie Crawford. Black and Puerto Rican cross-fertilization through rhythms, vocabulary, journal production, and the unifying sign "blackness" is especially well addressed in the collection. Cultural institutions, artists' collectives, art strikes, and philosophical musings on the role of "whiteness" in the "constructedness" of the black arts are all taken up in essays meant not simply to make us "remember." They also enrich, expand, and complicate our memories of a time in black artistic tradition when men and women occupied front lines of urban, intellectual, artistic struggle, and were not afraid to dream a revolution.

"Far from being the 'shortest and least successful' movement in African American cultural history, as Henry Louis Gates, Jr., has provocatively claimed," writes one contributor to *New Thoughts*, "the decade-long Black Arts Movement has had a broad and enduring impact on African American literature. It has remade that literature as a blues-toned legacy—unabashedly invested in, and supremely conscious of, its own southern-born vernacular taproot, a jook-honed survivor's ethos of self-willed mobility, self-determined personhood, and bittersweetly lyric self-inscription" (Gussow, chap. 11). *New Thoughts on the Black Arts Movement* is a lyrical, blues-inflected bridge of critical memory that ensures our "fallen leaves" will not be forgotten; it is a volume that guarantees furious flowers of thought, creativity, theory, methodology, criticism, and critique will continue as the spirit work of our future. The collection is a glad addition to the "black light" in our canons of thought. It comes at just the right moment, when our faith so palpably needs renewing. *Ashe.*

NOTES ON CONTRIBUTORS

Houston A. Baker, Jr. is a native of Louisville, Kentucky. He received his B.A. (magna cum laude and Phi Beta Kappa) from Howard University. He received his M.A. and Ph.D. degrees from UCLA. He has taught at Yale, the University of Virginia, and the University of Pennsylvania. Currently, he is the Susan Fox and George D. Beischer Professor of English at Duke University. He is the editor of *American Literature*, the oldest and most prestigious journal in American literary studies. Professor Baker began his career as a scholar of British Victorian literature, but made a career shift to the study of Afro-American literature and culture. He has published or edited more than twenty books and is the author of more than eighty articles, essays, and reviews. His most recent books include *Turning South Again: Re-Thinking Modernism, Re-Reading Booker T* (Duke University Press, 2001) and *Critical Memory: Public Spheres, African American Writing and Black Fathers and Sons in America* (University of Georgia Press, 2001). He is a published poet whose most recent title is *Passing Over* (Lotus Press, 2000). He has served in a number of administrative and institutional posts, including the 1992 Presidency of the Modern Language Association of America. His honors include Guggenheim, John Hay Whitney, and Rockefeller Fellowships, as well as eleven honorary degrees from American colleges and universities.

Emily Bernard is an assistant professor in the English department at the University of Vermont. She is the editor of two books: *Remember Me to Harlem: The Letters of Langston Hughes and Carl Van Vechten (1925–1964)* (Alfred A. Knopf, 2001) and *Some of My Best Friends: Writings on Interracial Friendship* (Amistad/HarperCollins, 2004).

Lee Bernstein is an assistant professor of history at SUNY New Paltz specializing in crime and punishment in U.S. history and culture. He is the author of *The Greatest Menace: Organized Crime in Cold War America* (University of Massachusetts Press, 2002).

He is currently at work on a book titled "'America is the Prison': A Cultural History of Prisons in 1970s America" (University of North Carolina Press, forthcoming).

LISA GAIL COLLINS is Class of 1951 Associate Professor in Art History and Africana Studies at Vassar College. She is the author of *The Art of History: African American Women Artists Engage the Past* (Rutgers University Press, 2002). She is also co-author (with Lisa Mintz Messinger) of *African-American Artists, 1929–1945: Prints, Drawings, and Paintings in the Metropolitan Museum of Art* (Metropolitan Museum of Art, in association with Yale University Press, 2003). Her essays appear in *Chicago Art Journal, Exposure, Feminist Teacher, Colors, Rutgers Art Review*, and *International Review of African American Art*.

MARGO NATALIE CRAWFORD is an assistant professor of African American literature and culture in the department of English at Indiana University. *Rewriting Blackness: Beyond Authenticity and Hybridity* is forthcoming from Ohio State University Press. She is now completing *Mother to Son: Gwendolyn Brooks and Haki Madhubuti* (Third World Press), a reevaluation of what the "mother tongue" meant in Black Arts cultural nationalism.

ERINA DUGANNE received her Ph.D. in 2004 from the department of art and art history at the University of Texas at Austin. She received her B.A. from Reed College. She is currently the Mellon Postdoctoral Fellow in the History of Photography in the Art Department at Williams College.

ADAM GUSSOW is an assistant professor of English and southern studies at the University of Mississippi. A professional blues harmonicist (please don't say "white bluesman"), he spent twelve years performing and recording with "Satan and Adam," a Harlem-based duo. His books include *Mister Satan's Apprentice: A Blues Memoir* (Pantheon, 1998) and *Seems Like Murder Here: Southern Violence and the Blues Tradition* (University of Chicago, 2002). His current project is entitled "Dreams of Beloved Community: Racial Healing in Contemporary America."

ROD HERNANDEZ is a writer and scholar specializing in twentieth-century American literature and culture, particularly the work of ethnic authors and urban literary communities. His articles have appeared in *The Américas Review, Callaloo*, and *XCP: Cross Cultural Poetics*. He is an assistant professor of English at California State University, Dominguez Hills.

KELLIE JONES is an assistant professor of history of art and African American studies at Yale University. Her recent publications include "(un)Seen and Overheard: Pictures by Lorna Simpson," in *Lorna Simpson* (Phaidon, 2002) and "Tracey Rose: Post-Apartheid Playground," in *FRESH: 7 Young South African Artists at the South African National Gallery* (2003). Her writings have also appeared in *NKA, Artforum, Flash Art, Atlantica*, and *Third Text*. She is currently at work on a book on African American artists in Los Angeles in the 1960s and 1970s.

MARY ELLEN LENNON received her Ph.D. in the history of American civilization from Harvard University in 2002. Her research centers on American movements of social protest. She now teaches in Harvard's History and Literature Program.

ALONDRA NELSON teaches African American studies and sociology at Yale University. She is co-editor, with Thuy Linh N. Tu, of *Technicolor: Race, Technology and Everyday Life* (New York University Press, 2001) and editor of *Afrofuturism: Speculative Imagery, Futurist Themes and Technological Innovation in the African Diaspora* (Duke University Press). She is presently at work on a manuscript about late-twentieth-century African American health advocacy around issues of genetic disease, medicalized models of social unrest, and reproductive rights, titled "Black Body Politics: African American Health Social Movements and Biomedical Knowledge."

CHERISE A. POLLARD is an assistant professor of English at West Chester University of Pennsylvania. Specializing in late-twentieth-century African American literature and cultural studies, she has written articles and presented her research at many national and international conferences on a range of topics, including the sexual politics of neo-blaxploitation films, working-class issues in black women's poetry, and the complexities of representing black bondswomen's experiences in recent historical novels. A poet, she is a member of Cave Canem.

JAMES SMETHURST is an associate professor in the W.E.B. Du Bois Department of Afro-American Studies at the University of Massachusetts-Amherst. He is the author of *The New Red Negro: The Literary Left and African-American Poetry, 1930–1946* (Oxford University Press, 1999) and *The Black Arts Movement: Literary Nationalism in the 1960s and 1970s* (University of North Carolina Press, 2005). He is also the co-editor of *Left of the Color Line: Race, Radicalism, and Twentieth-Century Literature of the United States* (University of North Carolina Press, 2003).

CHERISE SMITH is an assistant professor in the department of art and art history at the University of Texas at Austin. She received her Ph.D. from Stanford University where she wrote a dissertation titled "En-Acting 'Others': Ethnic, Gender, and Racial Performance in Works by Adrian Piper, Eleanor Antin, and Anna Deavere Smith." She has worked in a number of museums, curated several exhibitions, and authored essays that appear in *Fotofile*, *Museum Studies*, and *Let My People Go: Cairo, Illinois 1967–1973: Civil Rights Photographs* (Southern Illinois University Press, 1996).

LORRIE SMITH is professor of English and American studies at Saint Michael's College in Colchester, Vermont. She writes and teaches courses on race and culture, African American literature, American poetry, and the literature of the Middle Passage. Her essay is part of a book-in-progress entitled "'Report from Vernacular Valleys': Post-Sixties Black Poetry and the Public Sphere."

WENDY S. WALTERS has published articles in *TDR* and has work forthcoming in *Crossing Waters, Crossing Borders* (Duke University Press). Recent poems have been published in or are forthcoming in *The Seneca Review, The Yalobusha Review, Sou'wester, Spinning Jenny, American Poetry Journal, Nocturnes (Re)view,* and *Callaloo*. Ms. Walters has received grants from the Rhode Island School of Design (RISD), the Mary Cary Flagler Charitable Trust, the Smithsonian Institution, and the Ford Foundation, and participated in residencies at MacDowell, Cave Canem and Yaddo. She is an assistant professor of English at RISD.

MICHELLE JOAN WILKINSON completed her Ph.D. at Emory University, where her primary area of research was black and Latino cultural studies. Prior to her current position as an exhibition consultant at the Smithsonian American Art Museum, she was a postdoctoral fellow at the same institution. She has worked as a curatorial consultant at the National Gallery of Art and as editor and library coordinator at The Studio Museum in Harlem. From 1999 to 2002, she was an assistant professor of literature at Bard College. Ms. Wilkinson's articles and reviews have been published in *Revue Noire, Black Issues Book Review,* and *AHA! Hispanic Arts New.*

INDEX

NOTE: italicized numbers indicate illustration page references.

Abernathy, Billy. *See* Fundi
Abernathy, Sylvia. *See* Laini
Adal, 333
Adoff, Arnold, 360
Agee, James, 207n25
Agee, William, 103
Aguila, Pancho, 316n58
Ahmad, Muhammad, 76, 77
Alegría, Carmen, 333
Alegría, Fernando, 333
Alegría, Isabel, 333
Alexander, Kwame, 362
Algarín, Miguel, 319, 328
Allen, Samuel, 349
Allison, Bernard, 239
Allison, Luther, 237, 246
alternative arts/cultural institutions: African Free School, 39n4; AFRI-COBRA (African Commune of Bad Relevant Artists), 10, 15, 24, 44, 67n5, 290–292; Affro Arts Theater, 35, 88, 90n6; Afro American Association, 44; Art West Associated, 46, 53, 56; Art Workers' Coalition, 106, 107, 109, 110, 111; Association for the Advancement of Creative Musicians (AACM), 27, 44; Black Arts Council (BAC), 53–55, 56; Black Arts Repertory Theater/School (BARTS), 11, 15, 18n45, 24, 44, 76, 144, 227, 275, 277–278, 279, 282, 370, 373; Black Arts/West Theater, 76, 304; Black Emergency Cultural Coalition (BECC), 53, 70–71n51 105, 106, 301; Black House, 304; BLKART-SOUTH, 11, 18n45, 65, 88, 89n6; Boone House, 121; Boricua Artists Guild, 332n48; Brockman Gallery, 53, 55, 56; Center for Black Art, 86; Concept East Theater, 120; Detroit Artist's Workshop, 120–121; Feminist Art Program, 277–278, 280, 282, 283, 289; Free Southern Theater, 76, 77, 373; Gallery 32, 53, 55–56; Gathering of the Tribes, 352; Guerilla Art Action, 107; Hammonds House, 89; Harlem Cultural Council, 104–105; Heresies Collective, 285–286; Institute of the Black World, 86; Kamoinge Gallery, 201, 208n39; Kamoinge Workshop, 188–190, 207n23; MUSEUM,

alternative arts/cultural institutions (*continued*)
106; Museum of African American Art, 57–58; National Center of Afro-American Artists, 300; Neighborhood Arts Center, 52; Nommo collective, 352; Operation Discovery, Inc., 102; Organization of Afro-American Unity (OAAU), 17n15, 275; Organization of Black American Culture (OBAC), 11, 18n45, 25, 27, 35, 67n5, 76, 286, 287, 349, 373; Otis Art Institute, 46; People's Poetry workshops, 352; Queens Storefront Museum, 102; Recovery Theater, 304; Southern Black Cultural Alliance, 90n6; Spirit House, 11, 18n45, 24, 144, 282, 352; Studio Museum in Harlem, 101, 102, 103, 290, 297, 301; Studio O, 102; Studio Z, 62, 63; Sudan Arts Southwest, 88, 89n6; The Gallery, 53, 57–58; Umbra Poets Workshop, 14–15, 76, 319, 321; US Organization, 44, 45, 47, 65, 67n6, 94, 276; Watts Towers Arts Center, 48, 52–53; Watts Writers' Workshop, 46; Writers Club, 352; Weusi Nyumba ya Sanaa, 102. *See also* art institutions/museums

American Association of Museums, 102, 108, 109

American Indian Movement, 14

Amini, Johari, 122

Andrews, Benny, 105, 106, 297, 301, 302, 311

Anti-Vietnam War Movement, 14

Arnold, Kokomo, 245

art criticism: racial bias of, 93, 98

art institutions/museums: entrenched racism of, 93, 106. *See also* alternative arts/cultural institutions; "Harlem on My Mind"; entries for individual associations/museums

Art Strike. *See* Whitney Museum of American Art

Asim, Jabari, 351, 361

Atkins, Juan, 129

Aubert, Alvin, 122

Avotcja, 333, 340–343

Ayler, Albert, 227

Baca, Jimmy Santiago, 299

Bakari, Kitwana, 352, 357

Baldwin, James, 159, 263–264, 267, 353; *Tell Me How Long the Train's Been Gone*, 158–160, 163–164, 167, 168, 169, 171n16, 171–172n24. *See also* Baraka, Amiri

Ball, Marcia, 230

Bambara, Toni Cade, 65, 274

Banks, Mad Mike, 130

Baraka, Amina, 39n4

Baraka, Amiri (LeRoi Jones), 84, 121, 264, 349, 353, 365n11, 369, 371; black aesthetic and, 110, 173, 175; Black Arts Repertory Theater/School (BARTS) and, 18n45, 275, 279; black colleges/universities and, 77, 81, 83; blackness and, 10, 11, 165, 166–167, 317, 355; Black Power/cultural nationalism and, 5, 44, 76, 144, 269, 281, 315n51; the blues and, 228, 229, 231, 232, 233–234, 248; cross-generational connections and, 350, 360, 362, 373; Felipe Luciano and, 321, 326; as founder of Black Arts Movement, 225n33, 282; incarceration of, 303–304; Malcolm X and, 5, 151n47, 263, 270n29, 275, 276; music and, 152n54, 354; sexism/misogyny and, 176, 185n17; Spirit House and, 18n45, 39n4, 352; white power/whiteness and, 8, 10, 261, 266. *See also*, Baldwin, James; Black Power Movement; Neal, Larry

Baraka, Amiri (works of): *A Black Mass*, 18n35, 137–140, 143–148, 152nn58-59; "Black Art," 305; "The Black Arts Movement," 358–359; *Black Magic*, 16, 18n35; *In Our Terribleness*, 10, 11, 24, 29, 31, 35, 155, 156, 158, 162, 167, 169. 170; *Raise Race Rays Raze*, 258, 262, 304; "SOS," 16, 29, 258–259

Baraka, Ras, 351, 352, 357–358, 362

Barrett, Lindsay, 30
Bashir, Samiya A., 363
Battle, Joe Von, 117, 121
Baur, John I. H., 103
Baxter, Carolyn, 308
Beal, Francis, 274
Bearden, Romare, 97, 98, 100, 105
Beauvoir, Simone de. *See* Women's
    Liberation Movement
Bims, Hamilton, 236
Bin Hassan, Umar, 331n41
black aesthetic/"Black is Beautiful," 35,
    43, 94–95, 204, 240, 287, 290–292,
    318–319, 371; black female body
    and, 155, 162, 166, 167; "black light"
    and, 16, 30–34; black male body and,
    160–162, 167, 170; critiques of, 96;
    principles of, 95–96, 97, 98–100, 109,
    175; social/political responsibility and,
    96, 189, 371. *See also* Baraka, Amiri;
    Brooks, Gwendolyn; Karenga, Mau-
    lana Ron; Neal, Larry; Madhubuti,
    Haki
Black Arts Festival, 89
Black Christian Nationalists, 121
black colleges/universities: Alabama
    A & T, 80, 88; Atlanta University,
    78, 86; Central State University, 75,
    79, 82; Cheney Training School for
    Teachers, 75; Clark College, 86; Fisk
    University 78, 79, 81, 83, 88; How-
    ard University, 75, 80, 81, 82, 84, 88;
    Jackson State, 85, 88; Lincoln Univer-
    sity, 75; Morehouse College, 79, 86;
    Morgan State University, 75; Morris
    Brown College, 86; North Carolina
    A & T, 85; South Carolina State,
    85; Southern University, 79, 85, 88;
    Spelman College, 86; Tougaloo Col-
    lege, 77, 88; conservatism of, 78–79;
    Left intellectuals and, 79–80, 83; left-
    ist international students and, 81–82.
    See also Black Power Movement; Civil
    Rights Movement
Black Feeling, Black Talk, Black Judgement
    (Giovanni), 18n35, 173–174,
    179–180
Black Fire (Jones and Neal, eds.), 9, 11,
    12, 16, 30, 169, 170, 173–174, 176,
    178, 266
Black Liberation Army, 95
Black Liberation Front, 94
Black nationalism. *See* Black Power
    Movement
Black Panther Party, 4, 15, 44, 45, 65, 94,
    107, 240, 319
Black Poetry Festivals (Southern Univer-
    sity), 85
Black Power Movement, 4, 9, 85, 93, 94,
    240; Black Arts Movement and, 7, 76,
    318, 370–371; Black nationalism and,
    5, 6, 35, 120, 274, 275; Civil Rights
    Movement and, 76, 77; homopho-
    bia and, 12, 176; homosexuality and,
    159–160; Kerner Commission Report
    and, 3, 5; Malcolm X and, 275–276;
    parallel liberation movements and,
    14, 15; prisons and, 303, 304; sexism
    of, 12, 183; the sexual revolution and,
    159; the South and, 4, 84, 76–77;
    Women's Liberation Movement and,
    273, 278–279, 292, 293. *See also* black
    colleges/universities; Black Panther
    Party
Black Student Movement, 80, 82
Black Studies, 86
BlackWords, 359
Black Writers Conferences (Fisk), 79,
    83–84. *See also* black colleges/universi-
    ties
Blackstone Rangers, 349
Blauner, Robert, 97
Blayton, Betty, 111
Bloomfield, Mike, 235
Bohanon, Gloria, 56
Bond, Julian, 80
Bontemps, Arna, 83
Booker, Claude, 53, 55
Bourke-White, Margaret, 192
Boyd, Melba, 122
Boyd, Todd, 357
Broadside Press, 131, 349; founding/ori-
    gins of, 14, 44, 83, 121; literary vision
    of, 122–123; Motown Records and,

Broadside Press (*continued*)
118, 119, 120, 126, 128, 130. *See also*
Randall, Dudley
Brooks, Gwendolyn, 27, 30, 31, 34,
35, 121, 363; black aethetic/"Black
is Beautiful" and, 27–28, 36–38,
168–169, 170n5; "black light" and,
30–34; Black Power/Black Arts and,
27, 83–84, 349; Organization of Black
American Culture (OBAC) and, 18n45,
25; prison writers/writing and, 297,
309, 311; "The Wall," 27, 33. *See also*
Madhubuti, Haki; *Wall of Respect*
Brown, Ed, 82, 84
Brown, Elaine, 47, 65
Brown, H. Rap, 4, 84, 117, 371
Brown, James, 11, 25, 105, 231, 343
Brown, Sterling, 79, 80, 81, 84, 355, 373
Bullins, Ed, 11, 12
Bunker, Edward, 303
Burnham Louis, 80
Burroughs, Margaret, 80, 83
Bush, George Herbert Walker, 372
Bush, George W., 372
Butterfield, Paul, 235, 239, 240

Caldwell, Ben, 228
Caldwell, Erskine, 192
Campbell, W. Reason, 313n8
Canned Heat, 243
Cannon, Steve, 352
Cardenal, Ernesto, 333
Carmichael, Stokely (Kwame Ture), 3,
25, 82, 84, 246, 371
Cartier-Bresson, Henri, 201, 208n36,
218
Castillo, Otto Rene, 333
Castro, Fidel, 143
Catlett, Elizabeth, 55, 110
Césaire, Aimé, 275
Chandler, Dana, 110
Chapman, Abraham, 359
Charters, Samuel, 245
Chicago Black Arts Movement, 23, 27,
35, 38; photography and, 23, 30. *See
also* Brooks, Gwendolyn; Madhubuti,
Haki; *Wall of Respect*

Chicago, Judy (Judy Cohen/Gerowitz),
277–278, 280, 282, 285, 289; "female
imagery" and, 289–290; and *Woman-
house*, 282. *See also* alternative arts/
cultural institutions; Women's Libera-
tion Movement
Chicano Movement, 14
Christian, Barbara T., 333
Christmas, Edward, 29–30
Chuck D, 360
Civil Rights Movement, 46, 76, 77–78,
80, 82, 94
Clapton, Eric, 241
Clarke, John Henrik, 83, 143
Clayton, Willie, 248
Cleaver, Eldridge, 52, 138, 160, 165,
171n17, 263–264, 302, 330n14
Cleaver, Kathleen, 65
Cliff, Michelle, 167
Clifton, Lucille, 370
Cobb, Charlie, 84
Coleman, Ornette, 26
Coleman, Wanda, 47
Coltrane, John, 227, 234
Concholar, Dan, 55
Cone, James, 228, 232, 233
Congress of African Peoples, 88
Congress of Racial Equality (CORE), 3,
78, 81, 121
Conwill, Houston, 58, 60–61, 63, 65, 66
Conwill, Kinshasha, 60–61, 64, 65, 66,
71n61, 73n87
Conyers, John, 120
Copeland, Shamekia, 239, 247
Cortés, Felix, 320–321
Cortez, Jayne, 46, 47, 78, 228, 232
Cotton, Libba, 246
Cottrol, Robert, 191, 192, *192*
Cowherd, Darrell, 33
Cox, Courtland, 84
Crawford, Bob, *12*, 30, 35, *37*, 38; black
nationalism and, 155, 156, *156*, 157,
157, 170–171n8; blackness/black
beauty and, 158, *158*, 160–163, *161*,
162, *163*, *164*, 165, 169; the *Wall of
Respect/Wall of Truth* and, 25, 26, 27,
28, *29*, *34*, *36*

Crouch, Stanley, 47, 228, 232, 233, 236
Cruse, Harold, 143, 261, 262
Cruz, Victor Hernández, 15, 318, 321–325, 328–329, 331n35, 331n38, 331n40, 332n48, 333, 335–340
Cullen, Countee, 255–257, 260, 262, 263, 317
Cybotron, 129–130

Daaood, Kamau, 47
Dalton, Roque, 333
Danner, Margaret, 41n26, 80, 83, 120–121, 123, 349
Davidson, Bruce, 194, 195, *196*, 197, *197*, 198–199, 208n34
Davis, Alonzo, 46, 55, 71n55
Davis, Angela, 65, 228, 274, 302, 308, 310, 345
Davis, Benjamin, 82
Davis, Dale, 46, 55
Davis, Guy, 229
Davis, Ossie, 83
Davis, Thulani, 333
Debs, Eugene, 302
DeCarava, Roy, 24, 187–188, 205n2
Def Poetry Jam, 359
De Legall, Walter, 84
Dennis, Gene, 82
Dent, Tom, 18n45, 78, 81, 90n7, 228, 236, 319, 321, 373
DePillars, Murray, 5
Detroit: and *Blacktronic Science*, 127–128, *128–129*; commercial development in, 119; the Heidelberg Project and, 126–127
Detroit League of Revolutionary Workers, 121
Diggs, Charles, 120
Dixon, Melvin, 189
DJ Renegade, 355
DJ Spooky, 350
Dodson, Owen, 79
Donaldson, Jeff, 52, 85, 225n33; AFRI-COBRA and, 15, 290–291; black aesthetic/Blackness and, 10–11, 286; the *Wall of Respect* and, 24–25, 26, 27,
38, 39n6, 41n31, 42nn40-42. *See also* Brooks, Gwendolyn; Madhubuti, Haki
Dooley, Ebon, 78, 88–89
Douglas, Emory, 56, 57
Douglass, Frederick, 64
Draper, Louis, 188–189, 190–194, *191*, 206n11, 208n36
Drexciya, 130
Driskell, David, 54
Du Bois, Shirley Graham, 80
Du Bois, W.E.B., 78, 80
Dumas, Henry, 228, 232
Dunn, Donald "Duck," 235

Ebony magazine, 35, 211, 212, 213, 216, 222, 223n7, 224n12
Edwards, David Honeyboy, 229
Edwards, Melvin, 46, 60, 66
El Hadi, Suliaman, 331n41
Ellis bookstore, 35
Ellis, Thomas Sayers, 370
Ellis, Trey, 360
Ellison, Ralph, 336, 340
Emmanuel, James A., 122
Environmental Movement, 14
Espada, Martin, 320, 321, 322
Estes, Sleepy John, 246
Esteves, Sandra Maria, 328
Evans, Emory, 47
Evans, Mari, 80, 350
Evans, Ojenke, 47
Evans, Walker, 192, 193, *193*, 194, 207n25
Everett, Chestyn, 46, 66
Everett, Ron. *See* Karenga, Maulana Ron

Fabio, Sarah Webster, 81
Fabre, Geneviève, 320
Falcón, Angel, 320–321
Feminist Art Movement, 15
Fennar, Albert, 188, 206n11
Fergerson, Cecil, 53, 55
Figueroa, José Angel, 328, 332n48
Fisher, Rudolf, 168
Flores, Juan, 320–321, 322, 336
Flowers, Arthur, 228

Frankenstein, 139–140, 141, 146, 152nn57-58
Franklin, Aretha, 105, 231
Freedom Now Party, 121
Fuller, Hoyt, 18n45, 87, 95, 263, 349
Fundi (Billy Abernathy), 24, 30, 31, 33, 155, 158
Furious Flower Black Poetry Conference, 369, 370, 372

Galassi, Peter, 189
Gammon, Reginald, 221, *222*
García, Rupert, 333
Garon, Paul, 243
Garvey, Marcus, 25, 94
Gayle, Addison, Jr., 96–97, 173, 174, 175, 258, 260, 261
Gay Liberation Front, 107
Gay Liberation Movement, 14
Gee, Lethonia, 179
Ghent, Henri, 103, 104, 111
Gibson, Ray, 189
Gilbert, Derrick I. M. (D-Knowledge), 354, 362
Gilliam, Sam, 100, 101
Gilyard, Keith, 353, 357, 362
Ginsberg, Allen, 339
Giovanni, Nikki, 65, 83, 122, 173, 174, 262, 350; *Black Feeling, Black Talk, Black Judgement*, 18n35, 173–174, 179–180; the blues and, 228, 232; sexism/sexual imagery and, 12, 179, 180–181, 182–183. *See also* Sanchez, Sonia
Goldman, Albert, 239–240
Goncalves, Dingane Joe, 78, 154
Goodman, Paul, 299
Gordy, Berry, 123–124, 125, 130
Govan, Oswald, 84
Graham, Donald Lee (Le Graham), 83, 85, 88
Great Gatsby, The, 338
Great Migration, 65
Greene, Carroll, 53
Griffin, Ada, 265
Guggenheim Museum, 106
Guillén, Nicholás, 333
Gunn, Bill, 153n65

Guy, Buddy, 238, 246
Guyton, Tyree. *See* Detroit

Hammons, David, 52, 53, 55, 59, 60, 63, 65, 66, 73n83; conceptual art and, 58, 59–60, 61, 72n68, 72n79; *Injustice Case*, 53, *54*, 59
Harding, Vincent, 86
Harlem Renaissance/New Negro Movement, 259–260, 265, 268, 317, 371; black aesthetic/blackness and, 168, 256, 257, 258, 262; Black Arts participants' attitudes toward, 13–14, 261
Harper, Michael, 228
Harpo, Slim, 345
Harris, Corey, 229, 249n3
Harris, Trudier, 370
Hart, Kevin Youngblood, 247
Hassinger, Maren, 58, 61–62, 63, 65, 66, 73n83
Havens, Richie, 246
Hayden, Robert, 83, 84, 121
Henderson, David, 228, 321, 333
Henderson, Stephen, 85, 86, 87, 88, 175, 320, 360; black aesthetic and, 175, 353; the blues and, 228, 232, 248; and white appropriations of black culture, 234–235, 236, 238, 239–240, 247
Henderson-Holmes, Safiya, 363
Hendrix, Jimi, 241
Hernton, Calvin, 81, 85, 176, 235, 237, 238, 321, 373
Heron, Gil Scott, 360
Hewitt, Mary Jane, 58, 71n61
Hill, Z. Z., 248
Hinton, James, 187, 188, 204, 205n2
Hoffman, Abbie, 107
Hogu, Barbara Jones, 290, 291
Holiday, Billie, 25, 105
Hooker, Earl, 245
Hopkins, Lightnin', 237
House, Son, 234, 237
Hoving, Thomas, 104, 105, 107, 109
Howlin' Wolf, 237, 246
Huggins, Ericka, 302, 308
Hughes, Langston, 24, 121, 123, 247, 333, 339–340, 350; black vernacu-

lar and, 354, 355; homosexuality of, 265–266, 267; "The Negro Artist and the Racial Mountain," 38, 255–256, 257, 260, 262, 263, 268, 353

Hunt, Richard, 98, 99, 100

Hunter, Elliot, 26

Hurston, Zora Neale, 257, 355

Husock, Habel, 237–238, 244

Hutto, J. B., 246

Injustice Case (Hammons), 53, *54*, 59

Jaaber, Hajj Heesham, 281

Jackson, Esther Cooper, 80

Jackson, George, 302, 303

Jackson, John, 246

Jackson, Mae, 242

Jackson, May, 122

Jackson, Maynard, 88

Jackson, Suzanne, 55–56, 71n58

James, Skip, 245

Jarrell, Wadsworth, 85, 290, 291

Javitts, Jacob, 108

Jeffers, Lance, 79, 122

Jemison, Jan, 57

Jewish Museum, 108

Jim Crow laws, 66, 75, 84

Johnson, Charles, 129

Johnson, Jack, 110

Johnson, John, 224n11

Johnson, Lyndon B., 1, 4–5, 8. *See also* National Advisory Commission on Civil Disorders; Kerner Commission

Johnson, Roberta Ann, 303

Johnston, Percy, 84

Jones, Gayle, 228

Jones, LeRoi. *See* Baraka, Amiri

Jones, Sir Charles, 248

Joplin, Janis, 235, 238, 239, 240, 243

Jordan, June, 65, 274, 350, 352, 359–360, 362, 369

Joseph, Allison, 228

Julien, Isaac, 265

Kahn, Tom, 82

Kain, Gaylan, 325, 331n41

Karenga, Maulana Ron (Ron Everett), 44, 47, 188, 276; black aesthetic and, 194, 204, 220–221, 281, 285, 302; the blues and, 228, 231, 233, 243, 244, 248

Keil, Charles, 245

Kelley, Melvin, 83

Kelley, Robin D. G., 357

Kerner Commission, 5, 6–7; Report of, 1, 2, 8, 237

Kerouac, Jack, 339

Kgositsile, Keorapetse, 85, 88, 177

Killens, John O., 79, 83

Kilson, Martin, 96

King, Albert, 241

King, B. B., 229, 231, 237, 238, 243, 245, 246

King, Chris Thomas, 230–231

King, Martin Luther, Jr., 79, 110, 211, 302

King, Woodie, Jr., 120

Kitt, Eartha, 35

Knight, Etheridge, 95, 121–122, 232, 297, 309, 311, 350

Komunyakaa, Yusef, 228

Kramer, Hilton, 104

Kujichagulia, Imani, 308–309

Laedele X, 88

Laini (Sylvia Abernathy), 24

Lang, James A. 307–308, 310–311

Lang, Jonny, 238

Lansana, Quraysh Ali, 363

Last Poets/Original Last Poets, 15, 319, 321, 325, 331n41, 360

Laviera, Tato, 328

Lavong, Reggie, 232

Lawrence, Jacob, 98, 99, 100

Lay, Sam, 235

League for Industrial Democracy, 82

Lee, Alvin, 243

Lee, Don L. *See* Madhubuti, Haki

Lee, Russell, 24

Leigh-Taylor, Elizabeth, 56

Lewis, Elma, 300–301, 302, 311

Lewis, Fred, 102, 103

Lewis, Furry, 246

Lewis, Norman, 101

Lewis, Roy, 33

Lewis, Samella, 56–58, 71nn60-62

Lippard, Lucy, 278, 282–283, 283–285, 286, 287, 288

Lipscomb, Mance, 229, 246

Little Milton, 248

Llorens, David, 78

Lloyd, Tom, 97, 98–99, 100–101, 106, 109, 110, 111

Locke, Alain, 168, 260

Lockwood, Robert Junior, 238

Lomax, Alan, 245

Long, Richard, 87

Lorde, Audre, 85, 122, 155, 274, 350

Luciano, Felipe, 15, 19n56, 318, 321, 325–329, 331n41, 332n48

Lyle, K. Curtis, 47

Madhubuti, Haki (Don L. Lee), 16, 18n45, 23, 76, 78, 85, 121, 167, 309, 363, 371; black aesthetic/blackness and, 10, 11, 12–13, 28, 32–33, 36–38, 114n23, 168, 173, 175, 321, 359; "black light" and, 30–34; Gwendolyn Brooks and, 27–28, 349, 352; jazz/ the blues and, 228, 231–232, 234, 235, 238, 360; sexism of, 175, 184n12; Third World Press and, 14, 35. *See also Wall of Respect*

Magic Sam, 237, 245

Major, Clarence, 122, 306, 359

major, devorah, 363–364

Malcolm X, 64, 69n30, 105, 138, 141, 203, 301, 312; assassination of, 5–6, 144; Black nationalism/cultural revolution and, 4, 5, 6, 17n15, 25, 44, 95, 275–276, 371; incarceration of, 301, 302, 314n19. *See also* Baraka, Amiri; Nation of Islam; Neal, Larry

Maltheus, John, 168

March Against Fear, 3

Margolin, Bob, 238–239

Marjorie Cook Poetry Festival and Conference, 366n46

Martin Luther King, Jr. Memorial Center, 86

Marvin X, 122, 304

Mason, Philip Lindsay, 110

Matos, Luis Pales, 333

May, Derrick, 129

Mayfield, Julian, 185n21

McCannon, Dindga, 109–110

McDowell, Fred, 246

Medina, Tony, 350, 361, 363–364, 370

Melendez, Jesus Papoleto, 328

Mendel, Gregor, 140, 142

Meo, Yvonne Cole, 56

Meredith, James, 3

Metropolitan Museum of Art, 97, 104, 108, 109; "Harlem on My Mind" exhibition of, 104–106, 202, 301

Miles, Buddy, 235

Millett, Kate, 107

Milner, Ron, 83, 120, 349

Mitchell, Lofton, 83

Monroe, Arthur, 333

Montgomery, E. J., 56, 71n59

Moore, Jessica Care, 350, 370

Moreno, Dorinda, 343–345

Morgan, Robin, 286

Morganfield, Big Bill, 239

Morris, Robert, 107

Morris, Tracie, 360

Morrison, Toni, 65, 84, 165–166, 167, 228, 267, 364

Mos Def, 350, 360

Motown Records, 117–118, 119, 120, 123–126, 128, 130, 131

Mullen, Harryette, 228, 247, 360

Murguía, Alejandro, 333

Murray, Albert, 247

Museum of Modern Art (MOMA), 106–107, 108

NAACP Youth Council, 76

Nalija, 331n41

Nation of Islam (NOI), 64, 82, 121, 132n12, 301, 314n19; scientism of, 142–143; Yakub myth of, 138, 140–143, 144, 147, 150n18

National Advisory Commission on Civil Disorders, 1, 3, 8
National Association for the Advancement of Colored People (NAACP), 3, 121
National Urban League, 121
Neal, Larry, 76, 86, 112n5, 147, 279, 305–306, 350, 354; black aesthetic/blackness and, 16, 19n60, 30, 32, 95, 96, 155, 173, 175, 204, 205–206n7, 283, 285, 286–287, 292, 360; black colleges/universities and, 77–78, 81; *Black Fire* and, 178, 353; the blues and, 228, 232, 233, 241, 242, 243–244, 245, 248; cultural nationalism/revolution and, 7–8, 113n7, 193, 220, 260, 274; definition of the Black Arts Movement and, 137, 183n1, 261, 281–282, 318; Malcolm X and, 5–6, 276; sexism of, 175, 184n11. *See also* Baraka, Amiri; *Black Fire;* Black Power Movement
"Negro Artist and the Racial Mountain, The" (Hughes), 38, 255–256, 257, 260, 262, 263, 268, 353
Negro Digest/Black World, 35, 221, 223n7
Nelson, David, 325, 331n41
Ncngudi, Scnga, 56, 58, 61, 62–64, *63*, 65, 66
Neruda, Pablo, 333
New Negro Movement. *See* Harlem Renaissance
Newton, Huey P., 44, 165, 302, 303
Ngafua, Zizwe, 363
Nixon, Richard, 372
Non-Violent Action Group (NAG), 81, 82, 84
Nuriddin, Jalal, 331n41
Nuyorican Poetry Movement, 15, 319, 328

Odaro, 178
O'Hare, Kate Richards, 302
Oliver, Denise, 330n14
O'Reilly, Jane, 274
Ortiz, Ralph, 108

Oscer, Paul, 239
Outterbridge, John, 49, 50, 52, 58; Rag Man group, 50
Overstreet, Joe, 52, 225n33, 333
Oyewole, Abiodun, 331n41, 362

Pajaud, William, 46
Pan-African Congress, 121
Parker, Charles, 26
Parker, Franklin, 63
Parker, Junior, 237
Parks, Gordon, 218
Parks, Rosa, 120, 211
Parra, Violeta, 333
Patrick, William, 120
Patterson, Raymond R., 363, 369
Pell, Claiborne, 108
Perdermo, Willie, 350, 360
Perkins, Eugene, 95–96
Perkins, Pine Top, 238
Phillis Wheatley Bicentennial Festival (Jackson State), 85
Pietri, Pedro, 14–15, 328, 332n48, 333
Piñero, Miguel, 328
Plumpp, Sterling, 78, 122, 228
Pocho-Che, 334, 335, 346
Pool, Rosey, 80, 90n13
Porter, Allan, 190, 191, 193, 195, 199, 201, 204
Pound, Ezra, 358
Powell, Kevin, 350, 351, 352, 357–358, 362
Price, Sammy, 229
Priestly, Eric, 47
Prison Arts Movement, 15, 297, 298, 309–312
prisoners/prisons, 15
Prisoners' Rights Movement, 14
Purifoy, Noah, 48–49, *49*, 52, 53, 58, 69–70n33

Quarles, Benjamin, 373

race/racism, 3–4, 6, 8
Rachell, Yank, 229

Raitt, Bonnie, 243

Rambeau, David, 120

Randall, Dudley, 14, 80, 83, 123, 130, 309, 349, 360, 363. *See also* Broadside Press

Randall, Herbert, 197, 198, *198*, 199, *200*, 201

Reagan, Ronald, 372

Reconstruction, 75

Redding, Saunders, 83

Redmond, Eugene, 85, 228, 232, 350, 352, 360, 366n45, 370

Reed, Ishmael, 65, 228, 264, 321, 333, 350

Republic of New Africa, 121

Revolutionary Action Movement, 79

Ricks, Willie, 3

Riddle, John, 49–50, 52, 58, 70n36; *Ghetto Merchant*, 50

Ringgold, Faith, 32, 40–41n25, 110, 274, 297

riots/uprisings: Detroit, 1–2, 6; Newark, 1–2, 4, 6; Watts, 44, 45, 46, 48

Rivera, Louis Reyes, 355, 361, 362–363

Rodia, Simon, 48

RoHo, 63

Role Call, 16

Rosskam, Edwin, 24

Runagate Press, 352, 359

Rush, Otis, 237

Rustin, Bayard, 82

Saar, Betye, 46, 49, 50–52, *51*, 56, 58, 59, 274

Salaam, Kalamu ya, 14, 65, 350, 352, 357, 360, 362, 370; Black Power/civil rights Activism and, 77, 78; the blues and, 228, 231, 232–233

Sanchez, Sonia, 65, 76, 122, 309, 354, 355, 360, 369; Black Arts sexism and, 179–180, 181–182, 183; black male revolutionaries/poets and, 173, 174, 177–178; Black Power/civil rights activism and, 76, 78; cross-generational connections of, 350, 352, 361, 362; *Home Coming*, 173, 179–180; jazz/the

blues and, 228, 23. *See also* Giovanni, Nikki

Sarachild, Kathie, 279, 280

Saunderson, Kevin, 129

Schapiro, Miriam, 282, 284; and "female imagery," 289–290

Schoener, Allon, 105

Schulberg, Bud, 46

Schuyler, George, 256

Scott-Adams, Peggy, 248

Seale, Bobby, 76

Sease, Marvin, 248

Sellers, Cleveland, 84

Senghor, Léopold, 275

Sengstacke, Robert, 33, 204

Shahn, Ben, 127

Shakur, Tupac, 350

Shakur, Zayd, 303

Shange, Ntozake, 65, 274, 292–293, 362

Shepard, Kenny Wayne, 238

Shepp, Archie, 227

Simmons, Russell, 359

Simone, Nina, 26–27, 35

Sinclair, John, 228, 247–248

"66 Signs of Neon," 47, 48

Sleet, Moneta, Jr., 210, 211, 212–223, *214*, *215*, *216*, *217*, *218*, *219*, *220*, *222*, 224n8, 225nn27-28, 226n38. *See also Ebony* magazine

Smith, Bessie, 110, 230

Smith, Beuford, 189, 194–195, *195*, 197, 202–204, *202*, 208n33, 208n36, 208n40, 209n42

Smith, Bryant, 16

Smith, Marvin, 218

Smith, Morgan, 218

Smith, Welton, 169

Smith, W. Eugene, 218

SNCC Freedom Singers, 77

Snellings, Rolland, 170

Southern Black Cultural Alliance, 88

Southern Christian Leadership Conference (SCLC), 3, 77, 121

Spann, Otis, 235, 245

Spaulding, Val, 57

Spears, Alan, 362

Spellman, A. B., 9, 77, 81, 84, 85, 86–87, 88, 155, 228, 373
Spencer, Jon Michael, 228
Spriggs, Edward, 78, 89, 93, 102, 110
Steere, William, 108
Steinem, Gloria, 279
Stewart, James, 9, 11, 176, 221
Stinson, James, 130
Stone, Leroy, 84
Stuart, Alejandro, 333
Student Movement, 14
Student Nonviolent Coordinating Committee (SNCC), 3, 46, 76, 77, 78, 81, 82, 121
Sun Ra, 69n26, 137, 144, 145, 227
Szarkowski, John, 201

Tann, Curtis, 46
Tapscott, Horace, 47, 69n26
Taylor, Ed, 104
Taylor, Koko, 238
Tell Me How Long the Train's Been Gone (Baldwin), 158–160, 163–164, 167, 168, 169, 171n16, 171–172n24
Thelwell, Michael, 78, 84
Third World Communications (TWC), 334, 335, 340, 346
Third World Press, 14, 15, 16, 35–36, 352, 363. See also Madhubuti, Haki
Thomas, Lorenzo, 14–15
Thomas, Michael, Sr., 309–310
Thompson, James, 241–242
Thoreau, Henry David, 302
Thurman, Wallace, 262, 353, 354
Tolson, Melvin, 79, 83, 121
Touré, Askia Muhammad, 23, 38–39n1, 76, 77, 78, 321, 369, 370
Townsend, Henry, 229
Troupe, Quincy, 46, 65, 228, 232, 362
Truth, Sojourner, 64
Tshombe, Juno Bakali, 300, 301, 306–307
Ture, Kwame. See Carmichael, Stokely

Umbra magazine, 328, 333–334, 335, 346
Uncle Remus, 142

Vallejo, César, 333
VanDerZee, James, 105
Van Vechten, Carl, 262, 265–266
Vargas, Roberto, 333
violence: urban, 1–2
Voting Rights Act, 3

Waddy, Ruth, 46, 56
Walker, Alice, 65, 228, 273
Walker, Margaret, 79, 83, 121, 349, 363, 369
Walker, T-Bone, 237
Walker, William, 25
Wall of Respect, 11, 23, 24, 27, 30, 35, 38, 287; as collective enterprise, 25–26; mixed genres and, 29–30, 38; photographs/photography and, 27, 33–34; poems about, 27, 32–33; thematic categories of, 25, 26; Wall of Truth and, 34, 35, 38. See also Brooks, Gwendolyn; Donaldson, Jeff; Madhubuti, Haki
Washington, Timothy, 53, 55
Waters, Muddy, 25, 235, 237, 243, 246
Watts: as cultural center, 44–52; Towers of, 47–48
Watts Summer Festival, 47, 55. See also "66 Signs of Neon"
Wellburn, Ron, 235–236, 238, 239, 248
Wells, Junior, 237, 245
White, Charles, 46, 53, 55, 59, 68n20
Whitney Museum of American Art, 103, 104, 105, 106, 108, 111; Art Strike and, 107–109
Wideman, John Edgar, 41n27
Wilding, Faith, 280–281, 288–289
Wilkins, Rev. Robert, 246
Willi X, 310
Williams, Randy, 101,102
Williams, Robert F., 143
Williams, Sherley Anne, 228
Williams, William, 99, 101, 102
Williams, William Carlos, 325, 331n40
Willis, Deborah, 23, 39n2
Wilson, August, 228

Women's Liberation Movement, 14, 15, 273, 274, 275, 278–279, 279–280, 292, 293; feminism and, 274; Feminist Art Movement and, 273–274; Simone de Beauvoir and, 276–277, 278, 294n12, 294n17. *See also* Black Power Movement

Woodruff, Hale, 98, 99, 101

Wright, Jay, 85

Wright, Richard, 24

Young, Al, 228, 232, 236

Young, Kevin, 228, 247, 350, 370

Young Lords Party, 15, 107, 319, 325

Young People's Socialist League, 82